OBESITY
AND
WEIGHT
CONTROL

The Health Professional's Guide to Understanding and Treatment

Edited by

Reva T. Frankle, EdD, RD

Nutrition Consultant
Weight Watchers International
Jericho, New York

Associate Professor
Department of Community and Preventive Medicine
New York Medical College
Valhalla, New York

President
Frankle and Associates
Nutrition Consultants in Communication
and the Media
Somers, New York

Mei-Uih Yang, PhD

Obesity Research Center
St. Luke's-Roosevelt Hospital Center
New York, New York

AN ASPEN PUBLICATION
Aspen Publishers, Inc.

1988

Rockville, Maryland
Royal Tunbridge Wells

Library of Congress Cataloging-in-Publication Data

Obesity and weight control.

"An Aspen publication."

Includes bibliographies and index.
1. Obesity. I. Frankle, Reva T. II. Yang, Mei-Uih.
[DNLM: 1. Body Weight. 2. Obesity—prevention & control.
3. Obesity—therapy. WD 210 01146]
RC628.0229   1988   613.2′5   87-24111
ISBN: 0-87189-869-1

The authors have made every effort to ensure the accuracy of the information herein, particularly with regard to drug selection and dose. However, appropriate information sources should be consulted, especially for new or unfamiliar drugs or procedures. It is the responsibility of every practitioner to evaluate the appropriateness of a particular opinion in the context of actual clinical situations and with due consideration to new developments. Authors, editors, and the publisher cannot be held responsible for any typographical or other errors found in this book.

Editorial Services: Jane Coyle

Library of Congress Catalog Card Number: 87-24111
ISBN: 0-87189-869-1

Printed in the United States of America

1   2   3   4   5

To our mentor
whose wisdom and caring influenced our careers:

Orrea Florence Pye, Ph.D.
Professor Emeritus of Nutrition
Teachers College
Columbia University

Table of Contents

Contributors

Kelly D. Brownell, PhD
Obesity Research Group
University of Pennsylvania
Philadephia, Pennsylvania

Lisa Buckmaster, MS, JD
Department of Human Development and
    Family Life
University of Kansas
Lawrence, Kansas

C. Wayne Callaway, MD
Director, Center for Clinical Nutrition
Department of Medicine
George Washington University Medical
    Center
Washington, D.C.

Sharon Dalton, PhD
Department of Home Economics and
    Nutrition
New York University
New York, New York

Steven J. Danish, PhD
Professor and Chair
Department of Psychology
Virginia Commonwealth University
Richmond, Virginia

William H. Dietz, Jr., MD, PhD
Clinical Research Center
Massachusetts Institute of Technology
Cambridge, Massachusetts

Reva T. Frankle, EdD, RD
Nutrition Consultant, Weight Watchers
    International
Jericho, New York
Associate Professor
Department of Community and
    Preventive Medicine
New York Medical College
Valhalla, New York
President, Frankle and Associates
Nutrition Consultants in Communication
    and the Media
Somers, New York

M.R.C. Greenwood, PhD
Chairman, Department of Biology
Vassar College
Poughkeepsie, New York

Janet K. Grommet, PhD, RD
St. Luke's-Roosevelt Hospital Center
Weight Control Unit
New York, New York

Helen Hubert, PhD
Director
General Health Underwriting, Inc.
Washington, D.C.

Howard N. Jacobson, MD
Director, Institute of Nutrition
University of North Carolina
Chapel Hill, North Carolina

Harvey L. Katzeff, MD
Division of Endocrinology
Department of Medicine
North Shore University Hosptial
Manhasset, New York

John G. Kral, MD, PhD
Associate Professor of Surgery
Columbia University College of
    Physicians and Surgeons
Director of Surgical Metabolism
St. Luke's-Roosevelt Hospital Center
New York, New York

Diane R. Krieger, MD
Division of Endocrinology and
    Metabolism
Department of Medicine
Beth Israel Hospital
Harvard Medical School
Boston, Massachusetts

Lewis Landsberg, MD
Division of Endocrinology and
    Metabolism
Department of Medicine
Beth Israel Hospital
Harvard Medical School
Boston, Massachusetts

Idamarie Laquatra, PhD, RD
Nutritionist
H.J. Heinz Company
Pittsburgh, Pennsylvania

Carol A. Maggio, PhD
Obesity Research Center
St. Luke's-Roosevelt Hospital Center
New York, New York

William D. McArdle, PhD
Department of Health and Physical
    Education
Queens College
City University of New York
Flushing, New York

Anthony B. Miller, MB, FRCP(c)
Director, Epidemiology Unit
National Cancer Institute of Canada
University of Toronto
Toronto, Ontario

Carol J. Morton, MPS
Senior Service Designer
Weight Watchers International
Jericho, New York

Cheryl Nauss-Karol, PhD
Clinical Research and Development
Hoffman-La Roche Inc.
Nutley, New Jersey

F. Xavier Pi-Sunyer, MD, MPH
Obesity Research Center
St. Luke's-Roosevelt Hospital Center
Columbia University College of
    Physicians and Surgeons
New York, New York

Virginia A. Pittman-Waller, AB
Department of Biology
Vassar College
Poughkeepsie, New York

Jordon W. Smoller, AB
Harvard University Medical School
Boston, Massachusetts

Ann C. Sullivan, PhD
Director, Pharmacology I and II
Hoffman-La Roche Inc.
Nutley, New Jersey

Michael M. Toner, PhD
Queens College
Department of Health and Physical
  Education
City University of New York
New York, New York

Theodore B. Van Itallie, MD
Professor of Medicine
Columbia University College of
  Physicians and Surgeons
Director, Obesity Research Center
St. Luke's-Roosevelt Hospital Center
New York, New York

Joseph R. Vasselli, PhD
Obesity Research Center
St. Luke's-Roosevelt Hospital Center
New York, New York

Thomas A. Wadden, PhD
Obesity Research Group
University of Pennsylvania
Philadelphia, Pennsylvania

Mary Winston, EdD, RD
American Heart Association
Dallas, Texas

Judith Wylie-Rosett, EdD, RD
Department of Community Health and
  Medicine
Albert Einstein School of Medicine
Bronx, New York

Mei-Uih Yang, PhD
Obestiy Research Center
St. Luke's-Roosevelt Hospital Center
New York, New York

Foreword

Obesity is an old "disease" but it can only be properly understood and managed in the light of new scientific information. A great mistake of past generations of physicians and other health care professionals was to view obesity in grossly oversimplified terms—as a mere problem of overeating that could be cured by adherence to a low-calorie diet. The patient merely had to muster enough "will-power" or "character" to control his or her gluttony.

As a result of this oversimplification, obesity was neglected by the medical profession, and was generally regarded as a trivial problem unworthy of the attention of any sophisticated physician. Only recently has obesity come to be recognized as a labyrinthine and puzzling disorder or group of disorders ("the obesities"), with major health implications. Thus, there exists a sizable lag between the rapidly expanding body of new knowledge about obesity, and the professional application of such knowledge in its diagnosis, treatment, and prevention.

Retrospectively, it is shocking that a disorder afflicting some 26% of the adult American population and causing untold damage to the national health is, for the most part, still receiving unenlightened treatment by inadequately trained health care workers. It is only during the past few years that physicians and other health professionals have begun to organize sophisticated continuing medical education programs for those concerned with the treatment of obesity. Hopefully, this trend will lead to the development of a cadre of health professionals whose expertise in obesity will be comparable to that currently applied by their colleagues in the practice of subspecialties such as hematology, oncology, or gastroenterology.

In *Obesity and Weight Control*, the editors, Reva Frankle and Mei-Uih Yang, have assembled a remarkable array of chapters pertinent to obesity as a physiological phenomenon and as a clinical problem. The expertise of the contributing authors, who are outstanding investigators in obesity-related areas or experienced in some aspect of obesity management, or both, makes this an excellent resource for laboratory scientists, human nutritionists and practicing physicians.

Obesity and Weight Control is balanced. It does not neglect the scientific underpinnings of weight control. Most of the major research concerns in obesity are addressed in Part I: heredity vs environment, role of physiological regulation of body weight, endocrine factors in etiology and pathogenesis, energy metabolism and thermogenesis, body composition, and biologic adaptations to caloric restriction. The problem of treating obesity is thoroughly analyzed in Part II, with attention given to dietary management of obesity, behavior therapy, drug treatment, exercise therapy, and surgical intervention. In Part III, the special problems related to management of obesity during various stages of the life-span (childhood, adolescence, pregnancy, adulthood, and later life) are considered. Part IV covers management of obesity in nutrition-related diseases such as diabetes, coronary heart disease, and cancer.

To recapitulate, the professional management of obesity is badly in need of upgrading. Part of the problem stems from an unacceptably large gap between the "new knowledge" that is being rapidly generated about the subject, and the application of the relevant aspects of this body of information to the care and treatment of obese patients. The editors of *Obesity and Weight Control*, with their carefully selected team of expert authors, have contributed significantly to narrowing this knowledge/practice gap. Hopefully, *Obesity and Weight Control* and other educational efforts of a similar nature, will help instill a greater degree of professionalism into the weight-control field, thereby enhancing the care of America's large obese population. Such improved care is long overdue!

Theodore B. Van Itallie, MD
Professor of Medicine
Columbia University College of
Physicians and Surgeons
New York, New York

Preface

Several years ago Reva T. Frankle became involved in designing and teaching a course on obesity and energy metabolism for graduate nutrition students and first- and second-year medical students. As a public health nutritionist, registered dietitian, and nutrition educator, she sought a resource with a health promotion approach, a blend of scientific rationale and practical application that could be used by current and future practitioners alike. When a substantial search failed to produce such a resource, this book was written.

While scientists continue to search for clues in an attempt to unravel the mystery surrounding obesity, weight loss, and weight maintenance, the practitioner of weight management services must decide the type of therapy that can responsibly be offered to clients. Amid the numerous recommendations popularized by the media, fact must be distinguished from fiction. The purpose of this book is to aid practitioners in their decision-making efforts by providing an overview of the state of the art in the understanding and treatment of obesity. Part I addresses topics currently under investigation in the laboratory. Part II looks at intervention strategies and Part III, the life cycle. Part IV presents nutrition-related diseases for which obesity is a risk factor.

Both author/editors have been in the field of weight control for the greater part of their careers. Dr. Frankle had the invaluable experience of being a member of the New York City Department of Health Bureau of Nutrition in the early 1960s. Since then she has designed, implemented, and evaluated weight control programs delivered in medical center settings. More recently, as the Director of Nutrition for Weight Watchers International, she has been associated with community programs reaching overweight clientele in twenty countries.

Mei-Uih Yang has worked in the research setting, investigating metabolic rate, energy needs, body composition, and clinical studies at the Obesity Research Center, St. Luke's-Roosevelt Hospital Center. She has written many scientific papers that have appeared in refereed journals. In their work both authors realized the need for a practical handbook for the health professional.

xix

In summary, while this book represents a comprehensive, state-of-the-art source for understanding the possible etiology and consequences of as well as treatment for obesity, there is still much to learn to prevent obesity in future generations and to control or possibly cure those currently afflicted by it. We call for continued research into the possible causes of obesity and overweight. Because ''it's better to build children than to repair adults,'' we call for programs designed to prevent overweight and obesity, for a standard practice of reporting program outcomes so that intervention strategies can be compared among health professionals. Finally, we call for research to better understand weight maintenance and relapse prevention, to provide answers to the questions Morton raises: When does maintenance actually begin? What impact does being newly thin have on a person's ability to maintain his or her weight? How can adherence to suggested strategies be fostered in the long term? Is there a difference between weight loss and weight maintenance self-efficacy? These are subjects for on-going research.

Both authors are most appreciative of the fine contributors and their Aspen editor, Mike Brown, as well as of their patients and clients, who have taught them the vagaries of the treatment and outcome processes.

Reva T. Frankle
Mei-Uih Yang

Part I

Contemporary Topics in Weight Control: Scientific Rationale

Chapter 1

Weight Control: A Complex, Various, and Controversial Problem

M.R.C. Greenwood and Virginia A. Pittman-Waller

As might be expected, there is the greatest difference between the habits of different individuals. They vary from the girl who ate one orange, but explained that she had neither lunch nor dinner, to two young people who in one day consumed respectively in addition to their regular meals "one sandwich, four pieces of cake, a handful of popcorn, 1 lb box of popcorn, 2 handfuls of salted nuts, 2 pieces of candy," and "3 large pieces of candy, 16 small pieces of candy, 10 cakes, 1 cup of chocolate w/whipped cream." The last item, we are told, was taken simply for the sake of being sociable. . . .

A.L. MacLeod and M.A. Griggs
Dietary Study at Vassar College,
1917

The multitude and variety of eating disorders that afflict our society stand as striking testimony to the enormous problem that confronts the medical and public health communities today. Weight control is a multimillion dollar business, and treatment success is rare. From the extremes of obesity to anorexia, it is apparent that new information concerning causality is needed, as are innovative treatments.

Researchers have long known that weight is proportional to the adequacy of nutrition and to the degree of energy expenditure through physical activity. If this balance is upset by an increase in calories without a corresponding increase in activity, the weight gain attributable to increased fatness and obesity that follows may become apparent. This adiposity may have both health and psychosocial risks, but to appreciate it as a public health problem, obesity must be viewed in the contexts of both mortality and morbidity statistics and in terms of

Preparation of this manuscript and some of the work reviewed herein was supported by grant HD12637 from the National Institutes of Health. Bonnie Milne assisted in preparing the manuscript, James Brown provided graphics services, and Jerry Calvin provided photographic assistance.

relative risk, the mechanical difficulties it may cause and the psychosocial problems it evokes. In addition, new and unwanted side effects are inherent in its treatment.

We do not yet know what causes obesity, but there are at least two prevailing schools of thought (see Figure 1-1).

One school proposes that most obesity is the result of voluntary overingestion, and this notion has persisted as the dominant theory for decades. The proponents of this school, the PUSH school, believe that obesity is primarily a behavioral disorder, and thus they base nearly all of their treatment approaches on behavioral and dietary change. Given the extraordinary recidivism of people treated in such programs, it becomes increasingly apparent that this theory is not an adequate explanation, and that genetic or other factors are involved in the etiology of weight disorders.

Thus, support is growing for the second school of thought, the PULL school, related to the etiology of obesity. This school proposes that obesity results, at least in part, from inborn metabolic predispositions that generate false homeostatic signals leading to behaviors that sustain excess fat deposition. This school proposes that overfeeding behaviors are *caused* by the metabolic factors and are

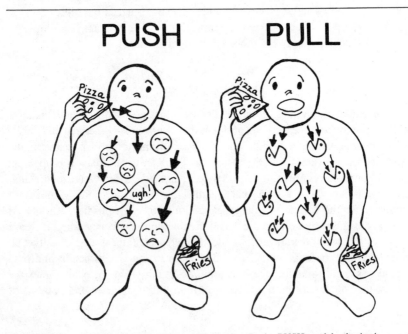

Figure 1-1 The PUSH and PULL Theories of Obesity. In the PUSH model, obesity is *caused* by voluntary pushing of excess nutrients into the body. In the PULL model, internal alterations *lead to* increased eating, but the increased eating is *secondary* to the primary internal disorder.

not themselves *causal*. Thus, while not so simple to address with current treatments, this theory proposes that as we understand the metabolic and genetic alterations leading to obesity, we may develop more successful treatments that are specific to individual problems.

THE DIMENSIONS OF OBESITY

Whatever the cause of obesity, its impact is increasing as a public health problem. For example, the *National Health and Nutrition Examination Survey II* (NHANES II) found that approximately 34 million adult Americans examined between 1976 and 1980 were overweight.[1] Severely overweight people numbered 10 to 12 million. The NHANES I data showed that between 1971 and 1974, 28.8 million adult Americans were obese and, among this group, 8.4 million were severely obese.[2] Thus, it may be that obesity increased over this decade.

The NHANES II data concerning the prevalence of being overweight are particularly noteworthy in view of sex, age, race, and poverty status (Figure 1-2). For example, in the NHANES II data, both white and black men between the ages of 25 and 55 years showed an increase in the prevalence of being overweight, which began to decrease in both races with increasing age. During the mid-decades (35 to 55 years), more black than white men were overweight (Figure 1-2). Furthermore, there is considerable sexual dimorphism in the prevalence of obesity. Overall, more women than men are obese, using our current criteria. The population of white American women becoming overweight steadily increases until the age of 65 years (Figure 1-2). In black American women, the prevalence of being overweight rises sharply from a significantly high 30% for the 10 years beginning at age 25 to almost 60% for the decade beginning at age 45 (Figure 1-2).

Generally, the prevalence of being overweight is higher among black women than white women, for any given age range. In fact, the prevalence of being overweight among black women between the ages of 45 and 55 years is twice as high as that of white women in the same age group. It is important to bear in mind that an economic variable may contribute to the propensity of black women to be overweight, since a considerable number of US blacks are below the poverty line. In contrast to the finding among women, American men have a slightly higher tendency to be overweight if they are above the poverty line than if they are below it. This phenomenon holds true uniformly among all age groups (Figure 1-2).

As mentioned previously, adult women below the poverty line show a propensity to be overweight. Thus, in American society, rich men tend to be overweight, while rich women tend to be thin. From a psychosocial standpoint, it

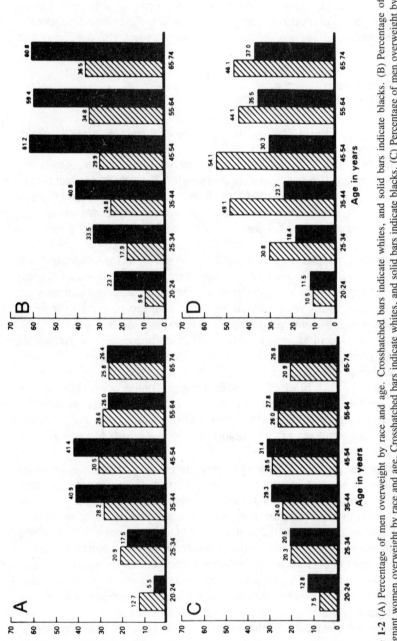

Figure 1-2 (A) Percentage of men overweight by race and age. Crosshatched bars indicate whites, and solid bars indicate blacks. (B) Percentage of nonpregnant women overweight by race and age. Crosshatched bars indicate whites, and solid bars indicate blacks. (C) Percentage of men overweight by poverty status and age. Crosshatched bars indicate poverty, and solid bars indicate nonpoverty. (D) Percentage of nonpregnant women overweight by poverty status and age. Crosshatched bars indicate poverty, and solid bars indicate nonpoverty. *Source:* Reprinted with permission from "Health Implications of Overweight and Obesity in the United States" by TB Van Itallie, *Annals of Internal Medicine* (1985; 103:983–988), Copyright © 1985, American College of Physicians.

is not surprising that women seem to be more adversely affected by obesity than men because an overweight woman is socially less accepted than a moderately overweight man.

Other mortality data are derived from the 1979 *Build Study*,[3] which examined the mortality risk of being overweight. In this study, the criteria for acceptable weight levels were taken from the 1979 Fogarty standards. The study showed that a body mass index (BMI) indicative of 20% to 25% above the body weight desired was associated with increased mortality. Further mortality data can be obtained from the 1979 American Cancer study,[4] which distinguished between smoking and nonsmoking populations. This study reported that underweight as well as overweight people had an increased mortality rate. While the overall findings showed less morbidity among nonsmokers, the same pattern was true: mortality was highest among severely underweight and overweight people. Thus, some degrees of being underweight are not necessarily associated with improved health, and being mildly to moderately overweight is associated with little increment in mortality.

It is important to examine and consider the evidence that associates obesity with increased mortality. However, it is equally important to note that some death rates may be highly underestimated since insurance companies may refuse to cover people who are severely overweight, diabetic, hypertensive, or have other serious medical complications. Furthermore, mortality data do not explain the etiology or the maintenance of the obesity. Therefore, it is now more common to examine the risk factors that seem to be linked with the development of cardiovascular disease or diabetes.

THE RISK OF OBESITY

Mortality data are useful for surveying the impact of obesity on a population, but they are of little use in predicting individual risk for death from heart disease, cancer, diabetes, or other pathologic conditions frequently associated with obesity. Thus, it is common to examine the prevalence of certain risk factors in groups of people. Among the risk factors for cardiovascular disease associated with obesity are hypertension and hypercholesterolemia. Impairments of glucose tolerance and plasma insulin regulation are common risk factors associated with diabetes. These risk factors are commonly increased in obese people and are reported to return toward normal with weight reduction. For example, in a study reported by Van Itallie[1] of the relation between overweight Americans and the risk for hypertension, the data showed that the relative risk for hypertension in overweight American adults between the ages of 20 to 75 years is 3 times the risk in nonoverweight people. In fact, the relative risk for hypertension is even greater among overweight Americans between the ages of 20 to 45 years. The likelihood of hypertension is 5.6 times greater in obese than in nonoverweight adults of the same age. Once past the age of 45, the relative risk in overweight people for hypertension decreases to approximately twice that in nonoverweight people in the same age group. However, the mechanism(s) whereby hypertension is associated with obesity is poorly understood, but may be related to increased insulin levels and glucose intolerance, which frequently develop in obese people over time.

Another risk factor often considered to be indicative of cardiovascular risk is a high total serum cholesterol level. The overall relative risk for hypercholesterolemia in obese people is 1.5 times higher than in those who are not overweight.[1] In the population of overweight Americans between the ages of 20 to 45 years, the relative risk for hypercholesterolemia is 2.1 times greater than in nonoverweight, same-aged peers. However, the association of being overweight with hypercholesterolemia may not always be concordant since the association is less in people 45 to 75 years of age.

Racial as well as age factors may be important in predicting relative risk. For example, overweight black men have a greater relative risk for high serum cholesterol levels. In addition, overweight men who are below the poverty line have an increased risk for hypercholesterolemia, and since more black men fall below the line than above it, it is quite possible that racial and economic factors are entwined.

The relative risk for diabetes among overweight compared with nonoverweight American adults is also increased.[1] In people aged 20 to 75 years, the risk for diabetes in those who are overweight is 2.9-fold that in the nonoverweight. In the population aged 20 to 45 years, the relative risk for diabetes in the overweight is 3.8 times that in the nonoverweight of comparable age. Between the ages of 45 and 75 years, the relative risk for diabetes decreases significantly, perhaps because those surviving into the older age groups are more resistant. While the relation of an *individual* risk factor to an *individual's morbidity and mortality* is not always directly related because so many other environmental, genetic, and cultural conditions may be involved, the detrimental impact of these risk factors and their association with mortality seem to be consistent with the most common causes of death among the overweight.

FAT DISTRIBUTION AND RISK

In the 1940s, Vague[5] noted that regional fat distribution, particularly in women, seemed to be correlated with specific risk factors, especially those associated with diabetes. Over the last few years, increased interest in the effects of regional fat distribution has opened up additional areas of investigation of aspects of metabolism and genetics related to morbidity in obese people.

As men become obese, the predominant distribution of this fat is in the abdominal, or central, area of the body. This distribution of obesity is sometimes referred to as *android*, or central, obesity (Figure 1-3). In women, however, there are two patterns of fat distribution. One is the abdominal, or android, distribution of fat, which is characteristic of men; the other is called *gynoid*, or peripheral, distribution of fat. This fat is typically distributed in the lower extremeties around the hip or femoral region, but it may also be distributed, to some extent, in the arms (Figure 1-3).

This gynoid, or peripheral, distribution of fat seems to be somewhat more benign than the abdominal distribution of fat. Fat distribution is frequently assessed by measuring the circumferences of the waist and the hip and computing the waist-to-hip (W:H) ratio. Normally, in women, the waist is smaller than the hip, and thus a normal W:H ratio is less than 1. In abdominal fat distribution, however, the waist measurement increases, while the hip measurement may remain stable or only slightly enlarged. This increasing W:H ratio is associated with the development of android, or central, obesity. In women, risk for impaired carbohydrate metabolism, and thus presumably diabetes, is correlated with this regional distribution of fat and not with the obesity per se.[6,7]

For example, as W:H ratios increase in obese women, plasma insulin and plasma glucose levels increase. Women equally obese but with normal W:H

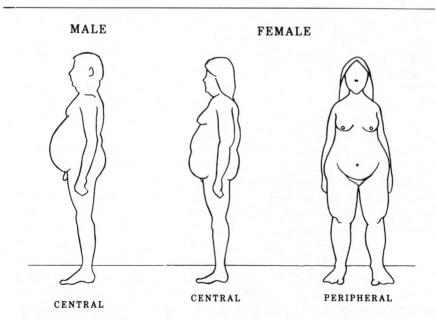

MALE   FEMALE

CENTRAL   CENTRAL   PERIPHERAL

Figure 1-3 Central Obesity in Men and Central and Peripheral Obesity in Women

ratios (gynoid obesity) do not show this impairment of glucose metabolism.[7] Such data argue strongly for regional fat distribution, rather than obesity per se, as a risk factor for diabetes in women. In men, abdominal distribution of fat seems to be important even in the absence of significant obesity; for example, even moderate accumulation of fat in the abdominal region increases the risk for hypertension.

Recently Rebuffe-Scrive et al[8] showed that the hip, or femoral, region of fat in women seems to be controlled by steroid hormones and reproductive experience. It is the hip, or femoral, fat that is primarily increased during pregnancy and presumed to be mobilized during lactation. Furthermore, it seems that the control of fat stores in this region is moderated primarily through the action of the fat-storing enzyme, lipoprotein lipase (LPL). The regulation of this enzyme during pregnancy and lactation may be responsible for the normal distribution of fat accumulation during pregnancy and lactation. Since many women report anecdotally that weight gain is associated with reproductive experience, the recent discovery that female fat stores are under sex-hormone control and are reproductively responsive may prove to be increasingly important in predicting those at risk for obesity associated with pregnancy or failure to lactate.

THE GENETIC FACTOR IN OBESITY

The association of morbidity and mortality not only with obesity per se but also with the distribution of fat may have a strong genetic component. Data[9] from genetic analyses strongly indicate that distribution of fat patterns may be inherited. Thus, it may be that the genetic factor is very important in the regional distribution of fat and has a dominant role in the associated risk for diabetes and other disorders. The remarkable concordance of the inheritance of fat patterns in obese and nonobese people was clearly shown in a study[10] of monozygotic and dizygotic obese twins.

In addition, the inheritability of BMI and body weight was shown in a report[11] on Danish adoptees and their biologic and adoptive parents. This study clearly illustrated that the association between the body weights of the adoptee and the biologic mother or father was highly statistically significant. The association between the body weights of the adoptee and the adoptive parents was unimpressive. Thus, physiologic and genetic, as opposed to behavioral, factors provide strong correlations in determining a person's body weight. Recognition of this concept is becoming increasingly important for understanding the etiology of obesity, and in determining approaches to rational treatments. Although it may be difficult to separate the genetics of regional distribution from environmental factors in humans, such interactions, while complicating approaches to treatment, provide directions for future research.

The role of genetics in determining adipose tissue development in humans is poorly understood. Although we know that monozygotic twins are more highly concordant in their fat distribution and fat development than dizygotic twins, we do not understand why. There are strong familial associations with obesity, but it is difficult to separate genetic from environmental factors. For example, obese children treated with aggressive measures such as caloric restriction or drugs have returned to their obese condition when followed-up many years later.[12] Such aggressively treated obese young children are frequently shorter than predicted, suggesting that the caloric restriction interfered with long-term linear growth, and that the biologic factors were dominant. Although we don't know all the factors that regulate fat cell development, we do know that abnormal adipose tissue development is essentially irreversible, and that genetic factors must have an important role in producing fat cells and in determining regional fat distribution. Consequently, treatments directed toward young obese people may need to be different than those used for obese adults.

THE ROLE OF ANIMAL MODELS IN UNDERSTANDING GENETIC AND ENVIRONMENTAL FACTORS IN OBESITY

It has been very difficult to obtain reliable data concerning the development of adipose tissue, both normal and abnormal, in humans. Thus, it is fortunate that animal models exist and have been employed to provide useful insights into both the etiology and the maintenance of the obese condition. One of the most valuable of these models is the genetically obese Zucker fa/fa rat. This rat inherits its obesity as a recessive trait. Thus, both parents must be carriers for the obese gene to be expressed in the offspring. The genetically obese Zucker rat is a particularly good model for early-onset obesity. In the fatty rat, even during the earliest postnatal stage, levels of adiposity are high. There are increases in fat cell size and number and in body fat in the absence of changed body weight or food intake. Such early shifts in the way energy is stored are mediated by LPL. An early and maintained increase in LPL seems to be the basis for the continued development of obesity and the later resistance to treatment.[13] Extreme treatments, such as lifelong food restriction,[14] exercise,[15] or removal of part of the large intestine (jejunoileal bypass surgery),[16] may normalize body weight but do not modulate obese body composition or excessive adipose tissue development.

Even when the genetically obese rat is fed the same number of calories as its lean litter mate from birth, the rat becomes obese. After 15 weeks of such feeding, the obese and lean rats weigh the same, but by 33 weeks, the obese rat outweighs the litter mate by at least 100 g. Obese rats restricted to the caloric intake and body weights of their lean litter mates have obese body compositions.

More than 50% of their body composition is fat. Thus, while body weight can be altered by various interventions, body composition (fatness) cannot.[14]

GENETIC OR ENVIRONMENTAL FACTORS AND TREATMENT CONSIDERATIONS

Since this complex genetic component is pertinent to human treatments as well, it is increasingly understandable why treating obesity is so very difficult. In a study of why diet therapy fails, Leibel and Hirsch[17] found that less than 3% to 5% of the patients who lost 13.6 kg (approximately 30 lb) or more could sustain such a weight loss for more than 2 years. They proposed that behavioral or metabolic factors, originally contributing to the development of obesity, may continue to operate after weight reduction. In support of this hypothesis, they noted that reduced-obese people require a lower caloric intake for weight maintenance than do weight-matched never-obese control subjects.[17] Furthermore, many formerly obese subjects, despite maintenance of more nearly "normal" body composition, have general dysphoria, depression, cold intolerance, hunger, and amenorrhea. The presence of these symptoms, normally associated with fasting in normal people, suggests that substantial weight reduction causes significantly marked alterations in behavior and metabolism.

Nonetheless, most studies in humans have not been able to separate potential "inborn," or genetic, factors from environmental factors. In fact, genetic predispositions and the environment may interact to produce a trigger for the response, and an interaction may be necessary for obesity to occur. Such an interaction might explain why some people with different "predispositions" respond to some reduced caloric diets or programs while others do not.

Over the past several years, it has become increasingly clear that the dieting-rebound cycle experienced even by normal-weight people, but especially by the obese, may have independent effects on obesity. This so-called yo-yo dieting may serve the purpose of enhancing metabolic adaptations to fasting and re-feeding such that it becomes increasingly more difficult for people to lose weight as a function of previous dietary experience. In studying this phenomenon, animal models have also been useful and illuminating. In one study,[18] three groups of rats were examined: (1) those who were eating normal laboratory chow, (2) those who were eating a highly palatable high-fat diet, and (3) those who had been eating the highly palatable high-fat diet and who were then dieted to normal weight twice and allowed to regain their weight. In this study, it was clear that the animals regained the weight faster than they lost it in both cycles. Food efficiency during the regain period was greater in the second cycle.

THE PSYCHOSOCIAL COST OF OBESITY

Aside from the difficulty obese persons have losing and maintaining the loss of excess weight, there are many psychosocial problems that accompany obesity. In the United States, there is a strong prejudice against obesity. Obese people often find themselves discriminated against in our body-conscious society. For example, Wadden and Stunkard[19] reported that prejudice against obese people could be found consistently in blacks and whites and in both rural and urban settings. In addition, emotional factors are closely related to obesity. At first it was thought that emotional disturbances caused obesity; now most investigators tend to think that the opposite is true, ie, that emotional disturbances are the consequences of obesity. The most common psychiatric disturbances of obese people are low self-image with disparagement of their body and an adverse, negative emotional reaction to dieting. Wadden and Stunkard[19] observed that women, adolescent girls, and morbidly obese people seem to suffer the most deleterious consequences of society's contempt for obesity.

Interestingly, it has been suggested that dieting may be partially responsible for the apparent nationwide increase in bulimia. There are as many health risks associated with being too thin as there are with being too fat; it is ironic that being "thin" rather than healthy is such a celebrated virtue. Bulimia is characterized by episodes of binge eating, followed by depressed mood and self-deprecating thoughts.[20] It is found in people of all weights, but especially in those of normal weight or who are anorexic. Only approximately 5% of obese people are bulimic, but no one knows how many formerly obese people may be bulimic. Prolonged dietary restriction may increase the risk for both negative emotional reactions and bulimia. Both bulimia and anorexia nervosa may mirror the American public's pervasive fear of obesity. At the core of both disorders, many investigators believe, lies an intense fear of becoming overweight and subsequently becoming the object of ridicule and prejudice that typically confront obese people.

As we gain a greater awareness of the heterogeneity of human weight disorders, we will be more capable of treating the various manifestations. Perhaps then we will be able to answer: Whom should we treat? How should we treat? What are appropriate weight goals? Among the obese, whom we should treat will depend on the identified associated risk factors as well as the family history of risk factors, such as diabetes, hypertension, and hyperlipidemia. The treatment approach should be based on the information gathered regarding dietary patterns, activity patterns, complicating conditions, and psychosocial resources and limitations.

The need to engage in considerable assessment of the patient before treatment may be somewhat discouraging to those who believe that obesity or other weight disorders are simple behavioral problems. However, increasingly, health professionals are becoming aware of the fact that obesity is a complex set of disorders that necessitate a range of treatments and rational matching of the person to the available treatments. Given the extraordinary recidivism rate for obese people and the lack of success of most of our current treatment in the hands of very talented professionals, it makes sense to imbue our approach to treatment with a genuine understanding of the problems faced by the obese person and to confront realistically the problems associated with lack of success. We must turn our efforts toward developing more creative and innovative approaches to treatment that emphasize the health-related aspects of both diet and exercise as opposed to the purely weight-related aspects of such treatments.

REFERENCES

1. Van Itallie TB: Health implications of overweight and obesity in the United States. *Ann Intern Med* 1985; 103:983–988.

2. National Center for Health Statistics, Obese and overweight adults in the United States, Washington, D.C.; U.S. Public Health Service; DHHS publ. no. 83-1680 (Vital and Health Statistics series 11, no. 230) (1983).

3. Society of Actuaries and Association of Life Insurance Medical Directors of America: *Build Study, 1979.* Philadelphia, Recording and Statistical Corporation, 1980.

4. Lew EA, Garfinkel L: Variations in mortality by weight among 750,000 men and women. *J Chronic Dis* 1979; 32:563–576.

5. Vague J: La differenciation sexuelle-facteur determinant des formes de l'obesite. *Presse Med* 1979; 30:339–340.

6. Kissebah AH, Vydelingum N, Murray R, et al: Relationship of body fat to metabolic complications of obesity. *J Clin Endocrinol Metab* 1982; 54:254–260.

7. Krotkiewski M, Bjorntorp P, Sjostrom L, et al: Impact of obesity on metabolism in men and women: Importance of regional adipose tissue distribution. *J Clin Invest* 1983; 72:1150–1162.

8. Rebuffe-Scrive M, Enk L, Crona N, et al: Fat cell metabolism in different regions in women. *J Clin Invest* 1985; 75:1973–1976.

9. Mueller WH: The genetics of human fatness. *Yearbook Phys Anthropol* 1983; 26:215–230.

10. Borjeson M: The aetiology of obesity in children. *Acta Paediatr Scand* 1976; 65:279–287.

11. Stunkard AJ, Sorenson TIA, Harris C, et al: An adoption study of human obesity. *N Engl J Med* 1986; 314:193–198.

12. Lloyd JK, Wolf OH, Whalen WS: Childhood obesity: A long term study of height and weight. *Br. Med J* 1961; 2:145–150.

13. Greenwood MRC, Vasselli JR: The effects of nitrogen and caloric restriction on adipose tissue, lean body mass and food intake of genetically obese rats: The LPL hypotheses, in *Nutritional Factors: Modulating Effects of Metabolic Processes.* New York, Raven Press, 1981.

14. Cleary MP, Vasselli JR, Greenwood MRC: Development of obesity in the Zucker (fafa) rat in the absence of hyperphagia. *Am J Physiol* 1980; 238:E284–E292.

15. Walberg, J, Greenwood MRC, Stern J: Lipoprotein lipase activity and lipolysis following swim training in obese and lean Zucker rats. *Am J Physiol* 1983; 245:R706–R712.

16. Greenwood MRC, Maggio CA, Koopmans HS, et al: Zucker *fafa* rats maintain their obese body composition ten months after jejunoileal bypass surgery. *Int J Obes* 1982; 6:513–525.

17. Leibel RL, Hirsch J: Diminished energy requirements in reduced-obese patients. *Metabolism* 1984; 33:164–170.

18. Brownell KB, Schraeger E, Stellar E, et al: The effects of repeated dieting on metabolism and food efficiency. *Physiol Behav* 1986; 38:459–464.

19. Wadden TA, Stunkard AJ: Social and psychological consequences of obesity. *Ann Intern Med* 1985; 103:1062–1067.

20. Agras WS, Kirkley BC: Bulimia: Theories of etiology, in Brownell KD, Foreyt JP (eds): *Handbook of Eating Disorders*. New York, Basic Books, Inc 1986.

Chapter 2

Mechanisms of Appetite and Body-Weight Regulation

Joseph R. Vasselli and Carol A. Maggio

INTRODUCTION

Basic Concepts

Perhaps the most basic question asked by investigators in considering the excess of body fat that defines the obese condition[1] is: What kind of disturbance of energy balance permits obesity to develop?[1] This chapter attempts to answer this question although, as we shall see, final answers remain speculative.

Energy Balance and the Set Point

A logical starting point for an analysis of body-weight regulation is the energy balance equation, which, simply stated, is

Change in energy stores = Energy intake − Energy expenditure.

If body weight represents the energy to be balanced, then the equation implies that body weight will be maintained at a stable value when the level of energy intake equals the level of energy expenditure. Of course, obesity will develop in a person when energy intake consistently exceeds energy expenditure.[2] This simple principle, as we shall see, leads to some complex questions.

First, the question immediately arises as to whether a regulatory system exists in the mature organism that is designed to maintain body weight at some fixed level. In fact, a good deal of empirical data, showing that the body weights of animals and humans remain remarkably stable over extended periods of time,

Preparation of this manuscript was supported by grants DK25141 and DK37918 from the National Institutes of Health. The authors thank Dr. Anthony Sclafani for his helpful comments on this manuscript.

seem to suggest exactly this.[3] Accordingly, the assumption of an active regulatory system for body weight operating around a fixed value, or "set point," has become the starting point for many analyses of potential disorders that may lead to obesity,[4,5] and is the basis of a good deal of research attempting to demonstrate body-weight regulatory mechanisms.[6] The hypothesis of a body-weight set point with an active regulatory system implies, of course, that under constant environmental conditions, people will maintain their weights within relatively narrow limits. The great diversity of human body weight, however, and the significant weight changes seen in many people during adulthood suggest that if set points exist, they do so over a wide range. Moreover, consistent with a set point hypothesis, it is unnecessary to assume that obesity is the result of a regulatory disorder. One need assume only that body-weight set points exist and are maintained at higher levels in obese people.[7]

Second, if a disorder of the mechanism controlling body weight is assumed, then the question arises as to how the disorder is expressed. An imbalance leading to excess caloric storage can be created by increased caloric intake in the face of normal levels of expenditure, unchanged caloric intake with reduced expenditure, or a combination of both these factors.[3] One can see quickly that overeating, metabolic rate changes, changes in the level of exercise, and interactions among these factors can all participate in excess weight gain. Finally, the question of the exact identity of the disorders leading to obesity has yet to be resolved.

What Is Disordered in Obesity?

Original hypotheses as to the disorders leading to obesity were relatively simple in approach. Overeating, viewed as a sustained imbalance on the input side of the energy equation, was the primary cause suggested by early observers,[8] although the complexity of the obese condition was recognized by some.[9] Accordingly, attention was initially focused on identifying potential excesses in the feeding behavior of the obese, and their psychologic basis. Evidence that the obese consistently overeat, however, relative to lean control subjects or reliably show enhanced preferences for sweet food items[10,11] is far from convincing. Thus, while it is true that surplus energy will lead to the deposition of excess body fat,[12] it is unclear that many obese people become so simply by means of caloric overconsumption. Newer behavioral notions stress motivational factors that prompt the obese to overeat under special circumstances.

Similarly, early analyses of biologic factors focused on the potential neural bases of overeating in the obese. The widely held hypothesis that an imbalance between two hypothalamic brain "centers" reciprocally controlling hunger and satiety[13] may underlie overeating and obesity[4] is now seen as an oversimplification.[14] Obesity stemming from endocrine imbalances was identified by early investigators,[9] but recognized as a relatively rare condition. Finally, although inactivity clearly is correlated with obesity, the view that excess body fat is the result of chronically decreased exercise may be applicable to only some obese people.[15]

Newer approaches to the causes of obesity stress that it is not a unitary disorder, but may involve alterations in one or more of the body's regulatory systems. These include the brain and its neurotransmitters, the gut and its peptides, the liver and its metabolic processes, the adipose tissue, and endocrine hormones. Thus, quite discrete disorders may underlie various types of obesity. The terms "appetite" and "hunger," usually distinguished in terms of preabsorptive *v* postabsorptive initiating stimuli,[16] are used interchangeably in the following discussion. To facilitate our analysis, we first consider the components of a simplified appetite–body-weight regulatory system.

A Simplified Regulatory Model

In considering the structure of hypothetical appetite and body-weight regulatory systems, workers in the area classically have inferred the existence of two regulatory components: A *short-term* component controls the onset and cessation of feeding on a meal-related basis. A *long-term* component monitors body-nutrient depletion and repletion over extended periods, and modulates intake such that body weight is maintained, with some fluctuations, within a relatively narrow range.[4,17] The two components, potentially having distinct mechanisms, may be assumed to interact in an additive way in performing regulatory corrections of body weight. Specifically, the potency of short-term satiety signals may be decreased or enhanced in accord with long-term regulatory influences reflecting the nutrient state of the organism.[18]

As indicated in Figure 2-1, feeding stimulated by both internal and external factors provides energy substrate to the body, the unused portion of which is stored primarily in depot fat. The body's fat mass is presumed to be the regulated compartment, since moderate fluctuations of adult body weight consist mainly of alterations of body fat. Extreme body-weight reductions, however, may result in the involvement of lean body mass as a regulated entity. The regulated compartment provides metabolic or neuronal signals that are reliable correlates of its size and which serve as error signals to a receptor having a reference value, or set point, for such signals. After "comparison" of the error signal with the reference value, presumably in the brain, the receptor initiates signals that ultimately provide stimulatory or inhibitory influences on the feeding mechanism. This is the long-term regulatory component of the system.

A short-term regulatory component, operating within a much more limited time frame, may also use error signals and a reference value (hypothetically, for example, in monitoring nutrient levels during a meal). However, in many cases, the passive accumulation of purely negative feedback stimulation, such as distension from increasing stomach volume, may suffice to inhibit feeding.

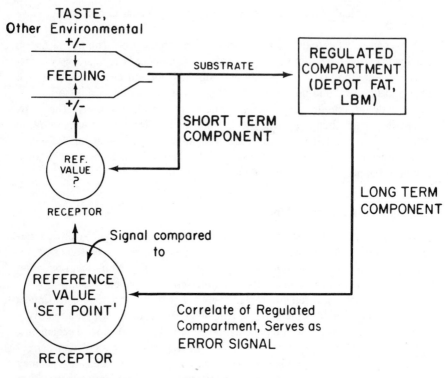

Figure 2-1 A Simplified Feeding–Body Weight Regulation Model

Signals controlling meal intake presumably arise from the gut, where newly introduced substrate is first sensed, but ultimately are processed by the brain. In our model, long-term and short-term feeding influences can summate or cancel each other, in accordance with the state of the gut and body fat stores. Their effects are integrated and expressed by the final common pathway, the feeding mechanism of the brain itself. Although this mechanism can be stimulated by external factors such as taste, temperature, and even psychologic events, the effects of feeding initiated in this way ultimately will be reflected in the body's regulatory system.

PHYSIOLOGIC SYSTEMS INVOLVED IN REGULATION

The Brain and Its Neurotransmitters

Earlier Notions

The "dual center" theory of feeding control evolved from extensive brain lesion and stimulation work focused on two specific areas in the hypothalamus, and potential interconnections between them.[13] According to the theory, impulses from the lateral hypothalamus (LH), or feeding center, initiate eating when incoming information signals nutrient depletion. As eating proceeds, feeding impulses are inhibited by stimulation from the ventromedial hypothalamus (VMH), or satiety center, which lies close to the brain's vascular bed and the cerebrospinal fluid (CSF), and can monitor rising nutrient levels. Support for this theory is found in the fact that destruction of the VMH by electrolytic lesion or other means leads to hyperphagia and obesity, while destruction of the LH leads to hypophagia and body-weight loss.[6]

The dual center theory was made considerably more powerful by the parallel development of the glucostatic hypothesis,[4] which identified the rate of glucose utilization by the tissues of the body as the error signal for the initiation or cessation of feeding. As a major tenet of the glucostatic hypothesis, insulin-sensitive glucoreceptors were posited for the VMH. Such receptors would directly reflect peripheral metabolic events, and make accurate feedback control by the VMH satiety center possible. However, as further experiments either directly or indirectly tested the assumptions of the dual center theory and the glucostatic hypothesis, it became clear that these notions, although appealing in explanatory and integrative power, were inadequate to represent the complexity of the neural and metabolic events controlling feeding.[14,19] Although the LH and medial hypothalamic area (MH) remain a focus of study for the regulation of feeding behavior, these areas today are seen as integrative components in a complex system of incoming and outgoing excitatory and inhibitory influences, mediated by a variety of neurotransmitters.[20,21]

A New Integrative Hypothesis

Interest has shifted to the paraventricular nucleus (PVN), located anteriorly and dorsally in the MH, as an integrator of satiety influences, and to the perifornical region of the hypothalamus (PFH), in the LH, as an integrator of feeding-stimulatory influences. A new hypothesis to explain the functioning of these areas centers on the fact that microinjections of norepinephrine (NE) into the PVN stimulate feeding, while microinjections of epinephrine and dopamine (DA) into the PFH inhibit feeding.[20,22] Since these areas have been identified as feeding-inhibitory and feeding-stimulatory, respectively, injections of these catecholamine (CA) neurotransmitters must exert inhibitory influences over the areas' normal function. Thus, according to the hypothesis, feeding and satiety are modulated by CA neurotransmitters acting endogenously in these brain areas. Indeed, discrete effects on the pattern of feeding, and specific influences on macronutrient appetites, have been proposed for each area.[23]

A considerable body of data now exists in support of this hypothesis. Depletion of NE in the PVN of rats results in a significant decrease of daily food intake on a long-term basis, involving a selective reduction of carbohydrate ingestion.[24] Moreover, the infusion of a satiety-inducing meal into the stomach of rats simultaneously inhibits NE release in the PVN, and enhances release of NE in the LH.[25] Finally, MH lesions centered in the PVN, as well as knife cuts of a tract exiting from the PVN and descending to the medulla, lead to hyperphagia and obesity, presumably because of the loss of feeding-inhibitory impulses normally originating in the PVN.[21] On the other hand, destruction of an ascending CA tract known as the ventral noradrenergic bundle, which terminates in the LH, also leads to hyperphagia and obesity, presumably in this case because of the release of this feeding-stimulatory area from CA inhibition.[20] This last observation, previously difficult to reconcile with notions of a satiety center located in the MH, is accommodated nicely by the newer hypothesis. Earlier VMH destruction, which was in general larger and less specifically targeted, probably resulted in obesity inducing damage to either or both of these hypothalamic systems.

The existence of other neurotransmitters that alter feeding when injected into the brain, however, indicates how complex the endogenous control of feeding may be.[26] Serotonin and its agonists, for example, inhibit feeding at MH sites, and seem to antagonize NE-induced feeding in the PVN specifically.[23] In turn, levels of brain serotonin are dependent on dietary intake of its amino acid precursor tryptophan, and also of carbohydrates, which enhance brain tryptophan uptake via their effects on insulin release.[27] The endogenous opioid peptides endorphin and dynorphin stimulate feeding when injected into the PVN, and an endogenous opiate system that provides tonic feeding stimulation but is antagonized by other neuropeptides has been proposed.[26] Finally, both endorphins and DA have been implicated as neurotransmitters in feeding-reward systems located in the hypothalamus.[22] It is important to emphasize that interconnections between the hypothalamus, cranial nerve nuclei, and brainstem areas[28] implicated in feeding control indicate that extensive integration of feeding-related information normally takes place in the brain.[29] It is clear that relatively minor alterations in this complex system can alter feeding behavior, and potentially body weight.

Signals from the Gastrointestinal Tract

In one of the earliest theories of food-intake regulation, the stomach was considered the locus of feeding control, with gastric contractions signaling the onset of hunger.[30] This theory fell into disfavor when no systematic relation could be detected between the occurrence of gastric contractions and reports of either hunger or feeding.[31] The gastrointestinal tract has again become prominent in theories of intake regulation, this time as a potential source of signals for satiety, or the inhibition of feeding.

Satiety is viewed as a complex process, which may involve both meal-related inhibitory signals and intermeal inhibitory influences.[32] Meal-related satiety signals are thought to arise in the gastrointestinal tract in response to the presence of ingested nutrients. The exact nature of these signals is unknown; however, several likely possibilities have emerged. First, in the stomach, satiety signals may be stimulated by the caloric properties of a meal or by simple distension resulting from gastric filling.[33] The process of gastric emptying, which involves feedback control of the stomach by the small intestine, may also participate in meal-related satiety.[34] As a meal empties from the stomach, intestinal receptors, activated by food-related stimuli, are thought to influence not only further emptying but also subsequent food intake. Interestingly, rapid gastric emptying, which may promote overeating,[35] is observed in some cases in obese animals[36] and humans.[37]

Second, behavioral[38] and electrophysiologic[39] evidence indicates that several types of receptors may encode information about ingested nutrients in the small intestine. These include osmoreceptors, which register changes in tonicity; tension receptors, which register changes in intestinal distension; and chemoreceptors, which are activated by specific nutrients. Recently described duodenal glucoreceptors, for example, may be involved in signaling satiety after carbohydrate-containing meals.[40] In addition, the existence of "calorie receptors" is suggested by demonstrations of precise feeding compensation in experimental animals in response to equicaloric preloads of various nutrients.[34]

Transmission of satiety signals from the gastrointestinal tract to the brain is believed to involve both neural and hormonal mechanisms. There is evidence that afferent impulses carried by the vagus nerve transmit signals from intestinal glucoreceptors,[39] and possibly from receptors for the intestinal hormone cholecystokinin (CCK).[41] In fact, several peptide hormones are known to be released when food-derived stimuli contact endocrine cells in the gastrointestinal tract. Much interest has centered on CCK since its administration has been shown to reduce meal size reliably in many species, including humans.[42] Administration of bombesin, a peptide found in the stomach, has also been shown to reduce meal intake effectively.[41] A number of other brain-gut peptides, such as somatostatin, glucagon, and neurotensin, are now being investigated as potential satiety-signaling agents.[43] The specificity of peptide-induced feeding inhibition and the conditions under which gut peptides such as CCK and bombesin participate in normal meal-related satiety remain to be determined.

Liver Metabolic Influences

After a meal, absorbed glucose is taken up by the liver and provides substrate for glycogen synthesis. The resulting availability of glucose in the liver may stimulate a hepatic glucoreceptor system, which in turn may signal the brain and result in prolonged satiety between meals.[40] Dependence of this system on the liver's glycogen content is indicated by the finding that hepatic infusion of glucose via the portal vein suppresses food intake in deprived animals but not in freely-feeding, presumably glycogen-replete ones. Since these effects are abolished by vagotomy, information concerning glucose availability in the liver may be conveyed by afferent fibers in the vagus nerve. The firing rate of hepatic vagal fibers has, in fact, been shown to vary as a function of the concentration of glucose in the portal blood.[44]

In an alternate "hepatostatic" theory of food-intake control, hepatic glucose metabolism is proposed as the source of signals triggering satiety and initiating feeding.[45] The critical event is viewed as alterations of the pyruvate level resulting from glycolysis in response to hepatic glucose uptake in the fed state (pyruvate surfeit), and liver glycogen breakdown in the fasting state (pyruvate deficit). Feeding occurs to replenish carbohydrate reserves and prevent the onset of gluconeogenesis, which is energy costly. Again, hepatic vagal fibers are identified as the relay for information to the CNS. In experimental preparations supporting this hypothesis, predicted effects are in fact abolished by vagotomy. In summary, in contrast to the more general role proposed for glucose in the earlier glucostatic hypothesis, glucose may have a specific role in signaling hunger and satiety in conjunction with the state of hepatic glucose metabolism.

A more general theory of the liver's role in the control of feeding has resulted from observations of the interchangeability of various metabolic fuels during states of energy depletion.[46] For example, feeding in response to insulin-induced hypoglycemia can be abolished not only, as expected, by infusions of glucose, but also by the ketone beta-hydroxybutyrate and by the sugar fructose, which does not cross the blood-brain barrier but is metabolized by the liver. Since all of the body's fuels ultimately are processed by the liver, the liver has been proposed as the ideal organ to monitor shifts in substrate flow occurring during energy surplus and deficit. Thus, feeding may be altered according to changes in the liver's overall metabolic status, which are sensed by metabolite receptors and transmitted via the vagus nerve to the brain. Indeed, all of these liver-based hypotheses rely on the presence of an intact vagus nerve to effect feeding control. However, although the effects of vagotomy are complex, the normal occurrence of hunger and relatively intact meal patterns have been reported in many cases in vagotomized humans and animals.[47]

Adipose Tissue Correlates

In addition to relatively short-term feeding control mechanisms associated with the gastrointestinal tract and liver, long-term regulatory signals have been proposed to arise from the adipose tissue. The notion that adipose tissue may regulate its own size through feedback signals to the brain that influence levels of feeding derives from early "lipostatic" hypotheses,[48,49] and from data indicating that total adipose tissue mass can be restored after lipectomy.[50] However, the nature of the signal(s) that reflects total lipid stores and permits alterations of feeding is yet to be determined. It is clear that signals conveyed to the CNS from adipose tissue are probably indirect since little or no afferent innervation of white adipose tissue has been identified.[51] Ideally, such signals would be a correlate of the amount of lipid stored in the tissue.[52] Two commonly considered candidate signals are glycerol and free fatty acids, breakdown products of lipolysis whose concentrations in blood increase as fat cells enlarge. Conclusive evidence for the role of such metabolites in the regulation of feeding has yet to be provided, however.

Recently, potential influences on feeding have been attributed to the size and number of the body's adipocytes. Adipocytes enlarge through the process of lipid filling, and correlational evidence relating feeding behavior to adipocyte size has been reported.[53,54] It has been proposed that as fat cells approach some maximal or "peak" size, an inhibitory influence on energy intake occurs, which results in decreased feeding. Conversely, when replete adipocytes are reduced in size, feeding may be stimulated to permit the cells to refill with lipid.[55]

It is now evident that the total number of fat cells may readily increase under appropriate dietary stimulation.[56] New fat cells are probably added in response to maximal enlargement of existing adipocytes, a process that seems to require an extended period of overeating. Such an increase of total adipocyte number would eventually exert additional feeding-stimulatory effects as the new cells begin to fill with lipid. Indeed, the tendency for adipocytes to achieve and maintain peak size suggests that adipocyte proliferation may result not only in a permanent elevation of body weight, but in the defense of that body weight, if necessary, through elevated caloric intake.[1] The possibility thus exists that as yet undefined correlates of adipocyte size and number modulate feeding so as to maintain lipid stores.

The genetically obese Zucker rat seems to be a good model of adipose tissue influences on feeding behavior. Data from our laboratory indicate that this rat may require higher levels of an adipocyte-derived signal to decrease feeding during development than its lean counterpart.[54] Moreover, in this obese animal, the rapid clearance of circulating triglyceride into adipose tissue, mediated by elevated activity of the enzyme lipoprotein lipase (LPL), may drive the hyperphagia characteristic of this animal during growth and in adulthood.[57] It is notable that LPL activity remains elevated in the Zucker obese rat despite therapeutic intervention, which may enable the animal to maintain its enlarged fat cell size and obese body composition despite significant weight loss. Interestingly, elevated LPL activity has been described in reduced-obese humans, and has been identified as one mechanism that may lead to weight regain in these people.[58]

Endocrine Mechanisms

Several theories of body-weight regulation involve a role for the endocrine hormones, either as direct feedback signals or as modulators of neural and metabolic processes responsible for feeding and energy expenditure. One prominent hypothesis in the first category identifies the level of insulin in the CSF as the error signal for the long-term control of body weight.[59] Starting with the observation that the level of circulating insulin is positively correlated with the body's adipose mass, the hypothesis asserts that a constant fraction of circulating insulin crosses the blood-brain barrier and accurately represents the size of adipose stores to hypothalamic areas capable of detecting CSF insulin. Hypothalamic centers, in turn, alter feeding in accord with a reference level of adiposity that the body attempts to maintain. According to this notion, increases of CSF insulin, reflecting increased adipose tissues, would signal reductions of feeding, while decreases of CSF insulin would prompt feeding. Since the introduction of this hypothesis, a considerable amount of supportive data have been generated, including the identification of insulin receptors in areas of the hypothalamus known to be involved in feeding control, experimental manipulations of the CSF insulin level and feeding, and the demonstration of altered CSF insulin levels and insulin binding in the brains of Zucker obese rats.[60,61]

Two additional hypotheses are based on complex interactions among the nervous system, endocrine hormone release, and peripheral metabolic processes. The autonomic-endocrine hypothesis rests on the fact that the MH and LH, via the splanchnic and vagus nerves, reciprocally control sympathetic and parasympathetic stimulation of insulin release, hepatic glycogen synthesis, fatty acid mobilization, and peripheral NE turnover.[62] These activities seem to be altered in favor of lipid deposition in many obese animal models. Moreover, feeding-stimulatory and lipogenic effects of the adrenal glucocorticoids greatly enhance the development of obesity. It is interesting to note that NE-induced feeding in the PVN is abolished by adrenalectomy.[63] A similar hypothesis concerning the etiology of obesity identifies as a primary cause a dysfunction of hypothalamic activity, which results in insulin oversecretion and related metabolic abnormalities such as enhanced hepatic glucose production and increased insulin resistance.[64] These two theories view obesity as a neuroendocrine disorder, potentially with a genetic basis.

BEHAVIORAL MECHANISMS INVOLVED IN REGULATION

External Responsiveness and Dietary Restraint

As mentioned earlier, the notion that the obese in general overeat compared with normal-weight people has received little experimental support. For example, one of the few positive reports found obese women to overeat only during a "dynamic" period of weight gain.[65] Several theoretical formulations have therefore emphasized the concept that eating behavior in the obese is characterized by motivational alterations that promote overingestion only under special circumstances. One of the earliest of such notions is the externality theory, which proposed that obese people eat primarily in response to food-related cues, such as sight, smell, and taste, rather than in response to internal physiologic stimuli, which govern ingestion in normal-weight people.[66] The externality concept was based on the notion that obese humans and VMH-obese rats have similar behavioral traits, and was eventually expanded to include hyper-responsiveness by the obese to all prominent external stimuli. A later modification of the theory proposed that a basis for the externality trait was a state of caloric deprivation, resulting from chronic dieting.[67] According to this view, calorically restricted obese people eventually fall below their set point for body weight and, as a result, become hyperemotional and hyper-responsive to external stimuli, like starved experimental animals.

The theory of externality has generated a considerable amount of research.[68] However, the relation of externality to the obese state does not seem so straightforward as originally assumed since external responsiveness has been observed in lean as well as obese people.[69] Consequently, the construct of dietary restraint was developed.[70] Dietary restraint, which is measured on a ten-item scale, describes a cognitively maintained effort to resist biologic urges to eat. In this case, over-responsiveness to external stimuli is assumed to be driven by the stress associated with continual dieting. While both lean and obese people may show restraint, the obese are assumed to have higher levels because of a constant struggle to control their body weight. Certain "disinhibiting" events may disrupt restraint and precipitate bouts of overeating, including bingeing followed by renewed dieting. Obese people do generally score higher in restraint, although, as a recent review concluded, their eating behavior is less responsive to experimental disinhibition than that of restrained eaters of normal weight.[71] Therefore, it was suggested that restraint may be a more appropriate construct for the analysis of disorders such as anorexia and bulimia.

Alterations of Palatability

Overconsumption of palatable, especially sweet-tasting, food items has been considered a prominent factor in the etiology of obesity.[16] While obese subjects may overconsume palatable foods under some experimental conditions,[10] numerous dietary surveys[65,72,73] have failed to detect reliable differences in the nutrient composition of diets ingested by obese and lean people. Likewise, studies[10] of taste perception have failed to uncover consistent obese-lean differences in pleasantness or intensity ratings of sweet solutions. Many palatable foods contain high levels of both fat and sugar, however, and recent studies[74] employing taste stimuli consisting of fat and sugar mixtures found that obese subjects preferred higher levels of fat and lower levels of sugar in such mixtures than normal-weight subjects. The use in these studies of sophisticated psycho-physical scaling techniques and complex taste stimuli, which approximate real foods, may help discern potential differences in the taste responsiveness of the obese, although the relation of such laboratory data to actual ingestion patterns remains to be determined.

As mentioned previously, obese people have been proposed to display increased sensory responsiveness as a result of chronic caloric deprivation.[67] In support of this notion, data indicate that the perceived palatability of ingestive stimuli may be affected by short- as well as long-term changes in a person's nutritional state.[75] In normal-weight people, pleasantness ratings of sweet stimuli have been observed to decrease with satiety induced by a preload. This "negative alliesthesia" disappears after weight loss and may be absent in the obese. It has thus been argued that taste reactivity is influenced by changes in body-weight status in order to maintain body weight at its set point.[75] Several reports have, in fact, noted that reduced-obese subjects prefer sweeter solutions and report higher pleasantness ratings in the fed state than was the case before weight loss.[76,77] Such data have been difficult to replicate and may depend on the method of weight loss.[77] Nonetheless, this phenomenon clearly warrants further investigation as a potential mechanism for the promotion of regain after weight loss.

Cephalic-Phase Responses

Finally, interactions between external stimuli and internal responses related to ingestion have been proposed to influence feeding behavior differentially in the obese. Specifically, food-related cues, particularly those of palatability, are proposed to alter an array of digestive and metabolic reflexes that occur before ingestion.[78] These so-called cephalic-phase responses are largely mediated by the vagus nerve; it has been suggested that their functional significance is to prepare digestive and metabolic processes for nutrient arrival.[79] In the obese, attention has focused on cephalic-phase release of insulin, a hormone whose administration increases food intake and weight gain via enhancement of nutrient deposition.[80] Thus, obese people have been hypothesized to display exaggerated cephalic-phase insulin secretion, which in turn promotes overingestion of palatable food items.[81] Viewed in this way, cephalic-phase insulin secretion serves as the physiologic mediator of external responsiveness. Indeed, exaggerated cephalic-phase responses were shown in the VMH-obese rat, which is hyperphagic on palatable diets.[78] The situation in obese humans is less clear-cut, with reports of cephalic-phase insulin secretion that is greater than[81] or comparable with that of lean humans,[82] or, in one case, undetectable.[83] Regardless of body weight, such responses are often small in magnitude, brief in duration, and highly variable.[84] The relation of cephalic-phase insulin release to feeding behavior remains controversial.

IMPLICATIONS FOR TREATMENT

Weight-Loss Therapies

It is clear that the regulation of feeding and body weight is multiply determined, with overlapping behavioral and physiologic systems apparently designed to maintain immediate and long-term caloric resources at relatively constant levels. It is this characteristic that renders attempts at appetite control and weight reduction so difficult. Therapies for the obese are targeted at every stage of the caloric ingestion-utilization process. Behavior modification programs in part alter the accessibility of food items; dietary fiber, anorectic drugs, and gastric surgery presumably reduce appetite or enhance satiety; low-calorie liquid diets bypass short-term control mechanisms entirely and more directly manipulate body weight; and exercise increases energy expenditure, diverting or mobilizing calories from storage.[85]

Most effective weight-loss therapies, however, lead to compensatory energy adjustments such as increased hunger and food intake, decreased metabolic rate, and/or reduced exercise levels. Of the potential treatments the practitioner can offer obese patients, the ideal one would, of course, manipulate the body-weight regulatory system so that equilibrium is achieved at a lower weight level. This alternative, clearly the most attractive, would also be the most difficult to implement.

Can the Regulatory System Be Manipulated?

Two treatments have been claimed to have set point–altering effects. The first is administration of the anorectic agents amphetamine and fenfluramine, members of the phenylethylamine class of compounds. The second is exercise.[91,92] We consider the case for fenfluramine, since the argument for its effects on the set point is somewhat better developed.

Studies indicate that rats treated with fenfluramine initially reduce food intake and body weight but upon weight stabilization increase intake to normal levels. Decreased body weight is maintained. Rats that are reduced in weight before drug administration show no intake reduction when treated, but maintain the reduced weight.[86] Thus the drug is hypothesized to act primarily by lowering the body-weight set point, and only secondarily to decrease appetite, if required, to effect a lowered weight level.[87] Several metabolic changes induced by fenfluramine, including decreased corticosterone release, increased insulin sensitivity, and decreased triglyceride synthesis, for which tolerance does not develop, may underlie the sustained body-weight reduction seen with the drug.[88] Long-term treatment of developing Zucker obese rats with fenfluramine decreases carcass lipid deposition as well.[89]

Two points should be made concerning these effects. First, while fenfluramine may act peripherally to enhance energy expenditure, and in this way shift the functional body-weight set point, it is unclear whether any central regulatory mechanism is genuinely altered by the drug. Second, if a shift in set point is induced by fenfluramine, it is temporary only. Withdrawal of the drug results in regain of the lost body weight. This has prompted some to suggest that the drug be used chronically in the treatment of obesity,[90] but the safety of such a procedure is not established.

REFERENCES

1. Vasselli JR, Cleary MP, Van Itallie TB: Modern concepts of obesity. *Nutr Rev* 1983; 41:361–373.

2. Garrow JS: The regulation of energy expenditure in man, in Bray GA (ed): *Recent Advances in Obesity Research*. London, Newman Publishing, 1978, vol 2, pp 200–210.

3. Bray GA: *The Obese Patient*. Philadelphia, WB Saunders Co, 1976.

4. Mayer J, Thomas DW: Regulation of food intake and obesity. *Science* 1967; 156:328–337.

5. Van Itallie TB, Gale SK, Kissileff HR: Control of food intake in the regulation of depot fat: An overview. *Adv Mod Nutr* 1977; 2:427–492.

6. Keesey RE: A set-point analysis of the regulation of body weight, in Stunkard AJ (ed): *Obesity*. Philadelphia, WB Saunders Co, 1980, pp 144–165.

7. Keesey RE, Corbett SW: Metabolic defense of the body weight set point, in Stunkard AJ, Stellar E (eds): *Eating and Its Disorders*. New York, Raven Press, 1984, pp 87–96.

8. Newburgh LH: Obesity; Energy metabolism. *Physiol Rev* 1944; 24:18–31.

9. Rynearson EH, Gastineau CF: *Obesity*. Springfield, Ill, Charles C Thomas Publishers, 1949.

10. Spitzer L, Rodin J: Human eating behavior: A critical review of studies in normal weight and overweight individuals. *Appetite* 1981; 2:293–329.

11. Vasselli JR: Carbohydrate ingestion, hypoglycemia, and obesity. *Appetite* 1985; 6:53–59.

12. Bray GA: Obesity: What comes first, in Angel A, Hollenberg CH, Roncari DAK (eds): *The Adipocyte and Obesity: Cellular and Molecular Mechanisms*. New York, Raven Press, 1983, pp 19–27.

13. Stellar E: The physiology of motivation. *Psychol Rev* 1954; 61:5–22.

14. Grossman SP: Contemporary problems concerning our understanding of brain mechanisms that regulate food intake and body weight, in Stunkard AJ, Stellar E (eds): *Eating and Its Disorders*. New York, Raven Press, 1984, pp 5–13.

15. Stern JS: Is obesity a disease of inactivity?, in Stunkard AJ, Stellar E (eds): *Eating and Its Disorders*. New York, Raven Press, 1984, pp 131–139.

16. Geiselman PJ, Novin D: The Role of carbohydrates in appetite, hunger, and obesity. *Appetite* 1982; 3:203–223.

17. Van Itallie TB, Smith NS, Quartermain D: Short-term and long-term components in the regulation of food intake: Evidence for a modulatory role of carbohydrate status. *Am J Clin Nutr* 1977; 30:742–757.

18. Panksepp J: Hypothalamic regulation of energy balance and feeding behavior. *Fed Proc* 1974; 33:1150–1165.

19. Novin D: The control of feeding: A reassessment, in Oomura Y (ed): *Emotions: Neuronal and Chemical Control*. Japan Scientific Societies Press, 1986, pp 3–13.

20. Hoebel BG: Neurotransmitters in the control of feeding and its rewards: Monoamines, opiates, and brain-gut peptides, in Stunkard AJ, Stellar E (eds): *Eating and Its Disorders*. New York, Raven Press, 1984, pp 15–38.

21. Sclafani A, Kirchgessner AL: The role of the medial hypothalamus in the control of food intake: An update, in Ritter RC, Ritter S, Barnes CD (eds): *Feeding Behavior: Neural and Humoral Controls*. New York, Academic Press Inc, 1986, pp 27–66.

22. Leibowitz SF: Hypothalamic catecholamine systems in relation to control of eating behavior and mechanisms of reward, in Hoebel BG, Novin D (eds): *The Neural Basis of Feeding and Reward*. Brunswick, Me, The Haer Institute, 1982, pp 241–257.

23. Leibowitz SF, Shor-Posner G: Brain serotonin and eating behavior. *Appetite* 1986; 7:1–14.

24. Shor-Posner G, Azar AP, Jhanwar-Uniyal M, et al: Destruction of noradrenergic innervation to the paraventricular nucleus: Deficits in food intake, macronutrient selection, and compensatory eating after food deprivation. *Pharmacol Biochem Behav* 1986; 25:381–392.

25. Myers RD, McCaleb ML: Feeding: Satiety signal from intestine triggers brain's noradrenergic mechanism. *Science* 1980; 209:1035–1037.

26. Morley JE, Levine AS: The central control of appetite. *Lancet* 1983; 398–401.

27. Fernstrom JD: Dietary effects on brain serotonin synthesis: Relationship to appetite regulation. *Am J Clin Nutr* 1985; 42:1072–1082.

28. Hyde TH, Eng R, Miselis RR: Brainstem mechanisms in hypothalamic and dietary obesity, in Hoebel BG, Novin D (eds): *The Neural Basis of Feeding and Reward*. Brunswick, Me, The Haer Institute, 1982, pp 97–114.

29. Sawchenko PE: Anatomic relationships between the paraventricular nucleus of the hypothalamus and visceral regulatory mechanisms: Implications for the control of feeding behavior, in Hoebel BG, Novin D (eds): *The Neural Basis of Feeding and Reward*. Brunswick, Me, The Haer Institute, 1982, pp 259–274.

30. Cannon WB, Washburn AL: An explanation of hunger. *Am J Physiol* 1912; 29:441–454.

31. Stunkard AJ, Fox S: The relationship of gastric motility and hunger: A summary of the evidence. *Psychosom Med* 1971; 33:123–134.

32. Van Itallie TB, VanderWeele DA: The phenomenon of satiety, in Bjorntorp P, Cairella M, Howard AN (eds): *Recent Advances in Obesity Research*. London, John Libbey & Co Ltd, 1981, vol 3, pp 278–289.

33. Deutsch JA: The stomach in food satiation and the regulation of appetite. *Prog Neurobio* 1978; 10:135–153.

34. McHugh PR, Moran TH: Calories and gastric emptying: A regulatory capacity with implications for feeding. *Am J Physiol* 1979; 236:R254–R260.

35. Hunt JN, Cash R, Newland P: Energy density of food, gastric emptying, and obesity. *Am J Clin Nutr* 1978; 31:S259–S260.

36. Duggan JP, Booth DA: Obesity, overeating, and rapid gastric emptying in rats with ventromedial hypothalamic lesions. *Science* 1986; 231:609–611.

37. Wright RA, Krinsky S, Fleeman C, et al: Gastric emptying and obesity. *Gastroenterology* 1983; 84:747–751.

38. Houpt KA: Gastrointestinal factors in hunger and satiety. *Neurosci Biobehav Rev* 1982; 6:145–164.

39. Mei N: Sensory structures in the viscera, in Ottoson D (ed): *Progress in Sensory Physiology.* Berlin, Springer-Verlag, 1983, pp 1–42.

40. Novin D, VanderWeele DA: Visceral mechanisms in feeding: There is more to regulation than the hypothalamus, in Sprague J, Epstein AN (eds): *Progress in Psychobiology and Physiological Psychology.* New York, Academic Press Inc, 1976, pp 193–241.

41. Gibbs J, Smith GP: Satiety: The roles of peptides from the stomach and the intestine. *Fed Proc* 1986; 45:1391–1395.

42. Smith GP: The therapeutic potential of cholecystokinin. *Int J Obes* 1984; 8:35–38.

43. Morley JE, Gosnell BA, Krahn DD, et al: Clinical implications of neurochemical mechanisms of appetite regulation. *Psychopharmacol Bull* 1985; 21:400–405.

44. Niijima A: Glucose-sensitive afferent nerve fibers in the liver and their role in food intake and blood glucose regulation. *J Auton Nerv Syst* 1983; 9:207–216.

45. Russek M: Current status of the hepatostatic theory of food intake control. *Appetite* 1981; 2:137–143.

46. Friedman MI, Stricker EM: The physiological psychology of hunger: A physiological perspective. *Psychol Rev* 1976; 83:409–431.

47. Novin D: The integration of visceral information in the control of feeding. *J Auton Nerv Syst* 1983; 9:233–245.

48. Kennedy GC: The role of depot fat in the hypothalamic control of food intake in the rat. *Proc R Soc Lond* [Biol] 1953; 140:578–592.

49. Liebelt RA, Bordelon CB, Liebelt AG: The adipose tissue system and food intake. *Progress in Physiological Psychology* 1973; 5:211–252.

50. Faust IM, Johnson PR, Hirsch J: Adipose tissue regeneration following lipectomy. *Science* 1977; 197:391–393.

51. Rosell S, Belfrage E: Blood circulation in adipose tissue. *Physiol Rev* 1979; 59:1078–1104.

52. Bray GA, Campfield LA: Metabolic factors in the control of energy stores. *Metabolism* 1975; 24:99–117.

53. Faust IM, Johnson PR, Hirsch J: Surgical removal of adipose tissue alters feeding behavior and the development of obesity in rats. *Science* 1977; 197:393–396.

54. Vasselli JR: Patterns of hyperphagia in the Zucker obese rat: A role for fat cell size and number? *Brain Res Bull* 1985; 14:633–641.

55. Faust IM: Nutrition and the fat cell. *International J Obesity* 1980; 4:314–321.

56. Faust IM, Johnson PR, Stern JS, et al: Diet-induced adipocyte number increases in adult rats: A new model for obesity. *Am J Physiol* 1978; 235:E279–E286.

57. Maggio CA, Greenwood MRC: Adipose tissue lipoprotein lipase (LPL) and triglyceride uptake in Zucker rats. *Physiol Behav* 1982; 29:1147–1152.

58. Brunzell JD, Greenwood MRC: Lipoprotein lipase and the regulation of body weight, in Curtis-Prior PB (ed): *Biochemical Pharmacology of Obesity.* Amsterdam, Elsevier, 1983, pp 175–199.

59. Woods SC, Porte D Jr: The central nervous system, pancreatic hormones, feeding, and obesity. *Advances in Metabolic Diseases* 1978; 9:283–312.

60. Woods SC, McKay J, Stein LJ, et al: Neuroendocrine regulation of food intake and body weight. *Brain Res Bull* 1980; 5:1–5.

61. Figlewicz DP, Dorsa DM, Stein LJ, et al: Brain and liver insulin binding is decreased in Zucker rats carrying the 'fa' gene. *Endocrinology* 1985; 117:1537–1543.

62. Bray GA: Integration of energy intake and expenditure in animals and man: The autonomic and adrenal hypothesis. *Clin Endocrinol Metab* 1984; 13:521–546.

63. Leibowitz SF, Roland CR, Hor L, et al: Noradrenergic feeding elicited via the paraventricular nucleus is dependent upon circulating corticosterone. *Physiol Behav* 1984; 32:857–864.

64. Jeanrenaud B: An hypothesis on the aetiology of obesity: Dysfunction of the central nervous system as a primary cause. *Diabetologia* 1985; 28:502–513.

65. Kulesza W: Dietary intake in obese women. *Appetite* 1982; 3:61–68.

66. Schachter S: Some extraordinary facts about obese humans and rats. *Am Psychol* 1971; 26:129–144.

67. Nisbett RE: Hunger, obesity, and the ventromedial hypothalamus. *Psychol Rev* 1972; 79:433–453.

68. Schachter S, Rodin J: *Obese Humans and Rats*. Potomac, Md, Erlabum, 1974.

69. Rodin J: Current status of the internal-external hypothesis for obesity: What went wrong. *Am Psychol* 1981; 36:361–372.

70. Herman CP, Polivy J: Restrained eating, in Stunkard AJ (ed): *Obesity*. Philadelphia, WB Saunders Co, 1980, pp 208–225.

71. Ruderman AJ: Dietary restraint: A theoretical and experimental review. *Psychol Bull* 1986; 99:247–262.

72. Maxfield E, Konishi F: Patterns of food intake and physical activity in obesity. *J Am Diet Assoc* 1966; 49:406–408.

73. Ries W: Feeding behavior in obesity. *Pro Nutr Soc* 1973; 32:187–193.

74. Drewnowski A, Brunzell JD, Sande K, et al: Sweet tooth reconsidered: Taste responsiveness in human obesity. *Physiol Behav* 1985; 35:617–622.

75. Cabanac M: Physiological role of pleasure. *Science* 1971; 173:1103–1107.

76. Grinker JA, Price JM, Greenwood MRC: Studies of taste in childhood obesity, in Novin D, Wyricka W, Bray G (eds): Hunger: Basic Mechanisms and Clinical Implications. New York, Raven Press, 1976, pp 441–457.

77. Rodin J, Moskowitz HR, Bray GA: Relationship between obesity, weight loss, and taste responsiveness. *Physiol Behav* 1976; 17:591–597.

78. Powley TL: The ventromedial hypothalamic syndrome, satiety and a cephalic phase hypothesis. *Psychol Rev* 1977; 84:89–126.

79. Nicolaïdis S: Rôle des réflexes anticipateurs orovégétatifs dans la régulation hydrominérale et énergétique. *J Physiol* [Paris] 1978; 74:1–19.

80. MacKay E, Callaway J, Barnes R: Hyperalimentation in normal animals produced by protamine insulin. *J Nutr* 1940; 20:59–66.

81. Rodin J: Insulin levels, hunger, and food intake: An example of feedback loops in body weight regulation. *Health Psychol* 1985; 4:1–24.

82. Simon C, Schlienger JL, Sapin R, et al: Cephalic phase insulin secretion in relation to food presentation in normal and overweight subjects. *Physiol Behav* 1986; 36:465–469.

83. Osuna JI, Pages I, Motino MA, et al: Cephalic phase of insulin secretion in obese women. *Horm Metab Res* 1986; 18:473–475.

84. Bellisle F, Louis-Sylvestre J, Demozay F, et al: Reflex insulin responses associated to food intake in human subjects. *Physiol Behav* 1983; 31:515–521.

85. Stunkard AJ: *Obesity*. Philadelphia, WB Saunders Co, 1980.

86. Levitsky DA, Strupp BJ, Lupoli J: Tolerance to anorectic drugs: Pharmacological or artifactual. *Pharmacol Biochem Behav* 1981; 14:661–667.

87. Stunkard AJ: Regulation of body weight and its implications for the treatment of obesity, in Carruba MO, Blundell JE (eds): *Pharmacology of Eating Disorders: Theoretical and Clinical Developments*. New York, Raven Press, 1986, pp 101–116.

88. Brindley DN: Phenylethylamines and their effects on the synthesis of fatty acids, triacylglycerols and phospholipids, in Curtis-Prior PB (ed): *Biochemical Pharmacology of Obesity*. Amsterdam, Elsevier, 1983, pp 285–308.

89. Beynen AC, Dekker D, van Tintelen G, et al: Body composition of obese rats fed the anorectic drug dexfenfluramine. *Nutrition Reports International* 1986; 33:491–497.

90. Hunsinger RN, Wilson MC: Anorectics and the set point theory for regulation of body weight. *Int J Obes* 1986; 10:205–210.

91. Donahoe Jr CT, Lin DH, Kirschenbaum DS, Keesey RE: Metabolic consequences of dieting and exercise in the treatment of obesity. *J Consult Clin Psychol* 1984; 52:827–836.

92. Young JC, Treadway JL, Balon TW, Gavras HP, Ruderman NB: Prior exercise potentiates the thermic effect of a carbohydrate load. *Metabolism* 1986; 35:1048–1053.

Chapter 3

Role of Hormones in the Etiology and Pathogenesis of Obesity

Diane R. Krieger and Lewis Landsberg

INTRODUCTION

Obesity is associated with many changes in endocrine function and endocrine function test results. The relation between these alterations and obesity is complex. Some of the endocrine changes of obesity are clearly secondary to the obese state itself; others may be the consequence of increased caloric intake. Identifying changes in endocrine function that are primary and that contribute to the development or maintenance of obesity is, therefore, problematic since primary changes may be subtle and difficult to distinguish from secondary ones. Classic endocrine dysfunction, such as hypothyroidism or hypercortisolism, is an infrequent cause of obesity in the general population, and in these cases the clinical picture is usually dominated by other characteristic features of the endocrinopathy.

The obvious cause of obesity is a chronic disequilibrium between energy intake and energy expenditure as set forth in the energy balance equation:

$$\text{Intake} - \text{Expenditure} = \text{Storage.}$$

At weight maintenance, when fat storage is stable, intake equals expenditure, and energy balance is achieved. It is obvious that the chronic disequilibrium between energy intake and energy expenditure that results in increased fat storage and obesity may result from either excessive intake or deficient expenditure. Since it has long been recognized that a variety of hormones affect either intake, expenditure, or both, an endocrine etiology for obesity has long been sought but

From Harvard Medical School and the Dana-Thorndike Laboratories, Department of Medicine, Division of Endocrinology and Metabolism, Beth Israel Hospital, Boston, MA 02215. Supported in part by USPHS grants AM20378, HL33697, HL37871, and AG00599.

never identified. Recent interest in the expenditure side of the energy balance equation, however, along with an increasing recognition of the potential importance of subtle regulated changes in metabolic rate have rekindled interest in the relation between hormonal status and obesity. For example, normal people differ in the range of dietary intakes over which energy balance can be maintained, and the difference cannot be obviously attributed to physical activity.[1,2] The argument that subtle alterations in metabolic rate contribute to obesity is strengthened by the recent finding of a genetic tendency to obesity[3] and by the demonstration of a familial association of low and high resting metabolic rates.[4] People with a "thrifty metabolic trait," or efficient metabolism, characterized by diminished thermogenic mechanisms, can withstand famine or starvation better than those with less efficient metabolism but are prone to obesity when faced with an abundant food supply. The search for a hormonal basis of obesity has intensified since hormones are known to influence metabolic rate and since the delineation of a hormonal contribution to alterations in metabolic rate in the obese has important therapeutic implications.

An additional problem in establishing an endocrine basis for obesity is the heterogeneous nature of the disorder. Etiologic factors involved in the development of one form of obesity may not be involved in others. Most studies have not segregated patients into appropriate subgroups, raising the possibility that meaningful changes in some patients may have been submerged by the inclusion of patients in whom the disorder is fundamentally different.

HORMONES AND THERMOGENESIS

Thermogenesis, or heat production, can be divided into two major compartments that are designated obligatory on the one hand and facultative on the other. These two compartments are divided into subdivisions that reflect diverse chemical processes and are regulated by different combinations of neural and humoral factors.[5] Obligatory thermogenesis represents the minimal heat produced by an organism maintained in the basal state. Basal or resting metabolic rate approximates this component. Obligatory thermogenesis has two major subdivisions. The first, referred to as essential thermogenesis, represents the energy produced by those reactions required to keep the organism in its basal state. Essential thermogenesis occurs in all living organisms. The second major component of obligatory thermogenesis, endothermic thermogenesis, is uniquely associated with the warm-blooded state. Endothermic thermogenesis represents an increment in metabolic rate that assures continuous stable heat production to maintain a constant body temperature and to permit thermoregulation by heat dissipation and heat production. The biochemical origins of endothermic thermogenesis are unclear, but it seems likely to represent a regulated increase in cellular respiration throughout the body. A major portion of endothermic thermogenesis depends on thyroid hormone;[6] catecholamines have a minor role.

Facultative thermogenesis represents heat produced in excess of that required to maintain the basal state. Unlike obligatory thermogenesis, it is highly variable and dependent on the external environment and the needs of the organism. Facultative thermogenesis is divided into several categories. The first is heat produced by skeletal muscle during exercise or shivering; catecholamines have only a permissive role in facilitating this type of thermogenesis. The second category is termed chemical thermogenesis to distinguish it from the thermogenesis that results from muscle contraction. It depends on the stimulation of specific exothermic reactions that use energy and produce heat. The adaptive form of chemical thermogenesis that occurs in the setting of cold exposure is designated nonshivering thermogenesis. More recently, an adaptive form of thermogenesis was identified in response to dietary intake and was designated dietary, or diet-induced, thermogenesis. This does not include specific dynamic action (or thermic effect of food), the heat produced during the metabolic disposition of ingested nutrient. Both nonshivering and diet-induced thermogenesis are regulated by the sympathetic nervous system (SNS). Thyroid and adrenal glucocorticoid may have permissive roles in this action.

SYMPATHETIC NERVOUS SYSTEM

The sympathoadrenal system consists of the adrenal medulla and the SNS. The adrenal medulla secretes the circulating hormone epinephrine, and the SNS innervates most body tissues so that norepinephrine (NE) (an adrenergic neurotransmitter) exerts its effect locally in the immediate vicinity of release. The sympathoadrenal system is of particular interest as a potential factor in the pathogenesis of obesity since (1) catecholamines have a critical role in the regulation of facultative thermogenesis, and (2) sympathoadrenal activity is profoundly affected by dietary intake.

Accurate assessment of SNS activity is problematic because only a small portion of NE released at nerve endings enters the circulation. Plasma and urinary NE, therefore, are only insensitive indicators of SNS activity.[7] In addition, neither urinary nor plasma catecholamine levels reflect the differing levels of sympathetic activity in various tissues. In rodents, SNS activity has been more closely estimated by measuring NE turnover in sympathetically innervated tissues. This technique uses injected labeled NE to assess transmitter renewal, which is proportional to neuronal activity. The use of this technique in laboratory rodents has established a relation between dietary intake and SNS activity.

The first determination of the influence of diet on SNS activity was made in 1977 with the demonstration that fasting and caloric restriction suppress the SNS in laboratory rodents.[8] The same seems to be true in humans. In both obese and lean human subjects, measurements of plasma NE levels and urinary NE metabolites during fasting and semistarvation point to a decrease in SNS activity.[9-12] While suppressing SNS activity in humans, fasting seems to stimulate the adrenal medulla modestly, as reflected by increased urinary epinephrine.[9,13] The concurrent suppression of sympathetic activity and the small increase in adrenal medullary activity are adaptive responses to starvation. When food is in short supply, metabolic activity decreases to conserve fuel. An increase in epinephrine, on the other hand, fosters substrate mobilization since the small increment in epinephrine output is sufficient to stimulate lipolysis during fasting[14,15] but insufficient to increase metabolic rate.[16]

The observation of the effect of fasting on SNS activity has led to investigations of the effects of various dietary components on sympathetic activity. High-calorie diets of mixed composition were shown to stimulate SNS activity in rats.[17] Similar observations were made in humans overfed a mixed diet for 10 days.[18] Again using the NE-turnover technique, a variety of refined carbohydrates were found to stimulate SNS activity in laboratory rodents.[19-23] SNS activity is increased by these sugars, even when total calories are not increased.[24] There is evidence that carbohydrate increases SNS activity in humans as well since the standard glucose tolerance test increases plasma NE in normal human subjects,[25-27] although the specificity of this response has been questioned.[28] Of greater importance is the fact that simultaneous infusions of glucose and insulin increase SNS activity in humans.[29-31] Dietary fat increases SNS activity in the rodent,[24] an effect demonstrable even when caloric intake is not increased.[24] The response of human subjects to fat has not been well studied, although a single high-fat meal is apparently without effect on plasma NE in human subjects.[27]

Protein seems to be different from sucrose and fat in its effect on the SNS in that it does not stimulate sympathetic activity.[32] Consequently, diets low in protein increase SNS activity since the relative proportion of carbohydrate and fat in such diets is higher.[33]

The fact that diet influences SNS activity means that the CNS must have a mechanism capable of assessing dietary intake and coupling it with sympathetic outflow. The signals linking dietary intake to SNS activity are not fully clarified. There is much evidence to suggest an important role for insulin-mediated glucose metabolism in sensitive neurons in the ventromedial hypothalamus.[29,34]

While the suppressive effect of fasting results in an adaptive energy-conserving decrease in metabolic rate, the stimulatory effect of overfeeding may also serve an adaptive function by allowing the dissipation of excess calories as heat. In a protein-deficient environment, an organism with this capacity could consume larger amounts of a low-protein diet necessary to satisfy basic nitrogen requirements. The excess calories would be dissipated as heat, and obesity would be avoided.

The significance of these diet-induced changes in SNS activity, therefore, lies in the connection between diet and energy expenditure. In rodents, the SNS participates in the control of facultative thermogenesis generated in response to diet and cold.[35,36] This heat seems to be produced by brown adipose tissue (BAT), an organ richly innervated by sympathetic nerves. The hypertrophy of BAT observed when rodents are exposed to cold or overfeeding[37] and the demonstration of alterations of SNS activity in BAT produced by dietary manipulation support a role for the SNS in dietary-induced thermogenesis. Although it is clear that catecholamines stimulate metabolic rate in humans,[38] a role for BAT has not been conclusively demonstrated.

The involvement of the sympathoadrenal system in dietary-induced thermogenesis suggests a role for this system in the regulation of body weight. The capacity to dissipate calories consumed in excess of need would confer resistance to the development of obesity. A defect in this ability could cause a predisposition to weight gain. Furthermore, adaptive decreases in SNS activity during therapeutic semistarvation could antagonize weight loss and reduce treatment effectiveness. There is much evidence that impaired sympathetic function in BAT explains the predisposition to obesity in rodent models of genetic obesity, particularly the ob/ob (obese) mouse and the fa/fa, or Zucker (fatty), rat.[39] The increased metabolic efficiency of these animals causes them to gain excess body fat on a normal intake.[39] The existence of genetic obesity in animals has led to a search for a similar "thrifty metabolic trait" in humans.

The most commonly studied animal model of genetic obesity is the ob/ob mouse. In addition to obesity, its defects include an inability to withstand cold, hyperinsulinemia, hyperphagia,[39] and inability to generate heat in response to overfeeding.[40] The impaired BAT responses to NE in this animal have been attributed in part to an impaired sympathetic drive.[41] The abnormal thermogenic activity predates the obesity, making it unlikely to be a consequence of either the obesity or the hyperphagia. Technical and conceptual limitations have made it difficult to establish the existence of a similar SNS-related thermogenic defect in obese humans. Of foremost importance is the lack of a technique for directly assessing SNS activity in humans. Methods currently employed to estimate SNS activity involve the measurement of urinary and plasma catecholamines; the limitations of these measurements, however, preclude the demonstration of a subtle defect.[7,42]

Since the SNS has a critical role in regulating adaptive thermogenesis, evidence of SNS involvement has frequently been inferred from evidence suggesting alterations in thermogenesis in obese animals and humans. While such inferences are clearly erroneous, the close association of catecholamines and the regulatory component of thermogenesis raises the possibility of adrenergic involvement in deficient thermogenic responses in obese animals and humans. In both the ob/ob mouse and the fa/fa rat, sympathetic outflow to BAT as well as BAT responses to normal stimuli are deficient.[41,43-45] In the ob/ob mouse, responses to both cold and dietary stimuli are altered; the fa/fa rat responds relatively normally to cold but abnormally to diet. In obese human subjects, no definite abnormalities of the SNS have been established; various reports[46] suggest that sympathetic activity may be normal, overactive, or underactive. Difficulty in accurately assessing sympathetic activity in humans, coupled with the likelihood that obesity is not a single homogeneous disorder, contributes to this uncertainty. Furthermore, although catecholamines clearly stimulate metabolic rate in humans,[38] the site of catecholamine-stimulated thermogenesis in humans is uncertain. While BAT comprises 2% to 5% of body weight in human neonates,[39] this tissue diminishes with age. The functional significance of BAT in adult humans remains uncertain,[30,39] although an important role has not been excluded.

Another problem in assessing sympathetically mediated thermogenesis in the obese is the difficulty inherent in accurately comparing the metabolic rates of lean and obese people. In the first place, metabolic rate is determined in part by body size and degree of adiposity. If metabolic rate is expressed per unit of weight, obese people exhibit a lower rate than control subjects. If it is expressed per unit of fat-free mass, the obese and the lean have similar metabolic rates.[47] Neither expression is entirely satisfactory since adipose tissue has a lower metabolic rate than lean body mass. Second, possible compensatory mechanisms, recruited to oppose a thermogenic defect in the obese, may confound a comparison between the lean and the obese if studies are carried out in the obese (compensated) state.

As a result, the available data comparing the lean and the obese with regard to thermic responses are confusing and contradictory. Metabolic rate has been reported to be low or high, as noted above, depending on the denominator employed to express caloric expenditure. When oxygen consumption (VO_2) in response to NE was measured in lean and obese people in an attempt to compare sensitivity with SNS stimulation, conflicting results were obtained. One report[48] showed a lesser rise in VO_2 with NE in the obese, with similar impairments found in the reduced obese. The failure of this response to normalize with weight loss has been used to support the hypothesis that a thermogenic defect underlies the obesity in some people.[48] Others[49] have refuted these conclusions by demonstrating comparable thermic responses to NE in the lean and the obese. The divergent results may reflect differences in the doses of NE infused,[49] as well as the heterogeneous nature of the obese population.

It is not now possible to state whether or not the obese have deficient sympathetically mediated thermogenesis. Recent studies[50,51] clearly raise the possibility that some obese people may have a defect in dietary thermogenesis and that such a defect, operative over a long period of time, could account for the development of obesity. It seems clear that dietary thermogenesis is reduced in at least some subpopulations of obese people, and since dietary thermogenesis seems to be mediated by the SNS,[30,31] this defect may involve sympathetic activity. Whether this is a defect in sympathetic activation, responsiveness to NE, or some other component of the thermogenic mechanism remains uncertain.

Pharmacologic stimulation of thermogenesis by adrenergic agonists has been well demonstrated in humans. Ephedrine, a drug known to suppress appetite, also has thermogenic properties.[52] In rats and mice, weight loss promoted by ephedrine has been thought to result from increased thermogenesis and not from decreased intake.[52] The thermogenic effects of this drug seem to increase over prolonged treatment, in contrast with the cardiovascular effects of ephedrine, which show substantial desensitization.[52] Methylxanthines, another class of drugs with thermogenic properties,[53] when administered with ephedrine were shown to be effective in increasing metabolic rate and lowering body fat in a mouse model of obesity.[53] Further study of the safety and efficacy of these treatments in humans is required.

THYROID HORMONE

The contribution of thyroid hormones to thermogenesis is difficult to separate from that of the SNS because the thyroid and the SNS are intimately related.[54] The thyroid gland itself is richly ennervated by sympathetic nerves. Thyroid hormone modulates tissue responsiveness to catecholamines, as hyperthyroidism is associated with increased responsiveness to the beta-adrenergic effects of infused catecholamines, and hypothyroidism is associated with a decrease in this responsiveness.[54] BAT, the main effector site for SNS-mediated thermogenesis, is rich in 5'-deiodinase,[55] the enzyme that controls the peripheral conversion of thyroxine (T_4) to triiodothyronine (T_3). NE influences enzyme activity in BAT[56] by an alpha-receptor mechanism.

One experimental method used in rodents to distinguish the impact of thyroid hormone on thermogenesis from that of the SNS is to measure and compare minimum oxygen consumption (MOC) and resting oxygen consumption (ROC). MOC represents thyroid-sensitive thermogenesis or obligatory heat production, while ROC is sensitive to diet-induced SNS activity and includes MOC.[57] In response to fasting, only the ROC diminishes.[57] The T_3 level does not influence this response to fasting,[58] consistent with a role for SNS withdrawal. MOC does not decrease with fasting, implying a major role of thyroid hormone in the regulation of basal metabolism.[58] The experimental use of beta-adrenergic stimulators and blockers supports the predominant role of the SNS and the facilitory role of thyroid hormone in mediating the response of metabolic rate to diet. T_3

is required for MOC response to isoprel, a beta agonist.[57] Beta blockade with propanolol inhibits the increase in metabolic rate induced by cafeteria-feeding rats as well as the increase in T_3 and metabolic rate in refed rats.[6] Beta blockade also decreases resting metabolic rate (analogous to ROC) in obese humans on a high-energy (but not on a low-energy) diet.[59]

An additional problem is the difficulty in determining subtle changes in thyroid function. Although gross hypo- or hyperfunction is easy to distinguish from normal function by simple assays of hormone levels, significant changes in the deiodination of T_4 to T_3 in particular tissues may not be reflected in altered plasma levels although they have significant effects on physiologic responses.

While thyroid hormone is the main endocrine regulator of essential thermogenesis, a more important role for thyroid hormone in the pathophysiology of obesity may involve its function as a facilitator of SNS-regulated facultative thermogenesis. Like the SNS, thyroid hormone is sensitive to dietary intake. Fasting produces a decrease in T_3, the metabolically active thyroid hormone,[60,61] that parallels the decrease in metabolic rate with fasting.[62] T_4 responds less consistently to fasting and was shown to increase[63] or decrease.[64] The decrease in T_3 results from a decrease in the peripheral conversion of T_4 to T_3.[65]

With overfeeding, the increase in metabolic rate is paralleled by an elevation in T_3.[62] T_4 is unaffected.[62] The T_3 response is determined by dietary composition as well as caloric intake.[62,63] While short-term overfeeding of all dietary components increases T_3[62] over the long-term, only carbohydrate has this effect in humans.[62] In refeeding studies, when starved obese subjects were refed hypocaloric diets, only mixed and carbohydrate diets elevated T_3, returning it to baseline.[63] Refeeding protein has no effect on T_3 in obese humans.[63]

Most evidence indicates that diet-induced changes of thyroid function are not the major cause of parallel changes in metabolic rate.[6,57] Rather, thyroid hormone seems to be permissive for the actions of the SNS in the adaptation of metabolic rate to nutritional state.[6,57] These diet-induced changes in the peripheral conversion of T_4 to T_3 parallel changes in sympathetic activity. Decreased peripheral conversion during fasting would potentiate the decrease in metabolic rate occasioned by SNS withdrawal. Conversely, increased peripheral conversion would augment the thermic response to increased sympathetic activity with overfeeding.

The effects of diet on the hypothalamic pituitary control of thyroid hormone production are less clear. A transient decrease in thyroid-stimulating hormone (TSH) is sometimes seen in the fasted obese,[63] but other studies[64] show no change. Despite the low T_3 level reached during fasting, a blunted response of TSH to thyrotropin-releasing hormone (TRH) is seen.[63] A similar blunted response is also observed with overfeeding.[62] These subtle alterations of hypothalamic pituitary function are of uncertain significance, but the blunted TSH response during fasting suggests a centrally regulated decrease in TSH output during caloric restriction.

A subtle defect in the facilitory effect of thyroid hormone on heat production may be one of the predisposing factors to excessive weight gain in a subset of the obese population. In the ob/ob mouse, although the defect in cold and diet-induced thermogenesis is explained by abnormalities in SNS-related thermogenesis,[41,44,45] when T_3 is administered, the ob/ob mouse exhibits an improved thermogenic response to NE and BAT responsiveness to cold.[6] It is possible that this rodent fails to respond to its normal levels of T_3, and this resistance contributes to insensitivity of BAT to NE in this model. That the ob/ob mouse responds to doses of T_3 that have no effect on lean mice further suggests at least a partial resistance to endogenous T_3.[6] This may be partially explained by a decrease in nuclear T_3 receptors seen in the liver and lung tissues of the ob/ob mouse.[66] Another possible thyroid-related thermogenic defect in this animal is its diminished sodium potassium–adenosine triphosphatase (ATPase) pump activity in liver, muscle, and BAT.[6] T_3 administration increases the amount but not the activity of this enzyme, suggesting partial resistance to T_3. This defect, however, is thought to have a small effect on overall thermogenesis and not to contribute to the animal's obesity.[6] Of greater significance is the recently described defect in the type II deiodinase present in BAT that is responsible for the peripheral conversion of T_4 to T_3 in this tissue.[67,68] Deficient local generation of T_3 may contribute to the poor thermogenic response of BAT to NE in the ob/ob mouse. The deiodinase deficiency, on the other hand, may be related in part to decreased SNS activity since treatments that increase SNS activity over time partially restore BAT thermogenesis.[41]

Vague similarities between thyroid function in the ob/ob mouse and in obese humans have been noted.[6] As in the ob/ob mouse, clinical euthyroidism has been observed in obese humans even when metabolic rate is low.[69] In the Pima Indian, a genetically homogeneous group prone to obesity, the decreased thyroid-sensitive red blood cell (RBC) sodium potassium–ATPase pump is inversely related to body weight.[70] Care must be taken in interpreting this finding, however, as a similar decrease is also seen in hyperthyroid people and in those with anemia or malaria.[70] It is still possible, however, that a partial refractoriness to T_3 or deficient conversion of T_4 to T_3 in some critical thermogenic tissue contributes to enhanced metabolic efficiency in obese humans.

Gross thyroid hypofunction is an infrequent etiology of human obesity, and thyroid function test findings are usually normal in obese humans.[71] Elevations in T_3 have been noted in some obese people and may be correlated with body weight.[72] These elevations in T_3 may represent merely high-calorie or high-carbohydrate intakes before the study.

Despite the uncertain relation between the thyroid and the etiology of obesity, thyroid hormones have been used for many years in the treatment of obesity. This treatment was shown to have serious adverse side effects and to be of questionable long-term effectiveness. Pharmacologic doses of T_3 or T_4 used alone or in combination with low-calorie dieting almost always cause an increased weight loss as compared with control subjects.[73] Since the heart is particularly responsive to thyroid hormone, the doses of T_3 or T_4 usually used to promote weight loss can have adverse cardiovascular effects, including tachycardia and elevations of systolic blood pressure.[74] There are also reports of atrial fibrillation and angina during treatment of obesity with thyroid hormone.[74] In one series,[75] 50% of the obese patients treated with thyroid hormone who had tachycardia were asymptomatic, implying that failure to sense the adverse physiologic effects of the treatment might prevent reporting and hence early diagnosis and treatment.

Other problems with thyroid treatment have been reported as well. First, weight loss was found to be unsustained when thyroid hormone was used.[74] This may be attributed to an increase in appetite, which may persist even after the drug is discontinued, or to an increase in fatigue, which leads to a decrease in physical activity.[74] Second, calcium balance may be disturbed during thyroid-hormone treatment. Increases in urinary calcium loss were reported after 3 weeks of high-dose T_3 treatment.[74] Even smaller doses of the thyroid hormone may potentiate the development of osteoporosis. This may be worrisome for those already on low-calcium diets for reducing.

The use of T_3 has been suggested as an adjunct to very-low-calorie diets to counteract some of the decrease in metabolic rate seen with semistarvation.[76] However, objections to this course of treatment have been raised because the increased weight loss with T_3 supplementation has been attributed to the loss of lean body mass rather than fat.[74,75] Bray et al[75] studied obese subjects on a low-calorie diet with 150 to 225 μg of supplemental T_3 and showed that more than 80% of the weight loss was accounted for by loss of protein. Lower doses (30 μg) of T_3 have been used in combination with small doses of T_4 and low-calorie diets.[76] While resting metabolic rate rose toward baseline with this regimen, nitrogen losses were not measured. In other reports,[76] nitrogen losses with low doses of T_3 were variable. The erosion of lean body mass may be prevented by supplemental protein[73] or anabolic steroids,[75] but these additions may reduce the rate of weight loss. It has been suggested that the decrease of T_3 during semistarvation serves an adaptive function by decreasing muscle proteolysis and sparing protein.[6] Replacement doses of T_3 may reverse this adaptive response, explaining the loss of lean body mass.

ADRENAL CORTEX

Observations that glucocorticoid excess leads to positive energy balance and deficiency leads to negative energy balance have led to the investigation of a role for glucocorticoids in the pathophysiology of obesity. A subtle relation between glucocorticoids and the regulation of body weight in rodents has begun to be elucidated by observations of the effects of removal of this hormone by adrenalectomy.[77-79] These observations show that glucocorticoids are required for the phenotypic expression of obesity in two rodent models.[80] Hyperphagia and weight gain in both the ob/ob mouse and the fa/fa rat are prevented by adrenalectomy and are restored by the administration of corticosteroids.[77,80] The difference in cortisol metabolism between lean and fa/fa rats does not seem to be linked to the hypothalamic-pituitary-adrenal axis, as morning and evening cortisol levels and ACTH levels are the same in both groups.[78] However, these animals seem to differ in their sensitivity to exogenous corticosterone.[78] While progesterone (an agent known to increase food intake) causes weight gain in both lean and fatty rats, treatment with corticosterone causes greater weight gain in the adrenalectomized fatty rat than in the adrenalectomized lean rat.[78] This leads to the suspicion that the fatty rat has an enhanced sensitivity to corticosterone.[78]

Adrenalectomy not only lowers food intake to normal[80] but also decreases metabolic efficiency in both genetically obese rodents.[77] The change in metabolic efficiency induced by adrenalectomy seems to be limited to dietary-induced thermogenesis.[80] In the fa/fa rat, adrenalectomy results in a decrease in metabolic efficiency primarily related to increases in VO_2 with feeding.[78] This increase in oxygen consumption is thought to be secondary to increased activity of BAT.[77] Similarly, adrenalectomy in the ob/ob mouse causes an increase in NE turnover in BAT, but does not reverse the hypothermia or reproductive abnormalities of this rodent.[80]

Thus, glucocorticoids may impair BAT sensitivity to diet-induced SNS stimulation.[77] In both types of genetically obese rodents, the normalization of NE turnover in BAT suggests that normalization of SNS activity occurs in the absence of glucocorticoids.[77] The relation between glucocorticoids and the SNS is further supported by observations that beta blockade prevents the increase in BAT mitochondrial activity in the adrenalectomized fa/fa rat.[77] This decreased diet-induced BAT thermogenesis in the fa/fa rat may result from corticosterone-dependent inhibition of SNS activation. While the mechanism for this is unclear, there are several possibilities, including inhibition of afferent dietary signals to the hypothalamus and inhibition of coupling of afferent information to sympathetic output.[77] The relation of adrenalectomy to a decrease in insulin levels in these genetically obese rodents has led to suggestions of insulin involvement in this mechanism.[77] Thermogenic properties of ACTH in rats have been reported,[81] and the possibility exists that the effects of adrenalectomy and corticosterone treatment may be attributable to secondary changes in ACTH release.[81]

Glucocorticoids may also have a role in the regulation of appetite and food intake. Adrenalectomy prevents the hyperphagia caused by injection of NE into the ventromedial hypothalamus[78] as well as the hyperphagia and weight gain in mice with gold thioglucose–induced necrosis of the ventromedial hypothala-mus.[79] Adrenalectomy also prevents the hyperphagia normally seen in the fa/fa rat and in diabetic mice.[78] Removing glucocorticoids in diabetic mice by adre-nalectomy reverses their insensitivity to gold thioglucose hypothalamic destruc-tion,[82] possibly by enhancing the sensitivity of these mice to low insulin levels.

While glucocorticoids seem to have a permissive role in both dietary-induced thermogenesis and the control of food intake in the CNS in animals, there is no evidence of a similar role in humans. There are, however, slight alterations in cortisol metabolism in the obese human that are generally thought to be secondary to the obese state.[83] In obese humans, cortisol production and clearance rate are elevated.[84] This is reflected by normal plasma cortisol levels and by an increase in the cortisol metabolite 17-hydroxycorticosterone. However, both cortisol pro-duction rates[85] and levels of 17-hydroxysteroids[86] normalize when corrected for body weight in the healthy obese. It has been suggested that accelerated cortisol metabolism may lead to a slight increase in ACTH output, causing an increase in cortisol production.[84] However, others argue that there is some impairment of the regulation of ACTH output rather than increased cortisol metabolism in the obese. The blunted action of methoximine, an alpha agonist and probable ACTH stimulant, is cited in support of this theory.[87]

These alterations in cortisol metabolism have implications for the laboratory evaluation of obese patients. The frequent association of obesity (particularly central) with diabetes and hypertension results in the assessment of these patients for Cushing's syndrome. The overnight dexamethasone suppression test, a useful screen for Cushing's syndrome, can show abnormalities in approximately 10% of the healthy obese.[86] This is probably a result of increased metabolism of the drug. In these cases, Cushing's syndrome can be ruled out with the standard 2-day dexamethasone suppression test during which adequate blood levels can be achieved. A reliable laboratory test for differentiating simple obesity from obesity secondary to Cushing's syndrome is the urinary free cortisol test.[86]

GROWTH HORMONE

Basal serum growth hormone levels are low in obese subjects.[84] Various stimuli of growth hormone release including sleep, arginine, L-dopa, exercise, hypoglycemia, and growth hormone releasing factor[88] elicit a blunted response in the obese.[89,90] This alteration in growth hormone output seems to be directly related to degree of adiposity.[88] Beta-adrenergic blockade with propranolol re-sults in normal growth hormone responsiveness to L-dopa in the obese.[90] This suggests an enhanced beta-adrenergic inhibition of growth hormone release in obesity of unclear significance.[90]

These abnormalities of growth hormone dynamics are generally regarded to be secondary to the obese state.[89,91] Weight loss usually produces a return of growth hormone responsiveness toward normal,[91] and overfed lean control subjects develop blunted growth hormone responses.[84] However, there is scanty evidence that growth hormone alterations reflect an underlying metabolic characteristic that precedes obesity.[92] Not all obese subjects regain growth hormone responsiveness with weight loss.[91,92] Some of this subgroup also fail to increase serum NE levels with hypoglycemia.[92] This suggests an alteration in hypothalamic control of growth hormone output as well as SNS activity that may be related to the predisposition to obesity.[92] Similarly, in the ob/ob mouse, growth hormone levels are low before the onset of obesity,[92] again suggesting that hypothalamic abnormalities precede rapid weight gain and may be linked to the thermogenic defects seen in this animal.

The physiologic significance of diminished growth hormone responsiveness is not clear. Linear growth is normal in obesity, probably as a result of normal somatomedin levels.[71] Production of this growth-promoting polypeptide is probably stimulated by the elevated insulin levels in obesity. The obese exhibit normal sensitivity to the calorigenic and lipolytic actions of growth hormone.[84] However, the elevated insulin–to–growth hormone ratio[93] seen in the obese may serve as a powerful force against weight reduction, as insulin promotes fat storage and growth hormone encourages lipolysis.

Growth hormone's calorigenic and lipolytic effects[94,95] have led to investigations of its use as a weight-reducing agent.[74] When added to a short-term regimen of T_3, it reduces nitrogen losses while increasing oxygen consumption, but weight reduction proceeds at a slower rate than with T_3 alone.[96] Long-term efficacy and safety have not been established. Potential problems include exacerbation of glucose intolerance and development of insulin resistance.[74]

INSULIN

Human obesity and many forms of experimental animal obesity are characterized by increased insulin levels, insensitivity to insulin, and decreased binding to insulin receptors. These abnormalities, although well recognized, are incompletely understood. The primary defect in insulin metabolism is not established. There are several possibilities. First, a decrease in insulin receptor number, with a concomitant decrease in insulin sensitivity, could result in compensatory increased circulating insulin.[97] Second, primary elevations in circulating insulin levels have shown to "down regulate" receptor number. (Conversely, decreasing insulin levels experimentally with streptozotocin or diazoxide increases receptor number in rats.)[98] Third, a defect in "postreceptor" or intracellular insulin metabolism has been proposed.[99] Other possible contributors to insulin resistance in the obese include decreased hepatic insulin clearance[100] and increased adipose cell size with associated insensitivity to insulin.[101-103] There is some evidence that the basic abnormality is different in different tissues,[97] with liver and muscle exhibiting decreased insulin binding and adipocytes exhibiting defective intracellular metabolism.

Hyperinsulinemia may be attributable in part to dietary influences,[104] with both calories and diet composition influencing the insulin secretory pattern.[104] Carbohydrate as well as fat stimulates increased glucose uptake by adipose cells.[105] In humans, hypocaloric diets are associated with low insulin levels when carbohydrate content is low, and normal insulin levels when carbohydrate content is high.[104] In rats, low-carbohydrate diets result in blunted insulin secretion.[104] Finally, starvation, both acute and chronic, results in increased insulin binding.[106]

Despite increased basal insulin levels and hyper-responsiveness to secretagogues,[104] most obese people have adequate insulin reserves and can maintain normal glucose uptake and metabolism. When reserve is insufficient, Type II diabetes mellitus develops. There is a greater incidence of diabetes with the android, or upper body, pattern of obesity. This body habitus is also associated with higher insulin levels, possibly related to the greater sensitivity of central fat cells to the effects of hormones on lipid deposition,[107] as well as to increased insulin resistance.

Since insulin resistance is reversible with weight loss and inducible with weight gain,[105] it is considered to be secondary to the obese state. In one rodent model of obesity, however, experimentally induced by a hypothalamic lesion, insulin excess may be causally related to weight gain.[108] In these rodents, hyperinsulinemia predates the obesity.[108] When their pancreatic beta cells are removed from vagal control and transplanted to other parts of the body, the hyperinsulinemia and weight gain are reversed.[108] This suggests that insulin is causally related to the weight gain. While hyperinsulinemia is a prominent feature of hypothalamic obesity in humans, a causal link has not been established.[71]

Insulin, nonetheless, through its relationship with the SNS, may have a role in the regulation of energy expenditure. The thermogenic response to NE is diminished in diabetic animals.[109] An increase in oxygen consumption is seen in diabetic cafeteria-fed rodents only if insulin is provided shortly before the measurement.[109] Nondiabetic animals do not exhibit an increase in oxygen consumption with insulin administration, perhaps because their endogenous insulin has sufficiently stimulated this response or, possibly, the development of hypoglycemia.

There is also evidence that insulin is a direct stimulator of the SNS in humans,[29] as plasma NE increases when insulin and glucose are infused simultaneously to maintain a normal glucose level.[29] Insulin is also known to cause an increase in heat production in humans.[30,31,110] This rise is prevented by propranolol, a beta-adrenergic blocker, again supporting the relation between insulin and the SNS.[110]

Finally, autopsy studies of the BAT of obese infants of diabetic mothers revealed abnormal BAT histology, indicating impaired function.[39] Maternal insulin levels may have induced this abnormality, illustrating a direct effect of insulin on BAT.

The high levels of insulin in obese subjects may excessively stimulate SNS activity and in turn contribute to the hypertension seen in these people. This hypothesis requires further study.[111]

CONCLUSION

Thus, the available evidence does not exclude a hormonally mediated defect in thermogenesis in some obese humans. Further studies require the identification of appropriate subgroups of obese people and the application of precise biochemical and physiologic techniques capable of distinguishing subtle defects in hormonal regulation. Such a defect in hormonally mediated thermogenesis might involve (1) decreased SNS activity, (2) impaired insulin-mediated thermogenesis, (3) primary hyperinsulinemia with associated stimulation of lipogenesis, and (4) deficient peripheral conversion of T_4 to T_3 in a thermogenically important tissue. These areas warrant further study in a reduced-obese population in whom the confounding effects of obesity itself can be avoided.

Whether or not hormonally mediated deficits in thermogenesis exist in the obese, it is clear that both suppression of sympathetic activity and diminished peripheral conversion of T_4 to T_3 during caloric restriction are associated with a decrease in metabolic rate and therefore diminish the effectiveness of low-energy diets and antagonize weight loss. Physiologic or pharmacologic modes of counteracting this conservative metabolic response may ultimately be helpful, as an adjunct to dieting, in the treatment of obesity.

REFERENCES

1. Miller DS, Mumford P: Gluttony: I. An experimental study of overeating on high protein diets. *Am J Clin Nutr* 1967; 20:1212–1222.

2. Sims EAH, Danforth E, Horton ES, et al: Endocrine and metabolic effects of experimental obesity in man. *Recent Prog Horm Res* 1973; 29:457–496.

3. Stunkard AJ, Sorensen TIA, Hanis C, et al: An adoption study of human obesity. *N Engl J Med* 1986; 314:193–198.

4. Bogardus C, Lillioga S, Ravussin E, et al: Familial dependence of the resting metabolic rate. *N Engl J Med* 1986; 315:96–100.

5. Nicholls D, Locke R: Cellular mechanisms of heat dissipation, in Girardier L, Stock MJ (eds): *Mammalian Thermogenesis.* London, Chapman & Hall, 1983, pp 8–49.

6. Himms-Hagen J: Thyroid hormones and thermogenesis, in Girardier L, Stock MJ (eds): *Mammalian Thermogenesis.* London, Chapman & Hall, 1983.

7. Landsberg L, Young JB: Assessment of sympathetic nervous activity from measurements of noradrenaline turnover in rats, in Joseph MH (ed): *Monitoring Neurotransmitter Release during Behavior.* Chichester, England, Ellis Horwood Ltd, 1986, pp 33–47.

8. Young JB, Landsberg L: Suppression of sympathetic nervous system during fasting. *Science* 1977; 196:1473–1475.

9. Young JB, Rosa RM, Landsberg L: Dissociation of sympathetic nervous system and adrenal medullary responses. *Am J Physiol* 1984; 247:E35–E40.

10. Jung RT, Shetty PS, Barrand M, et al: Role of catecholamines in hypotensive response to dieting. *Br Med J* 1979; 1:12–13.

11. Gross HA, Lake CR, Ebert MH, et al: Catecholamine metabolism in primary anorexia nervosa. *J Clin Endocrinol Metab* 1979; 49:805–809.

12. DeHaven J, Sherwin R, Hendler R, et al: Nitrogen and sodium balance and sympathetic-nervous-system activity in obese subjects treated with a low-calorie protein or mixed diet. *N Engl J Med* 1980; 302:477–482.

13. Palmblad J, Levi L, Burger A, et al: Effects of total energy withdrawal (fasting) on the levels of growth hormone, thyrotropin, cortisol, adrenaline, noradrenaline, T_4, T_3, and rT_3 in healthy males. *Acta Med Scand* 1977; 201:15–22.

14. Galster AD, Clutter WE, Cryer PE, et al: Epinephrine plasma thresholds for lipolytic effects in man: Measurements of fatty acid transport with (1-13C) palmitic acid. *J Clin Invest* 1981; 67:1729–1738.

15. Arner P, Engfeldt P, Nowak J: In vivo observations on the lipolytic effect of noradrenaline during therapeutic fasting. *J Clin Endocrinol Metab* 1981; 53:1207–1212.

16. Sjostrom L, Schutz Y, Gudinchet F, et al: Epinephrine sensitivity with respect to metabolic rate and other variables in women. *Am J Physiol* 1983; 245:E431–E442.

17. Young JB, Saville ME, Rothwell NJ, et al: Effect of diet and cold exposure on norepinephrine turnover in brown adipose tissue in the rat. *J Clin Invest* 1982; 69:1061–1071.

18. O'Dea K, Esler M, Leonard P, et al: Noradrenaline turnover during under- and over-eating in normal weight subjects. *Metabolism* 1982; 31:896–899.

19. Young JB, Landsberg L: Effect of diet and cold exposure on norepinephrine turnover in pancreas and liver. *Am J Physiol* 1979; 236:E524–E533.

20. Rappaport EB, Young JB, Landsberg L: Impact of age on basal and diet-induced changes in sympathetic nervous system activity of Fischer rats. *J Gerontol* 1981; 36:152–157.

21. Rappaport EB, Young JB, Landsberg L: Initiation, duration and dissipation of diet-induced changes in sympathetic nervous system activity in the rat. *Metabolism* 1982; 31:143–146.

22. Young JB, Landsberg L: Stimulation of the sympathetic nervous system during sucrose feeding. *Nature* 1977; 269:615–617.

23. Walgren MC, Kaufman LN, Young JB, et al: The effects of various carbohydrates on sympathetic activity in heart and interscapular brown adipose tissue (IBAT) of the rat. *Metabolism* 1987; 36:585–594.

24. Schwartz JH, Young JB, Landsberg L: Effect of dietary fat on sympathetic nervous system activity in the rat. *J Clin Invest* 1983; 72:361–370.

25. Young JB, Rowe JW, Pallotta JA, et al: Enhanced plasma norepinephrine response to upright posture and glucose administration in elderly human subjects. *Metabolism* 1980; 29:532–539.

26. Welle S, Lilavivathana U, Campbell RG: Increased plasma norepinephrine concentrations and metabolic rates following glucose ingestion in man. *Metabolism* 1980; 29:806–809.

27. Welle S, Lilavivathana U, Campbell RG: Thermic effect of feeding in man: Increased plasma norepinephrine levels following glucose but not protein or fat consumption. *Metabolism* 1981; 30:953–958.

28. Tse TF, Clutter WE, Shah SD, et al: Neuroendocrine responses to glucose ingestion in man: Specificity, temporal relationships, and quantitative aspects. *J Clin Invest* 1983; 72:270–277.

29. Rowe JW, Young JB, Minaker KL, et al: Effect of insulin and glucose infusions on sympathetic nervous system activity in normal man. *Diabetes* 1981; 30:219–224.

30. Acheson K, Jequier E, Wahren J: Influence of beta-adrenergic blockade on glucose-induced thermogenesis in man. *J Clin Invest* 1983; 72:981–986.

31. Acheson KJ, Ravussin E, Wahren J, et al: Thermic effect of glucose in man. *J Clin Invest* 1984; 74:1572–1580.

32. Kaufman LN, Young JB, Landsberg L: Effect of protein on sympathetic nervous system activity in the rat: Evidence for nutrient-specific responses. *J Clin Invest* 1986; 77:551–558.

33. Young JB, Kaufman LN, Saville ME, et al: Increased sympathetic nervous system activity in rats fed a low protein diet: Evidence against a role for dietary tyrosine. *Am J Physiol* 1985; 248:R627–R637.

34. Landsberg L, Young JB: Insulin-mediated glucose metabolism in the relationship between dietary intake and sympathetic nervous system activity. *Int J Obes* 1985; 9 (suppl):63–68.

35. Landsberg L, Young JB: Autonomic regulation of thermogenesis, in Girardier L, Stock MJ (eds): *Mammalian Thermogenesis*. London, Chapman & Hall, 1983, pp 99–140.

36. Landsberg L, Young JB: The role of the sympathoadrenal system in modulating energy expenditure. *Clin Endocrinol Metab* 1984; 13:475–499.

37. Rothwell NJ, Stock MJ: Diet-induced thermogenesis, in Girardier L, Stock MJ (eds): *Mammalian Thermogenesis*. London, Chapman & Hall, 1983, pp 208–233.

38. Katzeff HL, O'Connell M, Horton ES, et al: Metabolic studies in human obesity during overnutrition and under nutrition: Thermogenic and hormonal responses to norepinephrine. *Metabolism* 1986; 35:166–175.

39. Trayhurn P, James WPT: Thermogenesis and obesity, in Girardier L, Stock MJ (eds): *Mammalian Thermogenesis*. London, Chapman & Hall, 1983, pp 234–258.

40. Himms-Hagen J: Thermogenesis in brown adipose tissue as an energy buffer: Implications for obesity. *N Engl J Med* 1984; 311:1549–1558.

41. Himms-Hagen J: Brown adipose tissue metabolism and thermogenesis. *Ann Rev Nutr* 1985; 5:69–94.

42. Hjemdahl P: Measurements of plasma catecholamines by HPLC and the relation of their concentrations to sympathoadrenal activity, in Fillenz M, Macdonald IA, Marsden CA (eds): *Monitoring Neurotransmitter Release during Behaviour*. Chichester, England, Ellis Horwood Ltd, 1986, pp 17–32.

43. Triandafillou J, Himms-Hagen J: Brown adipose tissue in genetically obese (fa/fa) rats: Response to cold and diet. *Am J Physiol* 1983; 244:E145–E150.

44. Zaror-Behrens G, Himms-Hagen J: Cold-stimulated sympathetic activity in brown adipose tissue of obese (ob/ob) mice. *Am J Physiol* 1983; 244:E361–E366.

45. Young JB, Landsberg L: Diminished sympathetic nervous system activity in genetically obese (ob/ob) mouse. *Am J Physiol* 1983; 245:E148–E154.

46. Kush RD, Young JB, Danforth E Jr, et al: Effect of diet on energy expenditure and plasma norepinephrine in lean and obese Pima Indians. *Metabolism*, to be published.

47. Schutz Y, Bessard T, Jequier E: Diet-induced thermogenesis measured over a whole day in obese and nonobese women. *Am J Clin Nutr* 1984; 40:542–552.

48. Jung RT, Shetty PS, James WPT, et al: Reduced thermogenesis in obesity. *Nature* 1979; 279:322–323.

49. Katzeff HL, Daniels R: The sympathetic nervous system in human obesity. *Int J Obes* 1985; 9:131–137.

50. Jequier E: Energy expenditure in obesity. *Clin Endocrinol Metab* 1984; 13:563–580.

51. Jequier E, Schutz Y: Does a defect in energy metabolism contribute to human obesity?, in Hirsch J, Van Itallie, TB (eds): *Recent Advances in Obesity Research*. London, John Libbey & Co Ltd, pp 76–81.

52. Astrup A, Lundsgaard C, Madsen J, et al: Enhanced thermogenic responsiveness during chronic ephedrine treatment in man. *Am J Clin Nutr* 1985; 42:83–94.

53. Dulloo AG, Miller DS: The thermogenic properties of ephedrine/methylxanthine mixtures: Animals studies. *Am J Clin Nutr* 1986; 43:388–394.

54. Danforth E, Burger A: The role of thyroid hormones in the control of energy expenditure. *Clin Endocrinol Metab* 1984; 13:581–595.

55. Leonard JL, Mellen SA, Larsen PR: Thyroxine 5'-deiodinase activity in brown adipose tissue. *Endocrinology* 1983; 112:1153–1155.

56. Silva JE, Larsen PR: Adrenergic activation of triiodothyronine production in brown adipose tissue. *Nature* 1983; 305:712–713.

57. Danforth E Jr, Burger GA: Hormonal control of thermogenesis, in Cioffi, LA (ed): *The Body Weight Regulatory System: Normal and Disturbed Mechanisms*. New York, Raven Press, 1981, pp 107–114.

58. Wimpfheimer C, Saville E, Voirol MJ, et al: Starvation-induced decreased sensitivity of resting metabolic rate to triiodothyronine. *Science* 1979; 205:1272–1273.

59. Jung RT, Shetty PS, James WPT: The effect of beta-adrenergic blockade on metabolic rate and peripheral thyroid metabolism in obesity. *Eur J Clin Invest* 1980; 10:179–182.

60. Wilcox RG: Triiodothyronine, TSH, and prolactin in obese women. *Lancet* 1977; 1:1027–1029.

61. Visser TJ, Lamberts SWJ, Wilson JHP, et al: Serum thyroid hormone concentrations during prolonged reduction of dietary intake. *Metabolism* 1978; 27:405–409.

62. Danforth E Jr, Horton ES, O'Connell M, et al: Dietary-induced alterations in thyroid hormone metabolism during overnutrition. *J Clin Invest* 1979; 64:1336–1347.

63. Azizi F: Effect of dietary composition on fasting-induced changes in serum thyroid hormones and thyrotropin. *Metabolism* 1978; 27:935–942.

64. Carlson HE, Drenick EJ, Chopra IJ, et al: Alterations in basal TRH-stimulated serum levels of thyrotropin, prolactin, and thyroid hormones in starved obese men. *J Clin Endocrinol Metab* 1977; 45:707–713.

65. Vagenakis AG, Portnay GI, O'Brian JT, et al: Effect of starvation on the production and metabolism of thyroxine and triiodothyronine in euthyroid obese patients. *J Clin Endocrinol Metab* 1977; 45:1305–1309.

66. Guernsey DL, Morishige WK: Na$^+$ pump activity and nuclear T3 receptors in tissues of genetically obese (ob/ob) mice. *Metabolism* 1979; 28:629–632.

67. Kates AL, Himms-Hagen J: Defective cold-induced stimulation of thyroxine 5'-deiodinase in brown adipose tissue of the genetically obese (ob/ob) mouse. *Biochem Biophys Res Commun* 1985; 130:188–193.

68. Kaplan MM, Young JB: Abnormal thyroid hormone deiodination in tissues of ob/ob and db/db obese mice. *Endocrinology* 1987; to be published.

69. Miller DS, Parsonage S: Resistance to slimming: Adaptation or illusion? *Lancet* 1975; 1:773–775.

70. Klimes L, Nagulesparan M, Unger RH, et al: Reduced Na$^+$, K$^+$ -ATPase activity in intact red cells and isolated membranes from obese man. *J Clin Endocrinol Metab* 1982; 54:721–724.

71. Foster DW: Eating disorders: Obesity and anorexia nervosa, in Wilson JD, Foster DW (eds): *Williams Textbook of Endocrinology*. Philadelphia, WB Saunders Co, 1985, pp 1081–1107.

72. Bray GA, Fisher DA, Chopra IJ: Relation of thyroid hormones to body-weight. *Lancet* 1976; 1:1206–1208.

73. Lamki L, Ezrin C, Koven I, et al: L-thyroxine in the treatment of obesity without increase in loss of lean body mass. *Metabolism* 1973; 22:617–622.

74. Rivlin RS: Drug therapy: Therapy of obesity with hormones. *N Engl J Med* 1975; 292:26–29.

75. Bray GA, Melvin KEW, Chopra IJ: Effect of triiodothyronine on some metabolic responses of obese patients. *Am J Clin Nutr* 1973; 26:715–721.

76. Welle SL, Campbell RG: Decrease in resting metabolic rate during rapid weight loss is reversed by low dose thyroid hormone treatment. *Metabolism* 1986; 35:289–291.

77. York DA, Holt SJ, Marchington D: Regulation of brown adipose tissue thermogenesis by corticosterone in obese fa/fa rats. *Int J Obes* 1985; 9:89–95.

78. Yukimura Y, Bray GA, Wolfsen AR: Some effects of adrenalectomy in the fatty rat. *Endocrinology* 1978; 103:1924–1928.

79. Debons AF, Siclari E, Das KC, et al: Gold thioglucose–induced hypothalamic damage, hyperphagia, and obesity: Dependence on the adrenal gland. *Endocrinology* 1982; 110:2024–2029.

80. Bray GA: Integration of energy intake and expenditure in animals and man: The autonomic and adrenal hypothesis. *Clin Endocrinol Metab* 1984; 13:521–545.

81. Rothwell NJ, Stock MJ: Acute and chronic effects of ACTH on thermogenesis and brown adipose tissue in the rat. *Comp Biochem Physiol* 1985; 81A:99–102.

82. Debons AF, Krimky I, From A, et al: Diabetes induced resistance of ventromedial hypothalamus to damage by gold thioglucose: Reversal by adrenalectomy. *Endocrinology* 1794; 95:1636–1641.

83. O'Connell M, Danforth E Jr, Horton ES, et al: Experimental obesity in man: III. Adrenocortical function. *J Clin Endocrinol Metab* 1973; 36:323–329.

84. Glass AR, Burman KD, Dahms WT, et al: Endocrine function in human obesity. *Metabolism* 1981; 30:89–104.

85. Cheek DB, Graystone JE, Seamark RF, et al: Urinary steroid metabolites and the overgrowth of lean and fat tissues in obese girls. *Am J Clin Nutr* 1981; 34:1804–1810.

86. Crapo L: Cushing's syndrome: A review of diagnostic tests. *Metabolism* 1979; 28:955–977.

87. Laurian L, Oberman Z, Hoerer E, et al: Low cortisol and growth hormone secretion in response to methoxamine administration in obese subjects. *Israel J Med Sci* 1977; 13:477–481.

88. Kalkhoff R, Ferrou C: Metabolic differences between overweight and muscular overweight men. *N Engl J Med* 1971; 284:1236–1239.

89. Fingerhut M, Krieger DT: Plasma growth hormone response to L-dopa in obese subjects. *Metabolism* 1974; 23:267–271.

90. Barbarino A, De Marinis L, Troncone L: Growth hormone response to propranolol and L-dopa in obese subjects. *Metabolism* 1978; 27:275–278.

91. Ball MF, El-Khodary AZ, Canary JJ: Growth hormone response in the thinned obese. *J Clin Endocrinol Metab* 1972; 34:498.

92. Jung RT, James WPT, Campbell RG, et al: Altered hypothalamic and sympathetic responses to hypoglycaemia in familial obesity. *Lancet* 1983; 1:1043–1046.

93. Meistas MT, Foster GV, Margolis S, et al: Integrated concentrations of growth hormone, insulin, c-peptide and prolactin in human obesity. *Metabolism* 1982; 31:1224–1228.

94. Bray GA: Calorigenic effect of human growth hormone in obesity. *J Clin Endocrinol Metab* 1969; 29:119–122.

95. Evans ES, Simpson ME, Evans HM: The role of growth hormone in calorigenesis and thyroid function. *Endocrinology* 1958; 63:836–852.

96. Bray GA, Raben MS, Londono J, et al: Effects of triiodothyronine, growth hormone and anabolic steroids on nitrogen excretion and oxygen consumption of obese patients. *J Clin Endocrinol Metab* 1977; 33:293–300.

97. Olefsky JM: The insulin receptor: Its role in insulin resistance of obesity and diabetes. *Diabetes* 1976; 25:1154–1162.

98. Kahn CR: Role of insulin receptors in insulin-resistant states. *Metabolism* 1980; 29:455–466.

99. Crettaz M, Jeanrenaud B: Postreceptor alterations in the states of insulin resistance. *Metabolism* 1980; 29:467–473.

100. Smith U: Regional differences in adipocyte metabolism and possible consequences *in vivo*, in Hirsch J, Van Itallie TB (eds): *Recent Advances in Obesity Research: IV. Proceedings of the 4th International Congress on Obesity*. London, John Libbey & Co Ltd, 1983, pp 33–36.

101. Salans L, Knittle J, Hirsch J: The role of adipose cell size and adipose tissue insulin sensitivity in the carbohydrate intolerance of human obesity. *J Clin Invest* 1968; 47:153–165.

102. Stern J, Batchelor B, Hollander N, et al: Adipose-cell size and immunoreactive insulin levels in obese and normal weight adults. *Lancet* 1968; 2:948–951.

103. Sjostrom L: Adult human adipose tissue cellularity and metabolism. *Acta Med Scand* 544(suppl):1–52.

104. Grey N, Kipnis DM: Effect of diet composition on the hyperinsulinemia of obesity. *N Engl J Med* 1971; 285:827–831.

105. Salans LB, Bray GA, Cushman SW, et al: Glucose metabolism and the response to insulin by human adipose tissue in spontaneous and experimental obesity. *J Clin Invest* 1974; 53:848–856.

106. Kolterman OG, Saekow M, Olefsky JM: The effects of acute and chronic starvation on insulin binding to isolated human adipocytes. *J Clin Endocrinol Metab* 1979; 48:836–842.

107. Kissebah AH, Vydelingum N, Murray R, et al: Relation of body fat distribution to metabolic complications of obesity. *J Clin Endocrinol Metab* 1982; 54:254–260.

108. Inoue S, Bray GA, Mullen YS: Transplantation of pancreatic B-cells prevents development of hypothalamic obesity in rats. *Am J Physiol* 1978; 235:E266–E271.

109. Rothwell NJ, Stock MJ: A role for insulin in the diet-induced thermogenesis of cafeteria-fed rats. *Metabolism* 1981; 30:673–678.

110. Bennett T, Gale EAM, Green J, et al: The influence of beta-adrenoreceptor antagonists on thermoregulation during insulin-induced hypoglycaemia. *J Physiol* 1980; 308:26–31P.

111. Landsberg L: Diet, obesity and hypertension: An hypothesis involving insulin, the sympathetic nervous system, and adaptive thermogenesis. *Q J Med* 1986; 61:1081–1090.

Chapter 4

Energy Metabolism and Thermogenesis in Obesity

Harvey L. Katzeff

INTRODUCTION

Most people realize that obesity is produced by a caloric intake in excess of caloric expenditure. The equation

$$\text{Calorie intake} - \text{Calorie expenditure} = \text{Calorie excess}$$

is a basic law of thermodynamics and cannot be altered. In many people, chronic excessive caloric intake is the primary cause of obesity, but a subset of the obese store calories more efficiently than lean people. Scientists have hypothesized that the ability to be more metabolically efficient, ie, to be able to store a greater proportion of ingested calories as fat, confers on these people the ability to survive famines. In industrialized societies, in which energy expenditure is decreased and food is abundant, a genetic trait causing increased metabolic efficiency would predispose afflicted people to develop obesity and noninsulin-dependent diabetes mellitus.[1] In contrast, people who are genetically lean gain less weight during periods of overfeeding by expending a portion of the excess calories ingested as heat. Alterations of the activity of the sympathetic nervous system (SNS) and thyroid hormone metabolism in response to nutritional alterations may be responsible for this adaption.

This chapter reviews the knowledge of the possible differences between lean and obese people in energy expenditure and energy metabolism as they relate to the development and maintenance of obesity. The regulation of body weight with respect to food intake and energy expenditure is discussed. Last, strategies to prevent obesity by caloric restriction and maintenance of reduced weight are reviewed.

ENERGY METABOLISM

The Fed State

Humans, like all mammals, eat only for a small portion of the day. It is during the period 1 to 6 hours after each meal when calorie absorption exceeds calorie expenditure that storage of calories is possible. One frequently asked question is: Do obese people store calories differently than lean people after a given meal? This is a very complex question since calories may be stored as either carbohydrates (glycogen), proteins, or triglycerides (fat). The human body can store only a limited amount of glycogen; approximately 100 to 200 g. Glycogen stores in liver and muscle are filled within 48 hours of overfeeding. If a person then continues to ingest calories in excess of energy expenditure, these excess calories are stored as either protein or fat. Glucose theoretically can be used for fat synthesis (de novo lipogenesis), but this is energetically a very wasteful process and has not been recognized during normal feeding with the exception of total parenteral nutrition. Recently, investigators learned that oral and intravenous glucose ingestion stimulates the release of norepinephrine (NE) from the peripheral SNS via insulin release.[2,3] This release of NE is associated with a small rise in resting metabolic rate (RMR). Obese people are insulin resistant and have lower plasma NE levels after glucose ingestion, which may contribute to a lower thermic response to food.

During both fasting and feeding, protein synthesis and catabolism are continuous. It is only during the postprandial period that the rate of protein synthesis exceeds the rate of protein catabolism. Since the body is unable to store amino acids, the amino acids ingested in a meal are either metabolized to glucose or used for protein synthesis. The synthesis of new protein chains uses almost 24% of the energy content of the amino acids because it requires several adenosine triphosphate (ATP) molecules to make one peptide bond.

The regulation of protein synthesis is complex and multifactorial. One of the rate-limiting factors is the protein source ingested. Human beings must ingest the proper ratio of essential-to-nonessential amino acids to allow protein synthesis to occur at the maximum rate. If poor-biologic-quality protein (low in essential amino acids) is ingested, then less protein is synthesized, and the extra calories are stored as fat. This is uncommon in developed or industrialized nations, but does occur in undeveloped countries where the sources of protein are poor. This nutritional state is named *kwashiorkor*, or protein malnutrition, and leads to abnormalities in immunity, respiratory function, muscle strength, etc.[4]

During overnutrition of both protein and calories, protein synthesis proceeds at a maximum rate determined by genetic factors, exercise, and hormone levels. Genetic factors are important determinants of whether the excess calories ingested are used for protein synthesis or stored as fat. Genetic factors are also important in the regulation of exercise-stimulated protein synthesis. Exercise can stimulate protein synthesis and produce a marked increase in muscle mass, but there is considerable variability in the amount of muscle gained. Just examine the mess halls of the armed forces or professional football teams. The average caloric intake of army recruits can exceed 5,000 calories. Yet upon completion of training, the recruits have lost fat and have gained muscle mass. Similarly, players who would be considered obese by weight-to-height tables have only a small percentage of body fat and an extremely high muscle mass.[5]

Hormones also have an important role in protein synthesis. Anabolic steroids secreted by both the adrenal gland and testes, or converted from estrone in adipose tissue, are potent stimulators of protein synthesis. The lower concentrations in blood of these hormones is a major reason why women have lower muscle mass–height ratios than men. Exercising women can increase their muscle mass to a level equal to sedentary men with a strenuous exercise program, but the average woman has less muscle mass than the average man of the same height.[6] This is an important point to remember when the regulation of resting energy expenditure is discussed.

The concentrations of thyroid hormones, insulin, and insulin-like growth factors in blood are all dependent on the level of caloric intake, and the hormonal response to excess caloric intake differs between lean and obese people. Obese people frequently have increased plasma insulin increments in response to similar caloric challenges, and insulin is a potent stimulator of both protein and triglyceride synthesis. However, it is still not clear whether the increased insulin response to a meal alters the ratio of protein-to-triglyceride synthesis. Studies of triglyceride synthesis rates in vivo indicate that the increased concentration of insulin in blood accelerates triglyceride synthesis in obese people when compared with similar caloric intake in lean people.[7] Although insulin levels return to normal during weight loss, it is not known whether genetically preobese people have higher insulin levels or triglyceride synthesis rates than their genetically lean counterparts. Longitudinal studies in genetically preobese people (ie, Pima Indians) are presently underway and may provide answers to these questions.

There is a marked variability in the ratio of protein-to-fat that is synthesized during weight gain. People who spontaneously gain a high proportion of protein during overfeeding will alter their metabolism in two ways:

1. waste calories in the production of proteins rather than storage of triglycerides
2. increase their lean body mass.

An increase in lean body mass will produce a rise in the RMR of a given person. People who gain protein instead of fat mass during overfeeding will then expend a greater proportion of ingested calories than people who add only fat mass.

This difference in protein synthesis and lean body mass could produce differences in weight-gain efficiency.

Exercise not only increases energy expenditure but also alters body composition to increase energy expenditure further. It seems that women are less likely to gain lean body mass during overnutrition, unless they exercise, because of hormonal differences. Although differences in protein-to-fat accretion exist in obesity, present techniques are not sensitive enough to measure the increase in lean body mass during short-term overfeeding experiments. Thus, while the regulation of protein synthesis is possibly important in the pathogenesis of obesity, further research into protein synthesis and body composition during overfeeding using improved methods will need to be performed to understand the regulation of lean body mass.

The body stores of triglyceride are produced from two sources. The first is long-chain triglycerides, absorbed from the gastrointestinal tract and then attached to chylomicrons via the lymphatic system. This triglyceride is removed by the enzyme lipoprotein lipase (LPL) and is stored in adipose cells. The second source of triglyceride is the endogenous production of triglyceride from esterification of free fatty acids in the liver. These triglycerides are secreted into the blood attached to very-light-density lipoprotein particles and are also removed by adipose tissue LPL and stored in fat cells. While triglycerides absorbed through the gastrointestinal tract are simply stored as fat, the liver regulates triglyceride synthesis and, subsequently, the rate of fat deposition during the postprandial period.

Triglyceride synthesis in the liver is different between lean and obese people. One important difference is in the precursor pool required for triglyceride synthesis; the precursors, free fatty acids and glycerol, are present in greater quantities in obese people.[8] Also, triglyceride synthesis is dependent on the plasma insulin level, which is increased in obesity. These findings suggest that obese people synthesize more triglyceride during overfeeding compared with lean people because of a combination of a large precursor pool and increased insulin levels in blood.

In summary, in the postprandial period, both protein and triglyceride are stored in muscle and fat tissue to allow for survival during the fasting state. Protein and triglyceride storage is under multifactorial regulation including genetic factors, exercise, and hormonal responses to meals. Abnormal responses of insulin and the SNS to carbohydrate may alter the ratio of protein-to-fat storage and the thermic response to a meal. These factors can contribute to excessive fat deposition during periods of overnutrition.

Fasting State

While the elevated insulin levels of the postprandial period suppress glycogen and fat oxidation by the liver and adipose tissue 6 to 8 hours after a meal, when insulin levels decline, there is a shift in the metabolic fuels used by the body. During this time, in addition to the carbohydrate and fat ingested in the meal, previously synthesized fuel sources are used. Glycogen and protein are both converted to glucose to maintain the fasting blood glucose level. In addition, lipolysis in adipose tissue produces free fatty acids. During prolonged fasting or chronic severe caloric restriction, there is a marked decrease in protein catabolism and an increase in the relative proportion of free fatty acids used as an energy source. Studies[9] indicate that obese people are better able to tolerate prolonged caloric restriction by conserving lean body mass. Since the oxidation of free fatty acids is more efficient than the use of protein for gluconeogenesis, this will promote a lower rate of weight loss.

THERMOGENESIS

Thermogenesis is defined as the expenditure of calories as either work or heat and is usually divided into several components:

- resting metabolic rate (RMR)
- thermic effect of food (TEF)
- thermic effect of exercise (TEE)
- adaptive thermogenesis (AT).

Resting Metabolic Rate

Numerous scientists have studied the question: Do obese people expend calories in a different manner than lean people? One difficulty has been the appropriate yardstick with which to compare lean and obese people. Researchers have learned that the RMR measured after a 12-hour overnight fast is most directly correlated to the fat-free, or lean, body mass of a person.[10] Since overweight people have a greater lean body mass than lean people of similar sex and height, their RMR is greater. This does *not* mean, however, that their total daily energy expenditure is greater.

The concept that the RMR is proportional to lean body mass has renewed interest in the regulation of lean body mass. Generally, women have a lower lean body mass–height ratio than men.[6] In addition, aging produces a fall in lean body mass.[11] Women in the postmenopausal period have a greater fall in lean body mass compared with age-matched men, probably because men continue to secrete androgens. Exercise seems to help prevent the decline in lean body mass caused by aging in both men and women, but cannot reverse the process completely.

In addition to lean body mass, the RMR is regulated by the concentration and production rates of several hormones. The two most important are thyroid hormones, specifically triiodothyronine (T_3) and the peripheral SNS release of NE. Epinephrine, released from the adrenal glands in response to a stress stimulus, does not seem to be important in the control of RMR.[12]

Hypothyroidism has been a well-recognized cause of decreased metabolic rate. Although many obese patients blame an "underactive" thyroid gland for their obesity, data suggest otherwise. In numerous studies[13] of obese people who are weight stable, levels of both thyroxine (T_4) and T_3 are normal. In addition, hypothyroidism usually produces a decline in RMR of 10% to 15%. For an average woman weighing 60 kg, this is approximately 150 calories/day. In classic experiments by the German physiologist Neumann,[14] a change in the caloric balance of this magnitude produces a change in weight of just several kilograms until the new weight equilibrium between energy intake and expenditure is reached. This is because there is an increase in energy expenditure secondary to the increase in weight. Hypothyroid people may increase their fat mass, but hypothyroidism is not the cause of significant obesity. Hyperthyroidism increases energy expenditures and produces weight loss but produces a catabolic state in which a greater proportion of protein is lost than with caloric restriction alone.[15] For this reason, thyroid supplementation for weight loss is unsafe and should be avoided.

NE is also a potent stimulator of thermogenesis. NE acts by stimulating the breakdown of stored triglyceride into free fatty acids, which are then oxidized. NE also stimulates the breakdown of glycogen to glucose and its subsequent oxidation. After an overnight fast, the activity of NE may account for approximately 5% of the RMR.[16] Although initial studies suggest that sensitivity to NE is abnormal in obese humans, more comprehensive studies[17] indicate that NE sensitivity in the obese is normal during periods of both underfeeding and overfeeding as well as during weight maintenance. Studies[18,19] in obese men and women are conflicting as to whether NE secretion is abnormal during weight maintenance or altered nutritional states. Further studies are underway to determine NE action in lean and obese people. Another difference between lean and obese humans is a small but consistent difference in the respiratory quotient after an overnight fast.[20] The lower respiratory quotient of obese people is indicative of a higher proportion of free fatty acids and lipids as the energy source as opposed to carbohydrates in obese people. The clinical significance of a lower respiratory quotient in obese humans during weight maintenance is unclear, but the greater use of fat as an energy source during caloric restriction may help maintain lean body mass and prolong survival.

To summarize, the RMR in obese people during weight maintenance is apparently normal and proportional to the lean body mass of the person. In men and young women, obesity is frequently associated with an increase in lean body mass compared with age- and height-matched lean control subjects, and the absolute RMR is therefore elevated. Female sex and aging are each associated with a lower proportion of lean body mass and decrease the number of calories required to maintain weight. This indicates that the age-associated decline in RMR predisposes older people to weight gain if food intake is not decreased.

Thermic Effect of Food

The thermic effect of a mixed meal has both obligatory and facultative components. The obligatory component consists of energy expended for mechanical digestion, a secondary rise in cardiac output, and the thermogenic cost of synthesizing glycogen, proteins, and triglycerides in the postprandial period. The TEF was initially named *the specific dynamic action* and was thought to be attributable to the oxidation of protein alone. However, carbohydrate and fat as well as protein consumption produces elevations in the metabolic rate for several hours after a meal. The rise in metabolic rate is approximately 10% in response to glucose, 5% in response to fat, and 20% in response to protein. The lower thermic response to carbohydrate and fat ingestion is because less energy is required to store carbohydrate as glycogen, and fat as triglyceride than to synthesize peptide bonds between amino acids. The average meal contains approximately 40% fat, 40% carbohydrate, and 20% protein; the mean rise in energy expenditure above baseline is approximately 7% to 10% of the caloric content of the meal.

In addition to the obligatory cost of digesting and storing the ingested calories, several facultative processes stimulate thermogenesis in the postprandial period. Recent studies[2,3] have focused on the stimulation of the peripheral SNS by carbohydrate ingestion as a contributor to postprandial thermogenesis. Oral glucose administration and intravenous glucose-insulin infusions elevate plasma NE levels and increase metabolic rates to a greater extent than predicted by the metabolic cost of synthesizing glycogen from glucose. Acute propranolol administration decreases the thermic effect of both oral and intravenous glucose by approximately 20%, suggesting that beta-adrenergic stimulation in the postprandial state is a contributor to the thermic response to glucose in lean people.[18]

There have been numerous publications on the thermic effect of either glucose or a mixed meal in obesity, and although subject to much controversy, the data suggest that obese people have a slightly lower thermic response to food.[21] The difference in energy expenditure between lean and obese humans is small (1% to 2% of ingested calories), but over a period of years this caloric difference may be substantial. The lower thermic response to a meal seems to be proportional to the degree of insulin resistance present in a person. Insulin resistance also suppresses the plasma NE response to glucose. Obese people may have a lower

TEF because of facultative differences such as the insulin and NE response to a meal. Overfeeding worsens and weight loss improves these defects, suggesting that a lower thermic response is a secondary defect that helps maintain the obese state.

Thermic Effect of Exercise

The TEE is less controversial: it takes more energy for an obese person to walk or run compared with a lean person since the work performed is dependent on the total weight of the person. Bicycle riding is different from walking in that the work is external (moving the pedal against resistance), and the only difference between lean and obese people is the weight of their legs. During bicycle riding against zero resistance, obese people expend slightly more calories than lean people because of their larger leg mass. When pedaling against increasing grades of resistance (Figure 4-1), the increase in caloric expenditure (the slope: calories/work) is equal. Obese people are not more or less efficient when performing work. What is frequently true however is that they have an apparent economy of movement, which produces a lower caloric expenditure than lean people performing the same work. A classic study was performed with teenage girls, both lean and obese, who were playing volleyball together. In the study of their physical activity it was noted that the obese women had much less arm and leg movement during the game and expended fewer calories.[22] New research, using indirect calorimetry rooms to measure 24-hour energy expenditure, have developed the concept that spontaneous physical movement, "fidgeting," may be an important determinant of 24-hour energy expenditure.[23] The thermic effect of fidgeting was calculated as the total energy expenditure minus the sum of RMR plus TEF. People were placed in a room approximately 8 ft by 10 ft, given their meals there, and their 24-hour energy expenditure was measured. Since their ability to perform vigorous physical activity was restricted, their spontaneous physical movements, walking around the room, lying in bed, etc, were considered to be fidgeting. The results are fascinating: there were marked differences in degree of spontaneous physical activity between persons that accounted for up to 1,000 calories/day of energy expenditure. Thus it is possible for obese people with a higher RMR to have a lower 24-hour energy expenditure if they are less physically active, including fidgeting. Further work is indicated to support these findings, but they provoke interesting ideas for increasing energy expenditure during the day.

Other new work suggests that exercise in the postprandial period may expend more calories than either the TEF or similar exercise in the fasting state. This difference is small, and it is not known whether obese people also increase their energy expenditure during postprandial exercise.

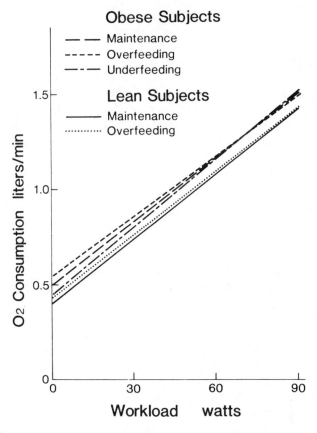

Figure 4-1 Increase in Caloric Expenditure with Increased Pedal Resistance

Adaptive Thermogenesis

Caloric Excess

The TEF is the acute response to caloric intake, and the AT is the chronic response to the level of caloric intake. It is the area of AT that has produced the major controversy and interest among obesity researchers. In 1902, Neumann[14] performed experiments on himself whereby he raised and lowered his daily caloric intake (500 to 1,000 calories) for several months at a time. He noted an immediate change in weight, but there was soon a stabilization at a new weight only several kilograms above or below the initial weight. He thought that his body adapted to the changes in caloric intake by either raising or lowering energy expenditure and named that process *luxus consumption*.[14] This theory fell into disrepute, but was revived and renamed *adaptive thermogenesis* in the 1960s after a series of overfeeding and cold acclimation experiments.

Sims and colleagues[24] at The University of Vermont overfed normally lean male prisoners for 4 to 6 months until the volunteers gained 25% of their initial body weight. These volunteers were not allowed to alter their exercise behavior, and yet there was marked variability in the level of caloric intake required to achieve the weight. The subjects then required an average of 2,700 kcal/m^2 to maintain their obese state compared with 1,300 to 2,100 kcal/m^2 for spontaneously obese men. The investigators concluded that normally lean men adapted to chronic overfeeding by increasing their energy expenditure during both overfeeding and their new obese state.

Overfeeding for 3 to 4 weeks produces several hormonal responses in lean men. Insulin secretion and insulin resistance both increase, the conversion of T_4 to T_3, its active metabolite, rises dramatically, and SNS activity may increase.[25] These changes have the effect of increasing both protein synthesis and thermogenesis. They also may increase metabolic pathways that expend calories but produce no useful work, the so-called futile cycles. But futile cycles have not been proven to expend significant quantities of calories.

In lean humans, RMR rises 7% to 10% within 10 days of overfeeding 1,000 to 1,500 calories/day.[17,18] This increase is greater than any conceivable increase in lean body mass and suggests that AT is present. Five obese women and one obese man were overfed 1,000 calories/day for 3 weeks, and the magnitude of the increase in RMR was lower than that observed in lean men. Obese and control lean Pima Indians had similar responses to overfeeding, but the rise in metabolic rate was lower than in lean whites.[26] These findings suggest that obese and genetically preobese people may have a smaller increment in RMR during overfeeding than normal people.

Overfeeding does not alter the TEF or the TEE in lean humans, but overfeeding may decrease the TEF in obese humans. Combining the differences in RMR and TEF observed during overfeeding of 1,000 kcal/day between lean and obese humans produces a difference of 200 calories/day in the 24-hour energy expenditure of lean humans. This difference is significant and could account for differences in metabolic efficiency during overfeeding.

In animals, researchers have learned that brown adipose tissue (BAT) is the organ responsible for AT. In mammals, it is located in the retroperitoneal space and near the spinal cord and constitutes less than 10% of total fat. Decreased activity of this tissue during overfeeding or cold adaptation is associated with obesity in the genetically obese ob/ob mouse and Zucker fatty rat.[27] There has been much speculation that decreased function of BAT may contribute to human obesity. Increased NE-induced thermogenesis, a marker of BAT metabolism, is present in normal incidence during overfeeding and cold adaptation and is not increased after 3 weeks of overfeeding in lean humans. Studies also indicated normal thermic responsiveness to NE in obese whites and Pima Indians, suggesting that BAT is probably not functionally important in the adaptation to short-term overfeeding in both lean and obese humans and is not the major site of AT in humans.

Caloric Restriction

The adaptive response to caloric restriction produces a fall in both plasma NE and insulin levels and a decrease in the production of T_3 from T_4. This is associated with a decline in the RMR out of proportion to a change in lean body mass. Although this adaptive response to underfeeding is beneficial during prolonged food restriction, ie, famine, it is counterproductive to an obese person attempting to lose weight by diet alone. The fall in RMR decreases the calories expended, limiting the quantity of fat mass lost.

Table 4-1 illustrates the dilemma imposed by restricting calories in order to lose weight. Shown is the caloric balance of an 80-kg woman before (period 1), during (periods 2 and 3), and after (period 4) a 1,000 calorie/day diet. She is sedentary and requires 1,900 calories/day to maintain her weight. The RMR is 1,250 calories/day (25 calories/kg of lean body mass), and the thermic effect of meals is 150 calories/day (8% of ingested calories). The energy cost of all physical movement is 500 calories/day. After 1 month on a 1,000 calorie/day diet (period 2) she has lost 6 kg of total body weight: 2 kg of lean tissue, 1 kg of water and salt, and 3 kg of fat mass. Note that at the end of period 2, the total energy expenditure has decreased to 1,547 calories/day. This is because of decline in the RMR of 203 calories/day. Additionally, there is a decrease in the

Table 4-1 Energy Balance During Moderate Caloric Restriction

Period	1	2	3	4
Day	0	30	60	65
Calories/Day	1,900	1,000	1,000	1,900
Weight (kg) - Total	80	74.0	72.0	72.0
- Lean Body Mass	(50)	(47.0)	(46.5)	(46.5)
- Fat	(30)	(27.0)	(25.5)	(25.5)
RMR (Kcal/Day)	1,250	1,047	1,023	1,163
TEF (Kcal/Day)	150	100	95	150
Activity (Kcal/Day)	500	400	380	450
Total Daily Caloric Expenditure	1,900	1,547	1,498	1,763

TEF because of a decrease in the calories ingested and a fall in spontaneous movement during caloric restriction.

During the second month of dieting (period 3), the difference between energy intake and output is just slightly more than 500 calories/day even though she may be rigorously adhering to the diet. Weight loss during this time period is much less since there are no further water and glycogen losses, and protein losses are held to a minimum. Her weight loss averages just 1.1 lb per week. It is easy to imagine the frustration and anger that dieters experience when after 4 to 8 weeks of adhering to a difficult program they lose just 1 lb/week. The longer a person restricts calories to lose weight, the less weight is lost.

When she stops restricting calories (period 4) she gains weight. There is an immediate increase in insulin and catecholamine secretion, which then produces sodium and water retention. Energy expenditure is still lower than in period 1 since the lean body mass and total mass are both lower. The decrease in lean body mass produces a lower RMR, and a decrease in total weight decreases the caloric cost of physical activity, unless there is a corresponding increase in exercise. The conclusions to be drawn from this example are upsetting to all overweight people:

- The longer one diets, the less one loses.
- Once a dieter, always a dieter.

There is only one path out of the cycle of dieting and recurrent weight gain. It is a change in life style to include daily exercise as an integral part of one's daily routine. Exercise alters the almost inevitable path toward recurrent weight gain after dieting by increasing energy expenditure. As shown in Figure 4-1, bicycle riding against resistance during caloric restriction expends a similar number of calories as during weight maintenance. Although the natural tendency during dieting is to decrease physical activity, and endurance is less than during weight maintenance, exercise is possible during caloric restriction. Of significance is the fact that the composition of the diet is important for endurance. A person's ability to ride a bicycle is markedly impaired when ingesting a diet containing no carbohydrate and improved when carbohydrate is substituted for fat. The level of T_3 in serum also decreases during carbohydrate restriction, and this decline may have a role in the decreased ability of muscle to perform endurance exercises.

Summary

Evidence exists that humans can increase or decrease energy expenditure in response to an alteration in food intake. These changes in energy metabolism act to maintain lean body mass at constant levels but can be overridden if changes in food intake are extreme. Humans who exhibit spontaneous morbid obesity may have difficulty increasing their energy expenditure during periods of over-feeding but have no difficulty decreasing energy expenditure during caloric restriction. These conditions make it difficult for obese people to lose weight and maintain weight loss. A defect only in AT is unlikely to produce significant weight gain. Decreased physical activity and abnormalities in the regulation of food intake need to be present for a significant degree of obesity to occur.

REGULATION OF BODY WEIGHT

When one considers the regulation of body weight, the equation of the con-servation of mass must again be considered:

$$\text{Calorie intake} - \text{Calorie expenditure} = \text{Weight change}.$$

The regulation of food intake is of obvious importance in any discussion of the pathogenesis of obesity, and a detailed discussion is beyond the scope of this chapter. Yet there are several points to remember: Studies of animals in their natural environment indicate that obesity is extremely uncommon. Labo-ratory animals and pets when given access to ordinary laboratory chow also do not exhibit obesity. It is only after ad libitum intake of highly palatable foods containing high percentages of fat and simple sugars that these animals increase their food intake.[28] Add to this increase in food intake a decrease in physical activity because of captivity or domesticity, and obesity develops in almost all animals studied. A similar situation has developed in humans. Paleontologists who studied humans before modern civilization also discovered that obesity was rare, food intake lower, and physical activity greater than in modern Western society. Evidence suggests that spontaneously obese people ingest calories more frequently because of palatability of the food rather than hunger alone, a similar finding in normal laboratory animals. Thus, in a portion of obese people, periods of hyperphagia lead to gain of both lean and fat mass.

While no significant differences have been detected during weight maintenance between lean and obese people with respect to the RMR per unit of lean body mass, the components of their 24-hour energy expenditure can differ signifi-cantly. Obesity can be thought of as one method whereby the body reaches equilibrium between caloric intake and expenditure. For example, consider two persons who have just completed adolescence, are of similar height and weight, and who both ingest 2,200 calories/day. Both have completed their growth processes and therefore require fewer calories. However, one person is more active than the other, expending 900 calories/day *v* 600 calories/day in physical activity. If the less physically active person continues to eat 2,200 calories/day because of habit or other psychosocial reasons, the following might occur: Subject A is in energy equilibrium and therefore weight stable; subject B, however, is expending 300 calories less per day and is storing those extra calories. Depending on the genetic makeup of this person, subject B can either:

- stimulate adaptive thermogenesis,
- increase physical activity, or
- gain weight until a new energy equilibrium is reached.

Remember that only increases in *lean* mass, not fat mass, produce an increase in RMR. Also remember that unless specific physical exercise is undertaken, ie, weightlifting, etc, people will increase both their fat mass and their lean body mass during weight gain. From animal studies, approximately one third of the excess weight is lean tissue and the remainder is added fat. Thus in order to reach a new energy equilibrium, subject B would have to gain 11 lb of lean mass and 20+ lb of fat mass. This would take between 12 and 24 months, depending on the ability to maintain physical activity as the person gained weight. Thus a combination of a mild increase in food intake, decreased physical activity, and a poor metabolic adaptation to overfeeding produced a 30+ lb weight gain. Yet, if subject B were studied at the new increased weight, the RMR would be equivalent, and no obvious cause for the obesity would be present. This is the difficulty in determining the pathogenesis of obesity in many people.

Body weight seems to increase with age until it peaks after the age of 65.[29] There are several possible explanations for this finding: The first is a decrease in physical activity. Young adult men who are athletic can expend literally hundreds of calories daily in sports such as basketball, soccer, and racquet sports, but as they grow older they frequently turn to less physically active recreation or pursuits. Women have similar problems, and they also tend to lose greater amounts of lean tissue after menopause. In addition, the physiologic changes of pregnancy include fat deposition to be used as a calorie source during breast-feeding. With the advent of formula feedings for infants, it is more difficult for women to lose weight after pregnancy if they do not breast-feed. Thus, numerous factors combine to decrease caloric requirements with increasing age, and if food intake does not decline, weight gain ensues.

Although there are several theories that discuss the role of the CNS in the regulation of weight, the premise on which they are based is simple. Obese people are unable to decrease their food intake when they are gaining weight. As noted, significant weight gain can occur during what is apparently normal food intake but decreased energy expenditure. The best treatment for obesity is, therefore, prevention. The only realistic method to accomplish weight loss is a change in life style to produce an increase in caloric expenditure and a change in diet to less calorie-rich foods.

REFERENCES

1. Neel JV: Diabetes mellitus: A thrifty genotype rendered detrimental by "progress"? *Am J Hum Genet* 1962; 14:353–357.

2. Welle SL, Lilavivat U, Campbell RC: Thermic effect of feeding in man: Increased norepinephrine levels following glucose but not protein or fat consumption. *Metabolism* 1981; 30:953–958.

3. Rowe JW, Young JB, Minaker KL, et al: Effect of insulin and glucose infusions on sympathetic nervous system activity in normal man. *Diabetes* 1981; 30:219–225.

4. Viteri FE, Torun B: Protein-calorie malnutrition, in Goodhart RS, Shils ME (eds): *Modern Nutrition in Health and Disease*, ed 6. Philadelphia, Lea & Febiger, 1980, pp 697–720.

5. Edholm OG, Adam JM, Healy MJR: Food intake and energy expenditure of army recruits. *Br J Nutr* 1970; 24:1091–1097.

6. Grande F, Keys A: Body weight, body composition and calorie status, in Goodhart RS, Shils ME (eds): *Modern Nutrition in Health and Disease*, ed 6. Philadelphia, Lea & Febiger, 1980, pp 3–34.

7. Bjorntorp P, Ostman J: Human adipose tissue dynamics and regulation. *Advances in Metabolic Diseases* 1971; 5:277–293.

8. Bagdade JD, Porte D, Bierman EL: The interaction of diabetes and obesity on the regulation of fat mobilization in man. *Diabetes* 1968; 18:759–772.

9. Keys A, Brozek J, Henschel A, Mickelson O, Taylor HL: *The biology of human starvation*. Minneapolis, University of Minnesota, 1950.

10. Ravussin E, Burnard B, Schultz Y, et al: Twenty-four hour energy expenditure and resting metabolic rate in obese, moderately obese and control subjects. *Am J Clin Nutr* 1982; 35:366–373.

11. Tzankoff S, Norris H: Effect of muscle mass decrease on age-related BMR changes, *J Appl Physiol* 1977; 43:1001–1006.

12. Landsberg L, Young JB: Fasting, feeding, and the regulation of sympathetic activity. *N Engl J Med* 1978; 298:1295–1301.

13. Danforth E Jr: The role of thyroid hormones and insulin in the regulation of energy metabolism. *Am J Clin Nutr* 1983; 38:1006–1017.

14. Neumann RO: Experimentelle beitrage zur lehre von dem taschlichen narungsbedarf des menschen unter besondeer. *Berucksichtiguang der Notwendigen Eiwessmenge Arch Hyg* 1902; 45:1–2.

15. Bray GA, Melvin KEW, Chopra IJ: Effect of triiodothyronine on some metabolic responses of obese patients. *Am J Clin Nutr* 1973; 26:715–721.

16. Landsberg L, Young J: The role of the sympathoadrenal system in modulating energy expenditure. *Clin Endocrinol Metab* 1984; 13:475–499.

17. Katzeff HL, O'Connell M, Horton ES, et al: Metabolic studies in obesity: During over- and undernutrition. *Metabolism* 1986; 35:166–175.

18. Welle S, Campbell RG: Studies of thermogenesis by carbohydrate overfeeding: Evidence against sympathetic nervous system activation. *J Clin Invest* 1983; 72:916–925.

19. O'Dea K, Esler M, Leonard P, et al: Noradrenaline turnover during under- and overeating in normal weight subjects. *Metabolism* 1982; 31:896–899.

20. Flatt VP: Biochemistry of energy expenditure, in Bray G (ed): *Recent Advances in Obesity Research*, 2. Westport, CT, Technomic Publishing Co, 1978, pp 211–228.

21. Jequier E, Schutz Y: New evidence for a thermogenic defect in human obesity. *Int J Obes* 1985; 9(suppl):1–7.

22. Johnson ML, Burke BS, Mayer J: Relative importance of inactivity and overeating in the energy balance of obese high school girls. *Am J Clin Nutr* 1956; 4:37–44.

23. Ravussin E, Lillioja S, Anderson TE, et al: Determinants of 24 hour energy expenditure in man: Methods and results using a respiratory chamber. *J Clin Invest*, 1986; 78:1568–1578.

24. Sims EAH, Danforth E Jr, Horton ES, et al: Endocrine and metabolic effects of experimental obesity in man. *Recent Prog Horm Res* 1973; 29:457–496.

25. Danforth E Jr, Horton ES, O'Connell M, et al: Dietary-induced alterations in thyroid hormone metabolism during overnutrition. *J Clin Invest* 1979; 64:1336–1347.

26. Katzeff HL, Daniels RJ: Sympathetic nervous system activity in man. *Int J Obes* 1985; 9(suppl):131–139.

27. Luboshitzky R, Bernadis LL, Goldman JK, et al: Brown adipose tissue metabolism in hypothalamic-obesity. *Metabolism* 1983; 32:108–113.

28. Rothwell NJ, Stock MJ: A role for brown adipose tissue in diet-induced thermogenesis. *Nature* 1978; 281:31–35.

29. Donald DWA: Mortality rates among the overweight, in Robertson RF (ed): *Anorexia and Obesity*. Edinburgh, RCP, 1973, pp 63–70.

Chapter 5

Body Composition and Resting Metabolic Rate in Obesity

Mei-Uih Yang

BODY COMPOSITION

Introduction

Most of our understanding of the composition of the human body is derived from direct chemical analyses of six cadavers (five men, one woman) reported between 1945 and 1956. The causes of death of these six adults (aged 25 to 60 years) included heart attack, uremia, arterial endocarditis, skull fracture, and suicidal drowning. The published data are summarized in Table 5-1. There is considerable variation among cadavers as seen from the wide range of values shown in Table 5-1. Nevertheless, these values provided a basis for developing indirect methods for measuring body composition in vivo.

Although chemical analysis is the most direct and precise method for the analysis of body composition, it is obviously not feasible to measure the body composition of a patient by direct chemical means. Various indirect methods have been developed for in vivo assessment. All of these depend, to some degree, on the assumption that the body consists of two components: fat and lean body mass. In other words,

Body weight = Fat + Lean body mass (including total body water)

If one of these two components is measured, the other component can be mathematically deduced from the difference between body weight (which can be measured easily and accurately) and the measured component.

It should first be made clear that there is a difference between fat-free mass (FFM) and lean body mass (LBM) (or lean body weight [LBW] or lean tissue). These two terms are often used interchangeably in spite of their different meanings.[5] *Lean body mass* refers to lean tissue in a living organism and includes a small amount of essential fat (perhaps as much as 3%), mainly within internal

Table 5-1 The Chemical Composition of Six Adult Cadavers and Fat-Free Mass

Reference	Sex	Age yr	Height cm	Total Weight kg	Body Composition				Fat-Free Mass			Cause of Death
					Fat %	Water %	Protein %	K mmol/kg	Water %	Protein %	K mmol/kg	
Mitchell et al,[1] 1945	M	35	183.0	70.6	67.9	12.5	14.4	—	77.6	16.5	—	Heart Attack
Widdowson et al,[2] 1951	M	25	179.0	71.8	61.8	14.9	16.6	56	72.5	19.5	71.1	Uremia
Widdowson et al,[2] 1951	F	42	169.0	45.1	56.0	23.6	14.4	56	73.2	19.2	72.6	Drowning
Forbes et al,[3] 1953	M	46	168.5	53.8	55.1	19.4	18.6	54	69.4	23.4	66.5	Skull Fracture
Forbes et al,[4] 1956	M	48	169.0	62.0	70.8	4.3	19.7	—	72.9	20.6	—	Bacterial Endocarditis
Forbes et al,[4] 1956	M	60	172.0	73.5	50.6	27.9	17.2	49	70.1	23.8	66.6	Heart Attack
Mean					60.4	17.1	16.8	54	72.6	20.5	69.2	

organs, bone marrow, and the central nervous system (CNS). In contrast, *fat-free mass* implies tissue devoid of all extractable fat, and this can only be measured through direct chemical analysis. Thus, FFM is an in vitro entity, and the term is more appropriately used with regard to direct carcass analysis. The nonfat compartment of a living organism (determined by indirect methods and which still contains a small amount of essential fat) is therefore properly termed *lean tissue*, or *lean body mass*, or *lean body weight*.

Methodology

Commonly Used Methods

Densitometry (Hydrostatic Weighing). The use of densitometry to determine body composition is based on the fact that at normal body temperature (37°C or 98.6°F), the density of body fat is 0.901×10^3 kg/m^3 and that of LBW is 1.097×10^3 kg/m^3. If body density is measured, the percent of body weight as fat can be calculated from a prediction equation such as given by Siri,[6] Keys and Brozek,[7] etc.

Body density is most commonly estimated from hydrostatic weighing by applying Archimedes' principle. The subject is asked to submerge, expire maximally, and remain as motionless as possible for few seconds while underwater weight is recorded. Because any air remaining in the lungs and gases trapped in the gastrointestinal tract, sinuses, etc (at the time of underwater weighing) contribute to buoyancy, these volumes must be considered. In general, gas other than in the lungs is small in quantity and can be ignored. However, residual lung volume is large and therefore must be measured and subtracted from the total body volume. It is usually estimated by means of the closed-circuit nitrogen-dilution technique with 100% oxygen as the tracer gas.[8] Body density and percent of body fat can then be calculated as follows:[6]

$$\text{Body density} = \text{Mass/Volume}$$
$$= (\text{Weight in air})/[(\text{Weight in air} - \text{Weight in water})/$$
$$(\text{Density of water} - \text{Residual volume})]$$
$$\% \text{ Body fat} = [(4.95/\text{Body density}) - 4.50] \times 100.$$

This method is well established and is commonly accepted as the "gold standard" in the study of body composition. However, the procedure is not without problems. The errors of body density are approximately 0.003 g/cc for children and 0.008 g/cc for adults.[9] As calculated by Roche,[10] this measurement error corresponds to 0.6 kg for children, 0.4 to 1.8 kg for men, and 2.3 kg for women with average body fat. Furthermore, the percent of fat may vary considerably depending on the prediction equation used. In a study of the body composition of young women, Young et al[11] employed five formulas to calculate fat content and found the value varied from 25% to 29% depending on the formula used. This finding is consistent with the observation of Lim and Luft[12] who studied a group of male adults. They found that the Siri[6] formula yielded results for fat content some 6% to 7% higher than did the Keys-Brozek formula.[7] If the average fat content for young men is 20%, then the discrepancy between the two methods of calculation is approximately 30%.

Although densitometry seems simple in theory, in practice there are a number of obstacles to overcome. First, one must convince subjects to submerge and remain underwater calmly until their underwater weight is recorded. This is particularly difficult if the subject is obese and therefore more buoyant. The procedure also requires an experienced operator with subjective but accurate judgment to perform the underwater weighing and residual lung volume determination.

Total Body Water. When calculating body fat using measurement of total body water (TBW), it is assumed that fat is stored in anhydrous form, and all the water in the body exists in lean tissue in a constant proportion. Direct chemical analysis of cadavers has revealed that fat-free weight contains 67.4% to 77.5% water, with a mean of 72.5%. This mean value is similar to the 73.2% water content obtained from chemical analysis of 50 eviscerated guinea pigs.[13] Thus, if TBW is known, body fat content can be estimated as follows:

$$LBM \ (kg) \ = \ TBW \ (L)/0.732$$
$$Body \ fat \ (kg) \ = \ Body \ weight \ (kg) \ - \ LBM \ (kg).$$

TBW is commonly determined by an isotopic dilution using either deuterium (^2H_2O), tritium (^3H_2O), or ^{18}O as a tracer. After the ingestion (or injection) of a known quantity of the tracer, 3 to 4 hours is needed for the tracer to equilibrate in the body. Any loss of the tracer through excretion should be collected quantitatively and subtracted from intake.

Although TBW can be measured fairly accurately, with a measurement error of $\pm 0.5\%$ to $\pm 2\%$,[14] the accuracy of estimating LBM from a TBW determination is affected by any disturbance in normal hydration such as dehydration, fluid retention, or disproportional increase in extracellular water associated with obesity. Furthermore, the estimate of TBW by dilution techniques may overestimate TBW up to 5.2% because of the exchange of tracer hydrogen with the nonaqueous (labile) hydrogen in the body.[15] Generally, the TBW method tends to yield values for LBM greater than those obtained from underwater weighing of obese people. It seems fair to conclude that the TBW procedure alone is not a suitable method for measuring body composition in obese patients or for determining changes in body composition during weight reduction.

Combination of Total Body Water and Densitometry. It has been suggested that a more reliable estimate of body composition would be obtained from a combination of body water and density measurements. A prediction equation was developed by Siri:[16]

% Fat = (2.057/Body density) − (0.786 × TBW/Body weight) − 1.286.

The rationale for the combined use of TBW and body density is that the combination of methods corrects for variation in the state of hydration and thereby reduces the error that derives from uncertainty about the hydration of LBM. But, as Siri[16] pointed out, this combination really does not eliminate the uncertainty about fundamental assumptions. Segal et al[17] measured the fat content of 75 people and found that the percent of body fat calculated from the combination of density and TBW did not differ from that determined by density alone. This is not surprising since their subjects were normal healthy volunteers with normal hydration. It would be more interesting to test this formula with a population who varied in hydration of LBM.

Total Body Potassium. On the assumption that 98% of potassium (K) in the body resides in lean tissue, and lean tissue has a constant potassium content, it is possible to estimate the quantity of lean tissue if the total body potassium (TBK) is measured.[18] Then, body fat can be easily calculated by the difference between body weight and lean tissue.

Lean tissue (kg) = TBK/(Potassium concentration/kg of lean tissue)

Based on direct chemical analyses of four cadavers, Forbes et al[19] proposed a constant of 68.1 mmol of potassium for each kilogram of human lean tissue. However, based on in vivo measurement by TBK counting and densitometry, Womersley et al[20] suggested 64.4 and 59.7 mmol of potassium per kilogram of lean tissue for men and women, respectively. More recently, when potassium counting was corrected for body geometry, higher values of millimoles of potassium, 71.8 for men and 60.8 for women, were reported by Pierson et al.[21]

The TBK can be measured in two ways: (1) by the ^{42}K dilution technique, which requires administration of a radioisotope (^{42}K), or (2) by a more convenient and rapid procedure using a whole body scintillation counter. The use of the whole body counter to measure TBK depends on the fact that the principal gamma ray activity in humans comes from a naturally occurring radioactive isotope of ^{40}K. It is also known that ^{40}K constitutes 0.012% of total potassium, regardless of its origin, which is composed of three isotopes: (1) ^{39}K (93.2%), (2) ^{40}K (0.012%), and (3) ^{42}K (6.8%).[22] Thus, it is possible to calculate TBK from ^{40}K measurement by a body counter. The counter varies from a single crystal detector (the least accurate) to 2π (180°) and 4π (360°, the most accurate) whole body liquid scintillation counters.

The whole body liquid scintillation counter is an expensive and intricate instrument, and only a few exist. The procedure of measuring subjects is rapid, convenient, and objective, and requires minimum cooperation from the patient (lying down in the counter for only a few minutes). However, its application in obese patients needs special attention. Colt et al[23] and Blahd et al[22] reported that ^{40}K radiation is attenuated in subcutaneous fat, causing a reduction in the counting efficiency for TBK measurement in obese patients. Appropriate corrections should be made for the geometry of the subjects by use of a calibration equation derived from measurement of ^{42}K.[21] The error of TBK measurement is reported to be $\pm 4\%$ for calibration standards, but in humans, it may be as much as $\pm 10\%$ if the geometry factor is not appropriately corrected.[21]

The TBK method has another limitation because of its assumption of the constancy of potassium content in lean tissue. Potassium content varies from person to person, is not uniform in various types of lean tissue, and is affected by the person's health, nutritional status, and age.

Anthropometric Measurements. Total body fat content can be estimated from measurements of circumferences and skinfold thicknesses at various strategic sites of the body using measuring tape and skinfold calipers. Anthropometry is based on the assumption that body fat is mostly accumulated under the skin as subcutaneous fat, which may also be related to internal fat.

The procedure for measuring skinfold thickness is to grasp a fold of skin and subcutaneous fat firmly with the thumb and forefinger, pulling it away from the underlying muscular tissue following the natural contour of the fatfold, after which the calipers are applied. The thickness of the double layer of skin and subcutaneous tissues is then read directly from the caliper dial and recorded in millimeters.

The most common places for measuring skinfold thickness are at the triceps, subscapular, suprailiac, abdomen, and upper thigh sites. All measurements are customarily made on the right side of the body, with the subject standing. A minimum of two measurements are made at each site, and the average value is used as the score for that site.

Numerous prediction equations have been developed to estimate the total body fat content from anthropometric data using either skinfolds alone or in conjunction with circumference measurements. Some investigators[24,25] have claimed that measuring one or two skinfold thicknesses at particular site(s) is as good as measuring at multiple sites in estimating total body fat content. Conversely, other investigators[26] consider that as many as 12 measurements (4 skinfolds, 6 circumferences, and 2 lengths) in addition to height and weight are necessary to obtain accurate estimations of body fat content. Since many of the anthropometric prediction formulas were developed with data collected from the normal-weight population,[9,27,28] their applicability to obese people may be questionable.

Durnin and Womersley[29] reported a linear relation between body density and the logarithm of the sum of the skinfold thicknesses of triceps, biceps, subscapula, and suprailiac. This relation was discovered from studies of 272 women and 209 men varying widely in age (16 to 72 years), body weight (51 to 122 kg), and body fat content (5% to 61%). From these findings, a table was constructed in which percentage of body fat corresponded to differing values for the total of the four skinfold thicknesses (biceps, triceps, subscapular, and suprailiac). The table is subdivided for sex and for age. The highest percentage of fat content in the table was 46% for men and 53% for women. The estimated error was within ±3.5% of body weight as fat for women and ±5% for men. At the present time, this table may be one of the best tools for estimation of body fat of the obese population in clinical settings if accurate measurements of skinfold thickness at the four sites can be obtained.

The equipment for this procedure is economical and can be easily used in clinical settings. Only minimal cooperation is required from the patient. However, the wide variation (low reproducibility) of the measurement at the same site by different operators and also with the same operator performing repeated measurements is common and most criticized. Its low reproducibility often makes the data collected less trustworthy. As with densitometry, skinfold thickness measurements also require careful and accurate judgment by an experienced operator. Moreover, measurements of skinfold thickness in grossly obese patients can be impossible, as quite often the thickness of the skinfold is greater than the capability of the jaws of the calipers.

To overcome this problem, ultrasonography was adapted to measure skinfold thickness. A lightweight portable ultrasound meter (Ithaco) is commercially available to measure the distance between the skin and fat-muscle layer. Therefore, the measurement is of a single fatfold unlike with calipers (double folds).

The probe (transducer) of the ultrasound meter is placed on the site of the skin surface. It emits pulses of high frequency sound waves that penetrate the skin surface. The sound waves pass through adipose tissue until the muscle layer is reached; the sound waves are then reflected from the fat-muscle interface to produce an echo that returns to the ultrasound unit. The time for sound wave transmission through the tissues and back to the receiver is converted to a distance score and displayed on a light-emitting diode (LED) scale. Although the ultrasound meter has no limit in measuring the thickness of fatfold and is based on proven scientific principles, it too requires an operator's experienced judgment for accurate and reliable readings. But because of its portability, and its basis on sound scientific theory, with additional technical refinement to overcome the problems with "layers" of fat separated by connective tissue, it may become the preferred choice over calipers for skinfold thickness measurement.

Body Mass Index. Ideally, obesity should be assessed by direct measures of the degree of fatness. However, all the in vivo methods for body composition discussed above are indirect, cumbersome, and, with the exception of anthropometric measurements, impractical to implement in a clinical setting. Accordingly, a body mass index (BMI) derived from weight (W) and height (H) is frequently used as an indirect correlate of obesity in human subjects. Frisancho and Flegel[30] using data from the US Health and Nutritional Examination I, 1971–1974,[31] compared the age-adjusted correlation coefficient of weight and various indices of obesity (W/H^2, W/H^3, W/H^p) with skinfold thickness at triceps and subscapula, and the sum of skinfolds for adults. It was found that W/H^2 or W/H^p explained 60% of the variability in body fat.

BMI has been used as an index and classification of obesity. Recently, the correlation between BMI (weight [kg]/height $[m]^2$) and total body fat (kg) was examined in 104 women and 24 men aged 14 to 60 years.[32] Total body fat was determined by densitometry, TBW, and TBK. In both sexes, density, water, and potassium gave progressively higher estimates of body fat (kg), and there were significant differences among the values obtained by the different methods. The average of the estimates by these three methods was taken to be the "true" value for each person. Regression of fat/H^2 on W/H^2 was 0.9555 for women and 0.943 for men. Prediction equations were developed based on these findings. Fat (kg) can be calculated from height and weight as follows:

- Women: Fat (kg) = $(0.713 \ W/H^2 - 9.74) \ H^2$
- Men: Fat (kg) = $(0.715 \ W/H^2 - 12.1) \ H^2$.

The authors[32] found that the measurement error was approximately 4.2 and 5.8 kg of fat for women and men, respectively. This magnitude of error is similar to that obtained with densitometry, TBW, and TBK. The prediction of body fat may be inaccurate in special groups, such as older people and very muscular athletes, but these are not groups for whom obesity is an important clinical problem. If these predictive equations prove to be valid, they will enable clinicians to evaluate a patient's fatness economically and easily.

Newer Methods

Total Body Electrical Conductivity and Bioelectrical Impedance Assessment. Both total body electrical conductivity (TOBEC) and bioelectrical impedance assessment (BIA) are new electrical methods that were recently applied to the assessment of body composition. Both procedures rely on the fact that lean tissue is far more electrically conductive than fat tissue in the body owing to the richer electrolyte content in lean tissue.

The TOBEC instrument (Dj Medical Instrument Corp) is an open-ended cylinder type of body counter, which differs from the TBK counter (closed). It is surrounded by a large solenoidal coil driven by a 2.5-MHz oscillating radio frequency current. The difference between impedance when the subject is inside the coil and when the coil is empty corresponds to the electrical conductivity of the subject (which is proportional to the LBM). The actual measurement takes less than 90 seconds.

Fewer than 10 years ago the first prototype HA-1 was built for measuring TOBEC in humans. Today, six or more second generation HA-2 instruments are being studied in many US institutions. A high correlation has been reported between TOBEC scores (signals of conductivity) and LBM estimated from body density. Segal et al[17] measured the body composition of 75 men and women varying widely in body weight (49 to 133 kg) and fat (5% to 55%), using densitometry, TBK, TBW, TOBEC, and BIA methods. A strong correlation ($r = .962$) was found between the percent of fat obtained by densitometry and by TOBEC. The validity of the TOBEC method for determining body composition in healthy human subjects has been confirmed on repeated occasions.[33]

In contrast to TOBEC, which is a uniform current induction method that measures total body electrical conductivity, BIA is a localized 50-kHz current injection procedure. It involves measuring total body resistivity, which is the inverse of conductivity. BIA makes use of the fact that impedance (resistance and reactance) to electrical flow of an injected current is related to the volume of a conductor (the human body) and the square of the conductor's length (height). The body resistivity (or impedance) can be measured by use of a four-terminal impedance analyzer. Sensor electrodes are conventionally placed over dorsal wrist and ankle, with signal electrodes placed at the proximal end of the metacarpals and metatarsals.

In the same population studied by Segal et al,[17] lean tissue was also estimated by BIA and compared with that determined by underwater weighing. Using the prediction equation provided by the manufacturer, it was found that with increasing obesity, BIA overestimated lean tissue as compared with that obtained from hydrostatic weighing. This is attributable to the fact that the BIA method of assessing body composition is based in part on TBW.

At present, the apparent advantages of both BIA and TOBEC methods over other procedures for measuring body composition include short assessment time, ease of use, subject convenience, and high reproducibility. Since these methods require no effort by the subject, except lying down, they might also be suitable for hospitalized patients. In addition, BIA is performed with a portable analyzer; one may foresee its popularity and wide usage in clinical settings. Because both methods are rather new, more research is needed to refine and validate the prediction equations developed. Their further application in body composition assessment also depends on their accuracy and sensitivity in detecting relatively small changes in body composition related to illness, supportive nutritional care, or therapeutic weight loss.

Total Body Nitrogen by Neutron Activation. All methods discussed above are indirect measurements of body composition. Advances in technology have made possible direct measurement of total body nitrogen (TBN) and thereby body protein (TBN $\times$ 6.25) in vivo. TBN can be measured by prompt gamma ray analysis. This technique involves the passage of neutrons through the trunk of the subject. Some of the neutrons are taken up by nitrogen atoms in the body, forming ^{15}N from ^{14}N and releasing gamma rays. Gamma rays are short-lived and, hence, must be measured at the same time as the passage of neutrons. The radiation dose to the patient is 30 to 50 mrem, and the measurement error of TBN is estimated to be 3% to 10%.[34]

TBN determined by neutron activation has been validated by direct chemical analyses. Knight et al[35] measured the TBN of two cadavers by both neutron activation and direct chemical analysis. The data obtained agreed within 2%.

Although this method provides an accurate and direct assay of body protein, it is unlikely that TBN will soon be available in regular clinical settings because of the high cost and relative rarity of the equipment. Nevertheless, the application of neutron activation to measure TBN provides the first direct in vivo measurement of body protein. TBN determination in conjunction with measurement of TBK, TBW, and bone ash (which is also estimated from total body calcium by neutron activation) offers an independent and complete assessment of LBM in vivo. The measurement error of body fat calculated as the difference between body weight and LBM is 2.7% to 5.1%.[36]

Other Methods

A number of new procedures are being studied for their usefulness in body composition research. For example, computer-assisted tomography (CT scan) has been used to investigate the distribution of deep fat (intra-abdominal) and subcutaneous fat. These two sets of fat depots cannot be separated by any of the methods discussed above. The CT scan can readily distinguish between adipose tissue and adjacent skin, muscles, bones, vascular structures, and intra-abdominal and pelvic organs by virtue of fat's distinctive low attenuation value. It has been reported that a single abdominal CT scan can give a good indication of fat content throughout the abdomen.[37,38] The error rate in predicting abdominal fat content from a single (L5) scan is estimated to be 10.7% for men and 8.4% for women.[38] The total time required for measurement is less than 15 minutes. However, because of the cost of CT scanners and their frequent use for clinical purposes, the technique is unlikely to be used routinely for body composition studies.

Other methods such as dual photon absorption (DPA), infrared interactance (IRI), nuclear magnetic resonance (NMR), etc are still early in development and validation for measurement of body composition. The determination of body fat by these procedures in clinical settings is unlikely to occur in the immediate future, and, therefore, discussion of these methods for body composition assessment is premature.

Body Weight, Frame Size, and Body Composition

Body Weight and Frame Size

There are many published tables that provide ideal or desirable weight for a person based on height and gender. Attributable in large part to publications from the Metropolitan Life Insurance Company, there is a widespread belief that body weight norms in adults should be related to frame size. Frame size is an ill-defined concept. Katch et al[39] found a significant difference between self-reported frame size and that appraised by investigators. An index of frame size should have no relation to adiposity since, like height, bigger-framed people are not necessarily fatter.

Frisancho and Flegel[40] examined the data of the US Health and Nutritional Examination Survey I of 1971 to 1974. They found that the elbow breadth, as compared with bitrochanteric breadth, and body weight, as compared with sum of skinfolds (triceps and subscapular), had the lowest correlation with adiposity and a low correlation with age regardless of sex or race. It seems that elbow breadth is the best indicator of frame size. A table of small, medium, and large categories of elbow breadth was established for adults depending on whether the elbow breadth was below the 15th (small), between the 15th and the 85th (medium), or above the 85th (large) sex-, age-, and race-specific percentiles for elbow breadth. In general, the elbow breadth of blacks is greater than that of whites in each frame category, and, as expected, men have significantly greater elbow breadth than either black or white women.

Elbow breadth can be measured with the spreading caliper. The examinee's right arm is extended forward perpendicular to the body. With the arm bent so that the angle at the elbow is 90°, with the fingers pointing up and the dorsal part of the wrist toward the examiner, the greatest breadth across the elbow is measured.

Body Composition

After deciding whether to incorporate frame size into relative body weight for a person, the clinician faces the even more difficult task of recommending an "appropriate" or "desirable" body fat content for the patient. It is interesting to note that values for "average" percentage of body fat reported in the literature vary depending on the type of research performed by the investigator. Scientists who are interested in sports medicine tend to set a lower "average" percentage of body fat than the ones who treat obesity. In the general population, body fat may range from 5% of body weight in wrestlers ready for competition to 50% or more in very obese people. Male athletes in peak condition have 5% to 15% body weight as fat; the female equivalent may have 15% to 20%.[41] Hannon and Lohman[42] suggest the upper end of this range, 15% for men and 22% for women, to represent the ideal body fatness for the average American. However, comparing body composition of obese and nonobese people, most investigators[43,44] included subjects who had body fat up to 20% for men and 25% for women in the control, nonobese groups. It may be reasonable to consider body fat of up to 20% for men and 25% for women as acceptable "average" values for normal-weight people.

A 70-kg nonobese man may have 20% fat and 80% lean tissue. The lean tissue consists of water (73.2%), protein (20.5%), minerals (5.4%), and a small amount of glycogen (0.9%), as shown in Figure 5-1.

Obesity and Lean Body Mass

Though obesity is generally defined as an excessive accumulation of fat, there is increasing evidence indicating that as obesity develops, lean tissue also increases. In 1964, Forbes[45] reported that lean tissue in obese children is greater than in nonobese peers. Subsequently, Drenick et al[46] also found an increase in lean tissue, as evidenced by the higher TBK content (calibrated with ^{42}K self-absorption) in their 49 obese adults (body weight ranging from 78 to 238 kg) over age- and height-matched nonobese control subjects.

James et al[47] assessed the body composition of 71 obese people (11 men and 61 women) and 26 normal-weight control subjects by skinfold thickness and TBK (calibrated with ^{42}K). They concluded that the excess weight accumulated by the obese over the normal-weight subjects was not pure fat, but was composed of 32% to 38% LBM and 62% to 68% fat. These numbers differ slightly from those reported by others. Webster et al[48] measured the body composition of 104 obese and normal-weight women by densitometry. They reported that the excess weight accumulated by the obese over the nonobese women consisted of 22% to 30% lean and 70% to 78% fat. They therefore proposed that, in the treatment of obesity, lean tissue loss should not contribute more than 22% of total weight lost.

More recently, Forbes and Welle[49] examined data on LBM in their and other published reports to address the question of whether obese children and adults have increased LBM. Since lean tissue is closely related to stature, the data were expressed as a lean:height ratio and compared. Their own data indicated that 75% of the obese had a lean:height ratio that exceeded 1 standard deviation (SD)

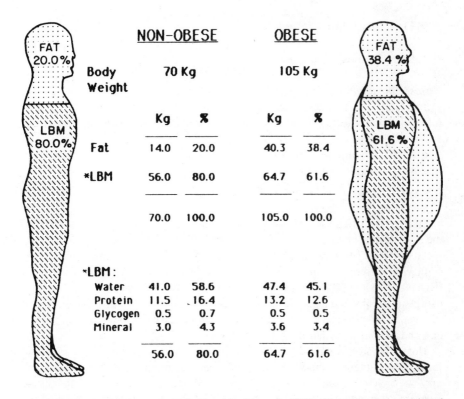

	NON-OBESE		OBESE	
Body Weight	70 Kg		105 Kg	
	Kg	%	Kg	%
Fat	14.0	20.0	40.3	38.4
*LBM	56.0	80.0	64.7	61.6
	70.0	100.0	105.0	100.0
*LBM:				
Water	41.0	58.6	47.4	45.1
Protein	11.5	16.4	13.2	12.6
Glycogen	0.5	0.7	0.5	0.5
Mineral	3.0	4.3	3.6	3.4
	56.0	80.0	64.7	61.6

Figure 5-1 Body Composition of a 70-kg Nonobese Man and a 105-kg Obese man. *Source*: Adapted with permission from *Intenational Journal of Obesity* (1978; 2:441–447), Copyright © 1978, John Libbey & Company Ltd.

of the mean for normal-weight subjects, and more than one half of them exceeded 2 SD. Extensive review of the literature confirmed their findings that, on average, obese subjects have a larger lean tissue mass than their nonobese peers, and that the lean component of the body accounts for a mean of 29% of the excess weight. This mean value is between the estimates of James et al[47] and Webster et al.[48]

Assuming that obesity is usually accompanied by increased lean tissue and contributes to approximately 23% of weight gained, a hypothetical body composition of a 105-kg man is proposed and shown in Figure 5-1 together with a 70-kg nonobese man. When the 70-kg man gained 50% (35 kg) of his body weight and increased it to 105 kg, both lean and fat tissues increased quantitatively. But when expressed as a percentage of body weight, body fat increased and lean tissue decreased.

RESTING METABOLIC RATES

Basal and Resting Metabolic Rates

Basal metabolic rate (BMR) can be defined as the minimum energy needed to maintain vital functions (heart, liver, kidney, and other organs and cellular metabolic processes). It is usually measured under the following conditions:

- 12 to 18 hours after the last intake of food
- patient lying awake and quietly in a thermally neutral environment
- patient relaxed and emotionally calm.

Since it is difficult to obtain these true basal conditions, it was proposed to measure resting metabolism instead of basal metabolism, and to determine the metabolic rate 2 to 4 hours after a light breakfast.[50] This resting metabolism is somewhat different from that defined in the Recommended Daily Allowances (RDAs).[51] In the RDA, resting metabolic rate (RMR) represents the average energy metabolism of a person resting in a comfortable environment, not engaged in any special physical activities. This rate may be measured at any time of the day and includes the thermic effect of food.

Most laboratories continue to measure RMRs under the conditions specified for BMRs, but term it the RMR with the understanding that true basal conditions may not have been established. Thus, the conditions under which the metabolic rates are assessed are standardized to some extent. The advantage of such standardization is obvious: it makes the comparison of results obtained from sequential measurements in a patient, or from one laboratory to another, possible and more interpretable.

Direct and Indirect Calorimetries

Although the RMR can be determined by a direct calorimeter, which directly measures heat production (changes in temperature), it is commonly measured by indirect calorimetry. The preference of indirect calorimetry over direct calorimetry is attributable to the cost and unavailability of direct calorimeters (only a few exist in the United States). In addition, direct calorimetry requires extensive time for equilibration and measurement.

Indirect calorimetry measures oxygen consumption and/or carbon dioxide production. From the rate of oxygen consumed and carbon dioxide produced, one can calculate the corresponding energy expenditure. The Benedict-Roth respirometer apparatus, which is a closed-circuit system, has been used since the turn of this century. In this method, a known volume of pure oxygen is supplied to the subject, and carbon dioxide is constantly removed as it passes through soda lime without being measured. The decrease in the gas volume in this closed system is related to the rate of the oxygen consumption, from which the metabolic rate is then calculated.

The commonly used indirect calorimeters are open-circuit systems. Several machines for indirect calorimetry have been developed and are commercially available. The subject inspires room air, and expired air is collected and analyzed for oxygen and carbon dioxide content. Normally, room air contains 20.93% oxygen and 0.003% carbon dioxide. The difference in content between room air and expired air is assumed to be consumed or produced by the subject. Newer systems usually have not only analyzers for oxygen and carbon dioxide but often come equipped with computers. Thus, the measurement of RMR can be accomplished in a short time. The most difficult task in obtaining reliable RMRs is proper preparation of the patient in a relaxed, postabsorptive condition.

All indirect calorimetry methods necessitate the collection and analysis of expired air. The use of a mouthpiece to collect the expired air requires less equilibration time, but has been criticized for causing discomfort. Such discomfort was found to cause a higher oxygen consumption than with a hood system or a respiration chamber.[52] However, others[53] compared the metabolic rate of young men using three means, ie, mouthpiece, mask, and hood system, to collect expired air; no significant difference among methods was observed.

Many factors may affect the RMR. For example, RMR decreases with age, and men have a higher RMR than women matched for age, height, and weight. Other factors such as body weight, body composition, diet, temperature, hormones, drugs, stress, and exercise may also affect the RMR. Some of these factors have been discussed elsewhere (see Chapters 3 and 4). Discussion here focuses on RMR with respect to body composition.

Body Surface Area, Lean Body Mass, Fat, and Resting Metabolic Rate

It is difficult to know the best way to express RMR. The problem lies in part in comparing the RMR of subjects of differing body composition and in part in defining what is "normal." Most find that RMR correlates best with LBM, which is an approximation of the respiring tissue mass. Other factors such as body weight to the two-thirds power (another estimate of metabolically active tissue), body surface area, and total body weight have also been used to express metabolic rate.

Generally, it is reported either as an absolute value (kcal/24 hr) or in relation to body surface area (kcal/m^2) so that it can be compared with reference values, eg, Harris and Benedict,[54] Boothby et al,[55] and Fleisch.[56] A RMR within 15% of the predicted reference value is usually considered "normal."

The definition of *normal* is based on the finding that the coefficient of variation of the BMR of normal healthy adults (without abnormal endocrine function) matched for age, sex, height and weight, or body surface area was 9%,[55] or 7.6% for men and 7.0% for women.[47] This result has been taken to mean that the appropriate limits for normality should be within ±15% to 20% (mean ± 2 SD) of the predictive metabolic rate.

Recent publications suggest that there is a wide variation in RMRs in obese as well as nonobese people. The probability of finding a person without any detectable endocrine abnormality who has a metabolic rate 20% different from expected is certainly not negligible.[57]

Standardization by LBM has been advocated by several groups.[58,59] Indeed, expressing RMR in terms of LBM eliminates observed differences between men and women and the apparent diminution of RMR with age in normal-weight people.[60,61] These studies assume that adipose tissue is metabolically inert. Studies of small numbers of obese subjects differ as to whether RMR is related more to LBM,[47,57,62] fat,[63] or both.[64,65]

Body Surface Area and Resting Metabolic Rate

Since heat is dissipated through the skin, RMR has been expressed per unit of body surface area (m^2). The body surface area of a person can be estimated from height and weight read directly from a nomogram or calculated with the following formula:[66]

$$\text{Body surface (m}^2) = 0.007184 \times \text{Height (m)}^{0.725} \times \text{Weight (kg)}^{0.425}$$

In 1940, Seltzer[67] reported the results of an investigation of the coefficients of correlation between basal oxygen consumption and various anthropometric measurements in 34 men, aged 20 to 38 years and weighing from 54.7 to 93.4 kg. Measurements included age, height, body weight, surface area, and circumferences of chest, waist at umbilicus, etc. It was found that basal oxygen consumption was highly dependent on body mass and surface area: the larger the gross measurements, the higher the oxygen consumption. Thus, it may be seen that surface area has the highest coefficient of correlation ($r = .505$), followed by stature ($r = .447$), body weight ($r = .412$), and the chest measurements.

The close relation between RMR and body weight, and RMR and surface area was also observed in 140 women studied by Dore et al.[57] These women varied in age, 16 to 68 years, and in weight, 56.9 to 162.3 kg. The variables most closely related to RMR were body weight (0.798) and surface area (0.787), followed by TBK (0.755) and age (-0.222).

Lean Body Mass and Resting Metabolic Rate

Similar to normal-weight people, the RMR of obese people is also found to be related closely to LBM. Halliday et al[62] reported a correlation coefficient of 0.844 between metabolic rate and LBM in 22 obese women aged 17 to 56 years and weighing 64 to 133 kg. However, a correlation of approximately 0.6 was found between fat and RMR. Further analysis of regressions of metabolic rate on lean and adipose mass suggested that the apparent relation of RMR and fat is largely attributable to the correlation between lean and fat tissue. The investigators[62] concluded that lean tissue is much more important than adipose tissue in explaining variation in RMR.

Fat and Resting Metabolic Rate

In contrast, Bray et al[63] reported that the metabolic rate was more closely related to fat mass than LBM in a group of 18 grossly obese women. They found that oxygen uptake was better correlated with body fat, weight, and surface area than with measures of LBM such as TBW, TBK, or creatinine. Body composition was measured by exchangeable potassium (by ^{42}K dilution) and TBW (by dilution of tritiated water) in 14 of 18 subjects. The time allowed for tracer to equilibrate in these morbidly obese subjects has been criticized as insufficient; therefore, the body composition determined may be inaccurate, and the finding may be questionable.[68]

However, similar findings that BMR correlates better with fat than with LBM were also reported by Miller and Parsonage.[69] They studied a group of 29 women who claimed difficulty in losing weight despite adherence to a reducing diet. These subjects were moderately obese (55 to 118 kg). Estimates of body fat were made with skinfold calipers. The correlation coefficient between BMR and fat content was 0.52, while that with LBM was only 0.33 (not statistically significant).It is interesting to note that correlation with fat was similar to that reported by Halliday et al.[62]

Lean Body Mass, Fat, and Resting Metabolic Rate

In 1983, we[65] reported that measurements of RMR in 202 obese people (154 women and 48 men) revealed that in both sexes there were significant univariate correlations between RMR and LBM, body fat, weight, fat cell weight, and fat cell number. Multiple regression analysis of these data showed that LBM and fat cell weight and number were significant predictors of RMR. However, the contribution of LBM was 3 to 5 times greater per kilogram than that of body fat.

The fact that the effect of body fat on RMR was highly significant in obese populations implies that although adipose tissue is known to be relatively inert metabolically, when the adipose mass accounts for a significant proportion of body weight, the relatively inert metabolism of adipose tissue accumulates and becomes an important contributor to total metabolic rate. Thus, it seems reasonable to conclude that in obese people, the RMR correlates highly with LBM and, to a lesser extent, with body fat.

Resting Metabolic Rate in Obese People

Numerous attempts have been made to establish whether obese patients have a metabolic abnormality that contributes to their obesity or accounts for their difficulty in weight reduction. The findings reported in the literature are varied and support all possible claims, that obese patients have low, normal, or high RMR, depending on how the comparison was made. The majority of obese patients have an increased RMR when it is expressed in kilocalories per 24 hours as compared with the expected values for normal-weight people of the same age, sex, and height. It is also reported that RMRs (kcal/24 hr) are within the range expected for their current obese weight.

Hoffman et al[64] compared the RMRs of 15 obese women with those of non-obese control subjects. The mean body weight and fat were 71 kg (SD ± 7) and 33.6% (± 3.4) for the obese, and 59 kg (± 8) and 20.4% (± 4.4) for the normal-weight group. The RMR was expressed in various ways and compared. It was found that the obese group had a significantly greater mean RMR than the control group when the values were expressed per 24 hours, per kilogram of lean body mass, or by oxygen consumption (ml/min). However, based on kilograms of body weight, the mean RMR of the obese group was significantly lower than that of the control group. The difference between the two groups diminished when the RMR was expressed per unit of body surface area (m^2).

Nelson et al[70] measured BMR in 142 people with varying amounts of body fat. The mean BMR for the obese patients was −0.6% of the expected value with a standard deviation similar to that for the normal population. The BMRs of 53 (65%) of the obese subjects fell within ± 10% of normal, 22 (27%) ranged between ± 10% to ± 20%, and only 7 had BMRs outside the ± 20% range. Thus the obese subjects had remarkably normal BMRs. The authors[70] concluded that the obese population had remarkably normal basal metabolism. The mean BMR and variability about the mean were nearly identical with those of normal-weight groups. Their data are in agreement with the earlier finding of Boothby and Sandiford[71] that BMR in obesity is normal.

Thus, if the actual measurement of RMR is not possible in clinical settings, the RMR can be predicted from body weight, height, age, and gender using prediction equations such as those provided by Harris and Benedict[54] as follows: RMR (kcal/24 hr) for

- Women: = 655.096 + 9.563 Weight (kg) + 1.850 Height (m) − 4.676 Age (yr)
- Men: = 66.473 + 13.752 Weight (kg) + 5.003 Height (m) − 6.755 Age (yr)

RMR varies considerably from person to person in the obese as well as the normal-weight population. In 72 obese patients studied by James et al,[47] RMR ranged from 1,050 to 2,410 kcal/24 hr. Of the 72, only 6 women had RMRs lower than that expected for their height, age, and obese weight. Thus, it should not be surprising that if the patient is adhering to a caloric intake less than the predicted RMR and is having difficulty losing weight, it will be quite possible that the patient may have an unusually low RMR without endocrine problems. In this case, the actual measurement of RMR is called for, and adjustment of prescribed calories may be necessary for successful treatment of the obesity.

Effect of Weight Reduction on Resting Metabolic Rate

One well-documented change occurring during weight loss through dieting is a dramatic reduction in RMR. In fact, this decrease in RMR is often greater than the decrease attributable to the weight loss. James et al[47] observed that several obese patients consuming either 360 or 680 kcal/day for 30 days had an RMR that fell to a subnormal value, even if their weight was still substantially in excess of the appropriate "desirable" range. However, after a period of weight maintenance, most returned to the predicted values.

Dore et al[57] reported that an excessive decrease in RMR during weight reduction may be curtailed by a slow rate of weight reduction. They reported that the metabolic rates of 19 severely obese women who lost an average of 30 kg in 1 year were still within the range predicted for their reduced weight. LBM contributed 26% (8.1 kg) of the total weight lost as determined by changes in TBK. The authors[57] concluded that if the weight loss is not rapid, the reduced weight will be associated with an RMR similar to that of people of similar weight who have not undergone massive weight loss.

Recently, Barrows and Snook[72] reported changes in RMR using various factors. Fifteen obese women, aged 30 to 54 years and weighing 66 to 104 kg, lost a mean of 19 kg while consuming 420 kcal for an average of 18 weeks. The mean weight loss was 1.1 kg/wk. The RMR decreased significantly from 1,692 to 1,334 kcal/day, 34.0 to 31.7 kcal/m^2/hr, and 1.5 to 1.4 kcal/kg of LBM per hour. The decline in RMR per 24 hours was 21% of the initial value and was similar to the 23% change in body weight. However, the magnitude of change in mean metabolic rates was very small, only 6.8%, when it was expressed per unit of body surface or LBM. This suggests that the change in RMR during weight reduction in an obese group cannot be explained totally by the reduced respiratory rate (improved efficiency) of metabolically active tissue, LBM. Unfortunately, data on changes in body composition were not reported, and, therefore, it is not possible to search for other factors that may also explain the changes in RMR.

Bortz[73] estimated that there is a reduction of 100 kcal/day in BMR for every 25 lb of weight lost in both men and women. This estimate is similar to the findings of James et al[47] who reported that an increase in weight of 20 kg is needed to achieve an increase in RMR of 800 kJ/24 hr (ie, 108 kcal/24 hr for every 25 lb of weight gain).

The rate of weight loss among obese women on a strictly controlled reducing diet was most closely related to their RMR, and this in turn was highly correlated with body weight.[74] As weight was lost, metabolic rate decreased, and thus it became more difficult for the reduced-obese person to achieve further weight loss or to maintain the reduced body weight. It is therefore of some practical importance to determine the component of body weight with which metabolic rate is best correlated.

If one believes that the RMR of obese patients is better correlated with their fat than with their lean tissue, then a reduction in fat (which is the objective of treatment) must inevitably cause a reduction in metabolic rate, and hence make further weight loss more difficult to achieve or sustain. However, if lean tissue determines metabolic rate, it is logical to seek a form of treatment that causes fat loss but spares lean tissue, and thus preserves a normal metabolic rate.

Effect of Exercise on Resting Metabolic Rate and Body Composition During Weight Reduction

It was reported in 1980 that exercise prevents the decrease of RMR that occurs during dieting in normal-weight volunteers consuming 800 kcal/day.[75] Since this report, exercise programs have been avidly promoted in the treatment of obesity. It is thought that the addition of exercise to the program of weight control may favorably modify the composition of weight loss and/or prevent the excessive reduction in RMR.

Zuti and Golding[76] compared the body composition changes of 25 women, 20 to 40 lb overweight, on a weight-reducing program. The program induced a caloric deficit of 500 kcal/day by reducing caloric intake (diet alone), by increasing energy output (exercise only), or by a combination of the two (diet plus exercise). The women were randomly assigned to one of the three regimens.

The amount of weight lost in the three groups was similar, 5.3 kg, 5.5 kg, and 4.8 kg for the diet alone, the diet plus exercise, and the exercise alone groups, respectively. However, body compositional studies performed at the beginning and end of the experiment showed that the diet plus exercise and the exercise alone groups lost fat but gained LBM. The diet alone group lost fat and LBM. It was a well-designed study in the sense that the size of the energy deficit was equal among the three groups. However, the findings are not convincing because the observed changes in LBM (0.5 to 1.1 kg) were small and still within the measurement error of any in vivo method for body composition determination including densitometry, which was used in this study.

The effect of exercise on RMR was investigated[77] in eight young women (mean body weight 70 kg). After 11 weeks of aerobic exercise (5 hr/wk) without any caloric restriction, the women lost a mean of 2.4 kg of body weight and 1.5 kg of fat. Exercise also induced a significant increase in RMR expressed as either kilocalories per minute or per kilogram of LBM. Again, the amount of fat lost may be significant statistically, but from a methodologic perspective, it may not be significant since the magnitude of the change, 1.5 kg, is still within the range of measurement error of densitometry.

In contrast, Heymsfield et al[78] reported that exercise in combination with caloric restriction induced a significantly greater reduction in RMR than that induced by caloric restriction alone. Eleven young obese women were assigned to either a 900-kcal regimen or a 900-kcal diet plus 350 kcal of exercise daily for 5 weeks. Body weight loss was 7.5 and 7.0 kg, and LBM loss was 2.2 and 2.6 kg for the diet plus exercise and the diet alone groups, respectively. The decrease in RMR (kcal/hr, kcal/kg, or LBM/hr) expressed as a percentage of initial values in the diet plus exercise group was twice that observed in the diet alone group. The significantly greater decrease in RMR observed in the diet plus exercise group might have resulted from the extra caloric expenditure (350 kcal/day) induced by exercise.

The literature investigating the effects of exercise on resting metabolism and/or body composition in an obese population during weight reduction are scanty and contradictory. Some of the reported changes or differences are small and still within the measurement error of the method used. Therefore, although the reported findings are statistically significant, they may be questionable.

SUMMARY

Most methods for in vivo determination of body composition are indirect and based on the assumption of certain constants, such as hydration of tissue, density of fat, etc. These factors, however, are not constant: they vary from tissue to tissue and change according to individual health status. In addition, each method has its own associated measurement errors. Thus, none of the methods currently used including densitometry, the commonly accepted gold standard, is error free. The measurement errors of various methods are shown in Table 5-2.

When reviewing data on body composition, especially in comparing differences between groups or between sequential measurements, one should keep in mind the magnitude of measurement error of the method used and be cautious in drawing conclusions about whether the differences are clinically significant.

The choice of methods and facilities for body composition measurement in a clinical setting is rather limited. It is unlikely that a regular clinic would install an underwater weighing facility or large, expensive equipment such as for TO-BEC. There is a need for validating and/or developing procedures that can be easily used in a clinical setting, and that can provide noninvasive, simple, convenient, and accurate measurement.

There is evidence that obesity is associated with increased LBM. LBM accounts for a mean of 23%[48] or 29%[49] of the excess weight that obese people accumulate over the normal-weight population. It is therefore recommended that in the treatment of obesity LBM should not constitute more than this proportion of total weight loss. This may be accomplished by a slower rate of weight loss.

The majority of obese people have RMRs appropriate for their obese weight but elevated when compared with predicted rates for matched nonobese people. This discrepancy diminishes when the metabolic rate is expressed per unit of LBM or body surface area. The choice of units for expressing metabolic rates depends largely on the intention of the clinician; total calories may be more

Table 5-2 Measurement Errors of Assessing Body Fat by Various Methods

Methods	Fat	Reference
Densitometry	2.5%	Lohman,[79] 1981
Total body water (TBW)	4.73%	Segal et al,[17] 1985
Densitometry and TBW	2.57%	Segal et al,[17] 1985
Total body potassium (TBK)	6.87%	Segal et al,[17] 1985
Total body electrical conductivity (TOBEC)	3.73%	Segal et al,[17] 1985
Bioelectrical impedance assessment (BIA)	6.10%	Segal et al,[17] 1985
Anthropometry Steinkamp et al,[26] 1965	8.49%	Segal et al,[17] 1985
Durnin and Womersley	2.3 kg for women 3.7 kg for men	Durnin and Womersley,[29] 1974
Total body nitrogen (TBN) by neutron activation	2.7%–5.1%	Cohn et al,[36] 1984
Body mass index (kg/m²)	4.2 kg for women 5.8 kg for men	Garrow and Webster,[32] 1985

useful than calories based on body weight (kcal/kg) or LBM (kcal/kg of LBM) in estimating energy expenditure and prescribing diets. On the other hand, when one compares the metabolic rates in different people or in one person on several occasions, it may be more meaningful to normalize the metabolic rate as kilocalories per kilogram of body weight, LBM, or body surface area. The RMR (kcal/day) accounts for 70% to 80% of daily energy expenditure of obese, sedentary people. It decreases with weight loss during the treatment of obesity, and thereby makes it more difficult to lose weight. Diet in conjunction with exercise has been touted to prevent this decrease in RMR, but the reported data are skimpy and contradictory. More research is needed to investigate the role of exercise and other factors in preventing the decrease in RMR associated with weight reduction in obese people.

REFERENCES

1. Mitchell HH, Hamilton TS, Steggerda FR, et al: The chemical composition of the adult human body and its bearing on the biochemistry of growth. *J Biol Chem* 1945; 158:625–637.

2. Widdowson EM, McCance RA, Spray CM: The chemical composition of the human body. *Clin Sci* 1951; 10:113–125.

3. Forbes RM, Cooper AR, Mitchell HH: The composition of the adult human body as determined by clinical analysis. *J Biol Chem* 1953; 203:359–366.

4. Forbes RM, Mitchell HH, Cooper AR: Further studies on the gross composition and mineral elements of the adult human body. *J Biol Chem* 1956; 223:969–975.

5. Behnke AR: Anthropometric evaluation of body composition throughout life. *Ann NY Acad Sci* 1963; 110:450–464.

6. Siri WE: Body composition from fluid spaces and density: Analysis of methods, in Brozek J, Henschel A (eds): *Techniques for Measuring Body Composition.* Washington, National Academy of Sciences, 1969, pp 223–244.

7. Keys A, Brozek J: Body fat in adult man. *Physiol Rev* 1953; 33:245–325.

8. Wilmore SH: A simplified method for determination of residual lung volumes. *J Appl Physiol* 1969; 27:96–100.

9. Wilmore SH, Behnke AR: An anthropometric estimation of body density and lean body weight in young women. *Am J Clin Nutr* 1970; 23:267–274.

10. Roche AF: Anthropometric methods: New and old, what they tell us. *Int J Obes* 1984; 8:509–523.

11. Young CM, Martin ME, McCarthy MC, et al: Body composition of young women. *J Am Diet Assoc* 1961; 38:332–340.

12. Lim TPK, Luft UC: Body density, fat and fat-free weight. *Am J Med* 1961; 30:825–832.

13. Pace N, Rathun EN: Studies on body composition: III. Water and chemically contained nitrogen content. *J Biol Chem* 1945; 158:685–691.

14. Halliday D, Hopkinson WI: Precise measurement of total body water using trace quantities of deuterium oxide. *Biomed Mass Spectrom* 1977; 4:82–87.

15. Culebras JM, Moore FD: Total body water and the exchangeable hydrogen in man. *Am J Physiol* 1977; 232:R54–R59.

16. Siri WE: The gross composition of the body. *Advances in Biological and Medical Physics* 1956; 49:239–280.

17. Segal KR, Gutin B, Presta E, et al: Estimation of human body composition by electrical impedance methods: A comparative study. *J Appl Physiol* 1985; 58:1565–1571.

18. Forbes GB, Hursch JB: Ages and sex trends in lean body mass calculated from ^{40}K measurements: With a note on the theoretical basis for the procedure. *Ann NY Acad Sci* 1963; 110:225–263.

19. Forbes GB, Gallup J, Hursh JB: Estimation of total body fat from potassium-40 content. *Science* 1961; 133:101–102.

20. Womersley J, Boddy K, King PC, et al: A comparison of the fat-free mass of young adults, estimated by anthropometry, body density and total body potassium content. *Clin Sci* 1972; 43:469–475.

21. Pierson R, Wang J, Thornton C, et al: Body potassium by four-pi ^{40}K counting: An anthropometric correction. *J Appl Physiol* 1984; 246:F234–F239.

22. Blahd WH, Cassen B, Ledered M, et al: Electrolyte metabolism by whole-body counting techniques with particular reference to muscle disease and obesity, in *Clinical Use of Whole-Body Counting*. Vienna, International Atomic Energy Agency, 1966, pp 169–186.

23. Colt EWD, Wang J, Stallone F, et al: A possible low intracellular potassium in obesity. *Am J Clin Nutr* 1981; 34:367–372.

24. Crook GH, Bennett CA, Norwood WD, et al: Evaluation of skin-fold measurements and weight chart to measure body fat. *JAMA* 1966; 198:157–162.

25. Seltzer CC, Mayer J: Greater reliability of the triceps skinfold over the subscapular skinfold as an index of obesity. *Am J Clin Nutr* 1967; 20:950–953.

26. Steinkamp RC, Cohen NL, Gaffey WR, et al: Measures of body fat and related factors in normal adults: II. A simple clinical method to estimate body fat and lean body mass. *J Chron Dis* 1965; 18:1291–1307.

27. Pollack ML, Hickman T, Kendrick Z, et al: Prediction of body density in young and middle-aged men. *J Appl Physiol* 1976; 40:300–304.

28. Wilmore JH, Behnke AR: An anthropometric estimation of body density and lean body weight in young men. *J Appl Physiol* 1969; 27:25–31.

29. Durnin JVGA, Womersley J: Body fat assessed from total body density and its estimation from skinfold thickness: Measurements on 481 men and women aged from 16 to 72 years. *Br J Nutr* 1974; 32:77–97.

30. Frisancho AR, Flegel PN: Elbow breadth as a measure of frame size for US males and females. *Am J Clin Nutr* 1983; 37:311–314.

31. Johnson CL, Fullwood R, Abraham S: Basic data on anthropometric measurements and angular measurements of hip and knee for selected age groups 1–74 years of age: United States, 1971–1975. *Vital and Health Survey No. 219*, US Department of Health and Human Services publication No. (PHS) 81-1669. National Center for Health Statistics, Hyattsville, MD, 1981.

32. Garrow JS, Webster J: Quetelet's index (W/H^2) as a measure of fatness. *Int J Obes* 1985; 9:147–153.

33. Van Loan M, Mayclin P: A new TOBEC instrument and procedure for the assessment of body composition: Use of Fourier coefficients to predict lean body mass and total body water. *Am J Clin Nutr* 1987; 45:131–137.

34. Beddoe AH, Hill GL: Review: Clinical measurement of body composition using in vivo neutron activation analysis. *J Parenteral and Enteral Nutr* 1985; 9:504–520.

35. Knight GS, Beddoe AH, Streat SJ, et al: Body composition of two human cadavers by neutron activation and chemical analysis. *Am J Physiol* 1986; 250:E179–E185.

36. Cohn SH, Vaswani AN, Yasumura S, et al: Improved models for determination of body fat by in vivo neutron activation. *Am J Clin Nutr* 1984; 40:225–259.

37. Borkan GA, Gerzof SG, Robbins AH, et al: Assessment of abdominal fat content by computed tomography. *Am J Clin Nutr* 1982; 36:172–177.

38. Grauer WO, Moss AA, Cann CE, et al: Quantification of body fat distribution in the abdomen using computed tomography. *Am J Clin Nutr* 1984; 39:631–637.

39. Katch VL, Freedson PS, Katch FI, et al: Body frame size: Validity of self-appraisal. *Am J Clin Nutr* 1982; 36:676–679.

40. Frisancho AR, Flegel PN: Relative merits of old and new indices of body mass with reference to skinfold thickness. *Am J Clin Nutr* 1982; 36:697–699.

41. Wilmore JH, Brown CH: Physiological profiles of women distance runners. *Med Sci Sports Exerc* 1974; 6:178–181.

42. Hannon BM, Lohman TG: The energy cost of overweight in the United States. *Am J Public Health* 1978; 68:765–767.

43. Barlett HL, Buskirk ER: Body composition and the expiratory reserve volume in lean and obese men and women. *Int J Obes* 1983; 7:339–343.

44. Ravussin E, Burnand B, Schutz Y, et al: Energy expenditure before and during energy restriction in obese patients. *Am J Clin Nutr* 1985; 41:753–759.

45. Forbes GB: Lean body mass and fat in obese children. *Pediatrics* 1964; 34:308–314.

46. Drenick EJ, Blahd WH, Singer FR, et al: Body potassium content in obese subjects and potassium depletion during prolonged fasting. *Am J Clin Nutr* 1966; 18:278–285.

47. James WPT, Bailes J, Daives HL, et al: Elevated metabolic rates in obesity. *Lancet* 1981; 1:1122–1125.

48. Webster JD, Hesp R, Garrow JS: The composition of excess weight in obese women estimated by body density, total body water and total body potassium. *Human Nutrition: Clinical Nutrition* 1984; 38C:299–306.

49. Forbes GB, Welle SL: Lean body mass in obesity. *Int J Obes* 1983; 7:99–107.

50. Durnin JVGA, Passmore R: *Energy Work and Leisure*. London, Heinemann Educational Books Ltd, 1967.

51. National Research Council: *Recommended Dietary Allowances*. Washington, National Academy of Sciences, 1980.

52. Tremoliere J, Carre L, Naon R: Interrelations between body weight level of vigilance and energy expenditure in subjects on various diets, in Apelbaum M (ed): *Energy Balance in Man*. Paris, 1973.

53. Segal KR: Comparison of indirect calorimetric measurement of resting energy expenditure with a ventilated hood, face mask, and mouthpiece. *Am J Clin Nutr*, 1987; 45:1420–1423.

54. Harris SA, Benedict FG: A biometric of basal metabolism in man, publication No. 279. Washington, DC, Carnegie Institution, 1919.

55. Boothby WM, Berkson J, Dunn HL: Studies of the energy of metabolism of normal individuals: A standard for basal metabolism, with a nomogram for clinical application. *Am J Physiol* 1936; 116:468–484.

56. Fleisch A: Le metabolisme basal standard et la determination au moyen du metabocalculator. *Helv Med Act* 1951; 1:23–44.

57. Dore C, Hesp R, Wilkins D, et al: Prediction of energy requirements of obese patients after massive weight loss. *Human Nutr Clin Nutr* 1982; 36C:41–48.

58. Keys A, Taylor HL, Grande F: Basal metabolism and age of adult man. *Metabolism* 1973; 22:579–587.

59. Miller AT Jr, Blyth CS: Lean body mass as metabolic reference standard. *J Appl Physiol* 1953; 5:311–316.

60. Tzankoff SP, Norris AH; Effect of muscle mass decrease on age-related BMR changes. *J Appl Physiol* 1977; 43:1001–1006.

61. Cunningham JJ: A reanalysis of the factors influencing basal metabolic rate in normal adults. *Am J Clin Nutr* 1980; 33:2372–2374.

62. Halliday D, Hesp R, Stalley SF, et al: Resting metabolic rate, weight, surface area and body composition in obese women. *Int J Obes* 1979; 3:1–6.

63. Bray G, Schwartz M, Rozin R, et al: Relationship between oxygen consumption and body composition of obese patients. *Metabolism* 1970; 19:418–429.

64. Hoffmans M, Pfsfer WA, Gundlach BL, et al: Resting metabolic rate in obese and normal weight women. *Int J Obes* 1979; 3:111–118.

65. Bernstein RS, Thornton J, Yang MU, et al: Prediction of the resting metabolic rate in obese patients. *Am J Clin Nutr* 1983; 37:595–602.

66. DuBois D, DuBois EF: A formula to estimate the approximate surface area if height and weight be known. *Arch Intern Med* 1916; 17:863–871.

67. Seltzer CC: Body build and oxygen metabolism at rest and during exercise. *Am J Physiol* 1940; 129:1–13.

68. Garrow JS: *Energy Balance and Obesity in Man*, ed 2. Amsterdam, Elsevier/North-Holland Biomedical Press, 1978.

69. Miller DS, Parsonage S: Resistance to slimming. Adaptation or illusion? *Lancet* 1975; 1:773–775.

70. Nelson RA, Anderson LF, Gastineau CF, et al: *Physiology and Natural History of Obesity*. 1972.

71. Boothby WM, Sandiford I: Normal values for standard metabolism. *Am J Physiol* 1929; 90:209–291.

72. Barrows K, Snook JT: Effect of a high-protein, very-low-calorie diet on resting metabolism, thyroid hormones, and energy expenditure of obese middle-aged women. *Am J Clin Nutr* 1987; 45:391–398.

73. Bortz WM: Predictability of weight loss. *JAMA* 1968; 204:101–105.

74. Garrow JS, Durrant ML, Mann S, et al: Factors determining weight loss in obese patients in a metabolic ward. *Int J Obes* 1978; 2:441–447.

75. Stern JS, Schultz C, Mole P, et al: Effect of caloric restriction and exercise on basal metabolism and thyroid hormone. *Alim Nutr Metab* 1980; 1:361. Abstracted.

76. Zuti WB, Golding LA: Comparing diet and exercise as weight reduction tools. *Physician and Sports Medicine* 1976; 4:49–53.

77. Tremblay A, Fontaine E, Poehlman ET, et al: The effect of exercise training on resting metabolic rate in lean and moderately obese individuals. *Int J Obes* 1986; 10:511–518.

78. Heymsfield SB, Casper K, Hearn J, et al: Rate of weight loss during underfeeding: Relation to level of physical activity. To be published.

79. Lohman TG: Skinfolds and body density and their relation to body fatness: A review. *Hum Biol* 1981; 53:181–225.

Chapter 6

Biologic Adaptations to Starvation and Semistarvation

C. Wayne Callaway

Understanding biologic adaptations to starvation and semistarvation is important because many dietary regimens for treating obesity have been based on moderately severe restrictions in caloric intakes, often combined with carbohydrate restriction.[1,2] Certainly, starvation is the fastest way to lose weight. However, starvation and semistarvation regimens are not without hazards, as tragically demonstrated by the several dozen deaths associated with liquid protein regimens a decade or so ago.[3] In addition, recent evidence suggests that severe caloric restriction actually predisposes to bingeing, on the one hand,[4] and a greater propensity to gain weight, on the other.[5] Thus, the following discussion can be seen as background for understanding the chapters on therapeutic diets that follow, and for understanding some of the frustrations and failure that many dieters have experienced repeatedly in the past.

The premises underlying this chapter can be stated simply: Starvation results in a series of adaptive changes that tend to conserve energy, glucose, and protein and, thereby, prolong survival in the face of inadequate caloric intake. Frequent starvation (or, semistarvation) leads to improvement in the adaptive responses, ie, with each dieting episode, the rate of weight loss is slower and, with return to normal eating, the rate of weight gain is more rapid. In addition, starvation predisposes to changes in appetite regulation, resulting in a tendency to overeat when food becomes available.

Such adaptations are associated with clinically significant side-effects, including changes in electrolyte balance; symptoms attributable to low levels of triiodothyronine (T_3); symptoms attributable to a functional autonomic neuropathy (because of low turnovers of norepinephrine [NE]); and symptoms probably secondary to alterations in central nervous system (CNS) neurotransmitters, including changes in mood, sleep, and perception.

Teleologically, one can conceive of such a composite of reactions as favoring survival, but at the cost of impaired performance of day-to-day functions. Second, not only is there an evolutionary ''memory,'' but there also seems to be an individual "memory" in that repeated starvation leads to improved efficiency in adapting and a greater tendency to binge once food becomes available.

HISTORICAL BACKGROUND

Although fasting has a long tradition, especially in various religious practices, the scientific study of the consequences of fasting can be dated from the 16th century, when Sanctorius (1561–1636) carried out a detailed series of metabolic balance studies, measuring rates of weight loss by combustion of energy stores and in evaporation. Sanctorius[6] showed that weight loss consists of sensible loss (feces and urine) and insensible perspiration. About 85 to 90% of this insensible loss was due to the vaporization of water; the remainder was due to the discrepancy between the amount of carbon dioxide exhaled and the oxygen absorbed.

Modern studies of fasting began with Benedict's classic studies of a professional faster, who was paid to undergo several prolonged fasts of up to 60 days each. Benedict[7] showed that the declines in metabolic rates with fasting were greater than could be accounted for by the loss of body mass alone. Furthermore, the decline in metabolic rate occurs acutely well before there is a significant loss in body weight.

One of the more moving human documents in the literature of this field is the collection of papers written by Jewish physicians[8] in the Warsaw ghetto in the late 1930s and early 1940s. In spite of extreme conditions, these heroic investigators documented a series of changes that occur in starvation, both among their neighbors and among themselves, using the limited technical facilities available to them. The papers themselves were hidden in various places, later smuggled to France, where they were published in French, and in the past decade translated into English.

The *Biology of Human Starvation*, the two-volume monograph that came from the Keys studies, remains the standard comprehensive reference in this field. During 1944 to 1945, Keys et al[9] studied extensively a group of young male conscientious objectors who volunteered to undergo chronic semistarvation in a research setting so that information could be obtained that would help in treating more effectively the victims of concentration and prisoner of war camps at the conclusion of World War II. One indication of the importance of this work is the fact that the monograph is still in print, nearly four decades after its publication.

In the mid-1960s, Cahill and a series of imaginative collaborators undertook a group of studies designed to elucidate the changes in hormonal control and energy substrates during starvation in obese women. Although various refinements have been added to the fundamental synthesis Cahill achieved, the synthesis itself still holds as the most useful framework for understanding hormonal-substrate interactions. In addition, Cahill and collaborators[10,11] made a number of original observations directly in humans, which were later confirmed in laboratory animals, including the fact that with prolonged starvation beta-hydroxybutyrate and acetoacetate (the so-called ketone bodies) can supply up to two thirds of the energy for the CNS, a critical adaptation in terms of glucose sparing.[12]

Recent work has focused on the control signals for the changes in metabolic rate, including changes in thyroid hormone metabolism and sympathetic nervous system activity. Work on the changes in fluid and electrolyte balance dates from the early 1960s, but unfortunately has not kept pace with studies of changes in the hormonal control of energy metabolism. Changes in appetite, in response to underfeeding, have been studied in the framework of the "restrained eater" paradigm, primarily in the past decade. Studies of neurotransmitter changes, at least in humans, remain in their infancy.

CONSERVATION OF ENERGY

During times of inadequate food, it is obviously to the organism's advantage to be able to conserve energy, ie, lower metabolic rate. Metabolic rate refers to the rate of oxidation of fuel substrates per unit of time and is usually measured by indirect calorimetry, that is, by measuring oxygen consumption and carbon dioxide production and calculating the energy equivalent (in calories or megajoules). Recently, the availability of direct calorimetry, whereby total heat production is measured, has stimulated a series of informative studies.[13,14] As far as adaptations to starvation are concerned, the results of indirect calorimetry and direct calorimetry are consistent.

Metabolic rate is dependent on a number of factors, primarily lean body mass (LBM).[14] Sex and age differences disappear when oxygen consumption is corrected for unit of LBM (ie, total body water, total body potassium, or other indicators of fat-free mass). There may also be genetic determinants of resting and postprandial thermogenesis; studies in this regard are still quite preliminary.

With caloric restriction, metabolic rate declines more rapidly than the decline in LBM, suggesting a true adaptation and energy conservation. The magnitude of this response can be dramatic. For example, in subjects with anorexia nervosa, metabolic rates were recorded that were one half the predicted values for healthy subjects of similar height, weight, age, and sex who were eating normally.[15] The survival value of this adaptation is illustrated by the fact that voluntary starvation in otherwise healthy young men can usually be sustained for slightly longer than 60 days.[7] In the absence of adaptive changes, one could calculate that the anticipated survival would be only approximately 3 weeks. Thus, the ability to lower metabolic rate in the presence of food scarcity allows one to triple survival.

The control mechanisms that allow for such adaptations are beginning to be understood. Initial studies focused on the conversion of thyroxin (T_3) to T_4, a process that occurs peripherally, primarily in the liver.[16] With caloric restriction and with carbohydrate restriction, there is reduced conversion of T_4 to T_3 and a decline in circulating T_3 levels. In most studies,[16,17,18] there is a corresponding increase in reverse T_3 (r T_3), at least transiently, which is now thought to be attributable to impaired metabolism of r T_3 rather than increased production. Thermogenically, T_3 is the active form of thyroid hormone; T_4 is inactive. Most observers feel that T_4 must be converted to T_3 before it is thermogenically active.

The decline in T_3, however, does not explain the magnitude of the decline in metabolic rate. Providing exogenous T_3 to someone who is already adapted to starvation results in an increase in ureagenesis and urinary nitrogen losses,[19] with only a minimal increase in metabolic rate.[20] It now seems that the more important control mechanism is probably a decline in the turnover of norepinephrine (NE).

Landsberg and Young[21], in particular, have documented a decline in NE turnover in a variety of organs in response to starvation, caloric restriction, and carbohydrate restriction. Furthermore, using insulin-glucose clamp techniques, they[22] obtained evidence to suggest that insulin is the primary signal that controls the reduction in NE turnover in response to underfeeding and the increase in NE turnover in response to glucose infusion.

Interestingly, NE and T_3 seem to affect the body's response to each other. In part, this seems to be mediated by alterations in receptor responses.[23] For example, in hypothyroidism, there is reduced receptor binding to NE and reduced organ responsiveness to beta-adrenergic stimulation. In hyperthyroidism, the reverse is true. Thus, there would seem to be a synergistic effect of the combined reduction in T_3 and NE turnover, greater than could be accounted for by the changes in either hormone alone.

NE, T_3, and insulin seem to be the primary thermogenic hormones. All three have been implicated in regulating sodium potassium–adenosine triphosphatase (ATPase) activity, a process that accounts for up to 40% of resting energy expenditure.[24] In addition, T_3 seems to be necessary for the normal dose response to NE in experimental studies of brown adipose tissue (BAT).[25] In the presence of "permissive" amounts of T_3, there is a linear dose response in oxygen consumption, heat production, and fatty acid use in the mitochondria of BAT. T_3 alone does not produce such a dose response. In the absence of T_3, the response to NE is blunted. The role of BAT in adult humans is still poorly understood. There is widespread speculation that such mechanisms may have a significant role in the increase in metabolic rate after meals. This subject is discussed in greater detail in Chapter 4.

With repeated dieting, the rate of weight loss declines. Preliminary data[26] suggest that this is associated with a more rapid decline in T_3 production and NE turnover. How this "learned" response occurs is not yet clear. Nevertheless, it would certainly seem to have further adaptive survival value for the organism exposed to repeated famines.

CONSERVATION OF GLUCOSE

Some tissues can use either glucose or fat as a primary fuel (eg, muscle, liver). Others are entirely dependent on glucose (erythrocytes and, perhaps, part of the renal tubule). The brain is primarily dependent on glucose, but can use ketone bodies (beta-hydroxybutyrate and acetoacetate) when they are available. Free fatty acids do not cross the blood-brain barrier well and, therefore, cannot directly supply a source of fuel for the brain.

Some tissues are insulin-dependent in that they require insulin for facilitating glucose uptake. These include muscle and fat cells, especially. Other tissues, such as the liver, are sensitive to insulin in terms of intracellular metabolism but do not require insulin for glucose uptake. The brain has insulin receptors, and isolated areas of the brain seem to be insulin sensitive; such areas of the hypothalamus, in particular, are thought to be involved in appetite, autonomic nervous system, and temperature regulation. However, glucose uptake by the brain, in general, is not insulin-dependent.

Given the requirement for glucose of red blood cells, the renal medulla, and the brain, it is not surprising that the liver has the capacity to synthesize glucose by recycling carbon moieties of three or more carbons, including pyruvate, lactate, glycerol, and amino acids. The kidney and the gut also seem to be potentially gluconeogenic. All three tissues (liver, kidney, and gut) contain glucose-6-phosphatase, the enzyme required to dephosphorylate glucose-6-phosphate and thereby release free glucose to the circulation.

With acute starvation, glycogenolysis provides the major source of circulating glucose. As starvation progresses, gluconeogenesis from amino acids becomes the primary source. In addition, the efficiency of recycling of pyruvate, lactate, and glycerol increases. As starvation continues, hepatic production of ketone bodies provides an alternative source of fuel for the brain, thereby sparing glucose and, indirectly, amino acids.

PROTEIN METABOLISM

Alanine is the major amino acid gluconeogenic precursor for the liver. Alanine is produced, primarily, in muscle, by transaminating an amino group from other amino acids to the 3-carbon pyruvate. In essence, alanine is an aminated pyruvate. From the muscle, alanine serves to transport ammonia to the liver, where the nitrogen can be deaminated and incorporated into urea or reaminated onto other carbon skeletons to form other amino acids. During starvation, alanine use by the liver increases. However, with the decline in insulin level and the reduced peripheral uptake of glucose (along with, perhaps, a decline in muscle glycogen), there is less pyruvate available in the muscle cell to be transaminated to alanine. Therefore, alanine release from muscle declines. With prolonged starvation, circulating alanine levels decline progressively. Availability of alanine then becomes the rate-limiting step for hepatic gluconeogenesis. Infusion of alanine into someone who is already starving results in a prompt increase in hepatic gluconeogenesis and ureagenesis.

Transamination of amino groups to alpha-ketoglutarate, and to glutamate, continues to occur. The end product is glutamine, which is released from muscle and which can serve as a source of both ammonia and glucose in the kidney. The ammonia (NH_3) is vital to regulation of acid-base balance in that release of NH_3 into the renal tubule can buffer the excess hydrogen ions (H^+) being delivered from the keto acids, beta-hydroxybutyrate and acetoacetate. In the absence of ammonia production, the excess hydrogen ions are exchanged for sodium and potassium, thereby depleting essential electrolytes.

In keeping with the theme of conservation, it is of interest that the kidney can then recycle the carbon moiety from the glutamine, glutamate, or alpha-ketoglutarate to produce glucose that can then be exported to other tissues. Acidosis and intracellular hypokalemia both stimulate ammonia production and renal gluconeogenesis. With prolonged starvation, nearly one half of the urinary nitrogen can be accounted for by ammonia, most of which is produced in the kidney itself. Indeed, the ratio of urinary urea to urinary ammonia can be used as an indirect indicator of the relative importance of hepatic gluconeogenesis and renal gluconeogenesis from amino acids, namely, alanine and glutamine, respectively.

CHANGES IN WATER AND ELECTROLYTES

Glycogen and protein are highly branched ("tree-shaped") molecules. Each is surrounded by water of hydration. For every gram of glycogen or protein, there are approximately 3 g of water in the cell.

Glycogenolysis and proteolysis (as occur with starvation and, especially, carbohydrate deprivation) result in the release of roughly 3 g of water of hydration for every gram of glycogen or protein hydrolyzed. This release accounts for much of the initial weight loss in patients who undertake very-low-calorie diets. It also explains the greater degree of weight loss seen in low-carbohydrate diets as compared with mixed carbohydrate-fat regimens.

Along with the water loss, however, is a loss of intracellular electrolytes including potassium, phosphorus, magnesium, and calcium. Total body depletion can occur even in the presence of normal serum concentrations of these electrolytes. With refeeding, as serum insulin levels increase and as glucose is transported back into the cell, water and electrolytes are also shifted from extracellular to intracellular compartments. This sudden shift can account for potentially fatal electrolyte imbalances, leading to cardiac dysrhythmias, muscle cramps, and other symptoms.

It is likely that the release of water of hydration does not account entirely for the initial diuresis of fasting. As mentioned, the keto acids provide an excess of hydrogen ions to the renal tubule. Initially, at least, some of the hydrogen ions are exchanged for sodium and potassium, thereby fostering natiuresis, kaluresis, and an associated diuresis.

Other mechanisms may be involved. Little is yet known about the role of atrial naturietic peptides. Likewise, little is known about the direct effects of insulin on the kidney. Insulin does stimulate sodium reabsorption, and it seems to oppose cyclic-AMP mediated hormones, including parathyroid hormone and glucagon. Cyclic-AMP levels do rise during starvation, and, in animal models, AMP infusion does result in a prompt naturiesis, kaluresis, and diuresis. So far, however, no systematic study of AMP and its effects on fluid and electrolyte balance has been carried out in fasting subjects.

With prolonged starvation, adaptations occur that predispose to refeeding edema. Early studies by Spark et al.[27] showed that maximum sodium reabsorption by the renal tubule could be achieved after 7 to 10 days of total starvation. Semistarvation could be expected to require longer periods of time before this mechanism would be fully operative. The net result, however, is that refeeding then can result in fluid retention, attributable not only to shifts from intravascular to intracellular compartments, but to actual intravascular overload and clinical edema (so-called starvation or refeeding edema). The mechanisms responsible for this clinical phenomenon have not been worked out. My speculation is that insulin is involved, since insulin has been shown to have a direct effect on the kidney, fostering sodium retention, water retention, etc. However, what is missing in this hypothesis is the hormonal signal that predisposes to the exaggerated effect of insulin on the renal tubule. Something is obviously causing a supraphysiologic adaptation, ie, more fluid is retained than is optimal under the circumstances.

Not only is refeeding edema potentially hazardous, but it is also a source of great confusion and frustration among patients who are dieting. For example, after any severely restricted diet is followed for a prolonged time, patients ''plateau'' or may even gain weight while still adhering to the low-calorie regimen. Often such patients encounter skepticism on the part of the therapist, who does not believe that the patient has continued to adhere to the diet. Furthermore, if the patient tries to go off the diet, there may be a substantial weight gain (as much as 5 kg in 24 hours), which is extremely discouraging. The time frame for the subsequent diuresis, which eventually does occur, is not well understood. With short-term semistarvation, usually the diuresis occurs within a few weeks. However, I have seen several cases of patients with persistent dieting and, as often happens, diuretic use who required 2 to 3 months to re-establish normal fluid balance after discontinuing the diuretics and being placed on a diet equivalent to their resting energy expenditures. Systematic studies of this phenomenon remain to be undertaken.

CLINICAL SYMPTOMS OF SEMISTARVATION

The foregoing discussion of physiologic adaptations to starvation can help us understand some of the symptoms patients experience after prolonged periods on low-calorie diets. The decline in metabolic rate (heat production) is associated with cold intolerance and, in extreme circumstances, with actual hypothermia. The decline in T_3 and in NE turnover are associated with bradycardia, hypotension, orthostatic hypotension (including dizziness and, occasionally, syncope), dry skin, dry hair, easy fatigue, and other symptoms of classic "hypothyroidism."

Constipation is quite common in patients who are starving. The pathophysiologic reason is not entirely clear, but certainly it is consistent with what is seen in hypothyroidism. Recently, Abell et al.[28] showed a variety of abnormalities, including delayed gastric emptying and dysrhythmias in gastric and small bowel electrical activity, associated with a blunted NE response after a meal. My interpretation of these findings is that there is a functional "autonomic neuropathy" involving the gut, leading to symptoms of gastroparesis, including easy filling, bloating, abdominal cramps and pain, with occasional episodes of intermittent diarrhea.

A variety of CNS abnormalities are also seen in starvation. For example, Keys and associates showed that there were abnormalities in sleep patterns, consisting of shorter amounts of time in the deeper levels of sleep and fatigue on awakening. There are also changes in perception, both of space and time. For example, varying the interval of sound and asking the subject to estimate the interval reveals that the starving subject is less able to estimate time accurately than the nonstarving subject. Interestingly, such findings have been found in obese patients after severe caloric restriction, even when they are still considered overweight. The conclusion I would draw from these studies is that it is the negative caloric balance and not the degree of body weight that is determining the adaptations.

Depression scores also increase with prolonged starvation. This is true both in experimental subjects[9] and in obese subjects[29] who starve. This finding is not so widely appreciated as it, perhaps, should be in regard to eating disorders. Patients with anorexia nervosa and bulimia are often depressed. It has not yet been determined to what extent this depression is secondary to the starvation (perhaps because of alterations in CNS neurotransmitters) and to what extent it may be part of the disease process itself. (My bias, as is apparent, is that much of the depression is secondary and could be corrected by adequate refeeding.)

A variety of less well-appreciated symptoms may also occur. For example, acrocyanosis is common in patients with anorexia nervosa. It is often misdiagnosed as Raynaud's phenomenon. I suspect it is merely a symptom of autonomic dysfunction; it resolves with refeeding and return of metabolic rate to normal. Other secondary phenomena, such as hypercarotenemia and hypercholesterolemia, are consistent with the functional "hypothyroidism" attributable to low T_3. Indeed, it is my current hypothesis that nearly all other signs and symptoms of semistarvation can be attributed to the adaptive decline in T_3 and NE turnover, both centrally and peripherally. Whether other neurotransmitters have a role, eg, serotonin depletion, remains to be determined.

THE RESTRAINED EATER

Undereating predisposes to bingeing. After World War I and World War II, it was commonly observed that as starving victims began to recover, some found it difficult to control their appetites. Caloric intakes of 4,000 to 5,000 calories/day were not uncommon. Many of the victims subsequently became obese. These findings were attributed to psychologic stress, an obviously significant factor in their experience.

What was largely overlooked were the "postexperimental" observations of Keys and associates[9] in their studies of conscientious objectors at the University of Minnesota. After cessation of the semistarvation regimen, some of their subjects experienced a similar increase in appetite. As they began to recover, they became more and more hungry. Subsequent follow-up showed that the subjects did not regain their weight to baseline, but actually regained approximately 5% more than their starting weight before the experiment. These findings were largely ignored until recently.

In the past decade, there have been a series of studies that may explain this rebound weight gain, prompted in part by the increase in eating disorders (or, at the minimum, increase in the *diagnosis* of anorexia nervosa and bulimia). Herman and Polivy,[30] in particular, have made major contributions to our knowledge. They have defined what they refer to as the *restrained eater*, a person who is always limiting his or her caloric intake.

When restrained eaters are placed in circumstances in which they are obligated to eat, they frequently overeat. This was most graphically illustrated by a now-famous set of experiments using women college students at Northwestern University.[31] A group of such students was asked to participate in what they were told was a test of taste perception. They were given different bowls of ice cream to eat and were asked to respond to a series of questions regarding flavor, texture, etc. What they were not told was that what was really being measured was how much ice cream they were eating. The ice cream bowls were on hidden scales, of which the students were not aware. Before being given the ice cream, the students were obligated to drink a milk shake, two milk shakes, or nothing. After the milk shake, the normal eaters ate less ice cream than they did on an empty stomach; after two milk shakes, they ate even less. The restrained eaters did just the opposite; after one milk shake they ate more ice cream and after two milk shakes they ate even more.

Herman and Polivy[30] have given their findings a psychologic explanation, namely, the restrained eaters have been forced to break their restraint and, therefore, it is more difficult for them to reimpose control. Since control is a major psychologic theme in our culture, the Herman-Polivy explanation carries great credence.

Similar findings can be found in animal studies. When animals are underfed, provision of a "preload" containing calories (especially sugar and alcohol) results in a greater consumption of food than provision of a noncaloric preload (such as water).[4] Such findings raise the question as to whether there is some biologic signal that is causing this increase in appetite when food becomes available to an animal that was previously underfed. As an endocrinologist, my bias, of course, is that such a signal must exist. It appears that the restrained eater pattern of eating does occur in animals in the wild. For example, during the summer, when ample small animals are available, wolves eat several times during the day and rarely, if ever, gorge themselves. In the winter, the wolves will attack and kill a large animal, gorge themselves, and lie down and go to sleep. If the wolf is then startled, it will get up and actually induce vomiting before running away.

It is not much of a stretch of the imagination to see this pattern of behavior as also being adaptive. In the presence of frequent famines, it would certainly be to the animal's advantage to have an "automatic" signal that increases food intake when food becomes available after a prolonged period of starvation.

SUMMARY

The adaptive changes that occur in response to starvation, semistarvation, and carbohydrate deprivation can heuristically be seen as having survival value. In the absence of adequate food, it is obviously advantageous to be able to reduce metabolic rate. Similarly, repeated starvation results in improved efficiency in adapting, which should also be of advantage long-term. The interpretation I have given to the restrained eater phenomenon, namely, that semistarvation predisposes to bingeing, can also be seen as teleologically useful. This interpretation is supported by observations of animals in the wild. The net result of these adaptations is that repeated dieting leads to greater and greater difficulty in losing weight, greater efficiency in gaining weight, and a tendency to overeat once food becomes available.

The other "costs" of these adaptations include abnormalities in fluid and electrolyte balance, leading to refeeding edema, on the one hand, and potentially lethal cardiac dysrhythmias, on the other. The decline in T_3 and NE turnover undoubtedly accounts for a host of symptoms, including cold intolerance, bradycardia, orthostatic hypertension, constipation, and other gastrointestinal dysfunctions, and perhaps even depression, fatigue, and sleep disturbances.

It is my belief that as these adaptations are more widely understood, physicians and nutritionists will be less inclined to recommend very-low-calorie regimens and will be more sympathetic in understanding the biologic factors involved in the frequent failures of dieting that many patients have experienced. Simply communicating such information to patients is often extremely helpful in removing some of the guilt and frustration they have accumulated. Indeed, I would go so far as to suggest that in the near future, we may look back on the era of low-calorie diets as the counterpart of the bleeding and purgings of the past: somewhat barbaric practices that uninformed physicians and nutritionists carried out on equally uninformed but well-meaning patients!

REFERENCES

1. Apfelbaum M: The effects of very restrictive high protein diets. *Clin Endocrinol Metab* 1976; 5:417–430.

2. Bistrian BR: Clinical use of a protein-sparing modified fast. *JAMA* 1978; 240:2299–2302.

3. Sours HE, Frattali VP, Brand CD, et al: Sudden death associated with very low calorie weight reduction regimens. *Am J Clin Nutr* 1981; 34:453–461.

4. Polivy J, Herman P: Dieting and binging: A causal analysis. *Am Psychologist* 1985; 40:193–201.

5. Blonz ER, Stern JS: Obesity and fad diets, in Ellenbogen L (ed) *Controversies in Nutrition.* New York, Churchill Livingstone, 1981, pp 105–124.

6. DuBois EF: *Basal Metabolism in Health and Disease.* Philadelphia, Lea & Febiger, 1936, p62.

7. Benedict FG: *The Influence of Inanition on Metabolism.* Washington, D.C.: Carnegie Institution of Washington (Publication No. 77), 1907.

8. Winick M (ed): *Polish Hunger Disease Study by the Jewish Physician in the Warsaw Ghetto.* New York, John Wiley & Son, 1978.

9. Keys A, Brozek J, Henschel A, et al: *The Biology of Human Starvation.* Minneapolis, University of Minnesota Press, 1950.

10. Cahill GF Jr.: Starvation in man. *New Engl J Med* 1970; 282:668–675.

11. Cahill GF Jr, Aoki TT, Rossini AA.: Metabolism in obesity and anorexia nervosa, in Wurtman RJ, Wurtman JJ (eds): *Nutrition and the Brain.* New York, Raven Press, 1979, pp 1–70.

12. Hawkins RA, Williamson DH, Drebs HA: Ketone-body utilization by adult and suckling rat brain in vivo. *Biochem J* 1971; 122:13–18.

13. Schutz Y, Bessard T, Jequier E: Diet-induced thermogenesis measured over a whole day in obese and nonobese women. *Am J Clin Nutr* 1984; 40:542–552

14. Ravussin E, Burnard B, Schultz Y, et al: Twenty-four hour energy expenditure and resting metabolic rate in obese, moderately obese, and control subjects. *Am J Clin Nutr* 1982; 35:366–373.

15. Stordy BJ, Marks V, Kalucy RS, et al: Weight gain, thermic effect of glucose and resting metabolic rate during recovery from anorexia nervosa. *Am J Clin Nutr* 1977; 30:138–146

16. Visser TJ, Lamberts SWJ, Wilson JHP et al: Serum thyroid hormone concentrations during prolonged reduction of dietary intake. *Metabolism* 1978; 27:405–409.

17. Azizi F: Effect of dietary composition on fasting-induced changes in serum thyroid hormones and thyrotropin. *Metabolism.* 1978; 27:935–942.

18. Vagenakis AG, Portnay GI, O'Brian JT, et al: Effect of starvation on the production and metabolism of thyroxine and triiodothyronine in euthyroid obese patients. *J Clin Endocrinol Metab* 1977; 45:1305–1309.

19. Bray GA, Melvin KEW, Chopra JJ: Effect of triiodothyronine on some metabolic responses of obese patients. *Am J Clin Nutr* 1973; 26:715–721.

20. Welle SL and Campbell RG: Decrease in resting metabolic rate during rapid weight loss is reversed by low dose thyroid hormone treatment. *Metabolism* 1986; 35:289–291.

21. Landsberg L, Young JB: Fasting, feeding and the regulation of sympathetic activity. *New Engl J Med* 1978; 298: 1295–1301.

22. Landsberg L, Young JB: Insulin-mediated glucose metabolism in the relationship between dietary intake and symmpathetic nervous system activity. *Int J Obes* 1985; 9(Suppl.2):63–68.

23. Burger AG: General comments on tissue sensitivity to thyroid hormones in starvation. *Int J Obesity* 1981; 5(Suppl.1):69–71.

24. Sweadner KJ, Goldin SM: Active transport of sodium and potassium ions: Mechanism of function and regulation. *New Engl J Med* 1980; 302:777–783.

25. Himms-Hagen J: Thyroid hormones and thermogenesis, in Girardier L, Stock MJ (eds:) *Mammalian Thermogenesis.* London; Chapman & Hall, 1983.

26. Brownell KD, Greenwood MRC, Stella E, et al: The effects of repeated cycles of weight loss and regain in rats. *Physiol & Behav* 1986; 38:459–464.

27. Spark RF, Arky RA, Boulter PR, Sudik CD, O'Brian JT: Renin, aldosterone and glucagon in the naturesis of fasting. *New Engl J Med* 1975; 292:1335–1340.

28. Abel PL, Malagenda JR, Lucas AR, Brown ML, et al: Gastric electromechanical and neuro-humoral function in anorexia nervosa. *Gastroenterology.* In press.

29. Stunkard AJ, Rush J: Dieting and depression reexamined: Critical review of reports of untoward responses during weight reduction for obesity. *Ann Intern Med* 1984; 81:526–533.

30. Herman CP, Polivy J: A boundary model for the regulation of eating, in Stunkard E, Stellar E (eds): *Eating and Its Disorders.* New York; Raven Press, 1984, pp 141–156.

31. Herman CP, Mack D: Restrained and unrestrained eating. *J Pers* 1975; 43:646–660; Behavior. *J. Abnorm Psychol* 1975; 84:666–672.

PART II

Weight Control: State of the Art Treatment

Chapter 7

Assessment of the Obese Person

Janet K. Grommet

In almost any endeavor, a prudent first step is to define the situation before initiating action. In a health care setting, the task is to define the health problem before proceeding toward a solution. Health care professionals are entrenched in this approach with such models as medical diagnosis and subsequent treatment or in initial patient interviewing and follow-up counseling.

Few would argue against patient assessment, ie, the process of defining the problem, as an initial step in providing health care. Yet obesity is frequently regarded as a generic condition and too often the "differential diagnosis" of obesity is glossed over. Without an attempt to clarify the problem and engage the obese person in defining the issues, treatment ensues based only on assumptions. Since overriding concerns in obesity treatment include commitment, compliance, motivation, recidivism, and resistance, perhaps a more concerted effort at initial assessment would maximize subsequent treatment. Assessment, in other words, can facilitate a better fit between problem and solution.

MULTIFACETED ETIOLOGY

The complexity of assessing the obese person stems from the multifaceted etiology of weight problems. Feinleib, for instance, notes " . . . body weight is determined by a complex interaction of genetic, cultural, and individual behavioral and psychological factors, all of which may have separate effects on health and longevity . . . ."[1] Whereas health professionals are trained in specific areas of expertise, eg, clinical nutrition, exercise physiology, family therapy, or internal medicine, obesity does not limit itself to academic lines. When assessment is unilateral, that is, limited to one line of inquiry, the person's weight problem may be construed as one dimensional, and subsequent interventions of treatment may be limited.

111

For example, Michael W (240 lb, 6'1'', age 26, married, lawyer) went to his internist because of lower back pain. Physical examination revealed no remarkable findings. The physician noted, however, that the excess weight was probably irritating the back and recommended weight loss, referring the patient to a local self-help group for weight control. Michael W did not follow through with the recommendation, indicating to his physician that the group met on the other side of town on Tuesday evenings and thus was not convenient for him. From this feedback the physician concluded that the patient was unmotivated to lose weight.

In another example, Keith G (260 lb, 5'10'', age 28, single, writer) is in psychotherapy dealing with emotional aspects of his overeating. The therapist has assisted him in understanding that, particularly when anxious, he attempts to calm or soothe himself by turning to food as opposed to confronting the cause of the anxiety. Occasionally during sessions Keith G dozes off, and the therapist suggests that he is perhaps resistant to looking at these issues.

Both of these fictitious cases indicate the limitation that can be placed on treatment when assessment is unilateral. In the first case, the patient had a physical problem, the side effect of excess weight. The physician's referral to a self-help group indeed seemed appropriate, but the patient did not follow through, allegedly because of lack of motivation. A fuller assessment, however, could explore what was actually preventing the patient from changing as opposed to dismissing him as unmotivated. In this fictitious case, Michael W perceived that the excess weight, although carrying the liability of lower back pain, offered an advantage of more presence or substance; and as the youngest member of his law firm, he derived an element of security from his physical size. The common unilateral approach, however, left the patient with an unresolved conflict, his weight problem, and no treatment.

In the second case, the patient presented with an emotional aspect of his weight problem, and the psychodynamic interpretation was indeed plausible. But again, a fuller assessment might have "teased out" the patient's so-called resistance. In this fictitious case, Keith was experiencing a physical effect of his excess weight, sleep apnea. His excess body weight compromised his lung capacity and was further exacerbated by sitting throughout sessions, resulting in his dozing off. In both cases, the ensuing treatment was truncated.

Patient assessment elicits a different line of inquiry from different professional vantage points. In assessing the obese patient, the internist relies on a medical history and physical examination to assess the patient's physical status. The internist may report weight history, family history of cardiovascular disease, perhaps an osteoarthritic knee, or a patient's borderline hypertension. From the vantage point of an exercise physiologist, the same patient may be seen as sedentary, having an arthritic knee related to an earlier injury. A clinical nutritionist might note the patient's tendency to avoid food throughout the day, resulting in a ravenous approach to dinner, or the high dietary fat intake juxtaposed with the family history of cardiovascular disease. And the psychotherapist might note that the patient's weight problem was adult-onset, beginning during college when establishing an independent life style.

Granted, the obese person has consumed more energy than expended, resulting in a caloric imbalance. But to evaluate this situation requires an assessment or delineation of problems and relevant issues to determine a plan for treatment. Thus, a multidisciplinary approach to assessment is proposed with the following components: (1) medical assessment, (2) nutritional and food behavior assessment, (3) physical activity assessment, and (4) psychosocial assessment.

MULTIDISCIPLINARY ASSESSMENT

A multidisciplinary approach to obesity is not guaranteed by any one staffing pattern. Although a health care team approach to assessment and treatment of obese people may be advantageous in that it assembles a broader base of expertise than any one person might have, multidisciplinary assessment of obese people need not entail an interview with numerous team members.

Assessment, in fact, can be expedited by administering entry questionnaire(s). As opposed to a unilateral assessment in which problems are identified in only one area, the multidisciplinary assessment frequently results in identifying an array of problems that can then be delineated in a problem list analogous to Weed's[2] approach to identifying a medical problem list. Such a delineation may result in referring a patient for adjunctive services if certain problems cannot be addressed in a weight control treatment program.

Nutrition and Food Behaviors

Self-reported food records are the traditional instrument for assessing food intake. In addition to customarily describing the food or beverage, the amount consumed, and the caloric value, food records may elicit information regarding the context or situation in which the food is eaten, eg, duration of eating, location and physical position while eating, presence of others and associated activities while eating, and mood state before eating. A sample of a comprehensive food intake record is shown in Appendix 7-A.

Food records in and of themselves, however, are essentially raw data and need to be further interpreted to bear on patient assessment. For example, nutrient analysis of the food records will allow assessment of the quantity of calories as well as the nutritional quality of the intake. Then, during treatment, gradual stepwise changes in food selections can be addressed to achieve a healthier eating style. A framework for implementing progressive changes is shown in Appendix 7-B.[3]

By summarizing the contextual data of food records over a block of time, the obese person can use the records to identify personal eating habits or behaviors. Levitz and Jordan's Analysis of Food Intake is an instrument that facilitates such a summary; an example is presented in Appendix 7-C, in this case a summary of a 7-day food record. The bar graph in Appendix 7-C summarizes frequency and temporal eating patterns, revealing this person's tendency toward frequent night eating. Examination of other categories indicates, for instance, a propensity toward snacking, in the bedroom, while lying down, while watching television. Furthermore, the person is frequently bored (before eating); reports minimal hunger; prefers snacking on baked goods, crackers, and deli meats; and tends toward significantly greater caloric intake on weekends than weekdays. Thus, the use of such a food analysis instrument provides more insight into the person's food behaviors than the mere recording of food intake.

Another approach to assessing food behavior includes self-administered questionnaires. Wollersheim's[4] Eating Patterns Questionnaire, for instance, poses approximately 60 questions addressing eating patterns and attitudes. For example, "Once you start eating, do you experience difficulty in stopping?" Each response is indicated on a five-point Likert scale, and scores can then be obtained for the following six factors of eating practices: (1) emotional and uncontrolled overeating, (2) eating response to interpersonal situations, (3) eating in isolation, (4) eating as reward, (5) eating response to evaluative situations, and (6) between-meal eating. (More recently, Gormally et al[5] modified the questionnaire, resulting in a shorter version.)

Another example of a self-report questionnaire is the Eating Behavior Inventory, developed by O'Neil et al,[6] which assesses behaviors, particularly food behaviors, associated with successful weight loss: (1) recording food intake and weight, (2) daily weighing, (3) refusing offers of food, (4) eating at only one place, (5) snacking, (6) eating slowly, (7) shopping from a list, and (8) eating in response to emotions. They reported high reproducibility of the instrument as evidenced by a test-retest correlation coefficient of $r = .74$ ($P < .01$) and results of several tests of validity including correlations between self-report and others' reports, internal consistency, and social desirability.

Initially, food records can be a valuable instrument for assessing nutritional status and identifying both adaptive and maladaptive food behaviors, and the obese person can subsequently use them as a self-monitoring tool during the course of treatment. Record keeping, however, is time-consuming. the questionnaire approach to assessment attempts to alleviate the repetitious or tedious aspect of record keeping by drawing on a body of questions that glean the essence of the person's food behaviors.

As with any questionnaire, for a food behavior questionnaire to be a valuable assessment tool, the questions must be valid, ie, well grounded, having conclusions correctly derived from premises, and reliable, ie, repeatable or reproducible. Although questionnaires offer the advantage of brevity, to date the questionnaires are limited to assessing food behaviors and are not designed to address nutritional quality. Thus, food intake records and the available food behavior questionnaires are not mutually exclusive assessment tools.

Energy Expenditure Assessment

When energy output or expenditure is equivalent to caloric intake, an individual is in energy balance, and body weight is consequently stable with neither significant gains nor losses. In the case of the obese person, however, caloric intake has exceeded energy expenditure for some time; this positive energy balance results in an accumulation of body fat and, consequently, excess weight (ie, an excess of 3,500 kcal theoretically results in 1 lb of body fat).

Data indicating that obese people may consume fewer calories than people of normal weight may initially seem implausible, but such an observation reflects only intake, not energy balance. Consider, however, that once a person is in positive energy balance and has stored this excess energy as body fat, the energy balance must become negative for the person to lose weight and return to the original body weight. If, for example, with the development of obesity the person has reduced energy expenditure, a reduction in food intake may simply be creating an energy balance but not the energy deficit necessary to lose the excess weight. (The complexity of energy balance is further addressed in Chapter 4.) The assessment of energy expenditure is thus valuable in that it encourages the obese person to focus on energy balance, ie, both intake and output, as opposed to focusing on food restriction exclusively.[7]

Furthermore, when only food intake data are available, recommendations for reducing caloric intake are necessarily general as they cannot be interpreted in tandem with energy expenditure. Consequently, there is a tendency to rely on blanket caloric prescriptions such as a 1,200 kcal or 1,000 kcal intake. However, by estimating energy expenditure as part of the initial assessment battery, an individualized caloric intake can be recommended. If, for example, energy expenditure assessment indicates that a person expends approximately 2,800 kcal daily, a 1,000-kcal reduction in calorie intake to 1,800 kcal/day could be recommended, resulting in a weight loss of approximately 2 lb in the course of 1 week. (Such calculations must be regarded as theoretical, recognizing that factors other than energy balance may affect actual body weight, for instance, body fluid shifts.)

Many obese people, although constantly focused on weight-loss attempts, frequently view the process of losing weight as an "all or none" proposition, ie, either on or off a diet. Generally, when the caloric intake recommended for weight loss is significantly lower than what the individual has recently been consuming (ie, a caloric deficit greater than 1,000 kcal/day), the person has difficulty sustaining the change for an extended period of time and thus "goes off the diet."[8] By estimating the energy expenditure in addition to assessing caloric intake, the recommended caloric intake may be not only individualized but frequently less restrictive, such as the 1,800 kcal recommendation in the example. Whereas this is not the only therapeutic approach to weight control, this strategy can potentially maximize the obese person's dietary compliance as it allows the person to focus on making behavioral changes as opposed to monitoring an unduly restricted caloric intake exclusively.

Methods for assessing energy expenditure include, for example, metabolic balance studies designed to quantify energy intake and changes in body weight or composition (considered *the reference standard method*), measures of oxygen consumption using a respirometer, heart rate/energy expenditure regression equations, and factorial methods that involve describing daily activities and coding them for energy cost for each factor or time period throughout the day. Of these methods the latter is recommended for clinical assessment of obese people as it involves the person in the assessment process and yet is less intrusive than the other methods, all of which require instrumentation and technician time. Borel et al[9] concluded that when compared with the metabolic balance study as the standard, the factorial method provided accurate estimates of energy expenditure; the method, for instance, overestimated energy expenditure in women by 4.74% and underestimated it in men by 1.65%, which was not statistically significant for either sex.

In using the factorial method, the time spent in various categories of activities is multiplied by the energy cost of the activity to determine energy expenditure in kcal/kg/24 hr. This value is then multiplied by the person's body weight to express expenditure in kcal/day. The sample log sheet shown in Appendix 7-4 factors the day into 15-minute segments, eg, 6:00–6:15 AM, 6:15–6:30 AM, 6:30–6:45 AM, etc. The predominant activity engaged in during each time segment is noted in the large box, and the corresponding energy cost of the activity is coded in the small box using a coding system such as the one shown in Table 7-1.

Coding systems are, of course, derived from basic research of energy costs of various activities and are reported in kcal/kg/min. Each category in a coding system represents a range of activities, and an approximate median energy cost for each category is then compiled as the coding system. The use of reported energy costs of various activities does not reflect the intensity at which a person performs an activity, but since the calculation of energy expenditure includes body weight, the fact that an obese person expends more energy than a normal-weight person, particularly in load-bearing activities such as walking (as opposed to swimming), is taken into account. Notable activity coding systems in the

Table 7-1 Table of Activities, Energy Costs, and Corresponding Categorical Values

Categorical Value	Examples of Activities	Energy cost in METS from various studies		Median energy cost used	
		Minimum	Maximum	METS	kcal/kg/15 min
1	Sleeping Resting in bed	1.0		1.0	0.26
2	Sitting: eating, listening, writing, etc	1.0	2.0	1.5	0.38
3	Light activity standing: washing, shaving, combing, cooking, etc	2.0	3.0	2.3	0.57
4	Slow walk ($<$ 4 km/h), driving, to dress, to shower, etc	2.0	4.0	2.8	0.69
5	Light manual work: floor sweeping, window washing, driving a truck, painting, waiting on tables, nursing chores, several house chores, electrician, barman, walking at 4 to 6 km/h	2.3	5.0	3.3	0.84
6	Leisure activities and sports in a recreational environment: baseball, golf, volleyball, canoeing or rowing, archery, bowling, cycling ($<$ 10 km/h), table tennis, etc	3.0	8.0	4.8	1.2
7	Manual work at moderate pace: mining, carpentry, house building, lumbering and wood cutting, snow shoveling, loading and unloading goods, etc	4.0	8.0	5.6	1.4
8	Leisure and sport activities of higher intensity (not competitive): canoeing (5 to 8 km/h), bicycling ($>$ 15 km/h), dancing, skiing, badminton, gymnastics, swimming, tennis, horse riding, walking ($>$ 6 km/h), etc	5.0	11	6.0	1.5

Table 7-1 continued

Categorical Value	Examples of Activities	Energy cost in METS from various studies		Median energy cost used	
		Minimum	Maximum	METS	kcal/kg/15 min
9	Intense manual work, high intensity sport activities or sport competition: tree cutting, carrying heavy loads, jogging and running (> 9 km/h), racquetball, badminton, swimming, tennis, cross country skiing (> 8 km/h), hiking and mountain climbing, etc	6.0	~15	7.8	2.0

Source: Adapted with permission from *American Journal of Clinical Nutrition* (1983; 37:466), Copyright © 1983, The American Society for Clinical Nutrition.

literature include those by Passmore and Durnin,[10] Katch and McArdle,[11] and Bouchard et al.[12]

Bouchard et al[12] also described using the factorial method based on logging activity for 3 days: 2 days being weekdays and the third being a weekend day. Based on test-retest experiments, they reported high reproducibility of the mean energy expenditure (in kcal) as evidenced by a correlation coefficient of $r = .96$ ($P < .01$); validity was assessed indirectly by correlating expenditure with measurement of physical working capacity (PWC). Interestingly, they concluded that the 3-day energy expenditure assessment was less time-consuming and less complicated than the more familiar 3-day food intake record.

Total energy expenditure can, of course, be partitioned into the components of basal metabolic rate and physical activity. Basal metabolic rate, the minimal energy needs for the body to maintain basic physiologic functions while in a waking state, actually accounts for the major portion of total energy expenditure; and an estimate of it is useful on several accounts in assessing obese people. First, for the obese person who frequently dismisses personal responsibility for body weight because of an allegedly low metabolic rate, assessment of basal metabolic rate can enable the person and the health professional to clarify the situation as opposed to working with assumptions. Because of the larger body size, an obese person may in fact have a higher absolute basal metabolic rate than a normal-weight individual of the same age and sex.

Perhaps more importantly, however, by assessing both total energy expenditure and the basal metabolic component, the role of physical activity can be poignantly addressed in subsequent treatment. For example, if a person's basal metabolic rate is estimated to be 1,500 kcal, and total energy expenditure is 1,725 kcal, the weight control treatment would more prudently focus on increasing physical activity than on caloric control exclusively since the total expenditure exceeds basal by only 225 kcal, or 15% in this case. As a rule of thumb, expending an additional 20% or less of basal calories classifies a person as sedentary. Ideally, to be moderately active the person would work toward expending 40% more than basal calories, or 600 kcal, for a total energy expenditure of 2,100 kcal. Methods for calculating basal metabolic rate including both direct measurement and handbook calculations are addressed in Chapter 5.

Thus, assessing total energy expenditure is useful in determining a realistic caloric intake for the obese person; furthermore, with an estimate of basal metabolic rate, physical activity can be estimated by difference (ie, total energy expenditure − basal metabolic rate = physical activity). Although many intellectually understand that effective weight control entails both decreased caloric intake and increased physical activity, quantification of these factors dissolves the mystery of weight loss.

Psychosocial Assessment

Stuart and Jacobson (*Redbook*, July 1986, p 104) indicate that most overweight people are not overeating in response to hunger but because it at least temporarily makes them feel better. In their three Cs, they offer a succinct explanation of why people overeat: (1) for comfort, (2) for control, and (3) to cope. For example, eating may stifle negative emotions such as anger, anxiety, boredom, depression, rejection, or loneliness and thus provide at least transient *comfort* for the individual. Or when home or job seems overwhelming, eating is an activity that is within the person's power or *control* and thus can ballast the person. Eating can also temporarily provide a sense of relief or support in order to *cope* with a stressful situation.

An underlying objective of psychosocial assessment of the obese person is for the patient and health professional to clarify the roles that food and body weight have in the patient's life. Thus, demographic information such as name, age, education, occupation, and living arrangements are but a prelude and not the essence of this assessment. Either in an intake interview or questionnaire form, the following are suggested lines of inquiry:

- noting past attempts, if any, at weight loss including when, weight change experienced, length of maintenance, why treatment terminated, problems encountered, if any
- noting reasons for wanting to lose weight including why interested in losing weight at this time

- considering how weight loss treatment will be different this time (assuming earlier attempts)
- identifying significant life event(s) that might be related to weight gain
- identifying any current lifestyle changes that might impede weight loss
- reflecting on how specific family members and friends feel about obesity
- considering if specific moods influence amount eaten or physical activity.

Responses to these leading questions may be further supplemented by standardized psychosocial instruments directed toward cognitive (ie, subjective thought processes) and affective assessment (ie, subjective feeling states). Cognitive processes, that is, thoughts or interpretation of statements and events, are influenced by many factors including past experiences; and in turn, a person's cognitions have a direct impact on both emotions and behaviors.

Measures of self-perception are one approach to assessing a person's cognitions. Crandall[13] evaluated 30 instruments classified as self-perception measurements and rank ordered them based on the quality of test construction factors such as sample size, reliability, and validity. Eppinger and Lambert[14] selected five high-quality instruments from this group with a view toward applicability in weight reduction and smoking cessation and gave the highest rank to the Tennessee Self-Concept Scale.[15] The test items on this scale reflect five general self-perception categories: (1) physical self, (2) moral-ethical self, (3) personal self, (4) family self, and (5) social self.

Without insight into an obese person's self-perception, the health professional can unknowingly set up the person for failure rather than success at weight loss. Poor self-perception, for example, carries the risk of possible relapse because of factors such as self-defeat expectancy.[16] Failure at weight loss can leave the person humiliated and lacking confidence and thus perpetuate the person's low perception of self. With the additional failure at weight control, the prospects for successful weight control diminish. Conversely, Leon and Rosenthal[17] reported that self-efficacy expectations before the start of treatment were significantly related to greater progress in weight control as measured at follow-up. Thus, several interventionist philosophies focus heavily on the person's thought processes, for example, Rotter's locus of control,[18] Ellis' rational-emotive therapy,[19] and cognitive restructuring within behavior therapy.

In addition to cognitive assessment, psychosocial assessment includes measures of affect. Thus, assessing mood and subsequently helping the obese person identify the relation between mood and food can be pivotal in subsequent treatment. In this regard, an available assessment instrument is the Profile of Mood States (POMS),[20] which consists of 65 adjectives, eg, relaxed, miserable, annoyed, alert, and forgetful; each is rated on a five-point scale. The results are analyzed into six mood scores: (1) tension-anxiety, (2) depression-dejection,

(3) anger-hostility, (4) vigor-activity, (5) fatigue-inertia, and (6) confusion-bewilderment.

On a more general level are measures of overall personality adjustment such as the Symptom Checklist 90-R (SCL-90-R)[21] and the Minnesota Multiphasic Personality Inventory (MMPI).[22] Attempts at using personality constructs as prognostic indicators of weight loss have not proved successful, but since these tests delineate individual traits and characteristics, they can be useful in treatment planning, particularly in better tailoring treatment strategies for the person.

Medical Assessment

The medical, or physiological, assessment is perhaps the best defined aspect of a multidisciplinary approach to assessing the obese person. Medical assessment includes both a medical history and physical examination as well as selected blood chemistry tests and urinalysis. This assessment defines the physical status, ie, medical diagnosis.

Bray and Teague[23] developed a branched decision-making algorithm specific to the physical examination of obese people, as shown in Figure 7-1. Underlying the physical examination is the appreciation that obesity is associated with a greater incidence of cardiovascular disease, diabetes, hypertension, certain cancers, and gallbladder disease.[24] Among other points, Bray and Teague's algorithm notes assessing for hypothyroidism. In an obese person on thyroid medication, the examining physician might also check blood chemistries to note if thyroid function test results are within the normal range and, if not, to adjust medication accordingly.

Several points can be noted in tailoring the medical history for the obese person. For example, the prudent examining physician will not only focus on symptoms of the conditions noted in the algorithm but will also take a detailed family history of these conditions, recognizing the cumulative risk of family history and obesity.

The medical history of an obese person should entail a weight history including interview questions pertaining to onset of weight problem, lowest adult weight, and highest adult body weight. Querying the person regarding prescription and nonprescription drugs is relevant in that weight gain can be a side effect of certain drug therapies, in which case alternative medication may be available. For instance, weight gain is frequently a side effect of tricyclic antidepressant medications. The examining physician can assess the appropriateness of diuretic therapy if it is being used by the obese person in an attempt to control body weight through fluid shifts and is jeopardizing electrolyte balance.

Comprehensive medical examination of the obese person should also include an estimate of body composition. (Methodology is addressed in Chapter 5.) Body

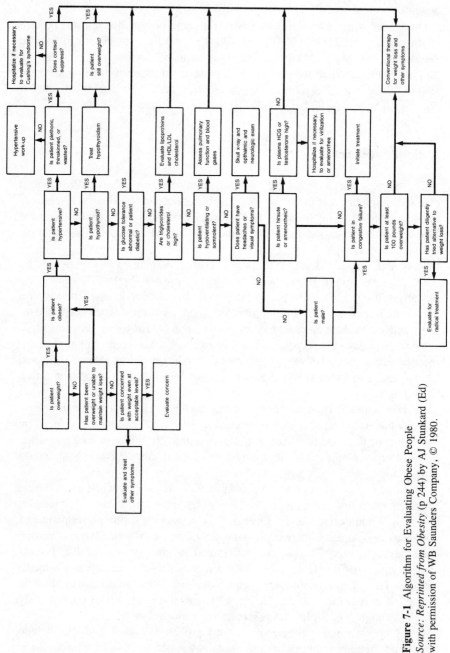

Figure 7-1 Algorithm for Evaluating Obese People

Source: Reprinted from Obesity (p 244) by AJ Stunkard (Ed)
with permission of WB Saunders Company, © 1980.

composition indicates the distribution of body weight between adipose, or fat, and lean body mass. An estimate of body composition helps focus the person on the concept of medically safe or high-quality weight loss, ie, mobilizing excess body fat stores and minimizing lean body mass loss.

Body composition data can also serve to validate the person's long-term weight goal. Some people establish long-term goals that may not be physiologically attainable or desirable, such as a weight loss goal that exceeds excess body fat. The sense of failing to achieve a goal can thus be averted and the composition data can be used to determine a revised goal.

SUMMARY

The multifaceted etiology of obesity necessitates assessing the incoming obese person from a broad but defined base. The proposed assessment strategy includes assessment of behaviors including food intake and energy expenditure, psychosocial assessment including cognitive and affective dimensions, and medical assessment to appraise physical status.

Comprehensive assessment such as this results in identifying an initial problem/issue list, which then influences treatment planning. Thus, as Storlie and Jordan[25] conclude, "A thorough evaluation process is recommended to pair appropriate treatment strategies with individuals." Although the assessment strategy so presented focused on initial evaluation, periodic assessment in the course of treatment provides for updating the problem/issue list and reformulating treatment if needed as noted in the guidelines for professional weight control programs proposed by the Fourth International Obesity Congress.[26]

Assessment ideally enhances the insight and understanding of both the health professional and the obese person and thus improves the treatment process.

REFERENCES

1. Feinleib M: Epidemiology of obesity in relation to health hazards, in *Health Implications of Obesity: National Institutes of Health Consensus Development Conference*. Washington, National Institutes of Health, 1985, p 36.

2. Weed LL: *Medical Records, Medical Education, and Patient Care*. Chicago, Yearbook Medical Publishers Inc, 1971, pp 25–48.

3. Franz M, Hedding BK, Holtmeier K., et al: *A Guide to Healthy Eating*. Wayzata, Minn, Diabetes Center Inc, 1985, pp 46–47.

4. Wollersheim JP: Effectiveness of group therapy based upon learning principles in the treatment of overweight women. *J Abnorm Psychol* 1970;76:462–474.

5. Gormally J, Rardin D, Black S: Correlates of successful response to a behavioral weight control clinic. *Journal of Counseling Psychology* 1980; 27:179–191.

6. O'Neil PM, Currey HS, Hirsch AA, et al: Development and validation of the eating behavior inventory. *Journal of Behavioral Assessment* 1979; 1:123–132.

7. Thompson JK, Blanton PD: The effect of dieting and exercise on metabolic rate. *Behavioral Medicine Abstracts* 1984; 5:5–8.

8. Polivy J, Herman, CP: Dieting and binging: A causal analysis. *Am Psychol* 1985; 40:193–201.

9. Borel MJ, Riley RE, Snook JT: Estimation of energy expenditure and maintenance energy requirements of college-age men and women. *Am J Clin Nutr* 1984; 40:1264–1272.

10. Passmore R, Durnin JVGA: Human energy expenditure. *Physiol Rev* 1955; 35:801–840.

11. Katch FI, McArdle WD: *Nutrition, Weight Control, and Exercise.* Philadelphia, Lea & Febiger, 1983, p 98.

12. Bouchard C, Tremblay A, Leblanc C, et al: A method to assess energy expenditure in children and adults. *Am J Clin Nutr* 1983; 37:461–467.

13. Crandall R: The measurement of self-esteem and related constructs, in Robinson JP, Shaver PR (eds): *Measures of Social Psychological Attitudes.* Ann Arbor, Institute for Social Research, University of Michigan, 1973, pp 45–67.

14. Eppinger MG, Lambert MJ: Assessment of habit disorders: A tripartite perspective in measuring change, in Lambert MJ, Christensen ER, DeJulio SS (eds): *The Assessment of Psychotherapy Outcome.* New York, John Wiley & Sons Inc, 1983, pp 387–389.

15. Fitts W: *Manual: Tennessee Self-Concept Scale.* Nashville, Counselor Recordings and Tests, 1964.

16. Sternberg B: Relapse in weight control: Definitions, processes, and prevention strategies, in Marlatt GA, Gordon JR (eds): *Relapse Prevention: Maintenance Strategies in the Treatment of Addictive Behaviors.* New York, The Guilford Press, 1985, p 524.

17. Leon GR, Rosenthal BS: Prognostic indicators of success or relapse in weight reduction. *Intl J Eating Disorders* 1984; 3:15–24.

18. Rotter JB: Some problems and misconceptions related to the construct of internal versus external control of reinforcement. *J Consult Clin Psychol* 1975; 43:56–57.

19. Ellis A, Harper RA: *A New Guide to Rational Living.* North Hollywood, Calif, Wilshire Book Co, 1979.

20. McNair DM, Lorr M, Droppleman LF: *Manual: Profile of Mood States (POMS).* San Diego, Educational and Industrial Testing Service-EdiTS, 1981.

21. Derogatis LR: *SCL-90-R Manual.* Baltimore, Clinical Psychometrics Research Unit, Johns Hopkins University School of Medicine, 1977.

22. Hathaway SR, McKinely JC: *Minnesota Multiphasic Personality Inventory Manual: Revised.* New York, The Psychological Corporation, 1967.

23. Bray GA, Teague RJ: An algorithm for the medical evaluation of obese patients, in Stunkard AJ (ed): *Obesity.* Philadelphia, WB Saunders Co, 1980, pp 240–248.

24. Van Itallie, TB: Obesity: Adverse effects on health and longevity. *Am J Clin Nutr* 1979; 32(suppl):2723–2733.

25. Storlie J, Jordan HA: *Evaluation and Treatment of Obesity.* New York, SP Medical & Scientific Books, 1984, p 114.

26. Altschul AM, Atkinson RL, Blackburn GL, et al: Proposed guidelines for professional weight control programs, in Hirsch J, Van Itallie TB (eds): *Recent Advances in Obesity Research: IV. Proceedings of the 4th Congress on Obesity.* London, John Libbey & Co Ltd, 1985, pp 268–270.

Appendix 7-A

Weight Control Unit
Food Intake Record

Date _____   Name _____

| Time | | | | Alone or | | | | M | | | |
Start	End	Place	Phy Pos	with whom	Assoc. Activity	M	H	/ S	Amount	Food or Beverage	Calories
6-11											
11-4											
4-9											
9-6											

Percent of entries filled out right before or after eating   0   25   50   75   100

Source: Henry A Jordan, Leonard S Levitz, and Gordon M Kimbrell, "Food Intake Record" From *Eating Is Okay*. Copyright © 1976 by Associates for Behavioral Education and S & R Gelman Associates Inc. Reprinted with permission of Rawson Associates, a division of Macmillan Inc.

Appendix 7-B

Food Pattern Progress Chart

Dietary Goal	Food Group	
		Level I
REDUCE FAT (especially saturated fats and cholesterol)	MEAT, FISH AND POULTRY	more than 8 oz./day
		high fat meats daily, smoked, cured, or pickled products
	EGGS	more than 5 egg yolks per week
	DAIRY PRODUCTS	whole milk and half and half only
		ice cream, sour cream, cheeses, processed cheese products, cream cheese
	FATS AND OILS	butter, shortening, lard, fried foods
		limited use of oils, creamy, cheese-based salad dressings, nondairy creams and whipped toppings, coconut & palm oil

Appendix 7-B   *continued*

REDUCE SUGAR	COMMERCIAL BAKED GOODS, PROCESSED FOODS, FAST FOODS	daily use, sweet desserts, chocolate, candies
	SOFT DRINKS	more than 7 soft drinks per week
	FRUITS & VEGETABLES	fruits canned in heavy syrup, fruit drinks, canned vegetables, deep fried vegetables
ACHIEVE OR MAINTAIN DESIRABLE BODY WEIGHT	CALORIES	consume calories greater than needed to maintain ideal body weight
INCREASE COMPLEX CARBOHYDRATES	COMPLEX CHO-FIBER	refined carbohydrates only, snack chips
REDUCE SALT	SALT	heavy table and cooking salt plus high sodium foods, cream soups, canned soups, salty condiments
REDUCE CAFFEINE	CAFFEINE	more than 52 oz. (6½ cups) coffee, tea, pop, diet pop per day with caffeine
REDUCE ALCOHOL	ALCOHOL	more than 3 oz. per day

Source: Reprinted with permission from *A Guide to Healthy Eating* by Marion J Franz et al, copyright 1985, Park Nicollet Medical Foundation, 5000 West 39th Street, Minneapolis, MN 55416. The Food Pattern Progress Chart is copyrighted by SHAPE, a division of Park Nicollet Medical Foundation.

Food Patterns:		
Level II	Level III	Level IV
7-8 oz./day	eat 4-6 oz. of protein/day (meat, fish, poultry, cheese)	less than 4 oz./day; 16 oz or less of red meat/week
high fat meats 4-6 times/ week, partially trimmed meats	high fat meats 1-3 times/ week, increased use of fish and poultry	no high fat meats, completely trimmed meats

Appendix 7-B   *continued*

3-5 egg yolks per week	2 egg yolks or less per week, egg whites liberally	no egg yolks per week, egg whites liberally
2% milk	1% and skim milk	skim milk only
ice milk, yogurt, creamed cottage cheese	frozen dietary desserts, low fat yogurt, low fat cottage cheese, sherbet	skim milk yogurt, low fat and low cholesterol cheeses
margarine, limited use of fried foods	corn, sunflower, or safflower stick margarine, broiled, baked or roasted only	corn, safflower or sunflower tub margarine
"vegetable" oil, olive, peanut oils, shortening	corn, safflower, sunflower, or soybean oils only, vinegar oil based salad dressings	
3-4 time/week, sugar, syrup, molasses, honey	1-2 times/week limited for weight control	homebaked, modified goods only, limited for weight control
4-7 soft drinks per week	1-3 soft drinks per week	no soft drinks per week or sugar free soft drinks only
fruits canned in light syrup	fruits canned in natural juices or water, fresh fruit, fruit juices, fresh or frozen vegetables	
consume calories that maintain weight	reduce calories to attain ideal weight	consume calories and expend calories to attain and maintain ideal weight
primarily whole grain breads, cereals, snack crackers	increased use of lentils, dried peas, beans, fruits, vegetables, oatmeal, plain crackers, whole grain (bran, brown rice, bulgur, etc.) products, nuts, seeds, popcorn, rye wafers	
eliminate salt at the table, cut back on foods with visible salt	low use of salt in cooking, eliminate processed foods high in salt	eliminate table salt, cooking salt, plus high sodium foods
48 oz./day (6 cups)	32 oz./day (4 cups)	less than 20 oz. (2½ cups) coffee, tea, or diet pop per day without caffeine
3 oz./day	2 oz./day	1 oz. or less/day

Appendix 7-C

Sample
Analysis of Food Intake

WEIGHT CONTROL UNIT
OBESITY RESEARCH CENTER
ST. LUKE'S HOSPITAL CENTER

NAME *MABEL SACHS*

WEEK OF *SEPTEMBER 3, 1978*

EXHIBIT 7-3
ANALYSIS OF FOOD INTAKE

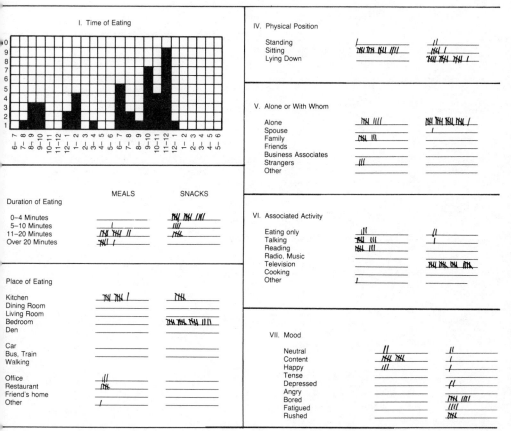

Appendix 7-C   *continued*

VIII. Degree of Hunger

0–2 (None to Mild)	ᵗᴴᴸ /	ᵗᴴᴸ ᵗᴴᴸ ᵗᴴᴸᵗᴴᴸ /
3–5 (Mild to Extreme)	ᵗᴴᴸ ᵗᴴᴸ ᵗᴴᴸ ///	ᵗᴴᴸ //

IX. Type of Food

Alcohol	ᵗᴴᴸ ///	
Sodas, reg		////
diet		
Coffee, Sugar	ᵗᴴᴸ ᵗᴴᴸ	
Cream/Coffeemate		
Candy, gum		///
Baked Goods, breakfast		ᵗᴴᴸ ᵗᴴᴸ // .
cakes, cookies, etc.	////	
Ice Cream, Pudding		
Jello, Sherbert		/
Jelly, Jam		
Crackers, Pretzels		ᵗᴴᴸ /
Potato Chips, etc.		////
Nuts		
Peanut Butter		
Bacon, Sausages	//	
(Butter) Margarine	ᵗᴴᴸ ᵗᴴᴸ	
Gravy, Sauces	///	
Oils		
Salad Dressings	///	
Mayonnaise		//
Breads, white	ᵗᴴᴸ ᵗᴴᴸ /	//
high fiber/whole grain		
Cereals, whole grain/bran		
Other Cereals	///	
Pastas		
Potato, Rice	////	
Beans, Legumes		

Starchy Veg. corn, peas		
Vegetables. raw	///	//
cooked	ᵗᴴᴸ	
Fruits. fresh		
canned		ᵗᴴᴸ
Fruit Juices	ᵗᴴᴸ /	
Beef. Lamb. Pork	ᵗᴴᴸ /	/
Poultry. Veal. Fish	//	
Canned Fish, Tuna. etc.	/	
Deli Meats, etc.		ᵗᴴᴸ //
Cottage Cheese	//	
Cheese	ᵗᴴᴸ	/
Eggs	//	
Milk, whole	ᵗᴴᴸ //	////
skimmed		
Yogurt	///	
Soups		
Condiments	//	

X. Total Caloric Intake

Sunday 4100 Monday 875 Tuesday 1250 Wednesday 146

Thursday 1800 Friday 1500 Saturday 2125

XI. Techniques

1. *KEEP food records ACCURATELY*

2. Fill out the ANALYSIS form

3. Not to EAT LYING down

4. To CONSOLIDATE SNACK AT 11 pm

Source: Source: Henry A Jordan, Leonard S Levitz, and Gordon M Kimbrell, "Analysis of Food Intake" from *Eating Is Okay*. Copyright © 1976 by Associates for Behavioral Education and S & R Gelman Associates Inc. Reprinted with the permission of Rawson Associates, a division of Macmillan Inc.

Appendix 7-D

Energy Expenditure Log

DATE: _____   NAME _____

	:00 / :15	:15 / :30	:30 / :45	:45 / :60
6am	sleep — 0	sleep — 0	sleep — 0	sleep — 0
7am	sleep — 0	grooming shower — 3	sleep — 3	dress — 3
8am	read newspaper — 2	read — 2	prepare to leave for work / walk to bus stop — 3	en route to work on bus (sitting) — 2
9am	walk from bus stop to office / walk around office — 1/2	desk work — 2	desk work — 2	walk around office / desk work — 1/2
10am	desk work — 2	desk work — 2	desk work — 2	desk work — 2
11am	desk work — 2	walk around office — 3	desk work — 2	desk work — 2
12AM	walk around office 3½ / desk work — 2	walk around office 3/4 / walk to restaurant — 2	sit in restaurant / eat lunch — 2	walk on street / Back to office — 4
1 p.m.	desk work — 2	desk work — 2	desk work — 2	desk work — 2
2 pm	meeting — 2	meeting — 2	meeting — 2	meeting — 2
3 pm.	walking around office — 3	desk work — 2	desk work — 2	desk work — 2
4 pm	desk work — 2	walk around office — 2	desk work — 2	desk work — 2
5 pm	walk to bus stop — 4	en route home on bus (standing) — 3	walking around grocery store — 3	grocery store, standing in line — 3

131

Appendix 7-D   *continued*

	:00 :15		:15 :30		:30 :45		:45 :60	
6pm	walking on street on write store	4	walking around house	3	read newspaper	3	reading	2
7pm	watch TV	2	TV	2	eat supper	2	reading	2
8pm	reading	2	reading	2	reading	2	walk around house	3
9pm	TV	2	TV	2	TV	2	TV	2
10pm	TV	2	TV	2	TV	2	TV	2
11pm	walk around house	3	undress for bed	3	lying down reading	3	lying down reading	1
12pm	resting	1	sleep	0	sleep	0	sleep	0
1am	sleep	0	sleep	0	sleep	0	sleep	0
2am	sleep	0	sleep	0	sleep	0	sleep	0
3am	sleep	0	sleep	0	sleep	0	sleep	0
4am	sleep	0	sleep	0	sleep	0	sleep	0
5am	sleep	0	sleep	0	sleep	0	sleep	0

Source: Courtesy of Weight Control Unit, Obesity Research Center, St. Luke's-Roosevelt Hospital Center, New York.

Chapter 8

Popular and Very-Low-Calorie Diets in the Treatment of Obesity

Jordan W. Smoller, Thomas A. Wadden, and Kelly D. Brownell

For several decades now, weight loss has been a national obsession. On any given day, at least 20% of the US population is dieting to lose weight.[1] The need for effective treatments for obesity is a very real one, given that 30% of adult American women and 25% of men are obese, as defined by a criterion of 20% or more above ideal body weight.[2] The health risks of obesity of this magnitude are well known and include diabetes, hyperlipidemia, hypertension, and cardiovascular disease.

When combined with behavior therapy, dietary interventions may be the most effective means of weight reduction.[3] Mildly obese people (20% to 40% overweight) have the luxury of choosing from among a staggering array of popular diets. For moderately obese people (41% to 100% overweight), more structured and aggressive dietary treatment is indicated.

Dieting is clearly not restricted to the obese, however. While the prevalence of obesity among women has reached 30%, a recent Nielsen survey[4] found that 56% of women aged 25 to 34 years were dieting to lose weight. A November 1985 Gallup poll further revealed that fully 90% of Americans would like to be thinner. In response to this demand, the proliferation of diet books, weight-loss gimmicks, and commercial clinics has reached such collective proportions that it is commonly referred to as the "diet industry."

Virtually all weight reduction diets share a common rationale: that weight loss results when energy output exceeds energy intake. The variations on this theme, however, are innumerable and range from bizarre fad diets to conservative medical regimens. This chapter reviews some of the dietary approaches available to mildly and significantly obese people. We begin with an analysis of popular reducing diets with particular emphasis on the issue of nutritional adequacy. We then consider the safety and efficacy of current very-low-calorie diets (VLCD) and conclude with a discussion of the psychologic sequelae of dieting.

DIETARY APPROACHES TO MILD OBESITY: POPULAR DIETS

Perhaps the only long-lived feature of popular diets is their short-lived popularity. The turnover of popular diet books is so rapid that between the writing and the publication of this chapter, a new generation will have dominated the market. Nevertheless, a discussion of some recent popular diets will illustrate the issues that are pertinent to the evaluation of self-administered regimens.

Nicholas and Dwyer[5] recently reviewed nine currently popular diets. Their analysis provides an excellent overview of the strengths and perils of such diets. The books, chosen on the basis of the frequency of their availability in major bookstores, included the following: *Aerobic Nutrition*,[6] *The Diet Center Program*,[7] *The Delicious Quick-Trim Diet*,[8] *Nutraerobics*,[9] *Fasting: The Ultimate Diet*,[10] *Dr. Abravanel's Body Type Diet and Lifetime Nutrition Plan*,[11] *The Over-30 All-Natural Health and Beauty Plan*,[12] *California Diet and Exercise Program*,[13] and *The Diet That Lets You Cheat*.[14]

In a marketplace flooded with competitors, the authors of such books clearly appreciate the importance of psychologic techniques for capturing and maintaining the dieter's attention. Table 8-1 catalogues the variety of techniques used in the books reviewed by Nicholas and Dwyer.[5] Claims of scientific breakthroughs and broad health benefits were frequently used to promote the diets. In some cases, unsubstantiated and even dangerous assertions were used to lure consumers.

Elaborate and rigid rules for food selection were often used in an attempt to promote adherence. This rigidity may have appeal to people who feel their eating habits are out of control. In some cases, dietary restrictions served no other discernable purpose than to distinguish the diet from others. Instead of focusing on calories, the real currency of weight control, several books emphasized the kinds of foods permitted.

Safety of Popular Diets

Two related issues are central to the assessment of any weight-reduction regimen: (1) safety, and (2) efficacy. In the realm of unsupervised popular diets, safety becomes the dominant concern. Specifically, the nutritional adequacy of some diets is questionable. In presenting the most recent Recommended Daily Allowances (RDAs) for nutrients, the Food and Nutrition Board concluded that "it is difficult to assure the nutritional adequacy of diets that are low in energy (less than 1800–2000 kcal)."[15]

Table 8-1 Psychologic Techniques Used in Popular Reducing Diets

Function and Technique	Description and Comments	Utilized By
Motivates dieter to embark on regime by: Gimmick marketing techniques	Informs dieter of a "new" remedy to the old problem of weight loss. Promotes special food, service, or other substance as vital to the diet.	Diet Center Program Over-30 All-Natural Health and Beauty Plan Diet That Lets You Cheat Dr. Abravanel's Body Type Diet and Lifetime Nutrition Plan Delicious Quick-Trim Diet Nutraerobics
Use of a famous name	The name of a well-known person or institution is used to give credibility to the diet.	Diet Center Program Over-30 All-Natural Health and Beauty Plan California Diet and Exercise Program Aerobic Nutrition Delicious Quick-Trim Diet Nutraerobics Fasting: The Ultimate Diet
"Scientific" and biochemical claims	Diet makes "new" scientific claims. Biochemical claims may be valid or unproven and speculative. Weight loss is likely due to a placebo effect that increases motivation or adherence if claims are not valid.	Diet Center Program Diet That Lets You Cheat California Diet and Exercise Program Dr. Abravanel's Body Type Diet and Lifetime Nutrition Plan Aerobic Nutrition Delicious Quick-Trim Diet Nutraerobics Fasting: The Ultimate Diet
Prophylactic claims	Diet is claimed to have other health promotional properties, such as reducing risks of chronic degenerative diseases and so on.	Diet Center Program Over-30 All-Natural Health and Beauty Plan Diet That Lets You Cheat California Diet and Exercise Program Aerobic Nutrition Delicious Quick-Trim Diet Nutraerobics Fasting: The Ultimate Diet

Table 8-1 *continued*

Function and Technique	Description and Comments	Utilized By
Stimulate adherence by: Fixed menus	No fixed calorie intake is specified. Fixed menus for each day place constraints on the number, kinds, and portion size of foods permitted. Exchange system provides general patterns of types and amounts of food permitted. The dieter is freed from temptation and possible misjudgments by clear instructions.	*Diet Center Program* *Over-30 All-Natural Health and Beauty Plan* *Diet That Lets You Cheat* *Dr. Abravanel's Body Type Diet and Lifetime Nutrition Plan* *Aerobic Nutrition* *Delicious Quick-Trim Diet*
"Crash" phase	Very low calorie levels are used initially to cause rapid weight loss, reward efforts, and encourage adherence. Other techniques such as ketogenic diets and fluid restriction may be used as well to encourage diuresis.	*Dr. Abravanel's Body Type Diet and Lifetime Nutrition Plan* *Delicious Quick-Trim Diet* *Nutraerobics* *Fasting: The Ultimate Diet*
Special foods or supplements	Special foods such as "health" or "natural" foods may be provided with claims that they assist weight loss; they have only placebo effects. Dietetic foods are slightly lower in calories than usual items. Dietary fiber such as bran or bulk producers may contribute to satiety but do not alter energy output.	*Diet Center Program* *Over-30 All-Natural Health and Beauty Plan* *California Diet and Exercise Program* *Dr. Abravanel's Body Type Diet and Lifetime Nutrition Plan* *Nutraerobics*
Reward and incentive foods	Built-in rewards such as candy, sweets, alcohol, and days off are used as incentives to adhere to the diet. While food	*Diet That Lets You Cheat* *California Diet and Exercise Program*

Table 8-1 *continued*

Function and Technique	Description and Comments	Utilized By
	rewards may provide rest from the restrictions of the diet, they may also promote nonadherence at other times.	
Unpalatable or monotonous foods	Altered taste, flavor, texture, temperature, color, or variety of foods may decrease palatability and thereby decrease food intake.	*Nutraerobics*
Eating rituals	Special order of eating foods, timing, cooking practices, or recipes may help satisfy dieter's sensory pleasure from food and need for routine.	*Delicious Quick-Trim Diet*
Special conditions on eating or availability of foods in the environment	Specifications on time, place, speed, or circumstances of eating and requirements for weighing, measuring, and recording foods eaten are employed. Social milieu or suitable emotional states for eating are outlined to assist dieters in overcoming problem eating behaviors.	*Fasting: The Ultimate Diet*
Monitoring by another person	Checks on adherence by another person may be helpful to some individuals.	
Groups	Provide social support and/or pressure for dieter.	*Diet Center Program* (if used in conjunction with commercial Diet Center group)
Cognitive techniques	Stress reduction techniques such as relaxation, meditation, yoga, and positive thinking may	*Diet Center Program* *Over-30 All-Natural Health and Beauty Plan* *California Diet and*

Table 8-1 continued

Function and Technique	Description and Comments	Utilized By
	improve adherence by decreasing stress or emotion-related overeating.	Exercise Program Dr. Abravanel's Body Type Diet and Lifetime Nutrition Plan Delicious Quick-Trim Diet Fasting: The Ultimate Diet

Source: From Handbook of Eating Disorders: Physiology, Psychology, and Treatment of Obesity, Anorexia, and Bulimia by Kelly D Brownell and John P Foreyt (Eds). Copyright © 1986 by Basic Books Inc, Reprinted permission of Basic Books Inc. Publishers.

Macronutrient Content

The macronutrient composition of popular regimens varies widely. Many regimens, such as the current high-carbohydrate diets, are designed expressly to highlight a particular macronutrient. A highly unbalanced distribution of dietary components can have serious consequences. Adequate protein intake is of particular importance because it is critical to the maintenance of lean body mass (LBM). Hypocaloric diets increase the need for protein because amino acids may be diverted from anabolic pathways and lost to gluconeogenesis. Prolonged depletion of protein can compromise cardiac muscle function with fatal consequences.[16]

Among the diets reviewed by Nicholas and Dwyer,[5] only the fast (Fasting: The Ultimate Diet[10]) qualified as a "low-protein" diet. Table 8-2 presents the caloric value and nutrient composition of these diets. Also included are the ratio of polyunsaturated–to–saturated fats (P:S ratio) and the cholesterol content.

Carbohydrates generally contributed the greatest share of calories to these diets, but nearly two thirds of the regimens provided less than 50% of calories from carbohydrates. More than one half of the diets were low in fat as defined by having less than 10% of calories from fats. Although this trend toward limited fat intake is laudable, the distribution of fats in some diets may be unhealthy. The American Heart Association has recommended a dietary P:S ratio of 1.0 for reducing the risk of coronary heart disease.[17] Table 8-2 shows that fewer than one half of the 27 separate regimens analyzed by Nicholas and Dwyer[5] achieved this level. While cholesterol content was at or below the recommended 300 mg level[18] in about one half of the diets, values ranged as high as 904 mg for Dr. Abravanel's Body Type Diet.[11] Similar concerns were raised by Fisher and Lachance[19] in their analysis of 11 different popular diets. None of these best-selling diets reached a P:S ratio of 1.0.

Table 8-2 Nutrient Composition of Popular Diets

	Calories	Protein[a]	Carbohydrate[a]	Fat[a]	P:S Ratio ≥ 1.0	Choles-terol ≤ 300 mg
Diet Center Program						
Conditioning	1,771	27	45	31	●[b]	
Reducing	983	32	41	30	●	
Stabilization	1,377	34	30	37		
Maintenance	1,396	28	47	29		
Over-30 All-Natural Health and Beauty Plan						
Basic	1,115	31	26	45	●	
Maintenance	1,524	27	40	37	●	
Diet That Lets You						
Cheat	1,319	21	53	30		●
California Diet and Exercise						
Program	1,312	25	48	31	●	●
Dr. Abravanel's Body Type Diet and Lifetime Nutrition Plan[c]						
G-Type:						
Basic weight loss	1,019	24	55	24		●
Last five pounds	1,029	19	54	33		●
Maintenance	1,217	25	59	19		●
A-Type:						
Basic weight loss	1,120	32	50	20	●	●
Last five pounds	986	28	62	15		●
Maintenance	1,248	26	48	29	●	●
T-Type:						
Basic weight loss	1,132	36	30	34		
Last five pounds	928	37	31	32		
Maintenance	1,431	29	45	28		
P-Type:						
Basic weight loss	1,046	38	45	19		
Last five pounds	1,163	32	32	39		
Maintenance	1,111	28	47	28	●	
Aerobic Nutrition	1,111	28	47	28		●
Delicious Quick-Trim Diet						
Basic	956	36	45	20		●
Variety	1,146	25	48	31	●	●

Table 8-2 *continued*

	Calories	Protein[a]	Carbohydrate[a]	Fat[a]	P:S Ratio ≥ 1.0	Choles-terol ≤ 300 mg
Vegetable	946	16	72	20	•	•
Liquid	915	28	64	9		•
Nutraerobics	607	18	59	24		•
Fasting: The Ultimate Diet	0	0	0	0	•	•

[a]Percent of calories.
[b]Bullets signify agreement with statements in column headings.
[c]Body types are assigned to the individual on the basis of a system devised by Dr. Abravanel that is neither widely accepted nor necessarily judged to be valid by physical anthropologists.

Source: Reprinted from *Handbook of Eating Disorders: Physiology, Psychology, and Treatment* (pp 122–144) by KD Brownell and JP Foreyt (Eds) with permission of Basic Books Inc, © 1984.

Micronutrient Content

Any person undertaking a popular diet must also be wary of micronutrient deficiencies. Regimens that do not provide sufficient quantities of even a single nutrient can have serious consequences if followed for extended periods of time. For example, inadequate intakes of potassium, magnesium, and trace elements have been implicated in sudden death after use of liquid protein diets.[20]

Deficiencies are of particular concern during periods in the life cycle when biologic processes are especially sensitive to nutrient requirements. Drastic perturbations in nutrient intake should be avoided during infancy, childhood, puberty, pregnancy, and lactation.[5] None of the diets reviewed by Nicholas and Dwyer[5] met the RDA standards for all vitamins and minerals. Remarkably, the use of recommended vitamin or mineral supplements did not always ensure sufficient micronutrient intake. Table 8-3 shows that deficiencies were most frequently encountered with iron, zinc, folacin, and vitamin B_6. Several diets were lacking in a variety of nutrients. For obvious reasons, *Fasting: The Ultimate Diet*[10] was nutritionally inadequate in all respects. The *Quick-Trim Diet*,[8] which provides roughly 1,000 calories in each of its four regimens, was deficient in most of the micronutrients surveyed.

This alarming nutrient insufficiency of many popular diets was independently substantiated by Fisher and Lachance.[19] Not one of the 11 programs they analyzed provided 100% of the US RDAs for vitamins and minerals. The best-selling *Beverly Hills Diet*[21] provided less than 80% of the RDAs for 10 of the 13 micronutrients studied.

Efficacy of Popular Diets

Although it has been estimated that less than 6% of available weight-loss diets are effective (*New York Times*, July 16, 1986, p C1), short-term weight losses are undoubtedly achieved by many regimens. Three periods in the progress of diet-induced weight loss can be differentiated: (1) initial loss of fluid weight, (2) short-term loss of body fat, and (3) long-term maintenance of weight loss. Popular diets tend to excel at the first two, but perform dismally at the third.

Anyone familiar with the marketing of popular diets has heard testimonials like "I lost 12 pounds in only 5 days!" If there is any truth to such claims, they can only refer to the initial loss of body water produced by many weight-loss diets. The composition of these diets is often geared to maximize diuresis. Diets that restrict sodium or fluid intake or promote intake of mild diuretics like caffeine-containing beverages may produce diuresis directly. Since carbohydrate consumption leads to water retention, low-carbohydrate diets will also result in substantial water loss. In addition, low-carbohydrate and VLC diets stimulate ketosis, which may induce diuresis.[5] Apart from its dehydrating effect, the chief danger of rapid fluid weight loss is its impact on dieters' expectations. After 1 to 2 weeks, fluid loss diminishes, and the dieter, accustomed to losing several pounds per week, may be disheartened by a sudden plateau of weight loss.[22]

As the duration of caloric restriction increases, the proportion of body fat in the weight lost will also increase. Since a substantial caloric deficit must be incurred to lose a pound of fat, this process is obviously more gradual than the initial fluid weight drop. Even under optimal metabolic conditions, when the dieter is finally burning a fuel mixture that is 96% fat, an energy deficit of 3,600 calories is needed for the loss of every pound.[23] Nevertheless, so long as energy expenditure exceeds energy intake, short-term weight loss can be expected.

Short-term losses are not an adequate criterion of success for the overweight dieter seeking a significant, sustained weight reduction. Unfortunately, a number of factors may subvert long-term success. Physiologically, caloric restriction is known to decrease the resting metabolic rate (RMR) of both obese and lean people. The decline begins within 24 to 48 hours of caloric restriction and may exceed 20% in only 2 weeks.[24–27] Besides diminishing overall metabolic rate, dieting produces a significant decrease in the energy cost of performing particular tasks.[27] This suppression of energy expenditure may be responsible for the plateau in weight loss that is commonly observed in dieters. As the body becomes more energy-efficient, a level of caloric intake that had produced weight loss previously may result in weight maintenance or even gain.

Weight gain is also likely if adherence to the diet diminishes. Diets that involve drastic changes in eating habits make long-term adherence difficult. Many popular diets achieve short-term success because the rigid monotony of their regimens discourages overeating and provides dieters with a break from their usual hab-

Table 8-3 Vitamin and Mineral Content of Popular Diets

	Vitamin A	Vitamin D	Vitamin C	Thiamin	Riboflavin	Niacin	Folacin	Vitamin B6	Vitamin B12	Calcium	Phosphorus	Absorbable Iron	Zinc	Nutrient Supplements Recommended
Diet Center Program														
Conditioning	A	–	M	A	A	A	A	–	A	A	A	A	–	yes
Reducing	A	–	M	–	A	A	–	–	–	A	A	–	–	yes
Stabilization	A	A	A	M	M	M	A	M	M	A	A	–	–	yes
Maintenance	A	A	A	A	A	A	A	–	A	A	A	–	–	yes
Over-30 All-Natural Health and Beauty Plan														
Basic	M	A	M	M	M	M	A	M	M	–	A	–	–	yes
Maintenance	A	A	M	M	M	A	A	M	M	–	A	–	–	yes
Diet That Lets You Cheat	A	A	A	A	A	A	–	–	A	A	A	–	–	
California Diet and Exercise Program	A	A	A	A	A	A	A	–	A	A	A	–	–	
Dr. Abravanel's Body Type Diet and Lifetime Nutrition Plan[a]														
G-Type:														
Basic weight loss	A	A	A	A	A	A	–	–	A	A	A	–	–	
Last five pounds	A	–	A	A	A	A	A	–	–	A	A	–	–	
Maintenance	A	A	A	A	A	A	A	–	A	A	A	–	–	
A-Type:														
Basic weight loss	A	A	A	A	A	A	A	–	A	A	A	–	–	
Last five pounds	A	–	A	A	A	A	–	–	–	–	A	–	–	
Maintenance	A	–	A	A	A	A	–	–	A	A	A	–	A	

T-Type:
  Basic weight loss
  Last five pounds
  Maintenance
P-Type:
  Basic weight loss
  Last five pounds
  Maintenance
Aerobic Nutrition
Delicious Quick-Trim Diet
  Basic
  Variety
  Vegetable
  Liquid
Nutraerobics
Fasting: The Ultimate Diet

yes

[a]Body types are assigned to the individual on the basis of a system devised by Dr. Abravanel that is neither widely accepted nor necessarily judged to be valid by physical anthropologists.

A = Adequate (80 percent or more of RDAs). I = Less than 80 percent RDAs). M = Megadose (10–100 times RDAs).

Source: Reprinted from *Handbook of Eating Disorders: Physiology, Psychology, and Treatment* (pp 122–144) by KD Brownell and JP Foreyt (Eds) with permission of Basic Books Inc, © 1986.

its.[3,5] In the long-run, however, these perturbations in eating patterns may be untenable. Indeed, Stunkard[3] noted that the entire concept of dieting can be criticized on psychologic grounds since "going on" a diet implies "going off" it and the resumption of old eating habits. Although long-term maintenance of weight loss is notoriously problematic,[28] the dieter's chances are certainly increased if eating habits are gradually reshaped to include foods that one can continue to eat indefinitely. Sadly, few popular diets include a comprehensive maintenance plan.

Classification of Popular Diets

We have seen that the safety and utility of popular diets vary widely according to their composition and usage. Although controlled trials of these diets are unavailable, Nicholas and Dwyer[5] have provided a valuable framework for evaluating their relative merits. A content analysis of the programs they reviewed yielded three categories: (1) reasonable regimens low in calories, adequate in nutrients, balanced in energy-yielding nutrients, scientifically objective in presentation, based on tested psychologic techniques, and straightforward in marketing practices; (2) questionable regimens that do not meet one or more of the preceding criteria; and (3) fad diets that present clear health hazards, are not administered under a physician's direction, advocate exaggerated or false theories, or whose marketing puts the consumer at unreasonable monetary risk.

Examples of Fad Diets

Nicholas and Dwyer[5] identified three fad diets among the nine programs they reviewed. *Fasting: The Ultimate Diet*,[10] which advocates self-initiated total fasts of varying duration, illustrates the dangers of many "crash" diets. Even medically-supervised fasting has been associated with severe complications including electrolyte imbalance, hepatic and cardiovascular dysfunction, and even death.[29–31] Nicholas and Dwyer[5] noted that *The Ultimate Diet*[10] ignores the need for vitamin and electrolyte supplements and promotes several dangerous myths about fasting. Adverse reactions such as headaches, nausea, and dizziness are referred to as healthy signs that the body is "ridding itself of toxins."[10] The book[10] makes an untenable distinction between starvation and fasting and seeks credibility in testimonials from historical figures who believed that fasting promoted physical and mental health. Finally, rapid weight loss produced by fasting is rarely maintained.[29] Since most of the initial loss is attributable to diuresis, a rapid weight rebound can be expected when eating resumes. The book does not recommend any long-term changes in eating or exercise habits.

The *Nutraerobics*[9] plan is based on a 600- to 800-calorie protein-sparing modified fast. The book provides general guidelines for designing the diet, but they are inadequate. When Nicholas and Dwyer[5] devised a regimen based on the book's recommendations, the result was deficient in ten vitamins and minerals. Even the highest quality VLCDs require strict medical supervision and may be subject to adverse side effects and poor weight-loss maintenance.

The outlandish claims that characterize many fad diets are exemplified by *Dr. Abravanel's Body Type Diet and Lifetime Nutrition Plan*.[11] The book is structured around a quasiendocrinologic theory of weight control that holds that (1) all persons have dominant glands (gonads, adrenal, thyroid, or pituitary) that determine the body's reaction to food, and (2) weight gain is attributable to "overworking" these glands. After identifying their body type and dominant gland, dieters follow a rigidly structured food plan designed to stimulate the "weaker" glands and give the dominant gland a rest. Nicholas and Dwyer[5] found the menus would be unbalanced, nutritionally deficient, and potentially dangerous if dieters were to follow the recommendation for long-term usage.

As bizarre as some diets seem to be, their very oddness may be a key to their popularity. By drastically altering eating patterns, they dramatize the dieter's effort to renounce old habits.[32] *The Beverly Hills Diet*,[21] one of the most popular fad diets of recent years, enticed dieters with clever pseudoscience and gourmet foods. The regimen was based on the author's exclusive discovery that enzymes in fruit can render other foods less fattening and that carbohydrate and protein digestive enzymes cannot work together. The first week's menu is restricted to fruit, from papaya to mango, and protein is not permitted until day 19 when steak or lobster may be eaten. With a protein content of only 7% and deficiencies in several vitamins and minerals, the diet is clearly inadequate.[19]

So-called diet aids generally fall into the fad category as well. These include a variety of commercially available products that allegedly promote weight loss by inducing physiologic changes or suppressing appetite. They may be distinguished from medically prescribed anorectic agents that clearly do produce short-term weight losses.[33] Unlike diet books, whose printed claims are protected from regulation by First Amendment rights, diet-related products and foods are subject to the jurisdiction of the Food and Drug Administration (FDA).[34] This jurisdiction was invoked against one of the most popular diet aids of recent years: starch blockers. Manufacturers claimed that the product contained enzymes that could prevent digestion and absorption of starch. Consumers were assured that they could eat as much as they wanted of their favorite starchy foods without fear of weight gain. Citing insufficient evidence, the FDA suspended the sale of starch blockers in 1982.[34]

The very real dangers posed by fad diets were painfully shown by the most notorious of them all: Linn and Stuart's *The Last Chance Diet*.[35] By 1978, the FDA[36] and the Centers for Disease Control[37] had received reports of more than 60 deaths related to the use of this "liquid protein" diet. Several factors have been implicated in these tragic outcomes.

The protein used in liquid protein diets was of poor biologic quality, consisting primarily of collagen and gelatin derivatives obtained from cowhide and other sources of connective tissue.[38] This inferior protein may have failed to provide adequate nourishment for the cardiac muscle, as suggested by autopsy findings of myocardial deterioration. Larger weight losses, lower initial body weight, longer duration of dieting, and pre-existing illness were associated with greater risk for sudden death.[20,39,40] Since liquid protein diets were deficient in calcium, magnesium, potassium, sodium, and other minerals, electrolyte disturbance was a likely cause of death by cardiac arrythmias. Unfortunately, many dieters received no medical supervision that might have identified and corrected such fatal imbalances.

Examples of Questionable Diets

Regimens that fit this designation are not as patently dangerous as fad diets but can nonetheless be faulted for certain inadequacies. For example, Nicholas and Dwyer[5] found that *The Delicious Quick-Trim Diet*[8] provided insufficient amounts of more than one half of the nutrients analyzed. The book makes a variety of unsupported claims and omits reasonable guidelines for weight-loss maintenance. *The Diet Center Program*,[7] based on the program offered at commercial Diet Center clinics, was also deemed questionable because of inadequate nutrition and untenable claims. Despite the fact that the book recommends calcium and vitamin C supplements, the program provides inadequate levels of seven other vitamins and minerals. Dieters are told that weight loss and maintenance are achieved by counting nutrients (rather than calories) and by controlling blood sugar levels.

The *Over-30* program[12] is based on the unsubstantiated theory that people over 30 years old are increasingly unable to metabolize starchy carbohydrate, resulting in fluid retention and weight gain. Without scientific basis, the diet excludes whole classes of foods while recommending vitamins in megadoses that could be toxic. While the recommended vitamin intake may be excessive, the diet was found to be lacking in important minerals. The regimen is also high in fat and low in carbohydrate, making it ketogenic and potentially associated with a number of adverse side effects.

The *Aerobic Nutrition* plan,[6] also considered questionable, makes apparently exaggerated claims about the diet's role in preventing chronic degenerative disease. Like other diets in this category, the program provides inadequate amounts of certain nutrients and gives minimal attention to the issue of maintenance.

Examples of Reasonable Diets

Although they may be harder to find, nutritionally adequate and scientifically reasonable diets do exist. Among the diets they reviewed, Nicholas and Dwyer[5] identified only two such programs: *The California Diet and Exercise Plan*[13] was credited for its emphasis on exercise as an adjunct to its moderately hypocaloric diet well suited to mildly overweight adults. The caloric content of the diet plans ranged from 1,200 to 2,800 calories, with menus becoming more liberal as physical activity is increased.

The *Diet That Lets You Cheat*[14] is another reasonable program. Again, caloric restrictions are moderate and incorporate a sensible degree of flexibility. The diet comprises three phases requiring progressive participation by the dieter in planning menus that do not exceed the caloric limits. The dieter is permitted to "cheat" by eating one 300-calorie "forbidden" food per week.

DIETARY INTERVENTIONS FOR MILD OBESITY: GENERAL GUIDELINES

The treatment of choice for mild obesity is a combination of caloric restriction and behavior modification.[3] While self-initiated popular diets may be the most commonly used means of weight control, many are inappropriate or incomplete. Any comprehensive dietary intervention should include the following three considerations.

Professional Evaluation and Supervision

Minimal medical supervision is needed when the dieter adheres to a nutritionally reasonable diet that promotes a gradual transition to sensible eating habits. At the very least, however, people should receive a complete medical screening to determine the degree and etiology of their obesity. Simple changes in eating patterns may be insufficient for those who are more than 40% overweight or those whose obesity is secondary to other medical conditions such as endocrinologic imbalances.

Medical screening may also identify people for whom significant caloric restriction is contraindicated, including pregnant and lactating women. Physicians and/or dietitians should evaluate the nutritional adequacy of a prospective diet for a given person. Specific nutritional needs will differ among people. For example, the protein and calcium provided by many popular diets may be inadequate for growing children; the iron provided is often insufficient for women of childbearing age.[5]

When prescribing a dietary program, practitioners should assess the patient's motivation. Many patients are ill prepared for the sustained commitment necessary to achieve and maintain weight loss; expectations are often unrealistic.

A psychologic evaluation should address this issue and should identify any pre-existing emotional difficulties that might be exacerbated by caloric deprivation.

Nature of the Diet

For reasons already discussed, programs that fall into the fad or questionable diet categories should be avoided. Patients who are planning to undertake a popular diet should be apprised of what to look for in selecting such a diet. Diets that promise quick weight loss by severely restricting calories, carbohydrates, salt, or fluids may chiefly promote diuresis, and early losses will be quickly regained when normal eating resumes. Diets that severely restrict any nutrients or food groups (with the exception of fats) are also cause for suspicion. The use of vitamin and mineral supplements may not guarantee nutritional adequacy with many such regimens.

More generally, diets that prescribe rigid menus, demand strict avoidance of various foods, or otherwise require drastic changes in eating patterns are ill suited to sustained weight reduction. Without built-in flexibility, long-term adherence becomes impossible, and dieting provides no more than a frustrating sense of failure. A sensible diet should also include a program for maintenance of weight loss. This component is critical; keeping weight off is much more difficult than losing it.

In summary, if "dieting" implies a drastic, time-limited change in eating patterns, the best diet may be no diet at all. Dietary interventions for mild obesity are best conceived as gradual changes in eating habits with a transition to foods that the person can continue to eat indefinitely. This means increasing the intake of complex carbohydrates, especially fruits, vegetables, and whole grains, and decreasing the intake of fats and simple sugars. In most cases, restricting caloric intake to 1,000 to 1,200 calories is sufficient to produce weight loss, with an adjustment to slightly higher levels for maintenance.

Adjunct Therapy: Behavior Modification and Exercise

To maximize long-term effectiveness, dietary interventions should include a program of behavior modification and physical activity. We have already noted the importance of modifying eating habits in ways that can be maintained indefinitely. This can be achieved by a comprehensive behavior modification program. Patients receive behavioral training in self-monitoring of eating behavior, control of eating cues, relapse prevention, and other established techniques (see Chapter 11). The combination of behavior modification and a 1,000- to 1,200-calorie diet consistently produces losses of 0.5 kg/wk or more, with losses as much as 14 kg in 25 weeks.[41]

Physical activity is another valuable adjunct to dieting for several reasons. Besides directly increasing caloric expenditure, exercise may prevent the loss of LBM that accompanies caloric restriction while enhancing loss of body fat.[42] Citing the increase in RMR that accompanies physical activity, some researchers[26,27] have argued that exercise may counter the decline in RMR that follows caloric restriction and weight loss. Since this decline in RMR is probably responsible for the plateau in weight loss common to dieters, exercise may increase the extent and duration of weight reduction. Physical activity may also promote adherence to dietary interventions by suppressing appetite and enhancing psychologic well-being.[42] Several studies[43–47] have shown that the combination of exercise and diet produces larger and better maintained losses than does exercise alone.

DIETARY APPROACHES TO MODERATE OBESITY: VERY-LOW-CALORIE DIETS

While a combination of behavior therapy and a 1,000- to 1,200-calorie diet is well suited to the treatment of mild obesity, more aggressive interventions are needed for the moderately obese who are at clear risk for health complications. The most effective dietary therapy for this population involves the use of VLCDs. These diets provide 300 to 600 calories daily and produce average weight losses of 20 kg in 12 weeks. By providing almost all of these calories in the form of protein, VLCDs seem to induce rapid weight losses without dangerous losses of LBM. In recent years, treatment with VLCDs has evolved sufficiently to become, in conjunction with behavior therapy, the treatment of choice for the markedly obese.

A Brief History

The use of VLCDs dates back to the early 1930s when Strang and colleagues[48,49] reported an average weight loss of 9.9 kg in 295 patients treated for 8 weeks with a 300- to 400-calorie diet. Despite these promising results, VLCDs were overlooked for many years. Research on fasting during the 1960s and 1970s led to their rediscovery.

In 1959, Bloom[50] reported an average weight loss of 8.4 kg among nine patients who fasted for 7 days. Psychologic adjustment to the fast was apparently favorable. In the following decade, other researchers[29] reported greater losses with longer periods of fasting.

Unfortunately, the promise of fasting was short-lived. Clinicians began to observe severe physical complications in their fasted patients. By 1970, at least five fasting-related deaths had been reported.[51-54] Although pre-existing illness may have contributed to several of these fatalities, the reports included the death of an obese but otherwise healthy young woman. Postmortem investigation in this case indicated that LBM had been lost from the heart.

At the same time, researchers were finding that weight lost by therapeutic starvation was quickly regained. In one series[55] of fasted patients, 78% equaled or exceeded their admission weight within 1 year of finishing treatment. As the disadvantages of starvation became apparent, researchers renewed their interest in VLCDs.

Nutritional Considerations in Very-Low-Calorie Diets

Protein Intake

Experience with fasting had shown that the chief danger in severe caloric restriction was the depletion of endogenous protein by its conversion to glucose (gluconeogenesis).[56] Protein malnutrition may impair cardiac, hepatic, renal, and pulmonary function.[57-59] Modern research on VLCDs has sought to produce large weight losses while minimizing losses of LBM through the provision of large amounts of dietary protein.

Changes in LBM have been measured indirectly by the method of nitrogen balance, with the assumption that maintenance of nitrogen balance can be equated with the preservation of LBM.[60] Investigators have disagreed about the amount of dietary protein required to achieve nitrogen balance during caloric restriction. Some patients have reportedly maintained nitrogen balance with as little as 31 g daily,[61] while others have failed to achieve it with 132 g daily.[62] These discrepancies illustrate the vast individual differences that may be observed in response to VLCDs. The existence of these differences underscores the need for careful medical supervision. Evidence that greater protein intake is associated with smaller losses of LBM suggests that practitioners should err on the side of prescribing too much rather than too little protein.[63]

The type of protein supplementation is also a matter of controversy. Current VLCDs are of two types. The protein-sparing modified fast (PSMF) developed by Blackburn, Bistrian, and colleagues[63-65] provides 1.5 g of protein per kilogram of ideal body weight. Protein is obtained from lean meat, fish, and fowl, consumed in three to four meals per day. No carbohydrate is permitted, and fat is restricted to that present in the protein source. The other approach relies on a milk- or egg-based powdered protein formula consumed as a liquid diet in three to five servings daily. These commercially prepared diets provide a daily ration of 33 to 70 g of protein, 30 to 45 g of carbohydrate, and approximately 2 g of fat.

The relative merits of these two formats have been debated. Proponents of PSMF argue that the diet teaches patients to handle conventional foods successfully, thus facilitating the transition from the diet to a pattern of controlled eating. Advocates of liquid diets contend that they facilitate adherence by removing the temptations of conventional foods. In addition, vitamin and mineral supplements are included in the preparation, thus reducing the possibility that patients will forget to use them.[66]

Although the two approaches produce similar weight losses, we have found that patients tend to report that PSMF is more acceptable and less disruptive of normal social eating. They also experience less hunger and preoccupation with food than do patients on liquid diets.[67] Indeed, patients reported significantly less hunger when consuming a PSMF than when consuming a preceding 1,200-calorie balanced diet. This therapeutic anorexia is often attributed to ketosis; however, research findings fail to confirm this claim.[29]

Since patients vary considerably in their response to these two diets, neither can be recommended categorically. Despite the evidence favoring the use of PSMF, some patients greatly prefer liquid formula diets because of their ease of preparation and lack of resemblance to other foods.

Carbohydrate Intake

Investigators disagree about the value of including carbohydrate in VLCDs. Those[66,68] who favor the use of carbohydrate point to its electrolyte-retaining effect, which minimizes the diuresis and consequent orthostatic hypotension associated with VLCDs. Most commercially prepared formula diets contain 30 to 45 g of carbohydrate.

Other researchers[69] claim that the substitution of carbohydrate for protein actually decreases protein-sparing, and they favor the exclusion of dietary carbohydrate. In the absence of carbohydrate, plasma insulin levels are suppressed, promoting ketosis and enhancing fat use. The ketones produced may replace glucose as an energy source so that gluconeogenesis is inhibited and LBM is spared.

Micronutrient Intake

VLCDs must be supplemented with vitamins and minerals. A multivitamin should be taken daily to meet RDA standards. Sodium intake of 5 g daily is required to counteract the marked loss of sodium resulting from diuresis. Even with this added salt intake, patients should drink a minimum of 1.5 L of noncaloric fluids to prevent dehydration. It is also crucial that adequate potassium intake (3 g daily) be maintained since it is necessary to ensure proper electrolyte balance and to achieve optimal protein-sparing.[70] An extra 400 to 800 mg of calcium may also be recommended in some cases.[64] Commercially prepared liquid formula diets (such as Optifast 70) may contain some or all of these supplements.

Clinical Use of Very-Low-Calorie Diets

Patient Population

VLCDs are appropriate for adults (aged 18 to 65 years) who are moderately (41% to 100% overweight) to morbidly (more than 100% overweight) obese as determined by standard height-weight tables.[71] These diets should not be undertaken by mildly obese people in whom the risks for serious untoward consequences are much greater.[16] For morbidly obese people who have failed repeatedly using VLCDs and other methods, gastric restriction surgery may be indicated.[72]

Medical evaluation of prospective patients generally includes a physical examination, medical history, electrocardiagram (ECG), chest x-ray study, a complete blood chemistry study, and a complete urinalysis. VLCDs are contraindicated in pregnant women and patients with cardiovascular or cerebrovascular disease, cancer, juvenile-onset diabetes, hepatic disease, renal failure, or severe psychiatric disturbance.

Administration of the Diet

Introduction of the VLCD is usually preceded by 2 to 4 weeks of a 1,200-calorie balanced diet. This preliminary period is useful in several respects. First, it allows patients some adjustment to caloric deprivation. Second, the gradual diuresis that results from this moderate restriction prevents the rapid sodium loss that would follow an abrupt introduction of the VLCD. Third, practitioners have the opportunity to assess adherence. Patients may be asked to record their food intake and to increase their physical activity during this time. Adherence to this phase of the program may predict adherence to the VLCD. Our research group found a strong correlation ($r = .67$) between weight lost during this preliminary period and total weight lost during a 6-month program that included 2 months of VLCD. Some researchers[73,74] believe that patients who adhere poorly to a 1,200-calorie diet should not proceed to the low-calorie phase.

Patients must be medically monitored at regular intervals once the VLCD is introduced. As with the initial medical evaluation, administration of the diet and medical monitoring may be done on an outpatient basis. The only exception is for Type II diabetic patients receiving 50 or more units of insulin per day; these patients must be hospitalized to be weaned from insulin.

During the low-calorie diet phase, blood tests must be conducted at least every other week to monitor electrolytes and other critical variables. A brief physical examination should be given at the same interval to check vital signs and monitor side effects. ECGs are indicated after every 12 kg of weight loss or every month on the diet.

For the first 2 weeks of dieting, some patients may experience fatigue and mild postural hypotension. The preliminary 1,200-calorie diet and the provision of salt and water during the VLCD should minimize these symptoms. Mild laxatives or fiber-rich low-carbohydrate vegetables may be added to control constipation. Women who become amenorrheic while dieting should receive a pregnancy test and should terminate the diet if pregnancy is confirmed. Practitioners may also observe cold intolerance, dry skin, and, rarely, brittle nails and hair loss; all of these symptoms remit when dieting ceases.

Rapid weight loss follows introduction of the VLCD. During the first week, losses of 2 to 4 kg are common. As diuresis subsides, the weight lost is primarily fat and averages 1 to 1.5 kg/wk for women and 1.5 to 2 kg for men, with even greater losses for heavier people.[75]

After the VLCD phase, a period of 2 to 4 weeks is devoted to refeeding. Milk and milk products, vegetables, cereals, and fruits are gradually introduced in this order. Carbohydrates, especially simple sugars, must be reintroduced slowly to avoid an abrupt gain of fluid weight.

Safety of Current Very-Low-Calorie Diets

VLCDs seem to be safe when the following four conditions are met: (1) the diet contains protein of high biologic quality; (2) the duration of dieting is brief (3 months or less); (3) use of the diet is restricted to patients who are 40% or more overweight and have no contraindicated physical conditions; and (4) patients receive careful medical supervision and proper micronutrient supplementation.

The liquid protein fad diets of the 1970s (discussed earlier) rarely met any of these conditions and were consequently associated with scores of fatalities. In contrast, the safety record of current VLCDs is impressive: no diet-related fatalities have been reported in more than 10,000 cases.

Effectiveness of Very-Low-Calorie Diets

The short-term effectiveness of VLCDs is, not surprisingly, dramatic and impressive. The eight major studies, including one by A. Palgi, MD (unpublished data, 1981),[68,74,76–80] summarized in Table 8-4, illustrate the large weight losses associated with these diets. Short treatments (4 weeks) produced losses of 7 to 10 kg,[68,78] while longer treatments (19 to 24 weeks) produced larger losses of 31 to 41 kg.[76,77] These weight losses are clearly superior to those achieved with other nonsurgical treatments for obesity, such as behavior modification, diet, and anorectic drugs. Only 10% of patients treated with conventional therapies ever achieve reductions of 20 kg,[81] the average weight loss for 12 weeks on VLCDs.

VLCDs are also effective in alleviating medical problems commonly associated with obesity. Large reductions have been reported for systolic and diastolic blood pressure and serum cholesterol and triglyceride levels; short-term control of adult-onset diabetes has also been shown.[29]

The long-term effectiveness of VLCDs is far less convincing. As Table 8-4 shows, studies that include follow-up indicate poor maintenance of weight loss. In this sense, weight losses achieved by VLCDs are no different from those achieved by fasts or popular diets: without instruction in maintenance, weight regain is inevitable.

In the case of VLCDs, maintenance must be addressed explicitly because it requires behavioral strategies very different from those used during the diet. Patients must learn to deal with foods that they were able to avoid while dieting. They must also learn how to reverse quickly the small weight gains that often follow the end of treatment.

To prepare patients for these and other contingencies, the dietary intervention should be combined with a program of behavior therapy. In this treatment co-alition, VLCD is used to induce a large rapid weight loss, and behavior therapy is used primarily to teach patients to maintain this loss.

Combined Treatment: Very-Low-Calorie Diet and Behavior Therapy

The feasibility and effectiveness of the combined approach were first shown by Lindner and Blackburn[74] and later confirmed by Wadden and colleagues[82] in a pilot study of 17 moderately obese women. Patients were treated for 6 months, including 2 months of VLCD.

Before the diet was introduced, patients were treated individually for 1 month, during which they consumed a 1,000- to 1,200-calorie balanced diet and received behavioral training in self-monitoring of eating behavior and increasing physical activity. During the second and third months of treatment, patients consumed a VLCD while receiving behavior therapy in weekly group meetings. The fourth month was devoted to refeeding, but patients continued to receive detailed behavioral training through the end of the sixth month. The behavioral component, designed specifically to promote strategies for maintenance, included traditional behavioral principles[83] as well as cognitive restructuring[84] and relapse prevention training (G.A. Marlatt, PhD, unpublished data, 1980).

As Figure 8-1 shows, patients lost an average of 20 kg (45 lb) in 6 months, the largest loss reported to date in a behaviorally oriented program. Moreover,

Table 8-4 Summary Analysis of Eight Major Studies Using Very-Low-Calorie Diets

Study	N	Subject Characteristics	Diet Regimen[a]	Mean Treatment Duration (Wk)	Mean Weight Loss (Kg)	Follow-up[b]
[c]Howard et al,[68] 1978	22	19F, 3M; M wt = 107.8 kg	Formula (31 g protein, 44 g CHO)	4	9.6	7 Ss stayed on diet 6 wk: M loss = 13.2 kg
	28 (22)[d]	25F, 3M at outset; M wt = 96.3 kg	Formula (same as above)	6	9.0	6 Ss stayed on diet 12 wk: M loss = 15.7 kg
McLean Baird and Howard,[78] 1977	38 (25)	30F, 8M at outset; ages 17–62; M wt (N=25) = 104.4 kg	Formula (25 g protein, 40 g CHO)	8	13.8	1 mo: M loss = 12.2 kg
Atkinson and Kaiser,[79] 1981	234	200F, 34M; M age = 37.9; M wt = 104.5 kg	Formula (1 g protein per kg IBW; .5 g sucrose per kg IBW)	variable; maximum of 12 wk on VLCD	18.7 (at 12 wk)	None
Tuck et al,[80] 1981	25	14F, 11M; M age = 40.7; M wt = 103.9 kg	Formula (Optifast)	12	20.2	None
Lindner and Blackburn,[74] 1976	67	57F, 10M; M age = 48; M wt = 93.6 kg	Formula (Ilentex P-20); training in nutrition and behavior modification	variable; M = 16.7	20.8 kg	12 mo: M loss = 18.4 kg; 18 to 24 mo: M loss = 14.5 kg
A. Palgi, MD, et al, unpublished data, 1981	668	564F, 104M; M age = 38.5; M wt = 98 kg	Animal protein (1.5 g protein per kg IBW); training in nutrition and behavior modification	variable; M = 17 wk on VLCD, preceded by 4 wk on balanced calorie diet	21	4.5 yr: 216 patients sampled, M loss = 6.6 kg

Table 8-4 continued

Study	N	Subject Characteristics	Diet Regimen[a]	Mean Treatment Duration (Wk)	Mean Weight Loss (Kg)	Follow-up[b]
[e]Vertes et al,[76] 1977	411	F; M age = 40; M wt = 109.6 kg	Formula (45 g protein, 30 g glucose)	variable; M = 23.8 wk	31.2	None
	119	M; M age = 40; M wt = 136.6 kg	Same as above	variable; M = 19.9 wk	37.6	None
Genuth et al,[77] 1974	45 (28)	F; M age = 42; M wt = 112.5 kg	Formula (45 g protein, 30 g glucose)	variable; M = 23 wk	32.5	22 mo: 56% of total (N = 75) regained 50% of weight lost
	30 (19)	M; M age = 44; M wt = 137.8 kg	Same as above	variable; M = 19 wk	41.1	

[a] All subjects were seen as outpatients except for 22 subjects in the study of Howard et al (1978). In the study of Genuth et al (1974), subjects were seen as inpatients for the first week, but as outpatients thereafter.

[b] All follow-up weights were calculated from pretreatment values.

[c] Number refers to listing in the "Reference" section.

[d] Number in parentheses refers to number of subjects remaining after attrition.

[e] Data presented here were calculated by Dr Vertes upon our request and do not fully correspond with those in the original publication.

Note: F = female. M = male. M = mean. IBW = ideal body weight. Variable = variable length of time. CHO = carbohydrate.

Source: Reprinted with permission from "Very Low Calorie Diets: their Safety, Efficacy and Future" by TA Wadden, AJ Stunkard, and KD Brownell, *Annals of Internal Medicine* (1983; 99:675–684), Copyright © 1983, American College of Physicians.

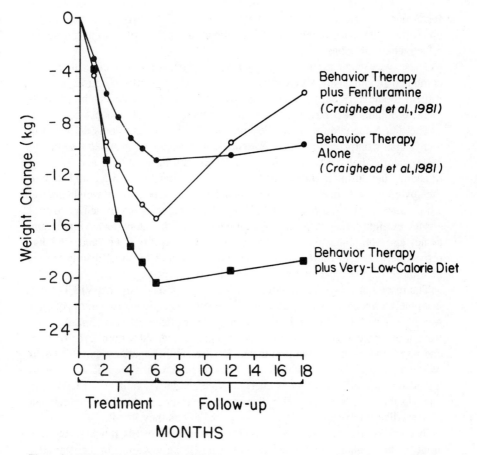

Figure 8-1 Weight loss (in kg) at the end of 6 months of treatment and 1-year follow-up for patients treated by behavior therapy plus VLCD,[74] in comparison with behavior therapy alone[85] and behavior therapy plus fenfluramine.[85] *Source*: Reprinted with permission from *Journal of Consulting and Clinical Psychology* (1984; 52:693), Copyright © 1984, American Psychological Association.

nearly 70% of the patients lost 18.2 kg (40 lb) or more, a goal achieved by only 10% of patients in conventional weight-reduction programs.[81] Most importantly, the emphasis on maintenance provided by the behavior therapy was effective. At 1-year follow-up, patients had regained an average of only 2.1 kg of their original loss.

These results are particularly striking in comparison with those of Craighead et al[85] who combined behavior therapy with another treatment modality, pharmacotherapy. As shown in Figure 8-1, patients who received this combination for 6 months regained 10.9 kg of their original 15.3-kg loss by 1-year follow-up. Unlike pharmacotherapy, VLCD treatment did not seem to compromise the effectiveness of behavior therapy.

These very encouraging results led to the first controlled clinical trial of combined treatment by VLCD and behavior therapy.[41] Fifty-nine (50 women, 9 men) moderately obese patients received either the 6-month combined treatment, 6 months of behavior therapy, or 4 months of VLCD alone.

The diet alone condition was designed to simulate treatment as delivered in a physician's outpatient practice. Patients in this program consumed a 1,000- to 1,200-calorie diet during month 1, the VLCD during months 2 and 3, and a refeeding diet during month 4, the final month. Patients in the 6-month behavior therapy group were instructed in traditional behavioral methods of weight control while they consumed a balanced 1,000- to 1,200-calorie diet of their choosing.

Mean weight losses at the end of treatment for the diet alone, behavior therapy alone, and combined treatment groups were 14.1 kg, 14.3 kg, and 19.3 kg, respectively. Losses for the combined treatment group were significantly greater than those for the other two groups, which did not differ.

The results of a 1-year follow-up confirmed the observation that VLCD alone is an ineffective long-term treatment. These patients regained two thirds of their weight loss (9.5 kg of a 14.1-kg loss) in the year after treatment, for a net loss from pretreatment of only 4.6 kg. No patients remained within 2 kg of their end-of-treatment weight, while at the other extreme, three patients exceeded their pretreatment weight by 2 kg or more. These dismal results provide an ominous lesson for the millions of consumers of commercially available VLCDs. Not only do they risk serious health complications from unsupervised dieting, but they are likely to regain weight almost as rapidly as they lost it.

In contrast, the behavior therapy group, who had lost as much as the diet alone group, regained only one half as much (4.8 kg v 9.5 kg) in the year after treatment. As expected, the net loss was greatest for the combined treatment group. Patients in this group regained only one third of their weight loss, remaining 12.5 kg below their pretreatment weights at 1-year follow-up.

PSYCHOLOGIC SEQUELAE OF DIETING

Finally, a word should be said about the psychologic complications associated with dieting. In 1957, Stunkard[86] reported that, among his patients, weight reduction was frequently accompanied by untoward emotional symptoms. By 1974, seven studies[87] had examined affective responses to dieting, and all found a high incidence of adverse emotional reactions. Only a decade later, however, Wing and colleagues[88] noted that six of ten behavioral studies reported improvements in mood, and none found untoward emotional responses to caloric restriction.

The apparent disappearance of negative emotional reactions to dieting in the literature of recent years has puzzled investigators. The discrepancy between earlier and later studies has been attributed to a range of variables.[89] Some researchers have claimed that adverse reactions were minimized by the smaller weight losses and group behavioral treatment that have characterized more recent studies.

We recently conducted a content analysis of the 35 existing studies of psychologic changes during weight reduction. Surprisingly, the hypothesized relations between affective response and the magnitude of weight loss or the nature of treatment were found to be largely unsupported. It seems that the emotional outcome observed in studies of weight reduction depends chiefly on the method by which mood is assessed. Researchers who relied on standardized paper-and-pencil tests reported benign mood changes, while those who used open-ended interviews reported untoward changes. Because the method of mood assessment is usually confounded with various treatment variables, the exact relation between dieting and mood change remains a mystery.

SUMMARY

Dietary interventions have an important part in the treatment of mild and moderate obesity. For mildly obese people, the treatment of choice is a combination of behavior therapy and a balanced 1,000- to 1,200-calorie diet. Although such diets may be found among commercially available programs, many popular diets are unsafe and ineffective. Careful evaluation of prospective regimens is required to assure nutritional adequacy and weight-loss maintenance.

Moderately obese people are most effectively treated with a combination of behavior therapy and VLCD. These diets produce large weight losses, averaging 20 kg for 12 weeks of treatment. Current VLCDs consisting of high-quality protein may be considered safe when used for periods of 3 months or less by healthy patients under strict medical supervision. Behavioral training in weight-loss maintenance must accompany VLCD treatment to prevent rapid weight regain.

REFERENCES

1. *Health United States*, US Dept of Health, Education, and Welfare publication No. (PHS) 80-1232. Government Printing Office, 1979.

2. National Institutes of Health Consensus Development Conference: *Health Implications of Obesity. Ann Intern Med* 1985; 103.

3. Stunkard AJ: Current status of treatment of obesity in adults, in Stunkard AJ, Stellar E (eds): *Eating and Its Disorders.* New York, Raven Press, 1984, pp 157–173.

4. *Who's Dieting and Why.* New York, AC Nielsen Co, 1978.

5. Nicholas P, Dwyer J: Diets for weight reduction: Nutritional considerations, in Brownell KD, Foreyt JP (eds): *Handbook of Eating Disorders.* New York, Basic Books Inc Publishers, 1986, pp 122–144.

6. Mannergert K, Roth J: *Aerobic Nutrition.* New York, Berkley Books, 1981.

7. Ferguson S: *The Diet Center Program.* Boston, Little Brown & Co, 1983.

8. Baker SS, Schur S: *The Delicious Quick-Trim Diet.* New York, Villard Books, 1983.

9. Bland J: *Nutraerobics.* San Francisco, Harper & Row Publishers Inc, 1983.

10. Cott A: *Fasting: The Ultimate Diet.* New York, Bantam Books, 1981.

11. Abravanel ED, King EA: *Dr. Abravanel's Body Type Diet and Lifetime Nutrition Plan.* New York, Bantam Books, 1983.

12. Martin E: *The Over-30 All-Natural Health and Beauty Plan.* New York, Bantam Books, 1982.

13. Wood P: *California Diet and Exercise Program.* Mountain View, Calif, Anderson World Books, 1983.

14. Parr RB, Bachman DC, Bates Noble H: *The Diet that Lets You Cheat.* New York, Crown Publishers Inc, 1983.

15. Food and Nutrition Board: *Recommended Dietary Allowances*, ed 9. Washington, National Academy of Sciences, 1980.

16. Van Itallie TB, Yang M-U: Cardiac dysfunction in obese dieters: A potentially lethal complication of rapid, massive weight loss. *Am J Clin Nutr* 1984; 39:695–702.

17. American Heart Association: Diet and coronary heart disease. *Circulation* 1978; 58:762A–D.

18. AMA Council on Foods and Nutrition and the Food and Nutrition Board of the National Academy of Sciences-National Research Council. Diet and coronary heart disease: A council statement. *JAMA* 1972; 222(December):1647.

19. Fisher MC, Lachance PA: Nutrition evaluation of published weight-reducing diets. *J Am Diet Assoc* 1985; 85:450–454.

20. Sours HE, Frattali VP, Brand CD, et al: Sudden death associated with very low calorie weight reduction regimens. *Am J Clin Nutr* 1981; 34:453–461.

21. Mazel J: *The Beverly Hills Diet.* New York, Berkley Books, 1982.

22. Van Itallie TB, Yang M-U: Current concepts in nutrition: Diet and weight loss. *New Engl J Med* 1977; 279:1158–1161.

23. Van Itallie TB: Dietary approaches to the treatment of obesity, in Stunkard AJ (ed): *Obesity.* Philadelphia, WB Saunders Co, 1980, pp 249–261.

24. Bray GA: *The Obese Patient.* Philadelphia, WB Saunders Co, 1976.

25. Garrow JS: *Energy Balance and Obesity in Man.* Amsterdam, Elsevier/North Holland Biomedical Press Inc, 1978.

26. Thompson JK, Jarvie GJ, Lahey BB, et al: Exercise and obesity: Etiology, physiology, and intervention. *Psychological Bulletin* 1982; 91:55–79.

27. Brownell KD, Stunkard AJ: Physical activity in the development and control of obesity, in Stunkard AJ (ed): *Obesity.* Philadelphia, WB Saunders Co, 1980, pp 300–324.

28. Brownell KD: Obesity: Understanding and treating a serious, prevalent, and refractory disorder. *J Consult Clin Psychol* 1982; 50:820–840.

29. Wadden TA, Stunkard AJ, Brownell KD: Very low calorie diets: Their efficacy, safety and future. *Ann Intern Med* 1983; 99:675–684.

30. Cahill GF, Owen OE: Body fuels and starvation. *International Psychiatric Clinics* 1970; 7:25–40.

31. Weinsier RL: Fasting: A review with emphasis on electrolytes. *Am J Med* 1971; 50:233–239.

32. Bruch H: *Eating Disorders.* New York, Basic Books Inc Publishers, 1973.

33. Stunkard AJ: Minireview: Anorectic agents lower a body weight set point. *Life Sci* 1982; 30:2043–2055.

34. Hodgson P: Review of popular diets, in Storlie J, Jordan HA (eds): *Nutrition and Exercise in Obesity Management.* New York, Spectrum Publications Inc, 1984, pp 1–16.

35. Linn R, Stuart SL: *The Last Chance Diet.* Secaucus, NJ, Lyle Stuart Inc, 1976.

36. Food and Drug Administration: Liquid protein and sudden death: An update. FDA Drug Bull 1978; 8:18–19.

37. *Liquid Protein Diets*, US Public Health Service publication No. (EPI) 78-11-2. Atlanta, Centers for Disease Control, 1979.

38. Van Itallie TB: Liquid protein mayhem, editorial. *JAMA* 1977; 240:140–145.

39. Frank A, Graham C, Frank S: Fatalities on the liquid-protein diet: An analysis of possible causes. *Int J Obes* 1981; 5:243–248.

40. Blackburn GL, Lynch ME, Wong SL: The very-low-calorie diet: A weight reduction technique, in Brownell KD, Foreyt JP (eds): *Handbook of Eating Disorders.* New York, Basic Books Inc Publishers, 1986, pp 198–212.

41. Wadden TA, Stunkard AJ: A controlled trial of very-low-calorie diet, behavior therapy, and their combination in the treatment of obesity. *J Consult Clin Psychol* 1986; 54:482–488.

42. Brownell KD, Rubin DJ, Smoller JW: Exercise and the regulation of body weight, in Shangold MM, Mirkin G (eds): *Women and Exercise.* Philadelphia, FA Davis, to be published.

43. Stern JS, Lowney P: Obesity: The role of physical activity, in Brownell KD, Foreyt JP (eds): *Handbook of Eating Disorders: Physiology, Psychology, and Treatment of Obesity, Anorexia, and Bulimia.* New York, Basic Books Inc Publishers, 1986, pp 145–158.

44. Martin JE, Dubbert PM: Exercise applications and promotion in behavioral medicine: Current status and future directions. *J Consult Clin Psychol* 1982; 50:1004–1017.

45. Gwinup G: Effect of exercise alone on the weight of obese women. *Arch Intern Med* 1975; 135:676–680.

46. Brownell KD: Behavioral, psychological, and environmental predictors of obesity and success at weight reduction. *Int J Obes* 1984; 8:543–550.

47. Dahlkoetter J, Callahan EJ, Linton J: Obesity and the unbalanced energy equation: Exercise vs eating habit change. *J Clin Psychol* 1979; 47:898–905.

48. Strang JM, McClugage HB, Evans FA: Further studies in the dietary correction of obesity. *Am J Med Sci* 1930; 179:687–694.

49. Strang JM, McClugage HB, Evans FA: The nitrogen balance during dietary correction of obesity. *Am J Med Sci* 1931; 181:336–349.

50. Bloom WL: Fasting as an introduction to the treatment of obesity. *Metabolism* 1959; 8:214–220.

51. Spencer IOB: Death during therapeutic starvation for obesity. *Lancet* 1968; 1:1288–1290.

52. Runcie J, Thomson TJ: Prolonged starvation: Dangerous procedure? *Br Med J* 1970; 3:432–435.

53. Garnett ES, Bernard DL, Ford J, et al: Gross fragmentation of starvation for obesity. *Lancet* 1969; 1:914–916.

54. Cubberley PT, Polster SA, Schulman CL: Lactic acidosis and death after treatment of obesity by fasting. *New Engl J Med* 1965; 272:628–630.

55. Swanson DW, Dinello FA: Severe obsity as a habituation syndrome: Evidence during a starvation study. *Arch Gen Psychiatry* 1970; 22:120–127.

56. Munro HN, Crim MC: The proteins and amino acids, in Goodhart RS, Shils ME (eds): *Modern Nutrition in Health and Disease*. Philadelphia, Lea & Febiger, 1980, pp 51–98.

57. Garnett ES, Barnard DL, Ford J, Goodbody RA, Woodehouse MA: Gross fragmentation of cardiac myofibrils after therapeutic starvation for obesity. *Lancet* 1969; 1:914–916.

58. Isner JM, Sours HE, Paris AL, Ferrans VJ, Roberts WC: Sudden unexpected death in avid dieters using the liquid protein modified fast diet. *Circulation* 1979; 60:1401–1412.

59. Keys A, Brozek J, Henschel A, Mickelson O, Taylor HL: *The Biology of Human Starvation*. Minneapolis, University of Minnesota Press, 1950.

60. Apfelbaum M: Effects of very restrictive high-protein diets with special reference to the nitrogen balance. *Int J Obes* 1981; 5:209–214.

61. McLean Baird I, Parson RL, Howard AN: Clinical and metabolic studies of chemically defined diets in the study of obesity. *Metabolism* 1974; 23:645–657.

62. Yang MU, Barbosa-Salvidar JL, Pi-Sunyer FX, et al: Metabolic effects of substituting carbohydrate for protein in a low-calorie diet: A prolonged study in obese outpatients. *Int J Obes* 1981; 5:231–236.

63. Blackburn GL, Bistrian BR, Flatt JP: Role of a protein-sparing modified fast in a comprehensive weight reduction program, in Howard AN (ed): *Recent Advances in Obesity Research*. London, Newman Publishing Ltd, 1975, pp 279–281.

64. Bistrian BR: Clinical use of a protein-sparing modified fast. *JAMA* 1978; 240:2999–2302.

65. Blackburn GL, Flatt JP, Clowes GH Jr, et al: Peripheral intravenous feeding with isotonic amino acid solution. *Am J Surg* 1973; 125:447–455.

66. Howard AN: The historical development, efficacy and safety of very-low-calorie diets. *Int J Obes* 1981; 5:195–208.

67. Wadden TA, Stunkard AJ, Brownell KD, et al: A comparison of two very-low-calorie diets: Protein-sparing modified fast versus protein-formula-liquid diet. *Am J Clin Nutr* 1985; 41:533–539.

68. Howard AN, Grant A, Edawards O, et al: The treatment of obesity with a very-low-calorie liquid-formula diet: An inpatient/outpatient comparison using skimmed milk as the chief protein source. *Int J Obes* 1978; 2:321–332.

69. Flatt JP, Blackburn GL: The metabolic fuel regulatory system: Implications for protein-sparing therapies during caloric deprivation and disease. *Am J Clin Nutr* 1974; 27:175–187.

70. Sapir DG, Chambers NE, Ryan JW: The role of potassium in the control of ammonium excretion during starvation. *Metabolism* 1976; 25:211–220.

71. Metropolitan Life Insurance Company. (1983 January–June). Metropolitan Height and Weight Tables. *Statistical Bulletin of the Metropolitan Life Insurance Company* 1983; 64:2.

72. Stunkard AJ, Stinnett JL, Smoller JW: Psychological and social aspects of the surgical treatment of obesity. *Am J Psychiatry* 1986; 143:417–429.

73. Bistrian BR, Hoffer LJ: Obesity, in Conn H (ed): *Current Therapy*. Philadelphia, WB Saunders Co, 1982, pp 444–447.

74. Lindner PG, Blackburn GL: Multidisciplinary approach to obesity utilizing fasting modified by protein-sparing therapy. *Obesity & Bariatric Medicine* 1976; 5:198–216.

75. Murray DC: Treatment of overweight: I. Relationship between initial weight and weight change during behavior therapy of overweight individuals: Analysis of data from previous studies. *Psychological Reports* 1975; 37:243–248.

76. Vertes V, Genuth SM, Hazelton IM: Supplemented fasting as a large scale outpatient program. *JAMA* 1977; 238:2151–2153.

77. Genuth SM, Castro JH, Vertes V: Weight reduction in obesity by outpatient semistarvation. *JAMA* 1974; 230:987–991.

78. McLean Baird I, Howard AN: A double-blind trial of mazindol using a very-low-calorie formula diet. *Int J Obes* 1977; 1:271–278.

79. Atkinson RL, Kaiser DL: Nonphysician supervision of a very-low-calorie diet: Results in over 200 cases. *Int J Obes* 1981; 5:237–241.

80. Tuck ML, Sowers J, Dornfeld L, et al: The effect of weight reduction on blood pressure, plasma renin activity, and plasma aldosterone levels in obese patients. *New Engl J Med* 1981; 304:930–933.

81. Asher WL, Dietz RE: Effectiveness of weight reduction involving 'diet pills.' *Current Therapy and Research* 1972; 14:510–524.

82. Wadden TA, Stunkard AJ, Brownell KD, et al: Treatment of obesity by behavior therapy and very-low-calorie diet: A pilot investigation. *J Consult Clin Psychol* 1984; 52:692–694.

83. Stunkard AJ, Berthold HC: What is behavior therapy? *Am J Clin Nutr* 1985; 41:821–823.

84. Mahoney MJ, Mahoney K: *Permanent Weight Control: A Total Solution to the Dieter's Dilemma*. New York, WW Norton & Co Inc, 1976.

85. Craighead LW, Stunkard AJ, O'Brien R: Behavior therapy and pharmacotherapy for obesity. *Arch Gen Psychiatry* 1981; 38:763–768.

86. Stunkard AJ: The dieting depression: Untoward responses to weight reduction. *Am J Med* 1957; 23:77–86.

87. Stunkard AJ, Rush J: Dieting and depression reexamined: Critical review of reports of untoward responses during weight reduction for obesity. *Ann Intern Med* 1984; 81:526–533.

88. Wing RR, Epstein LH, Marcus MD, et al: Mood changes in behavioral weight loss programs. *J Psychosom Res* 1984; 28:189–196.

89. Wadden TA, Stunkard AJ, Smoller JW: Dieting and depression: A methodological study. *J Consult Clin Psychol*, 1986; 54:869–871.

Chapter 9

Eating Management: A Tool for the Practitioner

Sharon Dalton

FOOD IS THE FOCUS IN EATING MANAGEMENT

The main argument of this chapter is that clients and practitioners benefit from an expanded food perspective rather than from a narrowly defined view of diet and a rigid pursuit of dieting in weight management.

First, a case is made for a planned and positive role for food as a tool in learning lifelong eating management skills. This is supported by evidence that "taste," broadly defined, is a primary reason for food choice. Long-term food management requires a working, practical knowledge of food characteristics, nutrient values, and factors that modify nutrient values, as well as marketing, preparing, and eating skills.

Second, a discussion of the problems with many diets suggests that "career" or chronic dieting among normal-weight and overweight people is itself a strong barrier to effective long-term weight management. Evidence is discussed that dieting leads to binge eating, and that constant dieting itself is a problem requiring intervention.

A third section suggests strategies for the nutrition practitioner to use in teaching eating management. Many strategies are based on behavior therapy principles and are planned to include food choices rather than to provide menus. Nutritionists are particularly equipped to use these strategies. They are distinguished from other weight-management professionals by two characteristics: (1) a working knowledge of the nutrient composition of food, and (2) a knowledge of food planning and preparation techniques that promote food acceptability, based on both nutrition and sensory qualities.

The final section addresses the practitioner's personal and professional responsibility in reducing the pressure to change the size, shape, and composition of our bodies through constant food manipulation. This includes attitudes toward food, dieting behaviors, and body size.

PERCEIVED TASTE IS BASIC IN FOOD SELECTION AND EATING MANAGEMENT

The central role of food in weight management is not supported by some professional approaches; popular diets often fail to reflect its long-term importance. Many diet programs are based on modified fasts and products containing an array of required nutrients. In skilled hands, these approaches have specific value, but do not emphasize food in learning and relearning behaviors. Very-low-calorie (VLC) product programs incorporate behavior management techniques at the food "reintroduction" stage, after a supervised period of VLC products exclusively. Some programs provide prepackaged food products as an essential part of their approach to limit choices. Diets in popular literature tend to de-emphasize the role of food by having a repetitive menu or by restricting food choices. Academic approaches, stressing only "nutrition education," illustrate the universal problem in changing health habits: the gap between knowledge and practice, or intentions and practice. Group programs, emphasizing only behavior modification, are also problematic in long-term effectiveness.

Nutrition, officially defined, is "the process by which food is selected and becomes part of the human body."[1] Nutrition, then, is the knowledge and behavior of food selection as much as it is the absorption and utilization (or storage) of nutrients. Flexible guidelines, based on a variety of choices, usually from food groups, with suggestions on how to adapt menus to cultural taste preferences and life style are important in weight management.

There is evidence that practical food guidance is valuable. A weight-control program for bank employees determined the most notable difference between successful and unsuccessful participants to be food practices that reduced calories but maintained palatability. These included substituting baking and broiling for frying, and eating smaller portions of highly acceptable food.[2]

Other studies[3,4] indicate that a variety of soup included in eating plans is highly correlated with weight loss and maintenance. Many strategies are suggested by weight-loss studies of high-fiber bread in diets,[5] or of a variety of fresh fruits, vegetables, and whole grains.[6] These foods were found to be acceptable and promoted satiety at low-energy intake levels. The evidence is that guided selection from the myriad of complex carbohydrate foods may promote effective weight management.

Why do we eat what we eat? The study of eating patterns is a complex undertaking. Models exist from economics, psychology, and consumer behavior. However, there is ample evidence that a major reason for food choice lies in its sensory properties.[7-9]

The sensory aspect of foods, coupled with internal signals, seems to condition appetite or satiety, and so determines what and how much is eaten. It is now clear that human eating habits are both cognitively and physiologically controlled. A perception and an awareness of the sensory and hedonic aspects of different foods are involved.[10] Rozin and Fallon[7] argue that these feelings or responses are acquired and form the major reason for food preference and acceptance. Foods that are liked or disliked are those deemed acceptable by the prevailing culture. They suggest that the second reason for food acceptance is "anticipated consequences," which could be pleasant or unpleasant feelings (satiation or nausea) or a delayed effect, which involves culturally transmitted knowledge about food ("it's good for me").

The important roles of both sensory appeal and health value are supported in a study by Dalton[9] comparing reasons for intended and actual food choices. "Sensory appeal" of food was the major food-choice determinant of both *actual* and *intended* food selections; "health value," "expediency," and "influence of others" followed. "Health value" was rated significantly lower in the actual selection, and also by those making different actual, compared with intended, food selections.

From cognitive and physiologic evidence, individual expectations of palatability are a leading factor in decisions to eat and what to eat.[11] Whether palatability responses distinguish overweight or obese from normal-weight people is unclear. Some studies indicate that overweight people tend to choose more good-tasting foods[12] and crave more dessert foods[13] than lean people. But other research shows that *both* lean and obese people respond to these situations. For example, the placement of highly palatable food in the front of cafeteria serving counters appealed to lean and obese people equally.[14] Misleading cognitive cues or false feedback regarding, for example, hunger and caloric density seem to exert a dominant influence on eating behavior, perhaps outweighing purely physiologic factors. Thus, related to our less than optimal understanding of whether weight variation affects food choice is the question: Do overweight people have more real or perceived hunger (or satiety)?[15] Nonetheless, whether food is consumed as a measure of taste responsiveness or "misresponsiveness," or whether eating is physically or cognitively controlled, food remains central to the process of eating management. The immediate sources of sensory conditioning of food preferences are at the table, in the kitchen, in the cafeteria, and among family and peers.

Although a basic premise of behavior modification is that food-related patterns are learned and can be relearned,[16] the success of behavior-change techniques in promoting weight loss and maintenance continues to be debated.[17] Hall et al[18] found the emphasis on correct food selection to be more responsible for weight loss than suggested behavior changes. Brownell and Wadden[19] strongly recommended that a behavior therapy program include nutrition education based on sensible eating. They did not include a specific diet but a flexible framework of food groups and caloric levels.

Suggested guidelines for a relearning approach, with a strong food focus, based on behavioral principles are:

- Identify and reinforce positive skills of acquiring, preparing, and eating a variety of acceptable, nourishing foods.
- Introduce carefully selected modified tastes requiring acquisition and preparation of new food skills.
- Reduce, but not necessarily extinguish, food practices involving so-called junk or guilt foods.

The important point is that past, present, and future perceived taste of food forms the basis of eating. Eating management ideally combines cognitive and behavioral learning principles, always with a focus on food.

EATING MANAGEMENT IS FOR MIND AND BODY

The premise of this section is that eating management creates a positive, flexible framework for dealing with food for life, and for health. Dieting is negative, restrictive, and temporary. Yet dieting is widespread and at least partially responsible for the compromised nutrient profile, the "restrained eater," the "creeping body fat-to-lean ratio" syndrome, and the "doomed to diet" metabolism.

Dieting Is Widespread

In the 1985 *National Health Interview Survey*, 46% of the women and 27% of the men surveyed were trying to lose weight, mainly by consuming fewer calories.[20] In a large, 1983 cross-sectional study[21] representative of the nonaged US population, 22% of the men and women were judged to be overweight by objective standards. However, 41% perceived themselves to be overweight (59% women and 29% men); more than one half of the 41%, mostly women, were dieting.[21]

The incidence of dieting is higher in specific groups. Grunewald[22] studied young college women, 18 to 24 years old. Of those studied, 18.1% had spent more than one half of the previous school year dieting (chronic dieters), 45.2% had dieted 50% of the time or less (periodic dieters), and 36.7% had not dieted. Among another sample of college women, 48% reported using a weight-loss program one or more times since college admission.[23]

In yet another study,[24] the majority of women with anorexic-like behaviors (31 of 77) and many of the problem-free ones reported that they were "always dieting," the mean ages at the first diet being 13.8 years and 15.1 years, respectively. Frequent dieting among adolescent girls begins as early as 10 years of age, with the reported incidence of periodic dieting ranging from 30% to 60%.[25,26]

Compared with the professional literature, market research surveys from industry suggest that dieting is even more common: 60% of all women diet, 25% continually and 35% sporadically, "as the need develops."[27] In fact, one "trend" report (*Newsweek*, April 14, 1985, p 5) noted a 2% drop among women (40% to 38%) and a 3% drop among men (30% to 27%) on a diet during any 2-week period between 1984 and 1985 "because dieting is now considered a normal way of life."

Determining the role and the consequences of widespread dieting is important in eating management.

Dieting and Compromised Nutrient Profiles

Recommended therapeutic dieting guidelines state that a diet must satisfy all nutrient needs except energy.[28,29] To be realistic, as well as fair, practitioners ought to compare the nutrient intakes of the mainly nondieting population, particularly women, with the nutrient evaluation of published weight-reducing diets.

The *Nationwide Food Consumption Survey 1977–78* findings[30] compared with the 1980 Recommended Dietary Allowances (RDA) indicated low intakes of calcium, iron, magnesium, and vitamin B_6 in the average 1,600-calorie daily food intake of women 19 to 34 years old. The 1985 *Continuing Survey of Food Intakes of Individuals*[31(pp 38–39)] indicated the same "problem" nutrients in the average 1,700-calorie intake of the same segment of women. Also low in 1985 were zinc and folacin, not studied earlier (Table 9-1).

The percentages of women represented in these data who reported being on a diet in 1977 were 11.5% and 15.8% in the 19 to 22 and 23 to 34 years age categories, respectively.[32] In 1985, 9.2% of women aged 19 to 34 years reported they were on low-calorie-weight-loss or low-fat diets.[31(p 57)] The nutrient intake of the dieters was not reported separately. However, nutrient intake per 1,000 calories, per individual, indicated the same problem nutrients as in diets of 1,200 to 1,500 calories.[31(p 46)]

Confirmation of low levels (less than 80% of the RDA, or below the low end of the estimated safe and adequate daily range) of calcium, magnesium, iron, zinc, copper, and manganese in food content and total diet was provided in the Food and Drug Administration's *Total Diet Study, 1982–1984*. Those most at risk for low intakes were young children, teenage girls, adult women, and older women.[33]

Table 9-1 Food Energy in Total Diet and Nutrient Intakes as Percentage of 1980 Recommended Dietary Allowances: Mean Per Individual in a Day, Spring 1977 and Spring 1985

Women: All Incomes by Age (Years)	Food Energy in Total Diet		Food Energy		Protein		Vitamin A		Ascorbic Acid		Thiamin		Riboflavin		Niacin	
	1977	1985	1977	1985	1977	1985	1977	1985	1977	1985	1977	1985	1977	1985	1977	1985
19–34	1,617	1,707	79	83	145	144	103	128	125	137	97	112	108	117	116	130
35–50	1,514	1,602	76	80	144	144	106	126	131	128	101	108	106	111	124	128

Women: All Incomes by Age (Years)	Vitamin B6		Vitamin B12		Calcium		Phosphorus		Magnesium		Iron		Vitamin E	Folacin	Zinc
	1977	1985	1977	1985	1977	1985	1977	1985	1977	1985	1977	1985	1985	1985	1985
19–34	60	63	118	158	74	81	121	128	69	72	54	63	98	52	60
35–50	59	59	126	154	64	75	115	123	74	72	59	60	96	49	59

Source: Nationwide Food Consumption Survey: Continuing Survey of Food Intakes by Individuals, USDA, Human Nutrition Information Service, Nutrition Monitoring Division, CSFII Report No 85-1, 1985; Nutrient Intakes: Individuals in 48 States: Year 1977–78, USDA, Human Nutrition Information Service, Consumer Nutrition Division, Report No 1-2.

A nutrient evaluation of 15 published weight-reducing diets found the nutrients most often below recommended levels to include thiamin, vitamin B_6, calcium, iron, zinc, and magnesium.[34] Except for thiamin, these are the same problem nutrients as those for most nondieting women.

Do compromised profiles mean that most women, including and especially dieters, have a compromised health status? Not necessarily. Dietary surveys only suggest groups at risk for poor nutritional status. When dietary and health status data (eg, the *National Health and Nutrition Examination Survey II*) coincide, a diet-related problem may exist. However, in the case of iron, a common problem nutrient for which sufficient data are available to assess both nutritional status and dietary intake, the overall prevalence of impaired iron status is low.[35] This is in spite of the substantial proportion of the US population, especially women, whose diets do not contain the full RDA for iron. The mean iron intake for women was 61% of the RDA in 1985 (Table 9-1).

Because the nutrient requirements for most people are less than the RDA, low intakes may not, in fact, indicate malnutrition. Low intakes, however, may indicate less than optimal nutritional health. Since it is difficult to assure nutritional adequacy of diets that are low in energy (less than 1,800 to 2,000 calories), dieters fall in the group with a reduced chance of optimal health.

Changes in food intake between 1977 and 1985 include a 60% increase in low-fat or skim milk use, which suggests a greater calcium intake. Yet, in 1985, only 24% of women were using these products. This is in comparison with the 54% using carbonated soft drinks, representing a 53% increase since 1977. One encouraging trend is that all women and children (1 to 5 years old) have dropped their fat intake 4% since 1977. Carbohydrate intake has increased approximately the same percentage. This is accounted for partially by increased grain product use alone, such as pasta and pizza, and in mixtures, such as stews, Mexican foods, and vegetables with rice.[31(pp 4–5)]

Two major points emerge from analysis of these data:

1. Regular food intake, especially that of women, does not satisfy all nutrient needs. This suggests the need for a realistic perspective in planning eating-management programs.
2. Food choices can and do change, probably in response to current information about potential health problems related to specific nutrients, eg, high-fat or low-calcium diets.

Eating management is charged with not only planning a program to promote weight loss and maintenance but promoting the use of foods containing the problem nutrients as well. This is a tall order. It requires goal setting based on progressive change measurements rather than on rigid criteria requiring 100% of nutrients or specific amounts of weight loss.

Progress should be measured in terms of:

- reduced chronic dieting and use of dangerous diets
- increased positive food selections, even when they fall short of a totally adequate diet
- improved concepts of dieting, eg, arresting weight gain is itself positive; arresting weight loss and regain is progress
- relearned, controlled use of guilt, "not allowed," and junk foods
- increased variety of nutrient-dense, calorie-controlled foods, eg, success is managing, not avoiding, favorite foods.

Dieting is Restrictive

Revising concepts of dieting is central in eating management. "Going on a diet" implies "going off" it. Dieting promotes self-defeating thoughts and behavior, which contribute to making dieting self-perpetuating. Berman[36] reports five frequently reported practices among dieters that call for revised concepts of dieting:

1. reward themselves for weight loss with a treat "off" diet
2. reward themselves for weight loss with a binge
3. "go off" diet if told they look terrific
4. "go off" diet if "undeserved" weight loss occurs
5. "go off" diet if "deserved" weight loss occurs.

The restricted nature of dieting tends to make habitual dieters into restrained eaters. Restrained eaters consciously restrict the amount, variety, and frequency of palatable foods consumed. They seem vulnerable to excessive eating when dietary restraint is interrupted by emotions or "preloads" of food. Herman and Polivy[37] showed that dieting changes the ability of both normal-weight and overweight people to respond appropriately in food situations, perhaps by affecting long-term weight-regulatory mechanisms. They argue that an overeating event for a restrained eater on a restricted calorie regimen triggers a "motivational collapse." There seems to be evidence, too, that restrained eaters salivate more when anticipating highly attractive food,[38] and that anticipation, or simply the presence, of appetizing food is sufficient to precipitate a breakdown of restraint.[39]

Particularly if they are identified as dieters, restrained eaters seem to be affected by the behavior of others. In the presence of unrestrained people eating normal amounts, restrained eaters exhibit "sensible" eating patterns; when left alone after such a "trigger event," they tend to revert to a binge, "counter-regulatory," pattern. Both restrained and unrestrained eaters are capable of sensible and aberrant eating behavior; they appear to differ only in the relative predominance of these patterns.[40] Related to restraint and dieting, but perhaps more common in obese than in normal-weight people, is sensitivity to disinhibition factors. A 51-item Three Factor Eating Questionnaire is currently used to study various aspects of restraint.[41] Dieting seems to be related especially to cognitive restraint.[41]

In response to the restraint problems caused by dieting, particularly sharpened by constant opportunities to preload in today's food environment, Brownell[42] suggested the use of behavioral techniques to minimize exposure to palatable foods. This, he says, is supported by the notion of "sensory specific satiety" in which repeated consumption of specific foods seems to enhance satiety for those foods.[43] However, one could argue that continual food deprivation by deliberate attempts to restrain eating makes food more reinforcing, as was shown by the classic studies of semistarvation.[44] The arbitrary labeling of food as "good" or "bad," or as guilt food, by dieters may also serve as a negative reinforcer. Identifying these evaluations is a priority in eating management. The notion of junk food is also common. Apparently, there is little difference in value assessments of food between obese and normal-weight people. Through multidimensional scaling of food perceptions, Drewnowski[45] found strong support for the popular attitude that "anything high-calorie cannot be good for you" in both groups.

These generalizations may have developed because food guides have traditionally not included high-calorie, low-nutrient-dense foods in a specific, guided category. Also, the nutrition community itself has not agreed on a definition for a "nutritious" food against which to judge foods according to their degree of usefulness.[46,47] There has been limited public nutrition education promoting the idea that food choices fall on a continuum of healthful characteristics, and that a given choice usually requires assessment based on an "advantage-disadvantage" ratio. The concept to teach is that junk foods are much less of a concern than junk diets. This means that a single food of low nutrient density is not necessarily junk, but many such foods taken together comprise a junk diet. Learning the nutrient characteristics of food in terms of, for example, fat is not for the purpose of avoiding all "empty calorie" or "fattening" foods but for selecting a variety of foods in controlled combinations.

The idea of a variety of foods is an issue in eating management. Variety is usually restricted in dieting to reduce total food eaten. And there is evidence to support this. Rolls'[48] work on "sensory specific satiety" indicates that exposure to a variety of palatable food is a problem. "As a food is eaten, its taste and appearance decrease in pleasantness, but the taste and appearance of other foods remain relatively unchanged."[48] As a result, "more is eaten during a meal consisting of a variety of foods than during a meal with just one of the foods, even if that food is the favorite."[48]

Defining *variety* as the number of unique food items and using National Food Consumption Study (NFCS) data, Smiciklas-Wright et al[49] found calories consumed increased with variety. For example, women who reported 1 to 15 items had a mean caloric intake of 858; those reporting 41 or more foods consumed 2,199 calories.

Following sound nutritional guidelines, nutritionists have traditionally promoted a variety of food choices to increase the likelihood of selecting an adequate diet. This presents several problems in addition to increased consumption. Since the average supermarket may contain 15,000 items, "variety" means an immense choice and confusion, particularly when coupled with the professional community's various interpretations of "variety." Is it foods from each major food group? Is it variety of preparation methods?[49] Defining "variety" and developing practical skills in selecting and preparing varied foods are crucial in successfully managing the constantly increasing array of palatable foods in our environment.

Sound nutrition and weight-control principles generally suggest a healthy eating pattern of three meals a day and planned snacks. Recommended guidelines specify that dietary manipulations, such as eating frequency, that claim to facilitate adherence or a higher metabolic rate, or to minimize hunger, must be supported by a rational hypothesis or scientific evidence.[28] One reason for recommending multiple meals and snacks in eating management is that the general US population is eating more often. In 1985, women and children averaged four, rather than three, meals a day, and obtained as much as 19% of their food energy from snacks, compared with 15% in 1977.[31(pp 7–8)]

Nibbling, currently called "grazing" in some US cities, has been studied in rats[50] and humans.[51–53] Data from both show that nibblers tend to have less body fat, are lighter in weight, and consume more total calories than counterparts who eat less frequently, weigh more, and consume less. This is evidence that eating infrequent, large meals favors lipogenesis; eating frequent, small meals does not. Infrequent meals may force intestinal adaptation requiring more food for satiety; between-meal hunger may also increase.[54] Supported by behavioral food skills that separate mindless, or automatic, eating from managed eating, eating more frequently is an important part of long-term eating management. It is a positive, rather than restrictive, guideline.

The evidence supports three practical approaches to counter negative dietary concepts and to solve the dilemma of planning a variety of palatable, nutritionally adequate foods that do not provide excessive calories:

1. Re-evaluate junk foods based on their contribution to the total daily diet.
2. Use favorite foods often, but in combination with a variety of less-liked, low-calorie foods.
3. Eat more frequently but more sensibly.

Dieting Is Fattening

Two related physical consequences of dieting argue against chronic dieting practices: decreased basal metabolic rate and increased cumulative body fat. In both obese and lean subjects, Garrow[55] reported that metabolic rate fell more rapidly with each dieting episode and that return to beginning levels took longer each time. Several researchers[56,57] have shown the adaptive change in energy expenditure that prevents further weight reduction.

Perhaps the most compelling argument against rapid weight loss followed by weight gain is the cumulative change in body composition.[58] The "yo-yo syndrome" strategy discussed in the next section provides a clear explanation, using a hypothetical model, of how dieting is fattening. Experts continue to discuss whether moderate degrees of being overweight in humans may be beneficial to health and, indeed, to survival.[59,60] There is no argument, however, in favor of body-weight fluctuations. The evidence suggests these guidelines: (1) prevent weight gain ("maintenance is progress"), and (2) arrest cyclical loss and regain.

Dieting Is Disappointing

The desire to achieve a more "ideal" body is a major reason for dieting. Body shape, or somatotype, and frame size are inherited characteristics. Endomorphs are likely to be heavier and to have a higher body mass index than ectomorphs. Dieting may reduce regional fat as part of overall fat loss, which may reduce health risk (as discussed in Chapter 1). But dieting does not change basic body shape from the android ("apple") to the gynoid ("pear") shape.[61] This is illustrated in Figure 9-1. The constant media connection between success and body size and shape is supported by the commercial interest in relating food products to body size. This is stiff competition for the practitioner, who, Hirsch[62(p 9)] suggests, ought to "remove guilt and dietary illusions" as a "refreshing and honest way to aid the obese." This is not easy. As practitioners, we need to seek ways to make honesty and reality not only refreshing but acceptable to the obese, the overweight, those of normal weight, and to chronic dieters.

THE PRACTITIONER IS A FOOD STRATEGIST

Guidelines for nutrition counseling in weight management are presented in Chapter 10 and in a related book by Snetselaar.[63] The strategies suggested here address the eating-management issues of focusing on food and revising dieting concepts discussed earlier in this chapter. They should be used by the practitioner together with a strong working knowledge of the appropriate counseling se-

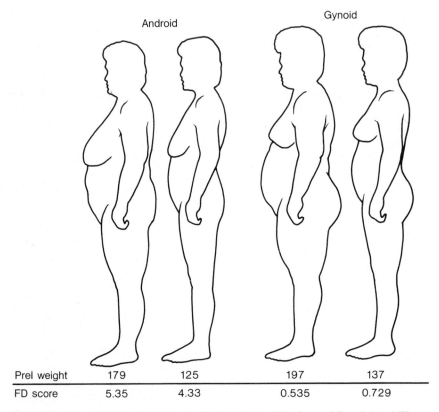

Prel weight	179	125	197	137
FD score	5.35	4.33	0.535	0.729

Figure 9-1 Effect of Weight Reduction on Fat Distribution (FD) Score of Two Selected Women
Source: Reprinted with permission from *International Journal of Obesity* (1978; 2:299), Copyright
© 1978, John Libbey & Company Ltd, London.

quence, of counselor and client roles, and of alternative diet-change behavior therapies.[64] These strategies rely on practice to provide positive reinforcing consequences, which, in turn, help maintain desirable thoughts and behaviors. Common elements of behavioral weight control form the foundation of these eating-management suggestions.

A strategy is more than just a specific activity or tactic. It is a comprehensive, planned approach, carefully chosen to change a selected behavior to one considered more desirable, based on current scientific information. A strategy should be simple, practical, and carefully supervised, either directly or through structured follow-up. The framework is flexible; whether the nutrition practitioner works with groups or individuals,[65] in a team with a behavior therapist, for periods longer than the suggested minimum of 4 months, or in weekly or biweekly meetings does not seem to affect overall effectiveness.[28] Food strategies may be more efficient and effective in groups for tasting and choosing combined with individual meetings to discuss special needs, review food records, and provide personal progress reinforcement.

These strategies are useful mainly with overweight and mildly obese persons (classified as 20% to 40% overweight), who comprise approximately 90% of the overweight population, and chronic dieters seeking to lose 10 to 15 lb. Stunkard[66] suggests more aggressive medical approaches for the remaining 10% of moderately and severely obese people.

Gathering and evaluating information on food and nutrition and then planning strategies are joint client and practitioner ventures. Some strategies are useful in the assessment and screening stage; others provide opportunities for practice and reinforcement. These should be considered and employed by the practitioner and client together, by the client alone, or in groups. Follow-up by the practitioner is important. The focus on food stresses its relationship as a means to the goal. Traditional dietary management focuses on a prescription from the counselor rather than individual goal setting. The benefits of client participation and self-direction in determining goals have been recognized by several researchers.[67] A comparison of prescription vs. goal setting in teaching two groups the US Dietary Goals and Guidelines did not indicate one method to be more effective than the other.[68] Yet there is evidence that learning to set and to implement goals is a skill-oriented task that requires practice to be effective.[69,70]

Practitioner goals are also important. Developing a daily food plan that is adequate in all nutrients may be as unrealistic as expecting all students in a class to earn an "A" every time. A realistic approach is based on positive changes. A "C" is progress for the student who earned a "D" yesterday. There are many reasons for differences in measurements of progress. For example, changes in body weight in response to food intake depend on several factors, including dieting methods and physiologic mechanisms such as thermic effects on feeding responses.[71,72] Success lies in the journey, not the destination.

Each strategy includes suggested objectives, activities for the client and the practitioner, progress measurement techniques, and supporting evidence and materials. They may be used in the order suggested or selectively, as needed. Strategies 1 and 2 are assessment strategies that provide foundation information.

Strategy 1: Mapping and Rating Eating History

Objectives:

- to identify food and eating patterns;
- to evaluate food patterns in meaningful ways using practical standards.

The client collects:

- all shopping receipts and restaurant checks,
- selected product labels,
- two special-event or weekend menus, and
- at least six daily food diaries over a 2- to 3-week period.

The practitioner develops:

- two 24-hour representative food profiles, using food models,
- a joint cafeteria visit, and
- the data provided by the client.

The client and the practitioner:

- determine the distribution of carbohydrate, protein, and fat using the Daily Calorie Distribution Worksheet or the Rate Your Plate Guide (Appendices 9-A and 9-B);
- identify at least three positive food choices and behaviors;
- identify one or two (maximum) food changes indicated by an analysis of energy nutrients; this change(s) may be in amount, frequency, or preparation method;
- agree on a specific progress measurement such as "selecting and using a reduced fat preparation method or reduced fat product 3 times a week"; this is preferable to a goal of "reducing fat from 43% to 40%" because it specifies the skill to be learned.

Snetselaar[63(p 88)] states that giving clients information on past positive performance can be reinforcing. Activities involving daily patterns such as differences between typical and traditional serving sizes benefit both the practitioner and the client.[73]

Strategy 2: Increasing Positive Food Selections

Objectives:

- to identify the relative importance of food choices;
- to determine the nutritional value of relative food choices;
- to increase positive food selections within the framework of preferred foods.

The client:

- categorizes each food in the food profile according to "favorite foods," "liked foods," or "so-so foods";
- categorizes "favorite foods" according to "anytime," "in moderation," or "now and then;" this categorization is based on the New American Eating Guide (Appendix 9-C);
- categorizes "liked foods" and then "so-so foods" according to "anytime," "in moderation," or "now and then."

The practitioner provides the criteria for placing each food in the suggested category based on nutrient content.

The client and the practitioner:

- determine the overall contribution of each food category (favorite, liked, so-so) to the calorie and nutrient profile;
- analyze adjustments in frequency, amount, or preparation methods to improve the nutrient profile using favorite foods.

Several food rating systems based on relative nutrient density (nutrient-to-calorie ratio) are available. The New American Eating Guide is one (Appendix 9-C). Tseng et al[74] propose a similar system, which is flexible enough to classify a food as nutritious if it contributes either large amounts of one or two nutrients, or small amounts of several nutrients. Both systems take into consideration certain "excessive" factors in foods. Guthrie[46] suggests that nutrient-oriented learning using food labels must complement but not replace food-oriented instruction and guidance. Visual materials illustrating the effect of fat and sugar dilution on the nutrient density of one food type such as milk products are useful (Appendix 9-D)[47]

Strategy 3: Mapping and Rating Dieting History

Objectives:

- to examine dieting patterns and behaviors;
- to rate dieting in terms of potential body changes and nutritional aspects.

The client:

- constructs a 1-year history of dieting according to diet type, duration, and weight change (Figure 9-2); (Snetselaar[63(pp 237–246)] provides a detailed weight history questionnaire);

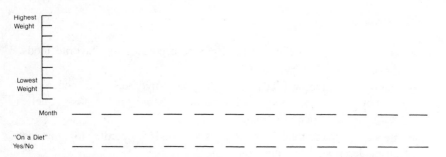

Highest
Weight

Lowest
Weight

Month

"On a Diet"
Yes/No

Figure 9-2 Client Weight Chart for Past Year

- constructs a retrospective weight history according to 5-year periods (Figure 9-3);
- completes the Restraint Scale (Appendix 9-E).[37(p 212)]

The practitioner determines the level of restrained eating.
The client and the practitioner:

- determine and predict the client's approximate body-fat status based on the "yo-yo" model (Appendix 9-F);
- rate selected diets using tools in strategies 1 and 2;
- determine positive aspects of dieting regarding both food choices and body changes;
- establish body shape and body size goals (see Figure 9-1);
- set progressive goals in terms of reduced fad diet use, weight maintenance, increased use of positive dietary guidelines, and reduced number of restraint behaviors.

The *Consumer Guide's Rating the Diets*[75] denotes two groups: (1) new quick weight loss diet programs, and (2) new life style diets. Rating criteria from 0

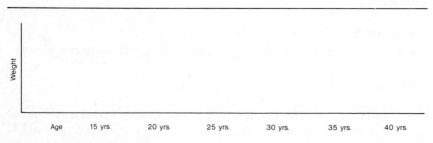

Weight

Age   15 yrs.   20 yrs.   25 yrs.   30 yrs.   35 yrs.   40 yrs.

Figure 9-3 Client Weight History

to 4 are outlined for each group. This guide may be useful for nutrition education. Life style diets are rated on effectiveness, nutritional balance, safety, and flexibility. Quick loss diets are rated on safety and effectiveness for approximately 3 weeks, even though they are unbalanced and low calorie.

Strategy 4: Deciding the Ground Rules

Objectives:

- to determine realistic eating management goals considering the client's view;
- to establish goals based on scientifically sound and practical principles.

The client:

- lists reasons for dieting relating to health, body size, and food goals; examples may be "increase energy level," "reduce hip size," "never eat bad foods," or "eat anything I want after I lose weight";
- rates each goal as realistic (R) or unrealistic (U).

The practitioner presents eating principles:

- Eating for pleasure is important in weight management.
- Recommendations for weight management are not different from nutrition recommendations for the general public.
- Lifetime diets are not complicated.
- Shopping and food preparation skills are important in eating management.

The client and the practitioner:

- discuss examples of each principle;
- use tools for evaluating fat in foods: *AICR Target Food Guide*,[76] Food Record Rating,[77] or The Fat Portion Exchange List.[78]

Cabanac[79] shows that in a conflict of motivations, food palatability is a sensory pleasure and serves as a potent drive of behavior. Taste forms a major part of this pleasure. Dwyer[80] argues that there is a misconception about the relation of modified diets and regular diets. They are based on the same principles. A reduction in the fat content of the American diet has been cited by the American Heart Association,[81] the National Academy of Sciences,[82] the US Senate,[83] and the American Cancer Society[84] as a means of reducing the risk of cardiovascular disease and certain cancers. These recommendations will also serve to reduce the likelihood of being overweight and obesity. deDennis et al[85] conclude that for the moderately overweight population, a general diet reduced in calories, especially fat, results in as good compliance as nonhazardous special VLC diets, drug programs, or complex behavioral programs.

Strategy 5: Relabeling Foods

Objectives:

- to determine connotations ("labeling") of foods;
- to change negative food labels into positive ones on the basis of frequency, variety, and amount of food use.

The client:

- categorizes food according to subjective labels such as "junk," "guilt," and "forbidden," using the 2-day food profile;
- determines the relative frequency of each food according to the Eating Guide (Appendix 9-C).

The practitioner determines the relative role of each category based on the frequency and situational use of each food.

The client and the practitioner:

- determine which foods require modification and/or relabeling;
- practice adaptive thinking: "I will never eat chocolate cake again," becomes "I will check the whole day of eating and plan if, when, and how much chocolate cake might fit. It may fit only once a week."

Snetselaar[63(pp 86–87)] discusses cognitive restructuring, thought stopping, shaping, and contracting as methods of eating management.

Strategy 6: Buying and Preparing Food

Objectives:

- to determine shopping and preparation patterns;
- to practice simple ways of modifying foods and recipes.

The client:

- collects frequently used recipes, food labels, or lists of ingredients, and itemized cash register receipts;
- identifies high-fat and high-calorie foods;
- selects two or three foods to modify.

The practitioner:

- demonstrates methods of reducing calories by broiling, chilling and removing fat from soups and mixed dishes, trimming fat, substituting low-fat for high-fat items;
- discusses taste responses with client.

The client and the practitioner review and practice selecting and preparing techniques.

The *Culinary Hearts Kitchen Instructor's Package*[86] from the American Heart Association includes a teacher's manual, handouts, recipes, and food and nutrition slides.

Two studies[87,88] report successful food modification using food preparation techniques.

Shopping with a list and shopping after a meal are two commonly employed behavioral weight-loss guidelines designed to reduce food purchases and therefore food consumption. Beneke and Davis[89] tested these methods by calculating calories in purchases and concluded that neither guideline is supported by evidence.

Strategy 7: Practicing Eating Management

Objectives:

- to prepare and taste modified foods such as reduced-fat, high-fiber, and other time-displacement foods;
- to select highly palatable foods together with a variety of other foods;
- to identify stages of hunger and satiety;
- to analyze feelings toward restrictive food situations.

The clients (this activity is effective and efficient in a group):

- prepare a variety of "starter" foods including soup and low-nutrient-dense foods identified as "junk" etc by group members.

- prepare a variety of calorie- and fat-modified foods;
- serve equal size and number of servings to everyone, except one or two persons who are served only cottage cheese or a liquid diet product.

The practitioner provides directions that include:

- checking hunger level at beginning, during, and end of meal;
- deciding, at the beginning of the meal, which food to leave on the plate.

The clients and the practitioner:

- discuss responses to those eating only liquid diets;
- recall responses and feelings regarding foods;
- role play modified food responses.

THE PRACTITIONER IS PART OF THE PROGRAM

A weight-management program based on society's current ideals of physical appearance rather than ability, health, and use of food is unrealistic.[90] Health professionals' attitudes toward overweight patients are often inconsistent and biased.[91]

Even Russell Baker, a man of ceaseless good humor, becomes exasperated at the prospect of dieting. In a column appropriately entitled "One Sacrifice Too Many" (*New York Times Magazine*, September 21, 1986, p 26), he writes: "I know about dieting. Know it's even harder than giving up smoking. I didn't go through the agony of giving up smoking so I could experience the higher agony of dieting. In many a fat man there is a thin smoker who finally ran out of willpower." Such frustration is shared by many Americans, for they know that dieting is not worth the sacrifice, the ongoing restraint, the everlasting exercise of will. Either it does not work well or it does not work at all. But Americans should know further that viable alternatives to dieting do exist, and that these are based on scientific strategies. There is a better way: not of weight control but of effective eating management.

REFERENCES

1. Society for Nutrition Education: Nutrition concepts and generalizations. *Journal of Nutrition Education* 1982; 14:1–2.

2. Kneip JK, Fox HM, Fruehling JK: A weight-control program for bank employees. *J Am Diet Assoc* 1985; 85:1489–1491.

3. Foreyt JP, Reeves RS, Darnell LS, et al: Soup consumption as a behavioral weight loss strategy. *J Am Diet Assoc* 1986; 86:524–526.

4. Jordan HA, Levitz LS, Utgoff KL, et al: Role of food characteristics in behavioral change and weight loss. *J Am Diet Assoc* 1981; 79:24–26.

5. Mickelsen O, Makdani DD, Cotton RH, et al: Effects of a high fiber bread diet on weight loss in college-age males. *Am J Clin Nutr* 1979; 32:1703–1709.

6. Duncan KH, Bacon JA, Weinsier R: The effects of high and low energy density diets on satiety, energy intake, and eating time of obese and nonobese subjects. *Am J Clin Nutr* 1983; 37:763–767.

7. Rozin P, Fallon A: The acquisition of likes and dislikes for foods, in Food and Nutrition Board: *What is America Eating?* Washington, DC, National Academy Press, 1986, pp 58–71.

8. Krondl MM, Lau D: Social determinants in human food selection, in Barker L (ed): *The Psychobiology of Human Food Selection* (Westport, Conn, AVI, 1982, pp 139–149.

9. Dalton S: Worksite food choices: An investigation of intended and actual selection. *Journal of Nutrition Education* 1986; 18:182–187.

10. Drewnowski A: Cognitive structure in obesity and dieting, in Greenwood MRC (ed): *Obesity: Contemporary Issues in Clinical Nutrition*. New York, Churchill Livingstone Inc, 1982, pp 87–101.

11. Booth DA: Acquired behavior controlling energy input and output, in Stunkard AJ (ed): *Obesity*. Philadelphia, WB Saunders Co, 1980, pp 101–143.

12. Witherly SA, Pangborn RM, Stern JS: Gustatory responses and eating duration of obese and lean adults. *Appetite* 1980; 1:53–63.

13. Wurtman JJ, Wurtman RJ, Growdon DG: Carbohydrate craving in obese people. *International Journal of Eating Disorders* 1981; 1:2–14.

14. Meyers AW, Stunkard AJ, Coll M: Food accessibility and food choice: A test of Schachter's hypothesis. *Arch Gen Psychiatry* 1980; 37:1133–1136.

15. Booth DA: How nutritional effects of foods can influence people's dietary choices, in Barker L (ed): *The Psychobiology of Human Food Selection*. Westport, Conn, AVI, 1982, pp 67–84.

16. Skinner BF: *Science and Human Behavior*. New York, Free Press, 1965, pp 64–66.

17. Jeffrey RW, Coates TJ: Why aren't they losing weight. *Behavior Therapy* 1978; 9:856–859.

18. Hall SM, Hall RG, Hanson RW, et al: Permanence of two self-managed treatments of overweight in university and community populations. *J Consult Clin Psychol* 1974; 42:781–786.

19. Brownell KD, Wadden TA: Behavioral and self-help treatments, in Greenwood MRC (ed): *Obesity*. New York, Churchill Livingstone Inc, 1983, p 51.

20. National Center for Health Statistics: Provisional data from the Health Promotion and Disease Prevention Supplement to the National Health Interview Survey: United States, Jan–March 1985. *Advancedata*, Nov 1985, pp 2–5.

21. Stewart AL, Brook RH: Effects of being overweight. *Am J Public Health* 1983; 73:171–178.

22. Grunewald KK: Weight control in young college women: Who are the dieters? *J Am Diet Assoc* 1985; 85:1445–1450.

23. Arrington R, Bonner J, Stitt KR: Weight reduction methods of college women. *J Am Diet Assoc* 1985; 85:483–484.

24. Thompson MG, Schwartz DM: Life adjustment of women with anorexia nervosa and anorexic-like behavior. *International Journal of Eating Disorders* 1982; 1:47–60.

25. Dwyer J, Feldman JJ, Mayer J: Adolescent dieters: Who are they? *Am J Clin Nutr* 1976; 20:1045–1056.

26. Storz NS, Greene WH: Body weight, body image, and perception of fad diets in adolescent girls. *Journal of Nutrition Education* 1983; 15:5–18.

27. Rowland KN: Dieting figures. *Calorie Control Commentary*, Fall 1983, pp 1, 5.

28. Weinsier RL, Wadden TA, Ritenbaugh C, et al: Recommended therapeutic guidelines for professional weight control programs. *Am J Clin Nutr* 1984; 40:865–872.

29. Munves E: Managing the diet, in Stunkard AJ (ed): *Obesity*. Philadelphia, WB Saunders Co, 1980, pp 262–275.

30. *Nutrient Intakes: Individuals in 48 States: Year 1977–78, Nationwide Food Consumption Survey 1977–78*, US Dept of Agriculture, Human Nutrition Information Service, Consumer Nutrition Division, Report No. 1-2. 1984, pp 1–439.

31. USDA, Human Nutrition Information Service, Nutrition Monitoring Division, *Nationwide Food Consumption Survey Continuing Survey of Food Intakes by Individuals*, Women 19–50 Years and Their Children 1–5 Years, 1 Day, NFCS, CSFII Report No. 85-1 (1985).

32. Rizek RL, Jackson EM: *Current Food Consumption Practices and Nutrient Sources in the American Diet*, Consumer Nutrition Center; Human Nutrition, Science and Education Administration (Hyattsville, Md, USDA, 1980, p 23.

33. Pennington JAT, Young BE, Wilson DB, et al: Mineral content of foods and total diets: The selected minerals in foods survey, 1982 to 1984. *J Am Diet Assoc* 1986; 86:876–890.

34. Fisher MC, Lachance PA: Nutrition evaluation of published weight-reducing diets. *J Am Diet Assoc* 1985; 85:450–454.

35. Woteki C, Johnson C, Murphy R: Nutritional status of the US population: Iron, vitamin C, and zinc, in Food and Nutrition Board, National Research Council, in *What Is America Eating?* Washington, National Academy Press, 1986, pp 25–26.

36. Berman EM: Factors influencing motivations in dieting. *Journal of Nutrition Education* 1975; 7:155–159.

37. Herman CP, Polivy J: Restrained eating, in Stunkard AJ (ed): *Obesity*. Philadelphia, WB Saunders Co, 1980, pp 208–225.

38. Klajner F, Herman CP, Polivy J, et al: Human obesity, dieting and anticipatory salivation to food. *Physiol Behav* 1981; 27:195–198.

39. Tobinson S, Hill AJ, Rogers PJ: Breakdown of restraint following the imagination of food but not after a highly palatable preload, abstracted. *Int J Obes* 1985; 9:89–91.

40. Herman CP, Polivy J, Silver R: The effects of an observer on eating behavior: The induction of sensible eating. *Journal of Personality* 1979; 47:85–99.

41. Stunkard AJ, Messick S: The three-factor eating questionnaire to measure dietary restraint, disinhibition and hunger. *J Psychosom Res* 1985; 29:71–83.

42. Brownell KD: The psychology and physiology of obesity: Implications for screening and treatment. *J Am Diet Assoc* 1984; 84:406–414.

43. Rolls BJ, Rowe EA, Rolls ET: How sensory properties of food affect human feeding behavior. *Physiol Behav* 1982; 29:409–413.

44. Keys A, Brozek J, Henschel A, et al: *The Biology of Human Starvation*. Minneapolis, University of Minnesota Press, 1950.

45. Drewnowski A: Food perceptions and preferences of obese adults: A multidimensional approach. *Int J Obes* 1985; 9:207–212.

46. Guthrie HA: Concept of a nutritious food. *J Am Dietetic Assoc* 1977; 71:14–19.

47. Wyse BW, Windham CT, Gaurth Hansen R: Nutrition intervention: Panacea or Pandora's box? *J Am Diet Assoc* 1985; 85:1084–1090.

48. Rolls BK: Experimental analyses of the effects of variety in a meal on human feeding. *Am J Clin Nutr* 1985; 42:932–939.

49. Smiciklas-Wright H, Krebs-Smith SM, Krebs-Smith J: Variety in foods, in Food and Nutrition Board, National Research Council: *What is America Eating?* Washington, National Academy Press, 1986, pp 126–140.

50. DeBont AJ: Influence of alterations in meal frequency on lipogenesis and body fat content in the rat. *Proc Soc Exp Biol Med* 1975; 149:849–854.

51. Bray G: Lipogenesis in human adipose tissue: Some effects of nibbling and gorging. *J Clin Invest* 1972; 51:537–547.

52. Fabry P, Tepperman J: Meal frequency: A possible factor in human pathology. *Am J Clin Nutr* 1970; 23:1059–1065.

53. Metzner HL: The relationship between frequency of eating and adiposity in adult men and women in the Tecumseh Community Health Study. *Am J Clin Nutr* 1977; 30:712–720.

54. Holeckova E, Fabry P: Hyperphagia and gastric hypertrophy in rats adapted to intermittent starvation. *Br J Nutr* 1959; 13:260–265.

55. Garrow J: *Energy Balance and Obesity in Man.* New York, Elsevier Science Publishing Co Inc, 1974, p 32.

56. Apfelbaum M, Bostsarron J, Lacatis D: Effect of caloric restriction and excessive caloric intake on energy expenditure. *Am J Clin Nutr* 1971; 24:1405–1409.

57. Djorntorp P, Yang MU: Refeeding after fasting in the rat: Effects on body composition and food efficiency. *Am J Clin Nutr* 1982; 36:444–449.

58. Brownell KD, Greenwood MRC, Stellar E, et al: The effects of repeated cycles of weight loss and regain in rats. *Physiol Behav* 1986; 38:459–464.

59. Stunkard AJ: Nutrition, aging and obesity: A critical review of a complex relationship. *Int J Obes* 1983; 7:201–220.

60. Reynolds MA, Ingram DK: Is thinner better? *Int J Obes* 1984; 8:285–287.

61. Ashwell M, Chinn S, Stalley S, et al: Female fat distribution: A photographic and cellularity study. *Int J Obes* 1978; 2:289–302.

62. Hirsch J: Dietary treatment, in Frankle RT, Dwyer J, Moragne L, et al (eds): *Dietary Treatment and Prevention of Obesity.* London, John Libbey & Co Ltd, 1985, pp 5–9.

63. Snetselaar LG: *Nutrition Counseling Skills: Assessment, Treatment, and Evaluation.* Rockville, Md, Aspen Publishers Inc, 1983.

64. Vickery CE, Hodges PA: Counseling strategies for dietary management: Expanded possibilities for effecting behavior change. *J Am Diet Assoc* 1986; 86:924–928.

65. Adams SO, Grady KE, Wolk CH, et al: Weight loss: A comparison of groups and individual interventions. *J Am Diet Assoc* 1986; 86:485–490.

66. Stunkard AJ: The current status of treatment for obesity in adults, in Stunkard AJ, Stellar E (eds): *Eating and Its Disorders.* New York, Raven Press, 1984, pp 157–158.

67. Evans RI, Hall Y: Social-psychological perspective in motivating changes in eating behavior. *J Am Dietetic Assoc* 1978; 72:378–381.

68. Mazzeo-Caputo SE, Danish SJ, Kris-Etherton PM: Dietary change: Prescription vs goal setting. *J Am Diet Assoc* 1985; 85:553–556.

69. D'Augelli AR: Healthy eating: A human development intervention perspective. *Journal of Nutrition Education* 1981; 13(suppl):S54–S58.

70. Ashwell M, Chinn S, Stalley S, et al: Female fat distribution—a photographic and cellularity study. *Int J Obes* 1978; 2:289–302.

71. Morgan JB: Weight reducing diets: The thermic effect of feeding and energy balance in young women. *Int J Obes* 1984; 8:629–640.

72. LeBlanc J: Thermogenesis in relation to feeding and exercise training. *Int J Obes* 1985; 9(suppl):75–79.

73. Krebs-Smith SM, Smiciklas-Wright H: Typical serving sizes: Implications for food guidance. *J Am Diet Assoc* 1985; 85:1139–1141.

74. Tseng RYL, Sullivan MA, Downes NJ: A proposed method for the nutritional rating of foods. *Journal of Nutrition Education* 1986; 18:67–74.

75. Berland T: *Rating the Diets.* New York, Signet Books, 1986.

76. *AICR Target Food Guide.* Washington, American Institute for Cancer Research. Washington, American Institute for Cancer Research.

77. Raab C, Tillotson JL: Food record rating for fat-controlled diets, in *Heart to Heart: A Manual on Nutrition Counseling for the Reduction of Cardiovascular Disease Risk Factors,* US Dept of Health and Human Services publication No. (NIH) 85-1528. Government Printing Office, 1983, pp 43–47.

78. Boyar AP, Loughridge JR: The fat portion exchange list: A tool for teaching and evaluating low-fat diets. *J Am Diet Assoc* 1985; 85:589–594.

79. Cabanac M: Preferring for pleasure. *Am J Clin Nutr* 1985; 42:1151–1155.

80. Dwyer JT: Nutrition education, in Food and Nutrition Board, National Research Council: *What is America Eating?* Washington, National Academy Press, 1986, pp 150–157.

81. Nutrition Committee of the American Heart Association: Rationale of the diet-heart statement of the American Heart Association. *Circulation* 1982; 65:839–854.

82. National Research Council Committee on Diet, Nutrition and Cancer: *Diet, Nutrition and Cancer.* Washington, National Academy Press, 1982.

83. US Senate Select Committee on Nutrition and Human Need: *Dietary Goals for the United States* ed. 2 Government Printing Office, 1977.

84. American Cancer Society: *Nutrition and Cancer: Cause and Prevention,* Special Report, *CA1984* 1984; 34:1–84.

85. deDennis SRK, Mitchell B, Shrago E: Efficacy of a general nutritional adequate low-calorie diet for weight reduction. *International Journal of Eating Disorders* 1986; 5:129–135.

86. American Heart Association: *Culinary Hearts Kitchen Instructor's Package.* Dallas, 1982.

87. Daniel-Gentry J, Dolecek TA, Caggiula AW, et al: Increasing the use of meatless meals: A nutrition intervention substudy in the multiple risk factor intervention trial (MRFIT). *J Am Diet Assoc* 1986; 86:778–781.

88. Richmond K: Introducing heart-healthy foods in a company cafeteria. *Journal of Nutrition Education* 1986; 18(suppl):S63–S65.

89. Beneke WM, Davis CH: Relationship of hunger, use of a shopping list and obesity to food purchases. *Int J Obes* 1985; 9:391–399.

90. Russ CS, Atkinson RL: Comments on the army weight control program: A critical view. *J Am Diet Assoc* 1985; 85:1435–1436.

91. Moynihan CM, Stark O, Peckham CS: Obesity in 16-year-olds assessed by relative weight and doctors' rating. *Int J Obes* 1986; 10:3–10.

Appendix 9-A

Daily Calorie Distribution Worksheet

DAILY CALORIE DISTRIBUTION

CURRENT AMERICAN DIET

U.S. DIETARY GOALS, 1977

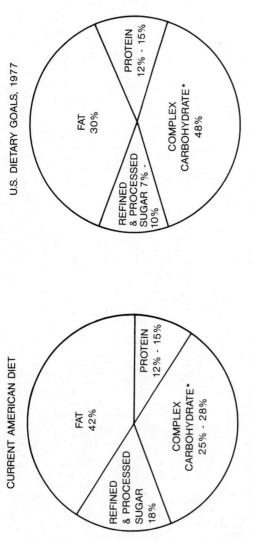

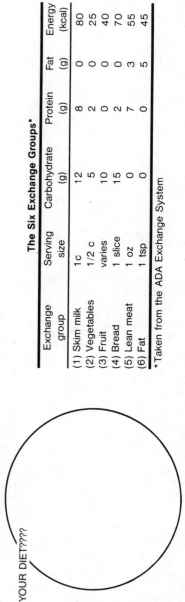

The Six Exchange Groups*

Exchange group	Serving size	Carbohydrate (g)	Protein (g)	Fat (g)	Energy (kcal)
(1) Skim milk	1 c	12	8	0	80
(2) Vegetables	1/2 c	5	2	0	25
(3) Fruit	varies	10	0	0	40
(4) Bread	1 slice	15	2	0	70
(5) Lean meat	1 oz	0	7	3	55
(6) Fat	1 tsp	0	0	5	45

*Taken from the ADA Exchange System

*Includes naturally occurring sugar in foods (fruits, milk, etc.)

YOUR DIET????

Food (1 Day)	Size and no. servings	Carbohydrate (gms.) complex/ nat. occ.	refined	Protein (gms.)	Fat (gms.)	Calories
Example 1-8 oz. gl. skim milk		12		8	0	80
1-8 oz. gl. whole milk		12		8	10	170
Sub Totals (gms)		X 4 =	X4 =	X4 =	X9 =	

Divide subtotals by total calories X 100   eg. $\dfrac{CHO\ Calories}{Total\ Calories} \times 100 = \%\ CHO\ Calories$

Percent calories from each Nutrient

Appendix 9-B

Rate Your Plate Guide

How to Use the Rate Your Plate Guide: We have assigned a number from 0–3 to each food recommended by the Dietary Guidelines, based on the relative amount of saturated fat, cholesterol, etc. (These figures are our estimates and are meant to be suggestive only.) You can rate your daily intake by adding up the number of servings of each group and multiplying it by the numbers shown. Then total up the points for each item. For saturated fat, cholesterol, sodium and refined sugar, the goal is to lower your daily points. For complex carbohydrates and fiber, the goal is to raise the number of points. Bear in mind that the use of highly processed snack foods like crackers, potato and corn chips, cakes and cookies will add considerably to your points for saturated fat and sodium. These foods should be used no more than once or twice a week.

Environmental Nutrition Newsletter's
Rate Your Plate Guide

Food Recommended by the Dietary Guidelines	Calories	Portion Size	Saturated Fat	Cholesterol
Fruits	40		*	*
Fresh		½ cup	0	0
Processed		½ cup	0	0
Vegetables	35			
Fresh		½ cup	0	0
Processed		1 cup	0	0
Whole Grains and Enriched Products	70			
Breads and		1 slice		
Cereals		½–¾ cup		
Whole grain			0	0
Refined			0	0
Pastas and		½ cup		
Rice		½ cup		
Whole grain			0	0
Refined			0	0
Milk and Milk Products				
Milk, whole	170	1 cup	2	1
skim	80	1 cup	0	0
low fat	135	1 cup	1	1
Cheese made with				
whole milk	200	2 ounces	2	1
skim milk	100–150	2 ounces	0	0
Plain yogurt made with				
whole milk	150	1 cup	2	1
skim milk	120	1 cup	0	0
Yogurt with added fruit	250	1 cup	as above	as above
Meat, Poultry, Fish, Eggs				
Fresh Meats				
Chicken and fish	165	3 ounces	1	2
Beef, pork and lamb	220	3 ounces	2–3	3
Cured Meats	250	3 ounces	2–3	2–3
Eggs	75	1 Med		3
Legumes, Nuts and Seeds				
Fresh	140	½ cup	0	0
Canned	150	½ cup	0	0

Appendix 9-B *continued*

Food Recommended by the Dietary Guidelines	Calories	Portion Size	Saturated Fat	Cholesterol
Fats, Oils				
Butter	45	2	1	0
Marg./ oils	45	1–2	0	0
Potato or Corn				
Chips, Snacks	180	10–15	2–3	0
Pastry, Cookies	150–300	2″ sq	2–3	1
Beverages, sweet				
carbonated	170	12 oz	0	0
*Amount in Food: 0–None or negligible 1–Insignificant 2–Moderate 3–Large	Suggested Rating Scale: Good Could be better		8 or fewer 10 or more	6 or fewer 8 or more

Food Recommended by the Dietary Guidelines	Sodium	Refined Sugar	Complex Carbohydrate	Fiber
Fruits	*	*	*	*
Fresh	0	0	2	2–3
Processed	0	2–3	2	0
Vegetables				
Fresh	0–2	0	3	1–3
Processed	1–3	0–1	2	1–2
Whole Grains and				
Enriched Products				
Breads and				
Cereals				
Whole grain	2	0–1	2–3	2
Refined	2	0–1	1	0–1
Pastas and				
Rice				
Whole grain	1	0	2	2
Refined	1	0	1	0–1

Appendix 9-B *continued*

Food Recommended by the Dietary Guidelines	Sodium	Refined Sugar	Complex Carbohydrate	Fiber
Milk and Milk Products				
Milk, whole	2	0	0	0
skim	2	0	0	0
low fat	2	0	0	0
Cheese made with				
whole milk	2	0	0	0
skim milk	2	0	0	0
Plain yogurt made with				
whole milk	2	0	0	0
skim milk	2	0	0	0
Yogurt with added fruit	2	2	0	0
Meat, Poultry, Fish, Eggs				
Fresh Meats				
Chicken and fish	1–2	0	0	0
Beef, pork and lamb	1–2	0	0	0
Cured Meats	3	0–1	0	0
Eggs		0	0	0
Legumes, Nuts and Seeds				
Fresh	0–1	0	2–3	2–3
Canned	2–3	1–2	2–3	2–3
Fats, Oils				
Butter	0	0	0	0
Marg/oils	0	0	0	0
Potato or Corn				
Chips, Snacks	3	0	1	1
Pastry, Cookies	1–2	3	1	0
Beverages, sweet				
carbonated	0	3	0	0
	18 or fewer	5 or fewer	18 or more	10 or more
	22 or more	8 or more	14 or fewer	8 or fewer

Source: Adapted with permission from *Environmental Nutrition Newsletter* (1980; 3:2), Copyright © 1980, Environmental Nutrition Inc.

Appendix 9-C

New American Eating Guide

	ANYTIME	IN MODERATION	NOW AND THEN

Group 1
 	
Beans,
  Grains,
  and Nuts
 	
four or more
  servings a
  day
	bread and rolls
	  (whole grain)
	bulgur
	dried beans and
	  peas
	  (legumes)
	lentils
	oatmeal
	pasta, whole
	  wheat
	rice, brown
	rye bread
	sprouts
	whole grain hot
	  and cold
	  cereal
	whole wheat
	  matzoh
		cornbread 8
		flour tortilla 8
		hominy grits 8
		macaroni and
		  cheese 1, (6), 8
		matzoh 8
		nuts 3
		pasta, except
		  whole wheat 8
		peanut butter 3
		pizza 6, 8
		refined, un-
		  sweetened
		  cereals 8
		refried beans,
		  commercial 1,
		  homemade in oil 2
		seeds 3
		soybeans 2
		tofu 2
		waffles or pancakes,
		  syrup 5, (6), 8
		white bread and
		  rolls 8
		white rice 8
			croissant 4, 8
			doughnut (yeast leav-
			  ened) 3 or 4, 5, 8
			presweetened break-
			  fast cereals 5, 8
			sticky buns 1 or 2, 5, 8
			stuffing, made with
			  butter 4, (6), 8

Appendix 9-B *continued*

	ANYTIME	IN MODERATION	NOW AND THEN

Group 2
 	
Fruits and
  Vegetables
 	
four or more
  servings a
  day
	all fruits and
	  vegetables
	  except those
	  listed at right
	applesauce (un-
	  sweetened)
	unsweetened
	  fruit juices
	unsalted vege-
	  table juices
	potatoes, white
	  or sweet
		avocado 3
		cole slaw 3
		cranberry sauce
		  (canned) 5
		dried fruit
		french fries, home-
		  made in
		  vegetable oil 2,
		  commercial 1
		fried eggplant (veg.
		  oil) 2
		fruits canned in
		  syrup 5
		gazpacho 2, (6)
		glazed carrots 5, (6)
		guacamole 3
		potatoes au gratin
		  1, (6)
		salted vegetable
		  juices 6
		sweetened fruit
		  juices 5
		vegetables canned
		  with salt 6
			coconut 4
			pickles 6

Group 3
 	
Milk Products
 	
two servings
  a day
	buttermilk
	  made from
	  skim milk
	lassi (low-fat
	  yogurt and
	  fruit juice
	  drink)
	low-fat cottage
	  cheese
	low-fat milk, 1%
	  milkfat
	low-fat yogurt
	nonfat dry milk
	skim milk
	  cheeses (6)
	skim milk
	skim milk and
	  banana shake
		cocoa made with
		  skim milk 5
		cottage cheese,
		  regular, 4%
		  milkfat 1
		frozen low-fat
		  yogurt 5
		ice milk 5
		low-fat milk, 2%
		  milkfat 1
		low-fat yogurt,
		  sweetened 5
		mozzarella cheese,
		  part-skim type
		  only 1, (6)
			cheesecake 4, 5
			cheese fondue 4, (6)
			cheese soufflé 4, (6), 7
			eggnog 1, 5, 7
			hard cheeses: blue,
			  brick, Camembert,
			  cheddar, Muenster,
			  Swiss 4, (6)
			ice cream 4, 5
			processed cheeses 4, 6
			whole milk 4
			whole milk yogurt 4

Appendix 9-C *continued*

	ANYTIME	IN MODERATION	NOW AND THEN
Group 4 Poultry, Fish, Meat, and Eggs two servings a day Vegetarians: nutrients in these foods can be obtained by eating more foods in groups 1, 2, and 3	FISH cod flounder gefilte fish (6) haddock halibut perch pollack rockfish shellfish, except shrimp sole tuna, water packed (6) EGG PRODUCTS egg whites *only* POULTRY chicken or turkey, boiled, baked, or roasted (no skin)	FISH (drained well if canned) fried fish 1 or 2 herring 3, 6 mackerel, canned 2, (6) salmon, pink, canned 2, (6) sardines 2, (6) shrimp 7 tuna, oil-packed 2, (6) POULTRY Chicken liver, baked or broiled, 7 (just one!) fried chicken, homemade in vegetable oil 3 chicken or turkey, boiled, baked or roasted (with skin) 2 RED MEATS (trimmed of all outside fat!) flank steak 1 leg or loin of lamb 1 pork shoulder or loin, lean 1 round steak or ground round 1 rump roast 1 sirloin steak, lean 1 veal 1	POULTRY fried chicken, commercially prepared 4 EGG cheese omelet, 4, 7 egg yolk or whole egg (about 3 per week) 3, 7 RED MEATS bacon 4, (6) beef liver, fried, 1, 7 bologna, 4, 6 corned beef 4, 6 ground beef 4 ham, trimmed well 1, 6 hot dogs 4, 6 liverwurst 4, 6 pig's feet 4 salami 4, 6 sausage 4, 6 spare ribs 4 untrimmed red meats 4 KEY: 1–moderate fat, saturated 2–moderate fat, unsaturated 3–high fat, unsaturated 4–high fat, saturated 5–high in added sugar 6–high in salt or sodium (6)–may be high in salt or sodium 7–high in cholesterol 8–refined grains

Source: Adapted from *New American Eating Guide*, which is available from the Center for Science in the Public Interest, 1501 16th Street, NW, Washington, DC 20036 for $4.25, copyright 1981.

Appendix 9-D

Effect of Fat and Sugar Dilution on Nutrient Density of Milk Products

Skim Milk (245 g)

	INQs	% STD
CALORIES	1.0	4.3
CALCIUM	7.8	33.5
ZINC	1.4	6.1
RIBOFLAVIN	6.7	28.6
VITAMIN B6	1.1	4.9
VITAMIN B12	7.2	31.0
PROTEIN	3.9	16.7
FAT	0.1	0.6
CHOLESTEROL	0.3	1.4
SODIUM	1.3	5.8

Lowfat Milk – 2% Fat (245 g)

	INQs	% STD
CALORIES	1.0	6.2
CALCIUM	5.4	33.2
ZINC	0.9	6.0
RIBOFLAVIN	5.3	32.7
VITAMIN B6	0.8	4.9
VITAMIN B12	4.8	29.4
PROTEIN	2.6	16.2
FAT	1.0	6.0
CHOLESTEROL	0.9	5.7
SODIUM	0.9	5.6

Whole Milk – 3.3% Fat (245 g)

	INQs	% STD						
			0	10	20	30	40	50
CALORIES	1.0	7.5						
CALCIUM	4.3	32.4						
ZINC	0.8	5.8						
RIBOFLAVIN	4.4	32.7						
VITAMIN B$_4$	0.7	4.9						
VITAMIN B$_{12}$	3.9	29.4						
PROTEIN	2.2	16.2						
FAT	1.4	10.4						
CHOLESTEROL	1.3	9.7						
SODIUM	0.7	5.5						

Lowfat Fruit Yogurt (245 g)

	INQs	% STD						
			0	10	20	30	40	50
CALORIES	1.0	12.5						
CALCIUM	3.3	41.4						
ZINC	0.9	11.3						
RIBOFLAVIN	2.9	36.8						
VITAMIN B$_4$	0.4	4.9						
VITAMIN B$_{12}$	3.1	38.4						
PROTEIN	1.7	21.6						
FAT	0.3	3.5						
CHOLESTEROL	0.2	2.9						
SODIUM	0.5	6.5						
SUGAR, ADDED	4.7	59.2						(59.2%)

Source: Reprinted with permission from *Journal of the American Dietetic Association* (1985; 85:1084), Copyright © 1985, American Dietetic Association.

Appendix 9-E

Revised Restraint Scale

1. How often are you dieting? Never; rarely; sometimes; often; always. (Scored 0–4)
2. What is the maximum amount of weight (in pounds) that you have ever lost within one month? 0–4; 5–9; 10–14; 15–19; 20 + . (Scored 0–4)
3. What is your maximum weight gain within a week? 0–1; 1.1–2; 2.1–3; 3.1–5; 5.1 + . (Scored 0–4)
4. In a typical week, how much does your weight fluctuate? 0–1; 1.1–2; 2.1–3; 3.1–5; 5.1 + (Scored 0–4)
5. Would a weight fluctuation of 5 lb affect the way you live your life? Not at all; slightly; moderately; very much. (Scored 0–3)
6. Do you eat sensibly in front of others and splurge alone? Never; rarely; often; always. (Scored 0–3)
7. Do you give too much time and thought to food? Never; rarely; often; always. (Scored 0–3)
8. Do you have feelings of guilt after overeating? Never; rarely; often; always. (Scored 0–3)
9. How conscious are you of what you are eating? Not at all; slightly; moderately; extremely. (Scored 0–3)
10. How many pounds over your desired weight were you at your maximum weight? 0–1; 1–5; 6–10; 11–20; 21 + . (Scored 0–4)

Source: Reprinted from *Obesity* (p 212) by AJ Stunkard (Ed) with permission of WB Saunders Company, © 1980.

Appendix 9-F

The Yo-Yo Syndrome

1. 115 lbs, 25% Fat

   Suppose that a 5'3" healthy 23 year-old woman weighs 115 pounds. The proportion of fat to lean body mass is normal: that is, 29 pounds of fat (25%) and 86 pounds of lean body mass. From this point on, she consumes 50 more calories per day than she burns off in daily activity.

2. 135 lbs, 34% Fat

   At the end of a four year period, our 27 year-old woman has gained approximately 20 pounds. She now tips the scale at 135 pounds, *but her body composition has changed*; she has approximately 46 pounds of fat (34%) and 89 pounds of lean body mass.

   Our hypothetical woman now wants to lose those 20 pounds. Summer is fast approaching and she wants to look good in her bathing suit. She can follow a sensible diet of 1200 calories per day expecting weight loss of 1½–2 pounds per week or 10–12 weeks to reach her goal. Wanting to lose weight faster, she joins one of the popular rapid weight loss plans that promises she can lose the 20 pounds in 6–8 weeks which she does by crash dieting on less than 650 calories per day. Nothing secret about it—she consumes less than she burns and she loses weight.

3. 115 lbs, 31% Fat

   But there is a catch: of the 20 pounds she lost, 10 pounds were fat, 5 water, and 5 muscle. Once again her body composition has been altered. Back at her original 115 pounds, as in phase 1, she is now *fatter* with 36 pounds of fat (31%) and 84 pounds of lean body mass (less lean body mass than she originally started with).

4. 135 lbs, 38% Fat

   Because she did not have a medical problem, our woman assumed any diet she went on would be acceptable as long as it took off the pounds. She didn't educate herself about behavior modification and lifestyle change in conjunction with her diet. When summer is over, she falls into her previous eating habits and slowly but surely over the year regains the 20 pounds she lost. She now weighs the same as before she dieted—135 pounds—*but something drastic has happened to her*. The 20 pounds she regains are not the same pounds she shed, rather she gains 15 pounds of fat and 5 pounds of water.

5. 115 lbs, 40% Fat

   If the same cycle is repeated for 3 more years with various diets, she might again weigh 115 pounds, but her body composition will be 46 pounds of fat (40%) and 69 pounds of lean body mass. Her body composition has dramatically changed in response to yo-yo fluctuations. Our slightly overweight female dieter, now 31 years old, is the victim of her unorthodox weight loss practices, and has become a metabolically-reduced body system which needs fewer calories to maintain itself.

6. + 10 lbs per year!

   If our hypothetical female's daily metabolic needs are reduced by just 100 calories per day because of her changed body composition and she consumes the same amount of calories as previously, she will gain 10 pounds per year!

   Our model female is no longer simply overweight, she is clinically obese. Her reduced amount of active lean tissue and slowed metabolic rate have plunged her into a vicious cycle of weight gain. She watches herself get heavier even as she consciously controls her calorie intake. At this point, she might say: "I can't avoid gaining weight. My metabolism is very low. I am not as lucky as other people who can eat and not gain a pound." *She is correct.*

Source: Adapted with permission from *RX Weight Control* (1984; 2:1), Copyright © 1984, Nutritional Management Inc.

Chapter 10

A Primer for Nutritional Counseling

Idamarie Laquatra and Steven J. Danish

INTRODUCTION

Dietary change is often considered a life style change because it impinges on more than simply eating behaviors. Often, the changes required alter a person's life well beyond the diet. For example, just one dietary change—reducing the habitual consumption of soft drinks—might involve:

- changes in shopping habits, to modify the routine purchase of drinks
- development of assertiveness skills, to handle well-meaning friends who expect a continued preference for soft drinks
- time management skills, as other beverages may not be so readily available as a conveniently located soda machine
- knowledge acquisition, concerning the nutritional content of soft drinks vs. other beverages
- some experimentation and emotional considerations, in finding a suitable replacement (S.J. Danish, PhD, et al, unpublished manuscript, 1984).

While any type of change is littered with obstacles, life style changes seem to be the most difficult to achieve. They can also be the most rewarding changes a person can make.

Dietitians spend a considerable amount of time trying to help people make dietary changes, often with dismal results. Frustration and disillusionment occur when practitioners find that people frequently do not follow their advice and continue to engage in behaviors that are contrary to good health.[1] The majority of research on adherence deals with patients' compliance with medical regimens. One third to one half of patients fail to follow fully the medical treatment prescribed by their doctor. Although scant, research on maintenance of dietary changes indicates that adherence to dietary regimens is notoriously low; in fact, it is lower than medical compliance.[2-4] What influences people to change their dietary behaviors, and more importantly, what maintains the changes once they are made? In this chapter, we provide a rationale and foundation for the counseling process. We also present a framework for helping clients set and achieve their dietary goals.

FACTORS THAT INFLUENCE ADHERENCE

The factors that influence adherence have puzzled investigators for years. Numerous variables have been studied in an effort to explain why people do and do not adhere to various types of prescribed treatments. These variables fall into five main categories: (1) the characteristics of the client, (2) the characteristics of the illness, (3) the characteristics of the clinical setting, (4) the quality of the interaction between the expert and the client, and (5) the characteristics of the prescribed regimen.

Characteristics of the Client

The client's age, gender, race, religion, family, ethnic background, and socioeconomic status do not consistently relate to adherence.[5-7] The educational level of the client is closely related to knowledge of the regimen prescribed, but not to adherence.[8] As an example that knowledge does not translate into permanent behavior change, consider the number of obese people who know more about dieting and the caloric content of foods than dietitians yet are not successful in implementing dietary change. Personality characteristics of clients have also been investigated, and these have not been predictive of adherence.[9] Adherence, therefore, cannot be viewed as a dispositional construct. Differences between those who do and those who do not adhere cannot be explained on the basis of specific characteristics of the client.

Characteristics of the Illness

Features of the disease are inconsistent and relatively unimportant determinants of compliance.[10] Although symptom occurrence is a factor in personal readiness to act, it is not sufficient for adherence.[11] A patient who recently suffered a heart attack embodies how the characteristics of the illness are related to adherence. Dietitians frequently see clients who are recovering from heart attacks. Often, these clients are willing to change, especially since the effects of their diets are so readily apparent. Yet as the client begins to feel healthier, enthusiasm about the reduced-calorie, low-fat, low-cholesterol diet wanes, and the client strays further and further from the goals originally set for dietary change. Unless there is near perfect correlation between dietary behavior and symptoms, compliance does not occur. An intermittant relation reinforces noncompliance.

Characteristics of the Clinical Setting

Conflicting evidence exists on the differences in adherence among clients who see private health practitioners *vs.* clients who use public health care facilities. Adherence levels were higher, lower, and no different when the two populations were compared.[12,13] Continuity of care seems to be the key, however, so that when clients are seen by the same health practitioner, adherence rates are higher. Interestingly enough, the amount of time clients must wait in the office before seeing the health professional does affect subsequent adherence to recommendations.[14] Long waits result in less adherence and failure to keep follow-up appointments.

While the continuity of care and waiting times are usually classified as characteristics of the clinical setting, they seem to be more related to the relationship between the expert, in this case, the dietitian, and the client. Following recommendations more closely if they are prescribed by the same health professional denotes trust or a type of bond between the expert and the client. Failure to comply with prescriptions when waiting times are long could be indicative of the client's feeling that the expert has little respect for time constraints, or that the importance of the client to the expert is minimal. Perhaps the conflicting findings related to private vs. public health care are therefore confounded by the quality of the expert-client interaction. If the interaction is good, private vs. public care may not be an issue at all.

The Quality of the Interaction between the Expert and the Client

Carl Rogers[15] described the core conditions of helping as empathy, genuineness, and unconditional positive regard. Empathy is the ability to perceive accurately the meaning and feelings of another person, and to communicate this understanding. Genuineness refers to the degree to which the counselor honestly communicates feelings toward the client. Unconditional positive regard, or warmth, is defined as the warm acceptance of the client without placing conditions on that acceptance. When the core conditions exist, the interaction that results between the expert and the client is of high quality.

The quality of the interaction indirectly influences adherence. Warmth, friendliness, and the ability to attend to concerns and expectations of clients increase their satisfaction with the counseling session.[16] In turn, satisfied clients are more likely to adhere to recommendations than dissatisfied clients. Responding appropriately to clients involves skills that can be learned. The skills require practitioners to listen closely to clients so that they can understand the dimensions of the problem from the client's viewpoint.

Characteristics of the Prescribed Regimen

Complex treatments are associated with lower levels of adherence.[17,18] When the regimen is complex, clients may become overwhelmed before they even begin to make changes, or they may start the regimen only to realize how much it interferes with their everyday schedule. *Contrary to what health practitioners hope, nutrition and health are simply not priorities to everyone,* and complex regimens can be viewed as too bothersome to follow. Additionally, therapeutic regimens are frequently designed with minimal input from the client. The diet is considered appropriate when it treats the problem under consideration; ie, low-calorie diets for the overweight, low-sodium diets for people with elevated blood pressure, exchange diets for people with diabetes. Clients usually assume a passive role in the development of these types of dietary schemes and are expected to assume an active role only when the diets are to be implemented. Clients need to be involved in the development of behavior-change strategies, since they will ultimately use only those procedures that suit their life style.[19]

It is evident that methods for encouraging and maintaining dietary change need to encompass two areas: (1) the interaction between the expert and the client, and (2) the design of the treatment. It is these two areas that form the basis of effective counseling.

WHAT IS COUNSELING?

Danish[20] described counseling as a two-part process: (1) the development of rapport, empathy, and a trusting relationship; and (2) the implementation of behavior-change strategies. The goals of each part differ. The goal of establishing an effective helping relationship is to learn about the nature of the problem from the client's viewpoint and to promote self-exploration by the client. In the second part of counseling, the goal is to help clients design specific, realistic behavior-change strategies that are within their perceived capabilities and that are directed at their problems.

Obviously, the first part of counseling is the foundation for the second. A counselor cannot initiate treatment and expect clients to change their behaviors until an effective relationship is developed and the counselor has a clear understanding of the problem. Attending to the second part of the counseling process without the strong foundation afforded by the first part results in dealing with the problem as being separate from the client, or worse yet, providing solutions to the wrong problems. As shown previously, behavior-change strategies designed under these circumstances are not likely to succeed.

The skills involved in the first part of counseling, developing a helping relationship, are packaged in a training program developed by Danish et al.[21] The program has been tested extensively and results in positive effects on clients, counselors, and the helping interaction. Dietitians and dietetic students have been successfully trained to use the skills in the program. In addition to increasing their repertoire of skills brought into the nutrition counseling session, the program encourages dietitians to develop a realistic philosophy about helping people change.

BUILDING THE FOUNDATION FOR BEHAVIOR CHANGE

Continuing Responses

The skills described as basic to the development of a high-quality interaction between the expert and the client are called "continuing responses." Continuing responses are the behaviors that are embodied in Roger's[15] construct of empathy. Continuing responses are statements that summarize or reflect the content or feeling presented by the client. The purposes of continuing responses are to communicate a willingness to help, to encourage the client to continue talking, and to clarify the problem. These responses help dietitians understand exactly what the problem is from the client's perspective. Listed below are three examples. Sometimes dietitians can summarize, in their own words, the *content* of what the client has said.

Client: I can easily eat low cholesterol, low–saturated fat foods at home, but when I visit my relatives, it's hard. They constantly push rich foods on me. I hate to always say no because I don't want to hurt their feelings, especially when they've prepared something special for me. I usually end up eating foods I don't really want at all.

Continuing Response: You just don't have as much control over your behavior when you're visiting relatives as you do when you're at home.

Client: It's impossible to follow my low-sodium diet now that my kids are living with me. I used to do so well. Now, when I shop and buy them chips or pretzels, I say to myself, "I won't eat this, it's for the kids." Once it's in the house, I end up eating it too.

Continuing Response: Sounds like your determination at the store melts once you bring the salty snacks home.

Client: I've lost 60 pounds since January, mostly by eating just one meal a day. Last week, I passed out in the lab and my boss sent me to the doctor. The doctor told me to eat small meals high in carbohydrates. I started to do that, but if I gain weight I'll just die. This is the first time I've ever been successful in losing weight on my own.

Continuing Response: You're so determined to succeed that you're almost willing to jeopardize your health.

When the client's statements are summarized, the dietitian develops a better understanding of the problem and situation surrounding the problem; when the dietitian focuses on the client's feelings, a better understanding of the client as a person occurs. To design effective behavior-change strategies both understandings are necessary. To understand the client's feelings, the dietitian labels the feeling that is evident in the client's voice or in what the client says. There are two steps involved: First, the dietitian pinpoints the feeling or *affect* expressed by the client. Second, the feeling is put into a complete sentence. Examples of such responses follow:

Client: I can easily eat low-cholesterol, low–saturated fat foods at home, but when I visit my relatives, it's hard. They constantly push rich foods on me. I hate to always say no because I don't want to hurt their feelings, especially when they've prepared something special for me. I usually end up eating foods I don't really want at all.

Continuing Response:

- Step 1: Client is feeling torn.
- Step 2: You feel torn because you want to control your eating, but you also don't want to disappoint your relatives.

Client: It's impossible to follow my low-sodium diet now that my kids are living with me. I used to do so well. Now, when I shop and buy them chips or pretzels, I say to myself, "I won't eat this, it's for the kids." Once it's in the house, I end up eating it too.

Continuing Response:

- Step 1: Client feels guilty.
- Step 2: Sounds as though you feel guilty about eating foods you know are high in sodium.

Client: I've lost 60 pounds since January, mostly by eating just one meal a day. Last week, I passed out in the lab and my boss sent me to the doctor. The doctor told me to eat small meals high in carbohydrates. I started to do that, but

if I gain weight I'll just die. This is the first time I've ever been successful in losing weight on my own.
Continuing Response:

- Step 1: Client is afraid of regaining weight.
- Step 2: You're afraid that eating the small meals will make you regain the weight you worked so hard to lose.

Continuing responses may feel uncomfortable to use for a number of reasons. First, previous training in dietetics has conditioned dietitians to use what the clients say to vault into a discussion of the diet. The approach we are describing forces the health practitioner to listen and respond to the client's statements rather than interjecting information and advice. This approach results in greater client satisfaction with the nutrition counseling session, and improved understanding of the dietary problem.

Another reason for the discomfort dietitians may feel when using continuing responses is the decreased amount of talking they ultimately do when using these skills. During workshops we[22] have conducted to teach this method, dietitians frequently say that they feel most comfortable when they are in control and doing most of the talking during a dietary counseling session. Of interest are the results of a study[23] that showed that counselors who talked most of the time during a counseling session were seen as unhelpful, inattentive, and nonunderstanding.

Finally, sometimes the hesitation to use the counseling skills is based on the fear that the wrong thing may be said. It is important to note that there are no right or wrong continuing responses. If the response made is not on target, the client will clarify. Recall that clarification is one of the purposes of using continuing responses. As with the development of any skill, practice smooths the rough edges and makes the skills come more naturally.

The following are thought questions:

- What is a continuing response?
- When do you think a continuing response would be appropriate?
- What type of continuing response would you make to the following clients?

Client: I really want to lose weight, but I just can't seem to do it on a permanent basis. I've tried a million diets, and I do lose weight, but I always go back to my old habits and regain what I lost plus more. I'm so tired of being fat.

Client: I dread the thought of having to eat out now that I have diabetes. How will I ever be able to choose what to eat? Restaurants don't prepare special foods for diabetics.

Client: The doctor says I have high blood pressure and that I need to watch my sodium intake. I don't feel sick at all, so why do I have to suffer with no salt?

Taking More Control: Leading Responses

"Leading responses" shift the responsibility for the direction of the counseling session to the dietitian, who begins the process of trying to resolve the dietary problem. Dietitians most frequently use two leading responses: (1) questions, and (2) advice. *Questions* are responses that seek to gather new information. There are three types of questions: (1) open, (2) closed, and (3) "why" questions. Open questions begin with the words "what" or "how," and usually cannot be answered with "yes," "no," or one or two words. Statements such as "tell me more about it" are considered open because they allow the client to explore freely. Closed questions can be answered with "yes," "no," or one or two words. They often begin with the following words: is, are, was, were, have, had, do, does, and did. Open questions are preferred to closed questions; however, it is recognized that there are times when closed questions are necessary. Unfortunately, dietitians, despite knowing better, tend to overuse questions and rely on them heavily during counseling sessions.[24,25] Note the difference between the open and closed questions below:

Closed question: Were you able to stick to your diet this week?
Open question: How did your diet go this week?
Closed question: Do you understand?
Open question: What questions do you have?

Recall that questions are used to gather *new* information. An error often made is asking a question when the answer is already known. Before asking a question, dietitians should first ask the question to themselves and see if they know the answer. If they do, they should rephrase the question into a continuing response. If this is done, the interaction will be both more effective and less time-consuming.

The last type of question is a "why" question. "Why" questions should be avoided because they tend to put clients on the defensive. When dietitians ask "Why?," clients may feel they need to come up with an excuse. Worse still, the "why" question will not result in any additional information when the answer is "I don't know."

The following are thought questions:

- What is the purpose of asking questions?
- Think of your last counseling session. How often did you ask a question when you already knew the answer?

Try to formulate an open question for the following client statements. Then change the questions into continuing responses.

Client: This is the fourth time I've been admitted this year with my blood sugar out of control. You don't have to explain the exchange system to me. I know the diabetic diet inside and out. But knowing it and following it are two different things. Have you ever tried to follow a specific eating pattern each day? It's not easy, I can tell you that.

Client: Things seem so easy when we plan them in your office. Unfortunately, when I'm alone and I start thinking about food, I lose my determination, and the long-term benefit of gaining weight or eating better seems to disappear. All I can think about is how fat I will feel if I eat.

Client: Watching the amount of saturated fat I eat is going to be difficult. I travel quite a bit and eat out most of the time. When I'm home, the easiest thing to do is to buy prepared food rather than making it myself.

Another leading response with which dietitians are familiar is advice. *Advice* is a response that provides a possible solution to a problem. Good advice may be about thoughts or acts not yet tried by the client. It is also specific and realistic. Advice should not be given until the dietitian has a very clear idea about what the problem is, what solutions have already been tried, and what solutions should be tried. If advice is given too quickly, without exploration into alternatives previously tried and without an understanding of the problem, the client will counter the advice with "Yes, but . . . ."

Client: I know I need to decrease the amount of soda I drink during the day, but I get so thirsty.

Advice: You might want to try iced tea to quench your thirst.

Client: Yes, but I like the carbonation in the soda.

Advice: Maybe you could switch to diet soda.

Client: Yes, but the diet sodas just don't taste as good to me.

Obviously, the dietitian needs to stop giving advice until there is an understanding of both the problem and the person with the problem. The responses we have described are not inclusive. Altogether, seven responses have been identified in the Helping Skills I Program[21] as representing the domain of possible responses in a helping interaction. These responses serve as the tools and foundation for building a helping relationship. However, for one to help another it is our belief that a problem-solving, behavior-change orientation must be established and implemented. The issue becomes, then, how do you use these responses to facilitate behavior change? To answer this question the health professional must develop a framework for understanding how and why change occurs.

A FRAMEWORK FOR BEHAVIORAL CHANGE

All too often, clients focus on the problems they are experiencing rather than on the positive outcomes they seek. Counselors, in turn, tend to dwell on these problems and inadequacies. Instead, we believe the focus should be on encouraging personal development and individual strengths. The message communicated is that clients must take an active role in changing their lives and that counselors should teach clients to "take the reins" in their lives.

While the idea of taking an active role in one's life can be easily understood and accepted, it is not so easily accomplished. Many roadblocks stand in the way. Often new skills must be learned, new information acquired, or new risks taken. But these roadblocks are not insurmountable, although they often seem so. Change occurs when people realize that the elimination of roadblocks is under their control, at least in many instances. When clients, for instance, learn how to set goals, they learn that they can approach their life in an active way. This produces a sense of self-confidence and control. They also learn that the choices they make and the plans they carry out make a difference. Future problems can be handled in a more carefully planned, goal-oriented way. Indeed, such a self-directed person plans ahead to prevent future problems. Self-development then becomes a constant, active process instead of a process of reaction to a problem.

This framework is embodied in the second training program, *Helping Skills II: Life Development Intervention.*[26] Six skills are taught: (1) goal assessment, (2) knowledge acquisition, (3) decision making, (4) risk assessment, (5) creating social support, and (6) skill development. The program has generic application to the training of all helping professionals. It has been used with dietitians on numerous occasions.[22] It is predicated on the assumption that dietitians work with *people* who have dietary problems, not just with dietary problems.

Goal Setting: An Essential First Step

A fundamental skill that forms the foundation on which all of the other skills in the program are based is "goal assessment." Through goal assessment, counselors help clients attain goals by breaking down complex behavior changes into a series of small, successive steps. This positive goal orientation focuses on the strengths of the client. Because the client has the freedom to decide what the goals are and is active in the process of setting them, commitment to change is fostered. There are four parts to goal assessment: (1) goal identification, (2) goal importance assessment, (3) goal roadblock analysis, and (4) goal attainment. Appendix 10–A is a guide for the goal assessment process, which we will now explain.

Goal Identification

The first step in goal assessment is goal identification. Goal identification involves changing the problem into a positive, specific goal. Once health professionals have a clear indication of what the client's problem is through use of continuing responses, they can help clients identify a goal by encouraging them to verbalize what they would like to do about the problem. Goals must be positive, specific, and under the client's control. An example of a problem and how to change it into an appropriate goal follows. Suppose the client is overweight and one problem in particular is heavy overeating at night, after dinner. A goal that is *not* a positively stated goal would be "I would like to avoid night eating."

When goals are not positively stated, the focus is on the negative, and much energy is wasted trying not to do something. Setting a negative goal almost always results in a negative outcome. Negative goals bring to mind the "allowed" and "avoid" dietary lists available at most hospitals and clinics. When clients see how many items they must avoid, they feel defeated before starting, even if they rarely eat the foods on the "avoid" list.

The goal must also be behaviorally stated. "I would like to control my night eating" does not include specific behaviors that indicate exactly what the client will do to achieve the goal. It is unclear what "control my night eating" means. The more behaviorally oriented the goal, the more likely it is that the goal will be achieved. It is the dietitian's task to help the client delineate exactly what will be done to achieve the goal. A rule of thumb when developing behaviorally stated goals is to answer the questions: What is the action to be taken? How many times will the action occur? When will the action occur? Under what conditions will the action take place?

Suppose the client decides that controlling night eating means eating a 300-calorie snack. Eating the 300-calorie snack, then, becomes the action to be taken. The client believes that the snack can be eaten (how many times) four evenings during the following week, (when) at 9 PM, (under what conditions) when he or she experiences hunger. The client's goal has therefore been transformed to something more tangible: "Four evenings during the next week, I will eat a 300-calorie snack at 9 PM."

Beware of goals that are not under the client's control. "I want my husband/wife to stop buying cookies" is a goal for someone else, not the client. The likelihood of achieving such a goal is slim.

Goal Importance Assessment

The second step of the goal assessment process is goal importance assessment. Dietitians need to ask, "To whom is the goal most important?" If the goal is more important to the physician or dietitian than it is to the client, the chances of the client achieving the goal are severely limited. Making dietary changes involves commitment and energy.

Unimportant goals are rarely, if ever, reached. Dietary goals often contain the word "should" or "ought to": "I should watch my weight"; "I really ought to start exercising." "Should" or "ought to" goals reveal a different level of commitment than goals clients want to achieve. When helping clients set goals, changing a "should" to a "want" will probably increase the chance of success.

Assessing the importance of the goal sets the responsibility for achieving the goal squarely on the shoulders of clients. Dietitians often express frustration and guilt when clients do not change. It is too often forgotten that the client has the ultimate responsibility for changing.

Goal Roadblock Analysis

The third part of goal assessment is the analysis of the obstacles or roadblocks that hamper goal achievement. Sometimes no obstacle stands in the way of goal achievement, and dietitians can immediately help clients develop steps for reaching their goals as soon as a goal is identified. At other times, one or a combination of the following roadblocks stand in the way: lack of knowledge, lack of skills, inability to take risks, and lack of social support.

A lack of knowledge means that clients are missing some information necessary to achieve the goal. Suppose the client who wanted to eat a 300-calorie snack did not know the caloric content of foods. The obstacle would therefore be a lack of knowledge.

A lack of skills can refer to either physical or mental skills. One can identify the roadblock as a skill deficiency when the client does not know *"how to."* For instance, the client may not know how to make a 300-calorie snack filling or enjoyable, and would need help in learning how to plan the snacks that could be eaten before achieving the goal. Other skills clients might need to be taught are becoming more assertive, making better decisions, learning to talk to oneself positively, and gaining self-control.

If the obstacle is an inability to take a risk, the client is *afraid* of something: afraid to fail because of past attempts at controlling caloric intake or afraid to hurt another's feelings by turning down an invitation for food from a friend. Helping clients assess the real risks involved gives them more power over the situation. If after assessing the risks and finding that the costs outweigh the benefits of achieving the goal, clients may decide to abandon the goal. Taking risks involves helping clients assess the risks and then to increase the benefits of an action and reduce the costs.

Another obstacle often encountered in dietary change is a lack of social support. Perhaps the client's spouse is overweight or underweight and is sabotaging efforts by being unsupportive. Client's may need help in finding other types of support or in soliciting support from friends.

When helping clients make dietary changes, the obstacle is frequently more than just a lack of knowledge. However, research[27] on counseling strategies used by nutritionists revealed that few practitioners use strategies other than information giving. The information-giving strategy is based on two tenuous assumptions: (1) if enough facts are communicated, clients will know what to do and behavior change will occur; and (2) if clients recognize that certain practices endanger their health, their behaviors will change.[1] Most of the time, these assumptions are simply not true.

It is important to recognize that giving information is important, but only when there is a lack of knowledge that interferes with clients achieving their goals. Usually, however, lack of information may be only one of the obstacles preventing behavior change. Also, even when the obstacle is a lack of knowledge, the amount of information given needs to be carefully considered. Patient education studies[28] have shown that within 5 minutes, patients forget half the information presented to them. Also, the more information given, the more is forgotten.[28]

If other obstacles inhibit the achievement of dietary change, why do dietitians rely on information giving as the primary counseling strategy? Most of the education dietitians receive throughout college is in the form of lectures. This type of learning mode is one that is most familiar, and it extends into the counseling situation. Additionally, dietitians rarely receive specific training in other behavior-change strategies, although efforts have been made to alter the situation.[29,30] More detail on how to help clients attain knowledge, develop skills, assess risks, and find support is given in the Danish and D'Augelli program.[26]

Goal Attainment

If no obstacle stands in the way, or once obstacles have been hurdled, dietitians can help clients specify exactly what steps they plan to take to achieve their goal. In Appendix 10–B, a sample plan is presented.

Once clients achieve the first goal, other goals can be set. Many times there are a number of small goals that must be achieved to reach an overall goal. For example, a person with a weight problem may set goals for controlling snacking behavior, reducing portion number and portion size, eating at social events, and dealing with boredom or anxiety.

Putting the Skills into Practice

One of the major reservations health professionals have against using the types of skills discussed in this chapter is lack of time. Any new skill requires an initial time investment until it "fits"; that is, until using the skill is a natural part of counseling. Also, although time constraints are a very real issue, it is time for health professionals to reassess their roles. We have so much more to offer beyond giving information.

Anyone can give information, but not everyone can work with people to effect dietary change. How much time is wasted giving people information they already know or cannot easily digest? Little research has been completed on the dietitian's use of time, but one study[31] in particular sheds light on the perspective of practitioners. In the study, timesaving tools, such as a 24-hour recall given before the client met with the dietitian, were introduced so that dietitians could have more time to spend with the client to work out a dietary strategy rather than asking routine questions. Much to the authors' surprise, the timesaving tool simply decreased total instruction time. The client did not realize the benefit of the timesaving device, because time saved was not transformed into more services for the clients. Clearly, the view of what constitutes nutrition counseling needs to be broadened. The following thought questions are presented with the hope that they will encourage dietitians to evaluate more critically their counseling sessions:

- During the counseling session, who did most of the talking?
- How did the client respond to the continuing responses you used?
- Could you have changed any of the closed questions to open questions?
- Did the client answer with "Yes, but" when you gave advice?
- What was the client's problem?
- What was (were) the roadblock(s)?
- Did you give information selectively or not at all if the obstacle to goal achievement was not lack of knowledge?
- What will the client do before returning for the next session?
- Does the client have a clear idea how to accomplish the goal set during the session?

It is not easy to change behaviors, especially dietary behaviors. It is also not a very fast process. Helping clients set and achieve goals is difficult, yet very rewarding. If skills are used that encourage clients to make and maintain change, dietitians will truly be fulfilling their roles as dietary change agents.

REFERENCES

1. Henderson JB, Hall SM, Lipton HL: Changing self-destructive behaviors, in Stone GC, Cohen F, Adler NE, et al (eds): *Health Psychology: A Handbook.* San Francisco,: Jossey-Bass Publishers, 1979, pp 141–160.

2. Cooper CA, DeLooy AE: The efficacy of energy-reduced diets in the treatment of obesity by dietitians. *Proc Nut Soc* 1978; 38:7A. Abstracted.

3. Holland WM: The diabetes supplement of the national health survey. *J Am Diet Assoc* 1968; 52:387–390.

4. West KM: Diet and diabetes. *Postgrad Med* 1976; 60:209–216.

5. Davis MS: Variations in patients' compliance with doctors' advice: An empirical analysis of patterns of communication. *Am J Public Health* 1968, 58:274–288.

6. Francis V, Korsch BM, Morris MJ: Gaps in doctor-patient communication: Patients' response to medical advice. *N Eng J Med* 1969; 280:535–540.

7. Morse W, Sims LS, Guthrie HA: Mothers' compliance with physicians' recommendations on infant feeding. *J Am Diet Assoc* 1979; 75:140–148.

8. Becker MH, Drachman RH, Kirscht JP: Predicting mothers' compliance with pediatric medical regimens. *J Pediat* 1972; 81:843–854.

9. Davidson P: Therapeutic compliance. *Canadian Psychological Review* 1976; 17:247–259.

10. Haynes RB: Determinants of compliance: The disease and mechanics of treatment, in Haynes RB, Taylor DW, Sackett DL (eds): *Compliance in Health Care*. Baltimore, The Johns Hopkins University Press, 1979, pp 49–62.

11. Kirscht JP, Rosenstock IM: Patients' problems in following recommendations of health experts, Stone GC, Cohen F, Adler NE, et al (eds): *Health Psychology: A Handbook*. San Francisco, Jossey-Bass Publishers, 1979, pp 189–215.

12. Charney E, Bynum R, Eldredge D, et al: How well do patients take oral penicillin? A collaborative study in private practice. *Pediatrics* 1967; 40:188–195.

13. Weintraub M, Au WYW, Lasagna L: Compliance as a determinant of serum digoxin concentration. *JAMA* 1973; 224:481–485.

14. Dunbar J: Adhering to medical advice: A review. *International Journal of Mental Health* 1980; 9:70–87.

15. Rogers CR: A theory of therapy, personality and interpersonal relationships, as developed in the client-centered framework, in Koch S (ed): in *Psychology: A Study of Science*. New York, McGraw-Hill Book Co, 1959, vol 3, pp 184–256.

16. Korsch BM, Gozzi EK, Francis V: Gaps in doctor-patient communication: I. Doctor-patient interaction and patient satisfaction. *Pediatrics* 1968; 42:855–871.

17. Hulka BS: Patient-clinician interactions and compliance, in Haynes RB, Taylor DW, Sackett DL (eds): *Compliance in Health Care*. Baltimore, The Johns Hopkins University Press, 1979, pp 63–77.

18. Stimson GV: Obeying doctor's orders: A view from the other side. *Soc Sci Med* 1974; 97:97–104.

19. Best JA, Bloch M: Compliance in the control of cigarette smoking, in Haynes RB, Taylor DW, Sackett DL (eds): *Compliance in Health Care*. Baltimore, The Johns Hopkins University Press, 1979, pp 202–222.

20. Danish SJ: Developing helping relationships in dietetic counseling. *J Am Diet Assoc* 1975; 67:107–110.

21. Danish SJ, D'Augelli AR, Hauer AL: *Helping Skills: A Basic Training Program*, ed 2. New York, Human Sciences Press, 1980.

22. Danish SJ, Lang D, Smiciklas-Wright H, et al: Nutrition counseling skills: Continuing education for the dietitian. *Topics in Clinical Nutrition* 1968; 1:25–32.

23. Kleinke CL, Tully TB: Influence of talking level on perceptions of counselors. *Journal of Counseling Psychology* 1979; 26:23–29.

24. Danish SJ, Ginsberg MR, Terrell A, et al: The anatomy of a dietary counseling interview. *J Am Diet Assoc* 1979; 75:626–630.

25. Laquatra I: *Helping Skills for WIC Nutrition Education Counselors*, dissertation. University Park, The Pennsylvania State University, 1983.

26. Danish SJ, D'Augelli AR: *Helping Skills II: Life Development Intervention*. New York, Human Sciences Press, 1983.

27. Glanz K: Strategies for nutrition counseling. *J Am Diet Assoc* 1979; 74:431–437.

28. Green LW: Educational strategies to improve compliance with therapeutic and preventive regimens: The recent evidence, in Haynes RB, Taylor DW, Sackett DL (eds): *Compliance in Health Care*. Baltimore, The Johns Hopkins University Press, 1979, pp 157–173.

29. American Heart Association. Heart to Heart: Nutrition Counseling for the Reduction of Cardiovascular Disease Risk Factors, Raab C, Tillotson JL (ed). US Department of Health and Human Services, Public Health Service, National Institutes of Health. NIH Publication No. 83–1528.

30. Snetselaar LG: *Nutrition Counseling Skills: Assessment, Treatment, and Evaluation*. Rockville, Md, Aspen Publishers Inc., 1983.

31. Pichert JW, Hanson SL, Pechmann CA: Modifying dietitians' use of patient time. *The Diabetes Educator*, Spring 1984, pp 43–46, 72.

Appendix 10-A

Goal Assessment Guide

I. Goal Assessment
   A. Describe the client's goal in positive, behavioral terms.

   _____

   _____

   B. To whom is the goal most important?

   _____client

   _____friend

   _____family

   _____someone else; if so, whom? _____

   C. Is the goal based on:

   _____realistic expectations

   _____wishful thinking

   _____other factors; if so, describe _____

   _____

   D. How will attaining this goal affect the client's life?   _____

   _____

   E. Do you think the client can achieve this goal?

   _____   yes   _____   no

   F. What are the realistic problems the client will face in trying to achieve this
      goal?

   _____

   _____

Appendix 10-A *continued*

G. Goal Roadblock Analysis. What is your understanding of the barriers the client must overcome to achieve this goal?

_____Knowledge roadblock. Describe. _____

_____

What does the client need to know? _____

_____

_____Skill roadblock. Describe. _____

_____

What skills does the client need? _____

_____

_____Risk-taking roadblock. Describe _____

_____

What risks does the client have to take? _____

_____

_____Social support roadblock. Describe. _____

_____

What social supports does the client need? _____

_____

_____Some combination of knowledge, skills, risk-taking, and social support.

Describe. _____

_____

II. Goal Attainment

A. Identify the steps using the Goal Ladder. Are the steps small and manageable? If not, divide the most complex step. More than ten steps is possible.

GOAL LADDER

Goal: _____

_____

Step   Time Frame (in no. of weeks or by date)

10 _____

9 _____

8 _____

7 _____

Appendix 10-A *continued*

6 _____

5 _____

4 _____

3 _____

2 _____

1 _____

B.   With what step(s), if any, is the client likely to have trouble? _____

_____

What kind of help will assist the client to overcome this trouble? _____

_____

Who can offer this assistance? _____

_____

Source: Adapted from *Goal Setting for Athletic Excellence* by Steven J Danish, unpublished manuscript.

Appendix 10-B

Goal Attainment

GOAL LADDER

GOAL: Four evenings during the next week, I will eat a 300-calorie snack at 9 PM

STEP	TIME FRAME
7. I will keep a journal of the snack I ate and the days I am able to do it.	
6. After finishing the snack and cleaning up, I will reward myself by listening to my favorite music for one-half hour.	
5. I will eat my snack at the dining room table.	
4. At 9 PM on the specified nights, I will set aside at least 15 minutes to enjoy my snack.	
3. Right after dinner, I will make my 9 PM snack and put it in the refrigerator.	Monday, April 20 Tuesday, April 21 Wednesday, April 22 Thursday, April 23
2. I will shop for the food to make the snacks.	Monday, April 20
1. I will plan four snacks that total 300 calories and choose the four nights to have the snacks.	Sunday, April 19

Chapter 11

Behavior Modification: The State of the Art

Lisa Buckmaster and Kelly D. Brownell

How useful is behavior modification? No single approach, including behavior modification, can be embraced as a guaranteed remedy for obesity. The complexity of this disorder argues against a simple model for its etiology and treatment. Current thought favors a biobehavioral model that involves the interaction of genetics, physiology, psychology, and cultural factors. Treatment is guided by a knowledge of metabolic and nutritional factors, with a strong emphasis on behavior change. This focus on behavior is grounded in social learning theory from which behavior modification is derived.

Behavior modification does show the most consistent positive results of any approach to weight loss. It is easy to conclude, therefore, that behavior modification is the treatment of choice for all people. This is not realistic, of course, because different people respond to different approaches. In this context, we wish to place behavior modification in perspective and to define its role in the world of weight-loss approaches.

We begin by introducing the reader to a biobehavioral model of obesity. After reviewing the changes in behavioral programs over the last two decades, we discuss the effectiveness of behavioral approaches and describe what we believe to be a comprehensive program for treating obesity. We then move to common clinical concerns including the maintenance of weight loss, methods for increasing weight loss, and attrition.

THE ART OF CHOOSING THE RIGHT TREATMENT

The clinician is faced with the choice of either (1) providing the intervention that works for the most people, or (2) matching a specific treatment to the person's needs. Science has yet to provide guidelines for matching treatments to persons. Consequently, inquiry has focused on the superiority of one treatment over another when treating *groups* of patients. In this contest, behavior modification is the winner, at least for treating the mildly obese. New physiologic theories are being advanced that may aid in the understanding of the etiology and treatment of moderate and severe obesity.

HOW PHYSIOLOGY MIGHT INFLUENCE THE CHOICE OF TREATMENT

Current physiologic theories may account for differences among humans in their ability to lose weight. Knowledge of these factors helps us appreciate the complexity of the problem and some of the interindividual variability so common in clinical settings.

The Biobehavioral Model

Physiologic factors may contribute a great part of the variance in explaining why some people are overweight, whether they can lose weight on conventional diets, and whether they can sustain weight loss once it occurs. For example, one study[1] from Sweden reported that 81% of the variance in weight loss in obese women could be explained by a combination of fat cell size and resting metabolic rate. The following theories shed light on the interplay between the physiology and the psychology of obesity.

Set Point Theory

Bennett and Gurin[2] and Keesey[3] postulated that humans, like animals, have a "set point" at which weight is held within a particular range. The amount of fat one carries is automatically regulated, and some people have more fat than others for genetic reasons.[4] The set point mechanism, which may receive information from fat cells, enzymes, hormones, etc, strives to maintain a given amount of weight, fat, lean body mass, or a related factor. Obesity results from a homeostatic process that acts to maintain body weight and fat at a high level. Attempts to lose weight are opposed by strong biologic processes. An obese person going on a diet to overpower the set point, or a thin person who overeats to gain weight, fights a difficult battle. Numerous studies[5] show a remarkable tenacity in human physiology to maintain a fairly constant weight range and a preordained amount of fat.

The set point theory has not been proven, so these ideas are speculative. Since there are many factors that *may* change the set point, the utility of the theory can be questioned. However, the notion that the body may regulate weight is helpful in approaching patients who consistently remain in specific weight ranges.

Fat Cell Theory

The amount of fat a person has is determined by the number and size of their fat cells. Enlarged fat cells are said to be *hypertrophic*, while *hyperplasticity* refers to an increased number of fat cells. Many people have both hypertrophic and hyperplastic obesity. It is possible to increase the number of fat cells after existing fat cells have reached a maximum size. With weight loss, cells reduce in size, but no cells are lost.[6]

There is a possibility that humans strive to achieve a specific fat cell size, and efforts to decrease the size below average result in lipid depletion. The cells may then actuate a physiologic mechanism to replenish the energy stores. The fat cell theory maintains that weight loss beyond the point at which cells reach normal size will be met with great resistance.

Here is where the set point and fat cell theories may merge. Set point may be determined by the size of fat cells, and the weight at which this occurs may depend on the number of cells. For example, consider two men each weighing 250 lb, one with a normal number of fat cells, which are enlarged, the other with an excessive number of fat cells, which are normal sized. For the hypertrophically obese man, weight loss and maintenance are possible since he can reduce his fat cell size and still sustain adequate lipid volume. However, the hyperplastic man already has normal-sized fat cells, and weight loss results in adipose cell depletion to below normal levels. Even if extraordinary motivation enables the hyperplastic man to overcome his set point, he will be physiologically prone to regain the weight later.

Consequently, from a treatment standpoint, it would be meaningful to reach the overweight patient before hyperplasticity sets in. Since biopsies are required to determine cellularity, this notion is currently of more theoretical than practical significance. This may change as research continues.

Weight Cycling Theory

Researchers have begun to study the "yo-yo" pattern in which weight is lost and regained many times. Recent findings point to an increased food efficiency in the organism, creating a "dieting induced obesity."[7]

The weight cycling theory hypothesizes that food efficiency increases as weight is lost, regained, and lost. This increased efficiency is manifested in each successive diet in slower losses, more rapid regains with each loss, and decreased resting metabolic rate. In essence, preliminary animal and human studies indicate that as one diets, the body compensates by losing weight more slowly with each diet, and less time is required to regain the weight once dieting ceases. Thus, with a decreased metabolic rate, the same body weight is maintained on fewer calories than was needed in predieting days. It is unknown whether prolonged weight maintenance and exercise produce an upward adjustment of the resting metabolic rate and a decrease in food efficiency in formerly obese patients.

Treatment Implications

What can be gleaned from these physiologic theories? The likelihood that obesity is a result of regulated, homeostatic processes that act to maintain body weight and body fat at a constant level, and that attempts to lower them are opposed by powerful biologic processes is relevant to the treatment of obesity. Experimental studies and clinical experience show how difficult it is to help patients lose weight and maintain their weight losses. These theories provide a rationale for this difficulty. The practitioner should be cognizant of these theories when approaching patients who do not lose weight on restricted intake or who readily regain when they resume or exceed normative caloric regimes.

Theoretically, the set point can be reset over prolonged periods of exposure to overeating of foods high in fat, variety, and sweetness,[5] and by exercise.[3] It may be helpful to focus on modifying the patient's diet composition to decrease high-fat and sweet food items. Increased activity would also be important. In keeping with the fat cell theory, early intervention would be preferable to waiting for hyperplasticity to occur, when treatment would produce markedly less effect. If the weight cycling theory is correct, it will be of utmost importance to make sure that the person's motivation is high before embarking on treatment. Otherwise, to expose the patient to repeated dieting may only make weight loss more difficult in the future.

CLASSIFYING OBESE PATIENTS

Classification schemes arose from the realization that obese patients differ in their response to treatment, cellular pathology, risk for disease, and long-term prognosis.[8] As more studies are done, it may be increasingly possible to classify obese people according to physiologic and/or psychologic variables. For now, classification schemes are based mainly on weight. Garrow[9] first proposed four weight classifications. Stunkard[8] later proposed three levels of obesity, based on severity, each with different implications for treatment. Table 11–1 illustrates this classification scheme.

The divisions in this scheme are somewhat arbitrary. As we learn more from physiologic research, patients may be labeled according to their resting metabolic rate, size and number of fat cells, or any combination of factors that aid in isolating appropriate treatment strategies.

Table 11-1 A Classification of Obesity Together with Prevalence, Pathology, Complications, Anatomy, and Treatment of the Three Types

Type	Classification of Obesity		
	Mild	Moderate	Severe
Percentage overweight	20–40%	41–100%	> 100%
Prevalence (among obese women)	90.5%	9.0%	0.5
Pathology	Hypertrophic	Hypertrophic, hyperplastic	Hypertrophic, hyperplastic
Complications	Uncertain	Conditional	Severe
Treatment	Behavior therapy (lay)	Diet and behavior therapy (medical)	Surgical

Source: Reprinted from *Eating and Its Disorders* (p 158) by A Stunkard and E Stellar (Eds) with permission of Raven Press, © 1984.

We believe that a comprehensive behavioral program that includes nutrition and exercise is important for *all* patients. For people less than 30% to 40% overweight, this program may stand alone. For heavier people, this approach may need to be combined with more aggressive approaches to weight loss.

BEHAVIOR MODIFICATION: A BRIEF HISTORICAL OVERVIEW

The origins of the use of behavior modification in treating obesity began with Ferster et al[10] in 1962. Self-monitoring and stimulus control were the mainstays of early behavioral programs and continue to be the backbone of many behavioral programs. An example of self-monitoring would be having the client keep daily records of calories and amount eaten. These records would then be checked by professionals to assess accuracy and detect problem areas. Stimulus control techniques typically include, but are not limited to, sitting in only one place when eating, not engaging in other activities while eating (eg, reading, watching television, cooking), eating from smaller plates, and storing food out of sight. The purpose of these techniques is to create patients' awareness of their intake and eating habits, and to structure their environment to minimize eating cues that might lead to excessive eating. Over time, techniques such as assertion training, relaxation, and token reward systems were added and then removed with little effect on weight loss.

Programs remained remarkably similar in nature and outcome for many years. A review[11] of behavioral studies up to 1976 found average post-treatment losses of 11.5 lb in programs of 8 to 12 weeks. A 1980 review[12] found average losses of 10.4 lb, with studies preceding 1974 showing a mean loss of 8.5 lb, and a loss of 9.4 lb in studies after 1978. These are quite stable results considering differences among studies in subject characteristics, cost, therapist training, and other factors that might influence outcome. It should be noted, however, that there is large variability among subjects' weight loss, a typical range of mean loss being from 2.4 to 18.9 lb in any given group.[12]

Brownell and Wadden[13] found that the only substantial change in the nature of the studies and outcome from 1974 to 1978 was the duration of follow-up, which increased from 15.5 weeks to 30.3 weeks. With the recalcitrant nature of obesity, the need for longer follow-up became a growing clinical concern. Along with longer-term follow-up measures, the average length of treatment increased from 8.5 to 9.4 weeks from 1974 to 1978, a trend that continues in more recent studies.

To summarize the first generation of behavioral studies, average weight losses were approximately 1 lb per week in programs lasting 8 to 9 weeks. These losses were maintained at follow-up. However, variability was usually greater at follow-up than after treatment, as some patients continued to lose large amounts while others regained.[14] These results are relevant mainly to subjects who are mildly overweight or who are the best responders to the behavioral approach. Given these results, findings from the second generation of behavioral studies are more impressive.

BEHAVIOR MODIFICATION TODAY

While early behavior modification consisted primarily of self-monitoring and stimulus control, today's behavior modification has a much broader scope. Emphasis on exercise has increased, as it aids in the maintenance of weight loss.[15] Social support and cognitive training seem to be clinically important, but there are only preliminary data showing that their inclusion augments effectiveness.

Table 11–2 shows the results of the second generation of behavioral studies with the more comprehensive approach. Along with a substantial increase in average weight loss from the 1984 studies (15.4 lb), as compared with 8.5 lb and 9.4 lb in the 1974 and 1978 studies, respectively, duration of treatment also increased. The question arises as to whether the greater weight loss resulted from better programs or simply from longer duration of treatment. Since the mean weight loss per week has not increased, longer treatment seems to be responsible for the better results.

Table 11-2 Summary of Data from Controlled Trials of Behavior Therapy Completed Before and During 1974 and During 1978 and 1984

	1974	1978	1984
Sample Size	53.1	54.0	71.3
Initial weight (lb)	163.0	194.0	197.0
Initial % overweight	49.4	48.6	48.1
Length of treatment (weeks)	8.4	10.5	13.2
Weight loss (lb)	8.5	9.4	15.4
Loss per week (lb)	1.2	0.9	1.2
Attrition (%)	11.4	12.9	10.6
Length of follow-up (weeks)	15.5	30.3	58.4
Loss at follow-up (lb)	8.9	9.1	9.8

NOTE: All values are means across studies.

Source: Reprinted from *Handbook of Eating Disorders: Physiology, Psychology, and Treatment of Obesity, Anorexia, and Bulimia* (p 182) by K Brownell and J Foreyt (Eds) with permission of Basic Books Inc, © 1986.

However, it is not known whether patients in earlier programs would have sustained the same total weight loss. The issues dieters confront in the course of treatment are different early and late in the programs. Cognitive techniques may be useful in the prevention of relapse and are, therefore, more suitable in later stages of therapy.[16] The added techniques may have the strongest influence during the maintenance phase of treatment.

Two salient differences exist between first and second generation studies. Mean weight loss increased (from 8.9 lb in 1974 to 15.4 lb in 1984), and follow-up is longer (58.4 weeks in 1984 *v* 15.5 weeks and 30.3 weeks in 1974 and 1978). Average follow-up weight loss has risen with longer follow-up.

Caution must be exercised when drawing conclusions from this summary. While the average weight loss during treatment is greater now, the percentage of initial weight loss maintained has declined somewhat. Regain at post-treatment follow-up in 1978 was only 0.3 lb. In 1984, subjects regained 5.6 lb. This could be attributable to passage of time, ie, if subjects in the first generation studies had been followed-up at 58.4 weeks, the weight regain might have been substantially different. Despite the fact that final weight loss at follow-up is slightly greater today, the course of weight fluctuation seems to be different. If greater initial losses followed by some regain has negative physiologic or psychologic effects, higher weight loss at follow-up may need to be examined from a different perspective. We can only speculate; this issue deserves further investigation.

THE EFFECTIVENESS OF BEHAVIORAL APPROACHES

The current comprehensive version of behavior modification results in a 1.0- to 1.5-lb loss per week during treatment. Treatment of more than 12 weeks indicates substantial weight losses. Perri and colleagues[14] reported an 18.9-lb average reduction in a 15-week program. Brownell and Stunkard[17] reported an 18.2-lb loss in 16 weeks, and Craighead et al[18] reported a 23.9-lb loss in a 24-week program. Jeffery and associates[11] reported losses of 21.9 lb, 26.3 lb, and 28.5 lb in 15- and 16-week programs using financial contracts in addition to the behavioral program. In a 25-week program, Wadden and Stunkard[19] showed a 31-lb loss.

These increased losses are quite impressive when contrasted with other approaches or with earlier behavioral programs. A 20- to 25-lb loss is the total loss needed for mildly overweight patients. Thus, behavior therapy may stand alone as the treatment for mildly obese patients. Notably, the long-term maintenance stands out when compared with the results from other approaches.[12] Two of the strengths of behavior therapy may be (1) its potential for long-term effects, and (2) its relatively low attrition rate. This suggests the possibility of combining behavior modification with other approaches to increase weight loss, (such as very-low-calorie diets [VLCD]) that may produce more dramatic losses.[13]

THE STATE OF THE ART: A COMPREHENSIVE MODEL FOR MANAGING OBESITY

In early behavior modification studies, the focus was on techniques directed solely at eating behavior, such as self-monitoring, stimulus control, slowing eating, and others. These techniques are only one part of what constitutes today's behavioral treatment for obesity. Behavior modification deals with all behaviors that affect weight loss, gain, and maintenance. The same principles that can be applied to eating (shaping, goal setting, self-monitoring for feedback, reinforcement, stimulus control, etc) can be used for changing exercise patterns, food selection, self-defeating thoughts, and garnering social support from others in the dieter's environment.

Five Factors in Weight Control

The essential five elements of (1) changing the act of eating, (2) nutrition training, (3) cognitive restructuring, (4) developing support systems, and (5) exercising have been integrated into a comprehensive weight control intervention program used by our group at the University of Pennsylvania. This program is designed to fit the clinical realities of treating obesity.

Behavior Modification of Eating Behavior

Traditional behavioral techniques are used to minimize excessive eating. These include, but are not limited to, self-monitoring, stimulus control, preplanning, slowing eating, disruption of eating chains, and substituting alternative activities. Self-monitoring and stimulus control were described above. Preplanning helps the client anticipate the "what, when, and where" of meals. For example, if the client decides to eat at 6:30 PM, at home, and has the proper ingredients available, the likelihood of eating other foods is decreased. Preplanning reduces the chances of impulsive eating. Slowing the act of eating allows the client to experience satiety before overeating. When eating because of boredom or fatigue persists, group members are taught to generate activities that would be reinforcing and would last long enough (10 to 15 minutes) to stave off boredom or fatigue temporarily.

Nutrition

Because improper dietary habits can lead to large losses of lean body tissue and other physical problems, nutrition is important for optimal weight reduction and maintenance. Our approach to nutrition emphasizes the four basic food groups. No foods are forbidden, as mandated abstinence only serves to enhance the desirability of food. It is important to allow patients to incorporate their food preferences into the weight-loss program. Otherwise, they revert to old eating styles, and quickly regain the weight lost on a more nutritious regimen.

Cognitive Training

Our program expands the early work of Mahoney and Mahoney[20] to include goal setting, coping with mistakes, and motivation. Strong emphasis is placed on attitudes in the later stages of treatment, when relapse prevention is of paramount concern.[16] The goal of treatment is to emphasize positive attitudes to enhance adherence to the life style, exercise, relationship, and nutrition parts of the program.

Social Support

Social support is a correlate of success in some weight studies[13] and can help maintain weight loss. Dieters learn to evaluate their social environment and determine whether anyone in the environment could aid or sabotage their efforts. Specific methods are taught for eliciting and rewarding support from others for esteem, information, motivation, and social companionship.

Exercise

Exercise is one of the few predictors of success in weight-loss programs. To engage a patient in exercise, the exercise must be enjoyable, or long-term adherence is improbable. This requires special sensitivity to the psychologic and physical concerns specific to obese people. It is essential to begin with a level of exercise that is reasonable, given a person's physical condition and attitudes about exercise. Activity should be monitored and reinforced through the program.

Program Materials and Structure

Given the comprehensive content of the program, our group[21] has devised a manual to convey this information to patients. Material is discussed in group meetings. The manual enables patients to review material between sessions, provides more detail than is possible within the time limits of meetings, and is a reference source once the formal program ends.

Group treatment is provided because of the social support gained from others in the group, and because of its cost-effectiveness. Based on clinical experience, optimal group size averages 8 to 12 patients. The program is designed to last 16 weeks, and follow-up data are gathered after termination of the intervention period.

CURRENT ISSUES IN BEHAVIOR MODIFICATION

Professionals commonly face three issues in treating the obese: the need to (1) increase weight loss, (2) increase maintenance, and (3) decrease attrition. Research is currently pursuing means to address these problems. The need for such research is apparent. While the usual 15- to 25-lb weight loss is useful for the mildly overweight, it is insufficient for the moderately obese person who needs to lose 50 to 100 lb. Additionally, although patients maintain two thirds of their weight loss at 1-year follow-up, some data suggest that patients may eventually approach pretreatment weights. Finally, attrition is a difficult problem.

Increasing Weight Loss

Techniques to increase weight loss include pharmacotherapy, VLCD, and social support. Social support seems to be more effective in maintaining weight loss than in increasing initial weight loss. The use of medications to increase weight loss often results in rapid initial weight loss. However, regain is equally rapid, even when combined with behavior modification techniques.[13] Consequently, at this time, pharmacology is not the answer to effective weight loss.

More promising for moderately and severely obese patients are VLCDs combined with behavior modification. A recent study by Wadden and Stunkard[19] indicated significantly greater weight loss with VLCDs than with behavior therapy alone. Those treated with behavior therapy or with behavior therapy plus VLCDs regained only one third of their weight loss as opposed to those treated with a VLCD alone who regained two thirds of their weight loss at 1-year follow-up. This suggests that more weight can be lost with a VLCD, and if combined with behavior therapy, there is twice the likelihood that a large percentage of the lost weight will be maintained at 1-year follow-up.

Increasing Maintenance

There is a real need for further research on the maintenance of weight loss. In response to this need, scientists have found that exercise, social support, and relapse prevention training are the most encouraging areas of investigation.

Exercise

Patients who exercise while engaged in a behavioral program maintain weight loss better than patients who do not (Chapter 12). Interestingly, it was shown[22] that patients who increase their energy expenditure by 200 to 400 calories with ordinary life style activities (eg, walking more, using stairs rather than elevators, etc) are more likely to maintain their weight loss than those participating in programmed aerobic activity, although this research was done with children. In modifying activity level, it is essential to begin with a level of exercise that is reasonable, given a person's attitudes about exercise and physical condition. As with eating, self-monitoring and reinforcement are important components of changing exercise behavior.

Social Support

Social support can decrease attrition from treatment, improve weight loss, and improve weight-loss maintenance.[23] The usefulness of social support is dependent on the dieter's view of who delivers the social influence and when. Social influence can have positive as well as negative effects. For example, the family could represent a source of stress and intimidation rather than a source of strength and intimacy. In examining the following three areas of potential social support, the clinician needs to assess on a case-by-case basis which types of social support would be most conducive to weight loss.

Family Support. In the treatment of obese adults, the role of spouses in the weight-loss process has been investigated. Findings are inconsistent. Mahoney and Mahoney[24] derived a social support index based on attendance and therapist reports of family cooperation. A positive relation was found between the index and weight loss. A literature review found that social support was a predictor of weight loss[25] and long-term success.[26]

The most promising results were found when spouses were trained with the dieter in a variety of techniques in a highly structured program that stressed mutual effort.[27] Separate manuals were provided to the spouses prescribing specific "spouse" behavior. Consequently, the spouse was an active participant rather than a passive spectator. Although initial weight loss did not differ among the trained couples' group and two other standard behavioral groups, the 6-month follow-up was telling. Patients in the couples' group had lost 30 lb, while in the two standard behavioral groups, where spouses were not included, the loss was only 19 lb and 15 lb. One third of the total weight loss for patients in the couples' group occurred after active treatment ended. Some studies have confirmed these findings, but others have not.[27] Treatment of childhood obesity in which a parent has an active role has met with positive results as well, as opposed to intervention in which parents are only peripherally involved.[28]

Therapeutic Support. External contingencies imposed in the therapeutic context are often thought to be a key factor in weight loss. Increased contact with the therapist seems to improve weight loss early in treatment but not during maintenance.[23] Research does not show an advantage to using booster sessions[18]; however, prolonged treatment (eg, extending two times the standard of 16 weeks) may result in increased weight loss.[13] Over time, transfer from external therapeutic control to internalized client control is the goal of treatment and prepares the client for potential relapse episodes.

Self-help groups. Peer support, although not systematically analyzed, is likely to be an important element of success in behavioral programs. In behavioral treatment in groups, peer support and empathy may be different from that provided by the therapist. Patients occasionally continue their meetings once the formal program has ended.

Perri and associates[14] followed patients in a "buddy group" that continued to hold weekly meetings, monitor each other's weight, and provide mutual problem solving and positive feedback after the end of treatment. Patients also had weekly contact with a therapist via telephone and mail. At 21 months' follow-up, the buddy group had maintained 10 lb of a 13.5-lb loss. In contrast, a group receiving only behavioral treatment and six booster sessions had regained all but 0.8 lb of a 12.4-lb loss. These results suggest an economical maintenance procedure consisting of peer support and patient-therapist contact by telephone and mail.

Relapse Prevention

As we increase our understanding of how physiologic, cognitive, behavioral, and social factors affect regain, maintenance should improve. It is unclear how these variables interact, because regain usually occurs after treatment has terminated. The patient is often seen again only after a significant regain.

Combining relapse prevention training with behavior therapy has produced significantly better maintenance results than behavior therapy or relapse prevention training alone.[29] The trend in relapse prevention is to distinguish between lapse and relapse. Lapse refers to a process (slips and mistakes) that may or may not lead to an outcome (relapse). In smokers, lapse is generally associated with situational factors, while relapse occurs with negative emotional states or stress events.[15] Whether the same findings are true with weight regain is undetermined.

Marlatt and Gordon[30] eloquently describe the process of relapse as follows: (1) patients find themselves in a high-risk situation in which they are exposed to the addictive stimulus (food, alcohol, etc); (2) they have no coping strategy to avoid the stimulus and simultaneously anticipate pleasure from its use; (3) they use the stimulus and feel guilt and loss of self-control; and (4) as a result of feeling an absence of self-control and that relapse has occurred, there is a greater likelihood of continued use of the addictive stimulus.

The goal of relapse prevention is to teach the patient to identify and cope with high-risk situations. In the event of transgression, the patient is taught to view the episode as a temporary "lapse," from which recovery is possible, rather than as a "relapse," which connotes failure and hopelessness.[16] Lapse and relapse are thought to occur in three stages of treatment: (1) at the onset, with motivation and commitment; (2) in initial change; and (3) during maintenance. Relapse prevention is also used in the beginning stages of treatment.

Attrition

Behavior modification can prevent dropout in early treatment. The dropout rate for medical treatment in general is as high as 80%, and attrition from self-help and commercial groups ranges between 50% and 80%.[12] Perhaps the greatest strength of behavior therapy for weight control is its lower attrition rate. In a review[12] of 17 studies with follow-up periods exceeding 6 months, dropout rates averaged 13.5%, ranging from 0% to 26%.

The problem of attrition can be addressed by manipulating aspects of the program and by carefully screening participants in the program. The screening process we implement requires that patients meet two stipulations: (1) they must lose at least 1 lb per week for 2 weeks in the screening phase; and (2) they must complete daily food intake forms for those 2 weeks. If these requirements are not satisfied, a 1-week period is allowed in which to comply; otherwise, they are not granted permission to enter treatment.

Without this screening process, people who qualify for treatment will often do poorly. Screening requirements, even though not rigorous, discourage the uncommitted from attempting to join and provide a concrete behavioral measure for the clinician to assess motivation. The participation of unmotivated patients can damage group morale. The major function of screening is to produce a motivated group to begin treatment and to enhance the likelihood of positive treatment outcome.

In manipulating the program itself, the deposit-refund system is standard treatment protocol. In addition to treatment charges, the patient deposits money that is refunded for attendance, weight loss, completion of records, or any behavioral condition deemed necessary for treatment. The amount of the deposit is determined by treatment costs and the financial status of the patient. An example of a deposit-refund system would be to require a $100 deposit in addition to a treatment fee of $200. One half of the deposit would be returned for attending 80% of the treatment sessions, with the remainder returned for attending 80% of the follow-up meetings.

The deposit-refund system seemingly discourages unmotivated people from entering treatment and encourages patients to remain once the program begins. An interesting review[12] of studies revealed an average attrition rate of 19.3% when deposits were not used and only a 9.5% attrition rate when they were. Hagen et al[31] systematically analyzed attrition according to the amount of deposit. Subjects made no deposit, a $5 deposit, or a $20 deposit. Those making a $20 deposit had a significantly lower dropout rate than the others, who did not differ.

In the effort to minimize attrition, it seems important to include a screening procedure and a deposit-refund system. By lowering attrition, relapse is prevented at two critical periods: (1) the stages of motivation and commitment, and (2) during initial behavior change.[16]

CONCLUSION

It is obvious to those with experience in treating the obese that treatment is more complex than simply applying common behavioral techniques like self-monitoring and stimulus control. Different categories of obese patients require different treatment approaches. New and more comprehensive behavioral approaches are showing greater weight losses over both the short- and long-term. There is reason to be optimistic, but not complacent. More research is needed to improve results.

REFERENCES

1. Krotkiewski M, Garellick G, Sjostrom L, et al: Fat cell number, resting metabolic rate, and insulin elevation while seeing and smelling food as predictors of slimming. *Metabolism* 1980; 29:1003–1012.

2. Bennet W, Gurin J: *The Dieter's Dilemma: Eating Less and Weighing More*. New York, Basic Books Inc Publishers, 1982.

3. Keesey RE: A set-point theory of obesity, in Brownell KD, Foreyt JP (eds): *Handbook of Eating Disorders*. New York, Basic Books Inc Publishers, 1986, pp 63–87.

4. Stunkard A, Sorensen T, Hanis C et al: An adoption study of human obesity. *N Engl J Med* 1986; 314:193–198.

5. Keesey RE, Corbett S: Metabolic defense of the body weight set-point, in Stunkard AJ, Stellar E (eds): *Eating and its Disorders*. New York, Raven Press, 1984, pp 87–96.

6. Bjorntorp P: Fat cells and obesity, in Brownell KD, Foreyt JP (eds): *Handbook of Eating Disorders*. New York, Basic Books Inc Publishers, 1986, pp 88–98.

7. Brownell KD, Greenwood MRC, Stellar E, et al: The effect of repeated cycles of weight loss and regain in rats. *Physiol Behav* 1986; 38:459–464.

8. Stunkard A: The current status of treatment for obesity in adults, in Stunkard A, Stellar E (eds): *Eating and Its Disorders*. New York, Raven Press, 1984, pp 157–174.

9. Garrow JS: *Treat Obesity Seriously: A Clinical Manual*. Churchill Livingstone Inc, London, 1982.

10. Ferster C, Nurnberger J, Levitt EB: The control of eating. *Journal of Mathetics* 1962; 1:87–109.

11. Jeffery R, Wing R, Stunkard A: Behavioral treatment of obesity: State of the art in 1976. *Behavior Therapy* 1978; 6:189–199.

12. Wilson GT, Brownell KD: Behavior therapy for obesity: An evaluation of treatment outcome. *Advances in Behavior Research and Therapy* 1980; 3:49–86.

13. Brownell K, Wadden T: Behavior therapy for obesity, in Brownell K, Foreyt J (eds): *Handbook of Eating Disorders*. New York, Basic Books Inc Publishers, 1986, pp 180–197.

14. Perri M, McAdoo W, Spevak P, et al: Effects of multicomponent maintenance program on long-term weight loss. *J Consul Clin Psychol* 1984; 52:480–481.

15. Epstein L, Wing R, Koeske R, et al: Effects of diet plus exercise on weight change in parents and children. *J Consul Clin Psychol* 1984; 52:429–437.

16. Brownell KD, Marlatt GA, Lichtenstein E, et al: Understanding and preventing relapse. *Am Psychol* 1986; 41:765–782.

17. Brownell K, Stunkard A: Couples training, pharmacotherapy, and behavior therapy in treatment of obesity. *Arch Gen Psychiatry* 1981; 38:1223–1229.

18. Craighead L, Stunkard A, O'Brien R: Behavior therapy and pharmacotherapy for obesity. *Arch Gen Psychiatry* 1981; 38:763–768.

19. Wadden TA, Stunkard AJ: A controlled trial of very low calorie diet, behavior therapy, and the combination in the treatment of obesity. *J Consul Clin Psychol* 1986; 54:482–488.

20. Mahoney M, Mahoney B: *Permanent Weight Control: A Total Solution to the Dieter's Dilemma*. New York, WW Norton & Co Inc, 1976.

21. Brownell K: *The LEARN Program for Weight Control*. Philadelphia, University of Pennsylvania Press, 1985.

22. Epstein LH, Wing RR, Koeske R, et al: A comparison of lifestyle change and programmed aerobic exercise on weight and fitness changes in obese children. *Behavior Therapy* 1982; 13:651–665.

23. Colletti G, Brownell KD: The physical and emotional benefits of social support: Application to obesity, smoking and alcoholism, in Hersen M, Eisler R, Miller P (eds): *Progress in Behavior Modification*. New York, Academic Press Inc, 1982, pp 109–178.

24. Mahoney M, Mahoney K: Treatment of obesity: A clinical exploration, in Williams BJ, Martin S, Foreyt JP (eds): *Obesity: Behavioral Approaches to Dietary Management*. New York, Brunner/Mazel, Inc 1976, pp 30–40.

25. Cooke C, Meyers A: The role of predictor variables in the behavioral treatment of obesity. *Behavioral Assessment* 1980; 2:59–69.

26. Miller P, Sims K: Evaluation and component analysis of a comprehensive weight control program. *Int J Obes* 1981; 5:57–66.

27. Brownell K, Heckerman C, Westlake R, et al: The effect of couples training and partner cooperativeness in the behavioral treatment of obesity. *Behav Res Ther* 1978; 16:323–333.

28. Le Bow M: *Child Obesity: A New Frontier of Behavior Therapy*. New York, Springer Publishing Co Inc, 1984.

29. Perri MG, Shapiro RM, Ludwig WW, et al: Maintenance strategies for the treatment of obesity: An evaluation of relapse prevention training and posttreatment contact by mail and telephone. *J Consult Clin Psychol* 1984; 52:404–413.

30. Marlatt GA, Gordon J: *Relapse Prevention*. New York, Guilford, 1985.

31. Hagen R, Foreyt J, Durham T: The dropout problem: Reducing attrition in obesity research. *Behavior Therapy* 1976; 7:463–471.

Chapter 12

Exercise in the Treatment of Obesity

F. Xavier Pi-Sunyer

Energy balance depends on equal intake and expenditure. To lose weight, one can either decrease intake, increase expenditure, or both. Until relatively recently, the emphasis in weight-loss programs was on diet, with low-calorie regimens being the treatment of choice. It has become increasingly clear, however, that dietary programs do not work for many people: the incidence of weight regain is very high.[1] In addition, particularly with very-low-calorie diets, there is concern that the weight being lost is not all fat but is very high in protein, so that the negative nitrogen balance created is too great to be acceptable.[2] In addition, since metabolic rate, both basal and during various daily activities, drops significantly with dieting, weight loss becomes more difficult as less calories are necessary to maintain weight.

Because of these problems, interest in exercise has grown in recent years. The promotion of exercise for the treatment of obesity was initially and is still primarily based on the premise that exercise generates extra caloric expenditure. However, there has also been a persistent suggestion that exercise may reduce food intake.

Exercise for the obese person has a third possible advantage: it may help reverse some of the risk factors that seem to be associated with obesity, such as hypertension, diabetes mellitus, and cardiovascular disease.

EXERCISE AS ENERGY EXPENDITURE

Americans have become inactive. This inactivity seems to be the price of technologically advanced societies. The ever-increasing use of labor-saving devices, from automobiles to electric egg beaters, has led to a gradual decrease of thermogenic activity. The decrease in activity, although it is difficult to quantitate, must be very large. Since 1900, for instance, obesity in the United States approximately doubled, while caloric consumption dropped 10%.[3,4]

The inactivity of Americans was highlighted in a report[5] comparing the caloric intake of 500 pairs of Irish brothers, one living in Boston and the other in Ireland, that found the brothers in America ate significantly less but were more obese, implying lower activity in the technologically more advanced society.

Not only is US society as a whole more sedentary, but people as they become more obese seem to become more inactive. Obese children were reported[6-9] to be less active than lean ones, and though not so many adult studies are available, they generally conclude that obese subjects are more inactive than lean ones.[10-12] However, some studies in children[13-16] and adults[14,17] found no differences. Most of these reports used rather crude measures of activity or self-report, so that the data are somewhat suspect. However, a strong case can be made for a difference in activity between the lean and the obese.

DOES EXERCISE INHIBIT FOOD INTAKE?

There has been considerable controversy over the effect of increased physical activity on food intake. There are three possibilities: food intake could (1) increase, (2) stay the same, or (3) decrease. If food intake increases, does it keep pace with expenditure so that body weight stays the same? If food intake stays the same, does this mean that exercise inhibits food intake, or does it mean that exercise has no effect on food intake and that food intake is regulated by other cues independent of activity? If food intake decreases, then a truly inhibitory effect of exercise on food intake could be invoked.

There have been few human studies of the effect of increased activity on food intake. The reason for this is undoubtedly that the accurate measurement over time of both energy intake and energy expenditure is very difficult and very expensive to do. Much of the data available are in rodents. The studies report a sexual dimorphism, with male rats decreasing food intake and losing weight and female rats maintaining or increasing intake so that they maintain or increase weight.

Crews et al,[18] Tsuji et al,[19] Pitts and Bull,[20] and Dohm et al[21] exercised male rats for periods of 28 to 106 days and compared their food intake with that of sedentary control rats. All found that caloric intake was lower in the exercised than in the control animals, and that the exercised animals were lighter in weight. A number of other investigators[22-25] published similar findings. However, it is interesting to note that female rats either do not change or actually increase their food intake and maintain their body weight[23,24] when exercise programs comparable with those given to male rats are introduced. The cause for this sexual dimorphism is unknown and warrants more research.

Some investigators have exercised rats on some days and not on others. In such studies,[25,26] food intake fell on exercise days and was close to that of control animals on rest days, with a net weight-reducing effect. Other investigators[26] subjected rats to isolated bouts of exercise and found not only that food intake decreased, but that the decrease correlated with the duration of the exercise period. Also, as the meal was fed closer to the end of the exercise period, the inhibitory effect increased.[26]

If humans are studied in a free-living condition, food intake must be measured by either self-report or a duplicates technique. Self-report requires food diaries. It is impossible to estimate the quantity of foods eaten precisely and determine the caloric content of each food item at the accuracy level required for calculating caloric balance equations. The weighing of duplicates circumvents the first problem, and bomb calorimetry of these duplicates circumvents the second, but these methods are so tedious that they are not feasible for the period of time required to resolve the exercise–food intake controversy. In fact, no such duplicate weighing studies have been done, attesting to the difficulty of the technique. With either estimates or duplicate weighing, another problem enters in, which is the very effect of focusing so much attention on the person's food intake. There is no way of knowing whether the very act of measuring in such a strict and compulsive manner alters the food intake amount and pattern.

With regard to the accurate measurement of the 24-hour energy expenditure, the difficulties are, if anything, even greater. One needs to measure essentially minute-to-minute expenditure. This can be done most accurately in a chamber calorimeter. But no one would be willing to stay in such a chamber for a significant period of time, and the enclosure would of itself limit activity and thus expenditure, so that a real-life situation could not be totally duplicated.

If a free-living state is used, activity diaries must be kept minute-to-minute. To keep these accurately over days while going about usual activities is difficult. It is because of these difficulties that few free-living studies that can be credited with accuracy are available on the effect of exercise on food intake over a long period of time. A review of the best of these studies is given below.

FOOD INTAKE STUDIES IN HUMANS

Free-Living Studies

Most exercise studies of obese people have been conducted with free-living people. While some studies measured food intake with dietary histories or food diaries, most used only body-weight changes as an indirect measure of food-intake behavior. As a result, accurate data on food intake and on changes in spontaneous activity that might compensate for the prescribed exercise are missing. Most of these studies lacked controls and did not have counterbalanced designs of exercise–no exercise periods.

In obese people, there is a lack of consistency in their response to exercise. In a study in which seven obese men combined running, calisthenics, isometrics, and weight training 5 days/wk for 8 weeks, Dempsey[27] reported a weight loss of 4.7 kg; 5.8 kg lost as fat and 1.1 kg gained as lean tissue. Since he documented no change in food intake, he assumed the weight loss was exercise-induced. This study can be interpreted as showing that exercise has no effect on food intake, that is, intake stays the same; or it could be interpreted as showing an anorectic response, that is, exercise would be expected to raise food intake to maintain equilibrium with expenditure, and if intake stayed the same, an inhibitory effect would be implied.

A report that comes to similar conclusions is by Dudleston and Bennion[28] in two obese young women who were exercised on bicycles and treadmills for 1 hr/day for 6 weeks and were compared with two sedentary control subjects. Weight dropped in the exercising women but food intake did not change.

There are, however, differing reports that indirectly suggest that exercise decreases food intake. Oscai and Williams[29] exercised five middle-aged obese men 30 min/day, 3 days/wk for 4 months, which resulted in a loss of 4.5 kg of weight and 3.6 kg of fat. Food intake was not measured. But calculation of the energy output and the weight loss suggests that food intake had to be inhibited to obtain as much weight loss as was reported. Boileau et al[30] obtained comparable results in 15 young obese men.

Gwinup[31] did a prolonged study in a group of women who walked 7 days/wk from 70 to 190 min/day for 1 year. Only 11 of the 34 women who started the study finished it. The women were told "to forego caloric restriction and begin an exercise program." Food intake was not measured. The 11 women lost a mean of 22 lb. It is unclear what was different between these 11 women and the dropouts. Possibly, however, the very act of committing to such an extended program implies a commitment to behavior change that may extend beyond exercise to other aspects of life-style, such as exercise, smoking, alcohol intake, etc. No such information is available in the study report. Thus, whether exercise per se, or other behavioral concomitants, had an effect on food intake is unclear in this study.

Dahlkoetter et al[32] investigated the effect on weight loss of exercise alone, diet alone, exercise and diet, and a control group. In this 8-week study, the exercise-alone group lost 6.1 lb, the diet-alone group lost 7.0 lb, the combined group lost 13.3 lb, and the control group lost no weight. The weakness of this study is that exercise was not carefully monitored and quantitated, so that it is unclear that equivalent amounts of exercise were done by the volunteers. Also, participants signed up because they wished to lose weight, so it is possible that the exercise group also dieted. It is not possible to calculate accurately whether the exercise-alone group decreased food intake.

A similar study was done by Weltman et al[33] in which 58 mildly obese men agreed to diet, exercise, diet and exercise, or act as a control subject for 10 weeks. Unlike the Dahlkoetter study, the exercise effect was disappointing, although it was relatively intense, consisting of walking at 3.5 mph 4 times per week for 45 min/day. Subjects who dieted lost 5.0 to 9.5 kg; those who exercised lost a disappointing 0.9 kg; and those who combined exercise and diet lost only 5.4 kg. This study was flawed because the subjects were not randomized into the groups. However, the effect of exercise alone or as an adjunct to diet was nil in this study.

Another disappointing report of the effect of exercise on weight loss is that of Krotkiewsky et al.[34] They studied a group of 58 obese women in Sweden, some of whom were hypertrophic but not hyperplastic (that is, fat cell size was enlarged but fat cell number was not elevated), and some of whom were both hypertrophic and hyperplastic (both fat cell size and number were elevated). They trained with jogging, calisthenics, and dancing for 6 months and were told not to worry about their diet. The hypertrophic patients lost approximately 0.5 kg/month, a rather small loss; the hyperplastic-hypertrophic patients did not lose any weight. The fact that these women either lost very little or did not lose any weight during this 6-month period of increased activity actually suggests they increased their food intake to keep their weight in equilibrium.

Leon et al[35] have the most successful report of weight loss in the literature. They studied ten healthy overweight young men 19 to 31 years old who volunteered for an exercise study. The only dietary advice was to eat whatever they wanted. The young men walked 5 days/wk for 90 minutes. They worked very hard, expending between 1,000 and 1,200 kcal/day, and lost 5.7 kg in 16 weeks. Interestingly, they lost 5.9 kg of body fat, and no lean body mass by body-density measurement. The investigators followed food and alcohol intake by 3-day dietary records at 4-week intervals during the study. Subjects initially ate more, and then less, so that by the twelfth week they were eating slightly below their sedentary amount. But if one calculates the energy balance equations and the weight loss produced, the numbers do not add up, suggesting that the dietary records were inaccurate and cannot be trusted. One can conclude from this study, however, that the men did increase intake while exercising, but not enough to maintain their weight at the sedentary level, and so lost a significant amount of weight.

Studies under Metabolic Ward Conditions

Because of the problems in studies with free-living people, investigators have used metabolic ward settings. Three such studies[36-38] are reported, but all subjects were lean. In these studies, the subjects seemed to increase food intake as exercise increased. There are difficulties with the studies, however. In two of them,[36,37] the volunteers underate in the sedentary period and ate more during the exercise period. But there was no crossover design, so a period or time effect cannot be ruled out. Also, the studies were very short, 5 to 7 days. It is doubtful whether adequate data on long-term food intake regulation can be obtained with such short time intervals.

Because of the lack of long-term studies under carefully monitored conditions, we did a series of studies[39–41] in lean and obese volunteers to try to resolve the issue. Because we wanted to measure food intake carefully, we brought volunteers into an institutional setting. We selected women whose weight had been stable for at least 6 months. They were recruited by being told that the aim of the protocol was to study the effect of physical activity on protein metabolism and nitrogen balance. They were warned that they would probably not lose weight and might even gain some. This was done to prevent the selection of volunteers who might wish to enter the metabolic unit to lose weight. We initially set up a protocol whereby subjects could maintain their weight during a sedentary period in the metabolic unit. It was a requirement of the study that they be in intake and expenditure equilibrium for the period. We could then manipulate expenditure by increasing activity and determine the effect on food intake.

To measure food intake, we used a platter method of food presentation previously developed by our colleagues for food intake studies.[42] The food was served individually to each volunteer in separate platters, each of which contained a triple portion of one food item. The volunteer could then eat as much or as little of each item as she wished. Food was covertly weighed before presentation and after eating. Food left on plates was also weighed. Energy balance was calculated as the difference between intake and expenditure.[39]

The volunteers were six women aged 22 to 61 who averaged 167% of ideal weight by Metropolitan height and weight tables. Each was studied for a total of 62 days.[43] There was an initial 5-day sedentary evaluation phase during which each person kept an activity diary, underwent body composition measurements, and was initiated to the measurement of oxygen expenditure by indirect calorimetry during various daily activities (resting, sitting, lying, standing, walking about). This period allowed us to calculate their usual sedentary 24-hour caloric expenditure and their 24-hour caloric intake at weight maintenance.

Three 19-day periods followed during which each subject was assigned randomly to one of three activity treatments: (1) sedentary, (2) mild exercise, or (3) moderate exercise. For the exercise periods, the subjects walked on a treadmill at a 2.5% grade. Subjects chose their rate of walking, and were given daily time assignments depending on their measured energy expenditure. During mild exercise, subjects had to expend 10% above their sedentary expenditure, and for moderate exercise they had to expend 25% above their sedentary expenditure.

This required an average of 39 min/day of brisk walking for the mild exercise period and 96 min/day for the moderate exercise period. The results of the study are shown in Figure 12-1.[43]

It can be seen that food was provided in an acceptable manner, so that energy equilibrium was maintained during the sedentary period. Mean daily energy expenditure rose significantly from the sedentary, to the mild, to the moderate exercise periods. Mean daily energy intake, however, was not significantly different between periods. It remained fixed whether the subjects were on sedentary, mild, or moderate activity. That is, intake seemed to remain independent of expenditure throughout the study. Since no compensatory increase occurred with exercise, a significant negative caloric balance occurred, so that patients lost weight over the period of the study.[39]

Because of the effect obtained in obese women, a similar study[41] was done in lean women. Five lean women between 21 and 51 years of age were studied who averaged 97% of ideal body weight. The protocol was identical with that described above. The results are shown in Figure 12-2.[41] Equilibrium of intake and expenditure was again attained during the sedentary period. But unlike in the obese women, this coupling of intake and expenditure was sustained during all three exercise treatment periods. That is, lean subjects compensated adequately for their increased energy expenditure and adjusted food intake upward accordingly. As a result, they maintained their weight and their body composition.

Why should lean and obese women respond differently to exercise? It is possible that the obese, since they have excess fat stores and enlarged fat cells, do not respond to food intake signals that stimulate the lean subjects to eat until these fat stores or fat cells have been depleted to a more physiologic level or size. It is also possible that obese women eat dysfunctionally, with factors other than the amount of energy expended taking predominance, factors such as palatability, variety, and availability of certain foods.

We have done preliminary studies[43] to test the effect of palatability and variety on food intake response during exercise. We studied four obese young men. They were asked to exercise at four levels, for 10 days each: baseline activity, 110% of baseline, 140% of baseline, and back to baseline. They were fed from platters as in the previous studies, but a great effort was made to prepare a great variety of gourmet foods. The results are shown in Figure 12-3.[43] It can be seen that expenditure was raised roughly as planned. However, once again, intake was fixed. But in this experiment intake was fixed much above expenditure, so that the subjects actually gained weight. The gourmet foods stimulated a much greater intake than the plainer fare the obese women had been served.

This suggests that the regulation of intake in obese people may be more closely tied to the sensory characteristics of the food available than to any specific expenditure signals triggered by the exercise activity. It is thus possible that

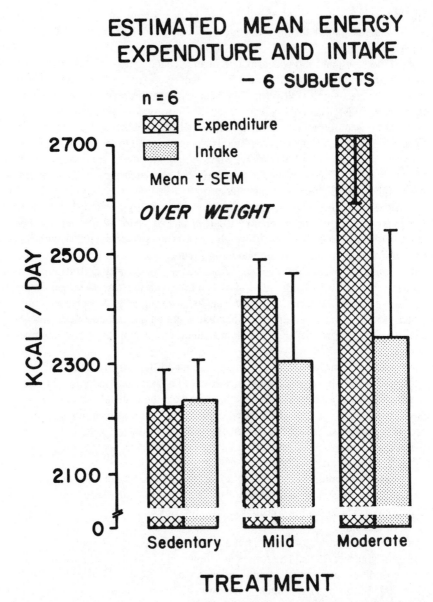

Figure 12-1 Mean energy expenditure and intake in six obese women over three 19-day periods in which they were either sedentary or exercised on a treadmill mildly (to 110% sedentary daily expenditure) or moderately (to 125% of sedentary expenditure). *Source*: Reprinted with permission from *Metabolism* (1985; 34:836–841), Copyright © 1985, Grune & Stratton Inc.

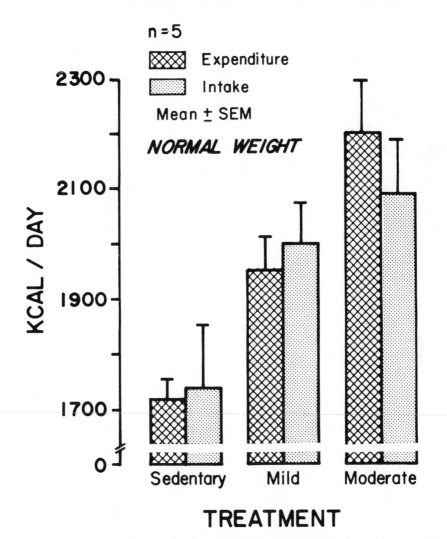

ESTIMATED MEAN ENERGY EXPENDITURE AND INTAKE

Figure 12-2 Mean energy expenditure and intake in five lean women over three 19-day periods in which they were either sedentary or exercised on a treadmill mildly (to 110% of sedentary daily expenditure) or moderately (to 125% of sedentary expenditure). *Source*: Reprinted with permission from *Metabolism* (1985; 34:836–841), Copyright © 1985, Grune & Stratton Inc.

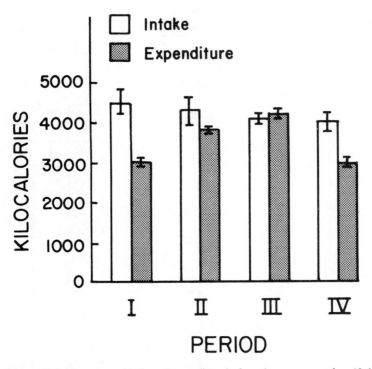

ENERGY INTAKE AND EXPENDITURE PER PERIOD

Figure 12-3 Mean energy intake and expenditure in four obese men over four 10-day periods in which they were either at a basal level of activity (I, IV) or their activity was increased by walking on a treadmill to a mild degree (to 110% of basal daily expenditure, II) or to a moderate degree (to 140% of basal expenditure, III). *Source*: Reprinted from *Recent Advances in Obesity Research* by J Hirsch and TB Van Itallie (Eds) with permission of John Libbey & Company Ltd, © 1985.

whatever cues come from exercise-derived signals are overwhelmed by food-derived signals in the obese. This fits in well with the concept of sensory-specific satiety described by Rolls et al,[44] which may be particularly strong in the obese.

In summary, our studies suggest that exercise is effective for weight loss in obese people. This is not because exercise has any particularly strong effect on food intake, but precisely because it seems to have very little effect in obese people. Since obese people, when they exercise, do not compensate for the increased energy expenditure of the activity by increasing food intake, they lose weight at a rate directly related to the amount of energy expended by the exercise.

It is important to understand that the energy expended by exercise is only that of the exercise itself. The statement is continually made that exercise raises metabolic rate for hours after the exercise bout and so helps burn energy while one is resting. There is little evidence for this at the levels of exercise that obese people generally do during weight-reduction programs.[45] Levels of resting energy expenditure are back to baseline within 40 minutes to 1 hour after the bout.

Finally, it is important to add that much more investigative work is necessary on the relation of exercise, food intake, and weight loss. There has been little research on the level of intensity of exercise and its effect on food intake. Intensity of the effort, kilocalories per minute, the amount of caloric load, and total calories of work done, need to be related more clearly to food-intake effects. Mayer et al[46] studied rats exercising at different rates for 1 hour, so that both intensity and amount of work increased in concert. Rats reached a level at which they became very fatigued and began to eat less and lose weight. This may be true also of humans. A level of exercise may be reached at which energy intake may decrease markedly. It is also possible that short but intense glycogen-depleting exercise could have a different effect than less intense but longer activity. The questions have been posed, but we have no answers as yet.

BENEFITS OF EXERCISE

There are other benefits of exercise to obese people besides the simple one of weight loss. Obesity tends to be associated with a number of conditions that increase both morbidity and mortality. These include diabetes mellitus, hypertension, and cardiovascular and gallbladder disease.

Obesity greatly enhances the risk of developing diabetes in susceptible people. Ninety percent of diabetic patients in America have type II maturity-onset diabetes, and of these approximately 85% are obese. The incidence of diabetes in a population greatly increases as it becomes overweight. The incidence falls when a population experiences food shortages or food rationing such as occurred in Europe during World War II. With diabetes come the possible complications of the disease, namely macrovascular disease, which is primarily manifested by coronary artery disease, and microvascular disease, primarily manifested by nephropathy, retinopathy, and neuropathy. There is strong evidence that exercise improves the diabetic condition in two ways: (1) indirectly through weight loss, and (2) by decreasing insulin resistance and enhancing insulin sensitivity, which enhances glucose transport and cellular postinsulin-receptor metabolic processes and tends to lower blood glucose levels. This can occur even in the absence of changes in weight or body composition.[47]

There has been some suggestion that insulin per se may be a risk factor for coronary artery disease, and it is well known that obese people have hyperinsulinemia. A high correlation has been found between hyperinsulinemia and coronary artery disease in prospective studies.[48] This correlation is independent of age, blood pressure, plasma cholesterol levels, and smoking.[49] With exercise, blood insulin levels are lowered,[50] and this effect persists for at least 72 hours after the exercise bout.[51] With regular chronic exercise, therefore, hyperinsulinemia can be lowered significantly, thereby decreasing any possible hazardous effect of hyperinsulinemia on cardiovascular disease.

The association of hypertension with obesity is a strong one. Numerous epidemiologic studies have reported that the incidence of hypertension rises with increasing weight, and that the risk increases with age. Hypertension, in turn, increases the risk for coronary artery disease, with consequent myocardial infarction and death. It is known that physically active people tend to have lower resting systolic and diastolic blood pressures.[52] This may be related to a decrease in peripheral vascular resistance or sympathetic tone.[53] The effect of exercise on hypertension is unclear, but there is suggestive evidence that blood pressure may be lowered, though studies are generally poorly designed and not well controlled.[54]

The association of obesity with cardiovascular disease in general has been a much debated point. Although obesity per se has not been accepted as a primary risk factor for cardiac disease and cardiovascular mortality, it seems to have a role through the exacerbation of other risk factors such as diabetes, hypertension, and hypercholesterolemia. A decrease in weight tends to improve all of these conditions and thereby decreases cardiovascular risk.[55] There is strong epidemiologic evidence that exercise lowers the risk of cardiovascular disease, not only by its effect on weight, but directly.[56]

The association between obesity and gallbladder disease is related to the supersaturation of bile in obese people. This predisposes to gallstone formation and subsequent inflammation of the gallbladder. Cholecystectomy is often required, and obese patients have a higher incidence of complications during surgery, including thrombophlebitis, pulmonary embolus, infection, wound dehiscence, and pneumonia. Exercise, by its effects on weight loss, can decrease the supersaturation of the bile and decrease the risk of gallstones and gallbladder disease.

In summary, even if it had no effect on food intake and weight, exercise would still be worthwhile for an obese person in that it diminishes a number of risk factors that lead to enhanced morbidity and mortality in overweight people. How to go about exercising is the subject of the next chapter.

REFERENCES

1. Stunkard AJ, Penick SB: Behavior modification in the treatment of obesity. *Arch Gen Psychiatry* 1979; 36:801–806.

2. Van Itallie TB, Yang MU: Cardiac dysfunction in obese dieters: A potentially lethal complication of rapid, massive weight loss. *Am J Clin Nutr* 1984; 39:695–702.

3. *Consumption of Food in the US in 1909–1952*, US Dept of Agriculture, Agricultural Handbook No. 62 (Suppl 1901). Government Printing Office, 1962.

4. Van Itallie TB: *Diets Related to Killer Diseases, Testimony before the Senate Select Committee on Nutrition and Human Needs*. Government Printing Office, Feb 2, 1977, vol 2, pt 2, *Obesity*.

5. Brown J, Bourke GJ, Gerarty GF, et al: Nutritional and epidemiologic factors related to heart disease, in Bourne GH (ed): *World Reviews of Nutrition and Dietetics*. Basel, Pitman Medical and Scientific, 1970, vol 12, pp 1–12.

6. Rose HE, Mayer J: Activity, caloric intake, and the energy balance of infants. *Pediatrics* 1968; 41:18–29.

7. Bullen BA, Reed RB, Mayer J: Physical activity of obese and non-obese adolescent girls appraised by motion picture sampling. *Am J Clin Nutr* 1974; 14:211–233.

8. Johnson ML, Burke MS, Mayer J: Relative importance of activity and over-eating in the energy balance of obese high school girls. *Am J Clin Nutr* 1956; 4:37–44.

9. Stephanik PA, Heald FL, Mayer J: Caloric intake in relation to energy output of obese and non-obese adolescent boys. *Am J Clin Nutr* 1959; 7:55–62.

10. Mayer J, Roy P, Mitra KP: Relation between caloric intake, body weight, and physical work: Studies in an industrial male population in West Bengal. *Am J Clin Nutr* 1956; 4:169–175.

11. Chirico A, Stunkard AJ: Physical activity and human obesity. *N Engl J Med* 1960; 263:935–940.

12. Bloom WL, Eidex MF: Inactivity as a major factor in adult obesity. *Metabolism* 1967; 16:679–684.

13. Stunkard AJ, Pestka J: The physical activity of obese girls. *Am J Dis Child* 1962; 103:812–817.

14. Maxfield E, Konishi F: Patterns of food intake and physical activity in obesity. *J Am Diet Assoc* 1966; 49:406–408.

15. Bradfield R, Paulos J, Grossman H: Energy expenditure and heart rate of obese high school girls. *Am J Clin Nutr* 1967; 24:1482–1486.

16. Wilkinson PW, Parklin J, Pearlson G, et al: Energy intake and physical activity in obese children. *Br Med J* 1977; 1:756.

17. Lincoln JE: Caloric intake, obesity, and physical activity. *Am J Clin Nutr* 1972; 25:390–394.

18. Crews EL III, Fuge KW, Oscai LB, et al: Weight, food intake and body composition: Effects of exercise and of protein deficiency. *Am J physiol* 1969; 216:359–363.

19. Tsuji K, Katayama Y, Konishi H: Effects of dietary protein level on energy metabolism of rats during exercise. *J Nutr Sci Vitaminol (Tokyo)* 1975; 21:437–449.

20. Pitts GC, Bull LS: Exercise, dietary obesity, and growth in the rat. *Am J Physiol* 1977; 232:R38–R44.

21. Dohm GL, Beecher GR, Stephenson TP, et al: Adaptations to endurance training at three intensities of exercise. *J Appl Physiol* 1977; 42:753–757.

22. Oscai LB, Mole PA, Brei B, et al: Cardiac growth and respiratory enzyme levels in male rats subjected to a running program. *Am J Physiol* 1971; 220:1238–1241.

23. Nance DM, Bromley B, Barnard RJ, et al: Sexually dimorphic effects of forced exercise on food intake and body weight in the rat. *Physiol Behav* 1977; 19:155–158.

24. Applegate EA, Upton DE, Stern JS: Food intake, body composition and blood lipids following treadmill exercise in male and female rats. *Physiol Behav* 1982; 28:917–920.

25. Oscai LB, Holloszy JO: Effects of weight changes produced by exercise, food restriction, or overeating on body composition. *J Clin Invest* 1969; 48:2124–2128.

26. Stevenson JAF, Box BM, Feleki V, et al: Bouts of exercise and food intake in the rat. *Appl Physiol* 1966; 21:118–122.

27. Dempsey JA: Anthropometrical observations on obese and non-obese young men undergoing a program of vigorous physical exercise. *Res Quarterly* 1964; 35:275–279.

28. Dudleston AK, Bennion M: Effect of diet and/or exercise on obese college women. *J Am Diet Assoc* 1970; 56:126–129.

29. Oscai LB, Williams BT: Effect of exercise on overweight middle-aged males. *J Am Geriatr Soc* 1968; 16:794–797.

30. Boileau RA, Buskirk ER, Horstman DH, et al: Body compositional changes in obese and lean men during physical conditioning. *Med Sci Sports* 1971; 3:183–189.

31. Gwinup G: Effect of exercise alone on the weight of obese women. *Arch Intern Med* 1975; 135:676–680.

32. Dahlkoetter J, Callahan EJ, Linton J: Obesity and the unbalanced energy equation: Exercise vs eating habit change. *J Consult Clin Psychol* 1979; 47:898–905.

33. Weltman A, Matter S, Stamford BA: Caloric restriction and/or mild exercise: Effects on serum lipids and body composition. *Am J Clin Nutr* 1980; 33:1002–1009.

34. Krotkiewsky M, Mandroukas K, Sjostrom L, et al: Effects of long term physical training on body fat, metabolism and blood pressure in obesity. *Metabolism* 1979; 28:650–658.

35. Leon AS, Conrad J, Hunninghake DB, et al: Effects of a vigorous walking program on body composition and lipid metabolism of obese young men. *Am J Clin Nutr* 1979; 33:1776–1787.

36. Warnold E, Lenner RA: Evaluation of the heart rate method to determine the daily energy expenditure in disease: A study in juvenile diabetics. *Am J Clin Nutr* 1977; 30:304–315.

37. Passmore R, Thomson JG, Warnock GM: A balance sheet of the estimation of energy intake and energy expenditure as measured by indirect calorimetry using the Kofranyi-Michaels calorimeter. *Br J Nutr* 1952; 6;253–264.

38. Durrant ML, Roystron JP, Wloch RT: Effect of exercise on energy intake and eating patterns in lean and obese humans. *Physiol Behav* 1982; 29:449–454.

39. Woo R, Garrow J, Pi-Sunyer FX: Effect of exercise on spontaneous calorie intake in obesity. *Am J Clin Nutr* 1982; 36:470–477.

40. Woo R, Garrow J, Pi-Sunyer FX: Voluntary food intake during prolonged exercise in obese women. *Am J Clin Nutr* 1982; 36:478–484.

41. Woo R, Pi-Sunyer FX: Effect of increased physical activity on voluntary intake in lean women. *Metabolism* 1985; 34:836–841.

42. Porikos KP, Booth G, Van Itallie TB: Effect of covert nutritive dilution on the spontaneous food intake of obese individuals: A pilot study. *Am J Clin Nutr* 1977; 30:1638–1644.

43. Pi-Sunyer FX: Effect of exercise on food intake, in Hirsch J, Van Itallie TB (eds): *Recent Advances in Obesity Research*. London, John Libbey & Co Ltd, 1985, pp 368–373.

44. Rolls BJ, Rowe EA, Rolls ET: How sensory properties of foods affect human feeding behavior. *Physiol Behav* 1982; 29:409–417.

45. Freedman-Akabas S, Colt E, Kissileff HR, et al: Lack of sustained increase in VO_2 following exercise in fit and unfit subjects. *Am J Clin Nutr* 1984; 41:545–549.

46. Mayer J, Marshall NB, Vitale JJ, et al: Exercise, food intake and body weight in normal rats and genetically obese mice. *Am J Physiol* 1954; 177:544–548.

47. Bjorntorp P: Effect of exercise and physical training on carbohydrate and lipid metabolism in man. *Adv Cardiol* 1976; 18:158–166.

48. Pyorala K: Relationship of glucose tolerance and plasma insulin to the incidence of coronary artery disease: Results from two population studies in Finland. *Diabetes Care* 1979; 2:131–141.

49. Ducimetiere P, Eschwege LK, Papoz JL, et al: Relationship of plasma insulin levels to the incidence of myocardial infarction and coronary heart disease mortality in a middle-aged population. *Diabetologia* 1980; 19:205–210.

50. Bjorntorp P, DeJounge K, Sjostrom L, et al: The effects of physical training on insulin production in obesity. *Metabolism* 1970; 19:631–638.

51. Schneider SH, Amorosa LF, Khachadurian AK, et al: Studies on the mechanism of improved glucose control during regular exercise in type 2 (non-insulin dependent) diabetes. *Diabetologia* 1984; 26:355–360.

52. Miall W, Oldham P: Factors influencing arterial blood pressure in the general population. *Clin Sci* 1958; 17:400–440.

53. Winder W, Hickson J, Hagberg A, et al: Training induced changes in hormonal and metabolic responses to submaximal exercise. *J Appl Physiol* 1979; 46:766–771.

54. Schneider SH, Vitug A, Ruderman N: Atherosclerosis and physical activity. *Diabetes Metab Rev* 1986; 1:513–553.

55. Kannel WB: Health and obesity, an overview, in Conn HL Jr, DeFelice EA, Kuo P (eds): *Health and Obesity*. New York, Raven Press, 1983, pp 1–19.

56. Kannel WB, Sorlie P: Some health benefits of physical activity: The Framingham Study. *Arch Intern Med* 1979; 139:857–861.

Chapter 13

Application of Exercise for Weight Control: The Exercise Prescription

William D. McArdle and Michael M. Toner

It is difficult to separate the causes of obesity into distinct categories because the mechanisms of excessive energy storage are complex and interrelated. It seems fairly certain, however, that the treatment procedures devised thus far, whether they be surgery, drugs, psychologic methods, or diets, either alone or in combination, have not been particularly successful in solving the problem on a long-term basis.[1] It is becoming increasingly clear that the lack of energy expenditure in daily physical activity is an important predisposing factor for obesity.[2] It is often observed that obese people eat the same or even less than leaner people over a broad age range as they become less active and slowly add weight.[3,4] In this regard, regular exercise, either alone or in combination with dietary modification, can have an important role in the prevention or treatment of obesity.

EXERCISE: AN IMPORTANT COMPONENT IN ENERGY BALANCE

When the number of calories ingested exceeds the daily energy requirement, the excess calories are stored as fat in adipose tissue. Conversely, for weight to be lost, an energy deficit must be created either by decreasing the energy intake (caloric restriction) or by increasing the energy output (exercising). To prevent an increase in body fat and maintain body weight, the weight-control program must establish an equilibrium between energy input and energy output.

Consider the sensitivity of energy balance in relation to the dynamics of weight gain or weight loss. Suppose caloric intake exceeds output by 100 kcal/day. Then the surplus number of calories consumed in 1 year would be 365 days $\times$ 100 kcal, or 36,500 kcal. Because 1 lb of adipose tissue contains approximately 3,500 kcal, this is equivalent to a gain of 10.4 lb of fat in 1 year. (Each pound of body fat is approximately 87% fat, or 454 g $\times$ 0.87 = 395 g; 395 g $\times$ 9 kcal/g = 3,555 kcal/lb.) On the other hand, if daily food intake is reduced only 100 kcal, and energy expenditure is increased 100 kcal by jogging approximately 1 mile each day (caloric deficit = 200 kcal/day), then the monthly caloric deficit would amount to a weight loss of 1.7 lb (approximately 6,000 kcal) of fat. This is the equivalent of a reduction of approximately 21 lb of fat in 1 year!

For men and women, combinations of exercise and caloric restriction, combined with appropriate behavior modification strategies and psychologic support, offer considerably more flexibility for achieving a negative caloric balance than either exercise or diet alone. In fact, the addition of exercise to the weight-loss program may actually facilitate adherence to the program, resulting in a more permanent weight loss compared with total reliance on caloric restriction,[5,6] and an enhanced psychologic status of the participant.[7]

Exercise and Caloric Expenditure

Physical activity has by far the most profound effect on human energy expenditure. World-class athletes nearly double their daily caloric output with 2 or 3 hours of hard training. In fact, most people can generate metabolic rates that are 6 to 8 times above the resting level during sustained large-muscle activities such as running, bicycling, and swimming. Tabled values for energy expenditure are available from which one can estimate the caloric cost of a variety of occupational, recreational, and sports activities.[8]

While many factors affect the energy expended during a particular exercise, the energy cost of most physical activities is generally greater for heavier people, especially in weight-bearing forms of exercise like walking and running, during which the person must transport body weight. Table 13-1 shows the energy expenditure during horizontal walking at speeds ranging between 3.2 to 6.4 km/hr for people who differ in body weight. These predicted values are generally accurate to within 8% to 15% of the actual energy expenditure for both men and women of different sizes. On a daily basis, therefore, estimates of energy expended in walking could be in error by 50 to 100 kcal, assuming that a person walks 2 hours each day. The important point is that in most forms of exercise the *total* calories expended by the heavier person are considerably more than by a lighter counterpart. With weight-supported exercise such as stationary cycling and swimming, the influence of body weight is evident though less extreme. Certainly, for moderately obese people with no physical limitations, weight-bearing forms of exercise can provide a considerable caloric expenditure.

Table 13-2 presents values for the net energy (NE = gross energy expenditure minus resting energy expenditure) expended during running for 1 hour at various speeds. Running speeds are expressed as kilometers per hour, miles per hour, and the number of minutes required to complete 1 mile at a particular running

Table 13-1 Prediction of Energy Expenditure (kcal/min^{-1}) Based on Speed of Walking and Body Weight[a]

SPEED		Body Weight												
mph	km/hr^{-1}	kg lb	45 100	54 120	64 140	73 160	82 180	91 200	100 220	109 240	118 260	127 280	136 300	145 320	155 340
2.0	3.2		2.0	2.4	2.8	3.2	3.6	4.0	4.4	4.8	5.2	5.6	6.0	6.4	6.9
2.5	4.0		2.3	2.8	3.3	3.7	4.2	4.6	5.1	5.6	6.0	6.5	6.9	7.4	7.9
3.0	4.8		2.6	3.1	3.7	4.2	4.7	5.3	5.8	6.3	6.8	7.3	7.8	8.4	8.9
3.5	5.6		2.9	3.5	4.1	4.7	5.3	5.9	6.4	7.0	7.6	8.2	8.8	9.4	10.0
4.0	6.4		3.2	3.8	4.6	5.2	5.8	6.5	7.1	7.7	8.4	9.0	9.7	10.3	11.0

[a]Predictive equation presented in *Guidelines for Exercise Testing and Prescription*, ed 3, American College of Sports Medicine, Lea & Febiger, Copyright © 1986.

Table 13-2 Net Energy Expenditure per Hour for Horizontal Running[a]

BODY WEIGHT		km/hr^{-1} [b]	7.0	8.0	9.0	10.0	11.0	12.0	13.0
		mph	4.3	5.0	5.6	6.2	6.8	7.5	8.1
		min per mile	13:82	12:00	10:43	9:41	8:46	8:02	7:26
kg	lb	kcal per mile							
50	110	80	350	400	450	500	550	600	650
58	128	93	406	464	522	580	638	696	754
66	146	106	462	528	594	660	726	792	858
74	163	118	518	592	666	740	814	888	962
82	181	131	574	656	738	820	902	984	1066
90	199	144	630	720	810	900	990	1080	1170
98	216	157	686	784	882	980	1078	1176	1274
106	234	170	742	848	954	1060	1166	1272	1378
114	251	182	798	912	1026	1140	1254	1368	1482
122	268	195	854	976	1098	1220	1342	1464	1586
130	286	208	910	1040	1170	1300	1430	1560	1690
138	304	221	966	1104	1242	1380	1518	1656	1794
146	321	234	1022	1168	1314	1460	1606	1752	1898
154	339	246	1078	1232	1386	1540	1694	1848	2002

[a]The table is interpreted as follows: For a 50-kg person, the net energy expenditure for running for 1 hour at 8 $km \cdot hr^{-1}$, or 5.0 mph, is 400 kcal; this speed represents a 12-min/ mile pace. Thus in 1 hour, 5 miles would be run and 400 kcal would be expended. If the pace were increased to 12 $km \cdot hr^{-1}$, 600 kcal would be expended during the hour of running.

[b]Running speeds are expressed as kilometers per hour (km/hr^{-1}), miles per hour (mph), and minutes required to complete each mile (min per mile). The values in italics are the net calories expended to run 1 mile for a given body weight, independent of running speed.

Source: Modified from data presented in *Exercise Physiology: Energy, Nutrition, and Human Performance*, ed 2, by WD McArdle et al, Lea & Febiger, Copyright © 1986.

speed. The boldface values are the net calories expended in running 1 mile for a given body weight. This energy requirement is fairly constant and independent of running speed. Thus, for a person who weighs 62 kg (136 lb) to run a 26-mile marathon requires approximately 2,600 kcal whether the run is completed in just over 2 hours or 4 hours. For a heavier person, the energy cost per mile increases in proportion to body weight. For example, if a 102-kg (225-lb) person jogs 5 miles each day at a comfortable pace, 163 kcal will be expended for each mile completed, or a total of 815 kcal for the 5-mile run. Increasing or decreasing the running speed simply alters the physiologic overload and duration of the exercise period; it has little effect on the total energy expended.

Regular Exercise, Fat Loss, and Body Composition

Regular aerobic exercise, especially when combined with dietary restriction, brings about greater reductions in body weight and a greater increase in functional capacity compared with dieting alone.[9] Of great importance is that exercise often provides protection against the significant loss in lean tissue observed with weight loss through dieting.[10,11] The effectiveness of the exercise program for weight loss is linked to the degree of fatness at the start. As a general rule, people who are obese lose weight and fat more readily than leaner counterparts. In addition, exercise stimulates improved function of various physiologic systems and may enhance the person's health status.[7,12]

Table 13-3 shows the effectiveness of regular exercise without dieting for weight loss. In this study, six sedentary obese young men exercised 5 days/wk for 16 weeks by 90 minutes of walking at each session. The men lost an average of approximately 13 lb of body fat, which represented a decrease in percent of body fat from 23.5% to 18.6%. In addition, physiologic fitness and exercise capacity improved, as did the level of high-density lipoprotein (HDL) and the ratio of high-to-low–density lipoprotein (LDL), which increased 15.6% and 25.9%, respectively.

Localized Fat Loss

The basis for attempts at localized fat loss or spot reduction with exercise is the belief that by exercising a specific body area, more fat will be selectively reduced from that area than if exercise of the same caloric intensity were performed by a different muscle group. In a practical sense, the advocate of spot reduction would recommend a large number of sit-ups for a person with an excessively fat abdominal area. It is believed that, in some way, disuse of a muscle group causes a disproportionate storage of local subcutaneous fat and, conversely, an increase in the muscle's activity facilitates a relatively great fat mobilization from these specific storage areas.

While the promise of spot reduction with exercise is especially attractive from an aesthetic standpoint, a critical evaluation of the research does not support this idea.[13] Comparisons were made, for example, of the circumferences and subcutaneous fat stores of the right and left forearms of high-caliber tennis players.[14] As expected, the circumference of the dominant or playing arm was significantfly larger than the nondominant arm owing to a modest muscular hypertrophy associated with the muscular overload provided by tennis. Measurements of fatfold thickness, however, showed that there were no differences between the arms in the quantity of subcutaneous forearm fat. Clearly, prolonged exercise of the playing arm was not accompanied by significantly reduced fat deposits in that arm.

Table 13-3 Changes in Body Composition and Blood Lipids in Six Obese Young Adult Men with a 16-week Walking Program

Variable	Pretraining[a]	Post-training	Difference
Body weight, kg	99.1	93.4	− 5.7[b]
Body density, $g \cdot ml^{-1}$	1.0444	1.056	+ 0.012[b]
Body fat, %	23.5	18.6	− 4.9[b]
Fat weight, kg	23.3	17.4	− 5.9[b]
Lean body weight, kg	75.8	76.0	+ 0.2
Sum of fatfolds, mm	142.9	104.8	− 38.1[b]
HDL cholesterol, $mg \cdot 100\ ml^{-1}$	32.0	37.0	+ 5.0[b]
HDL/LDL cholesterol	0.27	0.34	+ 0.07[b]

[a]Values are means.
[b]Statistically significant.

Source: Reprinted with permission from *American Journal of Clinical Nutrition* (1979; 33:1776), Copyright © 1979, American Society for Clinical Nutrition Inc.

Current knowledge of energy supply indicates that exercise stimulates the mobilization of fatty acids from the fat depots throughout the body, and the areas of greatest concentration probably supply the greatest amount of energy. There is simply no evidence that fatty acids are released to a greater degree from the fat pads directly over the exercising muscle. There is no doubt that a negative caloric balance created through regular exercise can significantly contribute to a reduction in total body fat. The fat, however, is not reduced selectively from the exercised areas but, rather, from total body fat reserves and from the areas of greatest fat concentration.

FORMULATING THE EXERCISE PROGRAM

Medical Screening

An integral aspect in formulating the exercise program is to determine the health status of the participant. In general, a moderate level of obesity (up to 130% of ideal body weight based on actuarial data from life insurance statistics) with no major coronary heart disease risks (elevated cholesterol levels, hypertension, cigarette smoking, abnormal ECG) poses no greater medical risk to participation in regular aerobic exercise than that in the general population.[15] However, in line with established and prudent recommendations for apparently healthy adults, it is recommended that obese people receive medical screening to establish overall health status before embarking on an exercise program.[16] For people above the age of 45, a maximum graded exercise test with a physician present is required. If the stress test is not administered to the apparently healthy younger participant, it is advisable to include in the screening an assessment of current fitness to evaluate physiologic responses (eg, heart rate, blood pressure) to exercise (eg, stepping, cycling, treadmill walking). Certainly for all those who begin exercising without a graded exercise test to maximum, the program should progress gradually, and the participant should be aware of unusual signs and symptoms.

For people with a greater than moderate level of obesity, a more cautious approach should be taken. These participants should be considered at risk for both cardiovascular and musculoskeletal complications.[17] Such people 35 years of age and older must be fully cleared in terms of health status, including evaluation by means of a graded exercise stress test up to maximum. Also, because obesity is frequently associated with certain psychologic disorders, the screening should also evaluate the emotional status of the participant.[18] An added benefit of the stress test is that it provides participants with an objective indication that they can perform strenuous exercise without harm or injury.

Aerobic Exercise: The Key to Weight Loss

When considering exercise for weight control, factors such as the specific form of exercise, the exercise intensity, frequency of participation, and the duration of each exercise session must be considered.

Continuous aerobic activities that activate a relatively large muscle mass such as walking, jogging or running, cycling, and swimming are ideal as the major component of a weight-loss exercise program. Many recreational sports and games are also effective in enhancing caloric output, although precise quantification and regulation of energy expenditure during such activities is difficult. Competitive sport activities may place the participant at unnecessary risk for injury. Rhythmic forms of sustained exercise burn considerable calories; favorably modify lipid metabolism, body fat, and blood pressure; and generally promote cardiovascular fitness. There is generally no selective effect among various forms of aerobic exercise; each is equally effective in altering body composition provided the duration, frequency, and intensity of exercise are similar.[19] What is most important is that each person participate in activities that are safe, pleasurable, and adaptable to any specific physical limitations. It is only when these criteria are met that there is a reasonable chance for sustained compliance on the part of the participant.

Walking

Walking is a safe, practical, and easily regulated way to start an exercise program for weight loss. For both walking and jogging, essentially no special equipment is required except for supportive and well-cushioned shoes to absorb shock and control the angle of the shoe as it strikes the ground. Walking, even at a rapid pace, is relatively gentle on the bones and joints. This is because there is no airborne phase as with running. Proper walking is achieved with a *heel-toe motion* with only moderate impact as the weight is gradually transferred to the ball of the foot.

Jogging or Running

Jogging or running, especially for the unconditioned and overweight, results in much greater impact, which can place an unnecessary strain on the knees, hips, and ankle joints.[20] It is estimated that during running the impact force when the foot hits the ground with each stride is equal to 2 to 3 times the runner's body weight. This would certainly increase the risk of orthopedic problems for the overweight engaged in exercise of long duration to increase caloric expenditure. For this reason, jogging would not be prescribed as the initial activity for the obese person. However, after the participant has been exercising for a period of time, has reduced body weight, and has experienced no orthopedic difficulties, jogging may be considered as a means of exercise. Slow jogging requires no complex skill. As with walking, large muscle groups of the body are exercised in rhythmic, continuous movement, and there is usually little localized muscle fatigue or cramping. Because the body weight is transported while walking or jogging, as opposed to swimming or stationary bicycling in which the body weight is supported, the number of calories burned is relatively high, especially for the overweight.

Stationary Cycling

There are a variety of stationary bicycles available with adjustable pedal resistance for convenient, well-regulated indoor exercise in the privacy of one's home. Because body weight is supported in bicycling, this exercise is often ideal for the overweight who, as a group, have compromised mobility and are susceptible to orthopedic problems, which may become magnified in weight-bearing exercise. A major complaint is that stationary cycling tends to become boring. This can be circumvented, however, by scheduling exercise during a favorite television program; one can even purchase an attachment to hold reading material during cycling. The use of a small fan can increase the effect of convective heat loss, which is generally minimal with this form of indoor exercise.

Water Activities

For many obese people, swimming and other forms of exercise in water such as aquatic aerobics and simulated jogging are ideal.[21] Body weight is supported by the buoyant force of the water. Consequently, there is little strain on bones and joints imposed by extra body weight, yet the increased resistance to movement provided by the water can add significantly to caloric output. Because the legs and arms are used in the rhythmic swimming movement, major muscles of the body are exercised. In addition, as heat intolerance is often a problem for the obese, the cool water is a pleasant environment in which to dissipate the metabolic heat generated by exercise. Furthermore, for the extremely obese, the weight-supported nature of swimming (and bicycling) may be desirable to counter the significant metabolic load imposed by weight-bearing exercise. In walking, for example, the energy cost for the extremely obese may be so great (because of body weight) that even a slow rate may place them outside their generally low physiologic capacity to sustain exercise.[22] In these situations, a weight-supported exercise program that includes swimming is ideal to bring the overweight person to a level of functional capacity so that a variety of physical activities may be effectively used.

Circuit Weight Training

By modifying the approach to standard-strength training methods so that heavy muscle overload is de-emphasized, it is possible to increase the caloric cost of exercise for effective aerobic training and weight control[23] while at the same time firming and moderately strengthening the major muscle groups of the body. Since a variety of muscles are exercised, it is likely that this form of exercise could have a significant effect in protecting the body from the loss of lean tissue frequently observed during weight reduction. A slight increase in muscle mass would also be a desirable byproduct by increasing the daily level of resting metabolism.

With this approach, called circuit weight training, the person lifts a weight that is 30% to 40% of peak strength (defined as the maximum weight that can be lifted only once). Different weight lifting exercises are performed in a pre-established exercise-rest sequence. In most programs, the circuit consists of 8 to 12 exercise stations. The weight is lifted 15 to 22 times for each exercise in a 30-second period. After a 15-second rest, the person moves to the next weight lifting station and so on until the entire circuit is completed. The circuit is repeated several times to allow for 20 to 30 minutes of continuous exercise. As strength increases, the weight lifted at each station also increases. The energy cost of such a circuit is usually similar to that achieved jogging at 5 mph[24] or participating in leisurely swimming or sports activity. Certainly, any program using weight lifting exercise for the obese needs to progress gradually and be carefully supervised to assume proper lifting technique and weight selection so as to optimize benefits and minimize the chance of injury.

The Exercise Prescription

Intensity of Exercise

The intensity of exercise is probably the most important factor for increasing aerobic fitness with training. For the overweight person, the key is to achieve a threshold exercise intensity for physiologic improvement yet focus on duration to magnify the caloric expenditure during each session.

The term "intensity of exercise" is quite relative because a considerable exercise stress for one person might be well below a training threshold for a highly conditioned person. Thus it is necessary to evaluate exercise in terms of the strain it places on the person's aerobic energy system. Consequently, it is necessary to evaluate a particular task and assign a training level in terms of the relative strain placed on each person.

Relative intensity is usually expressed as a percentage of maximum function, such as maximum aerobic capacity (max VO_2), maximum working capacity, or maximum heart rate (HR max). The most common expression is in terms of the exercise heart rate because heart rate reflects the overall strain on the cardiovascular system and is easily assessed at the wrist (radial artery) or neck (carotid artery). This practice of using the heart rate is also based on the fact that the percent of one's HR max and percent of max VO_2 are related in a predictable way regardless of gender or age, as shown in Table 13-4. The error in estimating the percent of max VO_2 from the percent of HR max, or vice versa, is approximately 8%. Because of the interdependence of the metabolic and cardiovascular systems, it is necessary only to monitor heart rate to estimate the relative strain on the aerobic machinery in the active muscles (percent of max VO_2). This, therefore, makes it possible to personalize an exercise program and regulate the intensity of exercise to keep pace with changes in the person's physiologic capacity.

As a general rule, aerobic capacity improves if exercise is of sufficient intensity to increase the heart rate to approximately 70% of maximum. This is equivalent to approximately 55% of max VO_2 or, for young adult men and women, a heart rate of 130 to 140 beats per minute with leg exercise like cycling, walking, and running. For people in relatively poor physical condition, the training threshold may be closer to 60% of HR max, which corresponds to approximately 45% of max VO_2.

To train at a predetermined percentage of HR max requires a knowledge of what the heart rate would be during near-exhausting exercise. Someone's actual

Table 13-4 Relation between Percentage of Maximal Heart Rate (percent HR max) and Percentage of Maximum Aerobic Capacity (percent max VO_2)

Percent HR Max	Percent Max VO_2
50	28
60	42
70	56
80	70
90	83
100	100

maximum heart rate can be determined immediately after 3 or 4 minutes of all-out running or stationary cycling. Generally, this procedure is inadvisable because such intense exercise is difficult, requires considerable motivation, and could be dangerous to those predisposed to coronary heart disease. However, HR max can be estimated as 220 beats per minute minus the person's age in years. In addition to the average age-adjusted maximum heart rates, Figure 13-1 illustrates the "training sensitive zone" that represents the threshold 70% and the upper level of 90% of HR max for each age group. Conditioning of the aerobic system will occur so long as the exercise heart rate is within this zone.

Clearly, exercise need not be strenuous to obtain positive results. An exercise heart rate of 70% of maximum represents moderate exercise that can be continued for a long time with little or no discomfort. This training level is frequently referred to as "conversational" exercise in that it is sufficiently intense to stimulate a training effect yet not so strenuous that it limits a person from talking during the workout. It is important to note that when working with overweight people in the initial phase of training, a lower intensity of exercise is desirable to reinforce favorable feelings about exercise and ease the person into the process of physiologic adaptation. In fact, if intensity is lowered to 60% of HR max, an extended duration of effort will still bring about a training response.

Suppose a 30-year-old man wishes to train at moderate intensity yet still be at or above the threshold level. A training heart rate would be selected that would be equal to 70% of the age-predicted HR max, or a target exercise heart rate of 133 beats per minute (0.70×190). For a 55-year-old woman, on the other hand, the target heart rate would be 116 beats per minute (0.70×166). By trial and error each person can arrive at a walking, jogging, or cycling speed that would produce the desired target heart rate.

In carrying out this trial-and-error procedure, the person should exercise moderately for 3 to 5 minutes, counting pulse rate for 10 seconds immediately afterward. If the exercise is not intense enough to produce the target heart rate,

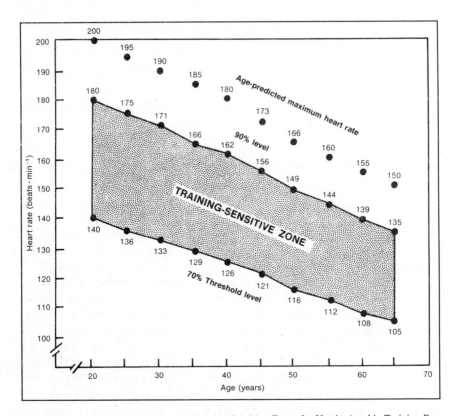

Figure 13-1 Maximal Heart Rates and Training-Sensitive Zones for Use in Aerobic Training Programs for People of Different Ages. *Source*: Reprinted from *Exercise Physiology: Energy, Nutrition, and Human Performance* (p 359) by WD McArdle et al with permission of Lea & Febiger, Copyright © 1986.

the same exercise should be repeated but at a faster pace. As cardiovascular fitness improves and the person starts to become "trained," the exercise heart rate will gradually decrease. It is common for the submaximal exercise heart rate to be lowered by 10 to 20 beats per minute as max VO_2 increases with training. To keep pace with improving aerobic fitness, the exercise level must be increased periodically to achieve the threshold heart rate or the target heart rate that has been established. A person who began training with slow walking must walk more briskly; this may gradually be replaced by jogging for periods of the workout and, eventually, continuous running to achieve the same relative exercise intensity as reflected by the desired target heart rate. If the progression in exercise intensity is not matched to training improvements, the exercise program essentially becomes a maintenance program.[25]

When exercise uses predominantly the musculature of the upper body, as in swimming or arm cranking, the relation between the percentages of HR max and max VO_2 is the same as in leg exercise. However, the HR max is approximately 13 beats per minute lower during arm exercise. Consequently, an adjustment must be made, and an average of 13 beats per minute should be subtracted from the age-predicted HR max values shown in Figure 13-1. Thus, a 25-year-old person wishing to swim at 80% of HR max would select a swimming speed that produced a heart rate of approximately 146 beats per minute (0.80) × (195 − 13). This would represent more accurately the appropriate training heart rate for upper-body exercise. If this adjustment is not made, a prescription for arm exercise based on a percentage of HR max for leg exercise would overestimate the appropriate training heart rate.

Frequency of Exercise

Training frequency is important when considering exercise for weight loss. Frequency is the means for distributing the calorie-burning effects of exercise throughout the week so that the amount of exercise in any one session is within the capability and comfort level of the participant. In a summary of six studies that investigated optimal training frequency,[26] it was observed that training 2 days/wk did not change body weight, fatfolds, or percent of body fat. Training 3 and 4 days/wk, however, had a significant effect. Subjects who trained 4 days/wk reduced body weight and fatfolds significantly more than the group that trained 3 days/wk. Reductions in percent of body fat, however, were similar for both groups.

Within the framework of available research, it appears that at least 3 days of training per week are required to change body composition through exercise.[27] There is indication that more frequent training may even be more effective in weight control. More than likely, this effect is the direct result of the added caloric output provided by the extra training.

Duration of the Exercise Session

Generally, the total energy expended is the most important factor that influences the effectiveness of the exercise program for weight control. In fact, a dose-response relation has been shown with weight loss being directly related to the time spent exercising.[14] Thus, an overweight person who begins with light exercise can accrue a considerable caloric expenditure simply by extending the duration of exercise. Furthermore, to condition the physiologic systems, the effects of a lower training intensity can be offset by extending the duration of the training session. From an energy standpoint, it is much better to continue in an activity for a prolonged period of time at a reasonable pace than to perform the same activity at maximum pace for a short time. A 150-lb person, for example, expends approximately 110 kcal while jogging 1 mile in 12 minutes. If continued for 3 miles, the total caloric output would be 330 kcal. If the same person runs only 1 mile, but at the fast pace of 5 minutes and 30 seconds, then only approximately 130 kcal would be burned. This effect of duration makes up for the inability (and inadvisability) of the previously sedentary obese person to exercise at high intensities. In a practical sense, adding 10 minutes to a 30-minute workout will burn 33% more calories.

Although it is difficult to speculate precisely as to a minimal level of energy expenditure for weight reduction and fat loss, it is generally recommended that the calorie-burning effect of each exercise session should be at least 300 kcal.[27] This can be achieved with 20 to 30 minutes of moderate to vigorous running, swimming, or bicycling or lower-intensity walking for 40 to 60 minutes. Exercise programs of lower caloric cost usually show little or no effect on body weight or body composition.

Program Monitoring

Careful and regular monitoring of exercise should be made in terms of frequency, duration, and physiologic response, as well as approximate calories expended and participants' subjective feelings. Pulse rate should be determined frequently in the early phase of the program as participants become familiar with their bodies' response to exercise. As training progresses, other clues such as breathing response and perceived exertion will be fairly accurate estimates of the relative exertion level.

Individualized Program

The program should be individualized to the specific needs and limitations of the participant and should always be formulated and modified against the background of previous medical history and physical testing. The program should also include exercises that will increase the chances of a long-term maintenance of an active life-style as well as assure adherence to the exercise program. Therefore, realistic exercise, fitness, and weight-loss goals for each participant must be established.

Basic Exercise Guidelines

Regardless of one's present physical condition, there are basic guidelines for an aerobic exercise program. These are especially important for an overweight person whose physical limitation of excess weight may be compounded by poor functional capacity because of a sedentary life style. The overweight person should be encouraged to join a highly structured exercise program that considers both the physiologic and the psychologic needs of the participant.

Start Slowly

The obese generally have considerably lower work tolerance than counterparts of normal weight.[22] Consequently, the initial stage of the exercise program for a previously sedentary overweight person should be developmental and should not include a high total energy output. Enjoyment and success should be key goals. In the first week or so, no more than 50 to 100 kcal should be burned per exercise session as the person is introduced to regular exercise. With steady progression in intensity and duration, the average participant should be able to expend 300 kcal per exercise session in 8 to 10 weeks.

In the early phase of conditioning, the participant should be urged to adopt long-term goals, personal discipline, and a restructuring of both eating and exercise behaviors. It is often counterproductive to include unduly rapid training progressions or prolonged exercise sessions, as many obese people initially show poor levels of fitness and a marked stress in their exposure to exercise. For example, it has been reported that extremely obese patients required 1 to 2 months of progressive exercise training before they could continually walk 2 miles.[27] If walking is the mode of exercise selected during the first few weeks, slow walking for 3- to 5-minute intervals should be replaced by longer periods of continuous walking. A buildup in intensity and duration must be gradual and progressive. At least 8 to 12 weeks may be required before observable changes in body composition occur, although more rapid changes have been reported with a combination of exercise and dieting in the severely obese in a clinical setting.[28] Behavioral approaches should also be used to cause meaningful life-style changes in physical activity. Walking or bicycling, for example, can replace the use of the auto, stair climbing can replace the elevator, and manual tools can replace power tools.

Warm-up

Before starting the conditioning phase of exercise, it is important to stretch the muscles gently and limber up for at least several minutes. The stretching exercises should be performed through the full range of joint motion. After stretching, there are numerous calisthenic exercises to provide the cardiovascular warm-up. The important point is to perform big muscle exercise in a rhythmic, moderate, and continuous manner to bring the heart rate to 50% to 60% of maximum. This helps ease the cardiovascular system into the more vigorous conditioning phase of the program and may reduce the risk of the abnormal ECG responses observed with sudden, vigorous exercise.[29]

Because of the actual encumbrance of large amounts of adipose tissue, it is important that the obese person not be placed for prolonged periods in a position that would hinder breathing movements during calisthenic or warm-up exercise. For example, a prolonged toe-touch in either the standing or seated positions or inverted cycling movements on the back often limit the normal ventilatory excursions for the obese and produce feelings of discomfort that would normally not accompnay such exercises.

Cool Down

After the conditioning phase of the exercise program, 5 or 10 minutes of progressively more mild exercise should be provided to allow metabolism to progress toward resting levels. More importantly, however, a gradual cool down prevents blood from pooling in the large veins of the previously exercised muscles. Furthermore, as obese people generally show greater heat stress during exercise compared with leaner counterparts, a sudden cessation of exercise could exacerbate the pooling of blood in the capacitance vessels of the periphery. Such venous pooling could bring about a reduction in venous return with a concomitant reduction in cardiac output. Insufficient blood flow may cause dizziness, nausea, and even fainting, while a reduced myocardial flow may precipitate arrythmias and trigger a dangerous cardiac episode.

Exercise in the Heat

Because of the relatively poor heat tolerance of the obese, special attention should be given to the temperature and humidity of the exercise environment as well as the hydration level and exercise attire of the participant. Participants should be encouraged to drink fluids before and at regular intervals throughout exercise. Exercise clothing should take maximum advantage of evaporative cooling. To this end, the clothing should be lightweight and loose fitting to provide for circulation of air between the skin and the environment. Cottons and linens permit vaporization of water, whereas clothing made of plastic or rubber retards the evaporation of moisture from the skin, thus preventing evaporative cooling. The body continues to sweat, however, forcing fluid reserves down and body temperature up. No benefits result and dangerous hypohydration can occur.

Special Considerations for the Extremely Obese

Although the research is limited, it does seem that the extremely obese (>150% of ideal body weight) can safely benefit in terms of functional capacity and their coronary heart disease risk profile from a highly structured program of regular aerobic exercise. It is noteworthy, however, that the extremely obese represent a special population with unique problems that must receive careful consideration when formulating an exercise program. Many of these people have abnormal psychologic profiles as well as specific physical limitations that may affect their compliance with a long-term exercise program. Orthopedic problems, low back pain, skin chafing brought on by the friction of movement, poor balance, poor response to both metabolic and environmental heat stress, low functional capacity, orthostatic hypotension, and poor psychologic perception of the exercise program are all factors to be considered in selecting exercise and formulating an appropriate rate of progression in exercise intensity. The unique problems that could affect exercise performance in the obese and practical solutions for each problem are presented elsewhere.[30]

REFERENCES

1. Johnson D, Drenick EJ: Therapeutic fasting in morbid obesity: Long term follow-up. *Arch Intern Med* 1977; 137:1381–1382.

2. Stern JS, Lowney T: Obesity: The role of physical activity, in Brownell KD, Foreyt JT (eds): *Handbook of Eating Disorders*. New York, Basic Books, 1986, pp 145–158.

3. Epstein LH, Wing RR: Aerobic exercise and weight. *Addict Behav* 1980; 5:371–388.

4. Keen H, Thomas BJ, Jarrett JR, et al: Nutrient intake, adiposity, and diabetes. *Br Med J* 1979; 1:655–658.

5. Stern JS, Lowney T: Obesity: The role of physical activity. *Handbook of Eating Disorders*, Brownell KD, Foreyt JT (eds). Basic Books Inc, 1986, pp 145–158.

6. Wing RR, Jeffery RR: Outpatient treatments of obesity: A comparison of methodology and clinical results. *Int J Obes* 1979; 3:261–279.

7. Lampman RM, Schteingart DE, Foss ML: Exercise as partial therapy for the extremely obese. *Med Sci Sports Exerc* 1986; 18:19–24.

8. McArdle WD, Katch FI, Katch VL: *Exercise Physiology: Energy, Nutrition, and Human Performance*, ed 2. Philadelphia, Lea & Febiger, 1986; pp 642–649.

9. Hagan RD, Upton SJ, Wong L, et al: The effects of aerobic conditioning and/or caloric restriction in overweight men and women. *Med Sci Sports Exerc* 1986; 18:87–94.

10. Moyer CL, Holly RG, Atkinson RL: Body composition changes in obese women on a very low calorie diet with and without exercise. *Med Sci Sports Exerc* 1985; 17:292–293.

11. Schteingart DE, Starkman MN, Lampman RN, et al: The physiologic and psychologic effects of exercise during weight reduction in obesity. *Psychsom Med* 1984; 46:75. Abstracted.

12. Lampman RM, Santinga JT, Savage PJ, et al: Effect of exercise training on glucose tolerance, in vivo insulin sensitivity, lipid and lipid protein concentrations in middle-aged men with mild hypertriglyceridemia. *Metabolism* 1985; 34:205–211.

13. Krotkiewski M, Mandroukas K, Sjostron L, et al: The effect of unilateral isokinetic strength training on local adipose and muscle tissue morphology, thickness and enzymes. *Eur J Appl Physiol* 1979; 22:271–281.

14. Gwinup G, Chevlam T, Steinberg T: Thickness of subcutaneous fat and activity of underlying muscles. *Ann Intern Med* 1971; 74:408–411.

15. Horton ES: Metabolic aspects of exercise and weight reduction. *Med Sci Sports Exerc* 1986; 18:10–18.

16. American College of Sports Medicine: *Guidelines for Exercise Testing and Prescription*, ed 3. Philadelphia, Lea & Febiger, 1986.

17. Foss ML, Strehle DA: Exercise testing and training for the obese, in Storlie J, Jordan HA (eds): *Nutrition and Exercise in Obesity Management*. New York, Spectrum Books, 1984; pp 93–121.

18. Brownell KD: The psychology and physiology of obesity: Implications for screening and treatment. *J Am Diet Assoc* 1984; 84:406–414.

19. Pollock ML, Dimmick J, Miller HS, Jr, et al: Effects of mode of training on cardiovascular function and body composition of adult men. *Med Sci Sports* 1975; 7:139–145.

20. Goodman CE, Waxman J: Jogging and obesity: Prevention of musculoskeletal injuries. *Obesity/Bariatric Med* 1984; 11:7–14.

21. Sheldhal LM: Special ergometric techniques and weight reduction. *Med Sci Sports Exerc* 1986; 1:25–30.

22. Foss ML, Lampman RM, Watt E, et al: Initial work tolerance of extremely obese patients. *Arch Phys Med Rehabil* 1975; 56:63–67.

23. Gettman LR, Ayers JJ, Pollock ML, et al: Physiologic effects on adult men of circuit strength training and jogging. *Arch Phys Med Rehabil* 1979; 60:115–120.

24. Gettman LR, Pollock ML: Circuit weight training: A critical review of its physiological benefits. *Phys Sportsmed* 1981; 9:44–60.

25. Hickson RC, Koster C, Pollock ML, et al: Reduced training intensities and loss of aerobic power, endurance, and cardiac growth. *J Appl Physiol* 1985; 58:492–499.

26. Pollock ML, Miller HS, Jr, Linnerud AC, et al: Frequency of training as a determinant for improvement in cardiovascular function and body composition of middle-aged men. *Arch Phys Med Rehabil* 1975; 56:141–145.

27. American College of Sports Medicine: Position statement on proper and improper weight loss programs. *Med Sci Sports Exerc* 1983; 15:ix–xii.

28. Foss ML, Lampman RM, Schteingart DE: Extremely obese patients: Improvements in exercise tolerance with physical training and weight loss. *Arch Phys Med Rehabil* 1980; 61:119–124.

29. Barnard RJ, MacAltin R, Cattus AA, et al: Ischemic response to sudden strenuous exercise in healthy men. *Circulation* 1973; 48:936–942.

30. Foss ML: Exercise concerns and precautions for the obese, in Storlie J, Jordan HA (eds): *Nutrition and Exercise in Obesity Management*. New York, Spectrum Books, 1984; pp 123–148.

Chapter 14

Pharmacologic Approaches to the Treatment of Obesity

Cheryl Nauss-Karol and Ann C. Sullivan

THERAPEUTIC GOALS AND RATIONALE

Obesity, defined as a body weight more than 20% above ideal, is a major health problem that results from an energy intake in excess of metabolic needs. The National Institutes of Health Consensus Development Conference[1] recently confirmed that obesity has adverse effects on health and longevity. Obesity also causes considerable social, psychologic, and economic stress.

Current methods of treating obesity are largely ineffective, especially if long-term results are considered. It is clear that a greater degree of efficacy is needed than has been achieved through dietary restriction (with or without the use of anorectics), behavior modification, and exercise regimens.

Safe and efficacious drugs are needed to accelerate weight loss and to prevent its regain once ideal body weight has been reached. These antiobesity drugs should be used as adjuncts to dietary restriction and exercise programs. Pharmacologic treatment of obesity, depending on its severity, may require intervention at one or more sites simultaneously to circumvent the multiple compensatory systems that work to maintain elevated body fat levels in obese patients. Thus, for severe forms of obesity, use of several drugs with different mechanisms of action may be required. Certain subtypes of obese patients may be most responsive to a particular type of mechanistic approach. These questions will remain unanswered until we have clinical evaluations of drugs with unique and different mechanisms of action.

Characteristics of the ideal antiobesity agent are:

- sustained reduction of body weight through a selective reduction of body fat stores

Donna Howe, Maggie Johnson, Cathy Muscara, and Lori Zielenski assisted in the preparation of this manuscript.

- prevention of rebound weight gain once other forms of therapy (caloric restriction, exercise, surgery) are no longer effective
- improved efficacy as an adjunct to caloric restriction
- no undesirable side effects or abuse potential.

The many possible sites for pharmacologic intervention can be grouped into three broad categories: agents producing (1) reduced energy intake, (2) decreased energy storage, or (3) enhanced energy expenditure. This chapter reviews marketed and experimental antiobesity drugs that seem to act by the following mechanisms: (1) appetite suppression, (2) inhibition of intestinal absorption of dietary carbohydrates and lipids, (3) suppression of lipid synthesis, and (4) thermogenesis stimulation.

APPETITE SUPPRESSANTS

Marketed Drugs

The traditional pharmacologic approach to treating obesity is the use of an anorectic agent as an adjunct to dietary restriction. Anorectic drugs currently available by prescription in the United States are listed in Table 14-1. Drugs affecting appetite can generally be categorized as primarily acting directly on the central nervous system (CNS) or at a peripheral site(s). Marketed anorectic drugs are phenethylamine derivatives, with the exception of mazindol, and all have a direct central site of action. These drugs presumably lower food intake

Table 14-1 Prescription Anorectic Drugs Currently Available in the United States

Generic Name	Proprietary Name	Drug Enforcement Administration Schedule
Amphetamine	Dexedrine, Obetrol	II
Methamphetamine	Desoxyn	II
Phenmetrazine	Preludin	II
Benzphetamine	Didrex	III
Phendimetrazine	Plegine and Others	III
Diethylpropion	Tenuate, Tepanil	IV
Fenfluramine	Pondimin	IV
Mazindol	Sanorex, Mazanor	IV
Phentermine	Fastin and Others	IV

by potentiating central dopaminergic, adrenergic, or serotonergic mechanisms. Amphetamine, diethylpropion, and mazindol seem to produce their anorectic effects through interaction with the catecholaminergic system,[2,3] while fenfluramine seems to act through a serotonergic mechanism.[4,5]

Chronic use of these drugs is restricted because of side effects, potential addiction liability, and the development of tolerance. Fenfluramine is a CNS depressant that can induce sedation and depression,[6] and should not be used in patients suffering from depression. All other anorectic drugs are CNS stimulants of varying degrees. Since most of these drugs structurally resemble the catecholamines, they may produce catecholamine-like side effects such as nervousness, insomnia, and tachycardia. Increased weight gain is often associated with withdrawal of anorectic agents.

To determine the efficacy of various anorectic drugs in weight reduction, the Food and Drug Administration reviewed data derived from more than 200 controlled double-blind studies of patients treated with all drugs marketed in the United States as anorectic agents in 1975.[7] Since no significant differences between anorectic drugs were noted, the data were combined and compared with placebo treatment. These results, based on 7,725 obese patients, indicate that, in general, use of an anorectic drug results in a rate of weight loss of 0.5 lb/wk more than that achieved by placebo. After 4 weeks of treatment, 68% of the drug group and 46% of the placebo group had lost an average of 1 lb/wk. Ten percent of the drug group as compared with only 4% of the placebo group had lost an average of 3 lbs (or more) per week during this time period. After completion of their treatment regimen (up to 12 weeks), 44% of the drug group and 26% of the placebo group had lost an average of 1 lb/wk. Two percent of the drug group and 1% of the placebo group had lost an average of 3 lbs (or more) per week. Efficacy was similar for all drugs evaluated.

More recently, the results of a series of double-blind clinical studies[8] using either phenethylamine or nonphenethylamine anorectics to assess weight reduction were evaluated. More than 5,000 patients were evaluated, and the duration of treatment ranged from 2 to 60 weeks. The findings were similar to those discussed above.[7] Efficacy was comparable with all drugs. In general, anorectic drugs produced an average weight loss of 0.6 lb/wk more than that achieved with placebo.

In summary, currently available centrally acting anorectics are useful as short-term supplements to weight-reduction programs employing nutritionally sound diets. Since all anorectic drugs seem to have comparable efficacy, there seems to be no justification for the use of schedule II anorectic drugs for antiobesity therapy. Recognition of the limitations of the currently marketed drugs has increased research in the discovery and development of novel anorectic agents that would be devoid of undesirable side effects and, therefore, safer for longer-term use.

Research Compounds in Clinical and Preclinical Evaluation

Anorectics Acting Through Serotonergic Mechanisms

The three antidepressants *fluoxetine, zimelidine,* and *femoxetine* are specific serotonin uptake inhibitors.[9] Antidepressant therapy, especially with tricyclic drugs, frequently results in weight gain. However, clinical studies with fluoxetine, zimelidine, and femoxetine have shown that their use in depressed patients causes either weight loss or no weight gain. A double-blind randomized crossover study[10] comparing 8 weeks of zimelidine treatment with 8 weeks of placebo treatment was done in 18 nondepressed obese female patients. Zimelidine produced a significantly greater weight loss (2.5 kg) and significantly decreased appetite as measured by subjective hunger ratings. Zimelidine seemed to be an effective antidepressant and had other useful properties, but a flu-like syndrome occurred in approximately 1.5% of patients.[11–13] Manifestations of this syndrome included fever and elevated hepatic enzyme levels, with probable hepatic damage. Because of these unusual but severe adverse reactions, the drug was withdrawn from the market in 1983.[9]

In an open-label 12-week study[14] of 21 obese patients, femoxetine produced an overall average weight loss of 3 kg, although the drug was more effective in patients under 45 years old. Subsequently, 81 obese patients were entered into a double-blind placebo-controlled study.[15] Average weight loss during the 16-week study was 5.3 kg and 1.5 kg for the treated and placebo groups, respectively. In both studies, the drug was well tolerated, and no dietary restraints were imposed. This degree of weight reduction was similar to that reported with marketed anorectics.

There are several reports[16,17] of weight loss associated with fluoxetine treatment in either depressed or nondepressed obese patients. With fluoxetine (20 to 80 mg/day for 6 weeks) treatment of depression, weight loss proportional to body mass index (BMI) was observed.[16] In a subsequent pilot study[16] of 120 patients, the fluoxetine (20 to 80 mg/day) group lost a mean of 4.5 kg, whereas the placebo group lost a mean of 1.4 kg during 8 weeks of treatment. Weight loss in the fluoxetine group was, again, proportional to the initial BMI.

In an analysis[18] of the safety data from more than 3,000 depressed patients who had been treated with fluoxetine (mainly at dosages of 20 to 80 mg/day), the following adverse effects were reported significantly more frequently than with placebo: nausea, nervousness, tremor, drowsiness, and excessive sweating.

In an 8-week study,[16] fluoxetine was given to nondepressed obese patients in set dosages ranging from 10 to 60 mg/day, or placebo. The 60-mg/day group lost a mean of 4 kg, while the placebo group lost a mean of 0.6 kg during the study. Lower doses had intermediate effects, and, again, weight loss was proportional to BMI. Fatigue and drowsiness increased in a dose-dependent manner, but there were no other statistically significant differences in adverse effects between the drug and placebo groups. In another study,[17] 150 nondepressed obese subjects were treated with either fluoxetine (mean dose 65 mg), benzphetamine (mean dose 97 mg), or placebo for 8 weeks. The groups receiving fluoxetine, benzphetamine, or placebo lost an average of 10.4 lb, 8.7 lb, and 3.6 lb, respectively. Subjects who reported carbohydrate craving at the beginning of the study lost more weight with fluoxetine than those without the craving. In rats, fluoxetine has been reported to decrease carbohydrate consumption selectively without affecting protein consumption.[16]

Opioid Antagonists

Opioid agonists, such as morphine, and endogenous opioids, such as beta-endorphin, stimulate food and water intake in animals. *Naloxone*, an opiate antagonist, has been reported to suppress food intake in animals and in both normal and obese humans.[19-22] However, naloxone has a short duration of action and must be administered intravenously (IV).

An orally active analog of naloxone, *naltrexone*, is a long-acting, potent narcotic antagonist to which tolerance does not develop.[23] When naltrexone was used as a narcotic antagonist, subjects reported a decrease in appetite.[24] Six of ten opiate-free volunteers also reported reduced food consumption after taking naltrexone.[25] However, in an 8-week outpatient study,[26] naltrexone at daily dosages of 50 and 100 mg had no significant effect on weight loss in obese male and female patients taken together. When the data were analyzed by sex, women taking naltrexone had a mean weight loss of 1.7 kg, whereas women taking placebo had a mean gain of 0.1 kg ($p<.05$). Naltrexone was generally well tolerated, but 6 of the 54 subjects completing the trial showed elevations in one or more liver function tests during naltrexone treatment.

Subsequently, a 10-week outpatient study[27] was performed in obese men and women using naltrexone at a daily dosage of 200 mg. Patients receiving naltrexone lost an average of 1.8 kg, while those on placebo lost 1.5 kg. This difference was not significant, and no sex effect was seen. In 3 of 21 subjects treated with naltrexone, liver transaminase levels were elevated to twice the baseline values. The authors concluded that naltrexone has no value for treating generalized obesity.

In another recent study,[28] naltrexone was administered to obese male inpatients in daily dosages ranging from 100 to 300 mg during a 28-day intensive crossover study. Results indicated a decreased daily caloric intake and modest weight loss with naltrexone as compared with placebo, but these effects were neither statistically significant nor dose-related. The study suggests that naltrexone was relatively ineffective in lowering food consumption and body weight in these obese men. As the authors[29] pointed out, several classes of opiate receptors have been recognized, and it seems likely that kappa receptors have a major role in opioid modulation of feeding behavior.[30] Since naloxone and naltrexone are reported to exert very little activity against kappa receptors,[31] this could explain their weak effects as anorectic agents.

Cholecystokinin

Cholecystokinin (CCK), an endogenous peptide known to stimulate gallbladder contraction and to release digestive pancreatic enzymes in response to a meal, has been studied as a possible short-term satiety signal.[32,33] Since the earliest report[34] of the satiating effects of CCK on rats, extensive work has been done both to confirm the initial observations and extend them to several other species,[32] including humans.[35-39]

Synthetic cholecystokinin-octapeptide (CCK-8) was used since this C-terminal octapeptide has the full spectrum of the biologic activity of CCK. In an early study,[36] 14 normal volunteers were given CCK-8 (20 ng/kg, 40 ng/kg, or 80 ng/kg) by intravenous (IV) or subcutaneous (SC) injection 10 or 20 minutes before a liquid formula test meal, respectively. One dosage level of test medication or placebo was given for 5 consecutive days in a randomized double-blind crossover manner. Although one of the five subjects receiving 20 ng/kg IV drank less formula ($p < .05$) during 5 days of treatment with CCK-8 than with placebo, there were no other significant changes in food intake. Both patients who received 80 ng/kg IV and one of the two who received 40 ng/kg IV experienced flushing, nausea, headache, diarrhea, and abdominal cramping. There were no side effects in the ten subjects receiving 20 ng/kg either IV or SC.

Three more recent trials[37-39] carefully examined the effects of IV infusion of CCK-8 on semisolid and solid food meals in lean and obese subjects. The results are encouraging and argue for a role of CCK in human satiety. In one trial,[37] 12 lean men received an IV infusion of either saline or CCK-8 (4 ng/kg/min) on each of 2 nonconsecutive days in a randomized double-blind crossover manner. Food intake of a semisolid meal was assessed by a universal eating monitor, which provides a sensitive measure of total intake, meal duration, initial rate of intake, and deceleration of intake by a continuous weighing of the food reservoir.[40] Administration of CCK-8 at the initiation of the test meal decreased meal size by an average of 122 g of a total of 644 g ($P < .05$) and decreased meal duration by an average of 1.53 minutes of a total of 9.37 minutes ($P < .05$). Five of the 12 subjects reported a "sick" sensation during CCK-8 treatment and not during the control period, but it was unrelated to satiety and was apparently mild. No other side effects were reported.

In a subsequent trial[38] the same design was used to study eight obese men. Infusion of CCK-8 decreased food consumption by an average of 125.5 g of a total of 977.2 g ($P < .05$) and decreased meal duration by an average of 2.6 minutes of a total of 12 minutes ($P < .05$). Response to a postmeal questionnaire indicated a higher incidence of a "sick" sensation during CCK-8 infusion. However, as in the previous study, this was not correlated with the satiating effects of CCK-8, and the effect was believed to be mild. There were no other side effects.

The effect of CCK-8 on ingestion of standardized sandwiches was assessed in 16 healthy volunteers who received single IV infusions of either saline or CCK-8 at a dosage of either 4.6 or 9.2 ng/kg/min in a randomized double-blind crossover design.[39] Subjects receiving the higher dosage reduced their sandwich intake by 50% ($P < .01$) and reported less hunger ($P < .02$). Those receiving the lower dosage reduced intake by 17% ($P < .05$) and also reported less hunger ($P < .05$). No side effects were observed.

In summary, the synthetic C-terminal octapeptide of CCK, CCK-8, seems to mimic the natural satiating effect of CCK. When administered by slow IV infusion to lean men and women and obese men, CCK-8 apparently brings about early termination of a meal, since subjects ate less as evidenced by a shorter meal duration. These effects were seen with dosages at which side effects were few and transient. Results with CCK-8 are encouraging, but the compound must be administered parenterally to be efficacious. It also has a short duration of effect. Therefore, CCK-8 alone has no practical use as an antiobesity agent. If an orally active, longer-acting analog of CCK could be developed, it could have utility as an antiobesity agent.

(-)-Threo-Chlorocitric Acid

Oral administration of (-)-threo-chlorocitric acid (chlorocitrate), a new anorectic agent, reduces food consumption dose-dependently in normal and obese rats and dogs.[41-43] Chronic treatment of rats with this compound resulted in a significantly lower rate of body-weight gain caused by a selective reduction of body lipid levels. No CNS stimulation was observed, and there was no development of tolerance, even after chronic treatment. The compound delays gastric emptying,[42] and its site of anorectic action is believed to be the upper gastrointestinal tract.

The effect of chlorocitrate on human eating behavior was recently examined in eight obese men in an 18-day inpatient study.[44] During the first 4-day single-blind phase, all subjects received placebo capsules three times daily (tid) to evaluate baseline food consumption and body weight, and to allow subjects to acclimatize to the metabolic ward. The 14-day treatment phase was double-blind, with each subject randomly assigned either active drug or placebo for the first 7 days, followed by the alternate treatment for the next 7 days. Ro 21–7716 at a dosage of 300 mg tid was administered 1 or 2 hours before each meal. Attractively presented food was available ad libitum, and intake was covertly monitored by use of the platter service method.[45] Consumption of a single test meal was measured by the universal eating monitor[40] during each treatment period. After receiving chlorocitrate at a dosage of approximately 8 mg/kg/day, these obese men gained an average of 1.6 kg less during the 7-day treatment than during the placebo period ($P < .02$). Food consumption was reduced by an average of 1,644 kcal/wk during drug treatment, but this difference was not significant. On the average, subjects ate less and had a slower initial rate of eating as measured by the universal eating monitor; but these results were not significant. No clinically significant adverse effects were observed. These data suggest that chlorocitrate has a significant antiobesity effect.

INHIBITORS OF INTESTINAL ABSORPTION OF DIETARY CARBOHYDRATES AND LIPIDS

Rationale

The major site of dietary nutrient absorption is the small intestine. A selective modification of the absorption of dietary lipid or carbohydrate through pharmacologic intervention would limit the availability of nutrients and create a chemical "bypass." The alteration of absorption could be regulated by drug dosage, and treatment could be readily discontinued if necessary to reverse the effect. Orally active nonabsorbable drugs that could suppress lipid or carbohydrate absorption would be particularly attractive. Expected side effects would be steatorrhea or carbohydrate intolerance produced by lipid or carbohydrate absorption inhibitors, respectively.

Inhibitors of Dietary Carbohydrate Absorption

The concept that a reduction in the digestion of dietary carbohydrates should diminish the postprandial glycemia, insulinemia, and triglyceridemia in patients with diabetes and/or obesity has stimulated research in this area.

Acarbose

Acarbose is the most extensively studied glucosidase inhibitor. This pseudotetrasaccharide potently inhibits maltase, sucrase, glucoamylase, and dextrinase.[46] In carbohydrate-loading experiments,[47] acarbose reduced the postprandial increase in circulating insulin and glucose levels in rats and humans. Acarbose also lowered the hyperglycemia and glucosuria of both insulin-independent and insulin-dependent diabetic patients.[48–50] During a recent 6-month study,[50] 600 mg/day of acarbose reduced insulin requirements in insulin-dependent diabetic patients by approximately 40%. In addition, high dosages of acarbose (1,500 mg/day) have been reported to help reduced-obese patients maintain their lowered body weight.[51,52] However, carbohydrate malabsorption symptoms are consistently reported with acarbose treatment. These unpleasant gastrointestinal effects may be a significant deterrent to widespread clinical use of the drug for the chronic treatment of obesity.

Bay m1099 and Bay o1248

Two new deoxynojirimycin derivatives, *Bay m1099* and *Bay o1248*, are potent alpha-glucosidase inhibitors. High doses did not produce carbohydrate maldigestion in rats, and both compounds seem to be nearly completely absorbed from the intestine.[53] Bay o1248 has a much longer duration of action than acarbose, and inhibits the intestinal degradation of starch and sucrose in rats even when administered 17 hours before carbohydrate loading. In rats, both compounds reduced food consumption, body weight gain, and fat-pad weight.

In a recent study,[54] nine healthy men ingested a 50-g sucrose load together with single doses of Bay m1099 (50 mg), Bay o1248 (10 mg), or placebo in a double-blind three-way crossover design. Both compounds significantly blunted the plasma glucose, fructose, and insulin peaks. Three of nine subjects with Bay m1099 and seven of nine subjects with Bay o1248 reported symptoms indicative of carbohydrate malabsorption (flatulence, abdominal discomfort). Breath hydrogen was increased with both drugs, also suggesting carbohydrate malabsorption. Since both drugs induced a significant delay in intestinal absorption of sucrose, they may be useful in treating diabetic patients in whom the slow absorption of carbohydrates is desirable.

AO-128

AO-128 is an alpha-glucosidase inhibitor and was recently reported to significantly lower serum triglyceride, glucose, and insulin levels and reduce body-weight gain in obese rats.[55] The reduction of body-weight gain was attributable to lower carcass lipid levels. In addition, the glucose intolerance normally apparent in these rats was ameliorated by AO-128.

The results of several clinical studies[55-57] have also been reported. When 14 male volunteers received a 2-mg dose and an additional 14 male volunteers received a 1-mg dose before lunch, the postprandial increases in serum glucose and insulin levels were suppressed in a dose-dependent manner.[56] When 20 male volunteers received 1 mg tid before meals for 3 days, the postprandial elevations in serum glucose and insulin levels were also reduced, except after the first breakfast.[56] Nearly all volunteers reported mild gastrointestinal symptoms (flatulence, distension, or diarrhea), but they were well tolerated.[56] The postprandial rises in serum glucose and insulin levels were similarly reduced in obese patients after a 2-mg dose of AO-128, and glucose tolerance improved in some obese diabetic patients after 2 weeks of treatment (3 mg/day).[57] Gastrointestinal symptoms were reported less frequently by obese than by lean people.[56,57] Two weeks of treatment with AO-128 at a dosage of 6 or 12 mg/day resulted in decreased body weight (1.5 kg) in three of five obese patients.[55]

Inhibitors of Dietary Lipid Absorption

Sucrose Polyester

Sucrose polyester (SPE) is a synthetic lipid that has physical and organoleptic properties remarkably similar to those of triglycerides.[58] Although not a classical inhibitor of lipid absorption, SPE cannot be hydrolyzed by pancreatic lipase, and therefore is nonabsorbable. SPE decreases the absorption of lipophilic substances like cholesterol by creating a persistent lipophilic phase in the intestine. Because of these qualities, SPE may have the two potential therapeutic benefits of lowering serum lipid levels and assisting in weight loss.

Several clinical studies were done with hypercholesterolemic,[59-62] normocholesterolemic,[62] or obese normocholesterolemic [63,64] patients in an effort to examine these possibilities. SPE interferes with cholesterol absorption in both humans and animals.[62,63,65,66] Indeed, the absorption of both exogenous and endogenous cholesterol seems to be reduced in normolipidemic obese patients.[63] In addition to reducing total serum cholesterol levels (mainly through a reduction of low-density-lipoprotein (LDL) cholesterol levels), SPE may also reduce serum triglyceride levels,[61,64] although not all authors report this result.

SPE seems more efficacious in lowering LDL cholesterol levels when simply added to a normal diet.[59-61] Substitution of SPE for 36 g of dietary fat resulted in a 4.1% weight loss after 30 days when coupled with a hypocaloric diet in five obese hypercholesterolemic women.[59] In a double-blind crossover inpatient study[64] designed to evaluate the effect of substituting dietary fat (60 g/day) with SPE, ten obese patients did not compensate for the caloric dilution by eating more, although this opportunity was available. Weight loss and subjective hunger ratings were similar during both 20-day treatment periods. Preliminary results of a second study[58] indicate that the five obese subjects studied may have compensated by eating more when SPE replaced 41 g of fat per day. SPE was generally well tolerated in all studies. To alleviate the anticipated interference in the absorption of fat-soluble vitamins, supplements could be taken.

Tetrahydrolipstatin

Results of preclinical studies[67,68] with tetrahydrolipstatin (THL), a potent and selective inhibitor of pancreatic lipase, have been reported. THL caused a specific dose-dependent inhibition of dietary triglyceride absorption in mice, squirrel monkeys, and dogs. Mice treated with the compound for 7 weeks gained significantly less weight than either pair-fed or ad libitum–fed controls. Fat absorption was reduced by 50% in the THL-treated mice.[67] Diet-induced obese rats treated with THL for 22 days lost 54 g of carcass fat and showed a 5-fold decrease in dietary fat absorption.[68] THL treatment also reduced serum triglyceride levels by 50% and retroperitoneal fatty acid synthesis by 25% in these rats.

INHIBITORS OF LIPID SYNTHESIS

Rationale

One of the metabolic changes sometimes associated with obesity in both humans and animals is increased fatty acid synthesis. In rodents, de novo fatty acid synthesis contributes significantly to lipid accumulation in adipose tissue,[69] although the importance of this contribution in humans is less clear. The true potential of an inhibitor of lipogenesis as an antiobesity agent may only be determined by clinical evaluation in obese humans. Many exploratory research studies have identified interesting compounds. However, the concept of inhibition of lipid synthesis as antiobesity therapy has not been evaluated in humans.[70]

Research Compounds

Ro 22-0654

Ro 22-0654 is an inhibitor of fatty acid synthesis that has antiobesity activity in the rat.[71] Chronic administration to both lean and genetically obese Zucker rats produced a significant reduction in body weight gain by a selective reduction in body fat. The efficiency of energy utilization was lowered in rats treated with Ro 22-0654, as the amount of weight gained per gram of food eaten was significantly reduced. A significant increase in fat oxidation has been shown in rats treated with Ro 22-0654.

Dehydroepiandrosterone

Dehydroepiandrosterone (DHEA) noncompetitively inhibits glucose-6-phosphate dehydrogenase, a key enzyme in generating the reducing equivalents required for fatty acid synthesis.[72–74] Chronic administration of DHEA prevented obesity in yellow (A^{vy}/a) obese mice without suppressing appetite and suppressed in vivo lipogenesis in liver.[75] Chronic treatment of Sprague-Dawley or lean Zucker rats with DHEA also decreased body weight gain without changing food consumption.[76,77] However, although chronic administration of DHEA reduces body weight gain in obese Zucker (fa/fa) rats as well, these animals do show a small decrease in food intake compared with control animals.[77] The lower food intake is presumed to be because of a smaller body size as it occurs only after the difference in body weight is evident.[77] Pair-feeding studies[78] indicate that the effects of DHEA on obese Zucker rats are independent of the small reduction in food intake that is seen. Decreased activities of glucose-6-phosphate dehy-drogenase and fatty acid synthase in liver and adipose tissue and decreased lipoprotein lipase activity in adipose tissue have been reported in obese Zucker rats after DHEA treatment.[79]

THERMOGENESIS ENHANCERS

Rationale

Obesity results from an imbalance between energy intake and output. In some people, hyperphagia may be the obvious cause of the imbalance, whereas in others a defective thermogenic capacity unable to adapt energy expenditure to a variable intake may have an important role.[80] The mechanisms of any ther-mogenic defects in humans are unclear; however, decreased sensitivity to the sympathetic nervous system (SNS) and insulin resistance are implicated. The possibility that some obese humans may have a defective thermogenic capacity, in addition to the known fall in energy expenditure after weight loss, has en-couraged the search for pharmacologic agents to stimulate thermogensis.

Studies of energy expenditure and body-weight regulation in rodents have emphasized the importance of brown adipose tissue (BAT). Under conditions of overfeeding mice and rats highly palatable diets, the major part of excess energy intake above maintenance is dissipated as heat through the sympathetic activation of BAT. In contrast, a thermogenic defect in BAT is involved in the development of genetic or hypothalamic obesity in mice and rats.[81]

The major function of BAT in rodents apparently is heat production; burning up calories either to provide the organism with needed heat (cold-induced non-shivering thermogenesis) or to maintain a state of energy balance (diet-induced thermogenesis). BAT is specialized for heat production and, therefore, is fun-damentally different from white adipose tissue, which is primarily a lipid storage site. After activation by the SNS,[82] BAT mitochondrial substrate oxidation be-comes uncoupled from adenosine triphosphate (ATP) formation.[83,84]

It seems that diet-induced thermogenesis has a smaller role in the control of energy balance in humans than in rodents. This may be related to the significant atrophy of BAT in adult humans.[85] This tissue is copiously distributed in newborns, including humans, hibernators, and cold-acclimated animals.[86] In adult humans, small deposits of BAT exist in a number of anatomical sites, especially in the interscapular and perirenal regions.[87-89]

The importance, if any, of BAT in human weight regulation is unknown. However, evidence suggests that individual differences in thermogenic responses may have a role in the maintenance of human body weight. Administration of norepinephrine (NE) to humans resulted in an increase in local skin temperature in regions where BAT deposits are know to occur.[89] Metabolic rates in lean, obese, or formerly obese women were tested in response to NE infusion. Although all subjects showed an increased metabolic rate, the response in the lean women was approximately double that in either of the obese groups.[90] The thermogenic response to glucose or a mixed meal was reduced in women with familial obesity.[91] When lean men with no family history of obesity were overfed for several months, they displayed a remarkable ability to adapt to increases in energy intake and still maintain body weight at a relatively normal level.[92]

Early Experience with Thermogenic Agents

Dinitrophenol and Aspirin

Dinitrophenol uncouples oxidative phosphorylation from respiration, thus causing heat production. At a dosage of 340 mg/kg/day, it significantly reduced body weight in obese humans,[93] and increased the feeling of warmth and sweating. However, the potent toxicity of this nonspecific uncoupling agent precluded its further use in humans. High doses of *aspirin* (20 mg/dL) also uncouple oxidative phosphorylation, resulting in elevation of oxygen consumption and heat production in both lean and obese subjects.[6] However, severe side effects such as tinnitus, prolonged bleeding, and gastrointestinal damage occur at these doses.

Thyroid Hormones

Some obese rodent models may be hypothyroid. Thyroid hormones increase the DNA and protein content of BAT; thus an enhanced thyroid activity in cold-adapted animals may augment the BAT hyperplasia.[86] It has been proposed that thyroid-stimulating hormone induces BAT activity.[94] Nutritionally induced alterations in thyroid hormone metabolism were reported in lean volunteers after overfeeding.[95,96] Overnutrition apparently increased the metabolic clearance and production rate of triiodothyronine (T_3) with no change in thyroxine (T_4) production. Thermogenesis and SNS activity, as shown by NE concentrations in plasma and urine, increased in overfed subjects.[97,98] Thyroid hormone metabolism also increased in cafeteria-fed rats, and these animals exhibited BAT hyperplasia.[99] In obese patients, thyroid hormones elevated oxygen consumption.[100,101] This increase in the basal metabolic rate can potentiate weight loss.

However, treatment with these agents causes serious side effects, including increased catabolism of protein, increased heart size, and modification of the chronotropic and inotropic properties of cardiac muscle.[6] The long-term success record of obese patients suggests that treatment with thyroid hormones is no better than dietary restrictions alone.[6]

Recent Studies of Thermogenic Agents

Caffeine and Nicotine

Drug-induced thermogenesis may be produced by several pharmacologic agents. *Caffeine* and *nicotine* are thermogenic substances commonly consumed in American society.[102] Caffeine stimulated metabolic rate in both lean and obese humans, but there was a greater oxidation of fat in lean subjects.[103] It has long been observed that average body weight in cigarette smokers is lower than in non-smokers,[104] and subjects giving up the habit gain an average of 8 kg.[105] More recently, cigarette smoking was shown to produce a significant increase of approximately 10% in 24-hour energy expenditure. This effect is presumably mediated, in part, by the SNS since urinary excretion of NE was significantly elevated during smoking.[106] These findings may explain the well-known weight gain occurring when people give up smoking.

Ephedrine

Ephedrine reduced body weight and fat in six different obese animal models when given SC or as a dietary admixture.[102,107,108] Oxygen consumption was elevated without a change in food consumption, no negative nitrogen balance was observed, and the compound was more effective in obese than in lean animals. Rectal temperatures were elevated by long-term treatment with ephedrine.

In humans, ephedrine increased total heat production, as measured by calorimetry,[102] or local heat production in areas known to typically contain BAT.[109] In an early clinical trial,[110] ephedrine-ethylenediamine was more effective in producing weight loss than either D-amphetamine sulfate or D-amphetamine sulfate with a barbiturate; 140 obese patients entered this study. After 1 month of treatment, average weight loss was 11.3 lb with ephedrine-ethylenediamine (18 mg/day), 7.7 lb with D-amphetamine (15 mg/day), and 3 lb with D-amphetamine (30 mg/day) plus pentobarbital sodium (45 mg/day). Patients taking placebo gained an average of 1.2 lb. All drugs were given tid 30 minutes before meals, and patients did not diet. No adverse effects were noted with ephedrine-ethylenediamine.

A combination of ephedrine and caffeine showed antiobesity activity comparable with that of diethylpropion[111]; 108 obese patients completed this study.

After 12 weeks of treatment, the median weight loss was 8.1 kg with ephedrine sodium (120 mg/day) and caffeine sodium benzoate (300 mg/day), 8.4 kg with diethylpropion (75 mg/day), and 4.1 kg with placebo. All drugs were given tid 30 minutes before meals, and patients were instructed in a 1,200-kcal/day diet. Sympathomimetic side effects such as agitation, tremors, and insomnia were reported more frequently with ephedrine and caffeine and caused four patients to drop out. No changes were seen in blood pressure or pulse, and symptoms were well tolerated.

In a more recent 3-month study,[112] ephedrine-hydrochloride was more effective than placebo for weight reduction in obese patients. Forty-six patients completed at least 1 month of the protocol and were included in the analyses; 31 patients completed the entire study. Final body-weight loss after 12 weeks of treatment averaged 10.2 kg with ephedrine (150 mg/day), 8.7 kg with ephedrine (75 mg/ day), and 8.7 kg with placebo. All drugs were given tid 30 minutes before meals, and patients followed a hypocaloric diet (1,000 to 1,200 kcal/day). The incidence of side effects (agitation, insomnia, giddiness, tremor, constipation) was higher in the group receiving the high dose of ephedrine. Symptoms were generally well tolerated and tended to disappear with continued treatment. The large weight loss seen in this study with placebo (8.7 kg in 12 weeks) is actually what differentiates it from previous studies. Overall weight loss with ephedrine was similar in all studies.

More recently this group[113] examined the effect of ephedrine in ten low-energy-adapted obese women. Patients received 2 months of treatment with ephedrine (150 mg/day) and placebo in this double-blind crossover study while continuing on their low-energy diets. Weight loss was significantly greater ($P < .05$) with the drug (2.41 kg) than with placebo (0.64 kg). Indeed, perhaps as the authors suggest, the drug might be useful in selected subgroups of obese patients who have a defect in thermogenesis.

Beta-Agonist Thermogenic Compounds

Three new thermogenic agents were recently described that markedly stimulated lipolysis and enhanced energy expenditure. *BRL 26830A, Ro 16–8714,* and *LY104119* seem to enhance thermogenesis by directly stimulating beta-adrenoceptors. Chronic administration of these drugs resulted in weight loss or reduced weight gain in several genetically obese rodent models (fa/fa rats, ob/ob mice, and A^{vy}/a mice), but not in their lean counterparts.[114–117] This reduction in body weight seems to be attributable to selective lowering of body lipid content. Whole body calorimetry studies suggest that heat production is elevated in obese rodents by these agents.[114–117] The thermogenic action of BRL 26830A and Ro 16–8714 seems to be partially mediated through BAT.[114–116] BRL 26830A has also been shown to increase energy expenditure in normal-weight human volunteers ingesting their usual diet.[118,119]

Recently, the effect of BRL 26830A in obese patients was evaluated in two clinical trials. In the first study,[118] 41 refractory obese women received BRL 26830A (50 mg qid) or placebo for 6 weeks in a double-blind random manner. Patients were given a high-fiber 1,000-calorie diet. This study showed no significant change in resting heart rate or blood pressure. However, 17 of the 20 subjects who received active medication reported a sensation of tremor or tremulousness. Although most patients tolerated this side effect well, two stopped treatment and a third temporarily suspended therapy because of severe symptoms. No other adverse reactions were reported. Weight change during the study was comparable in both groups. During the 6 weeks of active treatment, patients taking BRL 26830A lost an average of 0.2 kg, while patients on placebo gained an average of 0.3 kg. At the dose studied, BRL 26830A was ineffective in promoting weight loss in these refractory obese women.

In the second study,[119] 16 obese patients (14 women, 2 men) received BRL 26830A (50 mg qid) or placebo for 6 weeks in a double-blind manner. Thirteen patients were included in the final analysis. Each patient was given an individualized low-energy diet based on baseline energy expenditure that was followed for the 6-week treatment period and a 2-week follow-up period. During the 6 weeks of BRL 26830A administration, patients lost an average of 9.3 kg, while patients on placebo lost an average of 6.6 kg ($P < .01$). Even more interesting is the finding that overnight energy expenditure of the BRL 26830A group was maintained at baseline levels during the 6 weeks of dietary restriction, while that of the placebo group fell as expected. During the 2-week follow-up period of continued dietary restriction, the energy expenditure in the patients formerly treated with BRL 26830A also dropped. From these data it would seem that BRL 26830A facilitated weight loss in these obese patients through prevention of the usual drop in metabolic rate known to occur during continued dietary restriction. Further investigation is required to understand the apparent disparity between the results of these two studies.

The thermogenic effect of Ro 16–8714 was studied in six normal-weight males.[120] Energy expenditure was measured by indirect calorimetry before and for 6 hours after acute administration of Ro 16–8714 (5, 10, and 20 mg) or placebo in a randomized crossover design. Energy expenditure was significantly increased by 12%, 13%, or 16% and heart rate was significantly elevated by 12%, 28%, or 51% with doses of 5, 10, and 20 mg, respectively. Ro 16–8714 had a potent thermogenic effect in these lean men; but it was associated with tachycardia, indicating the need to discover compounds with which a greater separation of these effects could be obtained.

If a safe calorigenic agent able to correct inherent defects in thermogenic mechanisms and/or overcome the inevitable lowering of metabolic rate during caloric restriction could be identified, it would have significant potential for use as an antiobesity agent.

REFERENCES

1. National Institutes of Health Consensus Development Conference Statement: *Health Implications of Obesity. Ann Intern Med* 1985; 103:1073–1077.

2. Samanin R: Central mechanisms of anorectic drugs, in de las Heras FG, Vega S (eds): *Medicinal Chemistry Advances.* New York, Pergamon Press, 1981, pp 271–282.

3. Dobrzanski S, Doggett NS: The effect of propranolol phentolamine and pimozide on drug-induced anorexia in the mouse. *Psychopharmacology* 1979; 66:297–300.

4. Sullivan AC, Cheng L: Appetite regulation and its modulation by drugs, in Hatchcock JN, Coon J (eds): *Nutrition and Drug Interrelations.* New York, Academic Press Inc, 1978, pp 21–82.

5. Duhault J, Beregi L, du Boistesselin R: General and comparative pharmacology of fenfluramine. *Curr Med Res Opin* 1979; 6(suppl):3–14.

6. Bray GA: Drug therapy for the obese patient, in Smith LH, Jr (ed): *The Obese Patient.* Philadelphia, WB Saunders Co, 1976, pp 353–410.

7. Scoville BA: Review of amphetamine-like drugs by the Food and Drug Administration: Clinical data and value judgments, in Bray GA (ed): *Obesity in Perspective: Proceedings of the Fogarty Conference,* US Dept of Health, Education, and Welfare Publication No. (NIH) 75-708. Government Printing Office, 1975, pp 441-443.

8. Sullivan AC, Comai K: *Pharmacological treatment of obesity. Int J Obes* 1978; 2:167–189.

9. Lemberger L, Fuller RW, Zerbe RL: Use of specific serotonin uptake inhibitors as antidepressants. *Clin Neuropharmacol* 1985; 8:299–317.

10. Simpson RJ, Lawton DJ, Watt MH, et al: Effect of zimelidine, a new antidepressant, on appetite and body weight. *Br J Clin Pharmacol* 1981; 11:96–98.

11. Norman TR, Burrows GD, Marriott PF, et al: Zimelidine: A placebo-controlled trial in depression. *Psychiatry Res* 1983; 8:95–103.

12. Sawyer CN, Cleary J, Gabriel R: Possible hepatotoxicity of zimelidine. *Br Med J* 1983, 287–1555.

13. Nilsson BS: Adverse reactions in connection with zimelidine treatment: A review. *Acta Psychiatr Scand* 1983; 68(suppl):115–119.

14. Smedegaard J, Christiansen P, Skrumsager B: Treatment of obesity by femoxetine, a selective 5HT reuptake inhibitor. *Int J Obes* 1981; 5:377–378.

15. Smedegaard J, Christiansen P: Treatment of obesity with femoxetine in general practice. *Ugeskr Laeger* 1982; 144:938–942.

16. Levine LR: Weight loss associated with use of fluoxetine, abstracted. *Alimentazione, Nutrizione, Metabolismo* 1986; 7:21.

17. Ferguson JM, Feighner JP: Fluoxetine induced weight loss in non-depressed overweight humans, abstracted. *Alim Nutr Metab* 1986; 7:19.

18. Zerbe RL: Clinical studies of fluoxetine: A safety summary, abstracted. *Alim Nutr Metab* 1986; 7:22.

19. Trenchard E, Silverstone T: Naloxone reduces the food intake of normal human volunteers. *Appetite* 1983; 4:43–50.

20. Atkinson RL: Naloxone decreases food intake in obese humans. *J Clin Endocrinol Metab* 1982; 55:196–198.

21. Trenchard E, Silverstone T: A double-blind investigation of naloxone on food intake in normal human volunteers. *Int J Obes* 1982; 6:217–222.

22. Kyriakides M, Silverstone T, Jeffcoate W, et al: Effect of naloxone on hyperphagia in Prader-Willi syndrome. *Lancet* 1980; 1:876–877.

23. Meyer RE, Mirin SM, Altman JL, et al: A behavioral paradigm for the evaluation of narcotic antagonists. *Arch Gen Psychiatry* 1976; 33:371–377.

24. Smith D: Method for inducing anorexia. US patent application number 27,270, 1979.

25. Hollister L: Adverse effects of naltrexone in subjects not dependent on opiates. *Drug Alcohol Depend* 1981; 8:37–41.

26. Atkinson RL, Berke LK, Drake CR, et al: Effects of long-term therapy with naltrexone on body weight in obesity. *Clin Pharmacol Ther* 1985; 38:419–422.

27. Malcolm R, O'Neil PM, Sexauer JD, et al: A controlled trial of naltrexone in obese humans. *Int J Obes* 1985; 9:347–353.

28. Maggio CA, Presta E, Bracco EF, et al: Naltrexone and human eating behavior: A dose-ranging inpatient trial in moderately obese men. *Brain Res Bull* 1985; 14:657–661.

29. Chang KJ, Cuatrecasas P: Heterogeneity and properties of opiate receptors. *Fed Proc* 1981; 40:2729–2734.

30. Morley JE, Levine AS: The role of dynorphin-(1-17) and the kappa opiate receptors in the regulation of feeding. *Peptides* 1983; 4:797–809.

31. Egan TM, North RA: Both μ and δ opiate receptors exist on the same neuron. *Science* 1981; 214:923–924.

32. Gibbs J, Smith GP: Satiety: The roles of peptides from the stomach and the intestine. *Fed Proc* 1986; 45:1391–1395.

33. Smith G: The therapeutic potential of cholecystokinin, in Sullivan AC, Garattini S (eds): *Novel Approaches and Drugs for Obesity*. London, John Libbey & Co Ltd, 1985, pp 35–38.

34. Gibbs J, Young RC, Smith GP: Cholecystokinin decreases food intake in rats. *Journal of Comparative Physiological Psychology* 1973; 84:488–495.

35. Sturdevant RAL, Goetz H: Cholecystokinin both stimulates and inhibits human food intake. *Nature* 1976; 261:713–715.

36. Greenway FL, Bray GA: Cholecystokinin and satiety. *Life Sci* 1977; 21:769–771.

37. Kissileff HR, Pi-Sunyer FX, Thornton J, et al: C-terminal octapeptide of cholecystokinin decreases food intake in man. *Am J Clin Nutr* 1981; 34:154–160.

38. Pi-Sunyer FX, Kissileff HR, Thornton J, et al: C-terminal octapeptide of cholecystokinin decreases food intake in obese men. *Physiol Behav* 1982; 29:627–630.

39. Stacher G, Steinringer H, Schmierer G, et al: Cholecystokinin octapeptide decreases intake of solid food in man. *Peptides* 1982; 3:133–136.

40. Kissileff HR, Klingsberg G, Van Itallie TB: Universal eating monitor for continuous recording of solid or liquid consumption in man. *Am J Physiol* 1980; 238:R14–R22.

41. Sullivan AC, Guthrie RW, Triscari J: (-)-threo-Chlorocitric acid: A novel anorectic agent with a peripheral site of action, in Garattini S, Samanin R (eds): *Anorectic Agents: Mechanisms of Action and Tolerance*. New York, Raven Press, 1981, pp 143–158.

42. Sullivan AC, Dairman W, Triscari J: (-)-threo-Chlorocitric acid: A novel anorectic agent. *Pharmacol Biochem Behav* 1981; 15:303–310.

43. Triscari J, Sullivan AC: Studies on the mechanism of action of a novel anorectic agent (-)-threo-chlorocitric acid. *Pharmacol Biochem Behav* 1981; 15:311–318.

44. Heshka S, Nauss-Karol C, Nyman A, et al: Effects of chlorocitrate on body weight in obese men on a metabolic ward. *Nutrition & Behavior* 1985; 2:233–239.

45. Porikos KP, Sullivan AC, McGhee BM, et al: An experimental model for assessing effects of anorectics on spontaneous food intake of obese subjects. *Clin Pharmacol Ther* 1980; 27:815–822.

46. Puls W, Keup U, Krause HP, et al: Pharmacology of a glucosidase inhibitor. *Front Horm Res* 1980; 7:235–247.

47. Puls W, Keup U, Krause HP, et al: *Naturwissenschaften* 1977; 64:536–537.

48. Creutzfeldt W (ed): First International Symposium on Acarbose: Effects on carbohydrate and fat metabolism. International Congress Series, Amsterdam, Excerpta Medica, 1982, vol 54.

49. Johansen K: Acarbose treatment of sulfonylurea-treated non-insulin dependent diabetics: A double-blind cross-over comparison of an α-glucosidase inhibitor with metformin. *Diabete Metab* 1984; 10:219–223.

50. Dimitriadis G, Karaiskos C, Raptis S: Effects of prolonged (6 months) α-glucosidase inhibition on blood glucose control and insulin requirements in patients with insulin-dependent diabetes mellitus. *Horm. Metab Res* 1986; 18:253–255.

51. William-Olsson T, Sjöstrom L: Acarbose: A safe drug? *Current Therapeutic Research* 1982; 31:786–794.

52. William-Olsson T, Krotkiewski M, Sjöstrom L: Relapse-reducing effects of acarbose after weight reduction in severly obese subjects. *Journal of Obesity & Weight Regulation* 1985; 4:20–32.

53. Puls W, Krause HP, Müller L, et al: Inhibitors of the rate of carbohydrate and lipid absorption by the intestine, in Sullivan AC, Garattini S (eds): *Novel Approaches and Drugs for Obesity*. London, John Libbey & Co Ltd, 1985, pp 22–32.

54. Cauderay M, Tappy L, Temler E, et al: Effect of α-glycohydrolase inhibitors (Bay m1099 and Bay o1248) on sucrose metabolism in normal men. *Metabolism* 1985; 35:472–477.

55. Inoue S, Matsuo T, Ikeda H: Efficacy of a disaccharidase inhibitor, AO-128 in the treatment of obesity. The Fifth International Congress on Obesity, Jerusalem, Israel, Sept 14–19, 1986, p 50.

56. Matsuzawa Y, Kobatake T, Fujioka S, et al: Effect of a new α-glucosidase inhibitor, AO-128, on post prandial blood glucose and serum insulin levels in healthy male subjects. The Fifth International Congress on Obesity, Jerusalem, Israel, Sept 14–19, 1986, p 50.

57. Fujioka S, Kobatake T, Kawamoto T, et al: Effect of AO-128, a new α-glucosidase inhibitor, on carbohydrate metabolism in obese subjects. The Fifth International Congress on Obesity, Jerusalem, Israel, Sept 14–19, 1986, p 98.

58. Jandacek RJ: Studies with sucrose polyester, in Sullivan AC, Garattini S: (eds): *Novel Approaches and Drugs for Obesity*. London, John Libbey & Co Ltd, 1985, pp 13–21.

59. Glueck CJ, Jandacek RJ, Hogg E, et al: Sucrose polyester: Substitution for dietary fats in hypocaloric diets in the treatment of familial hypercholesterolemia. *Am J Clin Nutr* 1983; 37:347–354.

60. Mellies MJ, Jandacek RJ, Taulbee JD, et al: A double-blind, placebo-controlled study of sucrose polyester in hypercholesterolemic outpatients. *Am J Clin Nutr* 1983, 37:399–346.

61. Mellies MJ, Vitale C, Jandacek RJ: The substitution of sucrose polyester for dietary fat in obese, hypercholesterolemic outpatients. *Am J Clin Nutr* 1985, 41:1–12.

62. Fallat RW, Glueck CJ, Lutmer R, et al: Short term study of sucrose polyester, a nonabsorbable fat-like material, as a dietary agent for lowering plasma cholesterol. *Am J Clin Nutr* 1976; 29:1204–1215.

63. Crouse JR, Grundy SM: Effects of sucrose polyester on cholesterol metabolism in man. *Metabolism* 1979; 28:994–1000.

64. Glueck CJ, Hastings MM, Allen C, et al: Sucrose polyester and covert caloric dilution. *Am J Clin Nutr* 1982; 35:1352–1359.

65. Mattson FH, Jandacek RJ, Webb MR: The effect of a nonabsorbable lipid, sucrose polyester, on the absorption of dietary cholesterol by the rat. *J Nutr* 1976; 106:747–752.

66. St Clair RW, Wood LL, Clarkson TB: Effect of sucrose polyester on plasma lipids and cholesterol absorption in African green monkeys with variable hypercholesterolemic response to dietary cholesterol. *Metabolism* 1981; 130:176–183.

67. Hadvary P, Lengsfeld H, Barbier P, et al: Lipstatin and tetrahydrolipstatin, potent and selective inhibitors of pancreatic lipase. The Fifth International Congress on Obesity, Jerusalem, Israel, Sept 14–19, 1986, p 21.

68. Sullivan AC, Barbier P, Fleury A, et al: Studies on the antiobesity activity of tetrahydro-lipstatin, a potent and selective inhibitor of pancreatic lipase, abstracted. *Alim Nutr Metab* 1986; 7:47.

69. Leveille GA: *In vivo* fatty acid synthesis in adipose tissue and liver of meal-fed rats. *Proc Soc Exp Biol Med* 1967; 125:85–88.

70. Sullivan AC, Hamilton JG, Triscari J: Metabolic inhibitors of lipid biosynthesis as anti-obesity agents. *Biochemical Pharmacology of Obesity*. Curtis-Prior PB (ed): New York, Elsevier Science Publishers Inc, 1983; pp 311–337.

71. Triscari J, Sullivan AC: Antiobesity effects of a novel lipid synthesis inhibitor (Ro 22-0654). *Life Sci* 1984; 34:2433–2442.

72. McKerns KW, Kaleita E: Inhibition of glucose-6-phosphate dehydrogenase by hormones. *Biochem Biophys Res Commun* 1960; 2:344–348.

73. Marks PA, Banks J: Inhibition of mammalian glucose-6-phosphate dehydrogenase by steroids. *Proc Natl Acad Sci USA* 1960; 46:447–452.

74. Tsutsui EA, Marks PA, Reich P: Effect of dehydroepiandrosterone on glucose-6-phosphate dehydrogenase activity and reduced triphosphopyridine nucleotide formation in adrenal tissue. *J Biol Chem* 1962; 237:3009–3013.

75. Yen TT, Allan JA, Pearson DV, et al: Prevention of obesity in A^{vy}/a mice by dehydro-epiandrosterone. *Lipids* 1977; 12:409–413.

76. Cleary MP, Shepherd A, Zisk J, et al: Effect of dehydroepiandrosterone on body weight and food intake in rats. *Nutrition & Behavior* 1983; 1:127–136.

77. Cleary MP, Shepherd A, Jenks B: Effect of dehydroepiandrosterone on growth in lean and obese Zucker rats. *J Nutr* 1984; 114:1242–1251.

78. Cleary MP, Fox N, Lazin B, et al: A comparison of the effects of dehydroepiandrosterone treatment to *ad libitum* and pair-feeding in the obese Zucker rat. *Nutrition Research* 1985; 5:1247–1257.

79. Shepherd A, Cleary MP: Metabolic alteration due to dehydroepiandrosterone in the obese Zucker rat. *Am J Physiol* 1984; 246:123–128.

80. Jequier E, Schutz Y: New evidence for a thermogenic defect in human obesity. *Int J Obes* 1985; 9(suppl):1–7.

81. Levin BE, Sullivan AC: Regulation of thermogenesis in obesity, in Sullivan AC, Garattini S (eds): *Novel Approaches and Drugs for Obesity*. London, John Libbey & Co Ltd, 1985, pp 159–180.

82. Landsberg L, Young JB: Diet-induced changes in sympathoadrenal activity: Implications for thermogenesis. *Life Sci* 1981; 28:1801–1819.

83. Nicholls DG: Brown adipose tissue mitochondria. *Biochim Biophys Acta* 1979; 549:1–29.

84. Nicholls DG, Locke RM: Thermogenic mechanisms in brown fat. *Physiol Rev* 1984; 64:1–64.

85. Jequier E: Thermogenesis induced by nutrients in man: Its role in weight regulation. *J Physiol (Paris)* 1985; 80:129–140.

86. Rawls R: Obesity linked to metabolism in brown fat. *Chemical & Engineering News* 1981; 59:25–26.

87. Ricquier D, Nechad M, Mory G: Ultrastructural and biochemical characterization of human brown adipose tissue in pheochromocytoma. *J Clin Endocrinol Metab* 1982; 54:803–807.

88. Heaton JM: The distribution of brown adipose tissue in the human. *J Anat* 1972; 112:35–39.

89. James WPT, Trayhurn P: Thermogenesis and obesity. *Br Med Bull* 1981; 37:43–48.

90. Jung RT, Shetty PS, James WPT, et al: Reduced thermogenesis in obesity. *Nature* 1979; 279:322–323.

91. Shetty PS, Jung RT, James WPT: Effect of catecholamine replacement with levodopa on the metabolic response to semistarvation. *Lancet* 1979; 1:77–79.

92. Sims EAH: Experimental obesity, dietary-induced thermogenesis, and their clinical implications. *Clin Endocrinol Metab* 1976; 5:377–395.

93. Tainter ML, Stocton AB, Cutting W: Dinitrophenol in the treatment of obesity: Final report. *JAMA* 1935; 105:332–336.

94. Doniach D: Possible stimulation of thermogenesis in brown adipose tissue by thyroid-stimulating hormone. *Lancet* 1975; 2:160–161.

95. Danforth E: Dietary-induced thermogenesis: Control of energy expenditure. *Life Sci* 1981; 28:1821–1827.

96. Danforth E Jr, Horton ES, O'Connell M, et al: Dietary-induced alterations in thyroid hormone metabolism during overnutrition. *J Clin Invest* 1979; 64:1336–1347.

97. Burse RL, Goldman RF, Danforth E Jr, et al: Effect of excess carbohydrate (CHO) and fat intake on resting metabolism. *Fed Proc* 1977; 36:546.

98. Burse RL, Goldman RF, Danforth E Jr, et al: Effect of excess protein intake on metabolism. *Physiologist* 1977; 20:13. Abstracted.

99. Tulp O, Frink R, Sims EAH, et al: Overnutrition induces hyperplasia of brown fat and diet-induced thermogenesis in the rat. *Clin Res* 1980; 28:621A.

100. Gonzales-Barronco J, Schulte J, Rull JA, et al: Triiodothyronine versus placebo in obesity: Double blind crossover study, in Howard A (ed): *Recent Advances in Obesity Research*. London, Newman Publishing Ltd, 1975, vol 1, pp 386–388.

101. Hofmann GG, Schneider G, Strohmeier E, et al: Thyroid hormones in obesity: Thyroid function, effects on isolated fat cells of man and therapeutical application, in Howard A (ed): *Recent Advances in Obesity Research*. London, Newman Publishing Ltd, 1975, vol 1, pp 383–386.

102. Basel S, Karger AG, Miller DS: Thermogenesis and obesity, in Somogyi JC, deWijn JF (eds): *Nutritional Aspects of Physical Performance*. 1979, pp 25–32.

103. Acheson KJ, Zahorska-Markiewicz B, Pittet PH, et al: Caffeine and coffee: Their influence on metabolic rate and substrate utilization in normal weight and obese individuals. *Am J Clin Nutr* 1980; 33:989–997.

104. Sutherland WHF, Temple WH, Nye ER, et al: Adiposity, lipids, alcohol consumption, smoking and gender. *Am J Clin Nutr* 1980; 33:2581–2587.

105. Khosla T, Lowe CR: Obesity and smoking habits by social class. *British Journal of Preventive and Social Medicine* 1972; 26:249–256.

106. Hofstetter A, Schutz Y, Jequier E, et al: Increased 24-hour energy expenditure in cigarette smokers. *N Engl J Med* 1986; 314:79–82.

107. Massoudi M, Miller DS: Ephedrine, a thermogenic and potential slimming drug. *Proc Nutr Soc* 1977; 36:135A.

108. Yen TT, McKee MM, Bemis KG: Ephedrine reduces weight of viable yellow obese mice (A^{vy}/a). *Life Sci* 1981; 28:119–128.

109. Rothwell NJ, Stock MJ: A role for brown adipose tissue in diet-induced thermogenesis. *Nature* 1979; 281:31–35.

110. Kupersmith IH: Value of ephedrine-ethylenediamine as an appetite depressant: Comparison with D-amphetamine sulfate. *Current Therapeutic Research* 1960; 2:39–42.

111. Malchow-Moller A, Larsen S, Hey H, et al: Ephedrine as an anorectic: The story of the 'Elsinore pill.' *Int J Obes* 1981; 5:183–187.

112. Pasquali R, Baraldi G, Cesari MP, et al: A controlled trial using ephedrine in the treatment of obesity. *Int J Obes* 1985; 9:93–98.

113. Pasquali R, Cesari MP, Besteghi L, et al: Thermogenic agents in the treatment of human obesity: Preliminary results. The Fifth International Congress on Obesity, Jerusalem, Israel, Sept 14–19, 1986, p 50. Abstracted.

114. Arch JRS, Ainsworth AT: Thermogenic and antiobesity activity of a novel β-adrenoceptor agonist (BRL 26830A) in mice and rats. *Am J Clin Nutr* 1983; 38:549–558.

115. Arch JRS, Ainsworth AT, Ellis RDM, et al: Treatment of obesity with thermogenic β-adrenoceptor agonists: Studies on BRL 26830A in rodents, in Sullivan AC, Garattini S (eds): *Novel Approaches and Drugs for Obesity*. London, John Libbey & Co Ltd, 1985, pp 1–11.

116. Meier MK, Alig L, Burgi-Saville ME, et al: Phenethanolamine derivatives with calorigenic and antidiabetic qualities, in Sullivan AC, Garattini S (eds): *Novel Approaches and Drugs for Obesity*. London, John Libbey & Co Ltd, 1985, pp 215–225.

117. Yen TT, McKee MM, Stamm NB: Thermogenesis and weight control, in Sullivan AC, Garattini S (eds): *Novel Approaches and Drugs for Obesity*. London, John Libbey & Co Ltd, 1985, pp 67–78.

118. Chapman BJ, Farquhar D, Galloway S, et al: The effects of BRL 26830A, a new β-adrenoceptor agonist, in refractory obesity, abstracted. *Int J Obes* 1985; 9:230.

119. Zed CA, Harris GS, Harrison PJ, et al: Anti-obesity activity of a novel β-adrenoceptor agonist (BRL 26830A) in diet-restricted obese subjects, abstracted. *Int J Obes* 1985; 9:231.

120. Henry C, Schutz Y, Bückert A, et al: Thermogenic effect of the new β-adrenoreceptor agonist Ro 16-8714 in healthy male volunteers. The Fifth International Congress on Obesity, Jerusalem, Israel, Sept 14–19, 1986, p 49.

Chapter 15

Surgery for Obesity

John Kral

Obesity surgery is performed on the dual premise that obesity is a serious disease, threatening both quality and length of life, and that surgery can alleviate the disease, thereby improving quality of life and prolonging survival of the patient. There is hard evidence proving the seriousness of obesity and that the disease can be alleviated by surgery, at least for a longer period of time than with any other treatment, but there is no evidence that survival is improved after surgery.

The morbidity and mortality of obesity were recently summarized at a National Institutes of Health Consensus Development Conference.[1] Evidence of benefits of weight reduction has been presented in several published articles, lamentably fewer than those presenting diets, drugs, operations, or other means of reducing weight. The 1959 *Build and Blood Pressure Study*,[2] based on life insurance statistics, revealed a mortality ratio relative to normal-weight men of 102% for all overweight men who had reduced sufficiently to qualify for standard insurance. The Build study of 1979[2] showed a mortality ratio of 71% for all reduced men, but 110% for men who had been 25% or more overweight. Other risk-benefit or cost-benefit calculations of weight loss are not available, though it is reasonable to assume that ameliorization by weight loss of diabetes,[3] hypertension,[4] congestive heart failure,[5] and pulmonary insufficiency[6] is beneficial with respect to longevity, morbidity, and costs to society.[7]

Obesity of the degree justifying surgery is discouragingly difficult, if not impossible, to treat successfully over the long term by nonsurgical means. Even such potentially effective methods as jaw-wiring, intragastric balloons, or total or supplemented fasting fail in more than 90% of patients followed for a sufficiently long period of time. Surgery is also limited in its long-term efficacy, though it seems to be more successful than other modalities. The following is a presentation of indications, procedures, and results of surgical treatment of obesity.

INDICATIONS

Medical Indications

Since the early 1960s when obesity surgery began to be performed on a large scale, an arbitrary weight criterion for eligibility for surgery has been used to designate "morbid obesity," namely: *body weight at least 100 lb (45.4 kg) above "ideal" weight for height according to life insurance standards*. Even though all obesity by definition is "morbid"—it is a disease—and the weight criterion of 100 lb is arbitrary, it is likely that the risk in the vast majority of people for dying prematurely or developing life-threatening or debilitating conditions at this level of weight is extremely high. In fact, Drenick et al[8] reported a 12-fold increase in mortality in men who are morbidly obese compared with normal-weight men aged 25 to 34 years. It is noteworthy that men who are 5'11" (181 cm), corresponding to the upper 85th percentile of height of the American population, and weigh 100 lb above "ideal" are "only" 60% above ideal weight according to insurance tables. Nevertheless, this lesser degree of being overweight is associated with a considerable and geometric increase in the prevalence of morbidity and mortality compared with people of ideal weight.[9]

Indications for surgery must be individualized and can potentially cause controversy, particularly if the outcome of the surgery does not meet the expectations of patients and their family, members of the medical profession, or opportunistic attorneys. A weight of 100 lb above ideal weight and the presence of a life-threatening complication of obesity, proven to benefit from weight loss, is an *incontrovertible indication* for surgery in a patient in optimal condition to withstand surgery and anesthesia. The conventional indication, requiring only a weight of 100 lb excess, ie, without the presence of manifest complications, is more than justifiable in most cases, though theoretically patients may exist who can attain a normal life span without developing severe medical complications for whom surgery would entail a greater risk than the obesity itself.

With the significant improvement in the operative management of severely obese patients during the last 10 years and the development of safer procedures with respect to performance and potentially long-term side effects, it can be considered justifiable to widen the indications for intervention. Mortality and morbidity of surgery in obese patients in centers specializing in obesity surgery are so low as to approximate those of normal-weight patients having operations of comparable magnitude.[10]

Recently, the American Society for Clinical Nutrition[11] published guidelines for obesity surgery outlining criteria for eligibility, the role of the hospital, and briefing of the patient (informed consent). The guidelines accept complicated obesity, ie, with manifest comorbidity, at a body weight lower than 100 lb excess as an indiction for surgery, given the *refractoriness* of the weight to maintain a loss achieved by other means. Needless to say, if a patient has been able to lose a sufficient amount of weight, and keep it off, he is ineligible for obesity surgery and will probably not request it!

The issue of refractoriness is equivocal. In most texts, documented failure of weight-loss maintenance in treatment supervised by a physician has been a prerequisite for obesity surgery. Occasionally, some authors have proposed that previous successful weight loss be a prerequisite (proving the ability of the patient to cooperate), while others propose the opposite, ie, that patients must have been unable to lose by nonsurgical means in order to qualify. Another aspect of the same question is the requirement of a minimum duration of the morbidly obese state, traditionally 5 years. The reasoning behind this has never been explained or supported, though one might hypothesize that a more recent onset of severe obesity might be more amenable to nonsurgical treatment, though this has not been proven. Support for this proposal could be that only patients who have suffered for a sufficient duration are motivated enough to undergo obesity surgery. However, this should be fully addressed by requiring a sufficient degree of initial motivation, without burdening the patient with an arbitrarily chosen duration of suffering.

In the realm of medical indications for surgery, there is one further aspect that is difficult to define at our present state of knowledge. Latency or proneness to develop hazardous complications of obesity might well be considered an indication in patients whose excess weight is less than 100 lb or who have not yet developed the complication in question. Such "latent complicated obesity" should necessarily be refractory to qualify as an indication. Furthermore, markers for the later development of the complication(s) should be sufficiently validated in such patients.

Psychosocial Indication

An indication often perceived by the patient as very important, though more difficult to define in quantitative terms, is impairment of quality of life. It can correctly be claimed that such impairment constitutes a threat to mental health and thus qualifies as a "legitimate" health hazard, though criteria must be stringently defined to prevent abuse of this indication. Once again, refractoriness must be a requirement.

PROCEDURES

There are three principles for weight reduction that can be employed surgically: (1) restriction of intake by physical means, (2) malabsorption of ingested nutrients, and (3) voluntary reduction of intake by altered appetite regulation. They can overlap, and there are procedures that use more than one principle.

Gastric Restriction

The most common method by far is gastric restriction: by creating a small stomach pouch, the quantity of solid food that can be ingested at a single meal is limited. Furthermore, by making a small outlet through which the food must pass, a delay is imposed, which further limits the total nutrient delivery per day. *Gastroplasty* is the generic term used for any surgical reduction of gastric volume that does not alter the continuity of the gastrointestinal tract (Figure 15-1).

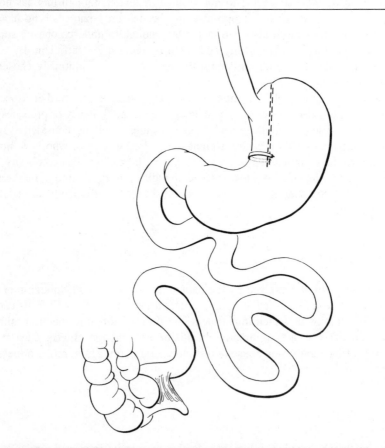

Figure 15-1 Vertical Stapled Gastroplasty. This procedure creates a 20-cc pouch with a band or ring to prevent stretching of the outlet, maintaining an inner diameter of 1 cm.

Many variations of gastroplasty have been used since it was first introduced in 1971. These mainly concern the position of the partitioning staple lines, horizontally or vertically, size of the pouch and outlet, and the method for reinforcing the outlet. One of the most recent techniques, gastric banding, does not involve stapling of the stomach proper, though the tight external band around the upper part of the stomach, acting as a waist, achieves a similar arrangement as the horizontal gastroplasty is considered obsolete.

Gastric bypass consists of a stapled partition across the top of the stomach creating a small (1.5 oz, 50 ml) pouch to which a limb of small intestine is connected. The rest of the stomach is thus closed off, draining its secretions into the duodenum and rendering the stomach inaccessible for diagnostic studies (Figure 15-2). Gastric bypass was the first of the restrictive procedures. It was introduced by Mason and Ito[12] in 1966 and used by Mason until 1980 in various versions. He abandoned the procedure since he felt that its method of action could be achieved more simply and safely by gastroplasty with a reinforced outlet. Proponents of the method, and there are many,[13-15] point out that gastric bypass has proven to be more effective than gastroplasty, because of malabsorptive and aversive components, through dumping of a hyperosmolar nutrient load into the upper intestine causing light-headedness, sweating, and palpitations.

The most extreme method of gastric restriction is folding the stomach to decrease volume and then *wrapping* it entirely with a mesh to prevent unfolding. This was introduced by Wilkinson and Peloso[16] in 1977 and has been performed by Wilkinson with variations in technique and material used for wrapping. The operation is more complex than gastroplasty, and concerns have been raised that it would be difficult to reverse the procedure should the need arise. Wilkinson[17] reports excellent long-term weight loss and relatively few side effects. The operation is currently being performed by surgeons at two other centers in the United States, who had not reported their results as of 1986.

The principle of wrapping the stomach to avoid stretching was used in a variant of the vertical gastroplasty in a very small series of patients followed for 3 years.[18] *Vertical gastroplasty wrap* used less foreign material than Wilkinson's operation and was less complex, requiring less dissection. It was abandoned since 30% of the patients did not lose weight, and there was a risk of mesh erosion over the long term in patients with successful weight loss.

Malabsorption

The oldest principle for treating obesity surgically is malabsorption. Originally, a large segment of the small intestine was removed in three patients, as described in 1951 by Henriksson[19] in Göteborg, Sweden. Since justifiable concerns were raised that the degree of weight loss was not predictable and that the operation

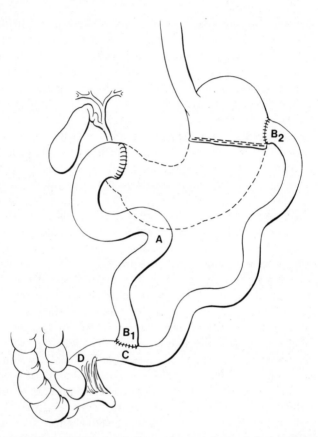

Figure 15-2 Gastric Bypass/Biliopancreatic Bypass. In gastric bypass, a horizontal stapled stomach pouch is attached to a loop of small bowel (B_2–C) so that food never enters the rest of the stomach. In biliopancreatic bypass, most of the stomach is removed, and the segment A–B_1 diverts bile and pancreatic secretions, which do not mix with food until it reaches the terminal ileum (C–D = 50 cm).

was irreversible, experiments were undertaken in dogs to develop a method to bypass a large segment of small bowel, leaving it "dormant" in the abdomen, rendering the operation reversible.[20] In this report, Kremen et al[19] described the first case of jejunoileal bypass in an extremely obese human patient. Subsequently, end-side *jejunoileal bypass* (Figure 15-3) was popularized by the late J.H. Payne of Los Angeles, who continued to perform the operation until shortly before his death in 1983. Tens of thousands of operations were performed in the United States alone, and several modifications were developed to try to achieve more efficient weight loss.

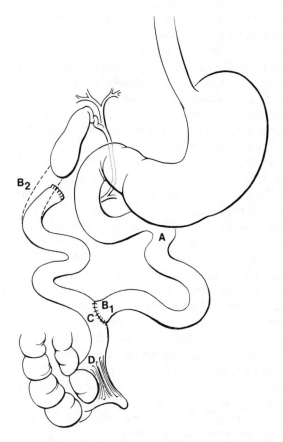

Figure 15-3 Jejunoileal Bypass/Biliointestinal Bypass/Duodenoileal Bypass. In jejunoileal bypass (end-side), the segment A–B$_1$ is 35 cm and C–D is 10 cm. In biliointestinal bypass, the "blind" stump B$_2$ is attached to the gallbladder. In duodenoileal bypass, A–B$_1$ is only 5 cm and C–D is 50 cm. Furthermore, an antireflux nipple valve is created just above C in the blind loop.

The mode of action of jejunoileal bypass was conceived to be malabsorption of a significant proportion of (over-) eaten calories, causing a nutritional deficit by expulsion in the stools. In fact, several clinical studies[21,22] verified in rat experiments[23,24] revealed that significant proportion of the caloric deficit was accounted for by decreased food intake, implying a regulatory mechanism as well as malabsorption. There is controversy whether the regulatory component relies on aversiveness or true satiety, though anecdotal evidence from patients who have had reversal of jejunoileal bypass implies that the operation in fact was aversive.

Numerous complications of jejunoileal bypass[25-27] have mainly been ascribed to the overgrowth of bacteria in the blind loop of terminal ileum, which initiates abnormal immune processes, absorption of toxic products of bacterial metabolism, and deficiencies. For this reason, different techniques have been developed to try to diminish the risk of bacterial overgrowth, thus improving the results of intestinal bypass. The methods in question have been evaluated from 4 to 10 years in different centers, fortunately without yet being disseminated to the broad practicing surgical community, as was the case with jejunoileal bypass.

Realization of the adverse effects of bacterial overgrowth of the blind loop has prompted development of various methods to avoid or diminish reflux into the blind loop. One strategy has been to construct fold or "valves" in the excluded loop, though no study has documented any benefit from such maneuvers. A different method was introduced by Eriksson[28] in 1976, *biliointestinal bypass*, in which he attached the jejunal stump of the blind loop of a conventional end-side jejunoileostomy to the gallbladder in an attempt to divert bile through the loop (Figure 15-3). Theoretically, the bile would stimulate peristalsis in the loop, helping it to self-empty, at the same time preventing overgrowth by the bacteriostatic action of the bile. Furthermore, reabsorption of bile in the bypassed segment would counteract bile spillover into the colon, which is a significant source of diarrhea. Eriksson has reported fewer side effects in patients undergoing this operation, including less flatulence, diarrhea, and arthritis, than in his historical control subjects having conventional jejunoileal bypass with a similar amount of weight loss. Others have shown a reduction in fecal fat and bile salts with the method,[29] though their long-term experience[30] and that of others[31] is limited with respect to the number of patients.

A different method for dealing with the blind loop was recently introduced by Gourlay,[32] of Vancouver, who performs an end-end jejunoileostomy (25 to 50 cm) and tacks the distal end of the blind loop into the antrum of the stomach as an *ileogastrostomy* (Figure 15-4). By April 1986, he had performed the operation in 152 patients, 50 of whom had been followed for 2 to 4 years. He, too, reported results superior to his historical control patients having end-end jejunoileostomy with ileocolostomy of the blind loop.

Still another method, the *duodenoileal bypass*, was introduced by Dorton[33] in 1981. It consists of an end-side anastomosis between the most proximal cuff of the jejunum (in essence, just distal to the fourth portion of the duodenum) and the distal 50 cm of ileum. An intussusception antireflux nipple valve is created in the bypassed segment just proximal to the anastomosis.

This operation is very similar to the original end-side jejunoileostomy with two important differences: (1) the distal loop of ileum is longer, increasing the absorptive capacity for critical nutrients; and (2) an antireflux valve prevents reflux into the blind loop, diminishing the risk of chyme stagnation with concomitant overgrowth of bacteria. The experience with this operation in two

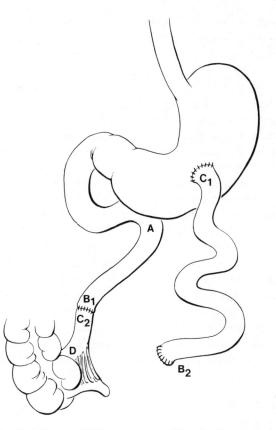

Figure 15-4 Jejunoileal Bypass with Ileogastrostomy. Jejunoileal bypass (end-end) with varying lengths of A–B$_1$ and C$_2$–D was formerly performed connecting C$_1$ to the large intestine. With ileogastrostomy, A–B$_1$ = 25cm, C$_2$–D = 50 cm, and C$_1$ is connected so it empties into the stomach.

centers in 57 patients followed for 2 to 5 years reveals similar, yet less frequent and less severe, side effects than those described in conventional jejunoileal bypass patients followed for a similar length of time.[33]

Combined Restrictive-Malabsorptive

Probably the most drastic operation in the field of obesity surgery is a procedure combining gastric restrictive features with maldigestion and malabsorption. *Biliopancreatic bypass* (Figure 15-2), introduced by Scopinaro et al[34] of Genoa, Italy in 1976, is the only operation performed in a large series of patients that is partially irreversible. It entails resecting all but 200 to 400 ml of the stomach, closing the duodenal stump as in Billroth II resection, and then creating a Rouxen-Y gastrojejunostomy with half of the small intestine as the Roux limb connected to the terminal ileum 50 cm from the ileocecal valve. Several versions of this operation with variable proportions of intestine and different sizes of gastric remnants have been used through the years. The patients operated on in Italy have generally been lighter than those in the United States. Weight loss has been extraordinary, though a fairly high frequency of nutritional complications has been seen. The operation has been adopted by several surgeons[35,36] in the United States who are reporting similar short-term results as the Scopinaro group.[37]

Recognizing the importance of a malabsorptive and/or maldigestive component of the gastric bypass for the superior weight loss compared with gastroplasty, several surgeons[38,39] have begun to use longer jejunal loops (see Figure 15-2) in gastric bypass operations. The most radical version of this type of operation is very similar to the Scopinaro biliopancreatic bypass and differs only in constructing a gastric bypass pouch instead of resecting the stomach. This allows the possibility of completely reversing the operation if required. It is too early to evaluate results of these operations, though extraordinary weight loss is to be expected. The main concerns are maintenance of an adequate nutritional state and monitoring for development of hepatic disease because of protein-calorie malnutrition. Blind loop overgrowth over the long term cannot be ruled out, and follow-up needs to evaluate any adverse effects of such overgrowth.

Regulatory Procedures

There are regulatory components to several of the described procedures in fact qualifying this surgery as "behavioral." In gastric restriction, fear of vomiting leads to aversive conditioning both with respect to eating behavior and dietary choices on the one hand, while a (comfortable?) sense of fullness simulates satiety, on the other hand, with positive reinforcement of consuming small quantities. As pointed out, the intestinal bypass procedures reduce food intake via poorly understood mechanisms, though delayed gastric emptying might contribute to this regulatory effect.

Some procedures have been conceived to be only regulatory. Electrolytic lesions of putative feeding nuclei in the hypothalamus were attempted in some patients reported in 1974, with only transitory effects and long-term failure.[40] Truncal vagotomy without drainage was attempted in a series of 21 patients with initially moderate effects,[41] though results over the long term have been discouraging.[43] Intestinal interposition, moving a segment of terminal ileum up to the proximal jejunum, has been attempted in five patients with poor and discordant results.[17]

In summary, it seems that regulatory procedures, proven effective in laboratory animals, are insufficient to achieve and maintain significant weight loss in human patients with morbid obesity. On the other hand, preliminary data imply that combining truncal vagotomy without drainage with vertical gastroplasty significantly enhances weight loss compared with gastroplasty alone.[43]

RESULTS

Weight Loss

There are four aspects to evaluating results of obesity surgery. The most obvious are the amount of weight lost and the duration of maintenance. From a medical standpoint, amelioration of complications and risk reduction (prevention) seem more important as measures of "success" of the surgery. Improvement in quality of life is the aspect most patients consider to be the most important, yet very few studies address this criterion of success.

Hardly any data document the natural course of morbid obesity, and no data document the natural course of surgical patients who have achieved and sustained significant weight loss. Consequently, there can be no definition of ideal weight for height or "goal" weight for a morbidly obese patient after surgery. Weight loss can be expressed as absolute loss or as loss of "excess weight." It seems reasonable to consider a loss of 100% of excess weight, bringing the patient down to ideal weight, as more successful than, for example, a loss of only 60% of excess weight. However, there is no evidence to support this, and it is conceivable that the former loss is less "healthy" than the latter, since it probably is associated with a greater degree of malnutrition.

Morbidly obese patients have a large frame,[44] and thus their ideal weight should be based on tables for large frames. Even though most of their excess weight is fat, they also have greater lean body mass and increased extracellular water. There is no definition of "ideal body composition" delineating the proportions of fat, lean, and water associated with lowest morbidity or mortality, but decreases in lean body mass have been shown to be detrimental, and being underweight is associated with increased mortality.[45] "Successful" weight loss after obesity surgery should ideally be achieved through reduction of fat without a dangerous loss of lean tissue. Several studies[46,47] have indeed shown reductions of fat with very little change in lean tissue, but the degree of total weight loss has been on the order of 60% of excess weight, and they have not included long-term follow-up of weight maintenance or morbidity or mortality. Obviously more data are needed to define an optimal or "goal" weight loss by surgery in morbidly obese patients. In practice, however, most operations fall short of achieving potentially hazardous weight losses: patients characteristically lose one third of their preoperative weight, corresponding to 55% to 65% of excess weight. It follows that the majority of patients will still weigh 135% to 145% of ideal body weight when they reach a plateau after surgery and obviously will still be obese.

Complications

Complications of obesity surgery are obesity-related or procedure-related. The latter are classifiable as operative complications or related to weight loss. The risks of anesthesia and surgery in obese patients were reviewed recently, and pulmonary, thromboembolic, cardiovascular, and wound complications were summarized.[10] Experience from the performance of obesity surgery has greatly lessened complication rates through such measures as prophylactic heparinization, routine use of antibiotics, chest physical therapy, and preoperative evaluation of cardiopulmonary status to reduce operative risk. The incidences of pulmonary embolus, thrombophlebitis, and wound dehiscence in pooled series of more than 1,000 obese patients are less than 1%, with rates of 4% to 6% for pneumonia-atelectasis and wound infection.[10] Even if these complications are considered obesity-related, they do differ depending on the operation performed.

Gastric restrictive operations have had more operative complications, mainly attributable to perforations of the stomach in all types of procedures and leaks from anastomoses in gastric bypass procedures. The malabsorptive operations are encumbered with long-term complications related to blind-loop and short-bowel syndromes, with deficiencies and problems related to bacterial overgrowth. It is important to keep in mind that the more efficient an operation is in terms of resultant weight loss and maintenance, the greater the potential for deficiencies. As gastric restrictive operations have become more efficient, and long-term results have become available, there are increasing reports[47-49] of nutritional sequelae of the operations.

Experience with the many complications of intestinal bypass, studied for more than 20 years, has provided information on how to treat and prevent complications. Take-down rates[50] of 15% to 25% in some series of jejunoileal bypass should be contrasted with the revision rate of 52% reported by Mason et al[51] in their first 69 patients with gastric bypass. Just as there have been modifications and improvements in gastric operations, there has been improvement in intestinal procedures.

Critique

The greatest difficulty in evaluating results of surgical treatment of obesity is the poor follow-up rate over the long term. Makarewicz et al[43] introduced the concept of the "hard follow-up rate," whereby *all* patients failing to return for outpatient check-up in spite of several reminders are considered failures with respect to weight loss.[52] This view is probably unduly pessimistic since many surgeons report patients with successful weight loss who have "surfaced" only after a long period of time. However, the failure rate among "no shows" undoubtedly is significantly higher than in patients keeping their appointments.

There are several reasons for dropout after surgery, one of which is shared with other obesity treatment modalities: failure to lose or maintain loss of weight. Other patients, and considerably fewer, do not return because they indeed feel so well as not to require visits to the physician. A third category, and much more troublesome, is patients with complications of surgery who dare not return for fear the surgeon will recommend take-down of the procedure, which would inevitably lead to regain of all weight. With the increasing availability of alternative operations and methods for revising procedures, it is expected that fewer patients will fail to return for follow-up for this reason.

Analyses of failures of weight loss have focused on technical shortcomings of the operations.[53] In intestinal bypass, failure of weight loss was attributed to the length of small intestine left in continuity whether by design (not bypassing a sufficient length of intestine) or by accident through difficulties in measuring small bowel or by reflux of nutrients into the bypassed loops. It is true that long-term adaptation of the in-continuity intestine leads to an arrest in the rate of weight loss and ultimately regain of weight, but long-term results of jejunoileal bypass have been more successful with respect to weight loss than gastric procedures.

Gastric restrictive procedures fail through enlargement of the stomach pouch, widening of the stoma, or disruption of the staple lines.[54] Even though these reasons for failure seem to be technical, they just as much represent *a conceptual failure*. The regulatory component of gastric restriction is insufficient to counteract overeating by obese patients, which leads to stretching of the pouch, erosion of stomal support, or frank breakdown of staple lines. Even in the absence of technical failures, there is a subgroup of patients who will "outeat" gastric restrictive procedures by selecting soft or liquid high-caloric-density foods, which are not effectively restricted by the gastric operations. This is shown by the 30% failure rate in patients with mesh wrapped around the gastroplasty preventing dilation and enlargement of the pouch (J.G. Kral, MD, unpublished data).

Since obesity is multifactorial and the eating behavior of morbidly obese patients varies immensely, it is unlikely that any single procedure ever will qualify as the method of choice. Effectiveness of weight loss is inimical to "good nutrition." An ideal procedure should achieve a selective reduction in body fat, sparing essential nutrients and maintaining lean body mass. Gastroplasties are the most benign operations, but are prone to long-term failure of weight loss. Intestinal malabsorptive procedures are more effective, and as a consequence more prone to deficiencies and long-term side effects. Conceivably, combinations of gastric restriction and malabsorption, performed concomitantly or sequentially (as in staged procedures) will be the solution to this serious disease.

SUMMARY

Surgical treatment is justified in patients with serious complications of obesity that has been refractory to nonsurgical treatment. It is also justified in severely overweight patients with a high likelihood of developing serious complications or even dying prematurely. Most surgical methods are more successful in achieving weight loss than other methods, though results over the long term are difficult to assess. It is important that the surgical candidate have realistic expectations with respect to weight loss (approximately one third of preoperative weight) and be fully cooperative with meticulous postoperative monitoring to detect potential deficiencies and other sequelae of the surgery. There are several surgical methods, and they differ significantly with respect to side effects and efficacy of weight loss. Surgical treatment of obesity must still be considered investigational, and considerable efforts must be made to ensure adequate follow-up to permit full evaluation of the different procedures. The most important area of investigation is characterization of surgical candidates to improve selection for surgery to avoid conceptual and technical failures, thereby optimizing outcome.

REFERENCES

1. *Health Implications of Obesity: National Institutes of Health Consensus Development Conference. Ann Intern Med* 1985; 103:977–1077.

2. *Build Study, 1979.* Chicago, Society of Actuaries and Association of Life Insurance Medical Directors of America, 1980.

3. Horton ES: Role of environmental factors in the development of noninsulin-dependent diabetes mellitus. *Am J Med* 1983; 75:32–40.

4. Reisin E, Abel R, Modan M, Silverberg DS, Eliahou HE, Modan B: Effect of weight loss without salt restriction on the reduction of blood pressure in overweight hypertensive patients. *New Engl J Med* 1978; 298:1–6.

5. Reisin E, Frohlich ED, Messerli FH, Dreslinski GR, Dunn FG, Jones MM, Batson HM Jr: Cardiovascular changes after weight reduction in obesity hypertension. *Ann Intern Med* 1983; 98:315–319.

6. Ray CS, Sue DY, Bray G, Hansen JE, Wasserman K: Effects of obesity on respiratory function. American Review of Respiratory Disease 1983; 128:501–506.

7. Lane DA, Lipscomb J, Eddy DM: A risk-benefit analysis of gastric obesity surgery, in Hirsch J, Van Itallie TB (eds): *Recent Advances in Obesity Research IV.* London, John Libbey & Co., 1985, pp 260–266.

8. Drenick EJ, Bales GS, Seltzer F, Johnson DG: Excessive mortality and causes of death in morbidly obese men. *J Am Med Assoc* 1980; 243:443–445.

9. Kral JG: Morbid obesity and related health risks. *Ann Intern Med* 1985; 103:1043–1047.

10. Pasulka PS, Bistrian BR, Benotti PN, Blackburn GL: The risks of surgery in obese patients. *Ann Intern Med* 1986; 104:540–546.

11. American Society for Clinical Nutrition Task Force: Guidelines for surgery for morbid obesity. *Am J Clin Nutr* 1985; 42:904–905.

12. Mason EE, Ito C: Gastric bypass and obesity. *Surg Clin North Am* 1967; 47:1355–1361.

13. Linner JH: *Surgery for Morbid Obesity*. New York, Springer-Verlag, 1984.

14. Flickinger EG, Pories WJ, Meelheim HD, Sinai DR, Blose IL, Thomas FT: The Greenville gastric bypass: Progress report at 3 years. *Ann Surg* 1984; 199:555–562.

15. Halverson JD, Zuckerman GR, Koehler RE, Gentry K, Michael HEB, DeSchryver-Kecskemeti K: Gastric bypass for morbid obesity: A medical-surgical assessment. *Ann Surg* 1981; 194:152–160.

16. Wilkinson LH, Peloso OA: Gastric (reservoir) reduction for morbid obesity. *Arch Surg* 1981; 116:602–605.

17. Wilkinson LH, Peloso OA, Milne RO: Gastric reservoir reduction. *Clin Nutr* 1986; 5:121–123.

18. Kral JG: Obesity surgery: State of the art, in Hirsch J, Van Itallie TB (eds): *Recent Advances in Obesity Research IV*. London, John Libbey & Co., 1985, pp 237–246.

19. Kral JG, Gortz L: Recent developments in the surgical treatment of obesity, in Enzi G, Crepaldi G, Pozza G, Renold AE (eds): *Obesity: Pathogenesis and Treatment*. New York, Academic Press, 1981, pp 255–259.

20. Kremen AJ, Linner JH, Nelson CH: An experimental evaluation of the nutritional importance of proximal and distal small intestine. *Ann Surg* 1954; 140:439–444.

21. Pilkington TRE, Gazet J-C, Ang L, Kalucy RS, Crisp AH, Day S: Explanations for weight loss after ileojejunal bypass in gross obesity. *Brit Med J* 1976; 1:1504–1505.

22. Condon SC, Jones NJ, Wise L, Alpers DH: Role of caloric intake in weight loss after jejuno-ileal bypass for obesity. *Gastroenterology* 1978; 74:34–37.

23. Sclafani A, Koopmans HS, Vasselli JR, Reichman M: Effects of intestinal bypass surgery on appetite: Food intake and body weight in obese and lean rats. *Am J Physiol* 1978; 234:E389–E398.

24. Kissileff HR, Nakashima RK, Stunkard AJ: Effects of jejunoileal bypass on meal patterns in genetically obese and lean rats. *Am J Physiol* 1979; 237:R217–R224.

25. Joffe SN: Progress report—Surgical management of morbid obesity. *Gut* 1981; 22:242–254.

26. Hocking MP, Kelly KA, Callaway CW: Vertical gastroplasty for morbid obesity: Clinical experience. *Mayo Clinic Proceedings* 1986; 61:287–291.

27. Adibi SA, Stanko RT: Perspectives on gastrointestinal surgery for treatment of morbid obesity: The lesson learned. *Gastroenterology* 1984; 87:1381–1391.

28. Eriksson F: Biliointestinal bypass. *Int J Obes* 1981; 5:437–447.

29. South LM, Littlewood A: Faecal bile salts after intestinal bypass, in Maxwell JD, Gazet J-C, Pilkington TRE (eds): *Surgical Management of Obesity*. London, Academic Press, 1980, pp 147–158.

30. MacFarland RJ, Gazet J-C, Pilkington TRE: A 13-year review of jejunoileal bypass. *Br J Surg* 1985; 72:81–87.

31. Wiklund B: Fate of weight: Ten-year observations after jejunoileal bypass for obesity. *Acta Chir Scand* 1982; 148:443–452.

32. Gourlay RH: Jejunoileal bypass with ileogastrostomy: An operation free of the complications associated with intestinal bypass. *Proceedings of the American College of Surgeons Postgraduate Course 2: Problems in Obesity Surgery.* Vancouver, April 13–17, 1986, pp 35–37.

33. Kral JG, Morton BA, Dorton HE: Duodenoileal bypass for morbid obesity. *Proceedings of the American Society for Bariatric Surgeons.* Iowa City, June 18–22, 1986 (abstract).

34. Scopinaro N, Gianetta E, Civalleri D, Bonalumi U, Bachi V: Biliopancreatic bypass for obesity II. Initial experience in man. *Br J Surg* 1979; 66:618–620.

35. Holian D: Biliopancreatic bypass: The American experience four years and more. *Proceedings Fifth Annual Symposium on Surgical Treatment of Obesity.* February 11–14, 1987, Universal City, California.

36. Wittig J: Reoperation and revision after biliopancreatic bypass. *Proceedings Fifth Annual Symposium on Surgical Treatment of Obesity.* February 11–14, 1987, Universal City, California.

37. Scopinaro N, Gianetta E, Civalleri D, Bonalumi U, Friedman D, Bachi V: Partial and total biliopancreatic bypass in the surgical treatment of obesity. *Int J Obes* 1981; 5:421–429.

38. Torres JC, Oca CF: Gastric bypass, lesser curvature and new developments with Roux-en-Y placement according to eating habits. *Proceedings Third Annual Meeting American Society for Bariatric Surgeons.* June 18–20, 1986, Iowa City.

39. Sugerman HJ: Influence of dietary habits in choice of weight reduction operation. *American College of Surgeons 14th Annual Meeting, Postgraduate Course 2, Problems in Obesity Surgery.* April 12–16, 1986, Vancouver, pp 51–54.

40. Quaade F, Vaernet K, Larsson S: Stereotaxic stimulation and electrocoagulation of the lateral hypothalamus in obese humans. *Acta Neurochirurgica* 1974; 30:111–117.

41. Kral JG, Gortz L: Truncal vagotomy in morbid obesity. *Int J Obes* 1981; 5:431–435.

42. Gortz L, Kral JG: A 5–8 year follow-up study of truncal vagotomy as a treatment for morbid obesity, abstracted. *Proceedings of the American Society of Bariatric Surgeons.* Iowa City, June 18–20, 1986.

43. Gortz L, Wallin G, Kral JG: Vertical banded gastroplasty with and without vagotomy. *Clin Nutr* 1986; 5:79–81.

44. Van Itallie TB: When the frame is part of the picture. *Am J Public Health* 1985; 75:1054–1055.

45. Lew EA: Mortality and weight: Insured lives and the American Cancer Society studies. *Ann Intern Med* 1985; 103:1024–1029.

46. Palombo JD, Maletskos CJ, Reinhold RV, Hayward E, Wade J, Bothe A Jr, Benotti P, Bistrian BR, Blackburn GL: Composition of weight loss in morbidly obese patients after gastric bypass. *J Surg Res* 1981; 30:435–442.

47. MacLean LD, Rhode BM, Shizgal HM: Nutrition following gastric operations for morbid obesity. *Ann Surg* 1983; 198:347–355.

48. Solomon H, Abarbanel Y, Berginer VM, Leff S, Trostler N, Roven J, Peiser J, Ovnat A, Charuzi I: Neurological deficits following gastric restriction surgery for morbid obesity. *Clin Nutr* 1986; 5:181–184.

49. Amaral JF, Thompson WR, Caldwell MD, Martin HF, Randall HT: Prospective hepatologic evaluation of gastric exclusion surgery for morbid obesity. *Ann Surg* 1985; 201:186–193.

50. Halverson JD, Schiff RJ, Gentry K, Alpers DH: Long-term follow-up of jejunoileal bypass patients. *Am J Clin Nutr* 1980; 33:472–475.

51. Mason EE, Lewis JW, Blommers TJ, Scott DH, Rodriguez EM, Bukoff ML: 1966–70 Gastric bypass in review, in Hirsch J, Van Itallie TB (eds): *Recent Advances in Obesity Research IV.* London, John Libbey & Co., 1985, pp 247–253.

52. Makarewicz PA, Freeman JB, Burchett H, Brazeau P: Vertical banded gastroplasty: Assessment of efficacy. *Surgery* 1985; 98:700–707.

53. Mason EE: Reoperations for obesity, in Mason EE (ed): *Surgical Treatment of Obesity.* Philadelphia, WB Saunders Co., 1981, pp 418–448.

54. Mason EE, Printen KJ, Hartford CE, Boyd WC: Optimizing results of gastric bypass. *Ann Surg* 1975; 182:405–414.

Chapter 16

Weight Loss Maintenance and Relapse Prevention

Carol J. Morton

INTRODUCTION

Over the past 15 years, considerable research has been conducted in an attempt to understand the etiology of obesity and to identify the techniques and processes that result in successful weight loss. While no definitive answers have been found, the understanding of the complex nature of this disorder is far better today than even a few years ago.

However, little attention has been focused on the issue of weight maintenance.[1] While most treatment programs have offered some type of maintenance support, with booster sessions after intitial treatment being the most frequently used,[2] it is only recently that weight maintenance has begun to receive the attention it deserves as a critical component of any weight-control program. Researchers are just beginning to understand the nature of the relapse process for addictive disorders in general and for obesity in particular, with Marlatt's relapse prevention model being the most fully defined maintenance strategy currently available.[3] Others have attempted to identify the correlates of weight maintenance. However, to date, very few factors seem to be correlated with long-term weight maintenance success. It is sad to say that more is unknown than known, and the fact remains that while only a small percentage of dieters will ever be successful in losing weight, an even smaller percentage will be able to maintain their weight loss for any length of time thereafter.[4]

While researchers continue to search for clues in an attempt to unravel the mystery surrounding weight maintenance, it is the practitioner of weight-control services who must decide the type of maintenance service that can be responsibly offered to clients. It is the purpose of this chapter to aid practitioners' decision-making efforts by providing an overview of Marlatt's relapse prevention model, identifying some of the weight-maintenance strategies currently being discussed and used by leaders in the field, outlining issues that practitioners need to take into account when designing a maintenance service, and suggesting one approach to offering such a service to clients that is based on my work with maintenance members of Weight Watchers over the course of 15 years.

AN OVERVIEW OF MARLATT'S RELAPSE PREVENTION MODEL

Marlatt's relapse prevention model[5] was originally developed as a general cognitive-behavioral model for use with a variety of addictive disorders. It is still in the preliminary stages of empirical evaluation to determine its effectiveness as a maintenance strategy.[3]

Relapse as a Process, Not an End State

Marlatt[5] hypothesizes that how people view the habit-change process can influence whether or not they ultimately return to baseline levels of the problem behavior.

If a person views relapse with an "all or nothing" mentality, then the person will interpret one instance of loss of control over the problem behavior to mean that control is totally and forever lost. The likelihood that this one brief lapse of control will be followed by a return to baseline behaviors is increased. However, if a person views relapse as a transitional process during which any lapse of control is viewed as a singular occurrence and something to be learned from, the person will be less likely to perceive that all has been lost, will be better equipped to deal constructively with a similar situation, and the likelihood of relapse will decrease.

Marlatt[5] advocates that relapse be viewed as a process rather than an end state because such a definition implies that learning and corrective action can be the outcomes of any lapse in control. This can then steer a person in the direction of positive change rather than relapse.

A Microanalysis of the Relapse Process

In order to gain control over a problem behavior, a person usually follows a specific set of rules (eg, abstinence for problem drinkers, controlled eating for dieters). While complying with these rules, the person experiences a sense of personal control or self-efficacy that continues until a high-risk situation is encountered. Marlatt[5] defines a high-risk situation to be any situation that poses a threat to a person's sense of being able to control the problem behavior. High-risk situations found to be especially prevalent among dieters are social situations and negative emotional states such as boredom and depression.[3,4]

If people can effectively manage the situation by using an appropriate coping response, they will continue to experience a sense of self-control. The likelihood that a lapse will occur is decreased, while the expectation that they will be able to cope effectively when confronted with a similar situation in the future is increased.

However, there may be times when the person may be unable to cope effectively with a high-risk situation because of either a lack of coping skills or because anxiety or fear block the response. This inability to cope leads to a decreased sense of personal control and a tendency to "give in" and indulge in the problem behavior. The result of this "I can't handle it" feeling is that when in a similar high-risk situation in the future, the person's expectation of being able to cope without indulging in the problem behavior will decrease and the urge to indulge will be given in to. The temptation to give in is increased if the person has what Marlatt[5] labels "positive outcome expectancies" regarding the effects of indulging in the problem behavior. This is when a person will anticipate the immediate positive effects of indulgence and forget or ignore the delayed negative effects (eg, weight gain or a full feeling in the case of overeating).

Feeling unable to cope with a high-risk situation teamed with positive outcome expectancies of the effects of the old coping behavior greatly increases the likelihood that an initial lapse will occur. Whether it develops into a total relapse will depend on how the person perceives the cause of the lapse and the reactions associated with its occurrence.

People who equate abstinence with success tend to have an all or nothing perspective. They are either totally in control of their behavior during abstinence or totally out of control. For example, in the case of a dieter, even one piece of what might be considered a "forbidden" food could be interpreted to mean that control has been completely lost. Any slip from this perfectionistic state is enough to violate the rule of abstinence. Once this occurs, it is irreversible. Marlatt[5] labels this transgression of absolutism the "abstinence violation effect" (AVE).

The intensity of a person's AVE is influenced by two factors. The first is cognitive dissonance. If people's view of themselves as abstainers or controlled substance users come in direct conflict with their behavior (indulgence), conflict and guilt are experienced. If people normally cope with conflict and guilt by indulging in the problem behavior, which for the dieter is eating, they may do so this time as well. They may also attempt to change their self-image so that it is more in line with their behavior. This reduces the dissonance associated with the slip from perfection. ("This just goes to show that I can't handle it! I knew I was meant to be fat all my life!") Regardless of which manner of coping with the dissonance the person selects, the result is the same: the probability that the lapse will escalate into a full relapse is increased.

The second factor is personal attribution. If people attribute the cause of the lapse to personal weakness rather than viewing it as a unique response to a particular situation, they are likely to view "lack of willpower" or some other internal cause as the reason for the lapse. This view increases the expectation of continued failure. ("What's the use! I have NO willpower!") Once again, the lapse is likely to develop into a full-blown relapse.

Marlatt[5] feels that, in many instances, the high-risk situation is encountered unexpectedly by the person. However, there are times when it seems as if it is the last link in a series of events that precede the first lapse. Upon close analysis, it also seems as if people have "set themselves up" to be in the high-risk situation, thereby planning their own relapse. They do this by making a series of apparently irrelevant decisions (AIDS), with each decision deliberately, even if unconsciously, placing them one step closer to the high-risk situation.

Why would a person deliberately set out to plan a relapse? Marlatt[5] states that one of the most common rationalizations used to justify a lapse is that the indulgence in the problem behavior is justified. He hypothesizes that the need to do so stems from a life style that is weighted down with a multitude of perceived "shoulds" (things a person feels must be done) and one in which there seems to be little room for pleasure. A person who lives such an unbalanced life style experiences an increased perception of self-deprivation. This results in the desire for indulgence and gratification to balance the disequilibrium. Use of the problem behavior results in immediate gratification, a "payoff" that outweighs the cost of any delayed negative effects. "I owe it to myself" is a common rationalization used to justify the planned indulgence. Somatically, the desire for indulgence is experienced as a craving or urge, with the person anticipating a positive effect once the urge has been given in to. Cognitively, through the use of rationalization and denial, the person then proceeds to make a series of AIDS, inevitably leading to a high-risk situation. The stage for relapse has been set.

Suggested Relapse-Prevention Strategies

To help prevent relapse once treatment has been completed, Marlatt[5] recommends a series of techniques for use with clients. His suggested maintenance program includes the following:

- identification of individual high-risk situations
- development of coping skills for high-risk situations
- practice in coping with potential lapses
- development of cognitive coping strategies for use immediately after a lapse
- development of a more balanced life style.

A detailed discussion of the various techniques and their application throughout the treatment process can be found in Marlatt and Gordon's *Relapse Prevention*.[5]

Application to Obesity

Several studies have begun to test relapse prevention with dieters. One study by Abrams and Follick[6] and another by Sternberg[4] found long-term results improved by adding relapse prevention techniques to standard behavioral programs in a worksite and a clinical setting, respectively. However, a study by Collins et al[7] subsequently failed to replicate Sternberg's[4] results. Another study by Perri et al[8] tested nonbehavioral, behavioral, and behavioral plus relapse prevention techniques in conjunction with post-treatment continuing therapist contact by mail and telephone. They found that the relapse prevention program boosted long-term results *only* when teamed with continuing therapist contact.

Since the relapse prevention model as applied to the treatment of obesity is still in the early stages of empirical evaluation, it is too early to draw any conclusions regarding how effective it is as a maintenance strategy. In the interim, however, the following should be taken into consideration by the weight-control practitioner wishing to use relapse prevention techniques with clients:

A relapse can occur either during weight loss (eg, a person fails to follow program requirements thereby failing to lose weight) or after weight loss (eg, as indicated by weight regain). Relapse prevention can, therefore, be used during both the weight-loss and weight-maintenance treatment process.

Controlled food use as opposed to abstinence is the goal of obesity treatment. Since "controlled food use" is difficult to define, a more subjective definition of an initial lapse may be warranted; the following two definitions are offered:

1. an instance of unplanned or uncontrolled eating in which a person consumes more than expected
2. eating that is not in accordance with a commitment to lose or maintain weight.[4]

ADDITIONAL MAINTENANCE STRATEGIES

While Marlatt's[5] relapse prevention model may be the most comprehensive maintenance strategy currently available, several other strategies have been identified as possibly contributing to successful weight maintenance. These strategies, which practitioners may wish to include in any maintenance treatment program, are as follows:

Exercise

Evidence is mounting that exercise is one of the few factors correlated with long-term weight maintenance.[1,9,10] Brownell et al[2] suggested that exercise may prevent relapse because it:

- becomes a positive addiction, serving as a positive replacement for the problem behavior
- may positively influence a person's self-concept, which may then generalize to the behavior-change process
- provides a peer group that supports healthy behavior
- removes a person to a safe setting.

Other reasons may include that exercise:

- becomes a constructive means for managing stress, tension, and other negative emotional states
- enables a person to consume a greater number of calories than otherwise would be possible.

Continued Self-Monitoring

Continued self-monitoring of either body weight or eating habits has been strongly advocated as an important maintenance strategy. Holmes et al,[1] in a study of obese patients at Wayne State University who had 40 lb or more to lose, found continued self-monitoring to be one of the three variables that predicted successful weight maintenance. Stuart,[11] in a study of Weight Watchers members, found that those who maintained their weight most successfully continued to use many of the techniques used to reach goal weight, one of which was food and behavior change monitoring.

Post-treatment Support

Booster sessions have been the most frequently used maintenance strategy. While their efficacy is uncertain, post-treatment support does seem to have a role in successful weight maintenance. Stuart and Guire[9] found that Weight Watchers members who continued to attend meetings after reaching goal weight in the same location and with the same lecturer were more likely to maintain their weight than those who did not. Holmes et al[1] found that clients most likely to maintain their weight loss were those who attended follow-up sessions. Perri et al[8] discovered that relapse prevention techniques aided weight maintenance only when teamed with post-treatment therapist contact. They[8] also suggested that booster sessions, as traditionally designed and implemented, may have failed for two reasons:

1. Three or four randomly scheduled sessions immediately after treatment may be insufficient to provide the support and advice necessary for weight maintenance.
2. Failure to maintain weight loss may not be the result of forgetting treatment techniques, the review of which has been the focus of the booster sessions, but rather a lack of motivation to sustain adherence.

Social Support

While social support has been suggested by many as important to weight maintenance, intervention attempts have produced inconsistent results.[2] Some studies have shown that the inclusion of spouses in weight-reduction treatment programs contributed to long-term weight maintenance; others have not.[12] However, Marlatt[5] proposed a social support component in his relapse prevention program, and Stuart[11] suggested the need to help mates of the newly thin to cope with the new social, job, and recreational opportunities that are available to their newly thin partners. What appears evident is that positive support from significant others in a client's life is more likely to foster long-term weight maintenance than lack of support, which can only make weight maintenance a more difficult process. It is, however, unlikely that any single approach to obtaining such support will work with all clients because of differences in the nature of their social relationships.[2]

Additional Strategies

Other strategies that seem to support weight maintenance include the following:[9,13]

- continuing use of specific strategies that were useful during weight loss
- setting a specific weight gain of no more than 3 to 5 lb as a sign of being overweight
- making life style changes, particularly in the areas of mood management and exercise
- including cognitive strategies that support clients' belief that they were instrumental in the attainment of their goal weight and that they have the ability to control their eating urges.

TREATMENT ISSUES

There are several issues surrounding weight maintenance that can affect treatment design and provision. Some are suggested by the literature, and others are based on my experience. It is important for practitioners to be aware of them and to take them into account when developing a treatment program.

Issue 1: When Does Maintenance Actually Begin?

Currently, there does not seem to be a consensus as to when weight maintenance as a phase in the weight-loss and control process actually begins. Most behavioral weight-control programs have been short-term courses in behavioral self-management, lasting 10 or 12 weeks. Usually, in such a short time, most participants have lost only a partial amount of the weight they need or desire to lose. Yet many researchers have defined maintenance as the client's ability to maintain the weight lost during treatment even though the client may be, and in most cases still is, in the process of losing weight.

Other researchers are beginning to identify weight maintenance as the period immediately after the client's attainment of a predetermined goal weight, with maintenance defined as the client's ability to maintain the goal weight. Weight Watchers and several other commercial diet organizations use this definition as well.

Needless to say, from the client's perspective, being actively involved in weight loss is not the same as attempting to stabilize and then maintain one's weight. While one may be the natural extension of the other, it is still in question whether the processes and strategies that promote weight loss also promote weight maintenance.

An agreed-upon definition of "weight maintenance" that distinguishes it from the weight-loss process is needed. Only then can a clear picture be obtained as to what factors truly affect the weight-stabilization process and ultimately lead to long-term maintenance.

Issue 2: What Impact Does Being Newly Thin Have on a Person's Ability to Maintain Weight?

While research is beginning to explore the strategies believed to contribute to long-term maintenance, little mention has been made of the impact that being newly thin has on a person's life. Even less attention has been focused on what type of support will be needed or desired during the first few months of weight maintenance if the person is to have a successful start. Yet it is this same time period that has been identified as being the one during which a majority of clients begin to relapse.[4]

If one looks at this time period from the client's perspective, one can almost understand why the relapse rate may be so high. Being thin may bring with it a new slim appearance and several other rewards. However, it can also be a time of unexpected stress as it is also a period of adjustment. Now that food is no longer the focal point of their life, the newly thin may experience the loss of friends for whom the basis of the friendship was eating. They may experience difficulty in seeing themselves as a thin person. Even the scale no longer reacts in the old familiar up and down manner! As time passes, the support and attention initially offered to the person by significant others begins to fade. Foods they originally thought could be given up forever begin to look inviting. The list could continue. Is it any wonder, then, that the thought "Is it really worth the effort?" may consciously or unconsciously run through the mind of the newly thin? If the answer is "No, it's not!", then there can be little expectation that the client will use even those techniques that may be identified as correlates of long-term weight maintenance.

Research is needed to explore what impact, if any, the adjustment process has on the newly thin, to identify the type of support needed during the process, and to determine whether providing such support correlates with long-term maintenance.

Issue 3: How Long Should Maintenance Treatment Last?

Arguments have been made for both short- and long-term follow-up treatment. Stuart,[11] recognizing the complex nature of obesity, advocated that treatment be offered both through the attainment of goal weight and through an initial maintenance period to bolster resistance to the pressure to return to one's original weight. Holmes et al[1] argued for extending treatment well into the maintenance period and suggested that this may mean a period of 6 months to 2 years for some clients. Termination of treatment would be based on the client's demonstration of competent use of self-control skills, maintenance of treatment goals for 2 months in succession, and the development of a support system to replace the treatment support group. Jordan and colleagues[14,15] suggested that it is unlikely that treatment can ever be terminated, as clients may need assistance during times of stress and as life circumstances change, as both can lead to an erosion of control.

On the other hand, however, cost efficiencies of extended treatment must be considered[3] as well as whether extended treatment during the maintenance period merely prolongs the time when the client will experience relapse.[2]

More research into the type and duration of the post-treatment contact required to promote long-term maintenance is warranted.

Issue 4: How Can Adherence to Suggested Strategies Be Fostered?

Lack of adherence to suggested strategies seems to be a contributing factor in relapse, especially when one considers the research findings that successful maintainers are more likely to continue using helpful weight-loss strategies than their less-successful counterparts. Perri et al[8] hypothesized that one of the reasons for the poor effectiveness of relapse-prevention techniques without therapist contact was that clients rationalized the instruction "to individualize the program" to mean the elimination of the critical strategies of exercise, self-monitoring, and stimulus control. They[8] also hypothesized that one of the reasons for the failure of booster-session participants to maintain their weight may be that they lack the motivation to sustain adherence to the techniques.

While the issue of adherence is appearing more and more in the literature, little research has been done to determine the factors that actually help sustain it. Martin et al[16] through a series of studies, attempted to identify the factors that fostered exercise adherence in normal, healthy, sedentary adults. Holmes et al[1] recommended that practitioners do whatever is necessary to help clients comply with self-monitoring. Jordan[17] suggested that an attitude toward food as something to be enjoyed rather than a taboo is important in fostering compliance with dietary guidelines, and that clients, therefore, need to incorporate some of their favorite foods into their dietary planning. Even Marlatt's[5] relapse prevention model can be viewed as a series of intervention techniques aimed at fostering adherence to certain self-control strategies.

Others[3,5,11] have attempted to address the issue through the individualization of treatment programs on the assumption that the more input clients have in their treatment goals and the strategies used to achieve them, the more motivated they will be to comply with the strategies and to achieve the goals. This approach is, in part, supported by the adult learning theory of Knowles et al,[18] the key points of which are discussed later.

Research is definitely needed in this critical area of adherence and motivation. In the meantime, how to foster clients' adherence to suggested strategies needs to be uppermost in the minds of all practitioners.

Issue 5: Is There a Difference Between Weight-Loss and Weight-Maintenance Self-Efficacy?

Much emphasis is now being placed in weight-loss research and treatment programs on self-efficacy. It is an important component of Marlatt's[5] model. Mitchell and Stuart,[19] in a study of Weight Watchers members who dropped out of the program before reaching goal weight, found self-efficacy to be the single most important factor in predicting success.

However, little mention has been made in the literature as to the extent to which people's belief in their ability to lose weight and control their urge to eat during the weight-loss process automatically extends itself into the weight-maintenance phase other than to suggest that it seems to be important that cognitive strategies be used to help clients believe they can control their urge to eat.[9,13]

It has been my experience in working with Weight Watchers members that while many successful members believe in their ability to lose weight and control their urge to eat during weight loss, this belief does not necessarily extend into the weight-maintenance phase; many members require support to cultivate this belief.

When viewed from the member's perspective, this lack of belief is understandable. While they may have been successful in losing weight, they may never have had a similar experience with regard to weight maintenance. In fact, many may have experienced repeated failures in this area for a multitude of reasons. Consequently, many newly thin people's belief in their ability to maintain their weight and to control their urge to eat on a long-term basis may be shaky at best. Unfortunately, the statistics regarding the success rate for long-term maintenance only serve to confirm that they may be justified in their doubts.

If self-efficacy is assumed to be a critical component of weight-loss success, it can be assumed that it is equally if not more important to long-term maintenance. How to help clients develop belief in their ability to maintain their weight, both initially and on a long-term basis, needs to be the subject of future research. In the interim, however, practitioners need to be aware that maintenance self-efficacy may be an issue for some of their clients and be prepared to incorporate into their treatment programs strategies aimed at helping these clients develop this belief.

ONE APPROACH TO A WEIGHT-MAINTENANCE PROGRAM

Program Specifications

The weight-maintenance program outlined here combines some of the latest thinking in the field regarding weight maintenance with my own 15 years of experience in providing maintenance services. It is designed according to the following specifications:

Definition

Weight maintenance is defined as beginning when clients have attained a predetermined goal weight as set by themselves in conjunction with the weight-control practitioner. It signifies that, at least for the time being, the weight-loss process has been completed, and clients are ready to begin stabilizing their weight.

Weight Maintenance Stages

While several researchers[2] have identified weight maintenance as being the final stage in the weight-loss process, it has yet to be isolated and analyzed in terms of its subcomponents. This stage, which in actuality is also the beginning of a lifelong endeavor for those who choose to maintain their weight, requires careful analysis to enable practitioners to intervene effectively in support of their clients' needs at each stage of the maintenance process.

This approach, therefore, is based on the concept that maintenance consists of a series of four substages, each of which has special treatment considerations:

1. decision to remain in treatment
2. management of the adjustment process
3. movement toward independence
4. acceptance of a lifelong commitment.

Maintenance Skills

While some of the skills necessary for weight maintenance are the same as those needed for weight loss, this approach recognizes that there are specific weight maintenance skills a person needs to understand and develop.

Duration of Treatment

The need for support will undoubtedly vary from client to client, with those who experienced early age of onset and greater degrees of obesity needing the greatest support and guidance[7] during stages 2 and 3. For these clients, stage 2 may last several months as might stage 3. For clients who have lost lesser amounts of weight and/or who experienced their first weight gains later in life, these two stages may be shorter, as there is less to learn and assimilate.

Frequency of Client-Practitioner Contact

Once a client decides to stay in treatment, weekly support needs to be offered throughout stage 2, though it can be offered more frequently on an as-needed basis. Support can begin to become less frequent during stage 3, with contact being provided only on an as-needed basis throughout stage 4.

Maintenance Self-Efficacy

Maintenance self-efficacy, which is defined as clients' belief in their ability to do what is necessary to maintain their weight, is viewed as being a separate issue from weight-loss self-efficacy, even though the former can build on the latter. The extent to which a client needs support in this critical area should be assessed on a client-by-client basis and then built accordingly into the treatment program.

Adult Learning Theory

This theory differentiates how adults and children learn. Its three key points, which have major implications for program design, are as follows:[18]

1. Adults do not learn for the sake of learning. They are motivated to learn when they experience a need to perform more effectively in life. They, therefore, enter a learning experience with a life-centered, task-centered, or problem-solving orientation to learning. Adults also have a great volume of life experience when they enter a learning situation. Consequently, they need to be treated as being capable of taking responsibility and being involved in the development of any learning plans. Finally, while adults do respond to some external motivation, the more important motivators are internal, such as improved self-esteem, better quality of life, greater self-confidence, etc.
2. Children, on the other hand, have little life experience that is of value as a learning resource. They come ready to hear what they are told they must learn. It is the teacher who has full responsibility regarding what is learned, when it is to be learned, and how learning is to occur. It is the learner's role to carry out the teacher's decision, with the motivation to do so coming from external pressures such as significant others, competition for grades, consequences of failure, etc.
3. The implications of these learning differences on program design include the importance of organizing adult learning around life experiences rather than content units sequenced according to the logic of the subject matter, and the importance of showing how each learning experience is relevant to the learner's life, tasks, or problems.

It is my belief that *one* of the reasons for the failure of clients to continue using the techniques that are part of most behavioral treatment programs may be that these short-term programs have consisted of a series of skills organized according to what seems to be a logical sequence of development and taught in isolation of the client's life experiences. Consequently, the following maintenance program has been based on the principles of adult learning theory.

Additionally, this program is based on the following three assumptions:

1. Clients were following reduced caloric dietary guidelines to attain their goal weight, and if they were on a liquid weight-loss diet, they will have

returned to solid food for at least several weeks before beginning maintenance.
2. Clients may or may not have participated in an exercise program while
   losing weight.
3. Basic behavioral self-management and relapse-prevention skills were taught
   during the weight-loss phase, which, in most cases, was long enough for
   clients to experience their high-risk situations. They could, therefore, use
   relapse-prevention techniques and receive practitioner feedback based on
   their real-life situations. Thus the need to construct an artificial relapse
   scenario, as advocated by Marlatt,[5] is eliminated.

A Maintenance Program

The following maintenance program uses the four stages of maintenance as
its framework and outlines the treatment considerations important for each stage.
Processes that can be used to carry out the treatment elements are not identified,
as it is felt that practitioners have the necessary counseling skills for delivery.

Stage 1: Decision to Remain in Treatment

The decision to maintain one's weight is a separate one from the decision to
lose weight and needs to be thought of as such by both clients and practitioners.
Clients frequently consider their job done once they have attained their goal
weight. Consequently, many do not appreciate what is required for and involved
in weight maintenance and, by extension, the need to remain in treatment.

Therefore, the purpose of this stage is for clients to understand the need for
and ramifications of continued treatment and to decide whether they will terminate or continue. Key information that needs to be presented and then discussed
with clients includes:

- the need for and benefits of continued treatment
- an overview of the proposed treatment program based on the particular
  needs of the client
- approximate duration
- cost implications.

Clients who decide to remain in treatment enter stage 2 of the program. Clients
who decide to terminate should leave with the understanding that the door is
always open should they wish additional support with their weight-maintenance
efforts. It has been my experience that many clients who decide there is no need
for maintenance support usually return after approximately 6 months once the

initial glamour of being thin has worn off and a few extra unwanted pounds have been regained.

Stage 2: Management of the Adjustment Process

The initial part of this maintenance program focuses on helping clients learn how to stabilize their weight. It is based on the premise that if the number of calories clients have been consuming has led to weight loss, then caloric intake needs to be adjusted if their weight is to stabilize. Clients who did not participate in an exercise program during the weight-loss process must decide if they will begin one, as their physical activity level will affect their caloric level. Additionally, the newly thin may need support in coping with experiences similar to those discussed earlier in this chapter.

The purpose of this stage, therefore, is for all clients to learn the skills necessary for weight stabilization and to receive the support they need for managing the adjustment process both in terms of weight stabilization and coping with being newly thin.

The seven weight stabilization learning and support areas that need to be presented and worked through with clients are:

1. establishing weight stabilization rather than weight loss as the goal for the next few weeks;
2. helping clients understand the impact that physical activity has on their caloric intake, determining whether physically inactive clients wish to begin such a program, and helping clients who decide in the affirmative to select a program that is right for them;
3. determining approximately how many calories clients need to regularly consume to stabilize their weight, taking into account their physical activity level;
4. identifying the wide range of foods and their caloric equivalents available to the client from which they may select their additional calories, some of which may be what clients consider to be favorite but forbidden foods;
5. helping clients who are ready to do so learn how to eat moderate portions of a few of their forbidden foods without losing control; this can be accomplished by encouraging clients to identify one food they would like to eat but are afraid of, identifying the control difficulties they have experienced in the past when eating this food, and, together, planning a strategy that draws on the skills clients have successfully used to control their eating during weight loss and that will increase the likelihood they will be able to eat a controlled portion of the food;
6. discussing clients' attempts to incorporate moderate amounts of forbidden foods into their eating and, using a problem-solving approach, helping them evaluate their success;

7. encouraging the continued self-monitoring of caloric intake and expenditure.

The four learning and support elements regarding coping with being newly thin include:

1. helping clients identify and cope with any unrealistic expectations they may have regarding what it means to be thin
2. helping clients see themselves as thin, rather than as fat or formerly fat
3. drawing out of clients the various changes they experience weekly and helping them manage them, if needed, as they occur
4. sharing in clients' joys and pleasures as they experience them.

Stage 3: Movement Toward Independence

The primary focus of this stage is to provide clients with the time necessary to assimilate what they learned in the previous stage and to deal with any unresolved issues to enable them to feel secure in their ability to maintain their weight effectively. This is especially important for clients who have been overweight much of their lives. Additionally, since clients cannot continue in treatment forever, they need to be prepared for eventual termination.

The purpose of this stage, therefore, is to help clients assimilate their learning and to prepare them for termination.

Five key areas of support for this stage are:

1. providing clients with continuing support for the assimilation of learning from the previous stage, eg, helping clients develop a deeper understanding of the need to adjust their caloric intake to compensate for any decreases in physical activity levels because of lack of desire, inclement weather, and seasonal activity level differences; ensuring that they know how to apply or adapt skills developed during the weight-loss process to new life situations as they encounter them; helping them strengthen mood management and relapse prevention techniques if needed, etc
2. dealing with unresolved, unrealistic "thin" expectations they may still harbor
3. encouraging the building of a support system to replace the practitioner or support group
4. helping any interested, significant others in the client's life deal with how the changes in their loved one's figure and behavior affect their relationship
5. preparing clients for termination.

Stage 4: Acceptance of a Lifetime Commitment

Successful weight maintenance is a lifelong endeavor. Currently, no cure for obesity exists, nor has it been determined that there exists a safe point beyond which weight maintenance is assured. If anything, recent research has indicated that, over time, people may experience weight gains during times of stress, and that motivation for weight control for most people probably increases or decreases in relation to their major life events.[15] My experience, both personally and professionally, supports Jordan and Canavan's[15] observations. Clearly then, to be successful at long-term weight maintenance requires hard work, constant vigilance, and a periodic redecision that being thin is really worth the effort.

Clients need to terminate treatment and enter this final stage with a realistic understanding that successful weight maintenance means a lifelong commitment to a process that can sometimes be difficult and other times a joy. To promise them anything else merely sets them up for unrealistic expectations regarding what is truly involved in weight maintenance, may contribute to decreased maintenance self-efficacy, and may lead to an eventual relapse.

Clients also need to understand that there may be times in the months and years ahead when they will need additional support for their maintenance efforts, and that it is perfectly natural both to feel this way and to seek help. They should also leave treatment and enter this final phase knowing how to recognize when they may need this support. Specific "warning" signals can be offered to help them more readily recognize this need:

- experiencing difficulty managing life's stresses or changes in life circumstances without overeating
- being 3 to 5 lb above their goal weight and experiencing difficulty in losing it
- feeling resistant to continued use of any techniques that were helpful in the past
- wondering if being thin is "really worth the effort" any more
- being ready to use some of the maintenance skills avoided in the past, eg, learning how to eat forbidden foods.

CONCLUSION

Much remains to be learned about the correlates of long-term weight maintenance. In the interim, it is hoped that this review will enable weight-control practitioners to take a positive look at how they can help support their clients' lifelong weight-maintenace efforts.

REFERENCES

1. Holmes N, Ardito EA, Stevenson D, et al: Maintenance of weight loss in a heavily overweight population, in Storlie J, Jordan HA (eds): *Behavioral Management of Obesity*. New York, Spectrum Publications Inc, 1984, pp 137–150.

2. Brownell K, Marlatt GA, Lichtenstein E, et al: Understanding and preventing relapse. *Am Psychol* 1986; 41:765–778.

3. Craighead LW: A problem solving approach to the treatment of obesity, in Hersen M, Bellack AA (eds): *Handbook of Clinical Behavior Therapy with Adults*. New York, Plenum Press, 1985, pp 229–267.

4. Sternberg B: Relapse in weight control: Definitions, processes, and prevention strategies, in Marlatt GA, Gordon JR (eds): *Relapse Prevention*. New York, The Guilford Press, 1985, pp 521–544.

5. Marlatt GA: Relapse prevention: Theoretical rationale and overview of the model, in Marlatt GA, Gordon JR (eds): *Relapse Prevention*. New York, The Guilford Press, 1985, pp 3–67.

6. Abrams DB, Follick MJ: Behavioral weight loss at the worksite. *J Consult Clin Psychol* 1983; 51:226–233.

7. Collins RL, Wilson GT, Rothblum E: The Comparative efficacy of cognitive and behavioral approaches in weight reduction. Paper presented at the Association for Advancement of Behavior Therapy, New York, 1980.

8. Perri MG, Shapiro RM, Ludwig W, et al: Maintenance strategies for the treatment of obesity: An evaluation of relapse prevention training and posttreatment contact by mail and telephone. *J Consult Clin Psychol* 1984; 52:404–413.

9. Stuart RB, Guire K: Some correlates to the maintenance of weight lost through behavior modification. *Int J Obes* 1979; 3:87–96.

10. Brownell K, Stunkard AJ: Physical activity in the development and treatment of obesity, in Stunkard AJ (ed): *Obesity*. Philadelphia, WB Saunders Co, 1980, pp 00.

11. Stuart RB: Weight loss and beyond: Are they taking it off and keeping it off?, in Davidson PO, Davidson SM (eds): *Behavioral Medicine: Changing Health Lifestyles*. New York, Brunner/Mazel, 1980, pp 00.

12. Wilson GT: Psychological prognostic factors in the treatment of obesity, in Hirsch/Van Itallie (eds): *Recent Advances in Obesity Research*. London, John Libbey & Co Ltd, 1985, vol 4, pp 301–311.

13. Gormally J, Rardin D, Black S: Correlates of successful response to a behavioral weight control clinic. *Journal of Counseling Psychology* 1980; 27:179–191.

14. Jordan HA: Motivational strategies, in Storlie J, Jordan HA (eds): *Behavioral Management of Obesity*. New York, Spectrum Publications Inc, 1984, pp 91–104.

15. Jordan HA, Canavan AJ: Patterns of weight change: The interval 6 to 10 years after initial weight loss in a cognitive-behavioral treatment program. *Psychological Reports* 1985; 57:195–203.

16. Martin JE, Dubbert PM, Katell AD, et al: Behavioral control of exercise in sedentary adults: Studies 1 through 6. *J Consult Clin Psychol* 1984; 52:795–811.

17. Jordan HA: Behavioral approaches to obesity treatment, in Storlie J, Jordan HA (eds): *Behavioral Management of Obesity*. New York, Spectrum Publications Inc, 1984, pp 1–18.

18. Knowles MS and Associates: *Andragogy in Action*. San Francisco, Jossey-Bass Publishers, 1985, pp 1–24.

19. Mitchell C, Stuart RB: Effect of self-efficacy on dropout from obesity treatment. *J Consult Clin Psychol* 1984; 52:1100–1101.

PART III

Weight Control in the Life Cycle

Chapter 17

Obesity and Pregnant Women

Howard N. Jacobson

INTRODUCTION

Obesity has long been considered a risk factor in pregnancy. Indeed, maternal preconception weight and weight gain during pregnancy are firmly established as major determinants of pregnancy outcome.[1] The very recent reports of Rosso[2] on underweight women and Abrams[3] on obese women make it most opportune to review our understanding of the effect of prepregnant weight on the course and outcome of pregnancy. From these and other studies, we can begin to formulate the likely direction assessment and management will take for obese women during pregnancy. It is hoped that clarification of these aspects will furnish a more informed base for nutritional advice for obese women as a part of their prenatal care.

BACKGROUND

In the late 1940s and early 1950s it was frequently recommended that the obese patient's gain in weight should be markedly restricted, and it was suggested by some that obese pregnant women should be made to lose weight.[4] These recommendations were outgrowths of the same kinds of concerns about pre-eclampsia that led to the then prevailing recommendations for routine restrictions in weight gain along with routine restrictions of sodium intake.

In the mid 1950s, alert to the associations of obesity with increased complications during pregnancy, we[5] attempted to determine whether weight could be safely reduced during pregnancy. Patients were accepted for study if the duration of pregnancy was between 16 and 30 weeks, the pregnancy was single, and obesity was present. The degree of obesity at the time of selection was estimated by subtracting the desirable pregnancy weight from the actual pregnancy weight. A desirable pregnancy weight for each woman was estimated by adding the usual weight gain per week during pregnancy, adjusted for her duration of pregnancy, to her desirable nonpregnant weight. By this technique, the obese women in the study averaged 47 ± 15.5 lb above desirable weight when first observed in the study clinic of the Boston Lying-in Hospital (BLIH).

A special clinic was established, and, at the first visit, a careful nutrition history was taken, and the patient was instructed as to the 1,500-calorie, 95-g protein diet she was to follow. She was asked to visit the clinic at 2-week intervals, and her diet was assessed at least once a month. If she reported a food consumption in excess of the study amount, or if there were uncertainties about whether she was consuming all the essential elements, she was eliminated from the study and placed on the regular prenatal diet used in the clinic.

This study found that (1) obesity was associated with increased complications during pregnancy, labor, and delivery, and with a substantial increase in perinatal mortality; (2) weight reduction during pregnancy and under these strict research conditions had no demonstrable adverse effect on the condition of the infant at birth or during the neonatal period; (3) the weight of obese women could, under such closely supervised conditions, be safely reduced during pregnancy. Weight control could indeed protect them from complications.

Some comments about this study should be made. First, it is still one of the very few in which careful dietary assessments were performed. In this regard, in an earlier study by Burke,[6] approximately one third of obese pregnant women had inadequate caloric intakes during pregnancy. As Burke[6] pointed out, "weight of patient per se does not reflect necessarily the general dietary intake and/or nutritional status of the patient." Second, extreme vigilance must be maintained to be sure that equal emphasis is placed on assurance that the patient is indeed eating all of the diet; this can be obtained only by frequent detailed interviews. These points are raised again here because it is still a common assumption that the obese pregnant patient consumes too much food during pregnancy when, in fact, the opposite may be the case. Finally, although we[5] showed that under rigorous research conditions pregnant women could be reduced, weight reductions during pregnancy were never shown to be either essential or desirable. Indeed, Tompkins and Wiehl[4] were quick to point out that at the Philadelphia Lying-in Hospital they could achieve the same desirable outcomes for the mother and her infant without resorting to restrictive and hence potentially harmful dietary intakes.

This early phase in the development of nutritional support for the obese pregnant woman culminated in the 1970 National Academy of Sciences report[7] that concluded: "Severe caloric restriction, which has been very commonly recommended, is potentially harmful to the developing fetus and to the mother and almost inevitably restricts other nutrients essential for growth processes. Weight-reduction regimes, if needed, should be instituted only after pregnancy has terminated." The report[7] emphasized that even for the obese young adolescent, "a modest weight gain should be permitted during pregnancy. . . ."

In short, the 1970s concluded with the recognition of the potential hazards of dietary restrictions during pregnancy. But it was not until the late 1970s and early 1980s that agreed-upon criteria for nutritional risk factors were adopted and which included obesity.

CURRENT STATUS

The importance of clarifying the influence of obesity on pregnancy outcome is emphasized by the repeated findings that a high proportion of women of childbearing age (approximately 18%) are very overweight and, hence, likely to be obese.[8] Guidelines[1] in use have selected 20% or more above the standard weight for height and age as the cutoff point for estimating the presence of obesity. Most studies[1] have found that the obese pregnant patient is at increased risk because of the association between obesity and such medical conditions as chronic hypertension, diabetes mellitus, and thromboembolism. Others[5] have also noted late pregnancy hemorrhage and an increased incidence of pre-eclampsia.

Abrams,[3] in a thorough review, noted that the rates of pregnancy complications reported for the obese have varied from place to place and over time: variations can be associated with geographic, urban-rural, and temporal factors. For these reasons, in order to interpret changes when found, information "should be collected from a comparison group similar to the study group with regard to time, location, socioeconomic status, etc."[3] In short, very few firm conclusions can be drawn about maternal obesity and pregnancy outcomes on the basis of the published reports.

NEWER STUDIES ON OBESITY AND PREGNANCY

The perinatal data base at the University of California, San Francisco, Department of Obstetrics, Gynecology and Reproductive Sciences, prospectively records data on the pregnancy course and outcome for all deliveries that occur at its affiliated hospital. Data on each patient are recorded at the first antenatal visit, at delivery, at maternal discharge, and at infant discharge. After verification for accuracy and internal consistency, the information on more than 300 variables is stored for further computer analyses. These favorable circumstances allowed Abrams[3] to "reappraise the hypothesis that obesity increases pregnancy risk by examining the incidence of perinatal complications in overweight women and women of ideal prepregnancy weight for height. An attempt was made to account for degree of obesity by categorizing the obese group into moderately overweight (120 to 135% of ideal pregravid body weight) and very overweight (greater than 135% of ideal pregravid body weight)."

Of the 2,901 women in the University of California study, 251 were very overweight, and 974 were moderately overweight. Very overweight women had increased rates of stimulated labor, cesarean section deliveries, hypertension, pre-eclampsia, diabetes mellitus, and postpartum hemorrhage. Moderately overweight women had only two complications, cesarean section delivery and excessive weight gain, at statistically significant rates as compared with the nonoverweight women. The very overweight women had heavier babies (3,590 g, average birth weight), which was not significantly influenced by weight gain during pregnancy. Abrams[3] pointed out that overweight increased with age, and that more women were delaying childbearing. "This suggests that more overweight women will become pregnant in the future."[3]

This landmark study[3] found that although perinatal mortality is not increased, very overweight women are at increased risk for complications during pregnancy. The risk for moderately overweight women is less dramatic.[3] The study[3] concluded that "These findings imply that classifying a woman 120–135% of ideal body weight as 'high risk' may be inappropriate, since the highest risk appeared in women greater than 135% ideal weight."

MODERN MANAGEMENT

Broberg et al[9] in a recent study on the effect of dietary advice on obesity in pregnancy used an 1,800- to 2,000-kcal diet. They found no ill effects for either the mothers or their infants. The women in the study gained only 6 kg in the final 24 weeks of pregnancy in contrast to the 14 kg gained by undieted women. This study reinforces the considered opinion that 1,800 kcal/day is as low as can be safely recommended in ordinary ambulatory settings. Nevertheless, we will need to become more skilled at individualized nutritional status assessments, as well as ongoing estimates of the extent of adherence or compliance with dietary recommendations, before we can make more informed judgments about benefits or risks of restricted diets for either mothers or their infants with any degree of assurance.

Anticipating the birth of a child is a very special time in a woman's life. A new life is being created. That means that the selection of a sound, healthy diet is more important than ever. As has been noted, pregnancy is not the time to plan for weight loss. It is a time, though, for careful and supervised control.

A time-tested program for controlled weight gain during pregnancy is The Quick Start Plus Program in the Weight Watchers handbook[10] as modified for pregnancy. The food plan is based on seven food categories with the number of exchanges and optional calories that allow for change and variety as shown in Table 17-1. Each of the three plans (pregnancy, lactation, and basic food plan) provides 45% to 50% of calories from carbohydrate, 20% to 25% from protein, and 25% to 30% from fat.

Table 17-1 Food Exchanges for Pregnancy and Lactation

Food Category	Pregnancy	Lactation	Basic Food Plan
Fruit	6 (at least 2 high vitamin C)	6 (at least 2 high vitamin C)	3
Vegetables	2 (at least)	2 (at least)	2 (at least)
Milk	4	6	2
Bread	5	5	2–3
Fat	3	3	3
Protein	8	10	6–8
Optional Calories	up to 550 weekly	up to 550 weekly	up to 550 weekly
NUTRITION INFORMATION			
Carbohydrate (g)	255	280	155
Protein (g)	90	120	65
Fat (g)	50	60	45
Cholesterol (mg)	300	350	300
Sodium (mg)	2100	2300	2000
Calories	1850	2150	1200

Source: Reprinted by permission of Weight Watchers International, Jericho, New York. Copyright © 1987.

General instructions include advisories about eating three meals a day, eating two protein exchanges (minimum) at both lunch and dinner, and drinking six to eight glasses of water. Average increased demand because of pregnancy calls for increased servings of fruit, milk, bread, and protein (as noted).

Regular or excessive consumption of alcohol is not recommended during pregnancy. Although concern has been expressed about caffeine consumption during pregnancy, there is no evidence of harmful effects when daily intake has been less than four to six cups of ordinary coffee per day.

Pregnancy is not the time to begin an exercise program other than a supervised prenatal exercise class. If a woman has been regularly exercising, she will probably be able to continue to do so in moderation. In any case, a physician should be consulted.

The Recommended Daily Allowances (RDAs) for all major vitamins and minerals are increased during pregnancy and lactation by roughly comparable amounts. It is generally assumed that these added needs will be met through a mother's consumption of her prescribed diet. Should she be unable to obtain an adequate diet or should doubts exist about the quality of her overall diet, a vitamin-mineral supplement equal to the RDA should be given.

In the event that routine vitamin and mineral supplementation is employed, there are two precautions that the woman needs to be reminded of: First, these supplements, although valuable, will not take the place of good basic foods and are only intended as supplements. Second, certain vitamins may be potentially dangerous to the fetus, for example, vitamin A, which is sometimes associated with bone deformities, and vitamin D, which may lead to kidney damage.[11]

THE FORESEEABLE FUTURE

It has long been recognized that dietary studies to estimate the amounts of foods and nutrients consumed are integral to sound interpretations of relations between dietary intakes and pregnancy outcomes. Nowhere is this more applicable than in the case of obesity and pregnancy. As emphasized above, extreme vigilance must be maintained to be sure that equal stress is placed on assurance that the patient is indeed eating all of the prescribed diet; this can be obtained only by frequent detailed interviews. But dietary intake interviews are traditionally time-consuming and must be performed by trained personnel, and their cost is high relative to the value of data usually obtained. In this regard, progress in the past 5 years has been dramatic, with regard to both conceptual issues and techniques for measuring dietary intakes.

Conceptually, it has become apparent that no single dietary standard will meet the needs of all those concerned with nutritional services for pregnant women.

This has led to the recognition of at least four already established and available alternative dietary standards:[12]

1. nutrient profiles for food procurement
2. nutrient density standards for menu planning and patient education
3. nutrient density standards for food labeling and related uses
4. food frequency patterns for use in patient screening and in collecting and assessing survey data.

There has been an even more rapid acceleration of progress in methodologies for collecting dietary intakes on large numbers of pregnant women under circumstances that meet the modern criteria of lowest cost, fast turnaround time, simplicity, and interpretability.

These modern advances are mediated by the increasing availability of computer-assisted techniques and the wider appreciation of the usefulness of historical or subjective data. Among the techniques that would seem to have the most promise in connection with a carefully controlled dietary program during pregnancy are:

- machine-readable food-frequency questionnaires
- touch-screen, interactive video devices suitable for clinics, offices, or other point-of-contact locations such as waiting rooms etc; this approach was field tested in North Carolina in 1985.[13]

The application of these kinds of computer-assisted techniques along with newly refined dietary standards should allow for a more reliable initial assessment of the woman's dietary pattern and then, in turn, individualized patient counseling, along with frequent monitoring of intakes to assure that the patient is indeed consuming the diet prescribed for her.

ESTIMATIONS OF FATNESS

Recognition of the importance of obesity coupled with the increasing recognition of the importance of both total weight gain during pregnancy and the pattern of weight gain calls attention to the need to be able to interpret body composition and weight gain in terms of its components (fat, fluid, etc) for the mother, the fetus, or both. Measurement of the contribution of lean body mass and adipose tissue is especially pertinent to nutritional assessment in overweight women.

For a long time, measurements of skin-fatfold thickness and arm circumference were the only means available for use with pregnant women. Nevertheless, the potential contribution of such noninvasive techniques as ultrasound has long been appreciated. Recent advances in technology give promise that devices that meet requirements for accuracy, reproducibility, cost, simplicity, and safety may soon be available for use in public health situations.[14]

MOTIVATION

Only in the past decade has there been acceptance of the importance of nutrition and the complexity of the reality of nutrition. Thus, there is no longer any credible dispute about the importance of a mother's diet in consort with the many other influences on pregnancy outcome. What remains to be shown convincingly

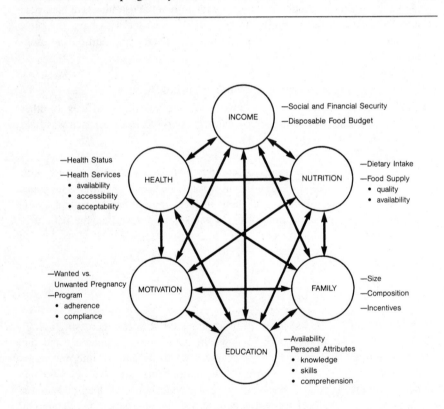

Figure 17-1 The seamless web of influences. *Source*: Adapted from *World Development Report* (p 69) by World Bank, ©1980. Adapted with permission of Oxford University Press Inc.

is that we can regularly improve pregnancy outcome with the aid of dietary measures once nutritional problems are accurately identified in pregnant women.

Similarly, the overly simplistic idea of treating nutrition as a single variable in its influence on the course and outcome of pregnancy has given way to a sounder appreciation of the reality of the factors that together shape the course and outcome of pregnancy. In this regard, the World Bank,[15] in summarizing its experiences worldwide in its attempts to improve pregnancy outcome, arrived at the concept of a "seamless web" of influences that must all be taken into account in plans and programs designed to improve the nutritional status of pregnant women. This concept, modified slightly,[16] encompasses the realities encountered by all who help provide services for pregnant women (see Figure 17-1). Further, it helps explain the frustrations to be expected when nutrition is treated as a single variable independent of other and, at times, potentially more profound influences.

That this is neither new nor disheartening was pointed out some 30 years ago by Burke[6] who expressed it this way: ". . . in any clinical and educational approach we have to be satisfied with having demonstrated that excellent overall prenatal care in which nutrition played an important part resulted in benefits to both mother and infant although we cannot say exactly what particular aspects of prenatal care produced these benefits."

REFERENCES

1. Food and Nutrition Board: *Nutrition Services in Perinatal Care*. Washington, National Academy of Sciences, 1981, p 72.

2. Rosso P: A new chart to monitor weight gain during pregnancy. *Am J Clin Nutr* 1985; 41:644.

3. Abrams BF: *Obesity, Weight Gain and Pregnancy Outcome*, thesis. Berkeley, University of California, 1985.

4. Tompkins WT, Wiehl DG: *Maternal and Newborn Nutrition Studies at Philadelphia Lying-in Hospital*. New York, Milbank Memorial Fund, 1955, p 77.

5. Jacobson HN, Burke BS, Smith CA, et al: Effect of weight reduction in obese pregnant women on pregnancy, labor, and delivery, and on the condition of the infant at birth. *Am J Obstet Gynecol* 1962; 83:1609.

6. Burke BS: *Discussion in the Promotion of Maternal and Newborn Health*. New York, Milbank Memorial Fund, 1955, p 177.

7. Food and Nutrition Board, National Research Council: *Maternal Nutrition and the Course of Pregnancy: Summary Report*. Washington, National Academy of Sciences, 1970, p 23.

8. Abraham S, Carroll MD, Najjar MF, et al: *Obese and Overweight Adults in the United States*, US Dept of Health and Human Services publication No. (PHS) 83-1680, National Health Survey Series 11, No. 230, Hyatttsville, Md, National Center for Health Statistics, 1983.

9. Broberg C, Gillmer MDG, Brunner EJ, et al: Obesity in pregnancy: The effect of dietary advice. *Diabetes Care* 1980; 3:476.

10. The Quick Start Plus Program, Weight Watchers International Inc, 1985, p 18.

Chapter 18

Childhood and Adolescent Obesity

William H. Dietz

Childhood and adolescent obesity constitutes a major health problem in the United States that is increasing in prevalence. Until recently, surveys that used a consistent methodology to measure fatness and that examined representative samples of children and adolescents were not available. In the mid-1960s, Cycles II and III of the National Health Examination Survey (NHES) provided triceps skinfold data on approximately 7,000 children aged 6 to 11 years (Cycle II) and 7,000 adolescents aged 12 to 17 years (Cycle III) representative of the noninstitutionalized population of each age group in the United States. Using a triceps skinfold greater than or equal to the 85th percentile for children and adolescents studied in NHES Cycles II and III as a baseline measure of obesity, we[1] examined the prevalence of obesity in children and adolescents studied in the first and second Health and Nutrition Examination Surveys (HANES I and II) conducted in the early and late 1970s. In this approximately 15-year interval, the prevalence of obesity increased by more than 50% in children aged 6 to 11 years and by approximately 40% in adolescents aged 12 to 17 years. Although the prevalence of obesity was greater in whites than in blacks in both surveys, the increases in prevalence were greater in blacks than in whites and greater in adolescents than in preadolescents.

These data indicate that obesity is now epidemic in children and adolescents in the United States. The data emphasize the need to develop effective means to prevent obesity and to treat it after it is established. In this chapter we discuss the risk factors associated with childhood and adolescent obesity that can be used to identify those at risk for the disease and those at whom preventive efforts should be directed. We then consider approaches to therapy.

RISK FACTORS ASSOCIATED WITH CHILDHOOD OBESITY

A variety of risk factors are associated with childhood obesity. These can be most easily separated into factors in the physical environment and those in the social environment. Host factors may also contribute to risk.

Physical Environment

Using data from NHES Cycles II and III, we[2] showed that season, region, and population density are associated with both childhood and adolescent obesity. In these surveys, the United States was divided into four regions of comparable population size. In each region, the population was further divided by population density into four subdivisions. These included large urban areas in which highly populated cities in each region were matched. For example, Atlanta in the Southeast was considered a large urban area, comparable in importance, population density, and socioeconomic status with Chicago in the Midwest or New York in the Northeast. Other divisions were large statistical metropolitan sampling areas (SMSA), smaller SMSAs, and rural areas. The sampling frame in every area but the Northeast provided data collected throughout the seasons of the year. Obesity was defined as a triceps skinfold equal to or greater than the 85th percentile for children of the same age and sex.

The odds ratios established from logistic regressions are shown in Table 18-1. This approach allows comparisons that are controlled for other potentially confounding associations. As shown in Table 18-1, obesity was most prevalent in the Northeast, followed by the Midwest, the South, and the West. Obesity was also significantly more prevalent in the winter than in other seasons. Finally, obesity was more prevalent in large urban environments than in areas of lower population density. The effects of the regional and seasonal variables were substantial, and caused an almost 3-fold variation in prevalence.

Table 18-1 Odds Ratios for the Effect of Variables in the Physical Environment on the Prevalence of Obesity

Season	Odds Ratio
Autumn	1.68
Winter	2.66
Spring	1.30
Summer	1.00
Region	
Northeast	2.89
Midwest	2.66
South	1.43
West	1.00
Population Density	
Large metro	1.42
Large SMSA	.91
Other SMSA	.78
All other	1.00

A variety of mechanisms could account for these variations. Clearly, inclement weather can cause variations in activity. In the Northeast, for example, children and adolescents are confined to indoor activities for long periods of the year. In addition, region and season could be associated with variations in the availability and cost of foods of low-caloric density such as fruits and vegetables.

Ethnicity may also be an important factor that affects prevalence. Other data[3] have shown that prevalence of obesity is directly related to the time immigrants have lived in the United States. The prevalence of obesity is greatest in first generation immigrants, and declines to the level of the general population by the third generation. Perceptions of excessive fatness may also be determined by ethnicity. Therefore, regional differences in prevalence could be accounted for by regional differences in ethnicity. Comparisons of prevalence in large readily identifiable ethnic subsets representative of the population that can be controlled for other confounding variables, such as Hispanics, have not been made.

A final explanation of the regional differences in the prevalence of obesity may be culturally based values of appearance. Children in the South and the West may spend more time in clothing that reveals their bodies, and may therefore be more sensitive to their physical appearance or more active in their efforts to control their weight.

Clearly, the magnitude of these effects is large. Studies that link these variables in the physical environment to the behavioral mechanisms that promote obesity will offer a variety of potential foci for preventive interventions.

Social Environment

A variety of social factors, most of which are in the family environment, are associated with childhood and adolescent obesity. The most widely recognized family variable associated with childhood obesity is parental obesity.[4] Data from the Ten State Nutrition Survey[4] indicate that the risk of childhood obesity rises in direct relation with parental obesity. The risk of childhood obesity is lowest in children with neither parent obese, greater when one parent is obese, and greatest when both parents are obese. These data, coupled with the resemblance in fatness between identical twins, have been used to argue that obesity is a hereditary trait. Likewise, recent data[5] from a comparison of adoptees with their biologic and adoptive parents revealed a significant trend between the body mass index (BMI) of adoptees and biologic parents that was not observed when adoptees were compared with their adoptive parents. However, in the latter study,[5] the prevalence of obesity among the adoptive and biologic parents of overweight and obese adoptees did not differ significantly. The study[5] therefore suggests that leanness or frame size, rather than obesity, is inherited. A more meaningful interpretation of the data is that a susceptibility to obesity may exist in children of obese parents, but that obesity can only result from the interaction of a susceptible host with a disease-producing environment.

Obesity is also related to a variety of other family variables. The levels of both parental education and socioeconomic class are directly related to the prevalence of obesity in children and adolescents.[4] These data are in contrast to findings in adult women for whom socioeconomic class is inversely related to the prevalence of obesity.

Family size is inversely related to the prevalence of obesity.[6] Among larger families, obesity in children is significantly less prevalent than in smaller families. Birth order also has a significant effect. Oldest and single children have a higher prevalence of obesity, as do younger children.

The behavioral mechanisms that account for the effects of variables in the family environment on the prevalence of obesity have yet to be specified. Nonetheless, these variables serve as risk criteria that enable the identification of children and adolescents at risk for obesity. Such families require careful attention to sources of excess energy intake or reduced energy expenditure.

One pertinent focus is fat intake. Over time, the prevalence of obesity has risen coincident with an increase in caloric intake derived from fat. Fat requires almost no energy for absorption and storage in adipose tissue, whereas almost 30% of the energy contained in carbohydrate is used in its digestion, conversion to fat, and storage as adipose tissue.[7] In addition, fat is more calorically dense than carbohydrate, insofar as it contains 9 kcal/g as opposed to 4 kcal/g in carbohydrate. These observations suggest that gram for gram, fat is considerably more "fattening" than carbohydrate. Furthermore, as a single dietary intervention, efforts aimed at reducing dietary fat intake may be the most effective steps to prevent the onset of childhood obesity.

A final family variable associated with childhood obesity is television viewing.[8] In the NHES, approximately one third of children studied in Cycle II aged 6 to 11 years were restudied in Cycle III when they were 12 to 17 years old. In each survey, questions were included regarding the time spent viewing television. In both Cycle II and Cycle III, time spent viewing television was directly related to the prevalence of obesity. Among adolescents, for each additional hour spent viewing television, the prevalence of obesity increased by 2%. Furthermore, when prior obesity was controlled in the 6- to 11-year-old cohort that was restudied during adolescence, time spent viewing television was the most powerful predictor of subsequent obesity. Time spent reading, listening to the radio, or in other leisure activities did not differ significantly in their effects on the prevalence of obesity. Furthermore, the effects of television viewing presisted when controlled for other confounding variables.

A number of mechanisms could account for this association.[9] The average American child aged 6 to 11 years watches approximately 25 hours of television per week. Time spent viewing television therefore accounts for more time than children spend in school or in any other activity except sleep. Therefore, time spent watching television represents a significant portion of time that is not spent in more energy-intensive activities. In addition, several anecdotal observations from our laboratory suggest that adolescents watching television expend less energy than when they are at rest doing nothing. Although these differences are small, over time they can account for a significant caloric imbalance.

In addition to reduced energy expenditure, television viewing may promote increased caloric intake. Characters on "prime time" eat almost 8 times per hour. The suggestive effects of the eating frequency that occurs on television, as well as the significant frequency of commercials that promote foods on children's television programs may account for the observation that snacking while watching television is directly related to the time spent viewing television. Television also affects snack choice. The more television a child views, the more likely the child is to consume the foods advertised on television. The foods advertised tend to be of high-caloric density, such as sugared breakfast cereals, candy bars, and foods sold in "fast food" chains. Because obesity rarely occurs among televised characters, the implicit message to children is that there are no consequences to eating as frequently as the characters on television, or consuming the foods that are advertised on television.

The association between the prevalence of obesity and television viewing suggests a causal relation. The association was consistent: it occurred in both cross-sectional samples and in the cohort studied longitudinally. Television viewing in the prospective study was temporally related to the onset of obesity. The relations were highly significant and persisted when controls for other potentially confounding variables were introduced. Finally, logical explanations existed that could explain the associations.

Although multiple family variables are associated with obesity, only television viewing has been linked to obesity in a causal fashion. Therefore, reductions in time spent viewing television and the consequent snacking behaviors that television viewing induce seem appropriate interventions for both the prevention and treatment of obesity.

Host Factors

In children and adolescents, the components of energy expenditure have rarely been examined. In our laboratory, we recently compared basal metabolic rate (BMR), the thermic effects of food, and the energy costs of activity in obese and nonobese adolescents. In contrast with the prevalent mythology, BMR in obese adolescents was significantly greater than in the nonobese, but did not differ significantly when normalized for lean body mass (LBM). During overfeeding of carbohydrate based on a constant proportion of BMR, the thermic effects of food were comparable in the two populations. The energy costs of activity did not seem to differ significantly.

Review of growth charts of obese children and adolescents indicates that rates of excess weight gain are 5 to 10 lb/year. These gains can be accounted for by an excess daily intake of between 50 to 100 kcal. Our comparisons of the components of energy expenditure in obese and nonobese adolescents suggest that if differences in energy expenditure exist, they will be undetectable using current methodologies. These observations also suggest that epidemiologic approaches to identify risk factors associated with obesity may provide a profile that could target those likely to develop the disease, and that preventive measures directed at small increments of excess caloric intake or reduced caloric expenditure may prove highly effective.

TREATMENT

The treatment of childhood obesity begins before the first encounter. In our clinic, it is mandatory that, in intact families, both parents accompany the child to the first clinic visit. From the outset, this stipulation indicates that we view the child's obesity as a family rather than an individual problem. This approach also means that the views of both parents with respect to the origin and therapy of their child's obesity can be solicited. In the case of the adolescent, it is our feeling that the value of the information gained from a family interview overrides the loss of the adolescent's privacy. Furthermore, only a family interview can determine if severe obesity provides a mechanism for keeping an adolescent at home with the family.

The history of obesity offers important information with respect to origin and complication. The more common diagnoses are shown in Table 18-2. A history of poor feeding and hypotonia in infancy followed by a ravenous appetite beginning at age 2 or 3 years suggests Prader-Willi syndrome. A careful dietary history with a modified food frequency assessment provides a rough estimate of the intake of fat, calorie-dense foods, and snack food choices. The family history reveals living arrangements, recent deaths, a family history of obesity, and other significant risk factors such as Type II diabetes mellitus, hypertension, or early atherosclerotic cardio- or cerebrovascular disease.

In the review of systems, indications of the complications of obesity should be sought. Headaches associated with neurologic symptoms or that are increasing in frequency and duration should prompt a search for an intracranial mass. Daytime somnolence suggests the Pickwickian syndrome, commonly caused by sleep apnea. Nocturia or enuresis may indicate Type II diabetes mellitus. Per-

Table 18-2 Diseases and Complications Associated with Childhood Obesity

	Signs or symptoms	Confirmatory tests
Prader-Willi syndrome	Truncal obesity, short stature, mild or moderate mental retardation, hypogonadism, short hands or feet	Chromosomal analysis, in some cases
Laurence-Moon-Bardet-Biedl syndrome	Mental retardation, hypogonadism, polydactyly, late blindness	Clinical diagnosis
Alstrom's syndrome	Nerve deafness, primary hypogonadism, early blindness, adult-resolution obesity	Clinical diagnosis
Cushing's syndrome	Violaceous striae, truncal obesity, buffalo hump, hypertension, short stature	Growth chart, cortisol, dexamethasone suppression test
Hypothalamic tumor (Fröhlich's syndrome)	Headache of increasing frequency or duration, ocular or neurologic abnormalities, nausea and vomiting	CAT scan
Pickwickian syndrome	Severe obesity, sleep apnea, daytime somnolence	Sleep study, arterial blood gas studies, pulmonary function tests, ECG
Slipped capital femoral epiphysis	Hip pain	Radiologic examination
Blount's disease	Tibia vara	Radiologic examination
Hypertension	Hypertension	Exclude renal or vascular cause
Diabetes mellitus	Polyuria, nocturia	Urinalysis
Keratosis nigricans	Keratosis nigricans	Clinical diagnosis

Source: Adapted with permission from "Childhood Obesity: Susceptibility, Cause and Management" by WH Dietz, *Journal of Pediatrics* (1983: 103:676–686), Copyright © 1983, The CV Mosby Company.

sistent or episodic hip pain should suggest the possibility of imminent slipped capital femoral epiphysis.

Measurements constitute the most important aspect of the physical examination. Plots of height and weight on growth charts permit an assessment of severity and can be used to show the time required for remission if weight maintenance can be achieved. Endocrine or congenital causes of obesity should be carefully sought in children or adolescents with heights below the 50th percentile or substantially lower than expected for midparental heights. The time required to achieve ideal body weight by weight maintenance also can provide a convincing argument for the need for weight reduction. Mid-arm circumference, tricep skinfold thicknesses, and mid-arm muscle circumference compared with existing tables provide relative measures of fat and LBM. Such measurements can be used as crude estimates of the composition of excess weight and the composition of weight lost. Because LBM is increased in childhood obesity, weight for height may underestimate ideal body weight. Therefore, as weight loss occurs, tricep skinfold measurements can be used to determine when the desirable level of fatness is achieved. Because fat distribution is a risk factor for cardiovascular complications, and central obesity accompanies Prader-Willi syndrome, the waist:hip ratio should be calculated.

Diseases and complications associated with childhood obesity are shown in Table 18-2. Because obesity is the leading cause of hypertension in children and adolescents, careful measurements of blood pressure are essential. In adolescents, a thigh blood pressure cuff may be necessary for accurate measurements. In hypertension consequent to obesity, blood pressure levels rarely achieve the magnitude of those found with pediatric hypertension from other causes.

Inspection of the skin may reveal a variety of associated conditions such as acanthosis nigricans (a risk factor for glucose intolerance), the violaceous striae of Cushing's syndrome or the intertriginous monilial infections. Evidence of self-mutilation, such as scabs on the fingers and hands, is common in the Prader-Willi syndrome.

A fundoscopic examination is essential to exclude papilledema. Strabismus, impaired tooth enamel, and dysathria are common in Prader-Willi syndrome.

Although other aspects of the physical examination should be completed, they rarely contribute to the assessment of cause or risk of complications.

Extensive laboratory studies are rarely helpful. We routinely perform a complete blood count and differential, a urinalysis to exclude diabetes, and a serum cholesterol determination. If the cholesterol level is elevated, a lipoprotein electrophoresis should be done. Bone ages are generally advanced, and determinations are unnecessary on a routine basis. However, in short children or adolescents, a delayed bone age may indicate an endocrine abnormality. Tests of thyroid or adrenal function are expensive and not routinely done unless the history or physical examination suggests an abnormality.

Finally, the risks of childhood and adolescent obesity should be thoroughly reviewed. Age of onset and severity are the two most important determinants of the risk of persistence. Families should therefore be counseled according to the severity of their child's obesity and age. We remind families that although complications such as diabetes and hypertension are unusual in childhood obesity, they are commonplace in adult disease, and successful treatment of childhood obesity prevents adult disease. We also discuss the elevations in low-density lipoproteins and reductions in high-density lipoproteins that accompany obesity in the context of cardiovascular risk.

Education

In studies of other chronic illness or health practices, education as a single intervention has proved of limited value. Obesity represents a similar circumstance. For example, in studies of other interventions, education alone is frequently the control intervention against which other therapies are compared.

In our experience, families of obese children and adolescents are frequently already aware of their practices that maintain obesity. Furthermore, many families are already well informed with respect to the caloric content of foods, the relevance of increased energy expenditure, and the consequence of persistent disease. Nonetheless, practitioners who treat obese children and adolescents should review with families the sources of the caloric imbalance that produce obesity, the role of television in the genesis of the caloric imbalance, and the adverse consequences of continuing disease. If parents are overweight, a therapeutic alliance may be initiated by a sympathetic review of their own difficulties, particularly if they were obese during childhood.

Because obese children and adolescents suffer substantial discrimination, both from anger in the family and the bias of peers, they are often highly defensive about their obesity and reluctant to listen to any but the most understanding and sympathetic practitioner. Under these circumstances, it may be helpful to review with the child or adolescent the social consequences posed by obesity. Common difficulties include teasing, name-calling, or ostracism by peers; difficulties finding clothes that fit; or, in adolescents, problems with getting dates. This approach constitutes education, but as an intervention, such a review only acknowledges problems that are eventually recognized, and does not provide a prescription for success.

Education for preadolescents is frequently misconceived as essential to therapy. For example, our earliest approaches to this problem began with an extensive program of education aimed at teaching the caloric content of food and the demonstration that since obesity is produced by an intake of energy in excess of caloric expenditure, weight loss could be achieved if energy expenditure exceeded intake. However, as we began to explore how our patients understood these processes, we recognized how abstract these concepts were. Most children understood that eating too much could make them fat. However, they were unable to comprehend food digestion, absorption, and the disposition of excess caloric intake as fat. Most perceived this process in concrete terms: if you ate a food high in calories, it went into your stomach, stayed there, and swelled out your stomach. Those who were somewhat more sophisticated understood that food somehow entered the bloodstream, but thought of the body as a bag of blood. Food went into the bag, and therefore went all over the body. This notion was supported by their observation that no matter where they cut themselves, they bled.

These observations suggest that intensive efforts at education directed at technical explanations of food consumption and the storage of excess calories as fat will not likely be successful. They also suggest that dietary programs that identify calorie-dense foods in a concrete fashion are probably better suited to the needs of preadolescents.

Behavior Modification

Behavior modification is reviewed elsewhere in this book in detail. Several pertinent modifications apply to children.[11,12] First, positive reinforcement by family and friends is considerably more effective than no or negative reinforcement. Second, parental involvement in the weight-reduction process seems to produce greater and more sustained weight losses than therapies aimed only at the child, or at the parent and child separately,[13] although some disagreement exists. Third, a variety of behaviors can serve as an appropriate focus for modification. These include behaviors such as eating rate, plate size, distractions during eating, and a focus on the food consumed. Exercise is also an important behavior that can be positively reinforced. Finally, time spent viewing television or snack choices can be altered through the use of reinforcements for other activities or choices. Additional detailed information regarding behavior modification in children and adolescents has been published elsewhere.[11-13]

Dietary Therapy

Dietary therapy remains the principal and most effective means to induce weight reduction. The goals of dietary therapy in children and adolescents are to produce fat loss, conserve LBM, and preserve growth. The diets used for children are shown in Table 18-3. Balanced calorie-deficit diets are the treatment of choice for younger children, preadolescents, and mildly to moderately obese

Table 18-3 Hypocaloric Diets for Obese Children and Adolescents

	Characteristics	Indication	Monitor
Balanced calorie-deficit diet	Deficit, one third of usual intake Reduced fat content (low-fat milk, elimination of high-fat luncheon meats, butter, gravy, salad dressing, fried foods)	All children Mild to moderately obese adolescents	Biweekly weight Monthly albumin, transferrin
Protein-modified fast	700 to 1,000 kcal/day Meat, egg, or cheese 1.5 g protein/kg ideal body weight/day Ad libitum salads and low-calorie dressing Daily supplements: Ca 800 mg/day, KCl 25 mEq/day, multivitamin with minerals	Severely obese Obese with morbid complication Need to monitor	Twice daily ketonuria Weekly weight for 2 wk, then Monthly electrolytes, Ca, P, Mg, lymphocyte count, C_3, transferrin, albumin
Protein plus carbohydrate	Same as protein-modified fast with 1.0 g carbohydrate/kg ideal body weight/day	Same as protein-modified fast Prolonged (>1 month) dietary therapy	Biweekly weight Monthly monitoring identical with protein-modified fast

Source: Adapted with permission from "Childhood Obesity: Susceptibility, Cause and Management" by WH Dietz, *Journal of Pediatrics* (1983; 103:676–686), Copyright © 1983, The CV Mosby Company.

adolescents. Highly restrictive diets should be reserved for severely obese adolescents or younger children in whom rapid weight loss is essential.

In young children, balanced calorie-deficit diets are the dietary therapy of choice. These diets are balanced with respect to the major food groups, but caloric intake is reduced by 25% to 30% below the usual intake. In practice, these deficits can best be achieved by reductions in fat intake. An advantage of this approach is that the usual pattern of food intake remains intact, but calories are reduced by the substitution of low- for high-fat foods. Use of a color-coded scheme for foods to identify those of high-caloric density has proved a simple and useful means to teach children which foods to avoid.[14] The goal of such diets is to achieve losses of 0.5 to 1.0 kg every 2 to 4 weeks.

We[15] recently observed reductions in growth velocity that were directly related to the amount of weight lost. Although no other adverse consequences were observed, and height velocities during weight reduction were still within the normal range, our observations suggest that calorie-deficit diets should be monitored carefully during periods of rapid weight reduction.

In severely obese adolescents, more restrictive dietary therapy may be warranted. We[16–18] have reviewed the indications and approach to the use of such diets elsewhere in detail. To summarize briefly, protein intakes between 1.5 and 2.5 g/kg of ideal body weight per day are required to achieve nitrogen balance. No data yet indicate whether protein is more protein-sparing than carbohydrate when protein intake equal to 150% of requirements is provided in adolescents. No clear advantage to ketotic diets has yet been shown in this age group. Finally, such diets must be monitored by experienced and competent professionals.

Exercise

The association of obesity with television viewing suggests that inactivity may have an important role in the genesis and persistence of obesity. Therefore, reductions in the time spent viewing television, regardless of the activities that are substituted, may increase the energy expended in activity.

As a single intervention, increases in activity rarely provide a caloric deficit large enough to achieve substantial weight reduction. When increased activity plus diet has been compared with diet alone, longer-term decreases in weight were observed in the group with added exercise.[19] When aerobic exercise was compared with participation in a wider variety of daily games and activities, the latter activities provided greater and more sustained weight losses than aerobic exercise.

Although limited, these data suggest that exercise is an important therapeutic adjunct to diet, and that the type of exercise is an independent variable that affects the rate, duration, and permanence of weight reduction.

Surgery

Only limited experience has accrued with respect to surgery as a treatment for adolescent obesity. Currently, we recommend surgery only for adolescents whose weight is more than 80% in excess of ideal, and only after other therapeutic interventions have failed. In this group, gastric bypass surgery has produced both notable successes and failures. To date, we have performed gastric bypass surgery in 12 patients, 3 of whom had Prader-Willi syndrome. In the latter group, weight regain has occurred in all three patients. Lasting remissions were subsequently achieved by residential placement of two of the three patients.

In nine other adolescent patients, the mean weight loss in the first 18 months after surgery was 30 kg. However, four patients were either lost to follow-up or regained most of the weight lost. Of the remaining five patients, one developed anorexia nervosa, two achieved ideal body weight, and two have maintained their weight losses although their obesity has persisted.

No major complications of surgery have occurred. In two patients, both of whom regained weight, relapse was accompanied by a relapse of their diabetes. Abdominal pain or vomiting commonly accompanies rapid or overeating. Patients quickly learn to chew their food well and to eat slowly to avoid these consequences. Sequential measures of body composition reveal that losses of LBM account for approximately 15% of the weight lost, but these losses are limited to the first 3 postoperative months and are repleted rapidly thereafter. No significant changes in lymphocyte counts or in serum albumin or transferrin levels have occurred.

Because experience with gastric bypass surgery in adolescents has been so limited, and because continuing attention to diet and psychosocial factors is required, this approach should only be used in the context of a more comprehensive therapeutic program.

TREATMENT FAILURE

Lack of motivation has frequently been cited as a reason for the failure of therapy. In our experience, lack of motivation is rarely a factor. Most patients and families are extremely concerned about the child's obesity, familiar with its consequences, and eager for weight loss to occur. More frequently, the attribution of lack of motivation stems from a failure to understand the adaptive role that obesity may have in families, and the extent to which families resist change.

Likewise, those who treat families are frequently frustrated at their lack of success and may blame their patients for the failures of the medical system to provide logical and comprehensive approaches to childhood obesity. Part of the difficulty may legitimately be attributed to those who treat the problem. Physicians and other medical professionals are not immune to the biases of their culture, and their refusal to deal directly with their patients' obesity may contribute to its persistence.

However, the most important difficulty found by those who treat obese children and adolescents is the temptation to assume responsibility for their patient's obesity. This temptation is a common consequence of the medical model, and a reasonable behavior in treating diseases amenable to pharmacologic or surgical approaches. However, in childhood obesity such an approach frees the family of their responsibility for the problem. On many occasions it may be more therapeutic to do nothing than to give directions to a family that is not prepared to hear or respond. Directions to such families may make the health professional part of the problem rather than part of the solution.

Finally, one homeostatic function of severe obesity may be to reduce conflict between parents. In these cases, failure to see the entire family and to understand disagreements between parents, particularly as they relate to therapy, may unwittingly remove the therapist from a neutral position into the corner of one of the parents. This alignment places the professional in an adversarial role rather than in a therapeutic alliance. Furthermore, such relationships may be so threatening that they severely compromise the likelihood of further weight-reduction attempts.

In the treatment of obesity, or in the failure of treatment, the role of the professional must be neutral. It is essential to explain the risks of childhood obesity and the consequences of its persistence. Advice and recommendations for change must be given in the context of the family environment, but failure should not be met with disparagement or frustration. Obesity is the family's problem, and is a chronic one. A negative response by the professional will only complicate the problem and add to the isolation and rejection that already exist. Therefore, the most important maxim of therapy is "First of all do no harm."

REFERENCES

1. Dietz WH, Gortmaker SL, Sobol AM, et al: Trends in the prevalence of childhood and adolescent obesity in the United States. *Pediatr Res* 1985; 19:198A.

2. Dietz WH, Gortmaker SL: Factors within the physical environment associated with childhood obesity. *Am J Clin Nutr* 1984; 39:619–624.

3. Goldblatt PB, Moore ME, Stunkard AJ: Social factors in obesity. *JAMA* 1965; 192:97–100.

4. Garn SM, Clark DC: Trends in fitness and the origins of obesity. *Pediatrics* 1976; 57:443–456.

5. Stunkard AJ, Sorensen TIA, Hanis C, et al: An adoption study of human obesity. *New Engl J Med* 1986; 314:193–198.

6. Ravelli GP, Belmont L: Obesity in nineteen-year-old men: Family size and birth order associations. *American Journal of Epidemiology* 1979; 109:66–70.

7. Flatt JP: The biochemistry of energy expenditure, in Bray G (ed): *Recent advances in obesity research.* London, Newman Publishing, 1978, vol 2, pp 211–228.

8. Dietz WH, Gortmaker SL: Do we fatten our children at the TV set? Television viewing and obesity in children and adolescents. *Pediatrics* 1985; 75:807–812.

9. Palumbo FM, Dietz WH: Children's television: Its effect on nutrition and cognitive development. *Pediatr Ann* 1985; 14:793–801.

10. Frisancho AR: New norms of upper limb fat and muscle areas for assessment of nutritional status. *Am J Clin Nutr* 1981; 34:2540–2545.

11. Epstein LH: Review of behavioral treatments for childhood obesity, in Brownell KD, Foreyt JP (eds): *Eating Disorders.* New York, Basic Books Inc Publishers, 1986, pp 159–179.

12. Brownell KD, Stunkard AJ: Behavioral treatment of obesity in children. *Am J Dis Child* 1978; 132:403–412.

13. Epstein LH, Wing RR, Roeske R, et al: Child and parent weight loss in family-based behavior modification programs. *J Consult Clin Psychol* 1981; 49:674–685.

14. Epstein LH, Wing RR, Steranchak L, et al: Comparison of family-based behavior modification and nutrition education for childhood obesity. *J Pediatr Psych* 1980; 5:25–36.

15. Dietz WH, Hartung R: Changes in height velocity of obese preadolescents during weight reduction. *Am J Dis Child* 1985; 139:705–707.

16. Dietz WH, Schoeller DA: Optimal dietary therapy for obese adolescents: Comparison of protein plus glucose and protein plus fat. *J Pediatr* 1982; 100:638–644.

17. Dietz WH: Childhood obesity: Susceptibility, cause and management. *J Pediatr* 1983; 103:676–686.

18. Dietz WH, Wolfe RR: Interrelationships of glucose and protein metabolism in obese adolescents during short-term hypocaloric dietary therapy. *Am J Clin Nutr* 1985; 42:380–390.

19. Epstein HH, Wing RR, Penner BC, et al: Effect of diet and controlled exercise on weight loss in obese children. *J Pediatr* 1985; 107:358–361.

Chapter 19

Weight Control for the Adult and the Elderly

Reva T. Frankle

INTRODUCTION

This chapter presents a definition of obesity, the prevalence of obesity, risk factors attributable to excessive body weight and fat, and a treatment plan addressing nutrition and diet, exercise, and behavior change and maintenance strategies. The nutrition-related diseases for which obesity is a significant risk factor are discussed in later chapters (see Chapters 20–23).

The field of obesity has been the subject of rigorous investigation by numerous scientists including physicians, biochemists, geneticists, physiologists, psychologists, nutritionists, endocrinologists, pharmacists, and others. Despite a tremendous amount of research since the mid-1950s, there is no one known mechanism for the cause of obesity. Obesity can no longer be defined as a disease of gluttony, as genetic, environmental, biochemical, metabolic, and physiologic factors are involved.

Overall, approximately 30% of adults 25 years or older are overweight, with more women (30%) than men (26%) overweight. People of all ages and weights from underweight to overweight want to lose weight. Just as more than 25% of all teenagers were on a diet in 1986, when women aged 65 to 86 years were asked what they would like to weigh, most said 10 lb less than their present weight.[1]

A review of growth charts for obese children and adolescents by Dietz (Chapter 18) indicated that rates of excess weight gain were 5 to 10 lb/yr, and that these gains could be accounted for by an excess daily intake of between 50 and 100 kcal. Likewise, most adult Americans between the ages of 25 and 50 years will gain 15 to 25 lb even if their eating habits do not change.

This means we enter our later years with a "creeping-up" of overweight. The Ten-State Nutrition Survey[2] found that approximately 50% of the women and 18% of the men over 60 years are obese. For those over 80 years, approximately 25% of the women and 15% of the men are obese. These figures imply elderly women are 2 to 3 times more likely to be obese than elderly men. The most likely explanation for this age-related increase in weight is that people tend to become less active with time, which results in a need for fewer calories. Also, body composition changes enter into the equation. A decrease in lean body mass (LBM) and an increase in body fat occurs with aging, resulting in a decrease in metabolic rate. Is this increase in weight and body fat deleterious to the health and longevity of our population? Data from the second National Health and Nutrition Survey[3] (NHANES II) showed a strong association between the prevalence of obesity and cardiovascular disease risk factors 5.6 times higher for the young (20 to 44 years old) overweight than for nonoverweight subjects in this group.

THE ADULT AND THE ELDERLY: WHO ARE THEY?

The adult population is segmented into five age groups in survey studies: 25–34, 35–44, 45–54, 55–64, and 65–74 years. Too often, the elderly are defined as "51 plus" or "65 plus." However, destined to become 13% of the population by the year 2000, growing from 51 million in 1985 to 56 million in 1995, representing one fifth of all Americans, this group is now being characterized by four market segments, each with projected growth patterns for the next decade, as shown in Table 19-1.[4]

The "older" group is keenly interested in maintaining a youthful appearance and are prime targets for exercise and health programs, including diet. This group, whose children have left home, is seriously considering retirement.

The "elderly" group resemble far younger people of past generations in their attitudes, education, use of leisure time, health, and marital status. They are more concerned than the general population with diet, salt intake, cholesterol, fried foods, and calories.

The "aged" fit the "senior citizen" image much better than people aged 65 to 74 years. With health often a problem for them and their mobility somewhat limited, the aged often require health care services and special care facilities. They are oriented to their extended families, are often lonely, and are concerned about financial security. For many, their fully paid homes are their most important assets.

People aged 85 years or older, the truly elderly, the "very old," are different from the rest of the mature market. They are not so independent as more youthful older Americans and may require support services to do everyday tasks. They lack mobility and require regular medical and hospital care. The needs of this group are not well understood, as this market has never before reached a size significant enough for marketers to investigate it closely. Some members of each segment of the adult and mature market are potential candidates for a weight-

Table 19-1 The Four Market Segments of the Adult Population

	1985 Million	1995 Million
The older population (55–64 yr)	22	21.5
The elderly (65–74 yr)	17	19
The aged (75–84 yr)	9	11
The very old (85 yr or older)	2.7	4

Source: Reprinted with permission from "Inside the Mature Market" by W Lazer, *American Demographics* (1985; 7:23–25, 48–49).

control program that offers a rational approach to modulating the energy equation with decreased caloric intake and increased energy expenditure to improve nutrition and physical fitness.

OBESITY: WHAT IS IT?

In relation to three national health surveys (the first National Health Examination Survey, 1960–62[5] [NHES 1], 6,257 men and women aged 20 to 74 years; the first National Health and Nutrition Examination Survey, 1971–74[6] [NHANES 1], 13,106 men and women aged 20 to 74 years; and NHANES II,[3] 11,864 men and women aged 20 to 74 years), *overweight* is defined as being a body mass index (BMI) at or higher than the 85th percentile for men and women aged 20 to 29 years studied between 1976 and 1980; *severe overweight* is defined as a BMI at or higher than the 95th percentile of the same 20- to 29-year-old referenced group. The rationale underlying the use of the 20- to 29-year-old reference population is that young adults are relatively lean, and that the increase in body weight that usually occurs as men and women age is attributable almost entirely to fat accumulation. Thus, the criteria used in the health surveys are defined statistically and are not derived from morbidity or mortality experience of the survey population. Body measurement data from these three national health surveys conducted by the National Center for Health Statistics make it possible to examine changes over time in the prevalence of overweight in the US population aged 20 to 74 years. In addition, NHANES II[3] provided data showing the relation of obesity and overweight to certain risk factors.

Whereas *overweight* is an increase in body weight above some arbitrary standard defined in relation to height, usually designated as a deviation 10% to 19% of the desirable weight, *obesity* refers to an abnormally high proportion of body fat (adipose tissue), resulting in a significant impairment of health. The excess fat accumulation is associated with increased fat cell size; in people with extreme obesity, fat cell numbers are also increased.[7] Adipose tissue is a normal constituent of the human body and serves the important function of storing energy as fat for mobilization in response to metabolic demands.

In order to determine whether a person is overweight or obese, there are several techniques for determining body composition described by Stock and Rothwell[8] (see Chapter 5). Visual observation and anthropometric evaluation is the best method suited to clinical settings. Anthropometric measurements involve determination of height, weight, and skinfold thicknesses.[9,10] There is a consensus that a measure of obesity is needed to overcome the subjectivity introduced by relying on visual inspection as an estimate of obesity.

For the diagnosis of obesity for adults 20 years or older, two methods have been proposed by the National Institutes of Health (NIH) Consensus Development Conference:[11]

1. estimation of relative weight (RW) calculated by dividing the measured body weight by the midpoint of the desirable weight for medium frame recommended in the 1959 and 1983 Metropolitan Life Insurance Company tables
2. calculations of body mass index:
   $$BMI = Body\ weight\ (kg)/Height\ (m)^2.$$

The BMI is a simple measurement highly correlated with other estimates of fatness. It minimizes the effect of height and is useful for descriptive or evaluative purposes.

It is noteworthy that the BMI, also known as the Quetelet index, originally proposed by Quetelet, a 19th century Belgian astronomer, has gained favor with the scientific community more than 100 years after his death. The major limitation of the BMI is that it is difficult to explain this mathematical index to patients and to relate it to weight that must be lost.

The BMI values, which correspond to 20% above desirable weight, are 27.2 and 26.9 for men and women, respectively, using the 1983 Metropolitan Height and Weight tables, and 26.4 and 25.8 for men and women, respectively, using the 1959 Metropolitan tables. The NIH consensus panel[11] recommended that physicians adopt this measure as an additional factor in patient assessment and that a nomogram be used to facilitate calculations of the BMI as shown in Figure 19-1.

In the 1983 Metropolitan Height and Weight tables, desirable weights for men and women in the shortest stature groups are 12 and 14 lb higher, respectively, than they were in 1959. It is recognized that such increased body weight may

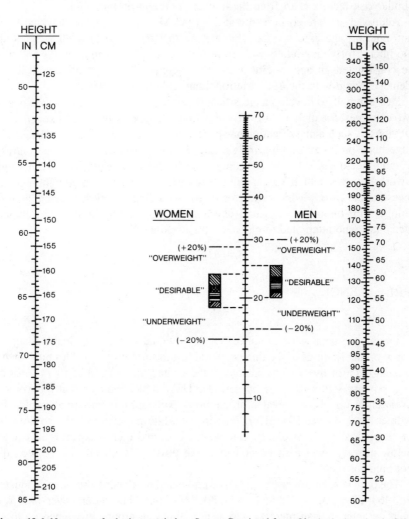

Figure 19-1 Nomogram for body mass index. *Source*: Reprinted from *Obesity in America* (p 6) by GA Bray, NIH Publication No. 79-359, November 1979.

contribute to high blood pressure, hypercholesterolemia, glucose intolerance, or similar risk factors apart from the impact of weight on mortality.

Andres et al[12] are concerned that the 1983 Metropolitan tables have erred by not entering age as a variable. Suggesting that the recommended weights are too liberal for young adults and too restrictive for persons in their 50s and 60s, he constructed an age-specific weight-for-height table (Gerontology Research Center) shown with the 1983 Metropolitan table in Table 19-2.

Past attempts to develop a classification system for obesity have taken one of two extremes, the dichotomous classifications "endogenous" vs. "exogenous." Obviously, such a classification has limited use. Multiple classification schemes have been proposed seeking insight into etiologic mechanisms or, in contrast, to subdivide obese subjects according to their degree of health risk. To this end, a workshop was held at Vassar College in 1982. The workshop brought together investigators from a wide variety of fields, including genetics, physical anthropology, cell biology, behavioral psychology, energy physiology, and clinical medicine, who attempted to classify "the obesities."

PREVALENCE

Prevalence data were compiled by the National Center for Health Statistics based on the findings of the three national health surveys.[3,5,6] Tables published[13] present data for overweight persons in the United States aged 25 to 74 years by sex, poverty status, and survey periods. These tables indicate that for women, overweight was more prevalent in the black population (approximately 60% for women aged 45 years or older) than in the white population (30% to 36% for those aged 45 years or older). Overweight occurred more frequently in women below poverty level than in women above poverty level, but this relation did not hold for men.

The prevalence of overweight can be compared for the three surveys conducted in 1960–62,[5] 1971–74,[6] and 1976–80.[3] No consistent pattern over time was seen for men, but an increase was seen within age groups in women up to 45 to 54 years, followed by a decline. The prevalence of severe overweight by age group was not significantly different for men and women over the three surveys.

Based on indices of body fat, studies of populations have shown that there is a continuous relation between RW or BMI and morbidity and mortality rates. Thus, it becomes important to establish ranges of these indices as guidelines for developing appropriate and effective approaches for the treatment and prevention of obesity. An important question needs to be addressed: What is the evidence that obesity has adverse effects on health and longevity?

Table 19-2 Comparison of the Weight-for-Height Tables from Actuarial Data (Bulid Study): Non-Age-Corrected Metropolitan Life Insurance Company and Age-Specific Gerontology Research Center Recommendations*

Height	Metropolitan 1983 Weights for Ages 25–59†		Gerontology Research Center Weight Range for Men and Women by Age (Years)‡				
	Men	Women	25	35	45	55	65
ft-in			*lb*				
4-10	⋯	100–131	84–111	92–119	99–127	107–135	115–142
4-11	⋯	101–134	87–115	95–123	103–131	111–139	119–147
5-0	⋯	103–137	90–119	98–127	106–135	114–143	123–152
5-1	123–145	105–140	93–123	101–131	110–140	118–148	127–157
5-2	125–148	108–144	96–127	105–136	113–144	122–153	131–163
5-3	127–151	111–148	99–131	108–140	117–149	126–158	135–168
5-4	129–155	114–152	102–135	112–145	121–154	130–163	140–173
5-5	131–159	117–156	106–140	115–149	125–159	134–168	144–179
5-6	133–163	120–160	109–144	119–154	129–164	138–174	148–184
5-7	135–167	123–164	112–148	122–159	133–169	143–179	153–190
5-8	137–171	126–167	116–153	126–163	137–174	147–184	158–196
5-9	139–175	129–170	119–157	130–168	141–179	151–190	162–201
5-10	141–179	132–173	122–162	134–173	145–184	156–195	167–207
5-11	144–183	135–176	126–167	137–178	149–190	160–201	172–213
6-0	147–187	⋯	129–171	141–183	153–195	165–207	177–219
6-1	150–192	⋯	133–176	145–188	157–200	169–213	182–225
6-2	153–197	⋯	137–181	149–194	162–206	174–219	187–232
6-3	157–202	⋯	141–186	153–199	166–212	179–225	192–238
6-4	⋯	⋯	144–191	157–205	171–218	184–231	197–244

*Values in this table are for height without shoes and weight without clothes. To convert inches to centimeters, multiply by 2.54; to convert pounds to kilograms, multiply by 0.455.

†The weight range is the lower weight for small frame and the upper weight for large frame.

‡Data from Andres.

Source: Reprinted with permission from "Impact of Age on Weight Goals" by R Andres et al, *Annals of Internal Medicine* (1985; 103:1030–1033), Copyright © 1985, American College of Physicians.

WHAT IS THE EVIDENCE THAT OBESITY AFFECTS LONGEVITY AND HEALTH?

Obesity, when measured by RW (actual weight as a percentage of average or desirable weight for a given height-age-sex group) has an adverse effect on longevity.[11] Convincing evidence of this has been evaluated[14] in data from NHANES II, four very large insurance company studies (1903–1979), the Framingham 30-Year Follow-up Study, the American Cancer Society study, and other smaller cohort studies. The findings indicate that below-average weights tend to be associated with the greatest longevity if such weights are not associated with concurrent illness or a history of significant impairment.[14]

The increase in mortality vs. RW is steeper in men and women under 50 years old than in older persons, and the increase with duration is also steeper. These findings suggest that particular attention should be paid to efforts to reduce weight in younger patients. Analysis of the Framingham Heart Study suggests that the duration of being obese has an important bearing on the putative relation between body weight and longevity (see Chapter 21). Thus, when the Framingham Study data were analyzed using a longer time interval between measurement of obesity and subsequent outcome, obesity was a significant predictor for cardiovascular disease, independent of age, cholesterol level, systolic blood pressure, cigarette smoking, left ventricular hypertrophy, and glucose intolerance. The conclusion from this study is that obesity is a long-term predictor of cardiovascular disease, particularly for younger people. In women, only age and blood pressure are more powerful predictors.

The location of body fat has emerged as an important predictor for the health hazards of obesity. Adipose tissue depots do not constitute a uniform organ; fat cells around the waist and flank and in the abdomen (android, or "apple-shaped" obesity) are more active metabolically and more detrimental to health than those in the thigh and buttocks (gynoid, or "pear-shaped" obesity). Sites of body fat predominance are easily measured by the ratio of waist to hip circumferences. High ratios are associated with higher risks for death and illness.[15] Studies suggest that the fat distribution may be a better predictor of mortality than BMI or RW. If confirmed, it may be important in the future to measure fat distribution in addition to using height-weight tables.

Experts continue to discuss whether moderate degrees of overweight may be beneficial to health. Andres et al[12] suggest that overweight in the elderly may be more protective than underweight. Their data indicate that older persons who were overweight no more than 130% of standard weight for height have less mortality and morbidity than do those whose weight ranges from 75% to 95% of the standard. However, data by Lew and Garfinkel[16] show overweight to be hazardous to the older person.

Lew and Garfinkel[16] report the mortality experience according to variations in weight among 750,000 men and women drawn from the general population in a long-term prospective study conducted by the American Cancer Society over the period 1959 to 1972. It is the first large-scale study of mortality by weight, based on sizeable numbers, to take the effects of smoking habits into account.

In general, the findings indicated that the lowest mortality was found among those close to average weight and those 10% to 20% below average weight. Mortality among men and women 30% to 40% heavier than average was nearly 50% higher than among those of average weight; among those more than 40% heavier than average, it was nearly 90% higher than among those of average weight.

The relation between obesity and altered glucose metabolism has been well established, and the development of noninsulin dependent diabetes mellitus (NIDDM) is closely linked to obesity (see Chapter 22). People with NIDDM are usually obese and older than 40 years at the time of diagnosis. The degree and duration of obesity seem to have roles in determining the risk for NIDDM or glucose intolerance. The reported risk for NIDDM is approximately 2 fold in the mildly obese, 5 fold in the moderately obese, and 10 fold in the severely obese.[17] People with diabetes as a group are much older than the general US population. The highest rate per thousand is 87.9% among males aged 65 to 74 years and 87.7% among women with an increase to 95.3% per thousand in women over 75 years of age.

FOR WHAT MEDICAL CONDITIONS CAN WEIGHT REDUCTION BE RECOMMENDED?

Weight reduction may be lifesaving for patients with extreme obesity, arbitrarily defined as weight twice the desirable weight, or 45 kg (100 lb) over desirable weight, or a BMI equal to or higher than the 95th percentile. In view of the excess mortality and morbidity associated with obesity, weight reduction should be recommended to people with excess body weight of 20% or more above desirable weights in the Metropolitan Height and Weight tables (using the midpoint of the range for a medium-build person).

Weight reduction is also highly desirable, even in patients with lesser degrees of obesity, in many other circumstances, including the following:

- NIDDM
- hypertension
- hypertriglyceridemia
- hypercholesterolemia.

In addition to the possible effects of obesity on mortality, obesity affects the function of many organ systems. For example, obesity increases the work of the heart,[18] and the enlargement of this organ is correlated with a rise in body weight. The cardiac output, stroke volume, and blood volume also increase with added weight; pulmonary function is impaired, endocrine function is moderated in the obese population, and abnormalities exist in the reproductive system with low levels of testosterone attributable to a reduction in circulating levels of sex-hormone binding globulin in men and abnormal menstrual cycles in women.[19]

The treatment plan recommended is one that encompasses nutrition and diet, exercise, behavior modification, a positive support system, and weight-control management strategies. As the author is currently Nutrition Consultant for Weight Watchers International, experiences with that program enter the discussion.

NUTRITION AND DIET

> "Nutrition is, historically, perhaps
> the most important contributor
> to man's successes
> against disease and disability."
>
> J. Michael McGinnis, MD
> Deputy Assistant Secretary for Health

Nutrition must be the cornerstone for a responsible weight-control program. Many reducing diets fail to give attention to nutritional adequacy. They often are grossly distorted with high protein, no carbohydrate, or with periods of bizarre intake (see Chapter 8).

There are many factors to be considered in the design of a successful weight-control food program. The proper distribution of energy intake among protein, fat, and carbohydrate, with adequate intake of the micronutrients, vitamins, minerals, and fiber, is important.

The Senate Select Committee on Nutrition and Human Needs[20] proposed recommendations for the American diet as seen in column 2 in Figure 19-2 (30% calories from fat, 12% from protein, and 58% from carbohydrate). Column 1 reflects the current US diet (1977) with 42% of the energy from fat, 12% from protein, and 46% from carbohydrate with 25% from refined sugar. Column 3 shows the Weight Watchers program. It should be stated that columns 1 and 2 are based on 2,400 calories and column 3 on 1,200 with actual protein in all three being approximately 65 g.

Nutrition specifically for the elderly is discussed in excellent review articles.[21,22] A number of factors affect nutrition in the elderly. These include physiologic changes in various organ systems, including achlorhydria and changes

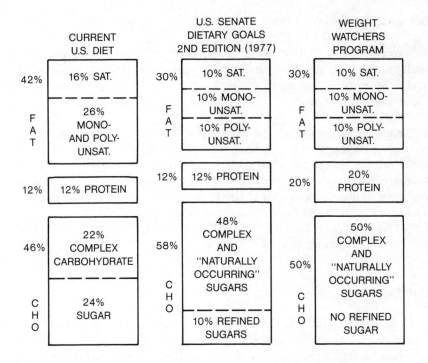

PERCENT CALORIES FAT, PROTEIN, CARBOHYDRATES

Figure 19-2 US Senate committee dietary goals and weight watchers program. *Source*: Adapted from *Dietary Goals for the United States*, ed 2, US Senate Select Committee on Nutrition and Human Needs, Government Printing Office, No. 052-070-04376-8, 1977.

in the absorption of nutrients, as well as altered mastication from loss of teeth or ill-fitting dentures. Loss of gustatory and olfactory sensation may also alter both appetite for food and thus consumption of nutrients. Vision and hearing loss, social isolation, and difficulties in mobility also contribute to nutrition-related difficulties. Physical infirmities or fears for physical safety may make it more difficult to shop for food. Apathy and depression owing to social isolation or grief and mourning may also militate against a healthy appetite. The use of prescription drugs that alter appetite also contributes to inadequate intakes. The incidence of chronic degenerative diseases rises with age; dietary factors may be relevant in their cause as well as in their treatment.

Energy and Calories

In recognition of the fact that energy needs decline progressively throughout adult life, the 1980 Recommended Dietary Allowances[23] (RDAs) record energy intakes for three age ranges of adults: 23 to 50, 51 to 75, and 76 plus years. Mean heights and weights with recommended energy intake are shown in Table 19-3.

The energy allowances for the two older age groups represent mean energy needs over these age spans, allowing for a 2% decrease in basal (resting) metabolic rate per decade and a reduction in activity of 200 kcal/day for men and women between 51 and 75 years, 400 kcal for women over 75 years, and 500 kcal for men over 75 years. NHANES II[3] has shown that the median kilocalorie intake for men in the 65 to 74 age group is 1,200 kcal, and for women is 1,415 kcal. This emphasizes the need for foods of higher nutrient density such as those provided in the prudent food plan discussed later.

Protein

An allowance of 0.6 g/kg/day of high-quality protein will cover the needs of almost all healthy people, or 0.8 g/kg/day for mixed proteins of the US diet. Since calorie intake per kilogram of body weight falls progressively with age, whereas the amount of protein per kilogram of body weight needed for nitrogen equilibrium is not reduced and may even increase, it is prudent to ensure that a weight-control plan provides at least 12% or more of the energy intake in the form of protein.

Fats

Dietary fat serves as a carrier for fat-soluble vitamins and provides essential fatty acids. Except for these needs, which can be met by a diet containing 15 to 25 g of appropriate food fats, there is no specific requirement for fat as a nutrient in the diet. Total fat intake, particularly in diets below 2,000 kcal, should be reduced so fat is not more than 35% of dietary energy,[23] or 30% as recommended by US Dietary Goals and Guidelines.[20]

Carbohydrates

A minimum of 150 g of digestible carbohydrate adequate to prevent ketosis should be provided daily. Foods such as fruits, vegetables, and whole grain

Table 19-3 Mean Heights and Weights and Recommended Energy Intake

Category	Age (yr)	Weight (kg)	Weight (lb)	Height (cm)	Height (in)	Energy Needs/Range (kcal)	Energy Needs/Range (MJ)
Women	23–50	46	101	157	62	2,000 (1,600–2,400)	8.4
	51–75	55	120	163	64	1,800 (1,400–2,200)	7.6
	76+	55	120	163	64	1,600 (1,200–2,000)	6.7
Men	23–50	70	154	178	70	2,700 (2,300–3,100)	11.3
	51–75	70	154	178	70	2,400 (2,000–2,800)	10.1
	76+	70	154	178	70	2,050 (1,650–2,450)	8.6

Source: Adapted from *Recommended Dietary Allowances*, ed 9 (p 23) by Food and Nutrition Board, National Research Council, with permission of National Academy of Sciences, © 1980.

cereal provide energy principally from carbohydrates and are generally good sources of vitamins and minerals.[23]

Dietary Fiber

Dietary fiber, water-soluble and water insoluble, is generally defined as the sum of indigestible carbohydrate and carbohydrate-like components of food, including cellulose, lignin, hemicelluloses, pentosans, gums, and pectins. Although dietary fiber is important, there is not a consensus for the specific level of intake. For the general population, water-insoluble fiber found in wheat, bran, and other grains is recommended. A moderate increase in the water-soluble fiber found in oats, barley, and dried beans have a beneficial effect as a dietary component in the treatment of high blood cholesterol levels and NIDDM. In view of the possible reduction in absorption of mineral elements, a very high intake of fiber is not recommended; a safe level is 20 to 30 g/day.

A RATIONAL APPROACH TO WEIGHT CONTROL

Dietary Treatment

Diet has been the mainstay of the treatment of obesity in past years, and the reduction of energy intake continues to be the basis of most successful weight-reduction programs. Evidence of this is the large array of popular diets reported in the press. Some of these "panacea" diets are named for a food: the Rice Diet, the Grapefruit Diet, or the Banana Diet; others carry a geographic connotation: Cambridge, Scarsdale, Southampton, and Beverly Hills.

A variety of modalities for dietary treatment have been proposed in a caloric taxonomy: fasting or zero calories, no longer considered appropriate because of dangerous loss of lean body tissue and reported death; very-low-calorie diets (VLCD) using protein supplements such as Cambridge, Optifast, and HMR providing 400 to 500 kcal/day; and the protein-sparing modified fasts consisting of lean poultry and fish plus vegetables providing approximately 600 kcal/day. Because of loss of LBM and possible electrolyte imbalances, the VLCD should be used in clinical settings under medical supervision. Moderate-low-calorie diets (MLCD) of approximately 1,000 to 1,200 kcal for women (1,500 kcal for men) are recognized as the safe caloric level for a slow progressive weight loss.[24] However, these MLCD may be either nutritionally unbalanced or balanced. The former, known as the Stillman, Beverly Hills, I Love New York, and the Atkins, to name a few, eliminate one of the basic food groups, are nutritionally unsound, and are not recommended.[25] A safe and rational approach to weight control offers a MLCD with all food groups represented, allowing for a nutritionally sound diet such as those prescribed by registered dietitions in private practice, in medical nutrition clinics, and in the Weight Watchers food plan. As Dalton reminds us (Chapter 9), eating for pleasure is important in weight management. Recommendations for weight management are not different from nutrition recommendations for the general public. Lifetime diets are not complicated. Shopping and food preparation skills are important in eating management for daily life and weight control.

The Weight Watchers Program

Although the author is well aware that there is no one method of weight management for all people, the method most likely to succeed for most people most of the time is the four-way approach:

1. a food plan based on the science and art of nutrition
2. a program of increased physical activity
3. a series of eating management skills (behavior change)
4. a positive support system.

The year 1988 marks the 25th year of operation for Weight Watchers International (WWI). In 1963, the founder, Jean Nidetch, weighing 214 lb, appeared at the New York City Department of Health Obesity Clinic and introduced the Bureau of Nutrition's Prudent Diet to her friends and neighbors. Now, Weight Watchers International conducts group meetings in 50 states and 21 countries, with more than 25 million enrollments to date. In any one week, more than 800,000 members around the world are attending 18,000 classes under the guidance of 10,000 group leaders.

Staff, formerly obese, are paid workers who follow a centrally conceived program, monitored professionally for effectiveness. One of the criteria for employment is that the group leader be a graduate of the program. Many were not successful the first time through the program, but all have reached goal weight and maintain their weight loss. They attribute their success to a changed life style, to family involvement, to new attitudes toward food, to the incorporation of new eating management skills, and, new to most, to a planned daily exercise routine for both staff people and members of their families.

Peer counseling brings together people for mutual problem solving and growth; members are encouraged to share their feelings, thoughts, and, if desired, personal experiences. It is the "high touch" needed to balance the "high tech" in today's society.

The strategies presented during the weekly meetings consist of the transfer of information, attitude changes, participant interaction, and educational materials to facilitate information exchange.[26]

Basic Considerations For A Weight-Control Food Plan

The following are nine basic considerations for a weight-control food plan:

1. energy deficit to allow slow, safe, progressive weight loss of 1 to 2 lb/wk
2. macronutrients (protein, carbohydrate, and fat) in amounts recommended by US Dietary Goals[20] (see Figure 19-2) and the recommendations of Dietary Guidelines for Americans[27]
3. micronutrients (vitamins and minerals) in amounts recommended by RDA[23]
4. an awareness of cholesterol, sodium, the P/S ratio, and fat sources; it is currently recommended that of the 30% of kilocalories from fat, one-third each should be saturated, monounsaturated, and polyunsaturated fats
5. key words: variety, moderation, portion control
6. an exchange system that presents foods of similar nutrient content within specific categories allowing for variety and portion control
7. optional calories: a daily allowance of extra calories that can be "banked" and/or "spent" to enhance recipe development and make possible the enjoyment of social situations such as dining out, brunches, and holiday fare, and foods not usually on weight-control plans
8. a weekly menu planner that outlines specific foods in specific amounts to provide structure to stay on course and at the same time freedom and flexibility for individual life styles
9. a system of individualization in the form of "Personal Choice Selections" to enhance adherence and to introduce maintenance strategies early in the weight-loss program.

Exchange System

Exchange categories are lists of food servings of similar nutrient content. This allows interchanging within each category and allows for variety along with portion control. The total daily exchanges in all seven categories for women and men are shown in Table 19-4.

With a working knowledge of the exchange system and the optional calorie category, people on a weight-loss regimen are able to make food choices that are traditionally not representative of weight-control dietary prescription: eggplant parmigiana, french toast, and chocolate mousse to mention a few. Thus, early

Table 19-4 Food Exchange Categories

FOR WOMEN (1,200 kcal)	*FOR MEN* (1,500 kcal)
Fruit 3	Fruit . . . . .4 to 6
Vegetables . . . . . . .2 (at least)	Vegetables . . . . . . .2 (at least)
Milk 2	Milk 2
Bread . . . . .2 to 3	Bread . . . . .4 to 5
Fat 3	Fat 3
Protein . . . . .6 to 8	Protein . . . . .8 to 10
Optional . . . . .up to 550 calories/wk	Optional . . . . .up to 550 calories/wk

*This food plan provides approximately 50% calories from carbohydrate, 20% from protein, and 30% from fat; 155 g of carbohydrate, 65 g of protein, 45 g of fat, 300 mg of cholesterol, and 2,000 mg of sodium.

Source: Reprinted with permission, Weight Watchers International, Jericho, New York, Copyright© 1987.

in their dieting experience, people learn they can live in the *real* world, experience *real* food choices, like *real* chocolate cake and candy kisses (550 optional weekly calories) and still lose weight.

Exercise

The lack of energy expenditure in daily physical activity is a predisposing factor for obesity. The successful prevention and treatment of obesity are dependent on an understanding of the energy balance systems and the incorporation of this knowledge into intervention strategies. Evidence suggests that exercise in conjunction with other treatments produces greater weight loss than do single intervention procedures. Regular exercise, either alone or in a combination with dietary modifications, can have an important role in the prevention and treatment of obesity.[28-31]

Epidemiologic data suggest a positive relation between inactivity and obesity. The prevalence of obesity has approximately doubled since 1900 despite a 10% reduction in caloric consumption. Evidence does not support the belief that overweight people generally consume more than do their leaner counterparts. Six studies found no significant difference in caloric intake between obese and nonobese populations, and five studies reported that the obese ate significantly less than did their nonobese peers.[32] Thus, contrary to popular belief, obese people have been reported to eat the same or even less than leaner people over a broad age range as they become less active and slowly gain weight.[33]

A frequent misconception about the role of exercise in weight-reduction programs is that an increase in physical activity results in an increase in appetite and caloric intake that equals the energy cost of the exercise. Woo et al[34] studied the effect of exercise on spontaneous caloric intake in obese women (mean 167% above ideal body weight) at three levels of caloric expenditure: one sedentary and two with treadmill exercise that increased daily expenditure to either 110% (mild) or 125% (moderate) of sedentary expenditure. Subjects selected their intake and did not change their intake level, which allowed for an energy balance during the sedentary period only. The difference between intake and expenditure between treatments was significantly different (sedentary 11, mild -114, and moderate -369 kcal/day). The balances observed with mild and moderate exercise were negative because there was no compensatory increase in caloric intake with increased expenditure.

An analysis of data generated from studies that involved monitoring caloric intake concurrent with programmed exercise training but without dietary interventions reveals an interesting relation between activity and intake.[32] Five of the seven studies reported decreases in caloric intake with exercise training or very small changes in caloric intake with exercise training. Most studies suggested a small lowering of consumption unless activity level was above the moderate range.

The mere addition of exercise to the weight-loss program may actually facilitate adherence to the program, resulting in a more permanent weight loss compared with caloric restriction alone,[35] while at the same time enhancing the psychologic status of the participant[36] with enhanced metabolic effects.[37]

Evidence is mounting that exercise may be one of the factors correlated with long-term weight maintenance.[38,39] Brownell et al[40] suggested that exercise may prevent relapse because it:

- becomes a positive addiction, serving as a positive replacement for the problem behavior
- may positively influence a person's self-concept, which may generalize to the behavior-change process
- provides a peer group that supports health behavior
- removes a person to a safe setting.

Other reasons may include that exercise:

- becomes a constructive means for managing stress, tension, and other negative emotional states

- enables a person to consume a greater number of calories than otherwise would be possible.

Effect on Body Fat and Lean Body Mass

Body fat is significantly affected by a program of prescribed exercise in both sexes at all age levels. Reductions in activity level are strongly correlated with body fat increases, even if caloric intake is significantly reduced.[41] The amount of fat loss depends on the specifics of the exercise and on the qualitative aspects of the body fat in the person.

It has been shown that if a person exercises during weight loss, the loss of fat is greater, and there is an increase in lean tissue. People losing weight by diet alone, in addition to losing less fat, lose lean body tissue.[29] On the basis of Gwinup's study, Zuti and Golding[42] recommended that any weight reduction program combine a lowered caloric intake with a good physical fitness program.

Current knowledge of energy supply indicates that exercise stimulates the mobilization of fatty acids from the fat depots throughout the body, and the areas of greatest concentration probably supply the greatest amount of energy (Chapter 13). There is no doubt that a negative caloric balance created through regular exercise can significantly contribute to a reduction in total body fat.

Exercise Prescription

In line with established and prudent recommendations for apparently healthy adults, it is recommended that obese people, especially the older obese, receive medical screening to establish overall health status before embarking on an exercise program.[43] For people over 45 years of age, a maximum graded exercise test with a physician present is required. Brownell[44] suggested the screening should include some evaluation of the emotional status of the participant as obesity may be associated with psychologic disorder impairment. An added benefit of the stress test is that it provides the participant with a positive indication that exercise can be undertaken without harm or injury. When considering the exercise for weight control, factors such as the specific form of exercise, the exercise intensity, the frequency of participation, and the duration of each exercise session must be considered (see Chapter 13).

Continuous aerobic activities that activate a relatively large muscle mass such as walking, jogging or running, cycling, and swimming are ideal as the major component of a weight-loss exercise program. Competitive sport activities may place the participant at unnecessary risk for injury. Rhythmic forms of sustained exercise burn considerable calories; favorably modify lipid metabolism, body fat, and blood pressure; and generally promote cardiovascular fitness. There is generally no selective effect among various forms of aerobic exercise; each is equally effective in altering body composition provided the duration, frequency, and intensity of exercise are similar. In Chapter 13, McArdle and Toner present a detailed discussion about exercise prescriptions: intensity, frequency, and duration. They stress that most important is that each person participate in activities that are safe, pleasurable, and adaptable to any specific limitations. It is only when these criteria are met that there is a reasonable chance for sustained compliance on the part of the participant.

Generally, the total energy expended is the most important factor that influences the effectiveness of the exercise program for weight control. Although it is difficult to speculate precisely as to a minimal level of energy expenditure for weight reduction and fat loss, it is generally recommended that the calorie-burning effect of each exercise session be at least 300 kcal.[24] At least 8 to 12 weeks may be required before observable changes in body composition occur, although more rapid changes have been reported with a combination of exercise and dieting in the severely obese in a clinical session.[45] Older men and women may improve their general physical fitness through systematic physical exercise.[46,47]

The Weight Watchers exercise plan recommends prolonged, low-to-moderate-intensity exercise coupled with the sound dietary guidelines of the food plan, resulting in a significant amount of safe weight loss. The exercises recommended to Weight Watcher clients, developed by McArdle, are those that engage the large muscles of the trunk and extremities that produce the highest energy requirement if continued for a prolonged period of time. The 1987 program offers five activities—walking, walking-jogging, stationary bicycling, outdoor bicycling, and swimming, plus special firming and toning exercises—at four levels that are specially suited to the individual member. Successful members report an increased level of maintenance caloric intake as a result of their newly acquired exercise program.

In summary, low-to-moderate exercise for the obese is one of the few factors correlated with long-term weight management with the following positive effects:

- reduced caloric intake
- increased metabolic rate
- favorable changes in body composition
- enhanced cardiovascular fitness
- reduced risk of heart disease
- increased longevity.

BEHAVIOR MODIFICATION

Though Stunkard would present new data in the early 1980s, in 1959 he summed up the effectiveness of treatment of obesity in what has become a classic and frequently quoted paper. ''Most obese persons will not remain in treatment.

Of those who do remain in treatment, most will not lose much weight, and of those who do lose weight, most will regain it."[48] This situation was radically changed in 1967 by the appearance of Stuart's[49] landmark paper on behavioral control of overeating in which he reported unprecedented therapeutic success using stimulus control procedures in the treatment of eight obese subjects. In 1975, Stuart became the psychologic director of Weight Watchers International and introduced their first behavior modification program.[50] Stunkard's[51] testimony to the Senate Select Committee on Obesity recognized Stuart's specific behavior change recommendations: "The application of the behavioral weight management program on such a large scale [Weight Watchers program in 21 countries] stands as one of the major social experiments of our time and the first approach to the control of obesity which is sufficiently broad to warrant description as a public health measure." The most commonly used elements of behavioral weight control, abstracted from the most widely read publications, appear in Table 19-5.[52]

Early techniques used in behavior modification programs for the treatment of obesity varied from one researcher to another. But most employed one or more of the following components: (1) self-monitoring of body weight and/or food intake; (2) implicit or explicit goal setting; (3) nutrition, exercise, and health counseling; (4) tangible operant consequences (reward and punishment); (5) aversion therapy; (6) social reinforcement in the form of therapist, group, or family support; (7) covert conditioning and cognitive restructuring strategies (the pairing of positive behaviors with pleasant scenes in the imagination); (8) self-presented consequences (self-reward, self-punishment); and (9) stimulus control procedures.[53] Today the approach is more positive, with emphasis on self-efficacy and relapse prevention (see Chapter 16).

With the advent of behavior modification, the ease of measurement based on weight-loss performance attracted researchers to the treatment of obesity. Interest in, and knowledge of, obesity was often secondary. Thus, many of the earlier assumptions on which behavioral treatment of obesity was originally based were found to be invalid. It was assumed, for instance, that obesity was a simple, learned disorder; that the obese were more susceptible to food cues than normal-weight subjects; and that teaching the obese to eat as their lean counterparts would produce weight loss.[54] But now obesity is known as a more complex disease entity. It is now understood that there are different "obesities" that will respond differently to different treatment methods. Current thought favors a biobehavioral model that involves the interaction of genetics, physiology, psychology, and cultural factors.[55–57]

Today, it is recognized that the treatment of obesity should be focused on the whole person rather than on the amount of adipose tissue: a holistic approach. Perhaps it is time to measure effectiveness in terms of the rehabilitation of the whole person, with their enhanced life style and self-esteem rating as higher indicators of success than merely pounds lost.

Table 19-5 Behavioral Principles of Weight Loss Cited in Books on the Subject

Principles	Books citing	Principles	Books citing
1. STIMULUS CONTROL		3. REWARD	
A. Shopping		1. Solicit help from family and friends	5
1. Shop for food after eating	3	2. Help family and friends provide this help in the form of praise and material rewards	5
2. Shop from a list	3	3. Utilize self-monitoring records as basis for rewards	5
3. Avoid ready-to-eat foods	3		
4. Don't carry more cash than needed for shopping list	2	4. Plan specific rewards for specific behaviors (behavioral contracts)	3
B. Plans		4. SELF-MONITORING	
1. Plan to limit food intake	4	Keep diet diary that includes:	
2. Substitute exercise for snacking	4	1. Time and place of eating	5
3. Eat meals and snacks at scheduled times	3	2. Type and amount of food	5
4. Don't accept food offered by others	2	3. Who is present/How you feel	5
C. Activities		5. NUTRITION EDUCATION	
1. Store food out of sight	5	1. Use diet diary to identify problem areas	5
2. Eat all food in the same place	5	2. Make small changes that you can continue	5
3. Remove food from inappropriate storage areas in the house	5	3. Learn nutritional values of foods	5

4. Keep serving dishes off the table — 4
5. Use smaller dishes and utensils — 3
6. Avoid being the food server — 2
7. Leave the table immediately after eating — 2
8. Don't save leftovers — 2

D. Holidays and Parties
1. Drink fewer alcoholic beverages — 2
2. Plan eating habits before parties — 2
3. Eat a low-calorie snack before parties — 2
4. Practice polite ways to decline food — 2
5. Don't get discouraged by an occasional setback — 2

2. EATING BEHAVIOR
1. Put fork down between mouthfuls — 4
2. Chew thoroughly before swallowing — 4
3. Prepare foods one portion at a time — 4
4. Leave some food on the plate — 4
5. Pause in the middle of the meal — 3
6. Do nothing else while eating (read, watch television) — 3

4. Decrease fat intake; increase complex carbohydrates — 4

6. PHYSICAL ACTIVITY
A. Routine Activity
1. Increase routine activity — 5
2. Increase use of stairs — 5
3. Keep a record of distance walked each day — 2
B. Exercise
1. Begin a very mild exercise program — 5
2. Keep a record of daily exercise — 2
3. Increase the exercise very gradually — 2

7. COGNITIVE RESTRUCTURING
1. Avoid setting unreasonable goals — 4
2. Think about progress, not shortcomings — 4
3. Avoid imperatives like "always" and "never" — 4
4. Counter negative thoughts with rational restatements — 4
5. Set weight goals — 4

Source: Reprinted with permission from *American Journal of Clinical Nutrition* (1985; 41:823), Copyright © 1985, American Society for Clinical Nutrition Inc.

If the treatment is to be effective over long periods, then it is important for patients in treatment to continue to perceive a gradual but regular loss of weight. For physiologic and psychologic reasons, a mild rate of weight loss is preferred. The modification of eating behavior needs to persist throughout weight loss and weight maintenance to become an established part of a person's life style. The management of obesity demands a treatment that can be employed forever. Furthermore, this treatment requires that that person take personal responsibility for initiating and maintaining treatment.

A great deal of emphasis is now being placed in weight-loss research and treatment programs on self-efficacy, the belief that one can successfully perform a coping behavior. Mitchell and Stuart,[58] in a study of Weight Watchers members who dropped out of the program before reaching goal weight, found self-efficacy to be the single most important factor in predicting success. If self-efficacy is assumed to be a critical component of weight-loss success, it can be assumed that it is equally if not more important to long-term maintenance. While many successful clients attending Weight Watchers meetings believe in their ability to lose weight and control their urge to eat during weight loss, this belief does not necessarily extend into the weight-maintenance phase (Chapter 16). While clients may have been successful in losing weight, some may not have had a similar experience with regard to weight maintenance.

Maintenance of weight loss is the crucial issue in the treatment of obesity. However, research in the development of effective maintenance strategies is only just beginning.[59] While the Weight Watchers program has offered special maintenance strategies with booster sessions after initial treatment, weight maintenance now receives increased attention early in the treatment during the weight-loss phase.

Morton (Chapter 16) reminds us that researchers are just beginning to understand the nature of the relapse process for addictive disorders in general and obesity in particular. She reviews Marlatt's[60] relapse prevention model, the most fully defined maintenance strategy currently available.

Based on more than 15 years of experience in the development and evaluation of the Weight Watchers program, Morton (Chapter 16) has outlined a series of four substages, each with its special treatment consideration, in the total approach to maintenance: (1) decision to remain in treatment, (2) management of the adjustment process, (3) movement toward independence, and (4) acceptance of a lifelong commitment.

POSITIVE SUPPORT SYSTEM

The Weight Watchers program, offered in a supportive group setting, provides an effective and safe modality for the treatment of obesity. Special meetings for elderly adults have been highly successful. Interviews with members attending special meetings for the elderly revealed the two most valued attributes to be the social setting and the supportive nature of the sessions. B. Kimmel (written communication, Aug. 1986) found that the bonding that takes place among group members of all ages carries over into their home and community setting. The leader of the group, trained in dynamics of group leadership, serves as an important role model for all members of the group. As a person who has triumphed over a problem behavior, the leader builds on personal experiences exploring the expanding of eating awareness, food management, self-efficacy, moods and feelings, social situations, and attitude changes. Members can join and/or resign from group participation with relative ease. During discussions of problem behavior, the leader attempts to stimulate the maximum possible interaction among members. This interaction helps members explore and resolve their questions and concerns about pertinent issues. Their active involvement helps build their commitment to the recommended steps and gives them opportunities for self-expression in a group, experiences that many members have never had before.

The Weight Watchers program creates new behavior by teaching modification of dietary patterns, a self-management plan, with reinforcement principles.[26] Each step in the dietary behavior chain has been broken into assignments and techniques, starting with buying behavior. Because people eat the food they buy, members are taught how to prepare menu plans and how to prepare shopping guides from the menu plans. How to shop is the focus of one skill builder; eg, if the husband is an impulse buyer, it is suggested that he stay home and let the family member who is not the impulse buyer do the shopping.

Food behavior is examined step-by-step, from shopping in the supermarket, to getting the food home, to storing the food, and to preparing the food. Other skill builders, not food oriented, that create new behavior deal with psychodynamics of weight loss, self-assertiveness, development of new interests, and ways to increase physical activity.

1990 OBJECTIVES FOR OUR NATION

The expected outcome of efforts directed toward the reduction of overweight in the US population is to help meet the 1990 Objectives for our Nation:[61] By 1990, the prevalence of overweight (BMI of 27.8 or higher for men and 27.3 or higher for women) in the US adult population should be reduced without impairment of nutritional status to approximately 18% in men and 21% in women.

This will require that public health issues and educational efforts associated with overweight and obesity be addressed. The *specific objectives* to be realized include:

- By 1990, 90% of adults should understand that to lose weight they must either consume diets lower in calories or increase physical activity, or both.
- By 1990, 90% of adults with acceptable weights will maintain their desired weight by adopting a nutritionally adequate caloric intake balanced with physical activity.
- By 1990, 90% of overweight adults should have adopted an appropriate balance of caloric intake and physical activity to achieve and maintain desirable weight.

The treatment and prevention of obesity in the adult and elderly offer a way to address nutrition-related diseases wherein obesity is a risk factor. Wellness programs including these components will help meet the 1990 Objectives For Our Nation leading to improved life style practices that will enhance the quality of life in later years.

REFERENCES

1. Czaka-Narins DM, Mead J, Kohrs MB, et al: Use of weight attitude guidelines with the elderly. *Fed Proc* 1983; 42:554.

2. *Ten-State Nutrition Survey, 1968–70*, US Dept of Health, Education, and Welfare publication No. (HSM) 72-8130, 1972. Atlanta, Centers for Disease Control.

3. National Center for Health Statistics: *Plan and Operation of the National Health and Nutrition Examination Survey, 1976–80*, Vital and Health Statistics Series 1, No. 15. US Department of Health and Human Services publication No. (PHS) 81-1317. Government Printing Office, 1981.

4. Lazer W: Inside the mature market. *Amer Demographics* 1985; 7:23–25, 48–49.

5. National Center for Health Statistics: *Plan and Initial Program of the Health Examination Survey*, Vital and Health Statistics Series 1, No. 4. US Public Health Service publication No. (PHS) 1000. Government Printing Office.

6. *Preliminary Findings of the First Health and Nutrition Examination Survey, 1971–72*. US Department of Health, Education, and Welfare publication No. (HRA) 74-1219-1. Government Printing Office, 1973.

7. Hirsch J, Batchelor B: Adipose tissue cellularity in human obesity. *Clin Endocrinol Metab* 1976; 5:299–311.

8. Stock M, Rothwell N: *Obesity and Leanness*. London, John Libbey & Co Ltd, 1982.

9. Durnin JVGA, Womersley J: Body fat assessed from total body density and its estimation from skinfold thickness: Measurements on 481 men and women aged from 16 to 72 years. *Br J Nutr* 1974; 32:77–97.

10. Frisancho AR: New standards of weight and body composition by frame size and height for assessment of nutritional status of adults and the elderly. *Am J Clin Nutr* 1984; 40:808–819.

11. National Institutes of Health Consensus Development Conference: *Health Implications of Obesity*. Statement of the 1985 NIH Consensus Development Conference on Obesity Volume 5, No. 9, Bethesda, MD: US Department of Health and Human Services.

12. Andres R, Elahi D, Tobin JD, et al: Impact of age on weight goals. *Ann Intern Med* 1985; 103:1030–1033.

13. *Nutrition Monitoring in the United States: A Report from the Joint Nutrition Monitoring Evaluation Committee*, US Dept of Health and Human Services publication No. (PHS) 86-1255. Government Printing Office, 1986.

14. Simopoulos AP, Van Itallie TB: Body weight and longevity. *Ann Intern Med* 1984; 100:285–295.

15. Bjorntrop P: Fat cells and obesity, in Brownell KD, Foreyt JP (eds): *Handbook of Eating Disorders*. New York, Basic Books Inc Publishers, 1986, pp 88–98.

16. Lew EA, Garfinkel L: Variations in mortality by weight among 750,000 men and women. *J Chron Dis* 1979; 32:563–576.

17. Salans LB, Knittle JL, Hirsch J: Obesity, glucose intolerance and diabetes mellitus, in Ellenberg M, Rifkin H (eds): *Diabetes Mellitus: Theory and Practice*, ed 3. New Hyde Park, NY, Medical Examination Publishing Co, 1983, pp 201–210.

18. Kotchen JM, Kotchen TA: Obesity and hypertension, in Frankle RT (ed): *Dietary Treatment of Obesity*. New York, John Libbey & Co Ltd, 1985, pp 137–145.

19. Bray GA: Obesity: Definition, diagnosis and disadvantages, in Truswell AJ, Wahlqvist ML (eds): *International Symposia on Nutrition and Obesity: The State of the Science. Med J Australia* 1985; 142(suppl):2–7.

20. US Senate Select Committee on Nutrition and Human Needs: *Dietary Goals for the United States*, ed 2, publication No. 052-070-04376-8. Government Printing Office, 1977.

21. Bidlack WR, Kirsch A, Meskin MS: Nutritional requirements of the elderly. *J Food Tech* 1986; 40:61–70.

22. Guthrie H: Nutrition for the elderly, in Lipsitz, Chermoff (eds): *Nutrition Elderly Symposium II*. New York, Raven Press, to be published.

23. Food and Nutrition Board, National Research Council: *Recommended Dietary Allowances*, ed 9. Washington, National Academy of Sciences, 1980.

24. American College of Sports Medicine: Position statement on proper and improper weight loss programs. *Med Sci Sports Exerc* 1983; 15:ix.

25. Fisher MC, Lachance PA: Nutrition evaluation of published weight-reducing diets. *J Am Diet Assoc* 1985; 85:450–454.

26. Frankle RT: Obesity a family matter: Creating new behavior. *J Am Diet Assoc* 1985; 85:597–602.

27. *Nutrition and Your Health: Dietary Guidelines for Americans*, ed 2, US Dept of Agriculture, US Dept of Health and Human Services, Home and Gardens Bulletin No. 232. Government Printing Office, 1985.

28. Stalones PM, Johnson WG, Christ M: Behavior modification for obesity: The evaluation of exercise, contingency management and program adherence. *J Consult Clin Psychol* 1978; 45:463–469.

29. Gwinup G: Effect of exercise alone in the weight of obese women. *Arch Intern Med* 1975; 135:676–680.

30. Dahkoetter J, Callahan EJ, Linton J: Obesity and the unbalanced energy equation: Exercise vs eating habit changes. *J Consult Clin Psychol* 1979; 47:898–905.

31. Hagan RD: The effects of aerobic conditioning and/or caloric restriction in overweight men and women. *Med Sci Sports Exerc* 1986; 18:87–94.

32. Thompson JK, Jarvie GJ, Lahey BB, et al: Exercise and obesity: Etiology, physiology, and intervention. *Psych Bull* 1982; 91:55–79.

33. Epstein LH, Wing RR: Aerobic exercise and weight. *Addictive Behav* 1980; 5:371–388.

34. Woo R, Gannser JS, Pi-Sunyer FX: Effect of exercise on spontaneous calorie intake in obesity. *Am J Clin Nutr* 1982; 36:470–477.

35. Miller PM, Sims KL: Evaluation and component analysis of a comprehensive weight control program. *Int J Obes* 1981; 5:57–66.

36. Lampman RM, et al: Exercise as partial therapy for the extremely obese. *Med Sci Sports Exerc* 1986; 18:19–24.

37. Sullivan L, Krotkiewski M: The role of exercise in the treatment of obesity, in Frankle RT (ed): *Dietary Treatment and Prevention of Obesity*. London, John Libbey & Co Ltd, 1985, pp 47–57.

38. Stuart RB, Guire K: Some correlates to the maintenance of weight lost through behavior modification. *Int J Obes* 1979; 3:87–96.

39. Brownell KD, Stunkard AJ: Physical activity in the development and control of obesity, in Stunkard AJ (ed): *Obesity*. Philadelphia, WB Saunders Co, 1980, pp 300–324.

40. Brownell K, Marlatt GA, Lichtenstein E, et al: Understanding and preventing relapse. *Am Psychol* 1986; 41:765–778.

41. Parizkova J: Body composition and lipid metabolism in relation to nutrition and exercise, in Parizkova J, Rogozkin A (eds): *Nutrition, Physical Fitness and Health*. Baltimore, University Park Press, 1978, pp 61–75.

42. Zuti WB, Golding LA: Comparing diet and exercise as weight reduction tools. *Physician and Sports Medicine* 1976; 4:49–53.

43. American College of Sports Medicine: *Guidelines for Exercise Testing and Prescription*, ed 3. Philadelphia, Lea & Febiger, 1986.

44. Brownell KD: The psychology and physiology of obesity: Implications for screening and treatment. *J Am Diet Assoc* 1984; 4:406–414.

45. Foss ML, Lampman RM, Schteingart DE: Extremely obese patients: Improvements in exercise tolerance with physical training and weight loss. *Arch Phys Med Rehabil* 1980; 61:119–124.

46. de Vries HA: Physiological effects of an exercise training program regimen upon men, aged 52 to 88. *J Gerontol* 1970; 25:325–336.

47. Astrand I: Aerobic work capacity in men and women with special reference to age. *Acta Physiologic Scandinavia* 1960; (suppl) 169:49.

48. Stunkard AJ, McLaren-Hume M: The results of treatment of obesity: A review of the literature and a report of a series. *Arch Intern Med* 1959; 103:79–82.

49. Stuart RB: Behavioral control of overeating. *Behav Res Ther* 1967; 5:357–365.

50. Stuart RB: *Act Thin, Stay Thin*. New York, Jove Publications, 1983.

51. United States Senate Select Hearings on Obesity. (1977). *Part II Diets Related to Killer Diseases*. Stunkard, p 90. Government Printing Office, 1977, p 90.

52. Stunkard AJ, Berthold HC: What is behavior therapy? A very short description of behavioral weight control. *Am J Clin Nutr* 1985; 41:821–823.

53. Stunkard AJ, Mahoney MJ: Behavioral treatment of the eating disorders, in Leitenberg H (ed): *Handbook of Behavior Modification and Behavior Therapy*. Englewood Cliffs, NJ, Prentice-Hall Inc, 1976, pp 45–73.

54. Wilson GT, O'Leary KD: *Principles of Behavior Therapy*. Englewood Cliffs, NJ, Prentice Hall Inc, 1980.

55. Blundell JF: Behavior modification and exercise in the treatment of obesity. *J Postgrad Med* 1984; 60(suppl):37–49.

56. Blundell JF, Hill AV: Biopsychological interactions underlying the study and treatment of obesity, in Christie MJ, Melbett OG (eds): *The Psychosomatic Approach: Contemporary Practice of Whole-Person Case*. New York, John Wiley & Sons Ltd, 1986.

57. Craighead LS: A problem solving approach to the treatment of obesity, in Hersen M, Bellack AA (eds): *Handbook of Clinical Behavior Therapy with Adults*. New York, Plenum Press, 1985, pp 229–267.

58. Mitchell C, Stuart RB: Effect of self-efficacy on dropout from obesity treatment. *J Consult Clin Psychol* 1984; 52:1100–1101.

59. Holmes N, Ardito EA, Stevenson D, et al: Maintenance of weight loss in a heavily overweight population, in Storlie J, Jordan HA (eds): *Behavioral Management of Obesity*. New York, Spectrum Publications Inc, 1984, pp 137–150.

60. Marlatt GA: Relapse prevention: Theoretical rationale and overview of the model, in Marlatt GA, Gordon JR (eds): *Relapse Prevention*. New York, The Guilford Press, 1985, pp 3–67.

61. Fisher KD, Bennett RB: *A Report of the Scientific Community's Views on Progression Attaining the Public Health Objectives for Improved Nutrition in 1990*. Bethesda, Life Sciences Research Offices, Federation of Societies of Experimental Biology, 1986.

PART IV

Weight Control and Nutrition-Related Diseases

Chapter 20

Heart Disease: A Review

Mary Winston

INTRODUCTION

The relation of nutrition to coronary disease has been the subject of scientific research for many years. More than 30 years ago, epidemiologists identified a number of risk factors strongly associated with coronary heart disease (CHD). Elevated plasma cholesterol, hypertension, and smoking are the most clearly established; however, obesity, diabetes mellitus, physical inactivity, and behavior patterns are also risk factors. Five of these are diet-related. The risk factor most closely associated with CHD is elevated plasma lipids (especially cholesterol), a condition known as hyperlipidemia or hyperlipoproteinemia.

HYPERLIPIDEMIA AND HYPERLIPOPROTEINEMIA

Hyperlipidemia (HLD) is defined as an elevation of plasma lipids that includes cholesterol, cholesterol esters, phospholipids, and triglycerides. They are transported in plasma as a part of macromolecular complexes named "lipoproteins." The five major families of plasma lipoproteins are chylomicrons, very-low-density lipoproteins (VLDL), intermediate-density lipoproteins (IDL), low-density lipoproteins (LDL), and high-density lipoproteins (HDL). Chylomicrons are produced in the intestinal mucosa from dietary fat and contain mainly triglycerides. Chylomicrons enter the systemic circulation through the thoracic duct and pass into the peripheral circulation where they come in contact with lipoprotein lipase (LPL), an enzyme located on the surface of the vascular endothelium.

After most triglycerides have been degraded by lipolysis, chylomicron remnants are returned to the circulation; these remnants are cleared rapidly by the liver. In addition, the liver produces triglyceride-rich lipoproteins (VLDL). VLDL triglycerides also are hydrolyzed by LPL and catabolized to smaller lipoproteins called "VLDL remnants." These remnants are found in both VLDL and IDL fractions. They are metabolic byproducts of chylomicron and VLDL metabolism. In normal humans, approximately one half of the VLDL remnants are removed by the liver. The remainder are degraded further to LDL, the major cholesterol carrier of plasma. LDL is cleared from plasma mainly by specific LDL receptors located on the surface of many types of cells. The liver probably is the major site of LDL clearance, but peripheral tissues also have the capacity to remove and degrade this lipoprotein. LDL thus can deliver cholesterol to peripheral tissues. Another lipoprotein, HDL, may have an important role in reverse cholesterol transport, ie, in transport of cholesterol from peripheral tissues to the liver where it can be catabolized.

When HLD is defined in terms of class or classes of elevated plasma lipoproteins, the term "hyperlipoproteinemia" (HLP) is used. The simplest nomenclature for defining the type of lipoprotein(s) present in excess is the phenotyping system of Fredrickson et al,[1] shown in Table 20-1. This system is widely used, but offers no information about the origin of the different types of HLP.

Three categories of causation have been identified: (1) genetic: premature atherosclerosis may develop in a person who inherits too much LDL cholesterol or too little HDL; (2) secondary to other diseases: diabetes mellitus, hypothyroidism, nephrotic syndrome, and renal failure have been observed to be associated with HLP; (3) dietary: the major dietary factors causing an increase in plasma lipoproteins in many people are obesity and/or habitually high intakes of saturated fats and cholesterol. A practical classification of HLP is to divide the various disorders into those causing mainly either hypercholesterolemia or hypertriglyceridemia. Low levels of HDL cholesterol are associated with increased risk for atherosclerotic disease, even in the absence of HLP.

Increasing evidence suggests that the protein components of the lipoprotein, apolipoproteins, have a key role in lipoprotein metabolism and may be important

---

Table 20-1 Nomenclature for Lipoprotein Phenotypes

Phenotype	Plasma lipoprotein present in excess
1	Chylomicrons
2a	LDL
2b	LDL + VLDL
3	Beta-VLDL*
4	VLDL
5	Chylomicrons + VLDL

*Beta-VLDL represents cholesterol-rich VLDL remnants

Source: Reference 1.

in the development of atherosclerosis. For this reason it is important to provide a brief explanation of their functions. Apoproteins are responsible for the transport of lipids and have been classified into five main groups: A, B, C, D and E.

1. Apo A-I and A-II: These are soluble in plasma and are readily transferred from one HDL particle to another. They may have a major role in removing excess cholesterol from the surface of cells.

2. Apo B-48 and B-100: Apo B-48 is the major structural apoprotein of chylomicrons and is necessary for the transport of fat out of intestinal cells. Apo B-100 is the major structural apoprotein of VLDL and LDL. It seems to have a crucial role in LDL metabolism and is the recognition site on LDL for interaction with LDL receptors.

3. Apo C: Apo C-II activates the enzyme LPL, which is responsible for the hydrolyses of triglyceride in plasma. Apo C-III seems to retard the catabolism of triglyceride-rich particles.

4. Apo D: It is associated with HDL and seems to be important in the cholesterol ester transfer complex.

5. Apo E: This series of apoproteins is required for normal catabolism of chylomicrons and chylomicron remnants. It likely participates in the conversion of VLDL to LDL.[2]

Knowledge of the association of nutrition, lipids, and lipoproteins with the atherosclerotic process comes from four sources: (1) prolonged observations of human populations (epidemiologic studies), (2) a multitude of experimental studies (animal models), (3) clinical studies, and (4) cellular pathology.

A large body of data from epidemiologic surveys, prospective, retrospective, between countries, and within countries, confirm the relation between plasma lipids (especially cholesterol) and the incidence of CHD.[3] Elevated plasma cholesterol is a particularly strong indicator of risk in young adult men.[4] Since most of the plasma cholesterol is carried in LDL, elevations of LDL are correlated with risk. The cholesterol ester is a major feature of all atherosclerotic plaques, and it is almost impossible to produce atherosclerosis in animals without first producing hypercholesterolemia. When hypercholesterolemia is reduced, atherosclerotic lesions regress.[5,6]

The crucial question, whether or not induced lowering of cholesterol levels in humans with established hypercholesterolemia will reduce risk of CHD, can only be answered by clinical trials. Absence of this type of evidence is attributable, in large part, to the complexities and expense involved in conducting such studies. Large numbers of subjects, an adequately randomized control group, a long period of time, a sustained lowering of cholesterol, and careful patient monitoring are needed.

Data from several clinical trials suggest that lowering of cholesterol can delay onset of CHD. The Oslo Heart Trial,[7] reported in 1981, is perhaps the best dietary study. Patients in the dietary intervention group lowered their cholesterol levels and maintained them 14% below those of the control group over a 5-year period. There was a 47% reduction in the incidence of myocardial infarction (MI) in the intervention group. Interpretation of the study is difficult because smoking cessation occurred in 25% of the intervention group v 17% in the control group. Nevertheless, the investigators[7] estimated that 60% of the reduction in incidence of MI was attributable to the difference achieved in cholesterol lowering in the two groups.

However, conclusive evidence of this benefit of reducing elevated cholesterol came from the Lipid Research Clinics Primary Prevention Trial.[8,9] This was a study of asymptomatic subjects (3,806 men, aged 35 to 59 years) with cholesterol levels above the 95th percentile. Both groups were given a modest cholesterol-lowering diet, but one received an ion-exchange resin, while the other received a placebo. It was the first study to show an overall reduction in MI and mortality attributable to cardiovascular disease specifically related to reduction in plasma cholesterol. The study provided the needed level of statistical significance on the efficacy of cholesterol reduction. Through the method of analysis it was shown that it was not the dosage of medicine per se but the cholesterol reduction that correlated best with coronary disease risk reduction. In those subjects taking the full drug regimen regularly, a 25% reduction in cholesterol was associated with a nearly 50% reduction in heart attack and heart death. Thus for every 1% reduction in plasma cholesterol, a 2% reduction in risk for fatal or nonfatal heart attack was achieved. Taken together with the accumulated body of scientific evidence, the study provides strong rationale for attempting to lower plasma cholesterol and LDL cholesterol in patients with hypercholesterolemia.

RATIONALE FOR NUTRITIONAL INTERVENTION

Dietary modification is the cornerstone of treatment for people with HLD. Before considering dietary intervention for HLD, it is useful to consider the effects of specific nutritional factors on lipid metabolism.

Cholesterol

Cholesterol is the most abundant of the animal sterols and is the only one absorbed in appreciable amounts by the intestine. The major sources of cholesterol in the usual American diet include egg yolks, meats, and fat in dairy products.

Human plasma cholesterol is carried largely in LDL and, to a lesser extent, in HDL and VLDL. Plasma cholesterol is derived from the diet and body synthesis. The average American consumes 400 to 500 mg of cholesterol per day. This is additive to the amount synthesized by the body, approximately 500 to 1,000 mg/day. It is believed that, on average, humans absorb a little less than one half of the cholesterol when consumed at rates in excess of 1 g/day. This cholesterol is incorporated into chylomicrons by the intestine, and these are metabolized by LPL, which primarily removes the triglyceride component. The residual remnant lipoprotein still containing most of the absorbed cholesterol is cleared by the liver. Thus most of the dietary cholesterol is rather quickly delivered to the liver where several effects may be observed. This increased cholesterol uptake may exhibit new cholesterol synthesis, increase sterol excretion in the bile as bile acids or as cholesterol, increase excretion of cholesterol from the liver as newly synthesized lipoproteins, primarily VLDL, or suppress specific receptors for LDL uptake and degradation. The latter two effects would tend to increase plasma lipoprotein cholesterol levels. In many people, the suppression of cholesterol synthesis is not sufficient to compensate for increased dietary intake, and the result is usually an increase in plasma lipoprotein cholesterol.

The relative content of the saturated and unsaturated fats in the diet affects the impact of dietary cholesterol. It has been shown[10,11] that in normal people consuming a diet with a polyunsaturated-to-saturated fatty acid ratio (P/S) of 0.4 or greater, the increase in consumption of cholesterol from 300 to 1,500 mg/day had no measurable effect on the lipoprotein cholesterol levels.

Beta-sitosterol is a plant sterol found primarily in soybean oil and cacao butter. In normal people it is absorbed only slightly by the intestinal tract and largely passes out in the stool. In pharmacologic doses, beta-sitosterol has been shown to have an hypocholesterolemic effect because of interference with the absorption of cholesterol. In some people with a genetic abnormality, beta-sitosterol is absorbed in much greater amounts than is customary so that it and other plant sterols accumulate in the blood and tissues. Under most conditions, the intake of plant sterols is not a significant factor in determining the plasma cholesterol level.

Dietary Fat

The relation between the amount and kind of fat in the diet and the effect on plasma lipid concentrations is well documented. Fat may be divided into three major classes identified by saturation and unsaturation characteristics. The term "saturation" refers to the content of hydrogen atoms on the available carbon skeleton of the fatty acids. The fat is saturated when every carbon contains its full component of hydrogen. All animal fats are highly saturated except those in fish and shellfish, and they are primarily polyunsaturates. Saturated fatty acids are not essential nutrients and can be synthesized in the body from acetate.

The second class of dietary fats is monounsaturated fatty acids present in all animal and vegetable fats. The only significant dietary monounsaturated fatty acid is oleic (18-1-omega-9), having one double bond at the w-9 position. Olive oil contains principally oleic acid.

Polyunsaturated fatty acids are the third class. They are important constituents of cellular membranes and serve as a substrate for the formation of different prostaglandins. They contain more than one double bond, and the most common examples are the omega-6 (18:2 linoleic acid) and the omega-3 (18:3 linolenic acid) series of fatty acids. Linoleic acid cannot be synthesized by the body, can only be obtained from dietary sources, and is, therefore, an essential fatty acid. It is found in vegetable oils such as corn, cottonseed, safflower, sunflower, and soybean. Both linoleic (omega-6) and linolenic (omega-3) acids are synthesized in plants and found primarily in the seeds. Linolenic is the major fatty acid in linseed oil. It is found in soybean oil and green leafy vegetables, but not in fish oils.

Eicosapentaenoic acid (EPA) (C-20-5, omega-3) and docosahexaenoic acid (DHA) (C-22-6, omega-3) are derived primarily from the phytoplankton and appear in the food chain as fish or shellfish. In general, the higher the fat content of the seafood, the greater the input of omega-3 fatty acids it contains. The highest fat fish with more than 5% body fat include salmon, mackerel, herring, anchovies, sardines, shad, albacore tuna, and trout. Medium-fat fish contain between 2.5% and 5% fat and include bluefin tuna, rockfish, halibut, mullet, red snapper, and swordfish. Low-fat fish contain no more than 2.5% fat and include cod, croaker, flounder, haddock, monkfish, sea bass, pike, and whiting. Shellfish are low in fat but contain relatively more omega-3 than other low-fat fish.

Mammalian tissue can use linoleic or linolenic acids to synthesize the longer chain and more highly polyunsaturated w-6 or w-3 fatty acids. These are not interconvertible and seem to have different effects on fat metabolism.

Saturated fats tend to elevate LDL cholesterol, and its effect on increasing plasma cholesterol is approximately twice as great as the impact of polyunsaturated fat on reducing cholesterol. Saturated fats that give the greatest effect in increasing plasma cholesterol are lauric (C-12); myristic (C-14), and palmitic acids (C-16); stearic acid (C-18) is much less effective.

Polyunsaturated fatty acids, in general, lower plasma cholesterol and concentrations of LDL. In most studies comparing the effects of the polyunsaturated and saturated fats, varying P:S ratios from 0.1 to greater than 8 have been used. Little additional effect occurs in plasma cholesterol by raising the P:S ratio above 2. Such changes can reduce LDL cholesterol by 10% to 15% in normal people, and as much as 25% in those with HLP. The mechanisms of these actions are not fully understood. One of the most controversial findings is that a negative cholesterol balance is created by increasing the content of cholesterol and bile acids excreted in the feces.[12] Others[13] have suggested that this effect is only transient. Longer-term studies[14,15] have shown an increase in the clearance rates of LDL in normal people and a decrease in synthesis of LDL in subjects with elevated LDLs.

The potential harmful effects of ingesting large amounts of polyunsaturated fat must be considered. Evidence exists to show that with increased neutral sterol excretion the bile is more litogenic.[16] In an autopsy study[17] done at the conclusion of a long-term clinical trial, the incidence of gallstones was increased as compared with the control group.

There is a great deal of concern about the threat of enhanced carcinogenesis in people who consume diets high in polyunsaturated fat. However, careful analysis of studies using such diets over many years has failed to establish such a relation.[7,18] Nevertheless, this possibility must not be overlooked, perhaps in part because of the accumulation of peroxides.

Currently, there is great interest in fish oils that are high in eicosapentanoic acid (EPA) and docosahexaenoic acid (DHA) (omega-3 fatty acids). Some studies suggest they may offer additional benefit over and above reducing plasma cholesterol and LDL levels. Unlike omega-6 oils, omega-3 reduce very low density lipoproteins (VLDL) and triglyceride levels. In a few dietary studies that included fish oil as the major source of fat, LDL cholesterol in normal people declined and HDL cholesterol was unchanged. From the standpoint of cardiovascular disease, these would be beneficial changes in the LDL:HDL ratio.

It seems that substances in fish-oil fatty acids change the composition of platelet lipids and decrease thromboxane A_2, a prostaglandin that stimulates platelet aggregation and eventually blood clotting.[19] Prostaglandins are produced in most body tissues and seem to have many functions in both physiologic and pathologic processes. There are different types of prostaglandins produced depending on the substrate available (EPA or archidonic acid). The other prostaglandinlike compound that affects platelet reactivity is prostacyclin. It, however, is a potent antiaggregator. Omega-3 fatty acids tend to inhibit the production of thromboxane A_2 more than they inhibit prostacyclin activity and are, therefore, considered to be antiaggregatory. However, in one study,[20] prolonged bleeding times were reported in one person, and a significant drop in platelets (without bleeding abnormalities) was observed in others.[20] Further research is needed to define better the fundamental biologic mechanisms that might involve fish oil and disease prevention.

Recent work[21,22] has suggested that monounsaturated fats may be as effective as those containing omega-6 fatty acids in reducing LDL without lowering HDL cholesterol levels. If these studies are confirmed, emphasizing replacement of saturated fats by monounsaturated fats may offer some advantage over the use of polyunsaturated fats.

Protein

The dietary treatment of HLD involves an increase in vegetable protein to compensate for the reduction in animal protein needed to achieve the recommended reduction in saturated fat and cholesterol. A nutritionally adequate diet including a well-balanced supply of essential amino acids can easily be provided by appropriate mixtures of vegetable proteins, together with an ample intake of low-fat dairy products. These are excellent sources of protein with little or no fat that also contribute to the daily requirement for calcium.

Carbohydrate

The reduction of calories from fat in the diet automatically indicates a need to increase calories from carbohydrate. Emphasis is placed on increasing complex carbohydrates from grains, cereals, vegetables, and fruit while reducing sucrose intake. Confusion exists regarding this recommendation because substitution of carbohydrate for fat causes a significant but transient rise in fasting triglyceride in VLDL concentrations. Long-term studies show that the elevation becomes apparent within a few days, reaching a maximum in 3 to 5 weeks. The plasma triglyceride and VLDL levels return to their initial value by 32 weeks.

The effects of different types of dietary carbohydrate on plasma lipids are uncertain. Earlier studies[23] reported that sucrose had a hyperlipidemic effect compared with glucose and starch. Subsequent investigations[24] have not always confirmed this. Nevertheless, it is appropriate to recommend a decrease in sucrose. Sucrose contributes to dental caries, is a source of unneeded calories that could contribute to obesity, and does not carry other nutrients such as vitamins, minerals, and protein as do other carbohydrate-containing foods such as fruit, vegetables, cereals, and grains.

Fiber

Dietary fiber, pectin, lignin, cellulose, and hemicellulose, found in complex carbohydrates are undigestible by the human gut. Fiber studies more than 20 years ago indicated their effect of lowering plasma lipid levels greater than might be expected from reductions in dietary fat and cholesterol. More recent studies[25] involving only water-soluble fibers have indicated the same. Examples of water-soluble fibers are oat bran, cooked pinto beans, white beans, and kidney beans.

Other examples are pectin found in nuts and the peel of apples and pears, and guar gum in seeds of the Indian legume, locust bean, and carob. However, the amounts of the latter required are unlikely to be consumed naturally. Overall it seems that the lowering of plasma cholesterol levels by fiber is a weak effect and has not been well separated from the obligatory changes in fat and digestible carbohydrate that accompany such diets. There are many benefits attributed to increased fiber intake including reduction in diverticulitis, hemorrhoids, appendicitis, and varicose veins. An increase in the consumption of fiber adds bulk to the diet, increases the sense of satiety, and obligates the addition of complex carbohydrates along with a lower consumption of fat and cholesterol.

Calories

Excessive caloric consumption resulting in obesity promotes HLD in some subjects, especially hypertriglyceridemia. Obesity is associated with an increase in total body synthesis of cholesterol,[26] elevated levels of VLDL and LDL, and a reduction in HDL.[27,28]

Weight loss decreases production rates of VLDL and thus lowers triglycerides. HDL levels should also rise. The effects on LDL are variable: weight reduction may cause an increase in LDL levels with familial-combined HLD. The reason for this is unkown. Body cholesterol pools take many months to equilibrate, and these changes in LDL metabolism may resolve with time.

Alcohol

Alcohol is used in the liver as a fuel-replacing fat. As a result, fat accumulates in liver cells and increased lipoproteins and ketone bodies are released into the bloodstream. The lipids are introduced into the circulation as triglyceride-rich VLDL. In subjects with hypertriglyceridemia the consumption of alcohol even in moderate amounts may exacerbate VLDL levels. A moderate consumption of alcohol may also raise HDL levels in some people.

The increased level of HDL cholesterol associated with alcohol consumption is not clearly associated with a reduced risk for vascular disease. Alcohol provides extra calories to the diet; is associated with traumatic death, liver disease, certain forms of cancer; and, in some persons, has serious social and physical consequences.

DIETARY TREATMENT OF HYPERCHOLESTEROLEMIA

For patients with hypercholesterolemia, the recommended diet is a progressive decrease in the intake of total fat, saturated fatty acids, and cholesterol (See

Table 20-2). The first phase of the treatment is a diet in which 30% to 32% of the calories are from fat, 45% to 50% are from carbohydrate (principally complex carbohydrates), and 20% are from protein. The fat should contain approximately equal amounts of saturated, monounsaturated, and polyunsaturated fatty acids. Each should contribute approximately 10% of total calories. Cholesterol should be below 300 mg/day. The objective is to gradually reduce intake of cholesterol to 100 mg/day and fat to 20% to 25% of total calories. This progressive reduction can occur in three phases, the first as described above. Phase 2 consists of approximately 25% of calories as fat (with equal amounts of the three types of fatty acids), 50% to 55% as carbohydrate, and 20% as protein, with 160 to 200 mg of cholesterol per day. Phase 3 consists of 20% of calories as fat (with equal amounts of the three types of fatty acids), 55% to 60% as carbohydrate, and 15% as protein, and 100 to 110 mg of cholesterol per day. Another principle of this diet is to achieve a desirable weight.

The degree to which intakes of saturated fatty acids and cholesterol are restricted will depend on the severity of the hypercholesterolemia, the willingness of the patient to adhere to the diet, and the response of each patient to each dietary phase. Not every person will need or be willing to proceed to phase 3. The importance of having a nutritious, appetizing, and overall balanced diet is emphasized.

The coexistence of other medical conditions must be considered when prescribing a diet for the individual patient. For example, people with renal failure or hepatic insufficiency may need to restrict protein intake. A decreased sodium intake may benefit the patient with hypertension. This diet is consistent with that of the American Diabetes Association for diabetic patients. For the non-insulin-dependent obese patient with diabetes, the importance of weight reduction must be emphasized.

There is uncertainty about the role of hypertriglyceridemia in causation of atherosclerosis. Available data suggest that some forms of hypertriglyceridemia are associated with more risk for CHD than others. People with high-normal

Table 20-2 Dietary Goals for Phases 1, 2, and 3

Phase	1	2	3
Fat	30%–32%	28%	20%–22%
Carbohydrate	45%–50%	50%–55%	55%–60%
Protein	20%	20%	20%
Cholesterol, mg	300	200	100
P/S*	1	1	1–2

*the ratio polyunsaturated fat to saturated fat

Source: American Heart Association, Dallas, Texas, 1986.

levels of triglycerides tend to have higher LDL levels than those with low-normal triglycerides; these higher concentrations of LDL should increase risk. In addition, elevated levels of triglycerides often are associated with lower concentrations of HDL, the latter another sign of increased risk. Thus, even if high-normal or slightly elevated triglycerides per se are not atherogenic, they may be a marker for factors contributing to atherosclerosis. These factors may be related to diet, and it may be possible to eliminate them by removing the offending nutrients from the diet. High intakes of saturated fats raise both VLDL and LDL. In overweight people, high intakes of total calories raise VLDL, enhance production of LDL, and lower HDL. Diets rich in carbohydrates increase triglycerides in some patients, a transitory effect since carbohydrates do not raise LDL. The actions of alcohol resemble those of carbohydrates; alcohol generally does not increase LDL and causes a paradoxical rise in HDL. Thus, the concern is mainly with saturated fats and obesity; attention to these factors takes priority.

The dietary recommendations for the patient with hypertriglyceridemia are the same as for the patient with hypercholesterolemia. Treatment should be initiated with phase 1 as described above. The basic goal of therapy is to reduce the overproduction of VLDL.

Primary hypertriglyceridemia often is compounded by obesity. When this occurs, weight reduction must be the first priority. Weight loss decreases production rates of VLDL and thereby lowers triglycerides. HDL levels should also rise. A second goal in dietary therapy of elevated triglycerides is to decrease intakes of saturated fatty acids. These fatty acids intensify lipoprotein overproduction, and they tend to raise LDL levels by interfering with LDL clearance. Dietary cholesterol should also be curtailed in patients with hypertriglyceridemia. A high-cholesterol diet raises the cholesterol content of VLDL and increases LDL levels. People with primary hypertriglyceridemia are often very sensitive to moderate amounts of alcohol. It may be necessary to eliminate it from the diets of some patients.

In some cases of hypercholesterolemia or hypertriglyceridemia, patients remain significantly hyperlipidemic despite maximal dietary modification. The decision to institute drug therapy must be made after evaluating the potential benefits *v* the risk of side effects.

Finally, the reasons for the linkage between low HDL cholesterol and CHD are unknown. Causes of decreased HDL cholesterol include poorly defined genetic factors, obesity, tobacco use, lack of exercise, hyperlipidemia (especially hypertriglyceridemia), certain drugs, and, occasionally, cholesterol-lowering diets. Whether reduction of HDL cholesterol by cholesterol-lowering diets enhances risk for CHD is unknown. It may be that a low HDL cholesterol is a significant risk factor for CHD only in populations in whom LDL levels are relatively high.

Several factors have been reported to increase HDL cholesterol including (1) weight reduction in obese subjects, (2) correction of hypertriglyceridemia,

(3) frequent, vigorous exercise, (4) cessation of smoking, (5) a moderate use of alcohol, and (6) use of estrogens. Alcohol, however, provides extra calories to the diet, may increase triglycerides, and, in some people, has serious social and physical consequences.

Final accomplishment of modifications in the fat and cholesterol content of the diet is signaled by the adoption of a "diet for life." If success is to be attained, changes must be made slowly. The enjoyment of a wide variety of foods whose flavors are enhanced by the skillful use of herbs and seasoning and low-fat cookery gradually becomes an everyday occurrence. The market abounds with several cookbooks featuring recipes for delicious low-fat foods. A few of these are listed in Appendix 20-A.

HYPERTENSION AND OBESITY

Many nutritional factors are associated with hypertension, another well-established CHD risk factor. There is little disagreement among scientists about the relation of body weight with arterial pressure in both hypertensive and normotensive populations. The mechanisms to explain the pathogenesis and pathophysiology of hypertension and obesity are poorly understood. Several suggestions have been made: (1) expanded blood volume; (2) elevated cardiac output associated with volume expansion; (3) associated increased sodium intake and increased vascular response to sodium; and (4) increased adrenergic participation in obesity-related hypertension. More recent evidence suggests that distribution of body fat has an independent contribution.[29]

Despite the unanswered questions and lack of explanation as to why pressure does not rise in all obese people, or why it is not reduced in all obese hypertensive people, there are many benefits to be gained from weight reduction. Cardiovascular morbidity and mortality will be reduced. For people receiving pharmacologic therapy for hypertension, the dosage may be reduced.

Sodium

Sodium is one of the major factors involved in hypertension. Although absolute proof of a cause-and-effect relation between sodium intake and elevated blood pressure is lacking, evidence of an association has accumulated from epidemiologic studies, animal experiments, and clinical trials.[30–32] Current scientific information supports a major role for sodium in the control of blood pressure and the development of hypertension. In people with established hypertension, restriction of dietary sodium can be an important part of treatment. It can minimize the need for drugs, such as diuretics, and thus reduce potassium loss. The applicability of a moderate sodium reduction in the general population is not accepted by everyone. However, many scientists[3] believe that lowering sodium intake has blood pressure-lowering effects in a wide range of the blood pressure distribution. Thus a more general preventive benefit might accrue affecting the majority of people.

Potassium

Epidemiologic evidence suggests that a possible explanation for the low blood pressure found in some unacculturated societies with low dietary sodium intake is their relatively high potassium intake. A recent review[33] of the role of dietary potassium in the treatment of hypertension lends support to the association. However, in the final analysis the available evidence is not convincing.

Calcium, Magnesium, and Trace Elements

The possible role of calcium in the prevention and treatment of hypertension has been the subject of intense research interest in recent years. This is not surprising when one considers calcium's involvement in cellular and molecular processes that produce muscle constriction in both hormonal and neurogenic interactions. Conflicting evidence exists from epidemiologic, experimental, and clinical studies, none of which implies cause and effect.[34–36]

The role of magnesium as a regulator of blood pressure has been the object of a few epidemiologic, clinical, and experimental studies. However, based on such limited evidence, it is premature to make recommendations about increased use of dietary sources of magnesium.

Little is known about the relation of trace minerals to hypertension. Fragmentary evidence exists relative to the role of cadmium, lead, selenium, copper, mercury, and zinc in the regulation of blood pressure and in the pathogenesis of hypertension.

Vegetarian Diet, Fat, Fiber, Protein, and Carbohydrates

Evidence[37] exists to suggest that a vegetarian diet may exert a lowering effect on blood pressure. A few studies[38] suggest it may exert a greater effect on systolic than on diastolic blood pressure. The blood pressure–lowering effect may be attributable to leanness of long-standing vegetarians, but there also seems to be a direct effect unrelated to body weight on sodium intake. Vegetarians tend to eat more polyunsaturated fat, dietary fiber, vegetable protein, potassium, and magnesium than do omnivores. They consume less total fat, saturated fat, cholesterol, and vitamin B_{12} than do omnivores and similar quantities of sodium, protein, and energy.

Some studies have shown that a low-fat diet, 25% of the calories from fat, seems to promote a lowering in blood pressure. Diet supplemented with fish oil and others in which a highly polyunsaturated fat was fed likewise seemed to promote a reduction in blood pressure.[39] In the final analysis, the role of unsaturated fat in reducing blood pressure has not been established.

Limited studies[40–41] have been done on the effects of dietary fiber on blood pressure. The results have been conflicting, some showing a lowering of blood pressure, others showing no effect.

The effect of protein feeding on blood pressure has not been studied in humans.

Some evidence[42] exists to show that sucrose increases blood pressure and glucose increases systolic pressure.

Other dietary nutrients have been examined in relation to blood pressure. These include total complex carbohydrate, combined fat and complex carbohydrate, frequency of fatty food consumption, proportion of linoleic fatty acid to fat, and frequency of consumption of sugar-containing food and dietary cholesterol. It was concluded that body mass index and regional fat distribution were the factors most strongly and consistently related to blood pressure.[43]

Alcohol

The evidence[44] for a direct pressor effect of ethanol continues to grow. When ingested chronically, moderate amounts of ethanol (45 to 70 g/day) will raise the blood pressure in normotensive and hypertensive people. Some data[45–46] show lower rates of coronary mortality among those who usually consume some ethanol each day.

Caffeine

Caffeine ingestion seems neither to keep blood pressure high nor to be associated with more hypertension.[47] It does, however, cause it to rise by 5 to 15 mmHg within 15 minutes after consumption of 150 mg of caffeine. The short-term effects are primarily mediated by an increase in cardiac output.

SUMMARY

In summary, available evidence indicates that recommendations for nutritonal intervention relative to control of hypertension must be restricted to weight control, alcohol restriction, and sodium restriction. Each of these modalities may independently control blood pressure, but may be effective in reducing the dosage of prescribed pharmacologic agents should their use be warranted.

REFERENCES

1. Fredrickson DS, Levy RI, Lees RS: Fat transport in lipoproteins: An integrated approach to mechanisms and disorders. *N Engl J Med* 1967; 276:32–44, 94–103, 148–156, 215–226, 273–281.

2. Grundy SM: Atherosclerosis: Pathology, pathogenesis and role of risk factors. *Disease-a-Month*, June 1983; pp 3–58.

3. Optimal resources for primary prevention of atherosclerotic diseases: Report of the Inter-Society Commission for Heart Disease Resources. *Circulation*, 1984; 70:157A–205A.

4. Wilson PW, Garrison RJ, Castelli WP, et al: Prevalence of coronary heart disease in Framingham Offspring Study: Study of lipoprotein cholesterols. *Am J Cardiol* 1980; 46:649–654.

5. Wissler RW: Principles of the pathogenics of atherosclerosis, in Braumwald E (ed): *Heart Disease: A Textbook of Cardiovascular Medicine*, ed 2. Philadelphia, WB Saunders Co, 1984, pp 1183–1204.

6. St Clair RW: Atherosclerosis regression in animal models: Current concepts of cellular and biochemical mechanisms. *Prog Cardiovasc Dis* 1983; 26:109–132.

7. Hjermann I, Velve BK, Holme I, et al: Effect of diet and smoking intervention on the incidence of coronary heart disease. *Lancet* 1981; 2:1303–1310.

8. The Lipid Research Clinics Coronary Primary Prevention Trial results: I. Reduction in incidence of coronary heart disease. *JAMA* 1984; 251:351–363.

9. The Lipid Research Clinics Coronary Primary Prevention Trial results: II. The relationship of reduction in incidence of coronary heart disease to cholesterol lowering. *JAMA* 1984; 251:365–374.

10. Ginsberg H, Lu NA, Mays C, et al: Lipoprotein metabolism in nonresponders to increased dietary cholesterol. *Arteriosclerosis* 1981; 1:463–470.

11. Schonfeld G, Wetztum J, Basich P: Effects of dietary cholesterol and fatty acids on plasma lipoproteins. *J Clin Invest* 1982; 69:1072–1080.

12. Grundy SM, Ahrens EH: The effects of unsaturated dietary fats on absorption, excretion, synthesis and distribution of cholesterol in man. *J Clin Invest* 1970; 47:1135–1152.

13. Nestel AJ, Havenstein H, Scott TU, et al: Polyunsaturated ruminant fats and cholesterol metabolism in man. *Aust NZJ Med* 1974; 4:497–501.

14. Shepherd J, Packard CJ, Grundy SM, et al: Effects of saturated and polyunsaturated fat diets on the chemical composition and metabolism of low density lipoproteins in man. *J Lipid Res* 1980; 21:91–99.

15. Turner JD, Lu NA, Brown WV: Effect of changing dietary fat saturation on low density lipoprotein metabolism in man. *Am J Physiol* 1981; 24:E57–E63.

16. Grundy SM: Effects of polyunsaturated fats on lipid metabolism in patients with hypertriglyceridemia. *J Clin Invest* 1975; 55:269–282.

17. Studevant RAJ, Pearce MI, Dayton S: Increased prevalence of cholelithiases in man ingesting a serum cholesterol lowering diet. *N Engl J Med* 1983; 288:24–27.

18. Levy RI: Consideration of cholesterol and noncardiovascular mortality. *Am Heart J* 1982; 104:325–328.

19. Goodnight SH, Harris WS, Connor WE: The effects of dietary omega-3 fatty acids on platelet composition and function in man: A prospective controlled study. *Blood* 1981; 58:880–885.

20. Goodnight SH, Harris WS, Connor WE, et al: Polyunsaturated fatty acids, hyperlipidemia and thrombosis. *Arteriosclerosis* 1982; 2:87–113.

21. Mattson FM, Grundy SM: Effects of monounsaturated fatty acids in lipoprotein levels in man. *Circulation* 1983; 68:111–187.

22. Grundy SM: Comparison of monounsaturated fatty acids and carbohydrates for lowering plasma cholesterol. *N Engl J Med* 1986; 314:745–748.

23. Little JA, McGuire V, Derken A: Available carbohydrates, in Levy RI, Rifkind BM, Dennis BH, Ernst N (eds): *Nutrition, Lipids, and Coronary Heart Disease*, vol. 1. New York, Raven Press, 1979, p 119.

24. Antonis A, Bershon I: The influence of diet on serum triglycerides in South African white and Bantu Prisoners. *Lancet* 1961; 1:3.

25. Anderson J, Story L, Sieling B, et al: Hypocholesterolemic effect of oat bran or bean intake for hypercholesterolemic men. *Am J Clin Nutr* 1984; 40:1146–1155.

26. Bennion LJ, Grundy SM: Effects of obesity and caloric intake on biliary lipid metabolism in man. *J Clin Invest* 1975; 56:996–1011.

27. Carlson LA, Ericasson M: Quantitative and qualitative serum lipoprotein analysis: I. Studies in healthy men and women. *Atherosclerosis* 1975; 21:417–433.

28. Garrison RJ, Wilson PW, Castelli WB, et al: Obesity and lipoprotein cholesterol in the Framingham Offspring Study. *Metabolism* 1980; 29:1053–1060.

29. Weinsier RL, Norris DJ, Birch R, et al: The relative contribution of body fat and fat pattern to blood pressure levels. *Hypertension* 1985; 7:578–585.

30. Page LB, Danion A, Moellering RC Jr: Antecedents of cardiovascular disease in six Solomon Islands societies. *Circulation* 1974; 49:1132–1146.

31. Oliver AJ, Cohen EL, Neel JV: Blood pressure, sodium intake and sodium related hormones in the Yanomamo Indians, a 'no-salt' culture. *Circulation* 1975; 52:146–151.

32. Limas C, Wesatrum B, Cohn JN: Effect of salt on the vascular lesions of spontaneously hypertensive rats. *Hypertension* 1980; 2:477–489.

33. Treasure J, Ploth D: Role of dietary potassium in the treatment of hypertension. *Hypertension* 1983; 5:864–872.

34. Garcio-Palmieri M, Costos R Jr, Cruz-Vidal M, et al: Milk consumption, calcium intake, and decreased hypertension in Puerto Rico. *Hypertension* 1984; 6:322–328.

35. McCarron D: Is calcium more important than sodium in the pathogenesis of essential hypertension. *Hypertension* 1985; 7:607–627.

36. MacGregor G: Sodium is more important than calcium in essential hypertension. *Hypertension* 1985; 7:628–640.

37. Rouse IL, Beilin LJ, Armstrong BK, Vandongen R: Blood pressure lowering effect of a vegetarian diet: Controlled trial in normotensive subjects. *Lancet* 1983; 1:5–9.

38. Sacks FM, Donner A, Castelli WP, et al: Effect of ingestion of meat on plasma cholesterol of vegetarians. *JAMA* 1981; 246:640–644.

39. Mortensen JZ, Schmidt EB, Neilson AH, Dyerbert J: The effect of 0-6 and 0-3 polyunsaturated fatty acids on hemostasis, blood lipids and blood pressure. *Thromb Haemost* 1983; 50:543–546.

40. Dodson PM, Beevers M, Fletcher RF, Pacy PJ, Bal P, Taylor KG: The effects of high fiber, low fat and low sodium dietary regimen on diabetic hypertensive patients of different ethnic groups. *Postgrad Med* 1983; 59:641–644.

41. Kelsay JL, Behall KM, Prather ES: Effect of fiber from fruits and vegetables on metabolic responses of human subjects: I. Bowel transient time, number of defecations, fecal weight, urinary excretions of energy and nitrogen and apparent digestabilities of energy, nitrogen and fat. *Am J Clin Nutr* 1978; 31:1149–1153.

42. McIntyre ML, Halden JM, Ahrens RA: Blood pressure changes caused by supplementing the diets of young adult volunteers with different amounts of sucrose (abstract). *Fed Proc* 1975; 34:911.

43. Final Report of the Subcommittee on Nonpharmacological Therapy of the 1984 Joint National Committee on Detection, Evaluation, and Treatment of High Blood Pressure. *Hypertension* 1986; 8:444–467.

44. Hennekens CH: Alcohol, in Kaplan NM, Stambler J (eds): *Prevention of Coronary Heart Disease*. Philadelphia, WB Saunders, 1983, pp 130–138.

45. Marmat MG: Alcohol and coronary heart disease. *Int J Epidemiol* 1984; 13:160–167.

46. Gordon T, Kannel WB: Drinking and mortality: The Framingham study. *Am J Epidemiol* 1984; 120:97–107.

47. Robertson D, Hollister AS, Kincaid D, et al: Caffeine and hypertension. *Am J Med* 1984; 77:54–60.

Appendix 20-A

Additional Resources

REFERENCES

1. Havel RJ (ed): *The Medical Clinics of North America*. Philadelphia, WB Saunders Co, 1982.

2. Recommendations for treatment of hyperlipidemia in adults: A joint statement of the Nutrition Committee and the Council on Arteriosclerosis, American Heart Association. *Circulation* 1984; 69:1065A–1090A.

3. Martin DW, Mayer VW, Radwell VW, et al: *Harper's Review of Biochemistry*, ed 20. Los Altos, Calif, Large Med. Pub., 1985.

4. Stanbury JB, Wyngaarden JB, Fredrickson DS, et al: *The Metabolic Basis of Inherited Disease*, ed 5. New York, McGraw-Hill Book Co, 1983.

SUGGESTED READINGS

1. Arntzenius AC, Kromhout D, Barth JD, et al: Diet, lipoproteins, and the progression of coronary atherosclerosis. *New Engl J Med* 1985; 312:805–811.

2. Bilheimer DW: Lipoprotein fractions and receptors: A role for Probucol? *Am J Cardiol* 1986; 57(Suppl):7H–15H.

3. Brown MS, Goldstein JL: A receptor mediated pathway for cholesterol hemostasis. *Science* 1986; 232:34–47.

4. Brunzell JD, Sniderman JD, Albers JJ, et al: Apoproteins band A-1 and coronary artery disease in humans. *Arteriosclerosis* 1984; 4:79–83.

5. Davidson MH, Liebson PR: Marine lipids and atherosclerosis: A review. *Cardiovasc Rev Rep* 1986; 7:461–472.

6. Kushi LH, Lew AA, Stare FJ, et al: Diet and 20-year mortality from coronary heart disease. *New Engl J Med* 1985; 312:811–818.

7. Optimal resources for primary prevention of atherosclerotic diseases: Report of Inter-Society Commission for Heart Disease Resources. *Circulation* 1984; 70:155A–205A.

8. Schaefer EJ, Levy RI: Pathogenesis and management of lipoprotein disorders. *New Engl J Med* 1985; 312:1300–1310.

9. Rudel LL, Parks JS, Johnson FL, et al: Low density lipoproteins in atherosclerosis. *J Lipid Res* 1986; 27:465–472.

10. WHO European Collaborative Group: European collaborative trial of multifactorial prevention of coronary heart disease: Final report on the 6-year results. *Lancet* 1986; 1:869–875.

COOKBOOKS

1. DeBakey ME, Gotto AM, Scott LW, et al: *The Living Heart Diet*. New York, Raven Press, 1984.

2. Eschleman R, Winston M (eds): *The American Heart Association Cookbook*, ed 4. New York, David McKay, 1984.

3. Roth H: *Deliciously Low*. New York, New American Library, 1983.

PATIENT AND NUTRITION COUNSELOR AIDS

1. *Eating for a Healthy Heart: Dietary Treatment of Hyperlipidemia*. American Heart Association, 1984 (patient manual).

Chapter 21

Obesity: A Predictor for Coronary Heart Disease[*]

Helen Hubert

Coronary heart disease (CHD) is caused by a complex interaction of genetic and life style factors that begin to exert their effects many years before disease diagnosis. Numerous epidemiologic studies in middle-aged populations have shown the importance of attributes such as elevated blood pressure, elevated blood lipids, and cigarette smoking in the etiology of this disease, and, as a result, intervention in high-risk people has been focused on reduction of risk factors with pharmacologic treatment, modified-fat diets, and programs for behavior modification. While such approaches to risk reduction are important and can decrease mortality, it is also clear that optimal preventive strategies will require modification of early markers for the development of CHD and its risk factors. The accumulated evidence strongly suggests that overweight or obesity is such a precursor to disease development and that prevention of CHD can be greatly promoted by the control of this attribute in overfed and sedentary populations such as those in North America. Some of the general reluctance to intervene directly in obesity in the clinical setting may be attributable to the confusion that exists concerning its relative importance in disease causation, not knowing how much weight is too much, and the lack of success often encountered in achieving long-term weight reduction.

However, it is known that within the general population, crude measures of obesity, such as increased weight relative to some standard or increased body weight for height, are linked to elevated blood pressure, blood lipids, and blood glucose,[1-5] and more importantly that dynamic relations exist in which changes in body weight over time are coincident with changes in these risk factors for disease.[6-10] Analysis of data from the Framingham Study[6] indicates that there are linear relations between change in relative weight in a middle-aged cohort

---

*Adapted with permission from *Annual Review of Public Health* (1986;7:493–502), Copyright © 1986 by Annual Review Inc.

and change in total serum cholesterol, systolic blood pressure, and blood glucose over 2-year intervals. In this population, weight gain had a detrimental effect on the risk factors in both men and women. For example, a 10% increase in relative weight, defined as a person's weight compared with the median for the person's sex-height group, was associated with increases in total cholesterol of 11.3 mg/dL in men and 6.3 mg/dL in women. The effect of the same weight gain on systolic blood pressure was 6.6 mmHg and 4.5 mmHg in men and women, respectively. These data further suggest that each 10% reduction in weight in men would result in a 20% reduction in coronary disease incidence, and each 10% increase in weight, a 30% increase in incidence. The effects of weight change on disease incidence would be similar, but less pronounced, in women.

While none of the large-scale clinical trials designed to measure the effects of risk factor reduction in middle-aged, high-risk populations in the United States included weight reduction as a specific treatment modality, there has been some attempt to look at the effects of weight change with respect to risk-factor change in these study cohorts.[11-14]

In the Hypertension Detection and Follow-up Program,[11] weight change over 2 years was related to the percentage of change in both systolic and diastolic blood pressure (Figure 21-1). The effects of weight change were evident in both the control group (referred care) and the experimental group (stepped care) who received intensive antihypertensive treatment. It is important to recognize that even with pharmacologic treatment, weight loss can have a significant impact on blood pressure reduction. Other data[15] from this study showed that weight reduction can improve the success of withdrawal of drug therapy in controlled hypertensive patients.

Results in the special intervention group of the Multiple Risk Factor Intervention Trial (MRFIT)[12] showed the detrimental effects of weight gain and the beneficial effects of weight loss on blood lipids and lipoproteins (Figure 21-2). The observed declines in triglycerides and total and low-density lipoprotein (LDL) cholesterol and increases in high-density lipoprotein (HDL) cholesterol with only moderate weight losses are impressive. Moreover, the effects of weight reduction on lipids were reported to be independent of the dietary and other interventions attempted in this study.

In the Lipid Research Clinics Primary Prevention Trial,[13,14] decreases in LDL cholesterol, influenced by weight reduction, were associated with reduced CHD incidence in both treatment and nontreatment groups, suggesting that weight loss may be an effective intervention strategy with or without drug therapy.

Most of the preceding discussion has centered on the effects of weight change in middle-aged populations. However, the development of optimal preventive strategies for CHD requires an understanding of the causes and implications of weight gain and loss in younger cohorts. While it seems that most of adult weight

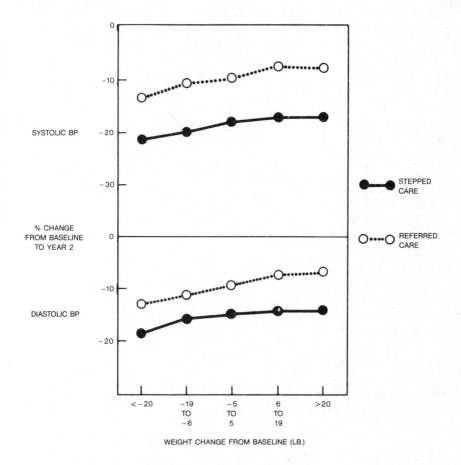

SYSTOLIC BP

% CHANGE
FROM BASELINE
TO YEAR 2

DIASTOLIC BP

STEPPED
CARE

REFERRED
CARE

WEIGHT CHANGE FROM BASELINE (LB.)

FD97 Bob5-15
Dress 1 & 2, Hel, Math

Figure 21-1 Percentage change in blood pressure (BP) and weight change from baseline to year 2 among Hypertension Detection and Follow-up Study participants. *Source:* Reprinted with permission from "The Relationship of Weight Change to Changes in Blood Pressure, Serum Uric Acid, Cholesterol and Glucose in the Treatment of Hypertension" by S Heyden et al, *Journal of Chronic Diseases* (1985; 38:284), Copyright © 1985, Pergamon Press Ltd.

gain occurs between the ages of 20 and 40 years, there is limited data during this age span to describe its effects either in the short- or long-term.

Figures 21-3 and 21-4 show the effects of weight change over 8 years in men and women aged 20 to 29 years who participated in the Framingham Offspring Study.[9] It is notable that more than 25% of this healthy, young-adult group gained 5 k or more, or more than 11 lb, during the 8-year observation period.

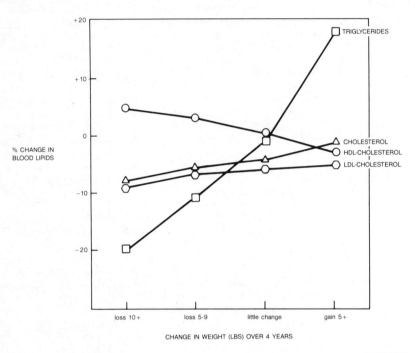

+20

+10

0

−10

−20

% CHANGE IN
BLOOD LIPIDS

TRIGLYCERIDES

CHOLESTEROL
HDL-CHOLESTEROL
LDL-CHOLESTEROL

loss 10+   loss 5-9   little change   gain 5+

CHANGE IN WEIGHT (LBS) OVER 4 YEARS

FD97 Bob5-15
Dress 1 & 2, Hel, Math

Figure 21-2 Percentage change in blood lipids by weight change in the MRFIT special intervention group. *Source:* Adapted with permission from *Preventive Medicine* (1981; 10:443–475), Copyright © 1981, Academic Press.

A pronounced relation between quintiles of change in body mass index (BMI), calculated as weight divided by height squared, and change in systolic and diastolic blood pressure is apparent over time (Figure 21-3). The effects on total cholesterol are also evident for both sexes, but there is a steeper gradient of cholesterol change with weight change in the men (Figure 21-4).

It is clear that weight gain had an adverse effect on lipoprotein profiles in this population, increasing LDL and very-low-density lipoprotein (VLDL) cholesterol and decreasing HDL cholesterol. Among men, the average change in LDL cholesterol was 19.3 mg/dL greater in the highest compared with the lowest quintile of change in body mass. Among women, the difference in change between quintiles was 8.8 mg/dL.

The detrimental effects of weight gain and the benefits of weight reduction were more pronounced at these younger ages than in the older Framingham participants. It is also significant that weight change in this young cohort was the strongest and most consistent correlate of blood pressure and lipid changes

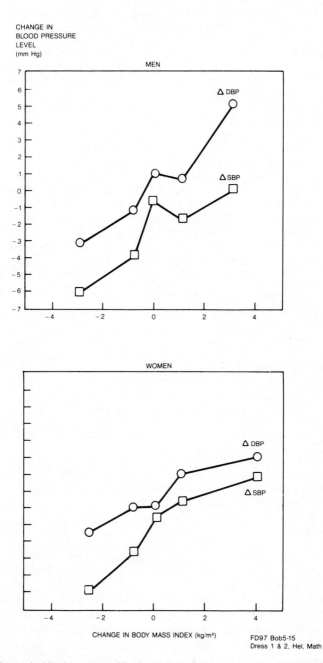

Figure 21-3 Change in blood pressure with change in body mass index in 20- to 29-year-old Framingham Offspring Study participants.

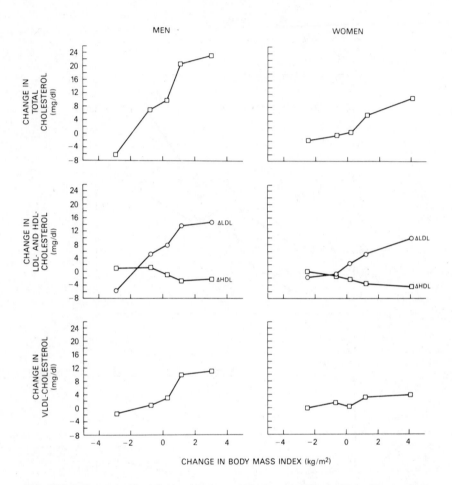

Figure 21-4 Change in blood lipids with change in body mass index in 20- to 29-year-old Framingham Offspring Study participants.

when compared with changes in other potentially modifiable life style related factors such as smoking, alcohol consumption, exercise, and oral contraceptive use.[9]

Recent studies[16–18] also have suggested that the distribution of body fat may have an important role in the development of coronary risk. Centrally located or upper-body obesity, in particular, has been associated with increased prevalence of hypertension and diabetes. It has been shown in some populations that the degree of upper-body fatness is a better predictor of coronary risk than other obesity measures.[19]

Despite the compelling evidence that increased body weight for height or obesity is directly associated with the development of an adverse coronary profile, and despite further data[20-25] suggesting its independent influence on other cardiovascular processes, considerable debate continues over the relative importance of obesity in the prevention of CHD. Controversy has been stimulated by epidemiologic studies that found no ''independent'' influence of obesity on coronary risk and by conclusions stating that excess weight is benign if it is unaccompanied by other risk factors for disease such as hypertension or hypercholesterolemia.[26-27] Attempts to compare the results from numerous studies sometimes conducted in very dissimilar populations and with very different methodologies have made consensus more difficult to achieve. Differences in duration of follow-up, definition and distribution of obesity in populations, cohort ages, criteria for disease, and concomitant life style, cultural, and genetic influences have complicated comparative analysis.

In light of such difficulties, this review focuses only on results from prospective studies in North American populations in which longitudinal observation was continued for a minimum of 4 years. Published reports of these studies,[26,28-37] conducted primarily in white male populations, present data that consistently show significant linear relations between some obesity measure and coronary morbidity or mortality on unadjusted analysis, that is, analysis that does not correct for the associations of obesity with other risk factors for disease (Table 21-1).

Relations are evident, for example, between BMI and myocardial infarction, sudden coronary death, and all coronary disease in the Manitoba Study,[30] between skinfold measures and all coronary disease in the Framingham,[29] US Railroad,[26]

Table 21-1 Obesity and CHD Incidence: Epidemiologic Study Findings Unadjusted for Other CHD Risk Factors

Significant Linear Relationship (P < .05)	No Significant Linear Relationship (P > .05)
Framingham population[20,21]	Minneapolis businessmen[31]
Manitoba Canadian Air Force[22]	Chicago Peoples Gas Co workers[32]
San Francisco longshoremen[23]	
Los Angeles civil servants[24]	
California employees[25]	
(Western Collaborative)	
Tecumseh population[26]	
US railroad workers[27]	
Boston VA (Normative Aging)[28]	
Chicago Western Electric Co workers[29]	
Pooling Project (5 groups)[30]	

and Western Electric studies,[36] and between percentage of desirable weight and myocardial infarction or sudden death in the 40- to 49-year-old participants in the Pooling Project,[37] which combined data from the Framingham, Tecumseh, Western Electric, Chicago Peoples Gas Company, and Albany studies. In the Manitoba Study,[30] for example, men whose BMI was 22.6 to 25.0 experienced almost twice the risk of CHD over 26 years compared with those whose BMI was less than 22.6. Risks at indices of 25.1 to 27.5 and 27.5 or more were 2.4 and 2.8 times those of leaner men. In the Framingham[28] population relative weights of 130% or more compared with those less than 110% were associated with 2 times the risk of CHD in men under the age of 50 years and 2.4 times the risk in similarly aged women.

In contrast to the overwhelming evidence supporting a linear relation, investigators[27] in Minneapolis found only a marginally significant association between skinfolds and disease. A significant U- or J-shaped relation between BMI and coronary mortality was reported in the Chicago Peoples Gas Company study.[38] In that cohort, mortality was increased in the lean as well as in the overweight men.

Results of multivariate analyses that are adjusted for the influence of other coronary disease risk factors reveal significant independent relations between obesity and outcomes, primarily in the younger cohorts studied (Table 21-2).[28,30,32,35,37] Even within the same populations, significant relations are evident only in those under 50 years of age and not at older ages. This age difference is observed in the Los Angeles,[32] Pooling Project,[37] and Boston VA[35] studies. The Pooling Project[37] data suggest that a 10% increase in relative weight would be independently associated with a 13% to 19% increase in disease incidence in 40- to 49-year-old men. It is particularly noteworthy that obesity in younger

---

Table 21-2 Obesity and CHD Incidence: Epidemiologic Study Findings Adjusted for Other CHD Risk Factors

Significant Linear Relationship (P < .05)			No Significant Linear Relationship (P > .05)		
Study	Duration (yr)	Age	Study	Duration (yr)	Age
Framingham[20]	26	av 44	Minneapolis[31]	20	av 52
Manitoba[22]			Chicago Peoples		
	26	av 31	Gas[32]	14	av 50
Los Angeles[24]	15	30–49	Los Angeles	15	50+
Pooling Project[30]	8.6	40–49	Pooling Project	8.6	50+
			Western		
			Collaborative[25]	8.5	av 47
			US Railroad[27]	5	40–59
Boston VA[28]	5	28–52 (av 43)	Boston VA[28]	5	53+

Framingham Study participants, ie, those under 50 years, still conveyed an increased risk of disease even when unaccompanied by borderline or definite hypertension, hypercholesterolemia, cigarette smoking, glucose intolerance, or left ventricular hypertrophy. These findings, in conjunction with those presented earlier, have strong implications for disease prevention.

On the one hand, it seems that obesity may lie near the beginning of the chain of events leading to disease causation and may operate, at least in part, through the well-recognized risk factors for disease. On the other hand, it is also apparent that obesity may exert an independent effect on the development of premature disease in younger cohorts observed over a sufficient period of time. Results of studies[20-25] showing an independent influence of obesity on cardiovascular hemodynamics, intravascular volume, left ventricular mass, fibrinolytic activity, and plasma fibrinogen concentrations suggest mechanisms through which obesity may operate independently to elevate risk. From any standpoint, obesity seems to be an important modifiable contributor to CHD risk.

To bring some of these issues into focus with regard to adult body-weight standards, Table 21-3 shows a comparison of the 1959 and 1983 Metropolitan Life Weight Tables at selected heights and medium build.[39,40] The largest differences in the tables occur at the shorter heights for men and women, at which increases equal 10 to 13 lb. While the 1983 weights may reflect minimum mortality in a highly selected insurance cohort, population studies[28,29] suggest that this percentage of weight gain would increase risk of CHD by approximately 10% for both men and women when all other risk factors remain constant. Risks would be further increased in the event that weight change adversely influenced blood lipids, lipoproteins, blood pressure, or glucose tolerance.

The suggestion that body-weight standards should be increased is worrisome, since statistics from national surveys already show increases in adiposity, unex-

---

Table 21-3 Metropolitan Life Insurance Company Weight Tables: Median Weights in Pounds (in Indoor Clothing) at Selected Heights and Medium Build

Height (in shoes)	Men			Women		
	1959	1983	Difference	1959	1983	Difference
5'5"	133	143	10			
5'9"	149	154	5			
6'1"	167	167	0			
5'0"				107	120	13
5'4"				120	131	11
5'8"				136	143	7

Source: Adapted with permission from *Statistical Bulletin of the Metropolitan Life Insurance Company* (1959; 40:1–11) and (1983; 64:1–9), Copyright © 1959 and 1983, Metropolitan Life Insurance Company.

plained by increases in stature, in American men and women. The population needs to understand the risks associated with such continuing trends. It is evident that leanness and avoidance of weight gain before middle age are advisable goals in the primary prevention of CHD for most American men and women. In addition, intervention in the well-established risk factors for disease should be accompanied by weight loss in the overweight person.

REFERENCES

1. Chiang BN, Perlman LV, Epstein FH: Overweight and hypertension: A review. *Circulation* 1969; 39:403–421.

2. Kannel WB, Gordon T, Castelli WP: Obesity, lipids, and glucose intolerance: The Framingham Study. *Am J Clin Nutr* 1979; 32:1238–1245.

3. Garrison RJ, Wilson PW, Castelli WP, et al: Obesity and lipoprotein cholesterol in the Framingham Offspring Study. *Metabolism* 1980; 29:1053–1060.

4. Noppa H, Bengtsson C, Bjorntorp P, et al: Overweight in women—metabolic aspects: The population study of women in Göteborg 1968–1969. *Acta Med Scand* 1978; 203:135–141.

5. Leren P, Askevold EM, Foss OP, et al: The Oslo Study: Cardiovascular disease in middle-aged and young Oslo men. *Acta Med Scand* 1977; (suppl 588).

6. Ashley FW, Kannel WB: Relation of weight change to changes in atherogenic traits: The Framingham Study. *J Chron Dis* 1974; 27:103–114.

7. Noppa H: Body weight change in relation to incidence of ischemic heart disease and change in risk factors for ischemic heart disease. *Am J Epidemiol* 1980; 111:693–704.

8. Criqui MH, Frankville DD, Barrett-Connor E, et al: Change and correlates of change in high and low density lipoprotein cholesterol after six years: A prospective study. *Am J Epidemiol* 1983; 118:52–59.

9. Hubert HB, Eaker ED, Garrison RJ, et al: Life style correlates of risk factor change in young adults: An eight year study of coronary heart disease risk factors in the Framingham offspring. *Am J Epidemiol*, to be published.

10. Borkan GA, Sparrow D, Wisniewski C, et al: Body weight and coronary disease risk: Patterns of risk factor change associated with long-term weight change: The Normative Aging Study. *Am J Epidemiol* 1986; 124:410–419.

11. Heyden S, Borhani NO, Tyroler HA, et al: The relationship of weight change to changes in blood pressure, serum uric acid, cholesterol and glucose in the treatment of hypertension. *J Chron Dis* 1985; 38:281–288.

12. Caggiula AW, Christakis G, Farrand M, et al: The Multiple Risk Factor Intervention Trial (MRFIT): IV. Intervention on blood lipids. *Prev Med* 1981; 10:443–475.

13. Lipid Research Clinics Program: Relationships between changes in diet and changes in total and low density lipoprotein cholesterol in hypercholesterolemic men: The diet plus placebo group of the Lipid Research Clinics Coronary Primary Prevention Trial, abstracted. CVD Epidemiol Newslett 1985; 37:29.

14. Lipid Research Clinics Program: Relationships between reductions in coronary heart disease and in low density lipoprotein cholesterol in hypercholesterolemic men: The diet plus placebo group of the Lipid Research Clinics Coronary Primary Prevention Trial, abstracted. CVD Epidemiol Newslett 1985; 37:28.

15. Langford HG, Blaufox MD, Oberman A, et al: Dietary therapy slows the return of hypertension after stopping prolonged medication. *JAMA* 1985; 253:657–664.

16. Kissebah AH, Vydelingum N, Murray R, et al: Relation of body fat distribution to metabolic complications of obesity. *J Clin Endocrinol Metab* 1982; 54:254–260.

17. Blair D, Habicht JP, Sims EAH, et al: Evidence for an increased risk for hypertension with centrally located body fat and the effect of race and sex on this risk. *Am J Epidemiol* 1984; 119:526–540.

18. Hartz AJ, Rupley DC, Rimm AA: The association of girth measurements with disease in 32,856 women. *Am J Epidemiol* 1984; 119:71–80.

19. Larsson B, Svardsudd K, Welin L, et al: Abdominal adipose tissue distribution, obesity, and risk of cardiovascular disease and death: 13 year follow up of participants in the study of men born in 1913. *Br Med J* 1984; 288:1401–1404.

20. MacMahon SW, Wilcken DEL, MacDonald GJ: The effect of weight reduction on left ventricular mass: A randomized controlled trial in young, overweight hypertensive patients. *N Engl J Med* 1986; 314:334–339.

21. Meade TW, Chakrabarti R, Haines AP, et al: Characteristics affecting fibrinolytic activity and plasma fibrinogen concentrations. *Br Med J* 1979; 1:153–156.

22. Alexander JK: Obesity and cardiac performance. *Am J Cardiol* 1964; 14:860–865.

23. Gordon ES: Metabolic aspects of obesity. *Adv Metab Disord* 1970; 4:229–296.

24. Feinleib M, Kannel WB, Tedeschi CG, et al: The relation of antemortem characteristics to cardiovascular findings at necropsy. *Atherosclerosis* 1979; 34:145–157.

25. Messerli FH, Sundgaard-Riise K, Reisin E, et al: Disparate cardiovascular effects of obesity and arterial hypertension. *Am J Med* 1983; 74:808–812.

26. Keys A, Aravanis C, Blackburn H, et al: Coronary heart disease: Overweight and obesity as risk factors. *Ann Intern Med* 1972; 77:15–27.

27. Keys A, Taylor HL, Blackburn H, et al: Mortality and coronary heart disease among men studied for 23 years. *Arch Intern Med* 1971; 128:201–214.

28. Hubert HB, Feinleib M, McNamara PM, et al: Obesity as an independent risk factor for cardiovascular disease: A 26-year follow-up of participants in the Framingham Heart Study. *Circulation* 1983; 67:968–977.

29. Hubert HB, Castelli WP: Obesity as a predictor of coronary heart disease, in Frankle RT, Dwyer J, Moragne L, et al (eds): *Dietary Treatment and Prevention of Obesity*. London, John Libbey & Co Ltd, 1985, pp 125–135.

30. Rabkin SW, Mathewson FAL, Hsu P: Relation of body weight to development of ischemic heart disease in a cohort of young North American men after a 26 year observation period: The Manitoba Study. *Am J Cardiol* 1977; 39:452–458.

31. Paffenbarger RS, Laughlin ME, Gima AS, et al: Work activity of longshoremen as related to death from coronary heart disease and stroke. *N Engl J Med* 1970; 282:1109–1114.

32. Chapman JM, Coulson AH, Clark VA, et al: The differential effect of serum cholesterol, blood pressure and weight on the incidence of myocardial infarction and angina pectoris. *J Chron Dis* 1971; 23:631–645.

33. Rosenman RH, Brand RJ, Sholtz RI, et al: Multivariate prediction of coronary heart disease during 8.5 year follow-up in the Western Collaborative Group Study. *Am J Cardiol* 1976; 37:903–910.

34. Chiang BN, Perlman LV, Fulton M, et al: Predisposing factors in sudden cardiac death in Tecumseh, Michigan: A prospective study. *Circulation* 1970; 41:31–37.

35. Glynn RJ, Rosner B, Silbert JE: Changes in cholesterol and triglyceride as predictors of ischemic heart disease in men. *Circulation* 1982; 66:724–731.

36. Paul O, Lepper MH, Phelan WH, et al: A longitudinal study of coronary heart disease. *Circulation* 1963; 28:20–31.

37. Pooling Project Research Group: Relationship of blood pressure, serum cholesterol, smoking habit, relative weight and ECG abnormalities to incidence of major coronary events: Final report of the Pooling Project. *J Chron Dis* 1978; 31:201–306.

38. Dyer AR, Stamler J, Berkson DM, et al: Relationship of relative weight and body mass index to 14-year mortality in the Chicago Peoples Gas Company Study. *J Chron Dis* 1975; 28:109–123.

39. Metropolitan Life Insurance Company: New weight standards for men and women. Stat Bull Metropol Life Insur Co 1959; 40:1–11.

40. Metropolitan Life Insurance Company: 1983 Metropolitan height and weight tables. Stat Bull Metropol Life Insur Co 1983; 64:1–9.

Chapter 22

Obesity and Type II Diabetes

Judith Wylie-Rosett

INTRODUCTION

Obesity is associated with inefficient use of the body's endogenous insulin, which is often accompanied by altered fuel metabolism. The noninsulin dependent form of diabetes may develop when the alteration in fuel metabolism is manifested by an elevation of blood glucose levels. Diabetes is a major health problem that leads to complications affecting almost every body system. The diagnosis and treatment of diabetes have been modified during the past few years.

This chapter discusses the relation between obesity and glucose intolerance focusing on clinical issues relevant to diet and nutrition. Various dietary and pharmacologic treatment approaches are presented, and therapies are discussed with respect to the management of clinical problems.

EPIDEMIOLOGY AND DIAGNOSTIC CRITERIA

The relation between obesity and altered glucose metabolism has been well established, and the development of noninsulin dependent diabetes mellitus (NIDDM) is closely linked to obesity.[1-5] People with NIDDM are usually obese and older than 40 years at the time of diagnosis. They present with relatively few of the classic symptoms associated with diabetes such as increased thirst and urination. Although they are not dependent on exogenous insulin for survival and are not ketosis prone, insulin therapy may be required if hyperglycemia persists in spite of other therapy or if any stress such as infection, surgery, or emotional trauma induces hyperglycemia.

According to the National Diabetes Data Group,[1] NIDDM, or Type II, diabetes can be diagnosed on the basis of a fasting plasma glucose level of 140 mg/dL or more, or on the basis of a glucose tolerance test in which two values are greater than 200 mg/dL. The diagnostic criteria for diabetes are listed in Appendix 22-A.

Based on information from the National Health Interview Survey,[4] there are 5.8 million people in the United States with a known diagnosis of diabetes, and the American Diabetes Association[5] estimated there may be as many as 5 million more people with NIDDM who have not been diagnosed. Between 80% and 90% of all people with diabetes have NIDDM, and some 60% to 90% of people with NIDDM are obese.[1]

Although obesity is the factor most strongly associated with the prevalence of NIDDM, it seems that family history is also an extremely important risk factor. Other variables are also associated with NIDDM. Known diabetes is relatively more common in women, low-income families, the less educated, inner-city residents, and the elderly. The prevalence of NIDDM in the United States is higher in the South and in several minority populations such as blacks, Hispanics, and American Indians. Women who have had gestational diabetes mellitus (GDM) or large-birth-weight infants are at increased risk for NIDDM.[4] In all of the groups *at risk*, the manifestation of overt diabetes is related to obesity.

OBESITY AS A RISK FACTOR FOR NONINSULIN DEPENDENT DIABETES MELLITUS

Obesity is generally associated with hyperinsulinemia. However, there is some confusion about the etiology of the relation between obesity and endogenous insulin production, and it is unclear whether excessive insulin production causes weight gain or whether excessive accumulation of body fat causes insulin resistance and thereby promotes increased insulin production. It has been established that approximately 50% to 60% of the obese have some degree of glucose intolerance.[5] However, many obese people do not show any impairment in glucose tolerance, leading to the question of why some obese people develop glucose intolerance while others do not.

It seems that obesity is associated with a decrease in the number and binding of insulin receptors in the body's tissues, and more insulin is required to allow glucose uptake by tissue. The development of diabetes is the result of a failure in the message that insulin transmits to cells with respect to the uptake and use of glucose.[5] If insulin production by the beta cells of the pancreas can compensate for this insulin resistance, normal glucose uptake and use in cells may be possible despite the abnormalities associated with the insulin receptors on the cell's surface.

Obesity History

The degree and duration of obesity seem to have roles in determining the risk for NIDDM or glucose intolerance. The reported risk for NIDDM is approximately 2 fold in the mildly obese, approximately 5 fold in the moderately obese, and approximately 10 fold in the severely obese.[5]

Studies[4,5] of the Pima Indian population have found a close relation between obesity and diabetes in the population under 35 years but not in the population over 35 years, possibly suggesting that the risk for diabetes diminishes with age in this population. However, the Pima Indians may not characterize the pattern for developing diabetes in other population groups. Obesity develops at a relatively young age in the Pima population, and the physiologic stress of weight gain in early adulthood may be more characteristic of Pima Indians than other populations. In most groups, the weight gain that often accompanies decreased activity after age 35 years,[5] or the so called middle-age spread, is associated with NIDDM.

Body Shape

Body shape has been suggested to determine the risk for NIDDM. Obese people who have relatively large waist measurements are reported to have a greater risk for NIDDM than do obese people with excess adiposity around the hips.[6,7] Excess fat accumulation around the waist is generally associated with middle-age spread and is seemingly inconsistent with the data from the Pima Indian population. Lifelong obesity and an increased number of fat cells may not characterize the Pima Indian population. It seems that they may have adult-onset weight gain at an earlier age. An increased fat cell size is characteristic of adult weight gain and is probably also associated with the deposition of excess fat around the waist. Irrespective of the pattern of weight gain, there is clearly a genetic predisposition for NIDDM that is characterized by insulin resistance of obesity and an inability to compensate by increasing insulin secretion. The inherited tendency for developing diabetes is manifested when the insulin resistance of obesity is not met by additional insulin production.

Family History

Family history is one of the factors most strongly associated with NIDDM. Studies[3,4] of monozygotic twins showed an almost 100% concordance for NIDDM diabetes, and it is virtually certain that if one twin develops diabetes the other twin will also develop diabetes within a few years.[2-4] The concordance rate in monozygotic twins for insulin dependent diabetes is less than 50%.[3] However, the gene loci for the inheritance of the insulin dependent form has been identified, and NIDDM does not have a specific marker, making the genetics poorly understood.

SCREENING AND POTENTIAL PREVENTION OF NONINSULIN DEPENDENT DIABETES MELLITUS

Identifying people at risk for NIDDM is relatively simple even though there is no specific genetic marker. People who should be screened include members of families with known NIDDM, the markedly obese, women with a morbid obstetrical history or a history of infants weighing more than 9 lb at birth, and all pregnant women between the 24th and the 28th week of pregnancy.[3] Generally, a fasting plasma glucose test is the most appropriate method for screening, and a value greater than 140 mg/dL is sufficient for diagnosis.[3] A glucose tolerance test is indicated only if the fasting value is between 115 and 140 mg/dL. However, in pregnant women, this criterion differs, and screening is of immediate concern.

GESTATIONAL DIABETES

Approximately 60,000 to 90,000 women with GDM give birth each year, and if this condition is not identified and aggressively treated it can result in increased perinatal risk. The term "gestational diabetes mellitus" is used to describe the glucose intolerance that develops or is first detected during pregnancy. GDM occurs in approximately 2% of pregnant women. Insulin resistance normally develops during the second or third trimester of pregnancy and is associated with the development of glucose intolerance in women at risk. Between 30% and 40% of women with GDM will develop overt diabetes within 5 to 10 years after parturition. The risk of developing subsequent NIDDM is associated with obesity.[3]

OTHER CATEGORIES OF GLUCOSE INTOLERANCE

The criteria for diagnosing various categories of glucose intolerance are listed in Appendix 22-A. The term "impaired glucose tolerance" (IGT) is used to classify people who have some impairment of glucose tolerance but do not have overt diabetes mellitus. The terms "chemical diabetes" and "prediabetic" have been used in the past to describe glucose intolerance but are no longer used because only approximately one third of people with IGT develop overt diabetes.[1,3]

TREATMENT

Dietary management is important in all types of diabetes, and it becomes an extremely high priority for the obese person who has NIDDM. Weight reduction is the choice treatment modality for such people, who are the vast majority of people with NIDDM. However, additional dietary modification such as decreasing dietary fat and increasing fiber and carbohydrate may be needed to achieve metabolic control.

A number of issues must be considered in establishing dietary recommendations for the management of NIDDM. Medication may be used in combination with dietary therapy.

Weight Reduction

Weight reduction is strongly recommended for the obese patient with NIDDM, but attempted weight reduction in these patients is frequently considered to be frustrating and may receive little emphasis in the health care plan. Weight reduction has been associated with an improvement in metabolic control,[8-12] and even a modest loss of 10 to 30 lb lowers blood glucose levels.[9,12] Therefore, the potential impact of even a rather modest weight reduction must be considered in planning the management of NIDDM. Very-low-calorie diets (VLCD) and fasting have been used to achieve a rapid reduction in blood glucose levels.[8,11] The use of a VLCD resulted in a dramatic reduction in fasting plasma glucose levels from 291 to 95 mg/dL when it was tested for 36 days in a small number of hospitalized patients.[8] This dramatic reduction is thought to be the result of a decrease in glucose output from the liver, increased sensitivity to insulin in the liver and in peripheral tissue, and a decrease in glucagon levels.[11]

Goals for Metabolic Control

The biochemical indices of metabolic control in the management of NIDDM are listed in Table 22-1. Normalization of blood glucose and lipids is considered to be of primary importance in the dietary management of diabetes. Individualization of the dietary prescription and nutritional counseling are strongly emphasized so that the prescription for a particular patient may differ from those listed if the dietary history, other medical problems, or problems in achieving

Table 22-1 Biochemical Indices of Metabolic Control: Top Limits

Biochemical Index	Normal	Acceptable	Fair	Poor
Fasting plasma glucose	115	140	200	>200 mg/dL
Postprandial plasma glucose	140	175	235	>235 mg/dL
Glycosylated hemoglobin	6	8	10	>10%
Fasting plasma cholesterol	200	225	250	>250 mg/dL
Fasting plasma triglyceride	150	175	200	>200 mg/dL

Adjust for normal values of laboratory.
Increase limits for elderly patients.

Source: Reprinted from *The Physician's Guide to Type II Diabetes (NIDDM): Diagnosis and Treatment* by H Rifkin (Ed) with permission of the American Diabetes Association Inc, © 1984.

metabolic control warrant deviation from the established composition recommendations.

Dietary Recommendations and Composition

The American Diabetes Association's Nutrition Recommendations and Principles for Individuals with Diabetes Mellitus: 1986[13] established the goals for dietary intake that consider the risk of complications and focus on achieving metabolic control. The goal established by the American Diabetes Association for the composition of the diabetic diet is shown in Table 22-2.

Protein

A wide range for protein intake is recommended to allow flexibility in dietary intake, but most patients will probably consume 12% to 20% protein. Reduction

Table 22-2 1986 Dietary Recommendations of the American Diabetes Association

Protein	12%–20%[†]
	(only 0.8 g/kg is needed)
Fat	25%–35%
Saturated	up to 10%
Unsaturated	approx 20%
Cholesterol	less than 300 mg
Carbohydrate	up to 50%–60%[†]
Fiber: approx 40 g (25 g/1,000 calories)	

[†]Composition may be altered to 25% protein and 45% carbohydrate in a diabetic patient not thought to be at risk for renal complications.

Source: American Diabetes Association, 1986.

of protein intake to 0.8 g/kg, or perhaps less, is emphasized for those considered at risk for renal complications.

Fat

Restricting dietary fat intake is considered to be a high priority as a means of reducing caloric intake and controlling blood lipids. An intake of 25% to 35% fat is considered a realistic goal in the management of diabetes, with an emphasis on the use of unsaturated fat. Restricting dietary cholesterol to less than 300 mg and replacing saturated with unsaturated fat is also recommended.

Carbohydrate

For many patients, an intake of 50% to 60% carbohydrate that includes primarily unrefined carbohydrate with fiber as an alternative to refined carbohydrate will be achievable, but for others this goal may need to be modified. Some who have achieved metabolic control will be able to consume a modest amount of sucrose without negatively affecting body weight or metabolic control.[13] But for others, this may result in a deterioration in control or excessive intake of high-calorie foods. An intake of 40 g of fiber with emphasis on soluble fiber is considered desirable. For the patient on a calorie-restricted diet, the recommendation is modified to 25 g/1,000 calories, and for some NIDDM patients who are trying to lose weight, increasing fiber intake in addition to decreasing caloric intake may be overwhelming and must be gradually introduced.

Fiber and the Glycemic Effect of Carbohydrate

The recommendation to increase dietary fiber is based on experimental studies[13-18] evaluating its effect on glycemic control and on epidemiologic evidence. A fiber-rich diet has been used to improve metabolic control, and some people with NIDDM have been able to discontinue medication.[14] More recent studies have evaluated the effect of specific fibers. Soluble fibers have greater viscosity and may delay gastric emptying and/or absorption time. Guar seems to have the most viscosity, but pectin, oats, and legumes also are highly soluble. The addition of fiber to the diet of the obese with NIDDM has been shown to improve metabolic control without any change in weight.[16] However, there is no recommendation to add purified fibers to the diet, and caution about the use of "noval" that are not from food sources is advised.[13]

The variability in the glycemic effect of carbohydrate-containing foods cannot be explained on the basis of fiber content or biochemical structure.[13,19-24] Research showing that "simple" carbohydrates do not have a greater impact on glucose than do some "complex" carbohydrates has led to a question about how carbohydrate-containing foods should be classified.[16,21-24]

The glycemic index has been used to categorize the postprandial glycemic impact of carbohydrate-containing foods using an equal amount of glucose (usually 50 g) as the standard.[22–24] White bread has been proposed as a new standard for comparison.[23] Factors that seem to influence or to be related to the glycemic impact of carbohydrate include the form of the food, fiber content, absorption rate, and release of glucose from the liver. Grinding some foods increases the glycemic impact, but for other foods grinding does not seem to be associated with any increase in postprandial glucose.

Table 22-3 lists the glycemic indices of some foods using 50 g of glucose as the standard for comparison. Legumes and dairy products have the smallest impact on glucose. All dairy products have a remarkably similar curve that seems to be independent of fat content. Vegetables with a high glycemic index may clinically have little impact on glycemic control because of the large volume required to make a significant contribution to intake.

Alternative Sweeteners

The American Diabetes Association[13] recommends that people with diabetes consider using a variety of sweeteners. Fructose and sorbitol do not raise blood glucose so much as sucrose does because insulin is not required for the early stages of their metabolism. However, the use of these nutritive sweeteners by the obese should be approached with caution. Aspartame and saccharin are considered sweeteners of choice for the obese with NIDDM because the caloric value of fructose and sorbitol is identical with that of sucrose. Most diet sodas use aspartame as the sweetener, and a few contain a blend of aspartame and saccharin. Aspartame has not been approved for use in baked goods, but is widely used in products requiring a relatively short cooking time on top of the stove.[25]

Sodium

A prudent approach to sodium intake is advised for the diabetic person.[13] Hypertension is commonly found in the obese with diabetes, and the elevation of blood pressure may be directly related to the obesity or may be a manifestation of a renal complication. Sodium restriction and/or weight reduction may be used to reduce blood pressure, and the addition of antihypertensive drugs is necessary if diet alone does not normalize blood pressure.

HEALTH PROBLEMS ASSOCIATED WITH NONINSULIN DEPENDENT DIABETES MELLITUS

People with NIDDM are at risk for various health problems associated with diabetes and/or its treatment. Both acute and chronic complications may de-

Table 22-3 Relative Glycemic Impact of Carbohydrate-Containing Foods

Exchange Group	Approximate Serving Size	CHO (g) per Exchange or Serving	Approx fiber (g) per Exchange	Glycemic* Index % (Based on 50 g CHO)	Relative† Glycemic Impact
Milk/Yogurt	8 oz	12	0	32–36	384–432
Vegetables	½ cup	5	2	64–92	320–460
Fruit	½ cup (¼ cup dried)	15	2	39–64	585–960
Starches					
Legumes	⅓ cup	15	5–6	15–40	225–600
Pasta/Buckwheat	½ cup	15	2	42–50	630–750
Cereal	½ cup cooked ¾ cup dry	15	varies (if whole grain)	49–80	735–1,200
Bread/Potatoes	½ cup	15	2 (if whole grain)	70–80	1,050–1,200
Rice	⅓ cup	15	2 (if whole grain)	66–72	990–1,080
Various Sources of Sugar					
Regular Soda	12 oz	40–50		59	2,360–2,950
Sucrose	1 teaspoon	5		59	295
Fructose	1 teaspoon	5		20	100
Honey	1 teaspoon	5		87	435

*Glycemic Index = $\dfrac{\text{Area under 2-hour glucose response curve for 50 g CHO as food}}{\text{Area under 2-hour glucose response curve for 50 g glucose}} \times 100$

†Glycemic Index × grams of CHO per exchange or serving of sugar

velop.[3] The health problems listed in Table 22-4 may be preventable, and metabolic control is thought to reduce the risk of complications. Hypertension and elevated blood lipids are associated with obesity and may increase the risk of the chronic complications.

Acute Complications

The risk of acute complications may be more subtle in NIDDM than in insulin dependent diabetes. When blood glucose is extremely high, dehydration and hyperosmolar coma can develop. This occurs infrequently in the *free-living population* with NIDDM unless an acute problem develops when the patient cannot tolerate liquids and/or has diarrhea associated with infection. Hyperosmolar coma is more likely to develop in the institutionalized patient who has difficulty with eating and drinking liquids. The acute complications of ketoacidosis and hypoglycemia that are usually associated with diabetes are much more common in NIDDM. The insulin resistance associated with obesity may have a role in reducing the likelihood of acute hypoglycemia in NIDDM patients including those who are treated with insulin even if the insulin dose is quite large. The patient who is treated with oral agents is not likely to develop hypoglycemia if a meal is missed or delayed and usually does not require snacks. However, severe hypoglycemia may occur if intake is significantly reduced for several days, or there is excessive alcohol consumption.

The treatment of hypoglycemia for the patient taking oral agents is more complex than for the insulin-treated patient. Many oral hypoglycemic agents

---

Table 22-4 Diabetic Complications

Acute
Hyperglycemia
    Ketotic
    Nonketotic (Hyperosmolar coma)
Hypoglycemia (side effect of therapy)

Chronic
Microvascular disease
    Retinopathy
    Nephropathy
Macrovascular
    Coronary Atherosclerosis
    Peripheral Vascular Disease
Neuropathic
    Peripheral Neuropathy
    Autonomic Neuropathy

---

have a long duration of action, increasing the risk for recurrent hypoglycemia. The treatment of hypoglycemia may require hospitalization for patients taking chlorpropamide (Diabinese), which has a 60-hour duration of action.[3]

Infection is a common problem associated with both insulin and noninsulin dependent diabetes. Infection increases the level of the hormones that counter-regulate the action of insulin, and, therefore, an infection often raises blood glucose levels. In addition, the resistance to infection is greatly diminished when the blood glucose level is high. Treating infection and hyperglycemia requires careful assessment and vigorous treatment of both problems.

Chronic Complications

The major chronic complications of diabetes are associated with the impact of the disease on the vascular and nervous systems. Diabetes affects both microvascular and macrovascular circulation.

Microvascular Complications

The microvascular changes primarily affect the eyes and the kidneys.[3] The primary cause of blindness associated with diabetes is retinopathy, which does not cause visual impairment until a relatively advanced stage is reached. Fortunately, much can be done to prevent the advanced changes in which there is a proliferative growth of new fragile blood vessels that are likely to hemorrhage and cause blindness. The progression of background retinopathy to proliferative retinopathy may be prevented through vigorously controlling blood glucose and blood pressure as well as using laser photocoagulation treatment to prevent hemorrhage.

Diabetic renal disease is also caused by changes in small blood vessels and affects approximately 20% of patients with NIDDM 15 years after diagnosis.[26] Vigorous treatment of blood glucose may prevent the microvascular change. Maintaining normal blood pressure has been shown to delay the progression of early renal disease.[3] Measurement of protein excretion is important in the early detection of diabetic renal complications and may be an indication for early protein restriction.[27] Proteinuria occurs earlier after diagnosis in patients with NIDDM than in patients with insulin dependent diabetes, but the development of overt renal disease is much more common in insulin dependent diabetes. Excretion of 3 g of protein or more is a clear indication for a renal workup. Protein restriction and modification of electrolyte intake are usually indicated. There is growing evidence that reducing protein intake before overt manifestation of renal complications may help prevent or delay the progression of kidney changes.

Macrovascular Complications

Macrovascular disease increases the risk for coronary heart disease (CHD), stroke, and peripheral vascular disease, usually manifested as intermittent claudication.[3] The risk for CHD doubles for the diabetic patient, but there is growing evidence that normalization of blood glucose and lipids may reduce the risk. The obese person is more likely to develop elevated lipid levels and elevated blood pressure in addition to the risk for NIDDM. Weight reduction is likely to improve all of these factors. Physical activity is recommended for improving blood glucose control and may improve blood pressure and peripheral circulation as well as burn calories. However, the person with peripheral neuropathy may not be able to increase physical activity because of limited sensation and the risk of injury.

Neuropathy

Autonomic neuropathy can affect the gastrointestinal tract and may result in gastroparesis.[3] If the gastroparesis affects the esophagus, the patient may experience vomiting, and if it affects the lower gastrointestinal tract, the patient may have constipation. Autonomic neuropathy of the gastrointestinal tract may require dietary modification to help treat the resulting vomiting, constipation, or diarrhea in addition to the medical treatment. The vomiting may result in a severely restricted dietary intake and weight loss, but the diabetic diarrhea may be socially debilitating with no associated weight loss. These problems are much more common in insulin dependent diabetes but should not be overlooked in the patient with NIDDM.

EDUCATION AND APPROACH TO THERAPY

The approach to therapy should consider the level of diabetic control, duration of diabetes, other health problems, diabetic complications, and the ability and willingness to learn information needed to provide self-care. The American Diabetes Association recommends staging patient education and counseling.

In the first stage, essential material is learned, and the later stage focuses on in-depth and continuing education.[28] The 1986 revision of the American Diabetes Association and American Dietetic Association Exchange List facilitates staging of education. There are two different educational tools: one is simplified and includes only basic information, and the other is suitable for in-depth education.[28-31]

Initial Educating and Counseling

The first stage is identified as the "survival," or initial, level and focuses on presenting basic information required to initiate behavioral change. For the obese patient with diabetes, this stage involves helping the patient identify obesity as a primary problem contributing to diabetes and developing an approach to treating the obesity. For the obese patient with NIDDM who has elevated blood pressure and/or lipid levels, this stage involves understanding that these health problems are interconnected and that losing weight is a common treatment approach. Accepting that reducing excess calories and fat rather than restricting carbohydrate as a primary treatment goal is an essential part of completing this stage.

In-depth Therapy, Education, and Counseling

The next stage is in-depth education and also involves the continuing education of the patient. The stage begins when the patient has adjusted to the diagnosis of diabetes and understands the importance of losing weight. However, the specific treatment approach may vary considerably. Several approaches can be used to reduce body weight in NIDDM, and individualization is essential. The goal of achieving metabolic control will facilitate selection of the approach.

For those with a fasting glucose level of less than 225 mg/dL, a modest loss may be enough to normalize fasting glucose and glycosylated hemoglobin levels. Most of the behavioral weight-reduction programs achieve an average loss of 10 to 30 lb,[9,10,12,32–34] and the American Diabetes Association[28] has established achieving a realistic weight loss or a "reasonable" body weight as the therapeutic goal.

The diabetic exchange system is probably the most commonly used approach to planning weight-reduction diets for people with NIDDM. Teaching the details of the diabetic exchange system is not appropriate before this in-depth phase. However, the exchanges may be introduced using a simplified tool earlier. The 1986 revisions of the exchange list have a slightly higher caloric value for starch and fruit to reflect more accurately the composition of commonly eaten foods in these categories.[29–31]

Fasting and very low calorie diets (VLCDs—less than 800 calories) can be used to reduce insulin resistance and improve metabolic control. Such a drastic approach is usually reserved for those who weigh more than 150% of the appropriate weight in established weight tables and who have fasting blood glucose levels that exceed 250 mg/dL. A liquid formula is often used, and the American Diabetes Association[3] cautions that the formula should be evaluated to ensure that it contains an adequate quantity of high-biologic-value protein (usually 50 to 60 g) and at least 30 g of carbohydrate. The VLCD or fast should be used as an initial treatment and therefore may be considered as part of the "survival" stage since another approach to dietary management will be needed after its use.

Achieving normal or desirable levels for blood glucose, blood pressure, and lipids is often difficult and may require a combination of therapies. If medication is used, the dietary approach still requires emphasis to achieve maximal pharmacologic efficiency.

SUMMARY

Obesity is strongly associated with insulin resistance, and the obese usually need higher than normal levels of blood insulin to maintain a normal blood glucose level. NIDDM can develop when the obese cannot produce enough insulin to meet the need imposed by the obesity. Criteria for diagnosing diabetes have been standardized, and many obese people have glucose intolerance without overt diabetes. Factors related to the development of diabetes in the obese include the degree of obesity, family history, distribution of body fat, gender, and age. The complications of diabetes can affect many body systems, and metabolic control seems to reduce the risk for developing these problems. Weight reduction is the primary treatment for NIDDM associated with obesity. There are several approaches to weight reduction used. Diabetes education and weight-reduction counseling should be staged to best meet the needs of the obese person with NIDDM. Resource materials to aid in this staging may be obtained from the organizations listed in Appendix 22-B.

REFERENCES

1. National Diabetes Data Group: Classification and diagnosis of diabetes mellitus and other categories of glucose intolerance. *Diabetes* 1979; 28:1039–1059.

2. Everhard J, Knowler WC, Bennett PH: Incidence and risk factors for non-insulin diabetes, in Harris M, National Diabetes Data Group (eds): *Diabetes in America: Diabetes Data Compiled 1984*, US Dept of Health and Human Services publication No. (NIH) 85-1468. Bethesda, Md, 1985, pp IV:1–35.

3. Rifkin H (ed): *The Physician's Guide to Type II Diabetes (NIDDM): Diagnosis and Treatment*. New York, American Diabetes Association Inc, 1984.

4. National Center for Health Statistics: Prevalence, inpact and impact of known diabetes in the United States, in *Advance Data from Vital Health Statistics*, US Dept of Health and Human Services publication No. (PHS) 86-1250. Hyattsville, MD, US Public Health Service, 1986, pp XXII:469–479.

5. Salans LB, Knittle JL, Hirsh J: Obesity, glucose intolerance and diabetes mellitus, in Ellenberg M, Rifkin H (eds): *Diabetes Mellitus: Theory and Practice*, ed 3. New Hyde Park, NY, Medical Examination Publishing Co, 1983.

6. Ohlson LO, Larsson B, Suardsudd K, et al: The influence of body fat distribution on the incidence of diabetes: 13.5 years of follow-up of the participants in the study of men born in 1913. *Diabetes* 1985; 34:1055–1058.

7. Kissebah AH, Vydelingum N, Myrray R, et al: Relationship of body fat distribution to metabolic complications of diabetes. *J Clin Endocrinol Metab* 1982; 54:254–260.

8. Henry RR, Wiest-Kent TA, Schaeffer L: Very low calorie diet therapy in obese non-insulin dependent diabetic and non-diabetic subjects. *Diabetes* 1986; 35:155–164.

9. Wing RR, Epstein LH, Koeske R: Long-term effectiveness of modest weight loss for type II diabetic patients, abstracted. *Diabetes* 1985; 34(suppl):90A.

10. Wing RR, Epstein LH, Nowalk MP, et al: Behavioral change, weight loss, physiological improvement in type II diabetic patients. *J Consult Clin Psychol* 1985; 53:111–122.

11. Henry R: Effects of weight loss on the mechanisms of hyperglycemia in obese non-insulin dependent diabetes mellitus, abstracted. *Diabetes* 1985; 34(suppl):90A.

12. D'Eramo G, Wylie-Rosett J, Hagan J: Intensity of education in Type II NIDDM: Effect on weight, glycosylated hemoglobin and knowledge, abstracted. *Diabetes* 1986; 35(suppl):49A.

13. American Diabetes Association: Nutritional recommendation and principles for individuals with diabetes mellitus: 1986. *Diabetes Care*, 1987;10:126–132.

14. Anderson JW: Physiological and metabolic effects of dietary fiber. *Fed Proc* 1985; 44:2902–2906.

15. Wheeler M (ed): *Fiber and the patient with Diabetes Mellitus: A summary and annotated bibliography*. Chicago: Diabetes Care and Education: Practice Group of the American Dietetic Association, 1983 (suppl. 1985).

16. Crapo PA: *Diet and Nutrition in Diabetes: A State of the Art Review*. Washington, DC, NDIC, US Dept of Health and Human Services, 1983.

17. Vinik A: Dietary fiber in the management of diabetes. *Diabetes Care*, to be published.

18. Ray TK, Mansell KM, Knight LC, et al: Long-term effects of dietary fiber on glucose tolerance and gastric emptying in non-insulin dependent diabetic patients. *Am J Clin Nutr* 1983; 37:376–381.

19. Wheeler M (ed): Diabetes mellitus and glycemic response to different foods: A summary and annotated bibliography. Chicago, Diabetes Care and Education: Practice Group of the American Dietetic Association, 1983.

20. American Diabetes Association: Glycemic effects of carbohydrates. *Diabetes Care* 1984; 7:607–608.

21. Crapo PA, Kolterman OG, Waldeck N, et al: Post-prandial hormonal responses to different types of complex carbohydrate in individuals with impaired glucose tolerance. *Am J Clin Nutr* 1980; 33:1723–1728.

22. Jenkin DJA, Wolever TMS, Jenkins AL, et al: The glycaemic index of foods tested in diabetic patients: A new basis for carbohydrate exchange favouring the use of legumes. *Diabetologia* 1983; 24:257–264.

23. Wolever TM, Nuttall FQ, Lee R, et al: Prediction of the relative glucose response of mixed meals using white bread glycemic index. *Diabetes Care* 1985; 8:418–428.

24. Jenkins DJA: Examination of the glycemic index in diabetes management. *Diabetes Care*, to be published.

25. Crapo P: The use of alternative sweeteners in the diabetic diet. *Diabetes Care*, to be published.

26. Herman WH, Teutsch SM: Kidney disease associated with diabetes, in *Diabetes in America: Diabetes Data Compiled 1984*, US Dept of Health and Human Services publication No.(NIH) 85-1468. Bethesda, Md, 1985, pp XIV:1–31.

27. Wylie-Rosett J: Examination of dietary protein in the management of diabetes. *Diabetes Care*, to be published.

28. Franz MJ: Nutrition education and counseling: The system and tools. *Diabetes Care* 1987;87:6–165.

29. Franz MJ, Barr P, Holler H, et al: Exchange lists: Revised 1986. *J Am Diet Assoc*.

30. American Diabetes Association & American Dietetic Association. *Healthy Food Choices*, Alexandria, Va, 1986.

31. American Diabetes Association & American Dietetic Association. *Exchange Lists for Meal Planning*, 1986.

32. Wing RR, Jefferies R: Outpatient treatment of obesity: A comparison of methodology and clinical results. *Int J Obes* 1979; 3:261–279.

33. Glanz K: Nutrition education for risk factor reduction and patient education: A review. *Prev Med* 1985; 14:721–752.

34. Hansen BC: Dietary considerations for the obese with diabetes. *Diabetes Care*, to be published.

Appendix 22-A

Diagnostic Criteria for Diabetes

NONPREGNANT ADULTS

Criteria for Diabetes Mellitus: Diagnosis of diabetes mellitus in nonpregnant adults should be restricted to those who have *one* of the following:

- A random plasma glucose level of 200 mg/dl or greater *plus* classic signs and symptoms of diabetes mellitus including polydipsia, polyuria, polyphagia, and weight loss

- A fasting plasma glucose level of 140 mg/dl or greater on at least two occasions

- A fasting plasma glucose level of less than 140 mg/dl *plus* sustained elevated plasma glucose levels during at least two oral glucose tolerance tests. The 2-hour sample and at least one other between 0 and 2 hours after the 75-gram glucose dose should be 200 mg/dl or greater. Oral glucose tolerance testing is not necessary if the patient has a fasting plasma glucose level of 140 mg/dl or greater.

Criteria for Impaired Glucose Tolerance: Diagnosis of impaired glucose tolerance in nonpregnant adults should be restricted to those who have *all* of the following:

- A fasting plasma glucose of less than 140 mg/dl
- A 2-hour oral glucose tolerance test plasma glucose level between 140 and 200 mg/dl
- An intervening oral glucose tolerance test plasma glucose value of 200 mg/dl or greater

PREGNANT WOMEN

Criteria for Gestational Diabetes: Following an oral glucose load of 100 grams, the diagnosis of gestational diabetes may be made if two plasma glucose values equal or exceed the following:

Fasting	1 Hour	2 Hour	3 Hour
105 mg/dl	190 mg/dl	165 mg/dl	145 mg/dl

CHILDREN

Criteria for Diabetes Mellitus: Diagnosis of diabetes mellitus in children should be restricted to those who have *one* of the following:

- A random plasma glucose level of 200 mg/dl or greater *plus* classic signs and symptoms of diabetes mellitus, including polyuria, polydipsia, ketonuria, and rapid weight loss

- A fasting plasma glucose level of 140 mg/dl or greater on at least two occasions *and* sustained elevated plasma glucose levels during at least two oral glucose tolerance tests. Both the 2-hour plasma glucose and at least one other between 0 and 2 hours after the glucose dose (1.75 g/kg ideal body weight up to 75 grams) should be 200 mg/dl or greater.

Criteria for Impaired Glucose Tolerance: The diagnosis of impaired glucose tolerance in children should be restricted to those who have *both* of the following:

- A fasting plasma glucose concentration of less than 140 mg/dl
- A 2-hour oral glucose tolerance test plasma glucose level of greater than 140 mg/dl

Source: Reprinted from *The Physician's Guide to Type II Diabetes (NIDDM): Diagnosis and Treatment* by H Rifkin (Ed) with permission of the American Diabetes Association Inc, © 1984.

Appendix 22-B

Resource Materials

National Diabetes Information Clearinghouse
Box NDIC
Bethesda, MD 20892
301-468-2162

Diabetes Care and Education Practice Group of the American Dietetic Association
430 North Michigan Avenue
Chicago, IL 60611
800-621-6469

American Association of Diabetes Educators
500 North Michigan Avenue, Suite 1400
Chicago, IL 60611
312-661-1700

American Diabetes Association, Inc.
National Service Center
1660 Duke Street
Alexandria, VA 22312
800-ADA-DISC
703-549-1500

International Diabetes Center
5000 West 39th Street
Minneapolis, MN 55416
612-927-3393

Joslin Diabetes Foundation
1 Joslin Place
Boston, MA 02215
617-732-2400

National Coalition for Recognition (NACOR)
1801 Rockville Pike
Suite 501
Rockville, MD 20852
301-468-6555

Chapter 23

Cancer and Obesity

Anthony B. Miller

INTRODUCTION

In this chapter, I consider the role of obesity in the causation of certain cancers from the viewpoint of epidemiology, "the study of the distribution and determinants (causes) of cancer in human populations." For obvious reasons, unless we are investigating a way to prevent cancer, we cannot determine the relation of a possible cause with a cancer by experimental means, thus epidemiology is largely an observational science. Yet it is largely through this mechanism, buttressed where possible by experiments in laboratory animals, that we have learned that various cancers may be influenced by dietary factors, and some by obesity. Most of the cancers in which obesity seems to have a role or may have a role are believed also to be endocrine dependent.

The cancers mainly considered in this chapter arise in the gallbladder, breast, endometrium, and ovary in women, and prostate in men. Of these, most information relates to cancers of the breast and endometrium.

Obesity is associated with affluence, and the cancers considered occur more commonly in technically advanced countries, are highly correlated in incidence, are correlated with the incidence of colorectal and, to a lesser extent, pancreatic cancer, and tend to be associated with higher socioeconomic status. All are generally regarded as associated in some way with diet and nutrition.[1]

OBESITY AND CANCER IN GENERAL

Although nearly all studies of obesity and cancer are directed to specific cancer sites, data on variations in mortality from cancer in general by weight among 750,000 men and women were available from the long-term American Cancer Society follow-up study.[2] Underweight men but not underweight women were found to have higher mortality ratios from all sites of cancer combined (Table

23-1). Overweight men consistently showed lower mortality ratios from all forms of cancer than overweight women, though in practice, both groups showed increased mortality from cancer. The male mortality in the group with a 140+ weight index category was one-third higher than those with a normal weight index, while the female cancer mortality in this overweight group was 55% higher than those in the normal weight index category.

The major contributor to the excess mortality in underweight men seems to have been cancer of the lung. This of course would also be a heavy-cigarette-smoking group. The major contributors to excess cancer mortality in overweight men seem to have been cancer of the stomach, cancer of the colon and rectum, and cancer of the pancreas (Table 23-2). None of these sites has been recognized as being associated with obesity in previous studies. For example, no association with excess weight 6 months before interview was noted in our own case-control study of diet and colorectal cancer. However, in that study a strong association with saturated fat consumption was noted.

For women, the major contributors to excess mortality in the overweight groups seem to have been cancer of the gallbladder and biliary passages, cancer of the breast, cancer of the endometrium and uterus unspecified, and possibly cancer of the ovary (Table 23-2). These sites are all believed to be associated with diet, particularly in the case of breast cancer, with excess fat in the diet.

GALLBLADDER CANCER

There have been few studies of the epidemiology of this site because of its relative rarity. However, there is a similarity in the incidence of gallbladder cancer with that of gallstones, while gallstones are themselves believed to be

Table 23-1 Mortality Ratios for All Sites of Cancer and All Ages Combined in Relation to the Death Rate of Those 90% to 109% of Average Weight

Weight Index (%)	Men	Women
Less than 80	1.33	0.96
80–89	1.13	0.92
90–109	1.00	1.00
110–119	1.02	1.10
120–129	1.09	1.19
130–139	1.14	1.23
140+	1.33	1.55

Source: Reprinted with permission from "Variations in Mortality by Weight among 750,000 Men and Women" by EA Lew and L Garfinkel, *Journal of Chronic Diseases* (1979; 32:563–576), Copyright © 1979, Pergamon Journals Ltd.

Table 23-2 Mortality Ratios for Selected Sites of Cancer for the Overweight Related to the Underweight (Weight Index Less Than 80)

Cancer Cause of Death	Sex	Weight Index	
		130–139	*140+*
Stomach	M	0.54	1.40
	F	1.70	1.39
Colorectum	M	1.70	1.92
	F	1.40	1.31
Gallbladder and ducts	F	2.65	5.26
Pancreas	M	0.63	1.35
	F	1.00	0.52
Breast	F	1.49	1.87
Endometrium	F	2.58	6.09
Ovary	F	1.02	1.90
Prostate	M	1.30	1.26
Kidney	M	1.42	NSD*
	F	1.65	1.81

*Not sufficient data.

Source: Reprinted with permission from "Variations in Mortality by Weight among 750,000 Men and Women" by EA Lew and L Garfinkel, *Journal of Chronic Diseases* (1979; 32:563–576), Copyright © 1979, Pergamon Journals Ltd.

associated with obesity. Nevertheless, the uniformly poor correlation of gallbladder cancer with other cancers associated with high-fat diets seems to militate against high-fat diets as a causal factor.[3] As no study of dietary factors and cancer of this site has been reported, however, it is not possible to do more than conjecture that the dietary factors associated with the production of gallstones, especially in relation to cholesterol metabolism and to obesity, and therefore particularly an excess of calories, may be relevant.

BREAST CANCER

In an early study of 632 white Americans and 1,253 hospital control subjects, Wynder et al[4] suggested that the stocky, in particular somewhat obese women, have a slightly higher chance of developing breast cancer than those of slimmer body build. However, Wynder[5] later pointed out that women in a low socioeconomic class have 3 to 4 times more obesity than women in a high socioeconomic class. After matching for socioeconomic factors, he found no clear association between obesity and breast cancer.

Brinkley et al[6] attempted an anthropometric evaluation of the possibility that breast cancer is associated with a particular body type. They included 150 patients with breast cancer and three comparison groups: (1) women with other cancers, (2) women with other diseases, and (3) normal women. Weight, height, sitting height, biacromial dimension, and biiliac dimension were measured. Various indices of these variables were calculated, a multivariate analysis conducted, and a discriminant function estimated. Weight and sitting height were among the variables significant in the analysis, and it was concluded that women with breast cancer tend to be more masculine in type.

In some of the centers in an international collaborative study, an association was found between height, weight, and breast cancer. In Athens,[7] for example, increasing risk was found with increasing height (H) and weight (W), and with the index W/H^2 (Quetelet's index). Adjustment for variables associated with height and weight (including schooling as an index of socioeconomic status) failed to abolish this effect. The authors[5] concluded that both height and weight have independent associations with breast cancer risk, the tallest and heaviest deciles of the population having almost twice the risk of the shortest and lightest deciles.

In Sao Paulo,[8] an association of increasing risk with increasing weight was found in women aged 50 years or older, and not in women aged 20 to 49 years. This association was reduced, but not abolished, when Quetelet's index was used to control for height.

In a parallel study in Taiwan,[9] there was a significant association of increasing risk with increasing weight, but not height. Women weighing more than 55 kg had more than twice the breast cancer risk of women weighing less than 45 kg. When the data were subdivided by age, there was a suggestion of a stronger effect of weight in women older than 50 years, but the effect in the younger women was not abolished.

A hypothesis that breast cancer in postmenopausal women was associated with obesity through a hormonal mechanism was proposed by de Waard and colleagues[10] based on cytologic studies of the vaginal smears of obese postmenopausal women that suggested continuing estrogenic activity. Obesity was defined as a body weight more than 25% above ideal weight. In women aged 55 years or older, 71% of those with breast cancer were obese compared with 54% of the control subjects, a significant difference.

De Waard et al[6] subsequently refined their hypothesis to postulate two types of breast cancer.[11] They suggested that one, occurring largely in premenopausal women, is connected with an endocrine imbalance in which the ovarian hormones are involved; the other, largely occurring in postmenopausal women, has as its major determinant altered hormonal homeostasis related to overnutrition. This hypothesis was supported by a prospective study[12] of 7,259 postmenopausal women. Increasing risk for breast cancer with increasing weight and increasing height was found, with women weighing 70 kg or more and 165 cm or more in height having 3.6 times the risk of women weighing less than 60 kg and less than 160 cm in height. However, using Quetelet's index as a measure of degree of overweight as a correction for height removed a large degree of the risk. Therefore de Waard[13] modified his hypothesis to postulate that body mass rather than overweight (obesity) was the risk factor.

In a further study, de Waard et al[14] evaluated the effect of weight and height on the age-specific incidence of breast cancer using data from The Netherlands and Japan. They suggested that approximately one half of the differences in incidence between Holland and Japan could be attributed to differences in body weight and height.

Support for the hypothesis of de Waard has come from a large study in California.[15] In premenopausal women, a lowered risk of breast cancer with a higher Quetelet's index (BMI) was found. In contrast, in postmenopausal women a markedly higher risk for breast cancer associated with an increased Quetelet's index was found. Further, although an estimate of weight gain between age 20 years and the interview showed little or no influence on breast cancer risk in the premenopausal women, it was strongly related to risk in postmenopausal women.

Elevated risk for breast cancer was found in those with a Quetelet's index of 21.5 or more. Comparing these women with those with an index of less than 21.5, and using the proportion of control subjects with an elevated index as an indication of their prevalence in the population, it is possible to calculate from this study that 18% of breast cancer in postmenopausal women may be attributable to obesity. This is equivalent to 12% of breast cancer at all ages.

Other studies, however, have not supported the de Waard hypothesis. Thus in one study of patients with breast cancer and control subjects aged 41 to 60 years in Finland,[16] little or no effect of height, weight, weight × height, or degree of overweight (Quetelet's index) on the risk for breast cancer was found. In a geographical correlation study[17] in Finland there was also no significant difference in height, weight, height × weight, and body mass index (W/H^2) in urban and rural population groups and in industrial workers. There were no statistically significant correlations between the size of the woman and breast cancer incidence. In Sweden,[18] another study found no difference in the distributions of height and weight or in two different indices for overweight. Wynder et al[19] in a second large study of breast cancer patients and control subjects in surgical services at the same hospitals also found no significant case-control differences for height, weight 2 years before diagnosis, or for Quetelet's index. In a study in Canada,[20] we found no association with height, and only a weak association with weight in postmenopausal women but not in premenopausal women. The positive association in postmenopausal women was almost restricted to women aged 70 years or older. We attempted to replicate this latter finding in women aged 65 years or older with breast cancer and population control subjects, but with essentially negative findings.

Nevertheless, in the long-term prospective study conducted by the American Cancer Society,[2] a significant trend of increasing mortality from breast cancer with increasing weight index was found. For those with a weight index of 140 +, there was a mortality ratio of 1.53 in relation to those 90% to 109% of average weight, in contrast to a mortality ratio of 0.82 for those with a weight index of less than 80 (the severely underweight). Thus the risk of death from breast cancer was nearly twice as great in the women who were heaviest compared with those who were underweight (Table 23-2).

Further, in US breast cancer screening program participants, there was increasing risk with increasing weight, but little effect of height when adjusted for weight.[21] Gray et al[22] also found that breast cancer incidence and mortality rates in different countries were correlated with height and weight, and with total fat and animal protein consumption. The anthropometric variables seemed to make an additional contribution to the effect of the dietary factors.

A particularly strong effect of overweight, increasing the risk of breast cancer in women aged 60 years or older but not in premenopausal or younger postmenopausal women, was reported from a study in Israel.[23] Even a recent decrease in weight seemed to be protective.

It seems likely that obesity in postmenopausal women makes an additional contribution to the risk for breast cancer over and above an effect of dietary fat. Thus, general population advice to maintain ideal body weight at all ages would seem appropriate.

Recently, it was suggested that treatment of obesity could well delay the rate of progression of advanced cancers of the breast and could even contribute to cure in a few people. Evidence for this hypothesis is not strong, though in at least one animal experimental study, it was noted that reduction of fat in the diet in animals that already had carcinogen-induced mammary tumors was followed by a reduction in the rate of growth of these tumors and improvement in the length of survival of the animals.[24] It was therefore proposed that the treatment of obesity should be evaluated in a controlled clinical trial of women with stage 2 (lymph node involved) breast cancer. Support for this suggestion has come from a follow-up of 300 of 400 cases in our case-control study of diet and breast cancer.[25] There was a clear association of body weight (and probably obesity) with survival, but not with estimated fat intake.

ENDOMETRIAL CANCER

Endometrial cancer has for some time been recognized as associated with obesity, largely through case series. This association has also usually, but not invariably, been confirmed in studies comparing weights of patients and control subjects. Thus Wynder et al[26] found that weight at ages 25 to 29 years and 50 to 59 years (as recorded at interviews) was significantly related to risk. The increase in risk was largely restricted to those 21 lb or more above average weight at ages 50 to 59 years. The highest risk was for women 51 lb or more overweight at either age. In addition, women who were tall (5 ft 6 in or more) and were also 10 lb or more above average weight had a higher risk than shorter women. They[26] suggested that the mechanism of action could be the unopposed retention of estrogens in obese women.

Elwood et al[27] also found that obesity was a risk factor in a study in Boston. They derived Quetelet's index from height and weight as recalled at least 2 years before the diagnosis of the cases. They found a trend of increasing risk with increasing relative weight, but a clear excess of risk (relative risk 1.9) only for the most obese women.

In contrast, a study in Manchester, England,[28] was interpreted as showing no association of endometrial cancer with obesity. In this study, consecutive patients with adenocarcinoma of the endometrium were age-matched with control subjects with nonmalignant disease drawn from the general surgical and medical wards of the same hospital division. Any patient known to be suffering from a condition specifically associated with obesity, hypertension, diabetes mellitus, or endocrine disorder was excluded from the control series. Unfortunately, the classification of obesity was based on such statements in the charts as "very thin, average weight, obese, grossly obese." On this basis, 34% of the patients were classified as obese, and 31% of the control subjects, a nonsignificant difference. It is difficult to accept this study as an adequate test of the hypothesis that obesity is associated with endometrial cancer. Apart from the rather poor data base, no attempt was made to present the data in categories of excess weight, it being relevant that the positive studies found excess risk for those at the upper end of the obesity scale.

However, two studies, both primarily directed to the association of endometrial carcinoma and exogenous estrogens, provide confirmatory evidence of the association of the disease with obesity. In a study[29] in which patients with endometrial cancer and control subjects were drawn from a retirement community, obesity was defined from data recorded in medical charts, or "when the usual weight was in excess of a standard upper limit for height in medium-frame women." A risk ratio of 1.5 for obesity was found for the entire group, and was 1.6 in matched users of any estrogens.

In the other study[30] patients with adenocarcinoma of the endometrium and matched controls drawn from the same institution with other gynecologic neoplasms were studied. Obesity was defined as "a weight of 130 percent or greater over upper limits of ideal weight for given height and medium frame." The risk of endometrial cancer associated with estrogen use was highest in patients without hypertension and obesity. Not only was obesity more prevalent in the patients with endometrial cancer who had not received estrogen, but the degree of obesity was considerably greater among those classified as obese. These observations add additional data to the hypothesis that obesity is associated with an increase in endogenous estrogen production and that this is the mechanism for the induction of endometrial carcinoma in the obese. However, in the nonobese, the use of exogenous estrogen results in a risk similar to that for the obese in the absence of exogenous estrogens.

Further support for the role of obesity in the etiology of endometrial cancer comes from the long-term American Cancer Society study.[2] Cancer of the endometrium showed the highest risk of any cancer studied with increasing weight index (Table 23-2).

OVARIAN CANCER

In contrast to breast and endometrial cancer, there is little evidence to support an association of ovarian cancer with obesity in spite of their correlation internationally, the correlation of ovarian cancer with dietary factors, and suspicions of common etiology. Lingeman,[31] in a review of the etiology of cancer of the human ovary, noted that "the hypertension-obesity-diabetes triad associated with high risk for adenocarcinoma of the endometrium has not been observed in patients with cancers of the ovary." Since then, of four case-control studies published that assessed obesity, three[32-34] specifically indicated no excess of risk in a total of 815 patients and 2,217 control subjects studied.

In a fourth study,[35] obesity was defined as "at least a 20% excess for a given height based on an ideal weight for a woman with a medium frame." It is notable that this definition seems to accept a lower degree of overweight as obesity than other groups. However, 23% of the patients and 13% of the control subjects were obese, as defined, the relative risk being 2.0.

Evidence that obesity may not be an important risk factor for ovarian cancer is derived from the American Cancer Society study[2] that showed no indication of a trend of increasing risk with increasing weight index, though the mortality ratio at a weight index of 140 or more was elevated (Table 23-2).

PROSTATE CANCER

As for ovarian cancer, prostate cancer has not generally been considered to be associated with obesity. However, of the various studies that have been conducted on the epidemiology of prostate cancer, two have reported data relevant to consideration of obesity.

In a study in New York, Wynder et al[36] found no differences between prostate cancer patients and control subjects in the distribution of weight or height.

Greenwald et al[37] collected follow-up information on Harvard University students on whom detailed physical and anthropometric measurements had been made upon their entry to college from 1880 to 1916. Of approximately 18,000 students examined, 268 were known to have died of cancer of the prostate by December 1967. Their characteristics were compared with those of 536 control subjects not known to have died of prostate cancer, selected from adjacent entries in the record books of the original examinations. No differences between groups were found in any of several anthropometric indices examined nor in a number of other body measurements.

In the American Cancer Society study,[2] although there was a slight increase in mortality ratios at weight indices of 120 or more, there was no evidence of a dose-response relation and no consistent trend (Table 23-2).

RENAL CANCER

There has been one study[38] that suggested an association of obesity with renal cancer in women but not in men. Some confirmation of this came from the American Cancer Society study[2] (Table 23-2), thus adding greater emphasis to the potential importance of obesity in increasing cancer risk in women.

SUMMARY

The conclusion that might be drawn from the long-term American Cancer Society follow-up study[2] that obesity increases the risk for cancer in general in both sexes is troubling, at least for men. This is because the cancers for which an excess mortality was noted for men were cancer of the stomach, cancer of the colon and rectum, and cancer of the pancreas, which have not been noted in the past as being associated with obesity and for which at least one (cancer of the colon and rectum) there is evidence from a case-control study[39] that weight is not of importance when dietary variables are taken into consideration. It must be born in mind that the American Cancer Society did not collect data in a form that would permit adequate control for the analysis of weight and cancer mortality for other variables that might be more relevant. Cancer of the colon and rectum and cancer of the stomach behave quite differently in different populations, and can be expected to have different etiologies. Indeed, all the evidence we have about their etiology points to a substantial difference between them. It has to be concluded, therefore, that obesity is not an important factor responsible for increases in cancer risk for men.

For women, however, in addition to the greater effect of obesity in the American Cancer Society study,[2] there is other evidence that at least for three cancer sites, cancer of the gallbladder, cancer of the breast, and cancer of the endometrium, obesity does increase the risk for cancer. The clearest direct evidence for this is for cancer of the endometrium, and a mechanism associating obesity with increased production of endogenous estrogens has been postulated. For cancer of the breast, the evidence is not so consistent, yet this is such an important cancer that it would be justifiable to evaluate further the effect of weight reduction in both reducing the risk for this cancer in women and, possibly, in increasing survival in women with pre-existing breast cancer. Although much of the effect of diet and breast cancer may be mediated through total fat consumption and not through caloric consumption and hence obesity, obesity may contribute to increased risk by an independent effect, which should not be ignored. We thus have some very good reasons for recommending to obese women that active measures should be taken to reduce their weight to ideal levels if they wish to reduce their risk of subsequent cancer occurrence and death. Indeed, the American Cancer Society study[2] suggests that additional benefit may accrue by reducing weight below that which might usually be regarded as normal.

There is increasing interest in the relation of diet and cancer, and ongoing pilot studies have been conducted in several centers that have shown that it is perfectly feasible, after individual counseling, to reduce dietary fat consumption from 35% to 40% of calories to as low as 20%. In addition, such women have increased their intake of whole grain products, fruits, and vegetables. An interesting additional effect, not specifically sought, has been weight reduction in many women. Although such studies will have to become much larger and prolonged to determine any effect of dietary modification and/or weight reduction on cancer incidence, they should be encouraged. We need not be too concerned if, as a result, we will be unable to determine unequivocally which component (reduction in total fat consumption, increase in dietary fiber, weight reduction) was largely responsible for any effect observed, as all can be confidently recommended as important steps to improved health.

REFERENCES

1. National Academy of Sciences: *Diet, Nutrition and Cancer*. Washington, National Academy Press, 1982.

2. Lew EA, Garfinkel L: Variations in mortality by weight among 750,000 men and women. *J Chron Dis* 1979; 32:563–576.

3. Fraumeni JF: Cancer of the pancreas and biliary tract: Epidemiological considerations. *Cancer Res* 1975; 35:3437–3446.

4. Wynder EL, Bross IJ, Hirayama T: A study of the epidemiology of cancer of the breast. *Cancer* 1960; 13:559–601.

5. Wynder EL: Identification of women at high risk for breast cancer. *Cancer* 1969; 24:1235–1240.

6. Brinkley D, Carpenter RG, Haybittle JL: An anthropometric study of women with cancer. *Br J Prev Soc Med* 1971; 25:65–75.

7. Valoras VG, MacMahon B, Trichopoulos D, et al: Lactation and reproductive histories of breast cancer patients in greater Athens, 1965–67. *Int J Cancer* 1969; 4:350–363.

8. Miller AB, Cole P, MacMahon B: Breast cancer in an area of high parity. *Cancer Res* 1971; 31:77–83.

9. Lin TM, Chen KP, MacMahon B: Epidemiological characteristics of cancer of the breast in Taiwan. *Cancer* 1971; 27:1497–1504.

10. de Waard F, Laive JWJ, Baanders, van-Haliwijn EA: On the bimodal age distribution of mammary carcinoma. *Brit J Canc* 1960; 14:437–451.

11. de Waard F, Baanders-van Halewijn EA, Huizinga J: The bimodel age distribution of patients with mammary cancer. *Cancer* 1964; 17:141–151.

12. de Waard F, Baanders-van Halewijn EA: A prospective study in general practice on breast cancer risk in post-menopausal women. *Int J Cancer* 1974; 14:153–160.

13. de Waard F: Breast cancer incidence and nutritional status with particular reference to body weight and height. *Canc Res* 1975; 35:3351–3356.

14. de Waard F, Cornelis JP, Aoki K, et al: Breast cancer incidence according to weight and height in two cities of The Netherlands and in Aichi Prefecture, Japan. *Cancer* 1977; 40:1269–1275.

15. Paffenbarger RS, Kampert JB, Chang HG: Characteristics that predict risk of breast cancer before and after the menopause. *Am J Epidemiol* 1980; 112:258–268.

16. Soini I: Risk factors of breast cancer in Finland. *Int J Epidemiol* 1977; 6:363–373.

17. Hakama M, Soini I, Kuosma E, Lehtonen M, Aromaa A: British cancer incidence: Geographic correlations in Finland. *Int J Epidemiol* 1979; 8:33–40.

18. Adami HO, Rimsten A, Stenkvist B, Begelius J: Influence of height, weight, and obesity on risk of breast cancer in an unselected Swedish population. *Brit J Canc* 1979; 36:787–792.

19. Wynder EL, MacGornack FA, Stellman SD: The epidemiology of breast cancer in 875 United States Caucasian women. *Cancer* 1978; 41:2341–2354.

20. Choi NW, Howe GR, Miller AB, et al: An epidemiologic study of breast cancer. *Am J Epidemiol* 1978; 107:510–521.

21. Brinton LA, Williams RR, Hoover RN, et al: Breast cancer risk factors among screening program participants. *J Natl Cancer Inst* 1979; 62:37–43.

22. Gray GE, Pike MC, Henderson BE: Breast cancer incidence and mortality rates in different countries in relation to known risk factors and dietary practices. *Br J Cancer* 1979; 39:1–7.

23. Lubin F, Rider AM, Wax Y, et al: Overweight and changes in weight throughout adult life in breast cancer etiology: A case-control study. *Am J Epidemiol* 1985; 122:579–585.

24. Wynder EL, Cohen L: A rationale for dietary intervention in the treatment of postmenopausal breast cancer patients. *Nutr Cancer* 1982; 3:195–199.

25. Newman SC, Miller AB, Howe GR: A study of the effect of weight and dietary fat on breast cancer survival time. *Am J Epidemiol* 1986; 123:767–774.

26. Wynder EL, Escher GC, Mantel N: An epidemiological investigation of cancer of the endometrium. *Cancer* 1966; 19:489–520.

27. Elwood JM, Cole P, Rothman KJ, et al: Epidemiology of endometrial cancer. *J Natl Cancer Inst* 1977; 59:1055–1060.

28. Fox F, Sen DK: A controlled study of the constitutional stigmata of endometrial adenocarcinoma. *Br J Canc* 1970; 24:30–36.

29. Mack TM, Pike MC, Henderson BE, Pfeffer RI, Gerkins VR, Arthur M, Brown SE: Estrogens and endometrial cancer in a retirement community. *N Engl J Med* 1976; 294:1262–1267.

30. Smith DC, Prentice R, Thompson DJ, Hermann WL: Association of exogenous estrogens and endometrial carcinoma. *N Engl J Med* 1975; 293:1164–1167.

31. Lingeman CH: Etiology of cancer of the human ovary: A review. *J Natl Cancer Inst* 1974; 53:1603–1618.

32. Joly DJ, Lilienfeld AM, Diamond EL, Bross IDJ: An epidemiologic study of the relationship of reproductive experience to cancer of the ovary. *Am J Epidemiol* 1979; 8:33–40.

33. Newhouse ML, Pearson RM, Fullerton JM, Boesen EAM, Shannon HS: A case-control study of cancer of the ovary. *Br J Preventive Social Med* 1977; 31:148–153.

34. Annegars JF, Strom H, Decker DG, Dockerty MB, O'Fallon WM: Ovarian cancer, Incidence and case-control study. *Cancer* 1979; 43:723–729.

35. Casagrande JT, Louie EW, Pike MC, et al: 'Incessant ovulation' and ovarian cancer. *Lancet* 1979; 2:170–173.

36. Wynder EL, Mabuchi K, Whitmore WF: Epidemiology of cancer of the prostate. *Cancer* 1971; 28:344–360.

37. Greenwald P, Damon A, Kermiss V, et al: Physical and demographic features of men before developing cancer of the prostate. *J Natl Cancer Inst* 1974; 53:341–346.

38. Wynder EL, Mabuchi K, Whitmore WF: Epidemiology of adenocarcinoma of the kidney. *J Natl Cancer Inst* 1974; 53:1619–1634.

39. Jain M, Cook G, Davis FG, Grace MG, Howe GR, Miller AB: A case-control study of diet and colo-rectal cancer. *Int J Cancer* 1980; 26:757–768.

Index